Voices for Equality

Voices for Equality

Ordain Women and Resurgent Mormon Feminism

Edited by
Gordon Shepherd, Lavina Fielding Anderson,
and Gary Shepherd

GREG KOFFORD BOOKS
SALT LAKE CITY, 2015

Copyright © 2015 Greg Kofford Books
Cover design copyright © 2015 Greg Kofford Books, Inc.
Cover design by Loyd Ericson

Published in the USA.

All rights reserved. No part of this volume may be reproduced in any form without written permission from the publisher, Greg Kofford Books. The views expressed herein are the responsibility of the authors and do not necessarily represent the position of Greg Kofford Books.

ISBN: 978-1-58958-758-8

Also available in ebook.

Greg Kofford Books
P.O. Box 1362
Draper, UT 84020
www.gregkofford.com
facebook.com/gkbooks

| 2019 | 18 | 17 | 16 | 15 | 5 | 4 | 3 | 2 | 1 |

Library of Congress Control Number: 2015945210

Contents

Preface:
The Contemporary LDS Church at a Crossroads on Gender Issues   vii
in the Twenty-First Century
Lavina Fielding Anderson

PART I
Conceptualizing the Issues of Gender and Equality in a Conservative Religious Faith

1. The Birth of Ordain Women: The Personal Becomes Political   3
   Lorie Winder Stromberg

2. Conflict and Change in Closed and Open Systems: 27
   The Case of the LDS Church
   Gordon Shepherd and Gary Shepherd

3. "The Greatest Glory of True Womanhood":   49
   Eve and the Construction of Mormon Gender Identity
   Boyd Jay Petersen

4. LDS Gender Theology: A Feminist Perspective   77
   Janice Allred

5. Egalitarian Marriage in a Patriarchal Church   103
   Kristy Money and Rolf Straubhaar

6. Trans-forming Mormonism: Transgender Perspectives   117
   on Priesthood Ordination and Gender
   J. Sumerau and Ryan Cragun

Part II
Historical and Cultural Context

7. Retrieving the Keys: Historical Milestones in LDS Women's   137
   Quest for Priesthood Ordination
   Margaret M. Toscano

8. Ecclesiastical Equality: Women's Progress in Contemporary Churches   167
   Mary Ellen Robertson

9. Ordination of Women: The Community of Christ Story   185
   Robin Kincaid Linkhart

Part III
LDS Organizational Structure and Ecclesiastical Dynamics

10. Organizational and Doctrinal Change   203
    in a Prophetic Religious Tradition
    Gregory A. Prince

11. Disciplinary Councils: Excommunication and Community   227
    in the Modern Church
    Robert A. Rees

12. Church Discipline and the Excommunication of Kate Kelly   241
    Nadine McCombs Hansen

Part IV
LDS Women in a Twenty-First-Century Church

13. The Great Lever: Women and Changing Mission Culture   259
    in Contemporary Mormonism
    Courtney L. Rabada and Kristine L. Haglund

14. An Insider Account of the Mormon Gender Issues Survey: 277
    Why We Did It and Why a Vocal Minority Hated It
    Brent D. Beal, Heather K. Olson Beal, and S. Matthew Stearmer

15. The Mormon Gender Issues Survey: 297
    A Quantitative Analysis of U.S. Respondents
    Ryan T. Cragun and Michael Nielsen

16. Finding the Middle Ground: Negotiating Mormonism and Gender   319
    *Nancy Ross, Jessica Finnigan, Heather K. Olson Beal,
    Kristy Money, Amber Choruby Whiteley, and Caitlin Carroll*

17. Mormon Feminists in Social Media: 335
    A Story of Community and Education
    Jessica Finnigan and Nancy Ross

18. What Ordain Women Profiles Tell Us   355
    about Mormon Women's Hopes and Discontents
    Gary Shepherd and Gordon Shepherd

19. From the Kotel to the Square: The Rhetoric of Religious Feminism   377
    Debra Elaine Jenson

Epilogue:
  Prospects for the Ordination of LDS Women   397
  in the Twenty-first Century
  Gordon Shepherd and Gary Shepherd

Appendix:
  Bibliography of Media Stories January 1, 2013–December 31, 2014,   401
  on Mormon/LDS Women, Ordain Women, and Kate Kelly
  Pamela A. Shepherd, compiler

Contributors   419
Index   425

Preface

The Contemporary LDS Church at a Crossroads on Gender Issues in the Twenty-First Century

Lavina Fielding Anderson

My daughter-in-law, Marina Capella, is a Stanford graduate and a board-certified pediatrician. In July 2014, she and my son moved to Carlsbad, California, where Marina was employed at a pediatric clinic. Shortly after they started attending their new ward (Carlsbad First), a new bishop was installed. In his opening address to the ward, he emotionally explained his lengthy history of callings in the Church and how earnestly he had anticipated his new calling.

Marina and Christian, in their first meeting with him, explained their own backgrounds, callings, and contributions, said that they had posted personal profiles on the Ordain Women website, and had flown up to Salt Lake City to participate in the first Ordain Women event in October 2013 when they and scores of other women and male allies asked, one by one, for admittance to the general priesthood section of conference, only to be refused. They asked the bishop directly if that was going to be a problem. He did not seem overly familiar with Ordain Women but assured them the stake presidency did not want it to be a problem. The second Ordain Women effort to again seek admittance to the priesthood session in April 2014 was again denied. Marina and Christian felt that the Church's decision to broadcast the priesthood sessions like all other sessions of conference and to declare the women's general meeting as the first session of general conference were steps in the right direction, but they found it disheartening when the Church took the extraordinary measure of closing Temple Square to the media. By then, co-founder Kate Kelly had been excommunicated on June 23, 2014, while threats against John Dehlin's membership resulted in his excommunication on February 8, 2015. Marina confronted her own feelings that her silence made her "complicit" in Church activities that she felt she could not support with integrity.

On Sunday March 1, Marina awoke early and felt impressed to write out a testimony that she wished to share with the ward later that day. Choosing to wait until she would be the last person to speak, she stood up. "I was terrified," she remembers. "My heart was racing, but I felt I had to do it." She introduced her testimony by saying that, as an act of personal authenticity, she had "considered resigning from the Church" but wanted to share some "deeply personal" beliefs that had brought her to this "painful prospect." At this point, speaking with tears in her eyes, she was taken aback when "a woman in the back of the chapel stood up and loudly proclaimed, 'You need to stop!' Marina "turned to the bishop and asked him if I needed to stop." He was startled, clearly paralyzed by this unexpected disruption. Marina says: "I decided I would probably stop to avoid further contention. I turned back to the audience, and the woman in the back again loudly proclaimed, 'You need to stop!'" Still standing at the pulpit and with tears running down her cheeks, Marina replied, "'We are called to mourn with those that mourn, and comfort those that stand in need of comfort. How dare you call yourself a Christian!" She returned to her seat next to my son and wept while the bishop abruptly brought the meeting to a close and his counselor bore a quick but firm "the Church is true" testimony to end the meeting.

A host of people, including the bishop, came up to her afterwards, hugged her, and apologized for what had happened. Some even said they wanted to know what she had planned to say.

The core of her undelivered testimony (quoted below with her permission) was a clear exposition of the paradoxical feelings fostered by the Church's gender policies and practices:

> I don't believe that the gendered segregation of leadership and priesthood responsibilities in this church is doctrine inspired by God. I think that gender, like race, is one of the MANY differences among us that conspire to divide us rather than unite us. In my professional life as a physician, I have been encouraged to use my talents to accomplish anything I desire to help advance human health. Yet, in this church, I see half of the members systematically excluded from opportunities for service based on their femaleness. I can help save lives in a hospital, but I cannot pass the bread of life to members in my ward. Young women can aspire to be CEOs of companies, but can't aspire to be a counselor in the bishopric. I recall our very own bishop, when he was called to the position less than a year ago, bear his testimony of how much he had longed to serve as a bishop, how he had looked forward to it for years. Why is this desire righteous in a man but sinful in a woman? How much more could the sister missionaries accomplish if they could give blessings and baptize members? There are some places in the world where female members far outnumber male members, but a branch or ward cannot be formed without a certain number of priesthood-holding males. How tragic that women should be denied access to a community of Saints solely because of a lack of male peers.
>
> ... If these problems are irrelevant to you, then I ask for your charity: all of us will have doubts and struggles some day, and these are mine. I also think that it is inevitable that in a community of Christians who believe in the sanctifying power of service, there will inevitably be some women who want to serve the world in a way other than motherhood, and these women will either need a chance to talk about these feelings, or need to forever struggle with feelings of inauthenticity and isolation in our congregations. The latter is the space I have occupied for the past decade.

Marina had continued from that point by describing the reactions of family and friends who had been affronted by her participation in Ordain Women:

> I have been told that if I don't believe 100% of the Church's teachings, I should just leave. I have been called an apostate. I have been accused of being power-hungry. I

have had the "motherhood-priesthood" argument explained to me in 100 different ways, none of which hold water in my view. . . . I tried fasting, praying, and studying scriptures and conference talks to try to understand how sexism can possibly be okay at church. I was in a state of spiritual agony for years trying to understand. It wasn't until I accepted the nagging thought that it *wasn't* okay that I felt at peace. Now, denying this fact would be going against what my mind, heart, and soul tell me to be true. Sadly, being true to myself in this way puts me in a very tentative place—one in which the threat of possible excommunication hovers constantly overhead.

Also left unspoken was Marina's conclusion—her powerful affirmation of faith: "Despite my unorthodox beliefs, I have an unshakable testimony of Jesus Christ, of his teachings, and of the love God has for each of us. I will never abandon that."[1]

An almost reflex reaction from those with whom she has shared this painful experience has been to ask about ecclesiastical reprisal. That same Sunday, she emailed the text of her testimony to the bishop. He responded ambiguously, assuring her that "it's okay" to have doubts and questions, but also warning her that they should not be discussed publicly and that he would have been obligated to stop her himself. She and Christian have continued to attend church, and Marina feels less inclined to consider resignation since she feels that her public stance relieves her conscience of feeling tacitly complicit in actions she cannot support.

This experience captures the ambiguities and ironies of the current status of the conversation on gender issues in the Church. It was another woman, who felt "prompted" to disrupt the meeting and reject Marina's sincere expression of belief and faith as invalid. The bishop sent a mixed message of acceptance but control. It is difficult to imagine a more vivid and precise message of the fears that haunt the possibility of discussion and—in fact—the absolute denial of Church meetings as a safe place in which respectful and thoughtful discussions of this issue can take place. It also underscores the lack of clarity in the Church's message to members. Ally Isom, Public Affairs senior manager for the Church, when pinned down by Doug Fabrizio's increasingly specific questions on NPR Radio West, was forced back from generalizations to specifics in claiming that such discussions are acceptable:

> Fabrizio: But what if you believe—as some women do—that it's time for the Church to give women the priesthood? Where do you express that?
> Isom: There are many avenues to express that and discuss that.
> Fabriozio: Where? In public?
> Isom: No one's questioning your ability to discuss it in a congregation, in a Sunday school class, in Relief Society class . . .
> Fabrizio: In a congregation? In a congregation a woman can stand up and say that?
> Isom: She can certainly have the conversation. In my Relief Society we can.[2]

---

1. Marina Capella, "Testimony," March 1, 2015, copy in my possession, used by permission.

2. Ally Isom, interviewed by Doug Fabrizio, NPR Radio West (Salt Lake City), June 15, 2015, full transcription by Alison Moore Smith, July 18, 2014, http://mormonmomma.com.

In the past few years, general conference has expanded to allow addresses by two members of the women's auxiliaries' presidents per conference, at least one prayer per conference offered by members from this same group, and the official, though somewhat awkward, designation of the women's general meeting as a "session" of conference. General Authorities have expressed appreciation for the contributions of women to their families and to the Church with complimentary accolades that have sometimes lapsed into sentimental and unconsciously patronizing language. From the other side, General Authorities have pared away at the male-priesthood boundary with varying degrees of success, clarifying that "priesthood holder" is not the same as "priesthood" per se, and trying to differentiate between the "power," "authority," and "blessings" of the priesthood, and the differences between priesthood exercised in the family and in the institutional Church.

Other essays in this anthology explore these developments and their relative significance; but the excommunications of Kate Kelly and John Dehlin, at least in part for his support of women's ordination and gay rights, was an exercise in drawing a line that has left men and women scrambling on both sides to determine their own position relative to that line. "If the Church can excommunicate Kate and John, then it could come after me" is one position. Another is costly compromises with conscience that some members have made to retain their place in their family and community life as "faithful" Latter-day Saints. For still others, such actions are "last straw" communications that have made them abandon the effort to find a way to negotiate a healthy—or even tolerable—relationship with the institution.

Landmark events in this on-going dynamic would fill a volume in themselves. Personal landmarks for me were a Sunstone presentation by Paul M. Edwards in the 1970s. Edwards, Temple School director of the Reorganized Church of Jesus Christ of Latter Days Saints (now Community of Christ), referred without emphasis to "a prophet . . . she . . ." I still remember the almost electric shock of hearing a prophet referred to with a feminine pronoun. This was a decade before that church's revelation, canonized in 1985 as Section 156 of the RLDS Doctrines and Covenants, extended priesthood ordination to women. Another unforgettable moment was worshipping with the local Community of Christ congregation in which a woman's voice, resonant and reverent, pronounced the blessings on the emblems of the sacrament. I pored over a photograph in its magazine of an ordinary baptism—but one in which the officiator was the grandmother of the child being baptized. Apostle Susan Skoor Oxley, now retired, and Robin Kincaid Linkhart, president of the Sixth Quorum of the Seventy, have been cherished guests in our home; and I have felt blessed by the courage and compassion they bring to their ministry. I see possibilities we, as Latter-day Saints, desperately need to learn from.

---

com/latter-day-saints-and-excommunication-kuer-radiowest-podcast-transcript/ (accessed March 1, 2015). Fabrizio is the long-time host and producer of Radio West and an active Latter-day Saint.

Many of the chapters in this book are fierce competitors for my "Most Favored" prize, Robin Linkhart's clear and courageous chronology about the long and difficult road that Community of Christ traveled to recognizes the giftedness of all members by broadening opportunities to serve ranks very high on my list. One of her most important messages is the cultural inertia of patriarchal systems, predictable religious resistance, the necessary grassroots struggle for change, but also the ultimate priesthood possibilities for contemporary women in a prophetic faith tradition. Particularly inspiring is her description of the deep listening required to hear past the clamor of tradition, argument, and counter-argument to hear God's call to live a purer gospel.

In larger Mormon society, I consider this book to be a third voice in an intensifying conversation. The first voice was that of Sheri Dew, president and CEO of Deseret Book, spelling out her position in *Women and the Priesthood*:

> I am not a feminist. But I am pro-progression, meaning that I am in favor of opportunities and experiences that allow for the personal development and growth of men and women alike—especially when those experiences are sanctioned by the Lord. . . .
>
> Although I can see ways in which the participation of LDS women in the Church could be further enhanced, if nothing changes in my lifetime in this regard, it won't affect my testimony one whit. I've had far too many witnesses that the gospel is true and that the keys, power, and authority of the Savior's kingdom have been restored to let organizational issues discourage me.[3]

Her book is a valuable doctrinal compendium of General Authority statements on the place of women and the role of priesthood, even though she is careful to clarify that she is not pronouncing on doctrinal questions. It draws deeply on quotations over time from General Authorities' conference statements and writings on various aspects of this troubling issue. Still, it continually falls back to the position that true believers cannot give any political or social problem the same emphasis as the love and atoning sacrifice of Jesus. The result is a curious disconnect between the two positions, with the implication that troubled or dissatisfied women are lacking full faith.

The second voice followed a year later with the appearance of Neylan McBaine's *Women at Church: Magnifying Women's Local Impact* (Salt Lake City: Greg Kofford Books, 2014). I consider her book to occupy a middle ground—the first half acknowledging the sources of genuine pain and confusion that gender issues have caused many Mormon women. McBaine usefully differentiates between policy and tradition, and comments several times on difficult policies: "This does not mean the alternate model our leaders are advocating is wrong. It means it is hard to understand and implement." In the second half of the book, she reports on encouraging examples of local creativity and accommodations that

---

3. Sheri Dew, *Women and the Priesthood* (Salt Lake City: Deseret Book, 2014), 2, 9.

open the door of priesthood leaders and women alike to explore avenues of expanded participation.[4]

Both Dew and McBaine are respectful, thoughtful, and moderate in tone. Certainly few readers will agree with everything that either writer says, but I think it is fair to say that nearly all readers can find material for reflection, careful consideration, and responsible dialogue through their conversations.

This book, *Voices for Equality: Ordain Women and Resurgent Mormon Feminism,* is the third book in as many years to explore this disquieting, yet immensely significant topic. Broader in scope than either Dew or McBaine's works, it is data driven, using a combination of sociological and historical analysis, political and theological explorations, and sometimes wrenching personal experiences. The results are a thoughtful examination how change occurs, and is resisted or even repelled, in a faith-based organization whose doctrinal foundations combine both intensely conservative traditions and a commitment to progressive change in an environment that assigns different and sometimes clashing roles to lay members and priesthood leaders. A professional lifetime of dealing with sociological examinations of religious movements on the part of Gordon and Gary Shepherd and other chapter scholars have moved this work beyond knee-jerk reactions or inflammatory rhetoric. Gender equality is an important discussion, and this book is a very significant voice in that conversation.

The book is organized in four sections. The first lays out the issues of gender and equality given the Church's conservative parameters, documents the rise of Ordain Women, and seriously examines gender theology from both an institutional and a feminist perspective. It also looks at the principles at work in couples striving for egalitarian marriages and explores the dilemma of the largely excluded demographic of transgender members of the Church. Part 2, after laying a solid historical foundation of gender issues in the nineteenth and the twentieth centuries, then devotes thoughtful attention to the turbulent and confusing status of current attempts to find ecclesiastical equality, with a steadying hand from Community of Christ officer Robin Linkhart, who has lived through and has helped shape that transition in her own faith community.

Part 3 gives earnest attention to the Church's ability and processes of change, then deals with the painful crossroads at which personal conscience and perceived institutional needs result in the Church's implementation of its most extreme measure of control—excommunication. Against this sobering background, Part 4 provides a data-rich analysis of contemporary issues—what the possible effects of more sister missionaries and expanded integration might prove, the controversial and enlightening survey on Mormon gender issues conducted in 2013, the impact of social media, and the activities of Ordain Women as both a response to and an agent in contemporary feminist activism.

---

4. Neylan McBaine, *Women at Church: Magnifying Women's Local Impact* (Salt Lake City: Greg Kofford Books, 2014), see, among others, 58.

The trend of this often bumpy history of gender relations in the Church is irresistibly but slowly moving toward equality. Perhaps one of the most encouraging signs is that the publisher, Greg Kofford Books, has positioned itself as a responsible, honest, and thoughtful platform—deliberately avoiding polarization and sensationalism. It provides a place in which Neylan McBaine's *Women at Church* and *Voices for Equality,* along with Sheri Dew's *Women and the Priesthood,* can engage this issue respectfully and insightfully—not as the last word, but as the next voice in this ongoing conversation.

PART I

Conceptualizing the Issues of
Gender and Equality
in a Conservative Religious Faith

Chapter 1

The Birth of Ordain Women: The Personal Becomes Political

Lorie Winder Stromberg

We rejoice that we are privileged to live in this season of the history of the Church when questions are being asked about the priesthood. There is great interest and desire to know and understand more about the authority, power, and blessings associated with the priesthood of God. —Linda K. Burton, LDS Relief Society general president, May 2, 2013[1]

For most of us, Ordain Women began with a simple acknowledgement—"I'm a Mormon, and I believe women should be ordained." This realization came long ago for some and much more recently for others. It was a bold assertion in a patriarchal church where the lay priesthood and its attendant administrative and decision-making authority—in Mormon terms, the "priesthood keys" of governance—were seen as a divine power bestowed only on men, enabling them to speak for God and preside over church and home. The formal theological and practical arguments that supported such an acknowledgement had been constructed by a handful of Mormon feminists over three decades. However, a significant social movement could not coalesce around the issue of women and priesthood ordination in Mormonism until a profound shift in attitudes and expectations about gender equality emerged—one sufficient enough to create a critical dissonance between Mormon women's lived experience and LDS cultural norms. There also had to be an effective, far-reaching social platform to facilitate communication and collaboration among enough of those troubled by the dissonance that they, through an alchemy of personalities and social networks, were compelled to confront it.[2] Both came together in early 2013 with the birth of Ordain Women.

I am a generation older than most of Ordain Women's other organizers, and my personal feminist narrative reflected an emerging feminist movement in Mormonism that coincided with a broader push for women's rights nationwide during the last decades of the twentieth century. Privately, I began to consider the possibility of women's ordination in the late 1970s and talk about it more openly in the 1980s. My initial feminist awakening occurred in 1973, when, as a student

---

1. Linda K. Burton, "Priesthood Power—Available to All," Address, Women's Conference, Brigham Young University, May 2, 2013.
2. See Margaret Toscano, "The Mormon 'Ordain Women' Movement: The Virtue of Virtual Activism," *Feminism, and Religion in the 21st Century: Technology, Dialogue, and Expanding Borders*, edited by Gina Messina-Dysert and Rosemary Radford Ruether (New York: Routledge, 2015), 153–66.

at Brigham Young University, I was invited to attend a meeting of the Utah Valley Chapter of the Women's Political Caucus and decided to support the Equal Rights Amendment (ERA). The ERA, which passed Congress in 1972 and was in the process of being ratified by the states, quite simply prohibited discrimination on the basis of sex. It was a few years, however, before I focused my new-found feminism on the sexual discrimination in my religion. In the early 1970s, a *Deseret News* poll indicated that over 60 percent of Utah Mormons supported the ERA. However, by the mid-1970s it seemed likely that LDS Church leaders might officially oppose the ERA. They did, at first informally in a December 1974 speech prepared for Relief Society general president Barbara Bradshaw Smith, and later more adamantly in an official First Presidency statement on October 22, 1976. Thereafter, support for the amendment among Mormons plummeted.[3] As an active, faithful Mormon, I took their concerns seriously and questioned my commitment to the controversial amendment. However, after reexamining all the arguments for and against the ERA, I decided I could not in good conscience adopt the Church's position. This process led me to examine other beliefs and practices, including the Church's patriarchal structure.

When I finished my master's degree in 1977, I moved to Boston, in part because I wanted to work with *Exponent II*, a Mormon feminist newspaper founded there in 1974 and still being published today. I needed to wrestle with both my Mormonism and my feminism among other LDS feminists. Through that association, I became acquainted with a network of Mormon feminists in Utah and Boston who were rediscovering Mormon women's history, sponsoring retreats and public forums, and publishing essays that challenged traditional LDS views of gender, history, theology, and social mores. By the time Sonia Johnson was excommunicated in December of 1979 for publicly challenging the Church's active opposition to the ERA, some of us were beginning to question its all-male priesthood policy.

Pivotal to the early public discussion on women's ordination were groundbreaking essays, such as Nadine Hansen's "Women and Priesthood," published in *Dialogue* in 1981,[4] Margaret Merrill Toscano's "The Missing Rib: The Forgotten Place of Queens and Priestesses in the Establishment of Zion,"[5] which was given at a Sunstone Symposium in 1984 and later published in *Sunstone* magazine, and Linda King Newell's "The Historical Relationship of Mormon Women and

---

3. D. Michael Quinn, "The LDS Church's Campaign against the Equal Rights Amendment," *Journal of Mormon History* 20, no. 2 (Fall 1994): 105–7, http://digitalcommons.usu.edu/cgi/viewcontent.cgi?article=1023&context=mormonhistory. This and all other internet sources cited in this chapter were live and available as of May 12, 2015.

4. Nadine Hansen, "Women and Priesthood," *Dialogue: A Journal of Mormon Thought* 14, no. 4 (1981): 48–57.

5. Margaret Toscano, "The Missing Rib: The Forgotten Place of Queens and Priestesses in the Establishment of Zion, *Sunstone*, July 1985, 17–22, https://www.sunstonemagazine.com/pdf/051-16-22.pdf.

Priesthood,"[6] published in *Dialogue* in 1985 with material from *Sisters in Spirit: Mormon Women in Historical and Cultural Perspective*.[7] Hansen, a former Relief Society president, had been very involved with Mormons for ERA and the League of Women Voters education arm and had helped expose the Mormon money flowing into Virginia to fight the amendment, so she was practiced in dissecting the flaws in anti-feminist rhetoric. Her essay openly—and hopefully—raised the question of ordaining Mormon women and responded to the historical and practical arguments against female ordination. Toscano, a classicist and then nascent feminist scholar, reinforced and expanded the theological arguments suggested by Hansen and referenced possible historical precedents for women's ordination in early Mormonism. Newell, who was doing research for her groundbreaking biography of Emma Hale Smith, co-authored with Valeen Tippetts Avery, explored the question of women exercising spiritual gifts, including their formerly sanctioned practice of giving blessings and its possible implications for reexamining Mormonism's exclusionary male priesthood policy. My first public presentation referencing women and priesthood was at a Sunstone Symposium in 1985 as part of a panel discussion titled "Since Sonia: New Directions for Women and the Church." I suggested that, if the Church did not seriously grapple with feminist issues, including the ordination of women, I feared a future Sunstone panel might be titled, "Since Sonia: Divergent Directions for Women and the Church."

Several more essays and collections that bolstered previous historical and theological arguments for the ordination of women to the priesthood appeared in the ensuing years.[8] The explosion of Mormon feminist scholarship was accompanied by the founding of various LDS feminist forums and advocacy organizations, including the Mormon Women's Forum (1988), the BYU student-initiated Committee to Promote the Status of Women (1988)—later renamed VOICE

---

6. Linda King Newell, "The Historical Relationship of Mormon Women and the Priesthood," *Dialogue: A Journal of Mormon Thought* 18 (Autumn 1985): 21–32.

7. Maureen Ursenbach Beecher and Lavina Fielding Anderson, eds., *Sisters in Spirit: Mormon Women in Historical and Cultural Perspective* (Urbana: University of Illinois Press, 1985).

8. D. Michael Quinn, "Mormon Women Have Had the Priesthood Since 1843," an expansion of his "Response," *Sunstone* 6 (September-October 1981): 26–27, http://signaturebookslibrary.org/women-and-authority-17; Margaret M. Toscano, "Put on Your Strength, O Daughters of Zion: Claiming Priesthood and Knowing the Mother," http://signaturebookslibrary.org/women-and-authority-18/ Jill Mulvay Derr, "An Endowment of Power: The LDS Tradition," *Dialogue: A Journal of Mormon Thought* 16 (Autumn 1984): 17–21; Carol Cornwall Madsen, "Mormon Women and the Temple," in *Sisters in Spirit*, 80–110; Margaret Merrill Toscano and Paul James Toscano, *Strangers in Paradox: Explorations in Mormon Theology* (Salt Lake City: Signature Books, 1990), 179–97; Maxine Hanks, ed., *Women and Authority: Reemerging Mormon Feminism* (Salt Lake City: Signature Books, 1992, http://signaturebookslibrary.org/840/; and Sonja Farnsworth, "Mormonism's Odd Couple," *MWF Quarterly* 2, no. 1 (March 1991): 1, 6–11, http://66.147.244.239/~girlsgo6/mormonwomensforum/wp-content/uploads/2011/04/MWFVol2Num1.pdf; rpt. in Hanks, ed., *Women and Authority*, http://signaturebookslibrary.org/?p=975.

(1989)—and BYU's Women's Research Institute (1993). These as well as independent LDS forums and publications, such as *Dialogue, Sunstone,* the Sunstone Symposia, *Exponent II,* and the *Mormon Women's Forum Quarterly,* provided invaluable, though by their very nature limited, platforms for the discussion of Mormon feminist issues and public advocacy.

Sadly, an institutional crackdown followed. In his April 1989 LDS general conference address, Apostle Dallin H. Oaks warned about "alternate voices . . . in magazines, journals, and newspapers and at lectures, symposia, and conferences."[9] A few years later, in May of 1993, Apostle Boyd K. Packer, speaking to the All-Church Coordinating Council, identified feminists, intellectuals, and homosexuals as significant dangers to the Church.[10] The following September, six prominent LDS scholars and feminists, most of whom had addressed the question of women and priesthood ordination, were excommunicated or otherwise officially disciplined. One of them, Lynne Whitesides, who, as president of the Mormon Women's Forum, "called for leadership roles to be opened to women" and was disfellowshipped, told the *New York Times,* "We are not trying to tear the church down. . . . Instead, we are trying to give Mormon women a reason to stay in the church."[11] There also emerged a split in the Mormon feminist community between those who wanted more expansive opportunities for women in the Church but stopped short of advocating for significant structural change and those who called for full structural equality. Female ordination was the flashpoint.[12]

The resulting fear of institutional, cultural, and familial reprisal among those engaged in Mormon feminist advocacy was predictable, especially when the excommunications of Mormon Women's Forum activists Janice Allred (1995) and Margaret Toscano (2000) followed. By 2003, that fearful reaction prompted *Salt Lake Tribune* religion writer Peggy Fletcher Stack to ask, "Where Have All the Mormon Feminists Gone?"[13] What Stack's article overlooked was the emergence of electronic lists. Mormon feminism was establishing itself online. Among the first LDS feminist lists were Lynn Matthews Anderson's

---

9. Dallin H. Oaks, "Alternate Voices," April 1989, general conference, https://www.lds.org/general-conference/1989/04/alternate-voices?lang=eng.

10. Boyd K. Packer, "Talk to the All-Church Coordinating Council." Text available at http://www.zionsbest.com/face.html

11. Dirk Johnson, "As Mormon Church Grows, So Does Dissent from Mormon Scholars and Feminists," October 2, 1993, http://www.nytimes.com/1993/10/02/us/as-mormon-church-grows-so-does-dissent-from-feminists-and-scholars.html.

12. "In Search of Mormon Feminism: A Conversation with Lorie Winder Stromberg," Feminist Mormon Housewives, April 20, 2005, http://www.feministmormonhousewives.org/2005/04/lorie-winder-stromberg/ (accessed 2, 2015); also see Margaret Toscano, "The Mormon 'Ordain Women' Movement: The Virtue of Virtual Activism," 154.

13. Joanna Brooks, "Mormon Feminism Is Back," Religion Dispatches, September 22, 2010, http://religiondispatches.org/mormon-feminism-is-back/.

Electronic Latter-day Women's Caucus—Plus Men (ELWC+)[14] and Maxine Hanks's Mormon Feminist Network, which created private forums for the discussion of feminist issues throughout the 1990s and into the next decade. They brought together a community of Mormon feminists in the United States, Canada, and beyond. That community—and the possibility for feminist activism—increased dramatically when Mormon feminism entered the rapidly expanding social media age, with public blogs like Feminist Mormon Housewives (FMH, 2004), Exponent (2005–2006) and Zelophehad's Daughters (ZD, 2005), and, eventually, associated Facebook groups. As LDS scholar Joanna Brooks wrote, the internet became "a major game changer for Mormon feminists. . . . [W]omen who may have once felt isolated in their congregations . . . found a safe space to communicate and collaborate."[15]

In 2004, I penned "Power Hungry," an essay that raised anew the question of women's ordination. It was published in *Sunstone* and shared on feminist blogs.[16] I had survived the purges of the 1990s—shielded by the immense integrity of my local Church leaders—and enjoyed the camaraderie of a burgeoning online community. The transparency and reach of the internet made Mormon feminists feel less subject to the possibility of institutional reprisal. Still, widespread support for women's ordination remained elusive, even among those who identified themselves as Mormon and feminist. Given the Church's hierarchical, top-down male leadership structure, priesthood and decision-making authority were so synonymous with maleness that it was difficult to imagine it could be otherwise, let alone suggest that women could appropriately play a part in facilitating such a change. Decidedly activist groups like Women Advocating for Voice and Equality (WAVE, 2010)[17] and All Enlisted (2012)[18] were formed to advocate for substantive feminist initiatives within Mormonism, but they stopped short of calling for female ordination.

In 2012, understandably frustrated by the lack of movement on the issue of women's ordination—but encouraged by a growing desire among Mormon feminists to take action on various initiatives—I began to write and speak routinely

---

14. Lorie Winder Stromberg, "The Sacred and the Mundane: Mormon Feminism on the Internet," *Mormon Women's Forum Quarterly* 7, nos. 1–2 (1996): 1–15, http://66.147.244.239/~girlsgo6/mormonwomensforum/wp-content/uploads/2011/10/MWfVol7Num12.pdf.

15. Brooks, "Mormon Feminism Is Back."

16. Lorie Winder Stromberg, "Power Hungry," *Sunstone* December 2004, 60–61, https://www.sunstonemagazine.com/pdf/135-60-61.pdf (accessed May 8, 215); rpt. in Feminist Mormon Housewives, April 14, 2005, http://www.feministmormonhousewives.org/2005/04/guest-post-power-hungry/.

17. See http://www.ldswave.org/?page_id=83.

18. For example, All Enlisted promoted a letter-writing campaign to ask that women be allowed to offer prayers in LDS general conference sessions, heretofore only offered by men. http://letwomenpray.blogspot.com/.

about women and priesthood ordination in discussions on Mormon feminist blogs and Facebook groups. The idea of women's ordination had to enter the realm of the thinkable and the familiar before it could enter the realm of the possible. Inspired by a February 3, 2012, Sunstone West Symposium presentation organized by *Exponent* blogger Caroline Kline—which featured feminist women religious from a variety of faith traditions—and aching for cohesive, coordinated activism on women's ordination in the Mormon feminist community, I wrote an *Exponent* blog post about the decidedly activist Roman Catholic Women Priests[19] and proposed a "Catholic/Mormon Dialogue on Women's Ordination." The dialogue was sponsored by the Women's Studies in Religion program at Claremont Graduate University in September 2012 and later reprised in March 2013 at the Sunstone West Symposium in Berkeley. Anticipating the dialogue, I also approached the women with whom I had collaborated a few years earlier to produce an online, feminist statement[20] in response to LDS Relief Society general president Julie B. Beck's troublingly regressive 2007 general conference address, "Mothers Who Know."[21] I asked them to help me prepare and mail an online petition to Church leaders calling on them to thoughtfully consider and earnestly pray about the question of women's ordination and the integration of women into the decision-making structure of the Church. Like the women at WAVE, I believed that what we conceptualized and called for as Mormon feminists had to be clearly stated, specific, and actionable. How could we realistically expect male Church leaders to respond to our nebulous hope for a more equitable church? We needed to document our desires.

Titled "All Are Alike unto God,"[22] the online petition, in solidarity with WAVE, also enumerated several interim measures—supported by egalitarian and complementarian feminists[23] alike—that could be implemented immediately by Church leaders to foster a more equitable religious community. Some of these initiatives included heightening the visibility of women and girls, using gender-inclusive language, including women regularly in all administrative councils, recognizing women as official witnesses at baptisms and temple weddings, and

---

19. Lorie Winder Stromberg, "Sacred Disobedience: Women's Call to Ordination," Exponent Blog, June 8, 2012, http://www.the-exponent.com/sacred-disobedience-womens-call-to-ministry/.

20. "What Women Know," http://whatwomenknow.org/.

21. Julie B. Beck, "Mothers Who Know," https://www.lds.org/general-conference/2007/10/mothers-who-know.

22. "All Are Alike unto God," http://whatwomenknow.org/all_are_alike/.

23. This theological concept, particularly prominent in conservative, Evangelical Christianity, Orthodox Judaism, and Islam, is that men and women have different, but complementary, roles. See Neylan McBaine, "To Do the Business of the Church: A Cooperative Paradigm for Examining Gendered Participation within Church Organizational Structure," an address given at the FAIR Conference in August, 2012, http://www.fairmormon.org/perspectives/fair-conferences/2012-fair-conference/2012-to-do-the-business-of-the-church-a-cooperative-paradigm.

calling women to perform interviews and pastoral counseling, particularly for girls and women who had been sexually abused. Such interim steps as well as others detailed in "All Are Alike unto God," the Let Women Pray initiative, and WAVE's list of simple, gender-inclusive changes, were important; but I believed the fundamental inequity of an all-male priesthood was such that anything less than ordination was insufficient. Too, an exclusive priesthood policy seemed at odds with what I understood to be foundational to Mormonism, namely, the expansive belief that God's power was not to be hoarded as if it were in short supply or reserved for an elite few, but must be shared and available to all who righteously sought it. Central to the LDS doctrine of deity and priesthood, I believed, was a simple truth I learned from a Christian scholar: Power used to control or dominate others would always burn itself out. Only power used to empower others was everlasting.[24] I also believed LDS doctrine supported a moral activism that held us responsible for our choice either to perpetuate inequality through silence and inaction or work for justice and equality.[25]

Given this narrative, it is not surprising that, when Kate Kelly telephoned in January of 2013 to propose a direct action related to women's ordination, I was willing to collaborate. At the time, Kate was an attorney with the Robert F. Kennedy Center for Justice and Human Rights in Washington, D.C., and her life was at a crossroads. Her work highlighted the dissonance between the equity for which she advocated daily in her secular life and the gender inequity she tolerated in her religious life. She could no longer justify inaction. Her parents, both LDS converts, operated with total parity in their marriage, and, like her mother, Donna, Kate assumed she would go to law school. Religiously orthodox and politically conservative, she went to Brigham Young University (1999–2006) and studied political science. In a religion class on the "Teachings of the Living Prophets," she was assigned a paper with the prompt, "What the Prophets Have to Say about . . ." She chose to research what Church leaders had said about women working outside the home. She read all the talks she could find on the topic and started to sob. She realized the life she wanted was incompatible with what she was reading.

Still, she tried to move forward. A self-described "intuitive feminist," Kate said she "intuited the power imbalance between those who went on missions and

---

24. See Scott Bartchy as quoted in Stromberg, "Power Hungry."

25. Mormon doctrine teaches that men and women are not mere instruments in God's hands, but co-actors with God. Chieko Okazaki, a counselor in the Relief Society General Presidency, wrote: "In most Mormon gatherings, if I were to ask who you are, particularly what your eternal identity is, many would answer, 'I am a child of God.' It is a beautiful answer shaped by the Primary song we have learned and loved for two generations. But that is not enough. Every living person is a child of God. But that's . . . not the ending point. The ending point is to become peers of God, friends of God, coworkers of God, adults of God." Chieko Okazaki, *Being Enough* (Salt Lake City: Bookcraft, 2002), 61.

those who didn't,"[26] and interrupted her studies to serve a mission for the Church in Spain. Her father, Jim, who, though twice a bishop, had not served a mission, was a "zealous missionary who gave copies of the Book of Mormon to people he met on the ski lift" and wrote a postcard to Kate every day of her mission. Equally zealous, Kate loved her mission (2002–2004). Because she worked with immigrants and those less fortunate, it also radicalized her politically. Too, she felt the unfairness of being passed over for leadership roles, though she was often more qualified than the male missionaries. She also came up against the glass wall of "loving and shepherding" the people she taught but whom, lacking priesthood ordination, she was unable to baptize.

When Kate returned to BYU to complete her studies, she met her future husband Neil Ransom, an anthropology major who campaigned for Ralph Nader, and Ashley Sanders, an English and philosophy major from Salt Lake City who, like Kate, entered BYU as a political conservative—indeed, "almost libertarian"[27]—but, frustrated by what she saw as a lack of honesty and transparency at BYU, became decidedly liberal and activist. Ashley, her roommate Chelsea Shields Strayer, an anthropology major who would later become active with Mormons for ERA and WAVE, and a group of their friends held a weekly discussion night where they explored a wide range of topics from hip hop to revolutionary movements. During this time, Ashley became a researcher for philosophy professor David L. Paulsen, who, with Martin Pulido, was working on a survey of historical teachings about Mother in Heaven that was later published in *BYU Studies*[28] and referenced in "Becoming like God," one of the Gospel Topics essays on the Church's website.[29] She was struck by the "paternalism of not talking about the divine feminine" in the Church and started debating the idea of a Mother God during their weekly discussion nights. Troubled by issues of free speech, censorship, and student government's lack of power and influence, several members of the discussion night group became student activists, staging successful demonstrations that attracted media coverage to the normally protest-free campus.[30] When it was announced that former Vice President Dick Cheney would be the commencement speaker their senior year, Ashley suggested that the

---

26. Kate Kelly, interviewed by Lorie Winder Stromberg, March 29, 2015, and April 9, 2015, digital recordings in my possession. Unless otherwise noted, all quotations attributed to Kate Kelly are from these two interviews.

27. Ashley Sanders, interviewed by Lorie Winder Stromberg, April 22, 2015, notes in my possession. Unless otherwise noted, all quotations attributed to Ashley Sanders are from this interview.

28. David L. Paulsen and Martin Pulido, "'A Mother There': A Survey of Historical Teachings about Mother in Heaven," *BYU Studies* 50, no. 1 (2011): 70–97.

29. "Becoming like God," https://www.lds.org/topics/becoming-like-god?lang=eng.

30. See, for example, Shinika A. Sykes, "Protesters Say BYU Squelches Free Expression," *Salt Lake Tribune*, April 1, 2006, http://archive.sltrib.com/article.php?id=3661938&itype=NGPSID.

group sponsor an alternative commencement. They raised $23,125, rented the then-McKay Center at Utah Valley State College[31] and invited Ralph Nader to speak. They also planned a protest during the official commencement.

When Ashley left BYU in 2007, she began working for the Sunstone Education Foundation and devoured books and articles on Mormon history and feminism. While she was troubled that Mormonism had abandoned its "visionary, communitarian roots," she was particularly struck by Margaret Merrill Toscano's "Are Boys More Important than Girls: The Continuing Conflict of Gender Difference and Equality in Mormonism." Published that year in *Sunstone* magazine,[32] Toscano's article deftly documented the LDS Church's structural gender inequality. Like others, Ashley questioned why women were excluded from priesthood ordination, which, since 1978, had been extended to all worthy men and boys in the Church over the age of twelve regardless of race. She shared her concerns with Kate and Neil, who married and eventually headed to graduate school in Washington, D.C.

While Kate was attending law school at American University Washington College of Law, most of her friends, including Ashley, decided they could no longer actively participate in the LDS Church. One, concerned about gender inequality, told Kate, "I became irrelevant to the Church, and so the Church became irrelevant to me." While she had a decidedly feminist sensibility, Kate was focused on law school and working for gender equity outside of the Mormon community. Ashley began to press the issue of gender inequality in the Church during her frequent discussions with Kate. By the fall of 2011, Ashley was a political organizer in Washington, D.C., working with Occupy DC Freedom Plaza, and often stayed with Kate and Neil. Chelsea Shields Strayer, having completed her graduate coursework at Boston University, moved to Baltimore with her husband Mike Strayer, where he attended Johns Hopkins and she associated with *Exponent II* co-editor Aimee Evans Hickman and blogged at Exponent. Weary of talking about gender inequality without taking action, Chelsea helped found WAVE in 2010, penning a particularly influential piece for the WAVE website that laid bare the structural gender inequality in the Church,[33] and became interested in working to pass the Equal Rights Amendment. She and Kate met through Ashley and attended the August 2012 "We Are Women" rally together in Washington, D.C., representing Mormons for ERA.

---

31. Brittani Lusk, "Students Talk about Idea behind Alternative BYU Commencement," *Herald Extra*, May 14, 2007, http://www.heraldextra.com/news/students-talk-about-idea-behind-alternative-byu-commencement/article_d989e6c3-fb59-58c5-9d1a-5eaa40dad690.html. Utah Valley State College became Utah Valley University in July 2008.

32. Margaret Merrill Toscano, "Are Boys More Important than Girls? The Continuing Conflict of Gender Difference and Equality in Mormonism," *Sunstone* June 2007, 19-29.

33. Chelsea Shields Strayer, "Ask a Feminist," LDS WAVE, http://www.ldswave.org/?p=402#comments.

Chelsea told Kate about her work in the Mormon feminist community. Kate had not participated much in Mormon feminist forums, online or otherwise; however, encouraged by Chelsea, she signed up for the annual *Exponent* retreat in New Hampshire in September 2012. While she enjoyed it, she thought too many of those in attendance "seemed satisfied with the status quo" and restlessly felt that there appeared to be "a lot of talking and not doing anything." By this time, Kate was working on global women's rights issues and found that her "orthodoxy increasingly clashed with [her] authenticity." She could no longer "sustain the disconnect" and decided she had to do something. Like Lynne Whitesides before her, she needed a reason for women to stay in the Church. Her activism was "a retention effort."[34] She was aware of All Enlisted's Wear Pants to Church campaign. However, she "thought it was a colossal waste of time" and decided not to participate. In a series of conversations with Ashley, Kate indicated that she "wanted total gender parity in the Church." Schooled in activism, Ashley advised Kate that whatever her goal, it had to be actionable. Ashley then pointed out that "the greatest indicator of structural inequality in the Church was women's lack of priesthood." In activist parlance, ordination had to be "the ask."

Convinced, Kate told Ashley she wanted "to do something big" and proposed dropping a banner calling for women's ordination over a balcony in a session of the April 2013 LDS general conference. She asked Ashley if she thought their activist friends from BYU would help her, initially envisioning that participating in such an action "might be terrifying to Mormons and only appeal to a few friends and radicals." The problem was that most of their friends were disillusioned and no longer active in the Church. Kate had what popular FMH blogger and podcast host Lindsay Hansen Park described as the "boldness, drive and naïve optimism of a Ralph Nader supporter."[35] What she did not have were enough contacts or credibility in the Mormon feminist community. Few knew who she was. Clearly, she needed to tap into the Mormon social media network. Kate thought about calling John Dehlin, who occasionally attended their BYU discussion nights and who had a significant online presence with the Mormon Stories Foundation. In early January of 2013, she decided to call John and ask him if he knew any Mormon women who might be willing to do the direct action.

John and I had talked about women's ordination on a number of occasions, and he knew about "All Are Alike unto God," which by the end of 2012 had been signed by hundreds of Mormons. He gave Kate my name and suggested that she also contact media-savvy Chelsea Robarge Fife, FMH blogger/podcast host Lindsay Hansen Park, FMH founder Lisa Patterson Butterworth, and Joanna Brooks, an LDS writer and academic who had become an articulate and highly

---

34. Peggy Fletcher Stack, "Mormons Launch Online Push to Ordain Women to the Priesthood," *Salt Lake Tribune*, April 4, 2013, http://www.sltrib.com/sltrib/news/56096212-78/women-church-priesthood-lds.html.

35. Lindsay Hansen Park, interviewed by Lorie Winder Stromberg, April 20, 2015, notes in my possession.

visible, though unofficial, media commentator during the so-called Mormon Moment—an intense period of interest in all things Mormon that accompanied Mitt Romney's 2012 bid for the U.S. presidency and the 2011 Broadway premiere of the hit musical *The Book of Mormon*. John also mentioned Kimberly Brinkerhoff and Stephanie Lauritzen, who had worked on the December 2012 Wear Pants to Church initiative to shine a light on gender inequality in the Church. The action was not just about the choice of Sunday apparel for the more than 1,000 women who participated. According to the *New York Times*, the event used "attire as a symbolic first salvo in a larger struggle over gender inequalities" with the hope that "the dialogue [would] now expand to include issues like the ordination of women."[36] That some of its organizers received death threats punctuated both the absurdity and the depth of resistance to feminist initiatives in Mormonism and generated national media attention.

Kate's telephone call to Lindsay Hansen Park garnered the names of at least two more women: FMH blogger and labor organizer Natalie Kelly and BYU student and Young Mormon Feminist blog founder Hannah Wheelwright, both of whom would become integral to the formation of Ordain Women. Hannah would also emerge as one of its most prominent spokespeople.

Hannah grew up on the East Coast in a large Mormon family. Precocious, she attended the Madeira School in McLean, Virginia. Though she often grew impatient with the incessant "stories of women who fought valiantly for their liberties"[37] that were told and retold at the elite, all-girls school, when she chose to attend BYU, she went with the expectation that the anti-feminist perspective her classmates associated with the LDS university was outdated. Hannah was deeply disturbed to find it was not. "I saw every stereotype about women placing the entirety of their self-worth on their status as a wife and mother, women accepting men as superior beings in both intellect and spirituality, women accepting the extent of their accomplishments in life to be restricted to their abilities to procreate. . . . I was enraged to see women actively perpetuating such limitations," she wrote.[38] One evening in 2011, Hannah pulled out her scriptures, which she had committed to reading in their entirety over the course of the school year. She read the passage in Genesis 3:16 where God tells Eve: "Thy desire shall be to thy husband, and he shall rule over thee." She stopped and knelt by her bed. She knew women were integral to God's plan but wanted to know if they "were somehow less."[39] As she struggled with the gendered messages she encountered and endured lectures from disapproving home teachers, she tried to

---

36. Timothy Pratt, "Mormon Women Set Out to Take a Stand, in Pants," *New York Times*, December 19, 2012, http://www.nytimes.com/2012/12/20/us/19mormon.html.

37. Hannah Wheelwright, "My Story," Young Mormon Feminists blog, July 12, 2012, http://youngmormonfeminists.org/2012/07/22/my-story/#more-15.

38. Ibid.

39. Hannah Wheelwright, Ordain Women Launch, April 6, 2013, https://www.youtube.com/watch?v=0CGrX67OH-0

disentangle what was doctrinal from what was cultural. She googled "feminism and Mormonism" and found Feminist Mormon Housewives as well as other sites, articles, and relevant books. It was in a discussion on FMH that Hannah first encountered Mormon women talking about female ordination. The more she studied the reasons given for why women should not be ordained, the more she believed ordination was essential.

In the summer of 2012, Hannah looked for feminist groups on campus where she could discuss Mormonism and gender issues. She found none, nor did she find a feminist Facebook group for BYU students. Given what she had heard about the uneasy relationship between the BYU administration and past groups, such as VOICE, she decided to start an off-campus discussion group, Provo Feminists, and, after a conversation with FMH's Lisa Butterworth, a blog called Young Mormon Feminists. She received a call in August from the *Salt Lake Tribune*'s Peggy Fletcher Stack, who had read the nascent blog and wanted to interview her for an article focusing on Mormon women seeking a middle ground toward greater equality. During the interview, Hannah stated, "Female ordination is the only ultimate signal of equality."[40] Such a bold, straight-forward assertion from a BYU student employed at the Church's Missionary Training Center stunned even the seasoned reporter. Lindsay had interviewed Hannah for FMH and knew of her public support for women's ordination. She told Hannah that a direct action had been proposed and suggested that Hannah contact Kate. Hannah was tentative at first. She had no idea who Kate was, but she was "gung ho about doing something."[41]

After Kate made the initial contacts, she scheduled the first "All Call," a group telephone call that included all who were interested in participating, on January 20, 2013. Kate had "little literacy in activism" but had exceptionally activist friends who were professional community organizers, including Katie Savage, Thelma Young, Renae Widdison, and, of course, Ashley. They explained how to organize direct actions, including structuring the necessary committees, planning for contingencies, and facilitating remote meetings, since we were all over the map geographically and had to do everything by telephone, email, or in online groups. The proposed action also needed a website to "put a human face" on the participants and "control the narrative."

The call itself was lengthy. It was focused primarily on facilitating an action in conjunction with the upcoming April general conference, less than four months away, and only secondarily on putting a plan in place for sustained collaboration and long-term work with other groups. Kate emphasized that group members were expected to participate, not just offer advice. She also purchased a few domain

---

40. Peggy Fletcher Stack, "Mormon Women Seeking Middle Ground to Greater Equality," *Salt Lake Tribune*, August 23, 2012, http://www.sltrib.com/54701143.

41. Hannah Wheelwright, interviewed by Lorie Winder Stromberg, March 25, 2015, digital recording in my possession. Unless otherwise noted, all quotations attributed to Hannah Wheelwright are from this interview.

names. We settled on OrdainWomen.org and began to talk about the website and committee assignments: communications/media, action, logistics/volunteers. Kate suggested that each participant do a personal video akin to those on the Church's "I'm a Mormon" site. Visitors to the website could click on each video and see that every action participant cared deeply about the Church and its members and wanted to help make it a more inclusive, equitable religious community.

I immediately loved the idea of an "I'm a Mormon, and I believe women should be ordained" campaign. Seeing the courage it took to post such personal profiles as a feminist action in and of itself, I thought we should accept submissions from any Mormon who was willing to go public with their support for women's ordination, whether or not they chose to participate in the action. Since I was technologically challenged, I also argued that we should allow people to submit written statements, accompanied by a photo or two, rather than require them to submit a video. Kate, focused on the action, resisted accepting submissions from anyone who did not plan to participate or was not a Mormon in good standing. The discussion continued in a private Facebook planning group, which Kate set up within a week after the initial call. A few of us, accomplished writer Holly Welker most insistently, argued that women like Lavina Fielding Anderson and Margaret Toscano had been excommunicated for speaking out on issues related to gender equity and women's ordination—the very things for which we were agitating. It seemed hypocritical to exclude them. What became the Ordain Women profile submission policy was lifted out of a comment I posted during that discussion: "We are not soliciting, nor do we support, diatribes against the Church of Jesus Christ of Latter-day Saints. We encourage thoughtful submissions on what the ordination of women would mean to you personally and/or for the institutional Church. We welcome those who are faithful Mormons, those who might return to the Church but for gender inequality, or those who care deeply about the Church and its members and are concerned about how gender inequality affects all of us." This discussion illustrates the collaborative decision-making that was foundational to the Ordain Women movement. So, too, is the fact that, by the end of the second All Call on January 27, 2013, we had abandoned the original action proposal.

It became clear almost immediately that there was significant resistance to the proposed action, with some questioning its effectiveness and others expressing concern about any action that might disrupt sacred space. As a professional labor organizer, Natalie, for example, thought our focus should be on building a sustainable movement that would mobilize Mormon women.[42] She was concerned that the banner drop was too militant for an initial action. Kate was understandably disappointed. She was committed to direct action and did not

---

42. Natalie Kelly, interviewed by Lorie Winder Stromberg, May 22, 2015, notes in my possession. For Natalie Kelly's thoughts on Mormon feminist activism during this time, see Nat Kelly, "Activism and FMH: Can We Change the Church," Feminist Mormon Housewives, February 26, 2013, http://www.feministmormonhousewives.org/2013/02/activism-and-fmh-can-we-change-the-church/.

want the nascent effort to devolve into yet another discussion group. We spent much of the second call brainstorming alternative actions. During the course of the discussion, one of the early organizers suggested we do something related to the priesthood session of general conference. A number of ideas were proposed before we settled on waiting as a group of women in the standby line for tickets to the all-male session. If we were admitted, we would attend. If not, there could be no better visual symbol of our exclusion. Either would make a significant statement. What we needed were women who shared our hope for ordination and were willing to stand with us.

We went to work on the website. Kate suggested we launch it on March 17, 2013, to mark the founding of the Nauvoo Relief Society. Kate's husband, Neil, enlisted the help of Jason Dilworth, a former missionary companion with expertise in topography and graphic communication. Together, Kate, Neil, and Jason came up with what they hoped would be a Mormon-friendly site design. Having collaboratively written the FAQ for the All Are Alike unto God website, it made sense for me to write the FAQ for the Ordain Women website with input from Kate and Michelle Weiner of Agitating Faithfully. We wanted the tone of the site to be clear, unapologetic, inclusively faith-affirming, and reasonable, and so we tweaked our mission statement in a series of emails back and forth. We approached those of our friends in the Mormon feminist community whom we knew supported women's ordination and asked them to submit a personal statement, or profile, that asserted: "I'm a Mormon, and I believe women should be ordained." Sensitive to the fear many felt in going public, we promised them that we would not launch the website unless we had at least twenty profiles. Caroline Kline shared my email soliciting a profile with the rest of the Exponent bloggers, many of whom were well known and trusted. That several of them decided to submit some of the first profiles lent Ordain Women significant early credibility in the online Mormon feminist community. The website launched with just over twenty profiles on the same weekend as Sunstone West, where Roman Catholic representatives Victoria Rue and Christine Haider-Winnett and Sunstone's Mary Ellen Robertson, Margaret Toscano, and I reprised the "Catholic/Mormon Dialogue on Women's Ordination" and informally announced the imminent birth of Ordain Women. When Kate clicked the website live on the opposite coast, many did not yet know that we already were planning the priesthood session action.

Word of the Ordain Women website spread rapidly throughout the Mormon blogs. The website received nearly 10,000 discrete hits in its first twenty-four hours. Its reasonable tone, the presence of profiles featuring women who were known and admired in the Mormon online community, and the simple boldness of declaring publicly, "I'm a Mormon, and I believe women should be ordained," were compelling. We expected to receive more submissions from our friends and contacts in the Mormon feminist community. And we did. Both stunned and moved by the website, respected Doves and Serpents blogger Heather Olson Beal, for example, not only submitted a profile, but soon shepherded volunteers with Chelsea Shields

Strayer, worked tirelessly in the leadership planning group, and, eventually, joined the Ordain Women Executive Board, as did Chelsea. In response to a FOX 13 News story titled "Feminists Call for LDS Church to Give Women the Priesthood"—which conflated the Catholic/Mormon dialogue with the launch of the Ordain Women website—Church spokesman Scott Trotter issued the following statement: "It is the doctrine of the Church that men and women are equal. The Church follows the pattern of the Savior when it comes to priesthood ordination."[43]

By the first week of April, the website had received over 100,000 hits, and the profiles more than doubled. Emboldened, many more who had been hesitant just a week or so before submitted profiles. What we did not expect, as news of the website went viral, was the variety of profiles that were submitted by Mormons we either had not contacted personally or did not know in the Mormon online community—including a currently serving bishop from the Midwest. Nancy Ross and Debra Jenson, two women who would become Ordain Women Executive Board members, were among them. Nancy, a professor of art history, said she "received a personal testimony of women's ordination a year before, [but] was told to wait." She had lurked for a long time on FMH and had not participated much until All Enlisted's December 2012 Wear Pants to Church action. When she saw a link to the Ordain Women website, she read everything. The site's tone was appealing to her, but "it looked so Mormony" that she sent an email to ask if it was legitimate. Both excited and anxious, she "had to act"[44] and immediately submitted a profile. A few months later, she joined the Ordain Women planning group and began helping the budding social media committee post profiles on the site. Debra, a professor of communication and member of her ward Relief Society presidency, had reactivated in the LDS Church when she was a teenager. She described herself as having a "firm testimony of Christ, loving Heavenly Parents," and the "sealing power of the priesthood," but as a girl she "chafed at what boys could do that she couldn't."[45] She "didn't begrudge men the priesthood"—she loved and admired her devout LDS husband and son—she just believed priesthood ordination should also be extended to women. Debra remembered reading a 1997 interview with President Gordon B. Hinckley. When asked by a reporter if the Church's exclusionary priesthood policy could change for women—much as it had for black men in 1978—Hinckley responded, "Yes. But there's no agitation for that."[46] Debra clung to that statement for fifteen

---

43. "Feminists Call For LDS Church to Give Women the Priesthood," Fox 13 Salt Lake City, March 21, 2013, http://fox13now.com/2013/03/21/feminists-call-for-lds-to-give-women-priesthood/.

44. Nancy Ross, Interviewed by Lorie Winder Stromberg, April 14, 2015, notes in my possession. Unless noted, all quotations attributed to Nancy Ross are from this interview.

45. Debra Jenson, Ordain Women Launch Event, April 6, 2013, https://www.youtube.com/watch?v=d5bAdVwVSQM.

46. Gordon B. Hinckley, interviewed by David Ransom, ABC Australia, November 9, 1997, http://www.abc.net.au/compass/intervs/hinckley.htm.

years, and then she saw the Ordain Women website. It was, she said, "an answer to years of prayer," not only for herself but for her daughters.

We were gratified by the reaction to the website. It had an appeal far beyond what we had anticipated. What Kate originally saw as a platform to facilitate a series of actions took on a life of its own. The website struck a chord. The profiles were powerful—many reflected the familiar Mormon discourse of testimony[47]— and women's ordination was being discussed throughout the Mormon online community and beyond. Margaret Toscano noted, the "brave women and men who first posted their testimonies placed their Church membership and status on the line because of their deep spiritual convictions about the need for women's ordination. Others quickly responded through online blogs and social media, with some expressing their support for the movement."[48] We felt a responsibility to honor the trust people put in us when they shared their souls. However, while we clearly stated on the website that Ordain Women intended to engage in direct action, we had no idea how many of those who trusted us with their profiles intended to participate in direct action, let alone knew what the term meant. And April conference was two weeks away. In a series of phone calls and emails, we decided that it was too soon after the launch of the website to effectively organize the priesthood session action for April. We needed time, not only to gauge the depth of our support, but also to let the idea of direct action percolate. We likewise needed to show that we had explored every other proper channel of communication with Church leaders—that without priesthood office or access, public advocacy was our only option. We put the priesthood session action on hold until the Church's semi-annual general conference in October.

Instead of the priesthood session action in April, we planned a formal Ordain Women launch event at the University of Utah student union on Saturday, April 6. The event was a substantive alternative to the semi-annual "Ladies Night Out" activities sponsored by Deseret Book, the Quilted Bear, and other craft venues in Salt Lake City during the Saturday priesthood session. Though on the East Coast, Kimberly Brinkerhoff, skilled in media relations, helped craft a press release and deftly coordinated interviews with news agencies before the launch. The event brought together Ordain Women organizers and supporters, many of whom had only met online, and attracted significant media attention. On Friday, April 5, the day before the launch event, the Church's newsroom uploaded an unusual video interview with the three presidents of the women's, young women's, and children's auxiliaries—Linda K. Burton, Elaine S. Dalton, and Rosemary M. Wixom, respectively—in which they addressed the role of women in the Church and the question of women and priesthood ordination. They asserted that women did not want the authority of the priesthood but were content with its blessings

---

47. Toscano, "The Mormon 'OrdainWomen' Movement," 158.
48. Ibid., 154.

and power.[49] Many saw the video as a direct response to news of Ordain Women's launch. Recognizing the wide reach of social media, Kate arranged for the launch to be filmed and uploaded onto the website.[50]

Organizers met on the Friday evening before Saturday's launch event for a leadership/action training that Ashley organized. It was also a chance to finalize the program for the launch and get to know each other offline. On Saturday, Kate, Hannah, and I spoke with the press, and we anxiously waited for the auditorium to fill up. Kate opened the launch with a brief introduction that included her own personal narrative. Mary Ellen Robertson, Margaret Toscano, and I gave more formal presentations that laid out the reasons and historical precedents for women's ordination, after which Debra—whom we really knew only through her profile—and Hannah spoke movingly about how they each had come to believe that women should be ordained. A question and answer period followed. More like a church meeting than a rally, the evening was both informative and galvanizing for the approximately 80-100 people present.

We prepared sign-up sheets, and a number of those present volunteered to help with future organizing, including Exponent blogger April Young Bennett and attorney Mark Barnes. Smart and articulate, April, who would soon join the Ordain Women Executive Board, crafted an influential multi-media presentation on historical precedents for women's ordination, kept the discussion on women's ordination alive in numerous blog posts, and became a thoughtful and reliable local spokesperson. Not unlike many of our supporters, Mark's participation in Mormonism was energized by Ordain Women and the possibility of women's ordination. His mother and uncle actively opposed the Church's pre-1978 exclusionary policy of denying priesthood to black men and temple participation to both black men and black women. Mark became a passionate and hard-working male ally, proved himself indispensable when it came to local logistics, and eventually joined the Ordain Women Executive Board. With tutoring from Joanna Brooks, we crafted simple, clear talking points to help us succinctly capture our message in media interviews. Kate and Hannah, who easily—and from all indications authentically—spoke with faith and optimism, emerged from the launch as seasoned, effective spokespeople.

In response to media requests from reporters covering the launch, the Church's Public Affairs department issued the following statement:

> There is nothing in the scriptures which suggests that to be a man rather than a woman is preferred in the sight of God, or that He places a higher value on sons than on daughters.
>
> The worth of a human soul is not defined by a set of duties or responsibilities. In God's plan for His children, both women and men have the same access to the guid-

---

49. Peggy Fletcher Stack, "Women Want Blessings of Priesthood, Not Authority, Say Mormon Leaders," *Salt Lake Tribune,* April 6, 2013, http://www.sltrib.com/sltrib/news/56114167-78/women-church-lds-leaders.html.

50. Ordain Women Launch Event Videos, http://ordainwomen.org/resources/.

ance of His spirit, to personal revelation, faith and repentance, to grace and the atonement of His Son, Jesus Christ, and are received equally as they approach Him in prayer.

The practice of ordaining men to the priesthood was established by Jesus Christ himself, and is not a decision to be made by those on Earth.[51]

It became clear with the launch event that we were in dialogue with the institutional Church—but only through the media. As we continued our efforts with Ordain Women, we repeatedly asked for meetings with the Church's hierarchy, through both informal channels and either hand-delivered or electronic letters. A number of us over the years had met with our local Church leaders to discuss issues of gender equity. However, they had no power to address or remedy Church-wide structural inequality and, stuck in a sort of Catch 22, most personal letters sent to the hierarchy were routinely sent back to stake or ward leaders. Following the massive Let Women Pray letter-writing campaign in January-March 2013, many in the Mormon feminist community were heartened that on April 6, Jean A. Stevens, first counselor in the Primary general presidency, became the first women in the Church's over 180-year history to pray in a session of general conference. It was certainly a step toward greater visibility for women. However, as Harvard historian and former *Exponent II* board member Laurel Thatcher Ulrich astutely told the *Salt Lake Tribune*, "I am sure this gesture ... was well meant, but it actually exposes rather than solves the problem."[52]

For Kate, "there is certainly a place for consciousness-raising in every single movement, but it is substantively different than activism. ... [A]ctivism is the use of direct action, like a demonstration, to openly confront a problem with the explicit goal of bringing about social change." Not all of us shared Kate's definition of what constituted activism. I saw many of the initiatives that came before Ordain Women as well as our own profiles as effectively activist, particularly given the reach of social media. Further, we grappled with the question as to what was appropriate "religious" as opposed to "political" action, particularly when, as April pointed out, political advocacy was seen as patriotic, while advocacy in a religious setting might appear disloyal. Later Nancy Ross prepared and administered surveys of those who participated in Ordain Women actions, either in person or by requesting that their name be carried by proxy. They revealed that well over 70 percent of respondents were active in the Church—an activity rate that most LDS wards would envy. That their commitment to the faith might be questioned was troubling. How—or whether—to translate direct political action into direct religious action became a running debate. Clearly, in choosing and executing the priesthood session action, we were negotiating that space. The

---

51. Brittany Green-Minor and Todd Tanner, "Mormon Group Pushes for Women to Get the Priesthood," Fox13 News, Salt Lake City, April 3, 2013, http://fox13now.com/2013/04/03/mormon-group-pushes-for-women-to-get-the-priesthood/.

52. Peggy Fletcher Stack, "So Are Mormon Women Really Making Progress? Views Differ," *Salt Lake Tribune*, April 9, 2013, http://www.sltrib.com/sltrib/blogsfaithblog/56131993-180/women-church-mormon-lds.html.csp.

question initially was whether to go public with plans for the action. It soon was clear that such an action would be hard to orchestrate privately. The question then became when to announce it publicly.

After the launch, Kate and I met in Washington, D.C., with representatives from the Women's Ordination Conference (WOC), a group founded in the 1970s to advocate for female ordination in the Roman Catholic Church. (See Chapter 19.) We hoped that continuing the public dialogue would shine a light on the exclusionary priesthood policies of both churches. We were also concerned about how gender inequality in religion negatively affected the lives of women throughout the world. In my Ordain Women profile, I had written: "We more readily recognize and decry inequity when it's blatantly abusive. But even discrimination that is subtle can negatively affect us in profound ways. To deny women access to decision-making authority in any community—religious or otherwise–opens up a space for the more extreme forms of discrimination and abuse that millions of women in the world endure." Why, I wondered, when we increasingly refused to tolerate discrimination in the secular world, did we accept it in our churches, shrines, synagogues, and mosques? At its best, I believed religion could help liberate rather than subjugate women.

With WOC, we decided to cosponsor an interfaith fast and social media campaign for gender equity in religion called Equal in Faith. Joined by Ordain Women Now from the Lutheran Church-Missouri Synod, we planned break-the-fast meetings in both Salt Lake City—organized locally by Debra and Mark—and Washington, D.C., on August 26, 2013, National Women's Equality Day, and invited women around the country to participate online. Over 400 joined us either virtually or at one of the venues. Faith-filled and inspiring, the events[53] animated Ordain Women supporters in Utah and Washington, D.C., and signaled that we might have the numbers we needed for the priesthood session action a little over a month away.

During a lively Ordain Women Sunstone panel on August 1, 2013,[54] we announced not only the Equal in Faith fast, but also the priesthood session action. We were committed. With well over a hundred profiles on our website, we went into full organizing mode for the October 5 action. Group calls and emails continued, while increasingly planning moved online to the Facebook group that Kate had set up in January. The original group of organizers expanded to include Mark, Nancy, Heather, Debra, Gabrielle Perri Crowley, Amber Choruby Whiteley, and Christy Ellis-Clegg, as well as three earnestly faithful women who would eventually join the OW Executive Board, BYU-trained psychologist Kristy

---

53. See EqualinFaith.org, http://www.equalinfaith.org/; Equal in Faith meeting video recording, St. Stephen's Episcopal Church, Washington, D.C., August 26, 2013, http://www.ustream.tv/recorded/37855947.

54. "Ordain Women," 2013 Sunstone Symposium, August 1, 2013, https://www.sunstonemagazine.com/test-symposium-podcast-2/.

Money, supremely organized Exponent blogger Suzette Smith, and Danielle Mooney, a Wellesley graduate in French cultural studies and colonialism.

Kate was emerging as the face of Ordain Women. In order to reflect the organization's desired collaborative structure and facilitate group decision-making leading up to the October 5 action, Kate suggested that we form an executive board in late September composed of herself, Hannah, Debra, April, Chelsea, and me.[55]

The action was planned with attention to every detail and contingency, complete with site and route plans, security, de-escalation and press training, crowd control, and even a dress code—Sunday best. Chelsea, Heather, Hannah, and Mark handled logistics and volunteers. Nancy[56]—now chair of the Social Media Committee—Christy, and Kristy kept an eye on the website, continued to post profiles, and put in place a plan to make use of social media platforms during the action. Kate set agendas and kept us all on task while Debra, April, Kimberly, Suzette, and I worked on messaging—the press release, talking points, and action-specific FAQs. Debra drafted a letter requesting 150 tickets to the priesthood session and hand-delivered a copy to the Joseph Smith Building, the Events Center, and the Ticket Office at Temple Square on Monday, September 16.[57] Church Public Affairs spokesperson Ruth Todd responded in a letter to Ordain Women on Tuesday, September 24: "It is the hope of the Church that the priesthood session will strengthen the men and young men including fathers and sons, and give them the opportunity to gather and receive instruction related to priesthood duties and responsibilities, much the same way parallel meeting are held for sisters, such as the general Relief Society meeting. It's for these reasons that tickets for the priesthood session are reserved for men and young men and we are unable to honor your request for tickets or admission."[58] While Ordain Women was denied tickets, the Church announced that, for the first time in its history, it would "offer the male-only priesthood session of the upcoming general conference over live broadcast television and in real time over the Internet."[59]

---

55. April Young Bennett, interviewed by Lorie Winder Stromberg, May 21, 2015, notes in my possession.

56. Pacing would later become an issue, both in personal toll and strategic planning. A number of board members stepped down in the months following Kate's excommunication. As chair of social media, Nancy Ross, for example, would spend up to forty to fifty hours a week in the run-up to an action. With two small children and on track for a tenured professorship, she found the pace unsustainable. Too, some of us struggled with the question of how to press the issue of women's ordination while allowing space for the institutional Church to respond.

57. Debra Jenson, "Ordain Women Submits Ticket Request to the Priesthood Session," Ordain Women, http://ordainwomen.org/ow_blog/page/13/.

58. Ruth Todd, Letter to Ordain Women, September 24, 2013, http://ordainwomen.org/wp-content/uploads/2013/09/Response-Letter-from-Ruth-Todd.pdf .

59. Joseph Walker, "LDS General Priesthood Meeting to Be Broadcast Live and Online for the First Time," *Deseret News*, Tuesday, September 24 2013, http://www.deseretnews.

We scheduled a participant training on Friday night, October 4, the eve of the action, and, again, waited for the room to fill up. There were always a handful of hecklers on the sidewalk outside Temple Square. Our numbers—and our message—had to be compelling and appropriately set us apart. Well over a hundred women had indicated on the Facebook event page that they were coming. The previous spring, I would have been satisfied with half that. When more than fifty showed up at the training, I relaxed. I think we all did. Kate and I spoke, and, recognizing Nadine Hansen and Margaret Toscano in the audience, acknowledged their work in articulating so long ago the inequity some in attendance were just beginning to voice. April, a practiced lobbyist, outlined ways of dealing with the press. Danielle, a seasoned feminist activist with All Enlisted, tutored us in de-escalation. Chelsea, the consummate anthropologist, expertly led us through the action's logistics—when and where to meet, what to wear, whom to ask should a question arise—as well as priesthood action etiquette—no signs, no banners, no chanting. This was not a protest; it was a plea. "The ask" was priesthood.

Nearly two hundred women and men walked with us from City Creek Park to Temple Square the following afternoon. One by one, we were turned away at the doors of the Tabernacle. We waited reverently in line, while boys barely out of grade school and men were ushered past us into the session. The images were poignant. They, of course, went viral.

Afterword

The lingering impact Ordain Women will have on Mormonism remains unclear. However, my sense is that LDS Church discourse on women and priesthood has shifted significantly since the birth of Ordain Women. First and foremost, questions are being asked and acknowledged, as President Linda K. Burton's address at the women's conference session on May 2, 2013, indicates: "We rejoice that we are privileged to live in this season of the history of the Church when questions are being asked about the priesthood. There is great interest and desire to know and understand more about the authority, power, and blessings associated with the priesthood of God."[60]

Church leaders are also openly admitting that some members are perplexed and troubled by the question of why only men hold the priesthood. Apostles Neil L. Andersen and M. Russell Ballard, and Sheri L. Dew, former second counselor in the Relief Society general presidency, admit that they ultimately do not know why men have the priesthood and women do not. Ballard, speaking at BYU's 2013 Campus Education Week Devotional, asked, "Why are men ordained to priesthood offices and not women?" His answer: "When all is said and done,

---

com/article/865586991/LDS-general-priesthood-meeting-to-be-broadcast-live-for-the-first-time.html.

60. Linda K. Burton, "Priesthood Power—Available to All," Women's Conference, Brigham Young University, May 2, 2013; printed in the *Ensign*, June 2014, https://www.lds.org/ensign/2014/06/priesthood-power-available-to-all?lang=eng.

the Lord has not revealed why He has organized His Church as He has."[61] In his October 2013 general conference address, Andersen posed the question as he heard it: "If the power and the blessings of priesthood are available to all, why are the ordinances of the priesthood administered by men?" His answer was to quote 1 Nephi 11: 17: "I do not know the meaning of all things."[62] Similarly, Dew, in her book *Women and the Priesthood*, writes: "Why aren't women eligible for priesthood ordination, anyway? . . . [W]e don't know."[63]

Priesthood and maleness are no longer accepted as synonymous. Heretofore, the term "the priesthood" was so commonly used to refer to men in the Church that asking most Mormon women if they wanted to be ordained was like asking them if they wanted to be men. A growing number of Church leaders, including Andersen and Ballard in their respective addresses noted above, have stated that men are not "the priesthood." Repeating the same message was Apostle Dallin H. Oaks in his April 2014 LDS general conference priesthood session address.[64] Uncoupling priesthood from maleness could be seen as an essential first step in extending full priesthood authority to all worthy adult members of the LDS Church.

Further, the terms "priesthood blessings," "power," "authority," "office," and "keys" are being parsed and distinctions drawn in ways that are certainly shy of validating female ordination but which attempt to be more inclusive of women. Late twentieth-century Church discourse responded to the women's movement primarily by asserting that both men and women enjoyed the blessings of the priesthood, even though women were denied ordination. Such attempts to deflect claims that an all-male priesthood was inequitable spawned rhetoric that occasionally bordered on the absurd. For example, Elder Bruce C. Hafen, speaking at the BYU Women's Conference in 1985, asserted: "The one category of blessing in which the role of women is not the same as that of men holding the priesthood is that of administering the gospel and governing all things."[65] More recently, Church leaders have asserted that women can access both the blessings and the power of the priesthood, particularly through LDS temple rituals. In an April 2013 video interview with the women general auxiliary presidents released

---

61. M. Russell Ballard, "Let Us Think Straight," Brigham Young University Campus Education Week Devotional Address, August 20, 2013, https://speeches.byu.edu/talks/m-russell-ballard_let-us-think-straight-2/ .

62. Neil L. Andersen, "Power in the Priesthood," LDS General Conference, October 6, 2013, https://www.lds.org/general-conference/2013/10/power-in-the-priesthood.

63. Sheri L. Dew, *Women and Priesthood: What One Mormon Woman Believes* (Salt Lake City: Deseret Book, 2013), 106.

64. Dallin H. Oaks, "Priesthood Keys and Authority," LDS General Conference, Priesthood Session, April 5, 2014, https://www.lds.org/general-conference/2014/04/the-keys-and-authority-of-the-priesthood?lang=eng.

65. Bruce C. Hafen, "Women, Feminism, and the Blessings of the Gospel," speech given at the Women's Conference, Brigham Young University, March 29, 1985, https://speeches.byu.edu/talks/bruce-c-hafen_women-feminism-blessings-gospel/.

a few weeks after the launch of the Ordain Women website, President Linda K. Burton said: "I don't think women are after the authority; I think they're after the blessings and are happy that they can access the blessings and power of the priesthood. There are a few that would like both. But most of the women, I think, in the Church are happy to have all the blessings."[66]

In her review of Dew's book, LDS scholar Valerie Hudson writes that "Dew's greatest contribution in this book . . . is her assertion that endowed women possess Godly power, or priesthood power."[67] Quoting Elder Ballard, Dew had asserted that, in the temple, both men and women are "endowed with the same power, which by definition is priesthood power . . . [and, once endowed] a woman has direct access to priesthood power for her own life and responsibilities."[68] Ballard's comment was reiterated in Oaks's address at the April 2014 priesthood session, a statement that Hudson termed remarkable: "The formula has always been that women are the beneficiaries of priesthood power, and so only 'share' it vicariously by being married to a man. . . . But Dew is plainly saying that endowed women have been given priesthood power in the temple, which power they can use to benefit others. In other words, for the first time it is being articulated that women are not simply passive recipients of divine power that has been coded male, but are able to hold and use divine power as agents without a male intermediary."[69] However, Hudson adds that, while Dew asks why it is that "women, unlike men, are not required to be ordained to the Melchizedek priesthood in order to enter the house of the Lord, though the ordinances performed there are all priesthood ordinances," Hudson notes that the question "is apparently a bridge too far for Dew and she does not answer it in her book."[70]

Increasingly, a distinction is being made between the "authority" and the "power" of the priesthood. Priesthood authority and power traditionally have been associated with priesthood office and thus are available only to men. Power now seems to be available to all, although it is not clear what having such a power means for women. In his April 2014 priesthood session talk, Oaks went further, asserting that women not only enjoy the blessings and the power of the priesthood, but they also exercise its authority in their callings. In the institutional Church, "priesthood authority is governed by priesthood holders who hold priesthood keys, and . . . all that is done under the direction of those priesthood keys is done with priesthood authority," explained Oaks. While women do not currently hold priesthood keys and office, Oaks asserted that both women and

---

66. "Top Mormon Women Leaders Provide Their Insights into Church Leadership," LDS Church Newsroom, released April 5, 2013, video transcript, http://www.mormonnewsroom.org/article/transcript-mormon-women-leaders-insights-church-leadership.
67. Valerie Hudson, "Book Review: Women and the Priesthood by Sheri Dew," *SquareTwo* 6, no. 3 (Fall 2013), http://squaretwo.org/Sq2ArticleHudsonDewBookReview.html.
68. Ibid.
69. Ibid.
70. Ibid.

men are recognized as having "the authority of the priesthood in their Church callings." He continued: "We are not accustomed to speaking of women having the authority of the priesthood in their Church callings, but what other authority can it be? When a woman—young or old—is set apart to preach the gospel as a full-time missionary, she is given priesthood authority to perform a priesthood function. The same is true when a woman is set apart to function as an officer or teacher in a Church organization under the direction of one who holds the keys of the priesthood. Whoever functions in an office or calling received from one who holds priesthood keys exercises priesthood authority in performing her or his assigned duties."[71] Again, as with the assertion that women have the power of the priesthood, we are still left wondering what it means for women to exercise the authority of the priesthood in their callings. Is a Relief Society president's authority actual or referred? Can she, for example, bless the women over whom she presides by the authority of the priesthood, which she exercises by virtue of the fact that she was called to her position by a male priesthood leader?

All of these rhetorical shifts move the conversation forward. In the end, however, such attempts reveal more than they satisfy.[72] Still, they signal an increased awareness among the LDS Church leadership that questions about women and priesthood ordination are legitimate and need to be seriously addressed. It is clear that Ordain Women has been a significant catalyst for such a discussion.

---

71. Oaks, "Priesthood Keys and Authority."

72. Laurel Thatcher Ulrich, quoted in Peggy Fletcher Stack, "So Are Mormon Women Really Making Progress? Views Differ," *Salt Lake* Tribune, April 9, 2013, http://www.sltrib.com/sltrib/blogsfaithblog/56131993-180/women-church-mormon-lds.html.csp.

Chapter 2

Conflict and Change in Closed and Open Systems: The Case of the LDS Church

Gordon Shepherd and Gary Shepherd

On June 23, 2014, Kate Kelly—Mormon feminist and the founder of Ordain Women, an activist group of LDS women—was excommunicated from the Church of Jesus Christ of Latter-day Saints. The all-male ecclesiastical council which judged her informed her that "[our] greatest desire has been to persuade you to desist from the course on which you have embarked so that you might remain in full fellowship in the Church while also protecting the integrity of the church and its doctrine. . . . We have approached this solemn and difficult task seeking only to know the Lord's mind and will. Having done so, our determination is that you be excommunicated for conduct contrary to the laws and order of the church."[1] For her part, Kelly professed continued devotion to her Latter-day Saint faith, describing herself as heartbroken by the council's decision against her but staunchly countering: "I've done nothing wrong and have nothing to repent. Once the church changes to be a more inclusive place, and once women are ordained, that's a place I'd feel welcome."[2]

Kelly's June excommunication followed Ordain Women's second public event supporting women's ordination at the LDS Church's April 2014 general conference at the historic Mormon Tabernacle in the center of Temple Square in Salt Lake City. The group had demonstrated previously at the October conference. Six months later, they had returned with twice as many followers, considerable advance publicity, and a rapidly growing website at which sympathetic supporters posted personal profiles expressing their reasons for favoring priesthood ordination of women. (Chapter 18 discusses how these profiles represent the hopes and discontents of contemporary Mormon women.)

In an interview following Kelly's excommunication, religious studies scholar Jan Shipps commented on the significance of Kelly's case to the press, observing: "It does more than excommunicate Kelly. It warns everybody." According

---

1. Quoted from a pdf copy of Kate Kelly's excommunication letter released by Ordain Women for online publication to the *Deseret News*, June 23, 2014, http://www.deseretnews.com/article/865605659/Ordain-Women-releases-LDS-bishops-letter-giving-reasons-for-Kellys-excommunication.html (accessed June 23, 2014).

2. Kate Kelly, quoted in the *Salt Lake Tribune*, June 24, 2014: "Kelly on Excommunication from Mormon Church: 'I've Done Nothing Wrong,'" http//www.sltrib.com/sltrib/news/58104587-78/church-kelly-women-ordain.html.csp (accessed June 24, 2014).

to Shipps, LDS Church leaders were implementing "boundary maintenance," using Kelly and other Mormon dissidents as examples to demonstrate how far Church members could go in questioning their faith's practices.[3] In a similar vein, Mormon scholar Armand Mauss commented that the message seems to be that "organizing pressure groups, and trying to cultivate a following for such groups, crosses a line that will trigger disciplinary action."[4]

Seven and a half months after Kelly's excommunication, Mormon podcaster John Dehlin was similarly excommunicated for "conduct contrary to the laws and order of the church"—specified in the ruling as publicly disseminating false teachings and charges against the faith via the internet and leading others away from the Church. While not faulting his local leaders, who were ecclesiastically responsible for the decision to deprive him of his LDS membership, Dehlin maintains that the real reasons for his excommunication had to do with his outspoken support for same-sex marriage and ordination of women to the priesthood and his refusal to censure his podcasts. In turn, LDS Public Affairs issued a statement denying Dehlin's claims; it averred that the particular decisions of LDS disciplinary councils—though guided by general Church principles and guidelines—are entirely in the hands of local Church officials, a claim often disputed by skeptical critics.[5] (The functioning of LDS disciplinary councils is examined in Chapters 11 and 12.)

In what follows, we (1) conceptualize the barriers to social change in relatively closed systems in contrast to open systems; (2) summarize the patriarchal priesthood structure of the LDS Church as an example of a relatively closed religious system; (3) describe alterations in modern Church policy as a process of "tension management" in response to accommodating pressures for religious change that come from larger cultural and societal trends outside the Church, especially in the context of competitive religious markets for growth-oriented religions; and (4) summarize the prospects of grassroots movements for greater gender equality and female ordination originating from *within* the conservative, patriarchal organization of Mormon ecclesiastical culture.

Closed Versus Open Social Systems

All human social systems cohere and operate on the basis of a normative structure which, among other things, establishes boundaries separating insiders from outsiders. Insiders are actors who occupy legitimately recognized statuses within a system that bestows upon them both rights and responsibilities. Insiders do not acknowledge that outsiders share mutual rights and responsibilities within their

---

3. Jan Shipps, as quoted in the *Huffington Post*, June 24, 2014, http://www.huffingtonpost.com/2014/06/24/kate-kelly-excommunication-activists_n_5525424.html.

4. Armand Mauss, as quoted in the *Provo Daily Herald*, June 24, 2014, http://www.dailyherald.com/article/20140624/news/140629326/ (accessed June 24, 2014).

5. For details of the news story and quotations concerning John Dehlin's excommunication, see the *Salt Lake Tribune*, February 10, 2015, http://www.sltrib.com/home/2163720-155/mormon-critic-john-dehlin-is-excommunicated (accessed February 10, 2015).

system. To a greater or lesser degree, system actors develop personal attachments to system norms and values that provide them with a social identity and collective sense of unity. Outsiders do not share the same social identity and sense of unity with insiders. Unity within a social system is, in fact, typically strengthened by boundaries that emphasize moral distinctions between insiders and outsiders. These moral distinctions generate contrasting conceptions which impute negative stereotypes to outsiders and their way of life while, in turn, insiders righteously proclaim the moral superiority of their own virtues and normative practices.[6]

How strict are the rules and their enforcement that define the structure of a normative system? How rigid are the boundaries that define people's identities and distinguish one social system from another in pluralistic environments? Empirical variations in the strictness of system rules and their corresponding boundaries point to the theoretical distinction between relatively closed and open systems.[7]

As a theoretical type, closed systems are characterized by their resistance to change, as well as the strictness of their rules and rigidity of their boundaries; they are relatively closed to outside influences while also resisting movements for change generated from within. Thus, closed systems are characteristically intolerant of internal diversity and dissent, which are kept under vigilant surveillance and suppressed both formally and informally. Closed systems lack institutional mechanisms for acknowledging the legitimacy of dissent and for accommodating internal differences within the system. The successful suppression of differences and dissent for lengthy periods of time increases the ultimate potential for disruptive and damaging conflict if and when grievances within the system reach a boiling point and burst the boundaries of repressive control.

In theoretical contrast, open systems are less rigid than closed systems; they are relatively tolerant of diversity and change and are open to change initiated both from within the system and through outside influences. Open systems have institutional mechanisms for accommodating differences and managing internal conflicts; they channel emerging conflicts in potentially constructive ways by legitimizing the expression of criticism and dissent that can be incorporated into a process of adaptive change. Thus, in contrast to closed systems, open systems are more likely to experience orderly rather than disruptive modes of change. In disruptive change, polarization intensifies and mutually hostile stereotypes that highlight moral distinctions between insiders and outsiders are reinforced, inhibiting peaceful accommodation and perpetuating social conflict.

---

6. The role played in conflict situations by the development of mutually hostile stereotypes in the form of contrast conceptions is analyzed by Tamotsu Shibutani in his classic text, *Social Processes* (Berkeley: University of California Press, 1986), chap. 15.

7. Lewis A. Coser makes and elaborates the theoretical distinction between closed and open systems in the study of conflict and social change in such works as *The Functions of Social Conflict* (New York: Free Press, 1956); "Social Conflict and the Theory of Social Change," *British Journal of Sociology* 8, no. 3 (1957): 197–207; and *Continuities in the Study of Social Conflict* (New York: Free Press, 1967).

Actual social systems in the context of human history are never completely open or completely closed. They do, however, vary substantially in the ways we have summarized. Systems themselves may undergo changes in the relative rigidity of their rules and boundaries over time, especially as a result of confronting different types of conflict. Both closed and relatively open systems may become more rigid and less tolerant when their leaders feel threatened by opponents. Thus, for example, open systems may retreat in the direction of greater closure when threatened by perceived enemies from either outside or inside the system.[8] On the other hand, when absorbing defeat at the hands of external enemies, previously closed systems may be forced to become more open.[9] Distinguishing the consequences of different types of conflict for the constriction or relaxation of system rules and boundaries is a necessary scholarly task for adequately understanding the scope and pace of social change in different human groups.

This said, it is in response to criticism of the existing normative order that originates from *within* a system that perhaps most clearly distinguishes open systems from closed systems. As previously noted, open systems are equipped to accommodate dissent and move toward constructive change while closed systems are not equipped to do so. Closed systems are more likely to view dissenters as disloyal to core system values and as actors whose challenging speech or disapproved activities threaten the authority and integrity of the prevailing normative order. Thus, rather than being regarded as persons with legitimate differences and the right to express them, dissenters in closed systems are stigmatized as defectors ("heretics" or "apostates" in religious systems) who must be quickly marginalized and punished. When labeled as defectors in closed systems, dissenters are both formally and informally deprived of their recognized rights and responsibilities within the system and are shunned or cast out as negative examples to deter others from being led astray. Authorities in closed systems become preoccupied with maintaining or strengthening the boundaries that exclude both outsiders and defectors, who in turn are redefined as outsiders, while sharpening more clearly a shared moral identity for those who persist in demonstrating their loyalty to the system.

---

8. Terrorist threats to the United States and its Western allies, for example, have intensified the debate between the need for greater homeland security surveillance and travel restrictions versus privacy concerns and personal liberty rights of free speech and mobility in a democratic society.

9. History abounds with examples of heretofore closed systems forced, through military conquest or political defeat, to become more open. Examples are the forced democratization of totalitarian Germany and Japan following their unconditional surrenders to Allied forces at the end of World War II, the abolition of slavery in the Confederate South following military defeat in the American Civil War, and 100 years later, the upending of legally sanctioned racial segregation in American civil law as a result of federal court decisions and a massive civil rights movement for political reform.

The LDS Church as a Relatively Closed Religious System

While many historical faith traditions have produced dogmatic and authoritarian churches, religions also vary in the degree to which they may be considered relatively closed or open systems. What kind of religious system is the Church of Jesus Christ of Latter-day Saints? Given the broad spectrum of denominations that flourish in contemporary America, and mindful of the transformative changes that nineteenth-century Mormonism underwent in the first half of the twentieth century preparatory to its global status as a flourishing missionary religion in the twenty-first century, it is nonetheless apparent that the modern LDS Church persists as a strict and relatively closed religious system with respect to its doctrinal rules, membership boundaries, and intolerance of internal dissent that criticizes or challenges priesthood authority. As sociologist Armand Mauss recently reminded the media: "The LDS Church is not a democratic institution and has never claimed to be. So such actions [e.g., public demonstrations organized by Ordain Women to press for the ordination of Mormon women] are interpreted by Church leaders as attempts to displace or undermine their legitimate authority over church policies and teachings."[10] The modern LDS Church retains a fundamental commitment to its foundational theocratic beliefs and has embraced a top-down, corporate model of echelon priesthood authority and organizational control that discourages grassroots innovation at the local, congregational level.[11]

As a relatively closed religious system, the LDS Church lacks any sanctioned policy or officially approved means for the expression of disagreement and the accommodation of internal dissent. As Lavina Fielding Anderson put the matter at a session of the Mormon Women's Forum Counterpoint Conference, "The vocabulary of disagreement is not a part of Mormon culture." Instead, for Mormons their vocabulary is ultimately "the vocabulary of obedience," an observation validated by the fact that there are no formal and valid modes or methods in the LDS Church for expressing minority views.[12] This, Anderson points out, is in contrast

---

10. Mauss, as quoted in a NBC news story, June 11, 2014, at http://www.nbcnews.com/news/us-news/mormon-womens-group-founder-kate-kelly-faces-excommunication-n129151 (accessed June 11, 2014).

11. Kristine Haglund attributes much of the contemporary stifling of LDS dissent and innovation at the grassroots level to implementation of the 1960s "correlation" movement of organizational reform that standardized all Church programs and decision making under a corporate model of priesthood echelon authority. See her essay at http://religionandpolitics.org/2014/06/25/banishing-dissent-the-excommunication-of-mormon-activist-kate-kelly (accessed June 25, 2014). For a summary analysis of the origins and implementation of the Church correlation movement, see James B. Allen and Glen M. Leonard, *The Story of the Latter-day Saints* (1976; rev. and expanded ed., Salt Lake City: Deseret Book, 1992), chap 5.

12. One important Church practice relevant to the question of expressing dissent is the ritual sustaining of LDS priesthood leaders at the annual and semiannual conferences of the

to Latter-day Saints' erstwhile cousins in the more open Community of Christ, who have ratified a document of dissent titled, "Faithful Disagreement."[13] (The lack of legitimate forms for member redress of grievances in the LDS Church is further addressed in Chapter 4 on gender theology and Chapter 12 on excommunication and disciplinary councils.)

At the same time, the Mormons' cardinal belief in modern revelation constitutes a theological mechanism of potentially tremendous flexibility for legitimating fundamental system change, if and when consensus concerning the need for change is achieved at the highest levels of ecclesiastical authority.[14] Historically, LDS authorities have claimed direct revelation as divine endorsement for certain momentous policy and organizational changes, such as abandoning its commitment to the practice of nineteenth-century polygamy and, in the twentieth century, lifting the ban on ordaining males of African descent to the priesthood. But these changes were also long resisted by Church authorities and occurred only after the accumulation of both tremendous internal and external pressures. (Several twentieth-century examples of policy change, and especially the reversal of the long-embraced priesthood ban on the ordination of black males of African ancestry, are examined in Chapter 11, which deals with LDS organizational and doctrinal change.)

Today, as a religious system competing for adherents in a global religious economy, the contemporary LDS Church is aggressively growth oriented,

---

entire Church and periodic stake conferences at the local level of Church organization. At these conferences, the presiding officer asks members for their sustaining vote in approving and upholding (nearly always) men who have been called to preside in various Church callings or positions. These are not votes in a conventional democratic sense. Almost always, voting is unanimous. The practice of collectively sustaining Church leadership periodically functions to reinforce the religious unity, loyalty, and shared commitment values of the Latter-day Saint community, not to provide a forum for discussion of disagreements or registration of dissent. The case of Byron Marchant who, at the October 1977 general conference, publicly dissented from sustaining the General Authorities to protest the exclusion of black men from priesthood ordination serves as a cautionary tale: Two weeks after his dissenting conference vote, Marchant was excommunicated by his local stake officials. Eight months later, the Church rescinded the priesthood ban. Marchant's membership, on the other hand, was never restored. See "Byron's Song," by Mark Barnes at http://ordainwomen.org/ow_blog/, accessed March 1, 2015).

13. Lavina Fielding Anderson, "Exploring the Community of Christ Document on Dissent," presented at the Counterpoint Conference, sponsored by the Mormon Women's Forum at the University of Utah, November 1, 2014, notes in authors' possession.

14. For analyses of revelation as a religious mechanism for social change, see Gordon Shepherd and Gary Shepherd, *Talking with the Children of God: Prophecy and Transformation in a Radical Religious Group* (Urbana: University of Illinois Press, 2010), and "Prophecy Channels and Prophetic Modalities: A Comparison of Revelation in The Family International and the LDS Church," *Journal for the Scientific Study of Religion* 48, no. 4 (2009): 734–55.

staunchly conservative, and theocratically committed to preserving the ultimate authority of its ecclesiastical hierarchy. For these reasons and others discussed below, the LDS Church should be classified as a relatively closed religious system that, while sustaining theological beliefs conducive to rationalizing significant system reforms, is predictably reluctant and slow to do so in actual practice. Most noteworthy for understanding increasingly contentious women's issues in the twenty-first century LDS Church, Mormonism's ecclesiastical structure embodies traditional principles of a patriarchal priesthood order. For readers who may be unfamiliar with this structure, we provide the following overview.

The LDS Church is a religious organization that depends upon highly active, lay participation in an episcopal system of male administrative authority. Similar to Catholic and Anglican churches, the LDS Church affirms the necessity of apostolic succession to priesthood authority. Unlike the former traditions, however, the LDS Church (1) features a *lay* priesthood of all "worthy" males, ages twelve and older (from which all women are excluded), and (2) bases its claim to apostolic succession on the twin doctrines of a Great Apostasy, which Mormons believe occurred after the deaths of the original twelve apostles, and the latter-day restoration of the primitive Christian Church through the prophetic agency of its founder, Joseph Smith Jr.[15] In the LDS ecclesiastical system, both males and females occupy numerous lay positions in the organizational programs of their church, but only males exercise priesthood authority in the administration of these programs and in policy-making councils. And only males are authorized to perform religious ordinances such as baptism, confirmation, marriages, healing, naming and blessing infants, bestowing patriarchal blessings in behalf of adults or young adults, ordaining other male priesthood holders, and consecrating ("setting apart") lay members to function in Church callings. Under male priesthood oversight, Mormon women are limited to leadership in women's and children's auxiliaries and teaching positions in these auxiliaries and also in the Sunday School and seminary program for teens.

At the base of the male ecclesiastical hierarchy in the LDS Church are bishoprics, each consisting of a bishop and his two counselors who preside over local congregations (the organizational equivalent of a parish) called wards. A designated set of wards (the organizational equivalent of a diocese), in turn, is presided over by a stake presidency consisting of a stake president and two counselors,

---

15. The idea of the "Great Apostasy" is a staple of Protestant ecclesiology in which, historically, the Roman Pope and Catholic Church were equated with the "Antichrist." It was the charge of ecclesiastical corruption and apostasy that justified the need for religious reformation and the consequent history of Protestant Christianity. Mormon ecclesiology is an innovative adaptation of Protestant doctrine that stresses the need, not for reformation, but for a total restoration of the original church and gospel of Jesus Christ. The Mormon version of the "great apostasy" (necessarily preceding the narrative of the Mormon restoration) is systematically expounded by James E. Talmage, *The Great Apostasy* (Salt Lake City: Deseret Book, 1983).

who appoint and consecrate ward bishops. In their turn, stakes are overseen by area authorities who consecrate stake presidents while also reporting to and being supervised by various quorums of LDS General Authorities, especially that quorum of men designated as the Twelve Apostles. The apostles counsel with the highest echelon of priesthood authority in the LDS Church, the First Presidency, consisting of the Church president and his counselors (usually two). The apostles constitute a self-selecting group, advancement to which is based on appointments made upon the deaths of previous apostles (who are consecrated for life) through discussion and consensus vote by existing quorum members. Individuals chosen as replacement apostles invariably have promising records of lengthy lay service and proven loyalty within the ranks of Mormon bishoprics, stake presidencies, area authorities, or other General Authority quorums.[16]

The rule of succession to become president of the LDS Church is based on seniority in the Quorum of the Twelve Apostles. Upon the death of a Church president, the senior apostle is elevated in his stead to become the new president and is at liberty to choose his own counselors in the First Presidency. The Church president is considered to be a living prophet whose official pronouncements and policy edicts (when approved and supported by his counselors in the First Presidency and the Quorum of the Twelve) are considered to be the revealed word and will of God to the restored Church of Jesus Christ in modern times.

Under the ultimate direction of its General Authorities, the daily operations of the LDS Church are administered and coordinated by a large, professional bureaucracy centered in Salt Lake City, Utah. The LDS bureaucracy is staffed by both men and women, but only priesthood-holding males occupy executive, decision-making positions. Many of these professional male administrators also occupy lay ecclesiastical positions in their local bishoprics or stake presidencies.

Theoretical Models of Change in Relatively Closed Systems

While upper-echelon authorities in closed systems are resistant to grassroots movements advocating internal system reforms, all social systems change over time, including relatively closed systems. If and when changes occur in closed systems, what are the social dynamics that emerge to cause them, and what is their pace, substance, and scope? Specifying these questions with regard to contemporary gender issues in the LDS Church, we may ask: What are the emerging social dynamics in which gender equality issues are increasingly being contested within the U.S. Mormon community? What are the ultimate prospects for comprehensive priesthood equality for LDS women in a conservative, relatively closed religious system that is bureaucratically headquartered in corporate America in the twenty-first century?

---

16. For a detailed historical description and analysis of the structure and functioning of the LDS Quorum of the Twelve Apostles, see D. Michael Quinn, *The Mormon Hierarchy: Origins of Power* (Salt Lake City: Signature Books, 1997).

Other chapters in this book describe and analyze various aspects of the Mormon faith that support our characterization of Mormonism as a relatively closed religious system: (1) its core theological doctrines pertaining to contested questions of gender and gender role responsibilities; (2) the ebb and flow of gendered consciousness and corresponding religiously enacted gender roles in Mormon history; (3) LDS ecclesiastical forms that structure the process of institutional change in a religion that staunchly adheres to belief in guidance through divine revelation imparted to male priesthood authorities and that safeguard orthodoxy through disciplinary councils conducted exclusively by men; and (4) attempts by male ecclesiastical officials to stay abreast of changing secular trends and technologies, especially those connected with the new social media and their capacity for generating and sustaining virtual community networks that are not easily regulated by traditional methods of social control.

In this chapter, we next summarize four theoretical models relevant to understanding Mormon history and institutions that are compatible with an analysis of reformative change within relatively closed systems.

Mauss's Tension Management Model in Response to External Pressures

In several publications, Armand Mauss has put forward a "tension management" model to explain institutional change in the contemporary LDS Church.[17] In this model, recruitment-oriented religions in relatively open, pluralistic societies must find ways to accommodate to the normative and legal demands of the larger society in which they operate while, at the same time, maintaining adherence to core beliefs and practices that set them apart from competitor religions. It is their distinctive theological beliefs and corresponding religious practices that are, of course, potential sources of tension between and among religious organizations and the institutions of law and government. The greater the distinctiveness or discrepancy between a particular religion's beliefs and practices and the normative standards of dominant groups in the larger society, the greater their tension will be. High levels of tension generate conflicts and the likelihood of repressive, dysfunctional consequences for minority religious groups when religious majorities perceive and label them as aberrant or morally offensive. Religious beliefs and practices that are essentially the same or very similar to those of other religious groups generate little or no tension but also deprive recruitment-oriented religions of any distinctive marketing appeal. Too much accommodation to the

---

17. Mauss's most important exposition of the tension management model is given in *The Angel and the Beehive: Mormonism's Struggle with Assimilation* (Urbana: University of Illinois Press, 1994). Other works in which Mauss expounds this thesis include: "From Near Nation to New World Religion," in Cardell Jacobson, Tim Heaton, and John Hoffman, eds., *Revisiting O'Dea's The Mormons: Persistent Themes and Contemporary Perspectives* (Salt Lake City: University of Utah Press, 2008); and *Shifting Borders and a Tattered Passport: Intellectual Journeys of a Mormon Intellectual* (Salt Lake City: University of Utah Press, 2012).

prevailing beliefs and practices of dominant groups promotes assimilation and the prospective extinction of an earlier, distinctive religious way of life.

In Mauss's analysis, a major challenge for religious authorities in pluralistic environments that permit a certain degree of religious diversity is finding and maintaining the right amount of tension (or what Mauss calls "optimum tension") between their own religious system and society at large. As already noted, too much tension produces repressive, dysfunctional consequences, while too little tension leads to assimilation and loss of a distinctive religious identity.

Applying these theoretical propositions to the Latter-day Saints, Mauss explicated his "retrenchment" thesis of modern Mormon development. After decades of pursuing a policy of deliberate assimilation in American society in the first half of the twentieth-century, he argued, the post-World War II LDS Church "retrenched" and began reversing course in an effort to preserve its religious and cultural distinctiveness. Mauss devoted most of his 1994 book to detailing mid-twentieth-century LDS retrenchment trends in scriptural literalism, corporate Church government, traditional gender role definitions, youth indoctrination, and political conservatism. Ironically, Mauss concluded that, in reversing its previous assimilationist posture in relationship to the normative and legal demands of American society, the contemporary LDS Church also had begun listing in the direction of conservative Protestantism and consequently was in some peril of losing its distinctive Latter-day Saint identity in the global religious economy.[18]

More recently, however, Mauss published a 2011 *Dialogue* article titled "Rethinking Retrenchment: Course Corrections in the Ongoing Campaign for Respectability." In this article Mauss reconsiders his retrenchment thesis and concludes that, for the past two decades, LDS General Authorities gradually have "introduced a series of changes in Church policy that have had the cumulative effect of pulling the pendulum of ecclesiastical culture back somewhat from the

---

18. In conjunction with the strident anticommunism of the Cold War era following World War II—and especially in reaction to the tumultuous social and political upheavals of the 1960s—LDS retrenchment ran parallel to a massive, conservative Christian backlash that was committed to reversing liberal social change. Conservative members of Protestant mainline denominations were unhappy with their clergy's support of the civil rights and anti-war movements of the 1960s. They also resisted the secular ideology of separation of church and state. Consequently, many were attracted to more conservative evangelical and non-denominational Bible churches that preached traditional morality, promoted evangelism, and threw their political support to candidates who opposed affirmative action policies in employment, secularization of public schools (e.g., busing as an instrument of racial desegregation and prohibition of prayer and religious texts), and especially the legalization of abortion. For analyses of the rise and relative decline of the historic mainline Protestant churches in contemporary America and the corresponding rise of the conservative Christian right, see Jason S. Lantzer, *Mainline Christianity: The Past and Future of America's Majority Faith* (New York: New York University Press, 2012), and Elesha J. Coffman, *The Christian Century and the Rise of the Protestant Mainline* (Cambridge, Mass.: Harvard University Press, 2013).

retrenchment mode and toward assimilation."[19] In Mauss's latest analysis, this partial reversal of retrenchment has occurred primarily in the areas of LDS scriptures and doctrinal exposition, gender and family policies, increased acceptance of homosexuality, and rapprochement with independent scholarship in Mormon studies. In these areas Mauss documents publicized organizational changes, Mormon advertising campaigns, policy announcements, media statements, and anecdotal evidence to support the conclusion that LDS authorities in recent years have begun relaxing the institutional strictures of retrenchment.

Mauss is careful to qualify his observations by saying, "I haven't yet gathered the kind of systematic data needed for reliable conclusions. Nor am I claiming here that there has been a wholesale rollback of the retrenchment policies, but only some relatively modest 'course corrections.'"[20] He concludes that the growth and strength of the Church periodically depend on these kinds of moderating adjustments in order

> to maintain an optimum level of cultural tension with the surrounding society, which itself is constantly changing. . . . [E]ach new retrenchment campaign seems to start from a more advanced stage of assimilation than the last one did, so that the ecclesiastical culture is never pulled all the way back to the tension level from which it started. . . . The end result is typically still a well assimilated religious community in the long term. In the short term, though, we might see the opposite—a strong retrenchment thrust followed by a partial retreat again toward assimilation, which is what I think has occurred during the past two decades.[21]

The language Mauss uses in extrapolating historical propositions concerning Mormon policy reforms from his tension management model of institutional change is compatible with our preliminary summary of conflict and change in closed and open systems. Thus, what Mauss refers to as "assimilation" phases of change in LDS ecclesiastical history correspond to the process in which a formerly closed system moves toward greater openness; his "retrenchment" phase corresponds with retreating movement toward greater system closure; and, as Mauss employs it, "modest course corrections" indicate tentative steps forward once more in the direction of greater openness.

If Mauss is right about the tentative softening of the LDS Church's mid-twentieth century retrenchment over the past two decades, it must now be asked if the 2014 excommunication of Kate Kelly, followed by John Dehlin's 2015 excommunication (along with reports of other disciplinary actions taken against Ordain Women supporters), signal the beginning of a new retrenchment era.[22]

---

19. Armand Mauss, "Rethinking Retrenchment: Course Corrections in the Ongoing Campaign for Respectability," *Dialogue: A Journal of Mormon Thought* 44, no. 4 (2011): 1–42.
20. Ibid., 4.
21. Ibid., 21.
22. In the media uproar surrounding John Dehlin's pending disciplinary council meeting, Mormon studies scholar Patrick Mason disputed the inference that the LDS Church is systematically cracking down on dissidents. "If there were a crackdown, we would be seeing

Whatever the case may prove to be, Mauss's analysis concentrates attention on the ecclesiastical leadership side of the LDS change equation, which arguably constitutes the single most important set of variables for understanding organizational change, if and when reform is instituted in relatively closed systems. At the same time, Mauss pays correspondingly less attention to the *membership* side of the change equation—to potential pressure for doctrinal or organizational change emanating from different segments of the membership base who are struggling to resolve theological teachings or current Church practices that appear irrelevant to contemporary problems or incongruent with real-life issues of equity and justice. How effectively are these kinds of internal strains communicated to upper echelon Church leaders, and how much influence do they actually exert on their collective thinking and willingness to modify current doctrinal interpretations and their application to long-established practices? While the modern LDS Church proactively manages its public image as a legitimate religious faith in the national and global religious economies through its professionally staffed Public Affairs Department, we must also ask: What normative mechanisms, if any, currently exist for effectively accommodating and managing *internal* tensions and divisions within the LDS Church?[23]

---

dozens or scores of these [excommunications] . . . You could say they [Dehlin and Kelly] are symbolic in some way, that it's the church drawing a line in the sand, but it's not an inquisition . . . There are thousands and thousands of Mormons who support same-sex marriage and women's ordination. They might get the cold shoulder or have an awkward conversation with their stake president, but they're not being excommunicated." Mason qtd. in http://www.nbcnews.com/news/us-news/mormon-podcaster-john-dehlin-bracing-excommunication-n301066 (accessed February 2015). On the other hand, there are numerous reports on the internet of Church members losing temple recommends and/or their Church callings (or being threatened with their withdrawal) because of their public support for Ordain Women. Debra Elaine Jenson, current chairperson of the Executive Board of Ordain Women, reported that, as of mid-January 2015, twenty people who have submitted OW profiles have been disciplined in this manner by their local Church authorities (http://ordainwomen.org/informal-discipline/), while many other cases go unpublicized. For many women who have been called to meet with local officials because of their support of Ordain Women, conversations with their bishops or stake presidents go far beyond "awkward" or merely getting "the cold shoulder." As one anonymous source reported, "The next thing I knew, I was being publicly shamed at church. Do you know what happens when your bishop publicly shames you at church? You start to have random visitors at your house calling you to repentance. You are shunned and you become an outcast to your community. . . . I lost my calling and everything that makes me want to stay at church." Unidentified woman quoted in http://www.the-exponent.com/no-discipline-cases-elder-oaks/ (accessed January 30, 2015).

23. It may be reasonably asked why, in an open religious economy, members whose values and most important concerns are not being adequately addressed by their chosen religion don't simply leave. Why stay? Large-scale member defections are, in fact, a major concern for contemporary, growth-oriented religions, including in particular the LDS Church. The family and personal histories of many supporters of Ordain Women,

In raising these questions, we remind readers that all closed systems strongly discourage grass-roots movements for reform and that organized reform movements in closed systems are likely to be labeled and treated as heretical rather than granted legitimate rights to criticize and advocate for change. This is especially true of dogmatic religions whose truth claims are enshrined in sacred texts that are seen as the product of divine revelation and whose authoritative interpretation is ceded to the inspiration of an ecclesiastical hierarchy. Closed religious systems embrace consensual moral assent to authoritative guidance and theological unity as the foundations of the faith community, while they typically repudiate the need for institutional mechanisms for legitimating dissent and accommodating internal differences among system constituents.

Finnigan and Stearmer's Model of Reform within Closed Systems

A theoretical model that emphasizes the dynamics of internal change in relatively closed systems in general, and in the LDS Church in particular, is offered by Jessica Finnigan and Matthew Stearmer.[24] In a way that closely parallels our characterization of closed systems, Finnigan and Stearmer identify and define what they call Hierarchical Conservative Settings (HCS). According to Finnigan and Stearmer's analysis, a specifically *religious* HCS exercises authority through a hierarchical ecclesiastical structure and its policies and normative practices are rooted in a literal, rather than an allegorical interpretation, of scriptural texts. HCS religious leaders' primary institutional function is conservative: namely, to preserve the integrity of both the religion's authority structure and its orthodox theological teachings. In an HCS religion, the conservative role of ecclesiastical leaders is most strongly supported by that category of church members which Finnigan and Stearmer call the "conservative core." Ecclesiastical leadership and the conservative core combine to maintain the doctrinal and organizational status quo in HCS religions. The conservative core in particular is resistant to change and constitutes an influential reactionary element in the HCS community in response to any dissent or perceived deviations from orthodoxy.

For internal, reformative change to take place in HCS religions, two different agents of change must emerge from the grass-roots membership: (1) individuals who propose alternative perspectives for interpreting core beliefs and their current policy applications—whom Finnigan and Stearmer call "alternative

---

however, are so deeply linked to Mormonism that it is very difficult for them to separate their identities from their LDS faith. Being Mormon is an essential part of who they are. They don't wish to leave the Church; they wish to remain an active part of it. They are true reformers who, by engaging in moral activism from the center of Mormon culture, aspire to facilitate the change of traditional religious practices that inhibit realization of what they envision as a more inclusive religious community.

24. S. Matthew Stearmer and Jessica Finnigan, "Radical Evolution: The Dynamics of Social Change and Innovation in Hierarchical Conservative Settings," copy of article draft in editors' possession.

narrative creators"—and (2) an "internal radical flank." The communication of alternative narratives in conjunction with the emergence of a radical flank serves to recast the meaning of problematic issues and expand the range of their putative solutions as traditionally expounded by ecclesiastical leaders and understood by the conservative core. By themselves, alternative narrative creators, who are typically intellectuals, scholars, and writers, cannot produce or influence substantive reform. At best, over time HCS leaders may respond to unauthorized alternative narratives by softening their own rhetoric and using some alternative language to reframe doctrinal interpretations and expositions of contested policies. At worst, HCS leaders, indignantly supported by the conservative core, may respond by repudiating and marginalizing the alternative narrator creators, whose reinterpretation efforts are perceived as heretical. In neither case do HCS leaders institute concrete policy reforms. If, however, a radical flank *also* emerges, the dynamics of internal reform coalesce and begin to stimulate renewed energy for institutional change. A true radical flank concerns itself not only with the language of alternative narratives but also with taking programmatic *action* to publicly articulate criticism and demonstrate its dissent from the status quo. In doing so, it creates public space for validating the expression of dissatisfaction and criticism of the traditionally conservative narrative, while also articulating and modeling more sharply defined goals of social change.

Since we are dealing with the prospects for internal reform in HCS religions, it is often difficult for outsiders to perceive the actions of an internal radical flank as being especially radical; those constituting that flank are radical only within the context of the HCS's own doctrinal rules, normative constraints, and disciplinary mechanisms for controlling dissent. Thus, for example, it is commonplace in democratic systems for citizens to assemble *en masse* in public places to rally, express grievances, chant brief slogans, wave placards, and publicly demonstrate their support for a wide range of civic causes. Even in Salt Lake City's relatively subdued civic life, such forms of dissent occur routinely on the spacious and well-lit steps of the State Capitol before flickering cameras. However, mere hundreds of organized Ordain Women supporters—estimates of the first march stood between 100–150, and of the second march as many as 350—without chanted slogans or banners, dressed in their Sunday best and encircled the Mormon Tabernacle on Temple Square in the heart of Salt Lake City to peacefully request and individually be denied standby tickets for admission to an all-male priesthood session. What might appear to outside observers as a relatively modest and polite protest was, within the context of Mormon culture, perceived by many Church members as an unprecedented and radical action. These women had audaciously defied official priesthood directives to not encroach on Church property during the semiannual conference of the Church for the purpose of dramatizing their cause and attracting critical media attention.

Mormon feminists and writers have operated for many years as Latter-day Saint alternative narrative creators, articulating in a variety of ways the need for greater gender equality in both Mormon culture and ecclesiastical programs of the LDS Church. Those years of perplexity, confusion, and unsatisfactory answers, if any, as they engaged Church leaders, helped clarify their message. The difference now, however, is that Ordain Women and its supporters have emerged very quickly as a twenty-first century radical flank organization. As an organized reform movement, Ordain Women is committed to planning and executing actions that compel interested publics to take notice, delimit the core issue at stake (female ordination to the priesthood), stimulate vigorous debate over this core issue, focus attention on the core message of equality and, in the process, gain increased support from moderate Mormons outside the conservative core. In doing this, they directly confront and challenge both the inspired wisdom of established Church policy and the ecclesiastical authority of current Church leaders.

A critical grass-roots challenge, expressed through organized action in contradiction to the policies and ecclesiastical leadership of an HCS religion, agitates the conservative core and polarizes public opinion. In the absence of effective alternative narratives for reframing divisive issues, leaders in solidarity with the conservative core predictably repudiate the actions of the internal radical flank. The episode passes to be remembered as, at best, an "irregularity." If, however, an alternative narration already exists, then the "radical" actions of the radical flank stimulate a much wider range of feasible possibilities for addressing divisive issues which the alternative narrative creators had previously articulated. At the same time, only when internal radical flank actions succeed in resonating with and symbolizing the frustrations of a significant segment of the membership base, which consequently communicates mounting concerns, are HCS leaders likely to perceive a genuine problem. Initially, leaders respond to emerging concerns by ignoring the narratives in which they are couched, then by redefining them as the concerns of only a marginal few, and ultimately by acknowledging that there is "a problem" but not a serious one.

In the LDS Church, several modest accommodations may be contemplated at this point. Church authorities concede a small but related issue—let a woman speak, for example, in general conference, or call the women's general meeting of the preceding weekend a full-fledged session of conference (and not just an appended "prefireside"), etc. Ritual talks expressing appreciation for the contributions of women flow over the pulpit, and an address with a slightly more ambitious theological content is propounded: that women performing ordinances in the temple are exercising priesthood authority; that in the absence of the husband, the mother must not defer to her teenage son to "preside" in the home, etc. These small steps, many of them constructed for their Public Affairs visibility, can either be woven into cultural rituals or be quietly forgotten if the ecclesiastical need seems to pass. *Only those periods of a community's history in which alternative narratives converge with the emergence of an internal radical flank are likely to compel the concerted attention of conservative organizational leaders.* This is especially true of HCS religions like the LDS Church, which are recruitment-oriented and committed to global expansion. The Church can ill afford to lose the commitment of some of its ablest and best-educated lay members who are unsatisfied with the standard (but lopsided) nostrum that priesthood "equals" motherhood and, instead, want to raise their children in a Latter-day Saint religion that reinforces genuine gender equality.[25]

Given a single, "radical" option sponsored by the internal radical flank, more moderate concessions—previously dismissed as unrealistic—may now seem like reasonable considerations to be seriously entertained by HCS leaders. The relatively radical change sought by the internal radical flank is not immediately realized but smaller, more intermediate changes are introduced by HCS leaders who are able to rationalize them by integrating alternative narrative language to reframe the interpretation and application of core doctrines. By reframing official Church narratives to justify modest policy changes, Church leaders are able to maintain doctrinal and ecclesiastical credibility for system stalwarts.

To summarize, in Finnigan and Stearmer's analysis, HCS religions are relatively closed systems resistant to change. The primary tasks of their ecclesiastical leadership are to preserve adherence to central, founding doctrines and enforce obedient compliance to the directions of top-echelon Church authorities. In performing these tasks, upper-echelon leaders are staunchly supported by a conservative core of lay members. If reformative modifications in Church policies and corresponding doctrinal interpretations are to occur as a result of *internal pressures* from the membership side of the change equation, two grass-roots agents of change must emerge: alternative narrative creators and a radical flank. The interactive presence of both alternative narrative creators and a radical flank is, in Finnigan's and Stearmer's analysis, a necessary condition for internal, reformative change in hierarchical, conservative religious settings.

Radke-Moss's Analysis of the Evolving Conversation between Mormon Traditionalists and Feminists

The somewhat abstract language of Finnigan and Stearmer's theoretical model of internal reforms in HCS religions is congruent with our earlier descrip-

---

25. For example, in the spotlight as prototypical of the "new young Mormon activists," LDS couple Kristy Money and her husband Rolf Straubhaar are described in a recent interview at thoughtfulfaith.org as a "feminist activist" and "social justice activist" respectively. According to the interview's introduction, they are "indicative of a new wave of educated Mormons . . . a quintessential young Mormon couple, fresh out of graduate school with young children, but full of ideas and dreams of a more expansive and inclusive vision of the faith that has their devotion." See http://athoughtfulfaith.org/category/iews on mormon-stories-2/ (accessed January 17, 2014). Arguably, these are the kinds of contemporary Mormons that the LDS Church needs and wants to keep in the fold rather than losing them and their children to disillusionment with constricting gender teachings and practices in Mormon ecclesiastical culture. Chapter 5 of this book features Money's and Straubhaar's views and experience modeling egalitarian marriage and gender roles for their children in a Latter-day Saint family.

tion of closed systems and also with more familiar terminology used in Andrea Radke-Moss's online *Patheos* article entitled, "Mormon Women, Traditionalists and Feminists: An Evolving Conversation."[26] Radke-Moss frames her analysis of contemporary changes in LDS gender policies and practices as the result of an evolving conversation between "traditional" Mormon women (who support strictly defined gender roles in the Church) and Mormon feminist women occupying different points on a spectrum between moderates (committed to earnest dialogue with male priesthood leaders concerning greater gender inclusiveness) and the activists of Ordain Women (committed to public demonstrations promoting the ultimate goal of female ordination through petitioning and challenging the Church's highest leaders to seek revelation). By drawing on this foundational Mormon model, with its roots in Joseph Smith's first teenage prayer in the Sacred Grove, petitioners have appropriated one of the most powerful elements of faith in seeking knowledge and generating changes. Given the current contentiousness about women's roles and status in the Church, LDS authorities have gravitated toward the moderates' proposals for greater gender inclusiveness while sternly rejecting Ordain Women's chief objective of ordination and, especially, the defiant public methods employed to attain it.[27] As characterized by Radke-Moss, "traditional" Mormon women make up an important part of Finnigan and Stearmer's conservative core while, roughly speaking, a number of "moderate" Mormon feminists have functioned as alternative narrative creators, with the active supporters of Ordain Women clearly constituting a radical flank.

Congruent with Finnigan and Stearmer's HCS reform model of internal change, Radke-Moss argues that the activist agenda of Ordain Women has opened up a substantially wider stretch of middle ground in the intensifying arguments over women's status and treatment in the LDS Church, rapidly expanding the "conversation" not only for traditional Mormon women but also for LDS priesthood authorities. As Radke-Moss puts it: "The highest levels of church leadership have been pulled into this urgent conversation about Mormon

---

26. See http://www.patheos.com/Topics/2014-Religious-Trends/Mormon/Mormon-Women-Traditionalists-and-Feminists-Andrea-Radke-Moss-071014.html (accessed January 2, 2015).

27. A prime example of more moderate proposals for change in LDS gender relations and practices, which seem increasingly reasonable to local priesthood authorities, is offered in Neylan McBaine's recent book, *Women at Church: Magnifying LDS Women's Local Impact* (Salt Lake City: Greg Kofford Books, 2014). McBaine argues that discriminatory practices with no basis in Church doctrine can and should be changed at the grassroots level of ward and stake organizations without the need for female priesthood ordination. She advocates cooperative strategies for doing this and eschews organized agitation or public demonstrations that provoke criticism of Church leaders. McBaine thus rejects both the goals of Ordain Women (priesthood ordination) and its methods (organized public dissent). At the same time, in a personal interview with us, McBaine acknowledged that OW's actions have forced more open discussion of gender issues and enabled the dissemination and consideration of her book in LDS Church networks.

women's relationship to priesthood, often in new and expansive ways," and that Ordain Women's advocacy "has brought discussions about gender in the Church from the margins to the center."

Softening their rhetoric in recent years on such issues as contraceptives, working mothers, women's pursuit of higher education, professional careers, and egalitarian parenting responsibilities, LDS authorities have also revised policies that allow greater gender inclusiveness in a number of ecclesiastical settings. Thus, for example, age eligibility for sister missionaries has been reduced from twenty-one to nineteen, not only generating an unprecedented surge in the number of proselyting Mormon missionaries serving worldwide but also deconstructing previous gender stereotypes and barriers to young women's recruitment into LDS missionary ranks on par with the kind of encouragement previously reserved for their male peers. (This topic is examined at length in Chapter 13.) Women are now called upon to offer prayers and speak at the annual and semi-annual general conferences of the Church. At general conference, women presidencies of the Young Women (teens), Primary (children ages eighteen months to twelve), and Relief Society (all women over age eighteen) auxiliaries are now seated on the dais alongside male priesthood authorities, In October 2014, a separate session of the general conference for all women over age eight has been instituted in purposeful symmetry with the all-male session general priesthood sessions. These changes may seem very small, but they also are unprecedented in Mormon history and appear to be directly correlated with unfavorable publicity concerning the discriminatory treatment of Mormon women stimulated by Ordain Women supporters and other feminist critics who claim continued attachment to their Mormon roots.

Expounding on what she sees as the expansive way in which LDS authorities are being pulled into the feminist conversation, Radke-Moss speculates about the implications of Apostle Dallin Oaks's October 2014 conference address on the Mormon doctrine in which he asked—and significantly left unanswered: "We are not accustomed to speaking of women having the authority of the priesthood in their church callings, but what other authority can it be?"[28] If the Church stipulates that women already exercise priesthood authority in their Church callings without ordination, Radke-Moss wonders what would bar LDS women in the future from greater inclusion in Church leadership positions such as Sunday School presidencies, ward and stake clerks, zone and district leaders in mission field organizations, or even counselors in bishoprics and branch presidencies.

It should be noted here that, in response to the ferment for change they appear to have accelerated, most Ordain Women supporters and other radical flank feminists applaud any forward progress being made but counter-argue that, in the absence of female ordination, Mormon women can never achieve true parity with men in the LDS Church.

---

28. Dallin H. Oaks, "The Keys and Authority of the Priesthood," https://www.lds.org/general-conference/2014/04/the-keys-and-authority-of-the-priesthood (accessed April 18, 2014).

Moderating changes in LDS authorities' rhetoric concerning women's issues, as well as incremental policy changes, may also be attributed to the kinds of leadership accommodation to secular, societal trends that Mauss identified in his "tension management" theory of modern Mormonism. Mormon authorities, especially in concert with the professionally staffed Public Affairs Department at Church headquarters, are sensitized to public opinion concerning perceptions of modern Mormonism as a mysterious and even aberrant religious faith.[29] Mitt Romney's two unsuccessful presidential campaigns clarified just how deep the misunderstanding ran. Public Affairs systematically has attempted to counter this perception by characterizing U.S. Mormons as typical Americans whose traditional family values are consistent with the views of other mainline conservative faiths in the American religious economy. Concurrently, Ordain Women's internal, radical flank commitment to female priesthood ordination has made modest LDS policy modifications seem cautiously compatible with growing gender egalitarianism in civil society. In the meantime, Church leaders' religious credibility with traditionalists has been preserved by continued insistence that priesthood ordination policies can be altered only through divine revelation and not through public agitation. (This, of course, was the same protective rhetoric initially employed by Church leaders when plural marriage and the exclusion of black men from priesthood ordination were objects of intense public opposition.)

Ordain Women's strategy has been to agree absolutely with the need for new revelation on the matter of female ordination but to fundamentally disagree that they are engaging in egregious methods. OW activists believe their methods are entirely consistent with their Mormon faith tradition by continuing to call for prayer from the General Authorities, to appear in public attired appropriately to worship with their brother men in priesthood meetings, and to share heartfelt testimonies about the spiritual growth they make in walking their "covenant path"—theme of the Young Women program in April 2014 but earlier introduced as a metaphor in the addresses of Mary N. Cook (April 2013), Carole M. Stephens (October 2013), Linda K. Burton (April 2014), Henry B. Eyring (October 2014), and Carol F. McConkie (October 2014). To them—a "radical flank" raising strong voices for equality—God will send revelation when the people righteously express their readiness to receive it and earnestly petition their authorized leaders to request it be given.[30] It is precisely this kind of willing-

---

29. In a 2011 national Pew survey, only 51 percent of respondents thought that Mormonism was a Christian faith, while the word most commonly picked by respondents to describe the Mormon faith was "cult." For a summary review of these survey results, see http://www.pewforum.org/2012/01/12/mormons-in-america-executive-summary/ (accessed April 21, 2014).

30. In his chapter on LDS organizational and doctrinal change in this volume (Chapter 10), Gregory A. Prince differentiates between "trickle-down" and "trickle-up" revelation to clarify the historical complexities of the Mormon revelatory process. By "trickle-down" revelation he means revelatory changes initiated by Mormonism's prophetic leadership, as

ness to publicly contest and even appear to instruct (however politely) prophetic priesthood authorities in their religious duties that strikes the conservative core as outrageous and intolerable. At the same time, persistent agitation by Ordain Women's radical flank actions is likely to continue paving the way for incremental changes in the direction of greater gender equality in LDS ecclesiastical culture.

Brayden King, Marie Cornwall, and Eric Dahlin's Analysis of the Logic of the Legislative Process

As a final helpful theory in exploring change in closed systems, Brayden King, Marie Cornwall, and Eric Dahlin's sophisticated analysis of the fifty-year political saga of the suffrage movement to win the vote for U.S. women offers some parallel understandings of the roadblocks confronting reform movements (even in democratically constituted systems) that complicate quick realization of their objectives.[31]

In what King, Cornwall, and Dahlin call the "logic of the legislative process," the political influence of organized reform movements (like the suffragists) is predictably greater at the earlier stages of the legislative process but substantially wanes thereafter as the political stakes rise, opposition intensifies, and movement resources typically dwindle. This is especially likely to be the case when the objectives of reform involve deeply entrenched cultural practices that enjoy the legal sanction of existing law (such as denial of political suffrage on the basis of race, gender, or religion). Thus, through careful statistical analysis of the suffragists' historical efforts from 1866 to 1918 to change voting laws through state legislatures, King, Cornwall, and Dahlin conclude that "legislators responded to suffragists by bringing the issue of woman suffrage to the legislative forum, but once suffrage bills reached the voting stage, differences in social movement tactics and organization did not have as great an impact." It is the "logic" of the legislative process—especially the mobilization of opposition and legislators' political need to satisfy the different demands of different constituencies in order to stay in office—that predictably retards the speedy realization of reformist goals

---

epitomized in the revelations of Church founder Joseph Smith. Prince argues, however, that over time, "the dynamics of change evolved in a different direction as more and more changes at the top were driven by changes effected at the grassroots level—that is, 'trickle-up revelation' became at least as important as 'trickle-down revelation,' until the correlation movement that began in the 1960s largely shut it down." It is the reinstatement of trickle-up revelation in the Mormon tradition that Ordain Women and their supporters advocate.

31. See Brayden G. King, Marie Cornwall, and Eric C. Dahlin, "Winning Woman Suffrage One Step at a Time: Social Movements and the Logic of the Legislative Process," *Social Forces* 83, no. 3 (2005): 1211–34. For related analyses, see Brayden G. King and Marie Cornwall, "Specialists and Generalists: Learning Strategies in the Woman Suffrage Movement, 1866–1918," *Research in Social Movements, Conflicts and Change* 26 (2005): 1–34, and Brayden G. King, "A Political Mediation Model of Corporate Response to Social Movement Activism," *Administrative Science Quarterly* 53, no. 3 (2008): 395–421.

in democratic systems. The fifty-year suffragists' battle showed a pattern of early successes, subsequent losses, and years of stagnation, but final victory as state legislatures gained sufficient national support to pass the Nineteenth Amendment to the U.S. Constitution, granting women the right to vote.

The apostles and First Presidency of the LDS Church are not, of course, a democratically elected, legislative body. United, however, they constitute the upper echelon priesthood body of a relatively closed religious system charged with responsibility for interpreting doctrine and formulating Church policy. In this system, are they not also political actors? As apostles prayerfully discuss religious questions and related policies in their ecclesiastical councils, are they not, like other human legislators, constrained in some sense by a political process which ultimately produces a religious consensus? To us, this conclusion clearly follows from the common observation that religious leaders (even prophets) are human; that however reliant they might be in their supplications for divine guidance, their judgments are not free from human caprice, foibles, or cultural prejudices.[32] It is the human side of LDS doctrinal and policy debates that makes political science analysis of the legislative process relevant to our attempts to understand the current and future impact of Ordain Women's organized efforts to gain priesthood ordination. If the past and analogous histories of reform movements (especially in relatively closed systems) teach us something, it is that meaningful reforms commonly come only after adherents pay a high price of lengthy and committed struggle against determined resistance. Furthermore, as the battle for the Equal Right Amendment has shown, there is no guarantee of ultimate success.[33]

Conclusion

The cultural and political matrix of both internal and external pressures for accommodating change in growth-oriented HCS religions that are situated in

---

32. Recent, official admission of human error and cultural prejudice in the LDS Church's 125-year policy of priesthood denial to males of African American descent stands as an epic case in point. The official acknowledgement is at https://www.lds.org/topics/race-and-the-priesthood. No author is identified nor date of posting; however, it was first accessed on December 10, 2013, according to web.archives.org (Wayback Machine). Both the reversal of this priesthood policy in 1978 and the current disavowal of its erstwhile theological rationale are a major point of reference and source of hope for Mormon feminists seeking priesthood ordination.

33. Winning the right to vote by amendment of the Constitution did not, of course, produce instant political equality for U.S. women who now, nearly 100 years later, must continue struggling to achieve full political parity with men at both the national and state levels of American government. Similarly, passage of the Civil Rights and Voting Acts of 1964 and 1965, did not put an end to racial discrimination in American political and civic culture. For a concise case study of the ongoing dialectic of African American enfranchisement and disfranchisement in Arkansas, both after the Civil War and, 100 years later, after passage of the 1965 Voting Rights Act, see John A. Kirk, "A Long Struggle," *Arkansas Times* 1, no. 22 (2014): 16–21.

relatively open, competitive religious economies—along with reactionary resistance to accommodation from the conservative core—combine to virtually guarantee complex and uneven historical trajectories, especially in the short run. In the *long run*, the benefit of hindsight allows scholars to discern larger patterns from the historical record and to assess more confidently the causes and consequences of bygone issues in bygone eras that, in turn, give rise to contemporary conflicts and the ultimate uncertainty of their future resolution.[34]

The theoretical models we have summarized for analyzing the impact of women's issues in the LDS Church predict incremental change in the short run, punctuated by convoluted starts and stops, breakthroughs and regressions, and seemingly contradictory developments. How long must the long run be to clearly discern the big picture of institutional change? Decades? Centuries? Given women's rapid twenty-first century secular advances in higher education, professional occupations, and leadership/management positions in both industry and government toward greater parity with men, how probable is it that the LDS Church will indefinitely resist gender parity in priesthood leadership and decision-making roles in its governing councils? And from the standpoint of this book, an important corollary question must also be asked: Given continued official resistance to its efforts, how probable is it that Ordain Women will continue to function as a cohesive, radical flank organization within LDS culture? Will OW activists sustain forward momentum in the years to come or will their moment quickly pass and be forgotten? How will historians 100 years hence view current OW activists and their supporters? As deluded heretics? As feminist heroines? Or as something in between? Our children's children will know the answer.

---

34. Concerning the long run, a religious leader and man of faith, the Reverend Martin Luther King, memorably declared, "The arc of the moral universe is long, but it bends towards justice." See Martin Luther King Jr., "Out of the Long Night," *The Gospel Messenger: Official Organ of the Church of the Brethren* 107, no. 6 (1958): 14. Ten years after his inspiring affirmation of the future of race relations in the United States, Dr. King was shot to death in Memphis, Tennessee, while lending his moral support to striking, African American sanitation workers.

Chapter 3

"The Greatest Glory of True Womanhood": Eve and the Construction of Mormon Gender Identity

Boyd Jay Petersen

Introduction

"The Family: A Proclamation to the World" offers Adam and Eve as the paradigmatic ideal family: "The first commandment that God gave to Adam and Eve pertained to their potential for parenthood as husband and wife."[1] Read by President Gordon B. Hinckley at the Relief Society general meeting on September 23, 1995, the document was almost certainly created for a distinctly political purpose. Most Latter-day Saints are not aware that when the Church issued "The Family: A Proclamation to the World," the institution was already deeply enmeshed in the political debate over same-sex marriage. The issue was on Church leaders' radar as early as 1984 when Elder Dallin Oaks drafted a memorandum outlining possible approaches the Church might take on the issue. Oaks was called as an apostle on April 7, 1984, and the memorandum is dated August 7, 1984, suggesting that it was one of his first assignments. In that memorandum, Oaks speculates that the Equal Rights Amendment may have been used to usher in gay marriage; and he also notes the potential "irony" inherent in the Church's issuing a statement against same-sex marriage: The Supreme Court case that established that marriage is between one man and one woman is the 1878 Reynolds anti-polygamy decision that quashed the LDS Church's practice of plural marriages.[2] In 1988 the Church hired a marketing firm to promote the Church's position in state legislatures and the U.S. Congress.[3]

---

1. The First Presidency and Council of the Twelve Apostles of the Church of Jesus Christ of Latter-Day Saints, "The Family: A Proclamation to the World," https://www.lds.org/topics/family-proclamation (accessed March 14, 2014).

2. Dallin H. Oaks, "Principles to Govern Possible Public Statement on Legislation Affecting Rights of Homosexuals," https://drive.google.com/folderview?id=0B1u3K43P-3JoNzNlY2IwNmMtMTMzYy00ZjM4LTgzMDgtNGVjZjljMThiY2Y4&usp=drive_web&hl=en&ddrp=1# (accessed May 12, 2015). See Laura Compton, "From Aloha to Ohana," May 15, 2015, http://rationalfaiths.com/from-amici-to-ohana/ (accessed May 16, 2015), for a cogent analysis of the social and legal background in which the proclamation was produced and first began to be used.

3. Richley Crapo, "Chronology of Mormon/LDS Involvement in Same-Sex Marriage Politics, Mormon Social Science Association, 1997, http://www.mormonsocialscience.org/2008/01/04/richley-crapo-chronology-of-mormon-lds-involvement-in-same-sex-

The Proclamation on the Family was released soon after the LDS Church had been denied standing by the Hawaiian Supreme Court in *Baehr v. Miike*, the first gay marriage case in the United States.[4] The document was then included in the amicus curiae brief that the Church filed in support of the case. The timing and subsequent use of the proclamation suggest it was designed for a destinctly political purpose: to demonstrate authoritatively that the LDS Church has a stake in the same-sex marriage debate. Indeed, a 1999 *Church News* article drew a distinction between Church-issued documents called "declarations," "statements," and "proclamations," stating that "generally, declarations and statements are directed at Church membership, whereas proclamations are meant to reach beyond the scope of Church membership."[5] Aside from being attached to the Church's amicus brief in the Hawaii case, on November 17, 1995, Utah Congressman Jim

---

marriage-politics/ (accessed May 12, 2015). See also Kaimipono David Wenger, "'The Divine Institution of Marriage': An Overview of LDS Involvement in the Proposition 8 Campaign," *Journal of Civil Rights and Economic Development* 26, no. 3 (2012), http://ssrn.com/abstract=2254634 (accessed May 12, 2015).

4. See *Baehr v. Miike, Justia US Law,* Justia.com http://law.justia.com/cases/hawaii/supreme-court/1996/18905-2.html (accessed May 6, 2015). In 1990 three same-sex couples sued the state of Hawaii for refusing them marriage licenses. After the circuit court dismissed the case, the couples appealed to the Supreme Court of Hawaii, which ruled that the government must show a "compelling public interest" in denying marriage to same-sex couples, and sent the case back to the lower court for further review. On February 14, 1994, the First Presidency of the LDS Church issued a statement declaring that "marriage between a man and a woman is ordained of God," signaling its opposition to "any efforts to give legal authorization to marriages between persons of the same gender," and urging members of the Church to "appeal to legislatures, judges and other government officials to preserve the purposes and sanctity of marriage between a man and a woman." A week later, the LDS Church's Hawaii Public Affairs Council announced its intention to petition the court to become a co-defendant in the Hawaii lawsuit. In that petition, the Church expressed fears that if same-sex marriages became legal the Church might lose its right to issue marriage licenses and that it might be subject to discriminatory lawsuits. However, the court rejected the Church's argument, stating that, since state laws force no minister to marry anyone, therefore any lawsuit filed against the Church would be considered frivolous. The Church appealed the court's decision and in January 1996, the Hawaii Supreme Court rejected the Church's appeal for standing. Around this same time, the LDS Church joined the Roman Catholic Church to form a lobbying group called Hawaii's Future Today. The Church statement was released on February 1, 1994, and is available at https://www.lds.org/ensign/1994/04/news-of-the-church/first-presidency-statement-opposing-same-gender-marriages (accessed May 12, 2015). It was reiterated in "Church Supports Call for Constitutional Amendment," *Ensign*, July 2006 available at https://www.lds.org/ensign/2006/07/news-of-the-church/church-supports-call-for-constitutional-amendment? (accessed May 12, 2015).

5. Julie A. Dockstader, "Proclamations, Declarations Clarify, Reaffirm LDS Doctrine," *Church News*, November 6, 1999 available at http://www.ldschurchnewsarchive.com/articles/36742/Proclamations-declarations-clarify-reaffirm-LDS-doctrine.html (accessed May 12, 2015).

Hansen read the proclamation into the record of the House of Representatives.[6] Four days later, President Hinckley and Apostle Neal A. Maxwell presented a copy to U.S. President Bill Clinton and Vice President Al Gore as they met in the White House to discuss ways to strengthen families.[7] In March 1997, Church representatives distributed the proclamation translated into Czech, English, French, Spanish, German, and Russian at UN World Congress of Families in Prague.[8] Framed copies of the proclamation have been presented to heads of state, foreign dignitaries, and high-ranking U.S. officials, including General Colin Powell, Texas Governor George Bush, Idaho Governor Dirk Kempthorne; presidents of Mexico, Italy, and French Polynesia; the prime minister of South Korea; the king of Tonga; and political leaders in Brazil and Australia.[9]

---

6. Compton, "From Aloha to Ohana."

7. Sheri L. Dew, *Go Forward with Faith: The Biography of Gordon B. Hinckley* (Salt Lake City: Deseret Book, 1996), 527. See also "News of the Church," *Ensign*, February 1996, available at https://www.lds.org/ensign/1996/02/news-of-the-church (accessed May 12, 2015).

8. "LDS to Be at World Congress of Families," *Church News* February 15, 1997, available at http://www.ldschurchnewsarchive.com/articles/29738/LDS-to-be-at-World-Congress-of-Families.html (accessed May 12, 2015); "Church Delegates Attend World Congress of Families," *Ensign*, June 1997, https://www.lds.org/ensign/1997/06/news-of-the-church/church-delegates-attend-world-congress-of-families (accessed May 12, 2015).

9. "Mission President Visits with Italian Leader," *Church News*, December 7, 1996, http://www.ldschurchnewsarchive.com/articles/27667/Mission-president-visits-with-Italian-leader.html (accessed May 12, 2015); Michael Leonard, "Apostles Meet with Prominent Media Leaders and Executives," *Church News*, February 8, 1997, http://www.ldschurchnewsarchive.com/articles/29556/Apostles-meet-with-prominent-media-leaders-and-executives.html (accessed May 12, 2015); "From around the World," *Church News*, December 20, 1997, http://www.ldschurchnewsarchive.com/articles/29539/From-around-the-World.html (accessed May 12, 2015); "News of the Church," *Ensign*, February 1998, https://www.lds.org/ensign/1998/02/news-of-the-church (accessed May 12, 2015); Christopher K. Bigelow, "Australia: Coming Out of Obscurity Down Under," *Ensign*, December 1998, https://www.lds.org/ensign/1998/12/australia-coming-out-of-obscurity-down-under (accessed May 12, 2015); "News of the Church," *Ensign*, June 2000, https://www.lds.org/ensign/1998/02/news-of-the-church (accessed May 12, 2015); "Solomon Islands Prime Minister Presented with Family Proclamation," *Church News*, February 11, 2011, https://www.lds.org/church/news/solomon-islands-prime-minister (accessed May 12, 2015); "South Korea," *Ensign*, August 2011, https://www.lds.org/ensign/2011/08/small-and-simple-things/south-korea (accessed May 12, 2015); "Tonga's LDS Note King's Birthday," *Church News*, July 11, 1998, http://www.ldschurchnewsarchive.com/articles/30890/Tongas-LDS-note-kings-birthday.html; "President Monson Dedicates Temple, Meets with Vice President in Brazil," *Liahona*, October 2008, https://www.lds.org/liahona/2008/10/news-of-the-church/president-monson-dedicates-temple-meets-with-vice-president-in-brazil (accessed May 12, 2015); Walter Cooley, "Hosts Give Warm Welcome to Visiting Dignitaries," *Ensign*, March 2006, https://www.lds.org/ensign/2006/03/news-of-the-church/hosts-give-warm-welcome-to-visiting-dignitaries (accessed May 12, 2015).

Furthermore, it has continued to be attached as an amendment to amicus briefs the Church has filed or been party to, including *Perry v. Schwarzenegger* (2010), *Commonwealth of Massachusetts v. United States Department of Health and Human Services* (2011), *Hollingsworth v. Perry* (2013), *Kitchen v. Herbert* (2013), *De Leon v. Perry* (2014), *Herbert v. Kitchen* (2014), and, most recently, *Obergefell v. Hodges* (2015).[10]

Likewise, the proclamation has been cited in many official public statements about same-sex marriage. When the U.S. Senate considered an amendment to the Constitution to protect marriage in 2006, the Church issued a supportive statement citing the proclamation, opposing gay marriage, and urging U.S. Mormons to "express themselves . . . to their elected leaders." Elder Russell M. Nelson quoted the proclamation in a speech at a press conference for the Alliance for Marriage at the U.S. Capitol building, and it was featured prominently in the controversial 2008 debate over California's Proposition 8, including in an LDS Newsroom commentary.[11] The Proclamation on the Family certainly motivated members of the Church to participate in the Prop. 8 campaign. Protect Marriage, a political action group opposed to same-sex marriage, estimated that Mormons contributed over half of the $40 million raised to support the amendment and represented between 80 to 90 percent of the early canvassing volunteers.[12] Even though the proclamation has not been accepted as scripture, it has nevertheless achieved authoritative status within the Church, having been fully integrated into Church curricula, periodicals, and General Authority discourses. (See Fig. 1).[13] The document is often given to young couples after their temple marriages, and some wards have supplied every individual or couple within its boundaries with a copy. Furthermore, with its official-looking layout and design, it invites special status as a material sign of Mormon devotion: members often decorate the walls of their homes with elegantly framed copies of the document, often with pictures of their family ensconced around it.

---

10. See Appendix for full citations.

11. "Religious Marriage Coalition," *Newsroom* April 24, 2006, http://www.mormonnewsroom.org/article/religious-marriage-coalition (accessed May 12, 2015); "Church Leader Speaks at the U.S. Capitol to Protect Marriage," *Newsroom* June 5, 2006 http://www.mormonnewsroom.org/article/church-leader-speaks-at-the-u.s.-capitol-to-protect-marriage (accessed May 12, 2015); "The Divine Institution of Marriage," Commentary, *Newsroom* 2008, http://www.mormonnewsroom.org/ldsnewsroom/eng/commentary/the-divine-institution-of-marriage (accessed May 12, 2015).

12. Jesse McKinley and Kirk Johnson, "Mormons Tipped Scale in Ban on Gay Marriage," *New York Times*, November 15, 2008, http://www.nytimes.com/2008/11/15/us/politics/15marriage.html?pagewanted=all&_r=0 (accessed May 12, 2015).

13. Significantly, in the *Preach My Gospel* manual, the proclamation is listed in boxes labeled "Scripture Study," thus equating the proclamation with scripture in the minds of missionaries in particular and Church members in general.

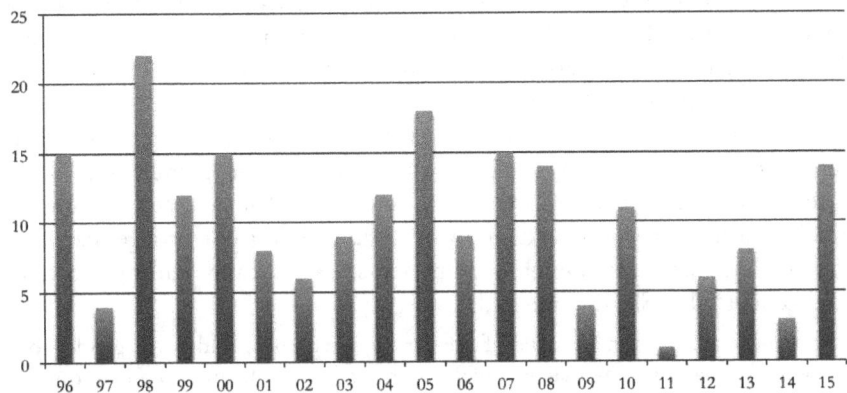

Figure 1. Frequency of the Proclamation on the Family in general conference addresses, according to BYU Corpus.

While the proclamation does not specifically address same-sex marriage—its first sentence states that "marriage between a man and a woman is ordained of God"—it also has a lot to say about gender roles. Feminists and gender studies scholars have often expressed bewilderment at the proclamation's insistence that *gender* is "an essential characteristic of individual premortal, mortal, and eternal identity and purpose."[14] Since sex is defined as the *biological morphology* of the individual (i.e., his or her reproductive organs), while gender is defined as the *performative conduct* of the individual (i.e., his or her dress and behavior), it seems strange to read that "gender," rather than "sex," is eternal. We are born with sex, but we learn to act according to gender norms. And gender norms are not consistent between cultures or throughout time.

It may well be that the authors[15] of the proclamation used the term "gender" as a euphemistic substitute for "sex," a word that has taken on the connotative

---

14. Prior to the early mid-twentieth century, "sex" was defined as either of the two categories (male and female) whereby humans and most other living things can be divided on the basis of their reproductive organs. Sex was a classificatory signifier, but not a signifier for copulation. According to the *Oxford English Dictionary*, "to have sex" (meaning to engage in intercourse) originates in D. H. Lawrence's 1929 poetry collection *Pansies*. Since that time, the word "sex" became synonymous with "sexual activity," and some people have come to use the word "gender" as a euphemism for the category marker "sex."

15. Although the First Presidency and Quorum of the Twelve have all signed the Proclamation, no one has said who actually wrote the document, and no author is credited. It was likely a committee project, like many recent statements issued by the Church. It does, however, show strong parallels, including allusions to and close paraphrases of Elder Boyd K. Packer's address, "For Time and All Eternity" delivered at the October 1993 general conference. In that discourse, Elder Packer states that God's plan requires "the righteous union of male and female" and asserts that "gender" existed prior to mortality in the preexistence. While he emphasized that men and women are equal in God's sight,

meaning of sexual acts.[16] So when the proclamation says "gender is eternal," we might assume that the Church really means "sex is eternal." However, it may also reflect a fundamental, perhaps unconscious, fear that gay marriage upsets the traditional gender roles of Western—particularly Mormon—culture. In a blog post on *Nursing Cleo*, a scholarly forum on gender and medicine, Tiffany K. Wayne wrote that, as she was listening to people at "protect marriage" rallies outside the Supreme Court in 2013, she came to the conclusion that their concern was not only their beliefs that homosexuality was sinful or that gay marriage may harm children, but that same-sex marriage presents a significant challenge to traditional gender roles. She commented:

> Same-sex marriage makes a lie of the very foundation of traditional gender roles. Same-sex marriages say that a woman can run a household, or that a man can raise a child. Same-sex marriage threatens the very foundation of what it means to *be* a woman/wife or be a man/husband. Who is in charge? Who will submit? Who will raise the children? Who is the man and who is the woman in the relationship? These are not questions of sex or sexuality; they are questions of gender. And when it comes to gender, same-sex marriage reveals the questions themselves as flawed.[17]

Same-sex marriage, in other words, unmasks the arbitrary nature of gender roles, calling them into question and destabilizing our long-held customs and beliefs about the essential nature of what it means to be male or female.

With its patriarchal structure, the LDS Church has a strong interest in shoring up the boundaries of traditional gender roles, and Eve has played a prominent role in that campaign. Institutional discourse about Eve is often prescriptive, holding Eve up as an model of ideal Mormon womanhood. In contrast, LDS

---

he also stressed that "both the scriptures and the patterns of nature place man as the protector, the provider," while woman is "the primary nurturer of the children." The Proclamation on the Family not only makes similar points but uses the same rhetoric. Interestingly, although Packer in his orally delivered address at the October 2011 general conference referred to it as a "revelation," the published version of his talk backtracked on this claim to "inspired counsel," continuing to leave its exact status somewhat uncertain—definitely not canonized but still highly authoritative.

16. Significantly, James E. Talmage, a Victorian who would have been too prudish to use a term like "sex" to communicate sexual intercourse, published his essay "The Eternity of Sex" in 1914, just prior to the usage change. But Talmage's essay essentially communicates the same message as the proclamation, except that he uses "sex" rather than "gender." As Talmage put it, "The distinction between male and female is no condition peculiar to the relatively brief period of mortal life; it was an essential characteristic of our pre-existent state, even as it shall continue after death, in both the disembodied and resurrected states." James P. Harris, ed., *The Essential James E. Talmage* (Salt Lake City: Signature Books, 1997), http://signaturebookslibrary.org/?p=14234. Talmage's article was originally published in the *Young Woman's Journal* 25 (October 1914): 600–604.

17. Tiffany K. Wayne, "Same-Sex Marriage Does Threaten 'Traditional' Marriage," *Nursing Clio*, April 2, 2013, http://nursingclio.org/2013/04/02/same-sex-marriage-does-threaten-traditional-marriage/ (accessed May 1, 2015).

women's personal, lived-religious descriptions of Eve often reflect their deepest longings, concerns, joys, and sadness. In this essay, after briefly considering the philosophical roots of Western gender roles, I explore how Eve has filled these dual prescriptive institutional and descriptive personal functions within Mormonism from the nineteenth century to the present. I believe this approach will demonstrate both the centrality of Eve in Mormon gender discourse and how the sometimes competing or even mutually incommensurate depictions of Eve have worked to construct and undermine Mormon women's gender identity.

The Origins of Gender Roles

Gender roles are as old as Western civilization itself and are, quite often, based upon significantly outmoded ideas about human biology and religious theology. Prudence Allen has argued that Aristotle not only "provided the foundation for the systematic advancement of knowledge" in Western culture, but also "for the intellectual roots of theories that distorted woman's identity" for millennia to come.[18] Aristotle believed men to be the ultimate realization of humanity. Women, in contrast, were defective, deficient, and deformed. He believed procreation involved an active, masculine element giving shape to a passive female element, as men provided the pattern for the fetus while women provided the matter out of which it was composed. He compared the process to creating cheese, "as rennet acts upon milk, for rennet is a kind of milk containing vital heat, which brings into one mass and fixes the similar material."[19] While we no longer accept the science behind Aristotle's reasoning, our words "father" and "mother" originate in this strange conception of biology: father is a cognate of the Latin *pater* which comes from the same root as "pattern"; mother is a cognate of the Latin *māter* which comes from the same root as "matter." Of course, the spiritual form provided by fathers was thought to be superior to the gross material substance provided by mothers.

The Greeks drew a sharp distinction between the public sphere of men (the *polis*), and that of women, the house (*oikos*). The *oikos* was the inferior realm of gross material infrastructure managed by women and slaves, whereas the male-controlled *polis* was, as J. G. A. Pocock writes, "the ideal superstructure in which one took actions which were not means to ends but ends in themselves."[20] (Significantly, our word "economics" comes from the Greek *oikos* and *nomos*, meaning "ordering of the household," and we have come to associate both the

---

18. Prudence Allen, *The Concept of Woman: The Early Humanist Reformation, 1250–1500* (Grand Rapids, Mich.: Eerdmans, 2002), 65. See generally Allen's Chapter 2, "Aristotelian Roots of Gender Identity in Academia."

19. Aristotle, qtd. in Marten Stol, "Embryology in Babylonia and the Bible," in *Imagining the Fetus: The Unborn in Myth, Religion, and Culture*, edited by Vanessa R. Sasson and Jane Marie Law (New York: Oxford University Press, 2009), 144.

20. J. G. A. Pocock, "The Ideal of Citizenship Since Classical Times," in *Theorizing Citizenship*, edited Ronald Beiner (Albany: State University of New York, 1995), 32.

world of economics and the world of politics with the male sphere outside of the home.) The view that men inhabit the public sphere of politics, economy, commerce, and law, while women inhabit the domestic sphere of child-rearing, housekeeping, and religious education carried on down through the Victorian era.

Bad theology further contributed to these twisted roles. From the time of the Jewish philosopher Philo of Alexandria in the first century and Augustine of Hippo in the fourth, well into the Middle Ages, the common interpretation of Genesis 1:26, where God proposed "let us make man in our image, after our likeness," was that that the male was created in the "image" of God, whereas woman was created after the image of man. By being both corporeal and woman, Eve was two steps removed from God, whereas Adam was only one. Ultimately, the bifurcation between the sexes resulted in the taxonomy shown in Table 1. Mormonism unavoidably adopted some of these gender roles from its surrounding culture.

The problem with the bifurcation of gender roles is that we inevitably value one side more than the other, paying lip service to one while the other gets promotions, raises, attention, and praise. Today, economists count every aspect of our economy: the GNP, GDP, and CPI; the DOW, Nasdaq, and S&P; manufacturing, government, and private sector job creation. They look at every imaginable measure of the production, distribution or trade, and consumption of goods and services. Yet none of these measurements take into account the value of work done in the home.[21]

Even though our understanding of biology is vastly different today than it was anciently and despite our modern rejection of sexist behavior, we continue to be influenced by antiquated ideas about gender roles. It is still common to hear men joke about how women are too emotional, or for both men and women to talk about how women are more nurturing. And while the women's rights movement of the 1970s made it politically incorrect to say things like "a woman's place is in the home," the notion that women should be more "domestic"—in charge of cooking, cleaning, washing, and caring for children—still flourishes within our contemporary society. Between 1970 and 2001, the percentage of families with an exclusive breadwinning father dropped from 56 to 25 percent in the United States.[22] Mormon families have been slower to follow this trend, with Mormon women twice as likely in 2008 to report they are housewives as non-Mormon women (26 percent vs. 13 percent); nevertheless, almost 50 percent of Mormon women work either full-time or part-time outside the home.[23]

---

21. Ann Crittenden, an economist who calculates the unpaid domestic contributions of (mostly) women in *The Price of Motherhood: Why the Most Important Job in the World Is Still the Least Valued* (New York: Metropolitan Books, 2001).

22. Sara B. Raley, Marybeth J. Mattingly, and Suzanne M. Bianchi, "How Dual Are Dual-Income Couples? Documenting Change From 1970 to 2001," *Journal of Marriage & Family* 68, no. 1 (February 2006): 11–28.

23. Rick Phillips and Ryan T. Cragun, *Mormons in the United States, 1990–2008: Socio-Demographic Trends and Regional Differences: A Report Based on the American Religious*

Table 1
Taxonomy of Gender Roles.

Man	Woman
• Active/stronger	• Passive/weaker
• Provide active element in procreation (form)	• Provide passive element in procreation (matter)
• Ruled by reason	• Ruled by passions
• Good judgment	• Deceived
• Fit for rule	• Fit to obey
• Dominant in the civic sphere	• Dominant in the domestic sphere
• Created in the image of God	• Created in the image of man

Compilation drawn from Allen, *The Concept of Woman*

Despite the fact that women have taken on more of the financial burden of raising their families, they still perform three times more of the household labor than men.[24] Many tasks, such as meal preparation, housecleaning, shopping for groceries, washing dishes, and doing laundry, are still considered "female" tasks. Combining their new responsibilities to help support the family with their traditional household tasks, many women are suffering from what researchers are calling "role overload," a stress factor that has a significant adverse effect on the mental and physical health of women.[25]

Realistically in a world economy, families will be forced to make further adjustments as these trends continue. Backlash often results when societal changes occur; feelings of insecurity inevitably accompany new roles and expectations. People tend to reinforce the traditional roles even as they are becoming more and more outdated and impossible to live. Yet the main problem with gender roles is that, for the most part, they are arbitrary. Take, for instance, the near-universal acceptance in the United States of baby colors: blue for boys and pink for girls. For centuries, most children, boys and girls, were dressed in practical white dresses that could be easily raised for diaper changing and easily bleached when diapers exploded. Pastel colors began to be introduced in the mid-nineteenth century; however, there was disagreement about which sex should wear which

---

Identification Survey 2008 (Hartford, Conn.: Trinity College, 2011), http://commons.trincoll.edu/aris/files/2011/12/Mormons2008.pdf (accessed May 13, 2015).

24. See, for example, Ganga Vijayasiri, "The Allocation of Housework: Extending the Gender Display Approach," *Gender Issues* 28, no. 3 (September 2011): 155–74; and Mylène Lachance-Grzela and Geneviève Bouchard, "Why Do Women Do the Lion's Share of Housework? A Decade of Research," *Sex Roles* 63, nos. 11–12 (December 2010): 767–80.

25. Keva Glynn, Heather Maclean, Tonia Forte, and Marsha Cohen, "The Association between Role Overload and Women's Mental Health," *Journal of Women's Health* 18, no. 2 (February 2009): 217–23.

color. A *Ladies' Home Journal* article in June 1918 said, "The generally accepted rule is pink for the boys, and blue for the girls. The reason is that pink, being a more decided and stronger color, is more suitable for the boy, while blue, which is more delicate and dainty, is prettier for the girl." Still others argued blonds should wear blue and brunettes should wear pink, while others argued that blue was for blue-eyed babies, pink for brown-eyed babies. In 1927, *Time* magazine provided readers with a chart documenting what the major U.S. stores felt to be the most appropriate colors for girls and boys. Filene's in Boston told parents to dress boys in pink, as did Best & Co. in New York City, Halle's in Cleveland, and Marshall Field in Chicago. It wasn't until the 1940s that industries settled on blue for boys and pink for girl—the standard of today. However, without really thinking about it, we assume it is monolithic and never-changing, something given, perhaps, by God to Adam and Eve in the Garden. It wasn't.[26]

Once it was considered shockingly unladylike for a woman to get an education or to vote. Nineteenth-century Mormon women were at the forefront of the suffrage movement and many sought an education. Nevertheless, no one would contradict Emily Spencer, a member of the first Relief Society founded at Nauvoo, when she wrote to the *Woman's Exponent* in 1875, stating that the women's rights movement had gone too far—that "to encourage women in wearing or imitating the dress of man is ridiculous."[27] History proves that a specific generation's expectations about gender behavior (or colors) are not eternal, unchanging, and universal, yet we assume concreteness in something that is arbitrary, universality in something that is localized, and timelessness in something that is utterly bound in time. Some gender roles made sense historically. Male dominance in upper body strength explains why men and women divided labor the way they did over the centuries. It's simply easier for a man than a woman to heft a bale of hay. Likewise, with women giving birth to children, it is logical that they would be concerned with creating a safe and comfortable "nest" for their children.

Yet across history and cultures, the specifics of gender roles are far from universal. Women were known as healers through the Middle Ages, until European universities (which excluded women) professionalized medicine and, at the same time, clerical and civil authorities began a campaign to brand women healers as witches.[28] Office clerical work was seen as men's work until World War II, when women picked up these tasks as men went off to war. When the men returned, however, the jobs were seen as "feminized" and clerks were renamed "secretaries" and "typists," and both the pay and the prestige for these jobs took a significant hit.

---

26. Jeanne Maglaty, "When Did Girls Start Wearing Pink?" Smithsonian.com. April 8, 2011, http://www.smithsonianmag.com/arts-culture/When-Did-Girls-Start-Wearing-Pink.html (accessed May 6, 2015).

27. Emily B. Spencer, "Answer to Inez," *Woman's Exponent* 4, no. 2 (15 June 1875): 16.

28. See, for example, W. L. Minkowski, "Women Healers of the Middle Ages: Selected Aspects of Their History," *American Journal of Public Health* 82, no. 2 (February 1992): 288–95.

Of course, in different cultures these gendered divisions of labor vary. In Saudi Arabia, women's roles are severely restricted, whereas women have served as ministers in the governments of Syria, Jordan, Egypt, Iraq, and Tunisia, and as vice president in Iran. Nevertheless, in the West, gender roles in work have traditionally followed an Aristotelian principle: public work is for men and private work is for women—even if it accomplishes much the same tasks: if it is work performed by or associated with males, it has prestige and high pay; if it is performed by or associated with females, it has less of both. Thus, men were chefs, while women were cooks; men were doctors, while women were nurses; men were professors, while women were schoolteachers. On rare occasions when women have had the primary role in a Western or Westernized government—Queen Elizabeth, Indira Gandhi, Golda Meir, Margaret Thatcher—they were mostly successful in so far as they led "like men"; they were not so much females-as-leaders as they were females-as-Honorary-Male-leaders. It is also significant that, despite the fact that women have been accepted in most every field in the United States, we have never had a female Commander in Chief.

Even the concept of marriage has evolved (thankfully). "For most of history it was inconceivable that people would choose their mates on the basis of something as fragile and irrational as love and then focus all their sexual, intimate and altruistic desires on the resulting marriage," writes Stephanie Coontz.[29] Anciently, marriage was a contractual exchange of woman as property, bought by the groom with a "bride price" to the father, and polygamy, concubines, and female slaves were often part of the norm. In the Middle Ages, marriage was used primarily as a way for nobles to create and maintain diplomatic ties between kingdoms. Marriages contracted by families, especially fathers, have been more common than marriages based on two people falling in love. As Justice Ruth Bader Ginsburg pointed out in the recent Supreme Court hearing in *Obergefell v. Hodges*, "marriage today is not what it was under the common law tradition," and until 1982 when Louisiana's "Head and Master Rule" was struck down, marriage in the United States could be defined as "a relationship of a dominant male to a subordinate female."[30]

Eve in the Nineteenth Century

The realities of frontier life and agrarian communities of nineteenth-century Mormonism required more fluidity within gender roles. Amy Hoyt and Sara Patterson have argued that pioneer femininity required a woman "who could work alongside her husband and support him as he carved civilization out of

---

29. Stephanie Coontz, *Marriage, a History: From Obedience to Intimacy, or How Love Conquered Marriage* (New York: Viking, 2005) 15.

30. *Obergefell v. Hodges*, Oral arguments, April 28, 2015, U.S. Supreme Court http://www.supremecourt.gov/oral_arguments/argument_transcripts/14-556q1_7l48.pdf (accessed May 14, 2015).

the wilderness."[31] Mormon masculinity was organized around the twin pillars of priesthood and polygamy. But with their husbands frequently away on missions, many Mormon women—whether monogamous or plural wives—were often left with the responsibility for both the sphere of domesticity and the sphere of commerce, keeping a home and keeping a career.

This did not stop nineteenth-century Church leaders from prescribing specific gender roles, and quite often they would cite Eve as a role model for Mormon women. Generally Latter-day Saints saw Eve in a different light than they do today. By partaking of the fruit, Eve fulfilled God's ultimate purpose; but being deceived, she did so inadvertently. James E. Talmage captured the standard nineteenth-century Mormon priesthood leaders' position on Eve in his 1899 book *The Articles of Faith*: "Our first parents are entitled to our deepest gratitude for their legacy to posterity—the means of winning title to glory, exaltation, and eternal lives." However, Talmage stressed, that while Eve "fulfill[ed] the foreordained purposes of God . . . she did not partake of the forbidden fruit with that object in view, but with the intent to violate the Divine command, being deceived by the sophistries of the serpent-fiend."[32]

Brigham Young believed that Eve was one of Adam's plural wives, whom he brought to this earth from a celestial sphere. In his sermons, he used Eve to caution women to remember their place in the home: "It is the calling of the wife and mother to . . . [labor] to make her home desirable to her husband and children, making herself an Eve in the midst of a little paradise of her own creating."[33] He also reminded women that "there is a curse upon the woman that is not upon the man, namely, that 'her whole affections shall be towards her husband,' and what is the next? 'He shall rule over you.'"[34] Young's counselor in the First Presidency, Heber C. Kimball, reminded Mormon priesthood holders that God "did not make the man for the woman but the woman for the man," but balanced this statement by admonishing, "If a man does not use a woman well and take good care of her, God will take her away from him and give her to another."[35]

Mormon women likewise held up Eve as a model for womanhood, but their attitudes were more varied and generally more generous. Eliza R. Snow called on a meeting of the Young Women's Retrenchment Association to abstain from "round dances," which she said "were originated by the adversary to lead to evil." To urge

---

31. Amy Hoyt and Sara M. Patterson, "Mormon Masculinity: Changing Gender Expectations in the Era of Transition from Polygamy to Monogamy, 1890–1920," *Gender & History* 23, no.1 (April 2011): 86.

32. James E. Talmage, *The Articles of Faith* (1899; rpt., Salt Lake City: Signature Books, 2003), 72–73.

33. Brigham Young, June 8, 1862, *Journal of Discourses*, 26 vols. (London and Liverpool: LDS Booksellers Depot, 1855–86), 10:28.

34. Brigham Young, September 21, 1856, *Journal of Discourses*, 4:57.

35. Heber C. Kimball, quoted by Helen Mar [Kimball] Whitney, "Scenes in Nauvoo, and Incidents from H.C. Kimball's Journal," *Woman's Exponent* 12, no. 5 (August 1, 1883): 34.

the sisters to take a strong stand, Snow asked, "As Eve led out in the evil, why should she not be the first in doing good?"³⁶ Citing the biblical injunction that Eve will be a "help meet" for the man, Phoebe Young, Brigham Young's daughter, stated, "It is not, then, our province to usurp the place, or do the work of our husbands, but to assist them, by every means in our power."³⁷ Almost twenty years later on the eve of Utah's statehood, Phoebe Young would articulate a strikingly different position: "Let not woman fear that she is overstepping the bounds prescribed by the Great Creator as the proper sphere of woman, for she was in the beginning created a helpmate for man and who will dare affirm she is out of place, because she shares his ambition and desires to assist in all great and worthy enterprises[?]"³⁸

Phoebe Young was not the first, nor was she the last, to interpret Eve's role more broadly. Emmeline B. Wells, writing under one of her numerous pseudonyms as Blanche Beechwood, saw the command to be a helpmeet and "a nearer conception of woman's mission and work" being fulfilled as the movement for women's suffrage allowed women to become "more thoroughly developed and highly educated." Beechwood continued, "Why should she not stand side by side with her brother, in all questions of interest for the common weal? For my part, I glory in the moral courage which arms woman with sufficient heroism to stand forth in her own defense, against any invasion upon her inherited rights and privileges."³⁹ Another writer to the *Woman's Exponent* saw Eve's role of "helpmeet" as "embrac[ing] all that was to be done, every requisition devolving upon mankind."⁴⁰ Eve's equality with Adam was stressed by M. E. Teasdale, who wrote, "Woman's sphere of usefulness is as great, and her influence as widely felt as man's. She was placed upon the earth with man to be his companion, his helpmate and his equal. 'She was not taken from his feet to be trampled upon by him, nor from his head to rule over him, but from his side to be equal with him; near his heart to be loved and cherished by him.'"⁴¹ Sarah Howard simply asked, "Do you think

---

36. "A Synopsis of Remarks, by Sister Eliza R. Snow, to the Young Ladies' Retrenchment Association of the 16th Ward," *Woman's Exponent* 3, no. 23 (May 1, 1875): 178.

37. Phoebe Young, "Woman's Voice," *Woman's Exponent* 4, no. 4 (July 15, 1875): 31.

38. Phoebe C. Young, "Ignorance and Superstition," *Woman's Exponent* 23, nos. 13–14 (January 1 and 15, 1895): 225–26.

39. Blanche Beechwood [Emmeline B. Wells], "Woman's Ambition," *Woman's Exponent* 4, no. 21 (April 1, 1876): 166.

40. E. A. Crane Waton, "Woman's Calling," *Woman's Exponent* 19, no. 4 (July 15, 1890): 27.

41. M. E. Teasdale, "Equality of Sex," *Woman's Exponent* 15, no. 24 (May 15, 1887): 185. This trope dates at least to the Middle Ages, but this particular version appears to be a paraphrase from Matthew Henry's Bible commentary, which states: "That the woman was made of a rib out of the side of Adam; not made out of his head to top him, not out of his feet to be trampled upon by him, but out of his side to be equal with him, under his arm to be protected, and near his heart to be beloved." *An Exposition of the Old and New Testament* (London: Joseph Ogle Robinson, 1828), 12. A decidedly different message comes from a Rabbinic midrash, where according to Genesis Rabbah 80:5, God says: "I will not create her

he would have created an inferior being for a helpmeet or companion for man, who had been created in the image of God[?]"[42] One woman even questioned the biblical record: "We are told in our earliest histories that man was made first, and that woman was so dependent on him, that even the first woman had to secure a start from man, and that afterwards she was placed in subjection to him, but this I doubt." She argued that women's subservience "never was a divine wish or expectation—was only a mundane retrogression that must first be checked before woman can attain her God-given position on [sic] strict equality with her liege lord, man."[43] Ida Peay reminded readers that God gave dominion to both Adam and Eve in Genesis 1:28: "God has always considered woman and commissioned her as he has man." She continued by calling for women's suffrage: "Man in his might and blindness has wrested from Eve's daughters their God-given rights in the dominion, hence this modern war which woman-kind is waging to obtain them back again. The struggle is surely divinely instituted and will ultimately succeed, for the world's problems to-day are sadly in need of the decisions of pure, high minded, God-fearing men and *women*."[44]

Eve in a New Century

As the Church moved to abandon polygamy between 1890 and 1910, it faced an identity crisis, forcing Latter-day Saints to confront the question of how to remain uniquely Mormon while assimilating into the larger American culture. Hoyt and Patterson argue that four pillars of Mormon manhood emerged to shore up that transition: a revised notion of priesthood, where the age of ordination was lowered to bring young men into Church activity sooner; a new adherence to the Word of Wisdom, where Mormon men were expected to fully abstain from tobacco, coffee, and alcohol; an increased expectation that young men would serve missions; and a new commitment to monogamous marriage. These four pillars set Mormon men apart and against the larger American culture.[45] Victorian society almost universally accepted the doctrine of "separate spheres," where women were guardians of home and hearth, and Mormons were no ex-

---

from Adam's head, lest she be swell-headed; nor from the eye, lest she be a coquette; nor from the ear, lest she be an eavesdropper; nor from the mouth, lest she be a gossip; nor from the heart, lest she be prone to jealousy; nor from the hand, lest she be light-fingered; nor from the foot, lest she be a gadabout; but from the modest part of man, for even when he stands naked, that part is covered." Quoted in Nehama Aschkenasy, *Eve's Journey: Feminine Images in Hebraic Literary Tradition* (Philadelphia: University of Pennsylvania Press, 1986), 44.

42. Sarah A. Howard, "Woman Suffrage," *Woman's Exponent* 22, no. 14 (March 15, 1894): 111.

43. D. P. Felt, "A Man's Advice about Woman Suffrage," *Woman's Exponent* 20, no. 10 (November 15, 1891): 73.

44. Ida S. Peay, "Taking a Stand for the Right," *Woman's Exponent* 41, no. 8 (June 1, 1913): 61; emphasis hers.

45. Hoyt and Patterson, "Mormon Masculinity," 72–91.

ception. As Susanna Morrill describes this concept, the "home-centered roles of mother and wife" were "seen as the glue that keeps society together."[46] Young Mormon women were tasked with guarding the virtue of young Mormon men. It was assumed that only men would hold the priesthood, that only they would be tempted to break the Word of Wisdom, and that only they would serve missions. Therefore young women were given the "enormous social burden" of protecting men's virtue.[47] Young Mormon women, like those of the larger Victorian culture, were taught to be righteous, talented, and desirable.[48]

Eve was frequently invoked to encourage women's positive influence over men. "Ever since Adam accused Eve in the Garden of Eden, men have been laying the blame of every great social wrong, in which both participated, on woman," wrote Wilhelmina Christafferson, but she went on to admit: It's "with a certain degree of justice." Women, Christafferson confessed, have immense power to influence the emotions of men. "It is needless to cite instances in proof of this; each one of us will readily call to mind instances of our own experience, and history will furnish others, of men, great men, men of strong character and exhibiting practical common sense in all the walks of life, who nevertheless became imbecile and acted like fools in cases where women were concerned." Women must acknowledge this powerful influence and "wield it openly and for good only."[49] Another wrote that "there are thousands of Adams to-day who smoke that vile weed tobacco, because some fair Eve has told them she admires the smell of a good cigar. Many a modern Adam has taken his first glass of wine because it was proffered by the beautiful jeweled hand of a modern Eve, and many a modern Adam reformed his habits and morals because some fair and lovely Eve, who is more to him than all the world beside, has told him that he *must do it*, or he can never occupy the same garden of Eden with her."[50]

Mary Anderson wrote that "if Eve had so much influence over her companion, should we not be careful how we use our influence over our companions, and associates by whom we are surrounded daily, for are we not all daughters of Eve[?]" Women must "use that influence which has been given her for a higher and better purpose," she argued.[51] "Ever since the days of mother Eve; woman's influence has been manifest for the advancement or retrogression of the people of the earth,"

---

46. Susanna Morrill, *White Roses on the Floor of Heaven: Mormon Women's Popular Theology, 1880–1920* (New York: Routledge, 2006), 20.

47. Hoyt and Patterson, "Mormon Masculinity," 83.

48. Ibid., 86.

49. Wilhelmina Christafferson, Letter to editor, *Woman's Exponent* 5, no. 3 (July 1, 1876): 19.

50. (Unattributed article), "Woman's Influence," *Woman's Exponent* 14, no. 15 (January 1, 1886): 114.

51. Mary Anderson, "An Answer to the Article Entitled 'Woman's Calling,'" *Woman's Exponent* 19, no. 6 (August 15, 1890): 42.

wrote Susie Armstrong; and "from that time until the present, woman by her influence has been more or less responsible, for the conditions of society."[52]

If Eve was culpable of leading Adam into sin, several writers argued, it is typically not the case for the woman to lead the man. "The old history of the Garden of Eden is repeating itself frequently. But in all recent repetitions of it, especially in political affairs, the Adam is the worst sinner. In ninety-nine cases out of a hundred he puts himself in the way of temptation, and in most of these he is saved from a fatal fall by his Eve."[53] Still another author saw men as the tempters. If women are called the "weaker sex," one author conceded, it is because of her "deep and pure love which gives her the lasting faith (of which men so frequently take the advantage) she being pure thinketh no evil, until her eyes are opened to see that she like 'Another Eve' has been deceived by Satan appearing in the form of man instead of a serpent."[54]

For Adelia B. Cox Sidwell, it was unfair to lay the blame for the fall on Eve. Condemned to wander in the garden for "untold centuries" with no female companionship, Eve must have longed for conversation, wrote Sidwell. "If I am allowed to judge Adam by most men of my acquaintance, he was probably very indifferent company, as men's conversational brilliancy is seldom exerted to any considerable extent for the benefit or entertainment of a wife." Suffering such isolation and being deprived of motherhood, woman's "crowning glory, comfort, joy," Sidwell continued, "who I ask can blame [Eve] for being discontent, and desiring a change in her monotonous existence? even though that change included Death!"[55]

Likewise, a woman writing under the name "Frances" stated that "the probability is if Adam had tasted [the fruit] first he would have kept the knowledge to himself and have not offered to share it with his companion." For Frances, Eve's inquisitive nature is only matched by her compassion. "She wished to share that which was good with her fellow-creature which is a credit to her, and certainly showed her to be actuated solely by motives of a purely unselfish and generous character."[56] Ruth May Fox contended that since Eve was blamed for the fall of humanity, "there has been a woman at the bottom of everything that savored of ill repute, but in the future there will be a woman at the bottom of everything that good [sic], not excluding good government."[57] Lucy M. Hewlings wrote, "If woman *was* foremost in the fall, she is first and foremost in every enterprise that has for its object the uplifting of humanity

---

52. Susie D. Armstrong, "Woman's Influence," *Woman's Exponent* 23, no. 18 (April 15, 1895): 254.

53. Ex. [pseud.], "A Vindication of Women," *Woman's Exponent* 5, no. 10 (October 15, 1876): 79.

54. R. [pseud.], "Woman," *Woman's Exponent* 5, no. 14 (December 15, 1876): 110–11.

55. Adelia B. Cox Sidwell, "Women of the Bible," *Woman's Exponent* 18, no. 17 (February 1, 1890): 136.

56. Frances [pseud.], "Woman," *Woman's Exponent* 20, no. 8 (October 15, 1891): 57.

57. R.M.F. [Ruth May Fox], "Lecture on Suffrage," *Woman's Exponent* 24, no. 6 (August 15, 1895): 41.

and the glory of God."[58] An unsigned editorial, likely written by Emmeline Wells, stressed Eve's role as the instigator of human progress: "Adam would probably have been content to remain in ignorance, but Eve, with woman's quick, keen perception, saw that the fruit of the tree of knowledge was pleasant to the sight and to be desired, and Adam was encouraged to eat of that which otherwise he might never have touched, because Eve offered it to him."[59]

Within the sphere of domestic life, Eve was seen as the role model for everything from raising a family to choosing appropriate clothing styles. As one woman wrote, the scriptures' teachings about Eve serve as "excellent instruction to the daughters of Zion," helping them "understand their true position" and purpose, to "keep the first great commandment given in the 'Garden of Eden,' viz. to multiply and replenish the earth."[60] Another woman, admonishing young women to learn how to cook, took a more comical tone: Eve "set us a worthy example" by "looking after, what she and Adam were to eat." And Adam partook, without "interfering with her domestic arrangements."[61] Sewing must be women's role, quipped M. C. Woods, "since our mother Eve must have used some sort of thread to sew the strings on her fig leaf apron."[62] "The domestic sphere is, of course, the theatre of woman's peculiar role, but did God intend her to be a domestic drudge?" asked Hannah Tapfield King. Toil is not mentioned in Eve's curse, she reminds readers. "That was especially man's punishment."[63]

Women not only looked to Eve for an example of how to keep their separate sphere in the home, but also, somewhat ironically, as an example of proper attire and as a critique of the vanity and folly of nineteenth-century women's fashions. Speaking of the "Idol of To-Day," Ruby Lamont, the pen name of Maria Miller Johnson, asked, "Does anyone suppose for a moment that Eve was supported by [a corset of] bones and steels? And that outrage to all modesty and beauty, that disgusting deformity of the human form and dishonor to God's handiwork and ourselves—the bustle! How must angels frown and demons laugh to see our sisters, the daughters of Zion! with that thing on to mock at and deform the shape that God has made!"[64] Citing the law given to Eve that "her husband should rule over her," Emily Spencer worried that for the woman's movement "to encourage women in wearing or imitating the dress of man is ridiculous." A woman responding to her did not discount how ridiculous it might be to dress like men

---

58. L.M.H. [Lucy M. Hewlings], "The Modern Esther," *Woman's Exponent* 25, no. 13 (January 1, 1897): 89.

59. "Woman's Influence," *Woman's Exponent* 14, no. 15 (January 1, 1886): 114.

60. I. P., "Woman's Voice," *Woman's Exponent* 16, no. 19 (March 1, 1888): 150.

61. Aunt Trudie, "Household Hints," *Woman's Exponent* 1, no. 17 (January 31, 1873): 131.

62. M. C. Woods, "Thread?" *Woman's Exponent* 25, no. 7 (October 1, 1896): 49.

63. Hannah T. King, "Woman an Institution," *Woman's Exponent* 14, no. 20 (March 15, 1886): 153.

64. Ruby Lamont [pseud. of Maria Miller Johnson], "The Idol of To-Day," *Woman's Exponent* 16, no. 3 (July 1, 1887): 17.

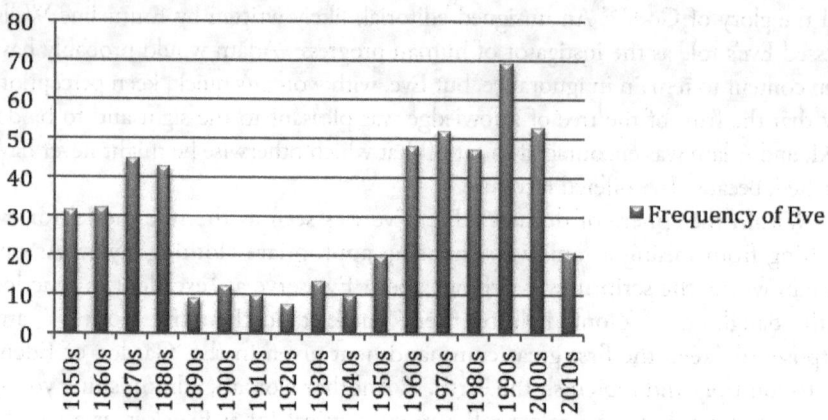

Figure 2. References to Eve in general conference addresses, 1850s–2010s.

but stated that she had not heard of "man's dress for woman, or anything approximating thereto, having been advocated among Latter-day Saints."[65] Mary Ann Pratt, on the other hand, looked to men's styles as a model for women's when she commented on the degrading influence of women's fashion: "Womankind should have respect for her fellow man, for as she looks upon him she sees the image of her Heavenly Father reflective. Man has not lost his original form as much as woman, he is not as much governed by fashion in dress as she is, in that which depresses the natural form."[66] Despite the fact that the only thing recorded in the scripture about Eve's apparel was that she and Adam wore fig leaves in the garden and that God made "coats of skins, and clothed them" (Gen. 3:7, 21) upon their expulsion therefrom, some women looked to Eve as an example of a dress code that was unostentatious and uniquely feminine.

Post-War Eve

General Authorities seldom spoke about Eve between 1890 and the 1950s. When she was mentioned, she was typically not being singled out for her unique role, but simply in passing as Adam's wife, and General Authorities have mentioned Adam many times more often than they have mentioned Eve. (See Figs. 2 and 3.) Indeed, as Carrie Miles has noted, talks in general conference only rarely discussed women's roles and only eighteen articles were indexed under the word "women" in the *Improvement Era* between 1891 and 1940, its first fifty years of

---

65. Emily B. Spencer, "Answer to Inez," *Woman's Exponent* 4, no. 2 (June 15, 1875), 16; Inez, "Eve's Curse: Is It Never to Be Removed?" *Woman's Exponent* 4, no. 3 (July 1, 1875): 22–23.

66. Mary Ann M. Pratt, "Woman's Vote," *Woman's Exponent* 19, no. 24 (June 15, 1891): 189.

Eve and the Construction of Mormon Gender Identity   67

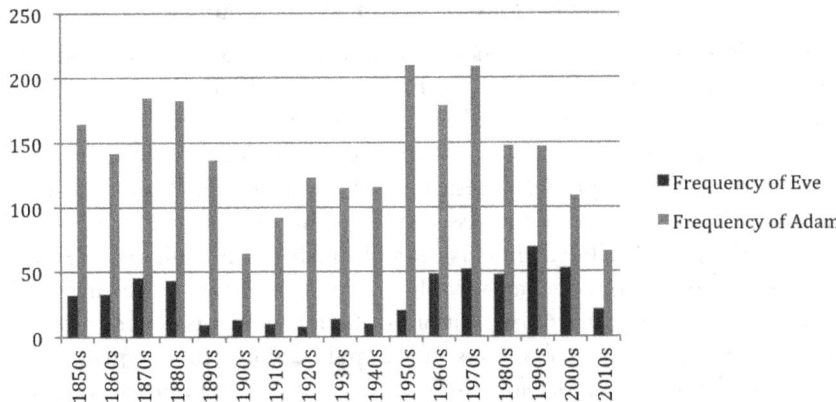

Figure 3. References to Eve vs. Adam in general conference addresses, 1850s–2010s.

publication.[67] One notable exception to this dearth of discourse about Eve was an address by President J. Reuben Clark, then first counselor to President George Albert Smith, delivered at the Relief Society general conference in October 1946. The talk veered between reverence for Eve and a strange sort of sexism. On the one hand he called Eve "radiant and divinely fair . . . the last created being" of the creation and suggested that Adam had prepared for her a "bridal home, . . . the Garden that from then till now has been the symbol of heaven on earth." But in contrast, Clark referred only to her role "to be a creator of bodies under the faculties given her by the Priesthood of God, so that God's design and the great plan might meet fruition." Clark continued, "This was her calling; this was her blessing, bestowed by the Priesthood. . . . From that day, when Eve thus placed first among her blessings the power to bear children, the greatest glory of true womanhood has been motherhood."[68] While motherhood is certainly a noble role, Clark stressed, it was bestowed by the (presumably male) priesthood. He does not recognize Eve's other roles: as the wise initiator of human progression, as a capable theologian who understood the importance of opposition in human development, or as an astute soul who discerned the Adversary.

---

67. Carrie A. Miles, "LDS Family Ideals versus the Equality of Women: Navigating Changes since 1957," in *Revisiting Thomas F. O'Dea's* The Mormons: *Contemporary Perspectives*, edited by Cardell K. Jacobson, John P. Hoffmann, and Tim B. Heaton (Salt Lake: University of Utah, 2008), 109.

68. J. Reuben Clark, "Our Wives and Our Mothers," address to the Relief Society general conference, October 3, 1946, in *J. Reuben Clark: Selected Papers on Religion, Education, and Youth*, edited by David H. Yarn (Provo, Utah: Brigham Young University Press, 1984), 60–61.

Eve and the Backlash to Second-Wave Feminism

The 1960s represented an upheaval in sexual mores and gender roles. The birth control pill was approved by the FDA in 1960; Betty Friedan published *The Feminine Mystique* in 1963; the Kennedy administration advocated women's rights as part of its New Frontier and established the Presidential Commission on the Status of Women, a proposal made by a Mormon, Esther Peterson (director of the U.S. Women's Bureau and Assistant Secretary of Labor in the Kennedy administration). LDS Church leadership and much of the rank-and-file membership began to perceive second-wave feminism as a threat to the family. The Church mounted a significant opposition to the Equal Rights Amendment and stressed traditional gender roles in discourses, publications, and manuals. Again, Eve was held up as a model for virtuous womanhood. Nevertheless, societal changes affected Mormons just as much as they affected the rest of the nation. More women began working outside the home and having fewer children.[69]

Calling motherhood a "sacred calling," Church president Spencer W. Kimball admonished women to not forgo children or marriage for careers. "Our beloved mother Eve began the human race with gladness, wanting children, glad for the joy that they would bring to her, willing to assume the problems connected with a family, but also the joys."[70] "In the beginning, Adam was instructed to earn the bread by the sweat of his brow—not Eve," stressed Apostle Ezra Taft Benson in 1981:

> Contrary to conventional wisdom, a mother's place is in the home! I recognize there are voices in our midst which would attempt to convince you that these truths are not applicable to our present-day conditions. If you listen and heed, you will be lured away from your principal obligations. Beguiling voices in the world cry out for "alternative life-styles" for women. They maintain that some women are better suited for careers than for marriage and motherhood. These individuals spread their discontent by the propaganda that there are more exciting and self-fulfilling roles for women than homemaking. Some even have been bold to suggest that the Church move away from the "Mormon woman stereotype" of homemaking and rearing children. They also say it is wise to limit your family so you can have more time for personal goals and self-fulfillment.[71]

After becoming Church president in 1987, Benson repeated almost verbatim much of this talk in a special fireside for parents. "In the beginning, Adam—not

---

69. Miles, "LDS Family Ideals," 114.

70. Spencer W. Kimball, "The Blessings and Responsibilities of Womanhood," *Ensign*, March 1976, https://www.lds.org/ensign/1976/03/the-blessings-and-responsibilities-of-womanhood (accessed May 2, 2015).

71. Ezra Taft Benson, "The Honored Place of Woman," October 1981 general conference, http://www.lds.org/general-conference/1981/10/the-honored-place-of-woman (accessed March 12, 2014).

Eve—was instructed to earn the bread by the sweat of his brow. Contrary to conventional wisdom, a mother's calling is in the home, not in the market place."[72]

A Parent's Guide, which the Church published in 1985, proposes Adam and Eve as ideal parents: "The relationship between a man and a woman is so significant that our Heavenly Father himself placed Adam and Eve together as husband and wife." Much of the advice the manual gives on rearing children is neutral, like its admonition to teach both daughters and sons "to seek opportunities to learn and to exploit every such opportunity fully. Girls and boys should learn all they can about every subject within their capabilities. They should nurture and develop their gifts (see D&C 46:11–26), striving always to achieve their full potential and to fill the measure of their creation (see D&C 88:19)." However, the pamphlet goes on to stress gender-specific roles for girls and boys: girls need to learn "the arts and sciences of housekeeping, domestic finances, sewing, and cooking," whereas boys should learn "home repair, career preparation, and the protection of women." The pamphlet stresses that the realities of the world—divorce, death of spouse, etc.—may necessitate some modifications. It goes on to state that men need to know some basic domestic skills and women may need to plan for a career, but it insists that "for all of the children of God, this life is primarily a probationary existence designed to prepare them for the eternal roles of husband and father, wife and mother."[73] The implication—that in the eternities husbands and fathers will be repairing homes, working in careers, and protecting women, while wives and mothers will be practicing "the arts and sciences" of cooking, cleaning, and sewing—seems rather odd.

Next to these rigid gender roles lies a competing, and many would argue contradictory, discourse about equality. For example, Ezra Taft Benson stated: "Adam and Eve provide us with an ideal example of a covenant marriage relationship. They labored together; they had children together; they prayed together; and they taught their children the gospel—together. This is the pattern God would have all righteous men and women imitate."[74] Emphasizing the need for couples to work together in their families, Elder Russell M. Nelson noted, "I presume another bone could have been used [to create Eve], but the rib, coming as it does from the side, seems to denote partnership. The rib signifies neither

---

72. Ezra Taft Benson, "To the Mothers of Zion," Pamphlet. Address delivered at the Fireside for Parents on February 22, 1987 (Salt Lake City: Church of Jesus Christ of Latter-day Saints, 1987). See also Lavina Fielding Anderson "A Voice from the Past: The Benson Instructions for Parents," *Dialogue: A Journal of Mormon Thought* 21, no. 4 (Winter 1988): 103–13, http://www.dialoguejournal.com/wp-content/uploads/sbi/articles/Dialogue_V21N04_105.pdf (accessed March 12, 2014).

73. *A Parent's Guide* (Salt Lake: The Church of Jesus Christ of Latter-day Saints, 1985), 26. Available at https://www.lds.org/bc/content/shared/content/english/pdf/language-materials/31125_eng.pdf (accessed May 12, 2015).

74. Ezra Taft Benson, "To the Elect Women of the Kingdom of God," in *Woman* (no editor or compiler identified) (Salt Lake City: Deseret Book, 1979), 291–92.

dominion nor subservience, but a lateral relationship as partners, to work and to live, side by side."[75] And Apostle Richard G. Scott called Eve Adam's equal, "a full, powerfully contributing partner."[76]

Equal Partner or "Complementing Differences"

In October 1993, Elder Boyd K. Packer spoke in general conference of the "complementing differences" between Adam and Eve, biological differences that allowed them to "multiply and fill the earth" as well as social roles that "are the very key to the plan of happiness." Men are to be "protector, the provider" while women are to be "the primary nurturer of the children." The contradiction of maintaining gender equality and patriarchal rule was later enshrined in "The Family: A Proclamation to the World," which echoed many of Packer's words. God's first commandment to Adam and Eve "to multiply and replenish the earth remains in force." While stating that fathers and mothers are "equal partners," it stresses separate gender roles for each: "fathers are to preside over their families in love and righteousness and are responsible to provide the necessities of life and protection for their families. Mothers are primarily responsible for the nurture of their children." Compared with the 1985 *Parent's Guide*, the Proclamation on the Family is much less specific at defining gender roles, and in many places it is even quite progressive. It begins by affirming that "all human beings—male and female—are created in the image of God" (there is no difference between women and men as there was for Philo and Augustine) and that "fathers and mothers are obligated to help one another as equal partners." Nevertheless, the basic taxonomy of differing gender roles is distinctly lopsided. Fathers are assigned three gender-specific roles: presiding, providing, and protecting. Mothers have only one: nurturing, and even it is given provisional status as only "primarily" theirs.

The proclamation's roles all sound similar to the Aristotelian model of gender roles, with men occupying the public sphere and women the domestic. As noted earlier, the motive for publishing the document appears to have been to establish the Church's position against same-sex marriage; however, it enshrines traditional gender roles in an unprecedented way which Church members seem to have accepted uncritically. (See Janice Allred's analysis of the Proclamation on the Family as the cornerstone of current gender theology in Chapter 4.)

Elder Bruce Hafen took a somewhat softer position about gender roles in his 2005 book on marriage: "The Victorian model treated women as dependent on their husbands. Today's liberationist model treats women as independent of their husbands and husbands as independent of their wives. But the restored gospel

---

75. Russell M. Nelson, "Woman—Of Infinite Worth," October 1989 general conference, http://www.lds.org/general-conference/1989/10/woman-of-infinite-worth. He is reverting to traditional imagery dating back at least to medieval times. See note 41.

76. Richard G. Scott, "The Joy of Living the Great Plan of Happiness," October 1996 general conference, http://www.lds.org/general-conference/1996/10/the-joy-of-living-the-great-plan-of-happiness (accessed March 12, 2014).

teaches that husbands and wives are interdependent with each other." Hafen invoked Adam and Eve: "In their life after the Fall, these interdependent partners worked together . . . they prayed and worshipped God together . . . and they taught their children together."[77]

In a subtly subversive talk given in the Relief Society general meeting of October 1999, Virginia Jensen, then first counselor in the Relief Society general presidency, spoke of how two birds—a swallow and a robin—built nests in her backyard. She detailed the pains both mother birds went through to build nexts, protect the eggs, and, eventually, feed their babies in their "daily vigil of *protecting* and *nurturing*" their brood. She went on to quote male Church leaders on the importance of work done in the home, stating, "Some think there are other uses of a woman's time and talents that are more important than the family." Then she emphasized that "prophets have been relentless in declaring that the role of homemaker is one of the most sacred and meaningful pursuits possible to man or woman."[78] So while affirming the traditional message that, as David O. McKay put it, "no other success can compensate for failure in the home,"[79] Jensen gently challenged the notion that gender roles are fixed. The mother birds both *protect* and *nurture*; the role of homemaker is noble for *both* men and women.

During the general women's session of the April 2015 conference, the twentieth anniversary of the Proclamation on the Family was highlighted with a special video presentation,[80] and the three women who spoke—leaders of the Primary, Young Women, and Relief Society—all stressed the importance of family. Bonnie L. Oscarson, the Young Women general president, described the proclamation as "our benchmark for judging the philosophies of the world" and issued a call for all Latter-day Saints to become "defenders" of the proclamation. Interestingly, however, Oscarson did not emphasize the strict gender roles enshrined in the document. Instead, she advised her audience to teach their children that "there is no greater honor, no more elevated title, and no more important role in this life than that of mother or father" and she challenged them to elevate the term

---

77. Bruce C. Hafen, *Covenant Hearts: Marriage and the Joy of Human Love* (Salt Lake City: Deseret Book, 2005), *Gospelink*, http://gospelink.com/library/document/131038 (accessed March 12, 2014).

78. Virginia U. Jensen, "Home, Family, and Personal Enrichment," October 1999 general conference, https://www.lds.org/general-conference/1999/10/home-family-and-personal-enrichment? (accessed May 13, 2015), emphasis mine.

79. Although McKay stated this twice over the pulpit, once in 1935 and again in 1964 (*Conference Report*, April 1935, 116), the saying actually comes from J. E. McCullough, *Home: The Savior of Civilization* (Washington, D.C.: The Southern Co-operative League, 1924), 42. See Russell Arben Fox, "About the McKay Quote …," Times and Seasons, March 11, 2004, http://timesandseasons.org/index.php/2004/03/about-the-mckay-quote/ (accessed May 13, 2015).

80. "The Family Is Ordained of God," April 2015 general conference, https://www.lds.org/general-conference/watch/2015/04 (accessed May 13, 2015).

"homemaker." "All of us—women, men, youth, and children, single or married—can work at being homemakers," Oscarson stressed.[81]

Just as in the nineteenth century, twentieth-century women have looked to Eve as a role model. And some of the most touching examples of how Eve exemplifies the lived experience of Mormon women are found in poetry. Reminiscent of Emily Dickenson's finest poetry, Carol Lynn Pearson's sparse "Eve's Meditation," is particularly poignant. Celebrating the divine words of Genesis 1:26, "Let us make man in our own image, male and female," Pearson's Eve deduces from the rest of God's creation the essential oneness of her union with Adam:

> Trunk and leaf
> Make the tree,
> Body and wing
> Make the bee.
>
> Gazing at the garden
> I cannot think it odd
> That you and I together
> Make the image of God.[82]

In a line from her poem "Tefnut," which celebrates the lives of goddesses and holy women throughout history, Penny Allen points to the central task Eve, Adam's helper, accomplished, moving Adam out of the Garden and, in so doing, unleashing human potential:

> What secrets did she insist on knowing
> When she took the fruit? Made to be a
> Helpmeet, she helped Adam out of Eden.[83]

A poem published in the Church's *Ensign* magazine in 1976 portrays Eve as Adam's companion in every sense of the word, working alongside him as he worked to subdue the "lone and dreary world."

> … she helped him
> tame the land, shared the aching length of days,
> the moisture-beaded brow. Endowed with knowledge now,
> she dared the thistled paths that pierced her spirit,
> strong in new-found peace.
> Pain-bent, she brought forth seed, sorrowing
> for those who erred, while guiding gently
> toward the light.

---

81. Bonnie Oscarson, "Defenders of the Family Proclamation," April 2015 general conference, https://www.lds.org/general-conference/2015/04/defenders-of-the-family-proclamation (accessed May 13, 2015).

82. Carol Lynn Pearson, "Eve's Meditation," *Beginnings and Beyond* (Springville, Utah: Cedar Fort, 2005), 125.

83. Penny Allen, "Tefnut," *Sunstone* 13, no. 6 (December 1989), 52. Republished in *Harvest: Contemporary Mormon Poems*, edited by Eugene England and Dennis Clark (Salt Lake City: Signature Books, 1989), 125.

The poem also depicts Eve as Adam's equal and goes on offer Eve as a model for all womanhood:

> Mother Eve,
> now reaching out through centuried time
> to me, a daughter of the latter day,
> you give your knowledge-gift
> entwined in shining strands of service
> and wrapped with dedication to eternal choice.
> Our sacred trust defined, you bridge eternity
> and set a jeweled precedent for me,
> and womankind.[84]

As this example shows, Mormon women of the twentieth century looked to Eve as a model of an independent, courageous, powerful, and liberated woman.

In "To Eve—With Empathy throughout the Years," Shirley Adwena Harvey imagines Eve's loss of both her sons, Abel to death, Cain to banishment.

> Gone—two sons of promise—
> One never to see tomorrow's dawn,
> Never to father generations.
> The other wrenched from you,
> Marked and cast out.

When the poet describes the pain "that tore heart and soul" one feels not only the grief of Eve, but of generations of women who have lost children. But the poem also offers comfort:

> There would be other dawns—and other harvests—
> With long hours of toil to fill empty days.
> Then slowly, surely, as pain gives way to faith,
> You feel God's love surround you,
> Warm as a shawl on your shoulders,
> And you hear His spirit whisper to your spirit
> That sometime—somewhere in eternity—
> A mother's heart will heal.[85]

Another poem depicts this same heartbreaking scene, emphasizing Eve's gift of healing and her developing understanding of death as the full pain of mortality sinks in. Speaking to Adam, Eve states:

> I am trying to understand.
> You said, "Abel is dead."
> But I am skilled with herbs

---

84. Martha Pettijohn Morrise, "Women, Look toward Eve," *Ensign*, March 1976, https://www.lds.org/ensign/1976/03/1976-eliza-r-snow-poetry-writing-contest-winners (accessed March 12, 2014).

85. Shirley Adwena Harvey, "To Eve—With Empathy throughout the Years," *Ensign*, July 1992, https://www.lds.org/ensign/1992/07/1992-eliza-r-snow-poetryverse-contest-winners (accessed May 13, 2014).

> Remember when he was seven
> The fever? Remember how—
> Herbs will not heal?
> Dead?

Eve then protests God's taking her sons from her:

> But God can't do that.
> They are my sons, too.
> I gave them birth
> In the valley of pain.

As the grief of losing her sons sinks in, Eve contemplates the word "multiply" in God's words in his commandment "to multiply and replenish the earth" as well as in the curse that he will "multiply thy sorrow."

> Abel, my son dead?
> And Cain, my son, a fugitive?
> Two sons
> Adam, we had two sons
> Both—Oh, Adam—
> multiply
> sorrow
> Dear God, why?
> Tell me again about the fruit
> Why?
> Please, tell me again
> Why?[86]

The question hangs in the air, with no answer forthcoming. And again, we sense that generations of mothers can empathize with Eve's pain and sorrow and the nagging questions about God's kindness and justice that persist in such tragic times.

Sarah Page's "Coring the Apple," which appeared in 2009, is strongly reminiscent of Robert Frost's sonnet "Never Again Would Bird's Song Be the Same." Frost's poem celebrates Eve as the creator of the soft eloquence of sound, coequal in her work to Adam's task of naming (creating words), the two abilities necessary, ultimately, for poetic production. But Page is not simply imitating Frost. While Frost honors Eve's (in fact all women's) gift of granting beauty to the world, Page celebrates Eve as a hero, as the shaper of divine destiny.

> I would like to ask Eve someday
> What she saw in the apple.
> Before she chose
> The fire-stung glory of mortality,
> Did she pause for even the space of a breath,
> Tremble at the bruise of pain, the sharpness of the briar?
> Perhaps she sensed the hope nestled star-like
> In the core of the fruit,

---

86. Arta Romney Ballif, *Lamentation and Other Poems* (n.p: Arta Romney Ballif, 1989), 3–6.

And so risked all she was for the quickening—
The promise of the seed dreaming deep in the loam.
I would like to ask Eve someday
What she saw in me.[87]

While Page's poem calls to mind Frost, it is also uniquely Mormon. She, like these other poets, sees Eve as a courageous woman, making a conscious choice, aware of the enormous stakes of that choice—but also seeing the limitless potential of future generations. It is common among Latter-day Saints to believe that, as he was suffering in Gethsemane and on the cross, Jesus thought about each of us personally and took upon himself each of our individual sins. But it is a unique insight to think that Eve was also aware of each of our lives and all of our potential when she took that fateful bite. These LDS poets recognize that, for Latter-day Saints of the twenty-first century, Christ is not so much the Second Adam as he is the Second Eve. For it is Eve who is celebrated for making the glorious decision to become mortal and wise, and it is Christ who transforms humanity from mortal to immortal, from wise to exalted. Even as she is still held up as a model of Mormon womanhood and traditional gender roles, a competing vision of Eve exists as the giver of life and knowledge.

Appendix:
Amicus Curiae Briefs and the Proclamation on the Family

- Amicus Curiae Brief of The Church of Jesus Christ of Latter-day Saints, *Baehr v. Miike*, No. 20371, Supreme Court State of Hawaii, filed August 1996, http://www.qrd.org/qrd/usa/legal/hawaii/baehr/1997/brief.mormons-04.14.97 (accessed May 12, 2015).
- Brief of Amici Curiae United States Conference of Catholic Bishops, et al., *Perry v. Schwarzenegger*, No. 10-16696, U.S. Court of Appeals for the Ninth District filed September 24, 2010, http://cdn.ca9.uscourts.gov/datastore/general/2010/10/25/amicus11.pdf (accessed May 12, 2015).
- Commonwealth of Massachusetts v. United States Department of Health and Human Services, et al., Nos. 10-2204, 10-2207, and 10-2214, U.S. Court of Appeals for the First Circuit filed January 27, 2011, available at http://www.usccb.org/about/general-counsel/amicus-briefs/upload/amicus-1cir-gill-2011-01.pdf (accessed May 12, 2015).
- Amici Curiae National Association of Evangelicals, et al., *Hollingsworth v. Perry*, No. 12-144, U.S. Supreme Court filed January 29, 2013, http://www.americanbar.org/content/dam/aba/publications/supreme_court_preview/briefs-v2/12-144_pet_amcu_nae-etal.authcheckdam.pdf (accessed May 12, 2015).

---

87. Sarah Page, "Coring the Apple," *Mormon Artist*, November 2009, 12, http://mormonartist.net/pdf/issueC1.pdf (accessed March 12, 2014).

- Brief of Amici Curiae United States Conference of Catholic Bishops, et al., *De Leon v. Perry*, No. 14-50196, U.S. Court of Appeals for the Fifth Circuit filed August 4, 2014, http://www.usccb.org/about/general-counsel/amicus-briefs/upload/DeLeon-Perry-Brief.pdf (accessed May 12, 2015).
- Brief of Amici Curiae United States Conference of Catholic Bishops, et al., *Kitchen v. Herbert v. Smith*, Nos. 13-4178, 14-5003, 14-5006, U.S. Court of Appeals for the Tenth Circuit filed February 10, 2014, https://archive.org/details/Gov.uscourts.ca10.13-4078Kitchen-v.-Herbert-Doc.-01019200417 (accessed May 12, 2015).
- Brief of Major Religious Organizations as Amici Curiae in Support of Respondents, *Obergefell v. Hodges*, Nos. 14-556, 14-562, 14-571, 14-574, U.S. Supreme Court filed April 2, 2015, http://www.supremecourt.gov/ObergefellHodges/AmicusBriefs/14-556_Major_Religious_Organizations.pdf (accessed May 12, 2015).

I have only found two amicus briefs with which the Church has been affiliated in some way that did not cite the proclamation: It was not included in the Brief Amici Curiae of National Association of Evangelicals, et al., *U.S. v. Windsor*, No. 12-307, U.S. Supreme Court filed January 29, 2013, http://www.americanbar.org/content/dam/aba/publications/supreme_court_preview/briefs-v2/12-307_blag_merits_nae-etal.authcheckdam.pdf (accessed May 12, 2015); and it was not included in the amicus brief filed by Hawaii's Future Today, a lobbying organization that received significant backing from the Church. In the latter, it is somewhat ironic that the brief relied, in part, on the Reynolds decision which invalidated LDS marriages of the nineteenth century. Footnote 11 reads, "Beyond its precedential value, the polygamy cases also should provide great concern from a practical point of view. Should this Court determine that the State of Hawaii possesses no compelling governmental interest supporting its current traditional marriage laws when weighed against challenges brought by homosexuals, it is very difficult to conceive of a compelling governmental interest which would save Hawaii's traditional marriage laws when weighed against a challenge by polygamists." Hawaii's Future Today Amicus Curiae Brief, *Baehr v. Miike*, No. 20371 Supreme Court State of Hawaii filed September 1996, http://www.qrd.org/qrd/usa/legal/hawaii/baehr/1997/brief.hawaiis.future.today-03.16.97 (accessed May 12, 2015).

Chapter 4

LDS Gender Theology: A Feminist Perspective

Janice Allred

As Mormon women voice their desire for priesthood ordination, they offer many reasons to explain why they see ordination as a good thing both for Mormon women and for the LDS Church. They affirm the value of equality and maintain that equality cannot be achieved in the Church until women are ordained. The ordination of women would strengthen the Church as it would allow and encourage women to develop and utilize their spiritual gifts and magnify their talents. Bringing women into Church governance would broaden the perspective of Church leadership, making Church governance more effective and more equitable. Women leaders would serve as role models for young women and encourage all women to see themselves as empowered, full participants in the family, Church, and community.

These are strong, cogent reasons that express the hopes and desires of many people, men as well as women, for equality in the Church. However, they are often dismissed by mainstream Church members as secular or feminist ideals that fail to take into consideration the gospel or the nature of God's plan for the Church and the family. The ideal of equality and the use of activism to achieve it are intrinsic to feminism. Activism gets attention when reasoned arguments do not. Mainstream members also view activism as a secular method that is inappropriate for bringing about change within the Church. But there are no channels within the Church for members to bring their concerns and questions to the top leadership. Individuals are not heard, but the concerted voices of activists speak loudly. Although Ordain Women uses activism in pursuing its goal of priesthood ordination for women, its members ground their activism in belief. Recognizing the sole authority of the First Presidency and Quorum of the Twelve to change Church doctrine and practice, women activists appealed to them, asking them to seek revelation from God concerning the ordination of women to priesthood. This appeal acknowledged the Church's teaching that these men are prophets who receive their authority and teachings from God. The failure of Church leaders to respond directly to Ordain Women and the excommunication of Kate Kelly, one of the organization's co-founders, have convinced many Mormons that the question of priesthood for women is closed.[1] However, the way of persuasion, long-suffering, and pure knowledge remains open.

---

1. John Dehlin, a longtime activist and advocate for more historical transparency, gay rights, and women's rights, among other causes, was summoned at about the same time to a high council court, but his court was delayed until February 2015. He was excommunicated.

The Power of Feminist Theology

Feminist studies seek to uncover and expose the ideas, structures, and mechanisms that disadvantage and oppress women. Their ultimate aim is to transform society, creating structures that promote equality and establish justice. A feminist theological investigation can examine the texts that support gender discrimination and see if they can be reinterpreted or rectified. It is important to give a strong theological defense for ordaining women to the priesthood and conferring all the rights of the priesthood on them. And, to be effective, this defense must be based on the scriptures and gospel doctrines. My studies of the scriptures have convinced me that it is possible to use them to show that receiving and participating in the priesthood is essential for full access to spiritual gifts and equality in the Church.

Equality is not only a feminist ideal. It is also foundational to democracies and valued in free societies. However, it is often misunderstood. Equality is not sameness. Diversity is a feature of reality and without it there would be no existence. The principle that grounds free societies is the belief that all human beings have intrinsic rather than utilitarian value and thus are of equal worth. The Declaration of Independence affirms the connection between equality and freedom: "We hold these truths to be self-evident, that all men are created equal, that they are endowed by their Creator with certain inalienable Rights, that among these are Life, Liberty and the Pursuit of Happiness—That to secure these Rights Governments are instituted among Men, deriving their just powers from the consent of the governed." Equality, then, is best promoted by honoring agency. The most basic right is freedom and all other rights arise from it. The ideal of equality calls us to seek for and work to establish justice in all human communities—the family, the workshop, the state, and the Church. Justice can be established only when human rights are protected.

Equality is also a feature of the gospel. The gospel of Jesus Christ is radically egalitarian. It is addressed equally to each person and invites all to come to Christ and partake of the goodness of God. The egalitarianism of the gospel arises from God's unconditional love manifested in the atonement of Christ:

> He doeth not anything save it be for the benefit of the world; for he loveth the world, even that he layeth down his own life that he may draw all men unto him. Wherefore, he commandeth none that they shall not partake of his salvation. (2 Ne. 26:24)
>
> ...for he doeth that which is good among the children of men; and he doeth nothing save it be plain unto the children of men; and he inviteth them all to come unto him and partake of his goodness; and he denieth none that come unto him, black and white, bond and free, male and female; and he remembereth the heathen; and all are alike unto God, both Jew and Gentile. (v. 33)

In his atonement, Christ makes himself equal to each of us, drawing us to him and offering us eternal life in and through him. In making himself equal to us, he makes us equal to each other. The principle of equality is a fundamental part of the gospel because the gospel message is predicated on it.

Gender and Gospel Teachings

In this chapter, I will examine the main scriptural texts and Church teachings that deal with gender. To establish my thesis, I will compare and contrast these teachings to the gospel of Jesus Christ. Jesus Christ is the foundation of the Church, and he tells us that his Church must be founded on his gospel (see D&C 33:11–13). Jesus gives a clear explanation of his doctrine in his ministry to the Nephites after his crucifixion and resurrection. First, he establishes his identity and authority: "Behold, I am Jesus Christ, whom the prophets testified shall come into the world. . . . I am the light and the life of the world. . . . I am the God of Israel, and the God of the whole earth, and have been slain for the sins of the world" (3 Ne. 11: 10, 11, 14). He then gives revelation about the unity and work of God as Father, Son, and Holy Spirit and tells us what we must do to inherit eternal life. We must have faith in him, repent of our sins, be baptized, and receive the Holy Spirit. The gospel message is simple. It is declared to us personally by our God and Savior. He finishes this explanation of his doctrine by declaring:

> Verily, verily, I say unto you, that this is my doctrine, and whoso buildeth upon this, buildeth upon my rock, and the gates of hell shall not prevail against them.
>
> And whoso shall declare more or less than this, and establish it for my doctrine, the same cometh of evil, and is not built upon my rock, but is built upon a sandy foundation, and the gates of hell stand open to receive such when the floods come and the winds beat upon them. (3 Ne. 11:39–40)

There are many true and important ideas and concepts that are not part of the gospel. Inspired writings and revelations from God may contain ideas and deal with topics not included in the doctrine of Christ. God gives us great freedom in seeking, exploring, and discussing them. But we must not establish them as his doctrine. This would limit our free agency and our ability to grow in truth and knowledge and could become the source of contention. The Church has the responsibility to teach the gospel, the doctrine of Christ. We may, as leaders and members, teach and discuss other ideas, but we should be very careful not to establish other teachings as doctrine.

The Adam and Eve Narratives

The Genesis account of Adam and Eve serves as a fundamental text for gender theology in the Abrahamic faith traditions, and feminist theologians in these traditions have worked with this foundational myth, reinterpreting, reconstructing, and even rejecting it. LDS theology sees the Creation and the Fall as essential elements in the plan of salvation. The doctrines of the Creation and the Fall have a narrative basis, and Adam and Eve are principal characters. Genesis contains two distinct accounts of the creation of Adam and Eve. The first account does not give precedence to either sex. The sexes are created simultaneously and together are given dominion over the earth and other living things:

And God said, Let us make man in our image, after our likeness: and let them have dominion over the fish of the sea, and over the fowl of the air, and over the cattle, and over all the earth, and over every creeping thing that creepeth upon the earth.

So God created man in his own image, in the image of God created he him; male and female created he them. (Gen. 1:26–27)[2]

In the second account, given in Genesis 2, the man Adam is created first and put into the Garden of Eden. God says, "It is not good that the man should be alone; I will make an help meet for him." God causes a deep sleep to fall upon Adam and creates a woman from one of his ribs. When God brings her to Adam, Adam says, "This is now bone of my bones, and flesh of my flesh: she shall be called Woman, because she was taken out of Man" (vv. 18, 21–23). This account of the creation of the Man and the Woman subordinates women in three ways. Adam is created first, placed in the Garden alone, given the commandment not to partake of the fruit of the tree of the knowledge of good and evil as a single person, and given the task of naming all the animals. Woman is derived from Man and created to be his helper. The Man names her, as he named the animals. Genesis 3 gives further symbols for women's subordination. The serpent tempts Eve, and she partakes of the fruit of the tree of the knowledge of good and evil, disobeying God's direct commandment. She then persuades Adam to partake of the fruit. This part of the story has been used to discredit the character of women. Because the Woman succumbs to the temptation of the serpent and then causes Adam to disobey God, women are seen as seducers who are themselves easily seduced, as vessels of sin, and as the weaker sex, morally as well as physically. (See also Chapter 3.)

When God discovers Adam and Eve's disobedience, he speaks to each of them. To the Woman he says, "I will greatly multiply thy sorrow and thy conception; in sorrow thou shalt bring forth children; and thy desire shall be to thy husband, and he shall rule over thee" (Gen. 3:16). To Adam he says, "Cursed is the ground for thy sake; in sorrow shalt thou eat of it all the days of thy life. . . . In the sweat of thy face shalt thou eat bread, till thou return unto the ground; for out of it wast thou taken: for dust thou art, and unto dust shalt thou return" (Gen. 3:17, 19). These words have furnished the rationale for the subordination of women to men and for different roles for men and women.

There are several ways these texts can be reinterpreted to minimize the subordination of women. LDS theology sees the Fall as an integral, even necessary, part of the plan of salvation. Eve does not foil the plan but actually initiates the fall into mortality, which is necessary for obtaining physical bodies, exercising free agency, experiencing the world of good and evil, and being tested in it.[3] Although

---

2. I have silently removed italics from quotations in the King James Version.

3. For a concise statement of the LDS view of the Fortunate Fall, see "The Fall of Adam and Eve," Chapter 6 in *Gospel Principles* (Salt Lake City: Church of Jesus Christ of Latter-day Saints, 1997), 31–34 and "The Fall of Adam" in the Bible Dictionary in the LDS edition of the Bible.

this interpretation does in some ways exonerate Eve of bringing evil into the world, it does not totally redeem her character. The Genesis text shows that she was deceived by Satan and hearkened to his voice rather than the commandment of God. According to this text, even if she fulfilled the will of God, she did so ignorantly, not because of wisdom. However, the most important problem with this interpretation is that it does not undo Eve's subordination to Adam, which is intertwined into the text in several ways, as has been shown.

One approach that can be taken is to give the text a critical and close reading, looking for ways to interpret the text in Eve's favor. The words of God to Adam and Eve after their partaking of the fruit are usually assumed to be a pronouncement of the punishment that God gives to each of them, which reflects the particular nature of their respective actions. Eve initiated their actions and led Adam into sin. Now Adam will rule over Eve. Further, there is an assumption usually made in this interpretation that Adam's ruling over, or presiding over, Eve is an eternal pattern. But we can interpret God's words as descriptive rather than prescriptive. Adam and Eve are entering into mortality, and God is describing the conditions of the fallen world. This is a world of sorrow in which men rule over women. The conditions of the Fall are not those of a righteous world. Men ruling over women symbolizes all forms of unrighteous dominion.

This line of interpretation can be further developed by looking closely at God's words to Adam. The conditions that God describes to Adam are human conditions, which all people are subject to: the necessity of working to sustain oneself, harsh physical conditions, and death. Adam, then, represents not only male persons but all people. This interpretation is supported in Genesis 5:1–2: "In the day that God created man, in the likeness of God made he him; Male and female created he them; and blessed them, and called their name Adam, in the day when they were created."

If Adam represents all of humanity, who does Eve represent? Adam does not call his wife Eve until after God describes the conditions of mortality. Before this he calls her simply "Woman." He was asleep when she appeared. Now his eyes are opened and he recognizes her. He does not name her; he recognizes her. She *is*, not *will be*, the "Mother of All the Living." In *Eve: The History of an Idea*, John A. Phillips states, "The Mother Goddess of ancient Near Eastern religions, by whatever name she was called, was honored and worshiped with the title 'the Mother of all the Living.'"[4] He points out that the name "Eve" is taken from a form of the Hebrew verb "to be." The Hebrew name for God, "Yahweh," is derived from this same verb. With Adam's recognition of Eve's name, God's words to Eve take on a new meaning: the Heavenly Mother, through her sacrifice, brings her children into a world of sorrow, pain, and death.

This identification requires us to reconfigure the myth in various ways. Mormons tend to see the story of Adam and Eve as happening in history. In call-

---

4. J. A. Phillips, *Eve: The History of an Idea* (San Francisco: Harper & Row, 1984), 3.

ing it a myth, I do not mean to deny that it is connected to real events. I mean to call attention to its archetypal dimensions and multi-layered scope. What is the time and setting of the events that take place in the Garden of Eden? Perhaps the accounts we have are made up of multiple strands representing different dimensions of the Creation and Fall, woven together to create a coherent narrative. The Genesis text says that God made coats of skin to cover the nakedness of Adam and Eve. Perhaps the nakedness of Adam and Eve symbolizes their lack of physical bodies and the coats of skin symbolize physical bodies. This would place the events as beginning in the preexistence and moving into mortality. Seeing the Adam and Eve story as simply occurring in history blinds us to its universal, representational aspects. My point here is not to argue for a particular interpretation of the Adam and Eve narrative but to show its complexity and the multiple meanings that can be drawn from its symbols. Like the Atonement, the Fall is not simply a historical event. Both are effected by God and have metaphysical dimensions which encompass multiple layers of reality.

The stories of Adam and Eve that we have in the scriptures function as myths in many ways. They affect the deepest levels of our psyches and influence the ways we structure reality. We cannot simply dismiss or disavow them. We must reread, restructure, reinterpret, and reimagine them, seeking to understand them in ways that are faithful both to the texts and our highest ideals. And we must remember that as followers of Christ, we are reborn into a new life. Although we remain subject to the conditions of the Fall, we are called to live according to the principles of the gospel. Men ruling over women is a condition of the fallen world. We should not duplicate it in Christ's church.

"The Family: A Proclamation to the World"

"The Family: A Proclamation to the World" supplies the most important text for gender theology in the contemporary LDS Church. Popularly called the "Proclamation on the Family," it was delivered to the Church by President Gordon B. Hinckley on September 23, 1995, at the general Relief Society meeting. In his preceding remarks, Hinckley said that it was "a declaration and reaffirmation of standards, doctrines, and practices which the prophets and seers of this Church have repeatedly stated throughout history."[5] Indeed the teachings of the proclamation can be found in numerous general conference addresses and other speeches given by General Authorities over a period of many years preceding its announcement.[6] Although its teachings were familiar, putting them in the form of an of-

---

5. Gordon B. Hinckley, "Stand against the Wiles of the World," *Ensign*, November 1995, 101; The First Presidency and Quorum of the Twelve Apostles, "The Family: A Proclamation to the World," ibid., 102.

6. Carolyn M. Wallace researched the topic of priesthood and motherhood in the LDS Church in 1978 and 1979. Her study, which uses many general conference addresses, gives a remarkably accurate view of the ideas later made official in the proclamation. See Wallace, "The Priesthood and Motherhood in the Church of Jesus Christ of Latter-day Saints," in

ficial proclamation inaugurated an increased emphasis on the family,[7] which, in the context of these teachings, has led to a widespread perception that the Church has a "doctrine of the family.[8] The Church spreads this message in speeches, publications, manuals, and missionary work and uses the concept of the eternal family as a way of identifying the Church in its public outreach.[9] However, the scriptures do not

---

Gender and Religion: On the Complexity of Symbols, edited by Carolyn Walker Bynum, Stevan Harrell, and Paula Richman (Boston: Beacon Press, 1986), 117–40. In her introduction to this book Bynum writes, "The Church of the Latter-day Saints, sometimes known as the Mormons, teaches that all spirits are created by a Heavenly Father and a Heavenly Mother and progress toward perfection in this life and beyond as members of human families. To Mormon adherents, the individual self has gender for all eternity, and this gender reflects a male/female division lodged at the heart of ultimate reality" (3).

7. A search in the BYU General Conference Corpus (www.lds-generalconference.org) shows that the family has always been a much discussed topic in general conference speeches. However, the number of citations of the word "family" increased markedly, first in the 1970s, then dropped in the 1980s, and again increased markedly in the 1990s. The first increase is probably connected to the inauguration of the feminist movement in the 1970s and the second to the publication of the proclamation in 1995. The number of citations has grown in each decade since then. A search for "eternal family" shows the same trend. There have been thirty-one citations of "proclamation on the family" since its announcement. The phrase "doctrine of the family" was not used before the 1990s, but has been used five times since then.

8. Speaking at the October 2011 general conference, Elder Boyd K. Packer announced that "The Family: A Proclamation to the World" was "an inspired document issued by the First Presidency and the Quorum of the Twelve Apostles, which taught that "in the premortal existence 'all human beings—male and female—[were] created in the image of God. Each is a beloved spirit son or daughter of heavenly parents, and, as such, each has a divine nature and destiny. Gender is an essential characteristic [and was established in that premortal existence]. Brackets in published address. Boyd K. Packer, "Counsel to Youth," https://www.lds.org/general-conference/2011/10/counsel-to-youth (accessed May 1, 2015). Significantly, in the October 2010 general conference, he had asserted that the proclamation "qualifies according to scriptural definition as a revelation, a guide that members of the Church would do well to read and follow." This statement was edited in the published version, to read, "It is a guide that members of the Church would do well to read and to follow." http://www.sltrib.com/sltrib/home/50440474-76/packer-church-speech-lds.html.csp (accessed June 22, 2015). In April 2011 he again referred to the proclamation as a revelation, this time citing teachings from the proclamation, but not naming it. This statement was allowed to stand in the published version. Boyd K Packer, "Guided by the Holy Spirit," *Ensign*, May 2011, 31.

9. The Church is increasingly identifying itself with the doctrine of the eternal family. A 2009 *Time* magazine article discussing the Church's involvement in passing Proposition 8 in California described the doctrine behind the Church's opposition to gay marriage. "The return to God is accomplished by heterosexually founded families, not individuals, and only as a partner in a procreative relationship can a soul eventually create spirit children." Marlin Jensen, then the Church historian, is quoted as saying, "The context for our being so dogged about preserving the family is that Mormons believe that God is their father

contain these teachings as part of the gospel message. The purpose of the proclamation seems to be to provide an authoritative source for the Church's teachings about gender, gender roles, sexuality, marriage, and the family since such sources cannot be clearly extracted from the scriptures. The language of the proclamation has a creedal quality in that it aims to give a clear statement of officially designated beliefs. Although the proclamation is clearly not a revelation from God, it functions as authoritative doctrine. Because it was issued by the First Presidency and Quorum of the Twelve and is frequently cited in general conference talks, most members regard it as official Church doctrine.[10]

A feminist critique of the proclamation reveals several problems. Religion structures reality. It provides an interpretation of the cosmos—of all that is. The proclamation defines a cosmology centered in the family. It states, "In the pre-mortal realm, spirit sons and daughters knew and worshiped God as their Eternal Father." The clear implication is that fatherhood gives the right to rule. The cosmology of the proclamation is thus patriarchal. Although the proclamation states that each human being is a "son or daughter of heavenly parents," it never names God as Mother or refers to her work. It is the Father's plan, his work; he rules. She is absent from the proclamation. Although it states that earthly fathers and mothers are "equal partners," it is clear that the heavenly parents are not.

The proclamation states, "Gender is an essential characteristic of individual premortal, mortal, and eternal identity, and purpose." The concept of genderedness is an important contribution of feminist thought. Gender is a fundamental feature of reality. Human beings are gendered, and human experience is gendered. Feminists have also defined and insisted upon a distinction between sex and gender. Sex is biological, but gender is culturally constructed. It is the meaning given to the masculine and the feminine. Cultures consider some roles and behaviors appropriate to women and others appropriate to men. Qualities and attributes may also be gendered. The proclamation does not make a distinction between gender and sex. Indeed, although sexuality is one of its main topics, it doesn't even use the word "sex." Instead, it uses "gender" to refer to biological sexual identity and "the sacred powers of procreation" to refer to sexual intercourse. The proclamation is on the cutting edge of contemporary thought in seeing gender as a fundamental aspect of reality, but it is profoundly reactionary in that it sees gender and gender roles as rigid and inflexible and as being either biologically or spiritually determined.

---

and that they have a heavenly mother and that eventually their destiny is to become like that." David Van Biema, "The Storm over the Mormons," *Time*, 22 June 2009, 51.

10. In the April 2015 general conference several speakers talked about "the doctrine of the family," drawing on or quoting from the ideas in the proclamation. L. Tom Perry asserted, "The entire theology of our restored gospel centers on families and on the new and everlasting covenant of marriage. In the Church of Jesus Christ of Latter-day Saints, we believe in a premortal life where we all lived as literal spirit children of God our Heavenly Father. We believe that we were, and still are, members of His family." L. Tom Perry, "Why Marriage and Family Matter—Everywhere in the World," *Ensign*, May 2015, 41.

Ironically, if there were no distinction between gender and sex, it would be unnecessary to promulgate the proclamation. If gender were not culturally, socially, and personally constructed, if it were determined and unchangeable, there would be no reason to prescribe gender roles or to set up ideals concerning the characteristics and purposes of each sex. If gender were fixed and determined by biology, there would be no need to demand that people fulfill their gender roles.

The proclamation's narrow view of sexuality excludes, marginalizes, and delegitimizes broad ranges of human experience. By reducing sexual expression to "the sacred powers of procreation," it denies importance to the broad meaning of sexuality and fails to address the many other important meanings that sex plays in people's lives. It fails to acknowledge the existence and intrinsic worth of people whose bodies do not fit into its male/female dichotomy. It doesn't deal with the problems faced by transgendered people. It fails to acknowledge the possibility of a sexual ethic based on consent, commitment, and the quality of relationships rather than institutionally rendered divine fiat. It fails to acknowledge that some of God's children are gays and lesbians and that they have a right to seek ethically responsible relationships that involve sex. It fails to define sexual abuse, to acknowledge its effects on people's lives, and to offer any help for victims' healing or perpetrators' repentance.

It might be objected that the proclamation, as a short document, cannot address these difficult issues. That may be true, but it does posit sexual expression as a fundamental part of eternal existence. It is best to avoid creedal statements about complex and difficult issues. The scriptures are not creedal. The texts about the nature of God, the nature of reality, human nature, and the principles of the gospel are rich, complex, and multilayered with images, symbols, and narratives that support a wide range of interpretations. Creeds attempt to limit interpretation. Texts inspired by the Spirit of God lead us into deeper understanding and new possibilities to explore.

The basic problem with the Proclamation on the Family is that it defines the family as the fundamental unit of society. The fundamental unit is the smallest part to which anything can be reduced. If the family, not the individual, is the fundamental unit of society, then the individual exists only as part of the family structure. This view denies intrinsic worth to the individual person. The person has utilitarian worth in the family unit only as he or she fulfills the roles assigned to him or her. Roles define the functions, responsibilities, and offices that people have in organizations or relationships with others. Roles are inherently unequal. This is apparent in the complementary role relationships of employer/employee, teacher/student, parent/child, and judge/accused. Since the proclamation defines rigid eternal roles determined by gender, it denies the fundamental equality of persons.

The proclamation declares, "By divine design, fathers are to preside over their families in love and righteousness and are responsible to provide the necessities of life and protection for their families. Mothers are primarily responsible for the nurture of their children." Presiding means being the president, being in the position of authority, being in charge, being in the leading role. Providing the necessities of life means having power over resources. Providing protection means exercising power to define and protect boundaries. The proclamation views power as belonging to men, but it fails to recognize or warn that power can be abused. The power to lead is also the power to oppress. The power to provide resources is also the power to withhold resources. The power to protect is also the power to injure. Nurturing is primarily giving, but it also requires resources and strength. In giving birth, a mother nurtures and protects her child with her own body, and in rearing the child she uses her spiritual, emotional, and intellectual resources. If the nurturing that a woman provides is not given willingly and not under her own control, then she is being exploited. It is servitude, not service.

Although both men and women are defined by their roles as fathers and mothers in the proclamation, the system is more pernicious for women because the roles specified for men identify powers which every person must possess. They define personhood or having agency. Free agency, which is fundamental in Mormon theology, requires a spirit that chooses for itself and a body in which and through which to act—power and resources. But the cosmology of the patriarchy sees the father as the primary source of power and resources. Motherhood, the role assigned to women, is a good role, but it is essentially a giving and sacrificial role. It must be freely chosen, and its responsibilities must be freely carried out. A mother must first be a person and must continue to be a person with desires, needs, other roles, purposes, and goals outside of her role as a mother.

The rigid gendered-determined role system of the proclamation establishes a domination-submission model of human relationships. This is established early in the proclamation which states: "Spirit sons and daughters knew and worshiped God as their Eternal Father." The child's role is to obey the Father. The domination-submission model is reinforced by giving primacy to roles rather than persons. Persons are defined by agency. Reducing them to roles subverts their agency. The proclamation defines a universe where men's destiny is to rule and women's destiny is to be exploited. Of course, in the real world, even in patriarchal systems, personal relationships and arrangements are more complicated. But paradigms have power, and ways of thinking influence how we act.

Complementarity and Gender

The concept of complementarity has been used to support the view that men and women have different but equally important roles to fill in the home, the Church, and in society. The argument identifies the complementary roles, affirms that each is necessary, and then concludes that, since the roles are equally important, they are equal. But the mere assertion of equality does nothing to achieve it. The view that men and women have complementary roles has a long history and is so widespread that it merits particular attention. In order to examine the validity of the view that strict gender roles are determined by cosmological reality and are part of God's eternal plan for his children, it is necessary to understand the principle of complementarity.

Lehi's teaching in the Book of Mormon about opposition in all things establishes the importance of this concept for Mormon theology. Lehi teaches that there is an opposition *in all things*. "Wherefore, all things must be a compound in one: wherefore, if it should be one body it must needs remain as dead, having no life, neither death" (2 Ne. 2:11). Here Lehi is speaking about the fundamental opposition that makes existence possible. This opposition is *in* all things. It is an opposition of harmony and balance. This is a teaching about the nature of reality—of all God's creations. Reality consists of interdependent, complementary pairs in balance with each other, each member of the pair depending on the other for its existence. Lehi's concept of opposition in all things can be called the principle of complementarity or polarity. It is fundamental to physical reality. Quantum mechanics describes a wave-particle duality at the subatomic level of matter. Its principle of complementarity states that, at the subatomic level, matter can be described as either particles or waves. The two ways complement rather than contradict each other, and quantum reality requires both states in order to be complete. Complementary particles, attracted to each other but never merging completely, are necessary to the existence of matter, giving it extension, duration, and complexity.

Thought also requires complementary pairs. The most basic pairs include same/different, self/other, one/many, giving/receiving, separating/joining, active/passive, and masculine/feminine or yang/yin. Complementary duality is also essential to the existence of a human being. A human being is created when primal intelligence is placed in a body of elemental light. According to Doctrine and Covenants 93, intelligence is the primary component of reality. It is differentiated into the complementary pair of truth and light (or spirit and element). Spirit, the active/conceptual force, and element, the formative/receptive force, cooperate in creation and all the processes of life. Agency is created by the union of spirit and body. "All truth is independent in that sphere in which God has placed it, to act for itself, as all intelligence also; otherwise there is no existence. Behold, here is the agency of man" (D&C 93:30–31). Our spirit forms the core of our being. It is the active, yang aspect of intelligence, our free agency, our will. The body is the yin part of the human being. The spirit chooses and the body gives form and stability to that choice. Body and spirit must be both differentiated and joined together to create an individual self with free agency. This opposition within a person creates individual existence.[11]

---

11. The concept of binary opposition is currently unfashionable in academic circles. I believe this is because many people fail to understand that there are three distinct forms of opposition. The first I call either-or opposition (also called binary or polar opposition). In this type, the binary elements must be completely distinct and separated, yet together they form a binary system. Examples are in/out, on/off, and negative/positive. This type of opposition is essential to logic, computer systems, and some physical processes. The second type consists of complementary pairs. This is the complementarity of harmony, balance,

It is important not to identify the masculine/feminine duality with a male person/female person duality. The yang/yin duality is within each person. The Genesis 1 account of the creation of humanity can be interpreted to show this. It plays with the single/plural, masculine/feminine dualities, separating and compounding them. "And God said, "Let us make man in our image, after our likeness." Here God is plural. "So God created man in his own image, in the image of God created he him; male and female created he them." Here God is singular and man is both singular and plural. Man (humanity, which consists of individual persons having male or female bodies) is created, each person bearing both the masculine and feminine principles. Both God the Father and God the Mother are the source of the masculine/feminine principle.[12]

How does the principle of complementarity relate to the ideal of equality? Both principles have both a metaphysical and an ethical dimension. The principal of complementarity is primarily metaphysical but it also has ethical implications. The members of a binary pair are mutually interdependent. One cannot exist without the other. Honoring the principle of complementarity requires us to seek harmony and balance, to recognize the worth of every aspect of creation, to look for and support hidden realities—the least, the little, the lost, the marginalized. One of the fundamental complementary pairs is self/other. We must esteem the other as ourselves—love our neighbor as we love ourselves, recognizing that her or his selfhood is equally precious, infinite, and eternal. Equality is primarily an ethical ideal formulated to deal with the phenomenology of difference. Reality is characterized by a multitude of differences. These differences characterize the natural world and arise naturally in human experience. The belief that each person is of equal value translates into the ethical imperative to esteem each person as we esteem ourselves. Thus, the ideal of equality and the principle of complementarity support the same ethical principle: love your neighbor as you love yourself, which, of course, is the primary ethical teaching of Jesus.

---

and interdependence where the concepts are dynamic, fluid, and interchangeable. They often work as both/and dualities. God is both just and merciful. Both male and female persons have both masculine and feminine attributes. The third opposition is antagonistic opposition. This is competitive opposition. It is not a necessary opposition and so is not really a binary or complementary opposition. It is not found in nature or logic but only in human reality when one member of the opposing pair seeks to dominate, overcome, exploit or destroy the other. The good/evil dichotomy falls into this category.

12. Gender and sex can be seen as a complementary pair analogous to the spirit/body duality. The spirit has agency, but the body conforms to physical and biological laws. The feminist distinction between sex as biological and gender as constructed is valid and important, but it is based on the more fundamental yang/yin component of reality. Gender/sex is not an either/or binary but a fluid complementary pair. Gender can be constructed in many ways. It is connected to, but not determined by, the biology of sex. The female body which conceives and gives birth to a child and the male body which provides sperm to impregnate the female furnish metaphors for constructing gender. The essential meaning of gender is difference itself. Difference is necessary for existence.

The most basic human interaction defined by complementarity is giving/receiving. Clearly every person must both give and receive, and there is always a giving in every receiving and a receiving in every giving. The principle of complementarity makes role reversal a necessary part of human interactions, but honoring the principle of complementarity requires us to actively seek to change roles. Since roles are inherently unequal, the ideal of equality also requires us to change roles. An ethics that values both complementarity and equality also obliges us to honor agency. Complementarity maintains the distinction between the members of its pairs. In relating to others, we maintain this distinction by honoring the other's agency. Since agency is essential to individual existence, intrinsic worth is tied to agency and promoting equality means working to secure and maintain human rights in all aspects of human life.

Because it defines rigid gender roles and identifies persons with their roles, the Proclamation on the Family defines an authoritarian cosmology which is not consistent with the gospel of Jesus Christ. It is significant that a document issued by the First Presidency and Council of the Twelve Apostles of the Church of Jesus Christ of Latter-day Saints proclaims a cosmology that excludes Jesus Christ. His teachings are recommended as promoting happiness in family life, but the one who is our Creator and Redeemer, whose spirit is in and through all things, whose atonement makes it possible for us to more fully receive the Spirit of God, is absent. The proclamation substitutes "the divine plan of happiness" for Christ's plan of salvation. "Plan of happiness" is used only twice in the scriptures.[13] The scriptures teach that following Christ and his plan of salvation leads one into a state of happiness, but the plan of salvation is primary. We cannot ignore the reality of sin, injustice, alienation, ignorance, poverty, war, oppression, environmental degradation, and death and guarantee happiness on the basis of obedience to gender roles. Sin and error come into the world because of free agency. Free agency is the ground of individual existence, which the proclamation overlooks. The gospel is addressed to each and every individual person. The good news of the gospel is that, through faith in Jesus Christ, we may be saved from sin and death. Because of the atoning power of his sacrifice, we may receive the love and enlightenment that will enable us to live in love, truth, freedom, and peace with others.

The purpose of my critique of the proclamation is not to reject or disavow the family. It is clearly part of God's creation, and the revelation that God is our Father-Mother is an important one. The problem is that the proclamation proclaims a cosmology inconsistent with the gospel of Jesus Christ with narrow, rigid, and creedal concepts. The new creation effected by the atonement redeems persons who are then empowered to create new structures, enabling them to live

---

13. Alma uses "plan of happiness" twice in his words to his son Corianton explaining the plan of salvation. He is emphasizing that the purpose of the plan of redemption or mercy is to bring about happiness. This is the discourse in which he declares, "Wickedness never was happiness." Mercy and justice are a complementary pair that cannot be separated. See Alma 42.

in love, truth, freedom, and peace in the kingdom of God. The family of the fallen world is also in need of redemption. However, the family, which at its best is based on love and service, giving and receiving, provides a model for relationships in God's kingdom.

Eternal Marriage

The Church's teaching that exaltation in the highest degree of the celestial kingdom is available only to a man and a woman sealed in the temple brings the concept of heterosexual marriage into the plan of salvation. Teaching that the temple marriage of a man and a woman is required for exaltation in the highest degree of the celestial kingdom is equivalent to positing separate paths of salvation for men and women. It is based on the idea that male persons and female persons are fundamentally different and that they must be inseparably joined in order to create a whole. As I have shown, this view subordinates women. Temple marriage as a requirement for the highest degree of glory also puts exaltation beyond the reach of homosexual persons, transgendered persons, and those who for various reasons do not marry. Holding out the possibility of having these disqualifications remedied in the next life minimizes the importance of this life and dismisses, even as it acknowledges, the suffering and experiences of these people in a Church defined by the proclamation.

The main text dealing with the degrees of glory is in Doctrine and Covenants 76. It proclaims the doctrine of universal salvation:

> And this is the gospel, the glad tidings, which the voice out of the heavens bore record unto us —
> That he came into the world, even Jesus, to be crucified for the world, and to bear the sins of the world, and to sanctify the world, and to cleanse it from all unrighteousness;
> That through him all might be saved whom the Father had put into his power and made by him;
> Who glorifies the Father, and saves all the works of his hands, except those sons of perdition who deny the Son after the Father has revealed him. (vv. 40–43)

According to Section 76, celestial beings are "just men made perfect through Jesus the mediator of the new covenant, who wrought out this perfect atonement through the shedding of his own blood" (v. 69). They "overcome by faith, and are sealed by the Holy Spirit of promise, which the Father sends forth upon all those who are just and true" (v. 53). Section 76 says nothing about temple marriage as a requirement for celestial glory. Concerning those who receive celestial glory it says:

> They are they into whose hands the Father has given all things—
> They are they who are priests and kings, who have received of his fulness, and of his glory;
> And are priests of the Most High, after the order of Melchizedek, which was after the order of Enoch, which was after the order of the Only Begotten Son.
> Wherefore, as it is written, they are gods, even the sons of God—
> . . . . and they are Christ's and Christ is God's. (vv. 55–59)

We can interpret "priests," "kings," and "sons" inclusively or exclusively. To interpret them exclusively would mean that there are no women in the celestial kingdom, unless they are assumed to be among the things possessed by their husbands. If we interpret these words inclusively, celestial women are priests of the Most High, kings in Christ's kingdom, and sons of God. This second possibility is consistent with the full equality that is characteristic of the celestial glory. The seeming exclusivity of the words is a problem, but the problem is embedded in the fallen world and cannot simply be solved with inclusive language. If the words "priestesses," queens," and "daughters" had been used, the full equality of the celestial kingdom would not be as clear since priestesses are not equal to priests, queens are not equal to kings, and daughters are not equal to sons *in this world*.[14] Inclusive language would have simply pushed the problem of subordination into the next world.

The LDS Church's emphasis on the eternal family has led to a corporate conception of salvation, but the gospel is addressed to the individual person. It is as individuals that we have faith in Christ, repent of our sins, are baptized, and receive the Holy Spirit, which enables us to be sanctified, enlightened, and grow in truth and light. Individual salvation and corporate salvation are brought together in Christ. He is the vine and we are the branches. Connected to him through the Holy Spirit, we are also connected to others. Eternal life is embodied and lived in community, and communities of love, freedom, truth, and equality are made possible by the work of Christ and the Holy Spirit, renewing, sanctifying, enlightening, and magnifying individuals who are then empowered to live peaceably together.

Although the teaching that temple marriage is required for exaltation has scant scriptural support, it is taught as doctrine. Only two texts support it, and both are problematic. The first is in Doctrine and Covenants 131:

> In the celestial glory there are three heavens or degrees;
> And in order to obtain the highest, a man must enter into this order of the priesthood [meaning the new and everlasting covenant of marriage];
> And if he does not, he cannot obtain it. (vv. 1–3)

The usual interpretation of verse 1, that there are three degrees in the celestial kingdom, is erroneous. The word "celestial" is being used here in its general sense to mean "divine" or "heavenly." It is not being used in its specialized sense to designate one of the kingdoms of glory. Verse 1 simply summarizes the content of the revelation of Section 76. There are three degrees of glory in the heavenly realm:

---

14. It is important to remember that inclusive language was not stressed before 1980. In the scriptures when "man" and "men" are used generically or in general statements, their primary meaning is inclusive. This is true even if the authors or speakers had androcentric images and concepts in mind. The words "All men are created equal" carry a universal meaning even if the signers of the Declaration were only thinking of male persons, and they have inspired people to strive for equality.

the celestial degree, the terrestrial degree, and the telestial degree. Section 76 makes it clear that there are no degrees of glory in the celestial kingdom. "And he makes them equal in power and in might, and in dominion" (v. 95). All receive of the fullness. Only in the telestial kingdom are there differences in glory (v. 98).

Verse 2 seems to state explicitly that marriage in the new and everlasting covenant is required for obtaining the highest glory, which is the celestial kingdom. The phrase "meaning the new and everlasting covenant of marriage" is enclosed in brackets in the official, canonized version. It is an interpretation of an unclear text. Section 131 is not a dictated revelation. It was taken from notes that William Clayton made in his journal of Joseph Smith's remarks to members of the Church in Ramus, Illinois. The bracketed material is not in the original notes but was added when the material was included in the 1876 edition of the Doctrine and Covenants.[15] Although these remarks are interesting, they do not have the same importance as direct revelations given to Joseph Smith that he had published during his lifetime.

The scriptural teachings concerning covenants are complex. I will just make a few points here. The order of the priesthood Joseph is referring to in verse 2 is probably the Melchizedek Priesthood. As I noted above, those who inherit the celestial glory are priests of the Most High after the order of Melchizedek. The "new and everlasting covenant" is "from the beginning," before creation (D&C 22:1; 49:9). It therefore originates within the Godhead and is the source of all the covenants God makes and seals. Jesus is the mediator of the new covenant and through him "all those who are just and true" are "sealed by the Holy Spirit of Promise" (D&C 76:53). This sealing is to God through the Spirit, and this is the primary meaning of eternal life.

Section 132 is the primary text supporting the teaching that temple marriage is required for exaltation, but this section is problematic for at least three reasons. First, it describes polygamy, not monogamy, as being required for exaltation, and the theology that developed to support polygamy subordinated women in many ways. Second, Section 132 is presented in the form of a revelation given in the voice of the Lord; but, like Section 131, it was not published by Joseph Smith as one of the revelations given to him.[16] Third, Section 132 contains many

---

15. Lyndon W. Cook, *The Revelations of the Prophet Joseph Smith* (Provo, Utah: Seventies Mission Bookstore, 1981), 291–93, 346.

16. Most of the revelations received by Joseph Smith were promptly recorded, entered into Revelation Book 1 or 2, and canonized during his lifetime. The *Evening and the Morning Star, Times and Seasons,* and the *Messenger and Advocate* published many of the revelations not canonized during Joseph Smith's lifetime. Most of the revelations not found in Revelation Books 1 and 2 are among the papers documented in the Documents and Journals volumes of the Joseph Smith Papers Project. The Joseph Smith Papers Project has not yet published the volume covering the years when Sections 131 and 132 were received. See Robin Scott Jensen, Robert J. Woodford, Steven C. Harper, Richard E. Turley Jr., and Riley M. Lorimer, eds., *The Joseph Smith Papers: Revelations and Translations*, 2 vols. (Salt Lake City: The Church

statements that are contrary to the gospel.[17] None of the other revelations in the Doctrine and Covenants has this problem. This is an extremely important point. The principles of the gospel and the plan of salvation are clearly taught in many revelations and scriptural texts and their concepts are intertwined and embedded in the texts in complex ways. The teaching that temple marriage is required for exaltation in the celestial kingdom is poorly attested and embedded in a problematic text containing material contrary to the gospel. There is no good reason to try to integrate this requirement into the plan of salvation. One way to deal with this text is to ignore it or take out the parts contrary to the gospel and the parts dealing with polygamy. The text which then remains contains teachings about sealings. Sealings are an important part of Mormon theology, but the text remains problematic because of its errors.[18] Let me make it clear that I am not calling into question the validity of temple sealings or the possibility of sexual relations and procreation in eternity. What I am trying to show is that temple marriage is not a condition for exaltation. Receiving temple sealings can be seen as a blessing available to those who inherit the celestial glory rather than as a requirement for exaltation in the celestial kingdom.

God the Mother

Theology deals with the relationship between God and humankind and must be based on revelation from God. The scriptures are a primary source for this revelation. Feminist theology must deal with the gender of God. "If God is male, then male is God," wrote Mary Daly, calling attention to the subordina-

---

Historian's Press, 2011), Michael Hubbard McKay, Gerrit J. Dirkmaat, Grant Underwood, Robert J. Woodford, William G. Hartley, Matthew C. Godfrey, Mark Ashurst McGee, and Brent M. Rogers, eds., *The Joseph Smith Papers: Documents*, 3 vols. (Salt Lake City: The Church Historian's Press, 2013–14), and Dean C. Jessee, Mark Ashurst-McGee, Richard L. Jensen, Andrew H. Hedges, Alex D. Smith, and Richard Lloyd Anderson, eds., *The Joseph Smith Papers: Journals,* 2 vols. (Salt Lake City: The Church Historian's Press, 2008, 2011). See also Cook, *The Revelations of the Prophet Joseph Smith.*

17. For example, v. 3 says that all who have the doctrine of polygamous eternal marriage revealed to them must obey it or be damned. The gospel message is not compulsory. The sharp distinction between exaltation and damnation that this verse (and others in Sec. 132) posits is contrary to the revelation of universal salvation.

18. The primary meaning of "to seal" is "to confirm," "to guarantee," "to authenticate," and "to make binding or eternal." The revelations teach that the Spirit of God, or the Holy Spirit of Promise, is the sealing power. The most important sealing is the sealing of persons to God, giving them eternal life. "Therefore, I would that ye should be steadfast and immovable, always abounding in good works, that Christ, the Lord God Omnipotent, may seal you his, that you may be brought to heaven, that ye may have everlasting salvation and eternal life" (Mosiah 5:15; see also D&C 76:53). This sealing underlies all other sealings. The only scriptural text that discusses sealings of persons to persons is Section 132.

tion of women in patriarchal religions, which consider God to be masculine.[19] Although most theologians in the Judeo-Christian tradition assert that God is beyond gender, the metaphors, images, and scriptural texts of these religions clearly present a male God. Some feminist theologians have dealt with this problem by searching for and calling attention to feminine metaphors, attributes, and images to complement the masculine representations of God, while others have insisted that a Goddess is needed to counterbalance the male God. Still others have argued that God must be androgynous. However, as I attempted to show in my discussion of the concept of complementarity, it is important to maintain the distinction between the members of a complementary pair. Although the complements are joined and interdependent, if the distinction between the two is lost, the more visible (yang) member of the pair tends to eclipse the less visible (yin) member. An androgynous god looks more like a male god than a female god. The female body is essential for maintaining the reality of a female deity.

The Mormon doctrine of embodied heavenly parents does acknowledge the individual existence of the Mother in Heaven; however she remains invisible, subordinate, and excluded from the Godhead. In other words, she is not herself God. President Hinckley's 1991 speech directing members not to pray to the Mother in Heaven[20] has had an enormous influence on discourse about the Heavenly Mother, effectively silencing members and impeding the development of a theology that includes her in the Godhead. The logic underlying this position is simple. Prayer is properly addressed to God. Therefore, if we cannot pray to the Heavenly Mother, then she must not be God. Joseph Smith's teaching that God the Father is an exalted Man who is the literal Father of our spirits—coupled with the teaching that exaltation in the highest degree of the celestial kingdom is only available to heterosexual couples sealed in the temple and developed with the underlying, unrecognized assumption that men are superior to women and the masculine is superior to the feminine—has led to the theology presented in the proclamation. This theology leads to a problem for Mormon feminists. If we reject the cosmology of the proclamation, do we have any support for belief in God the Mother?[21] If we retain it, how do we avoid the inequalities enshrined in the proclamation?

The Mormon belief that God is embodied furnishes sufficient grounds to posit the existence of God the Mother. The Genesis account of the creation of Adam and Eve in the image of God necessitates the existence of both a male and

---

19. Mary Daly, *Beyond God the Father: Toward a Philosophy of Women's Liberation* (Boston: Beacon, 1973), 19.

20. Gordon B. Hinckley, "Daughters of God, *Ensign*, November 1991, 100.

21. The proclamation is increasingly cited as the authority for the Mormon belief in a Mother in Heaven. For example, see Kevin L. Barney, "How to Worship Our Mother in Heaven (Without Getting Excommunicated)," *Dialogue: A Journal of Mormon Thought* 41, no. 4 (Winter 2008): 121, and David L. Paulsen and Martin Pulido, "'A Mother There': A Survey of Historical Teachings about Mother in Heaven," *BYU Studies* 50, no. 1 (2011): 73.

a female Creator God. The account focuses on the creation of the bodies of both the male and the female in the image of God. The importance of God's body is also revealed in the incarnation and resurrection of Jesus Christ. Revealed in scripture as the Creator, he was incarnated and resurrected in a male body. His body is eternal. We may look for his female partner in Creation.

One of the problems of the theology associated with the proclamation is that it fails to develop comprehensive teachings about the nature and work of God. Focusing exclusively on God as parent is as problematic for God the Father as it is for God the Mother. Earthly parentage may be in the image of heavenly parentage, and it does furnish a metaphor for our understanding of God, but the gospel message about the nature and work of God reveals God as Creator, Redeemer, and Holy Spirit. It reveals the transcendent, personal, and immanent aspects of God's being through the revelation of Jesus Christ. Understanding that Jesus Christ is the revelation of God to humanity is the key to developing a theology that includes both the masculine and feminine aspects of God. Jesus reveals God as a human person with a male body, and he completes an essential aspect of salvation as this human person endowed with the immanence and transcendence of God. The gospel message grounded in the equality of persons and the creation of male and female bodies in the image of the bodies of Mother/Father God together hold the promise of the revelation of the hidden Goddess who with Jesus Christ creates, redeems, sanctifies, enlightens, and empowers their children.[22]

Priesthood

The struggle for equality for Mormon women centers in priesthood. Exclusion from priesthood ordination and callings disempowers Mormon women and gives them a subordinate status in the Church. As an activist movement, Ordain Women rightly focuses on ordination for women. Without ordination

---

22. I have been working on such a theology for almost forty years and have found rich and plentiful scriptural resources. The theology that I have developed posits two members of the Godhead: God the Father and God the Mother united in and through the Holy Spirit. They are each Creator, Redeemer, Revelator, Sanctifier, and Comforter and have transcendent, personal, and immanent modes of being. The Eternal Father, as the Book of Mormon proclaims, is Jesus Christ, who comes into the world to redeem his people. See my "Jesus Our Mother" and "Toward a Mormon Theology of God the Mother" in *God the Mother and Other Theological Essays (*Salt Lake City: Signature Books, 1997), 20–68 and "The One Who Never Left Us," *Sunstone*, Issue 166 (March 2012): 62–69. See also Margaret Toscano's significant work: "Is There a Place for Heavenly Mother in Mormon Theology? An Investigation into Discourses of Power," in *Discourses in Mormon Theology: Philosophical and Theological Possibilities*, edited by James M. McLachlan and Loyd Ericson (Salt Lake City: Greg Kofford Books, 2007), 193–223, her "Put On Your Strength, O Daughters of Zion: Claiming the Priesthood and Knowing the Mother," in *Women and Authority: Re-emerging Mormon Feminism*, edited by Maxine Hanks (Salt Lake City: Signature Books, 1992), 411–37, and Margaret and Paul Toscano, "Godhead," Part II in *Strangers in Paradox: Explorations in Mormon Theology* (Salt Lake City: Signature Books, 1990), 25–104.

to priesthood and priesthood offices, women cannot achieve full equality in the Church. Feminist theology exposes and seeks to remedy the ideas and structures that contribute to inequality. Ordaining women to priesthood offices in an authoritarian structure will not lead to full equality for all people if priesthood itself structures inequality. The gospel of Jesus Christ is radically, at its very roots, egalitarian. In his atonement, Jesus Christ represents each person and invites everyone to believe in him and partake of the goodness of God. Priesthood, on the other hand, is associated with special rights, privileges, and powers. It creates hierarchy; it has been associated with lineage so that some lineages have been denied the priesthood. And priesthood is denied to all women in Mormondom. The Church, governed and structured by the priesthood, contains many inequalities. These inequalities arise, not just because women are denied full participation in the blessings and responsibilities of the priesthood, but also because the conception of priesthood which excludes women is not firmly grounded in the gospel of Jesus Christ. We need a better understanding of the nature and purpose of priesthood and how it is related to the gospel and the Church in order to address the root cause of inequality in the Church.

The gospel, the Church, and the priesthood are all centered in Christ, and they all have the same purpose: to bring the individual more fully into the presence of God and into the community of the Saints, there to partake of eternal life. The gospel message is that God himself came into the world to redeem his people from sin, injustice, ignorance, oppression, and death. By his atonement, he draws all people to himself. Salvation is through faith in him, repentance, baptism, and the reception of the Holy Spirit. The scriptures distinguish two parts of salvation, traditionally called justification and sanctification. In justification we are forgiven of our sins through faith in Christ, accepting his unconditional love or grace, and are brought into the community of the Church. In sanctification we grow in faith, love, and knowledge, becoming like God. Sanctification is through the Holy Spirit, which enlightens, strengthens, and brings us into unity in the community of Christ.

The main scriptural texts dealing with the nature and purpose of priesthood are Alma 13 and Sections 84 and 121 of the Doctrine and Covenants. Both Alma 13 and Section 84 connect priesthood to the process of sanctification. Alma teaches that receiving the priesthood consists of being called with a holy calling and ordained with a holy ordinance. He makes it clear that receiving the holy calling is based on having faith in Christ and his atonement, repenting of our sins, and following Christ faithfully. Receiving the holy ordinance then leads to sanctification in priesthood service. The calling is extended to everyone. It is not predestined. If being male were a qualification for the calling and ordination, then male spirits would be predestined to be able to qualify for the priesthood and female spirits would be predestined to be eternally excluded from the priesthood.

Section 84 links becoming sanctified with receiving the priesthood and making temple covenants. This revelation is given in the context of building the temple, which will be filled with the glory of the Lord, and with which priesthood is associated:

> [This] priesthood continueth in the church of God in all generations, and is without beginning of days or end of years. (v. 17) . . .
>
> And this greater priesthood administereth the gospel and holdeth the keys of the mysteries of the kingdom, even the key of the knowledge of God. (v. 19)

Because the revelation names many men who held this priesthood in ancient times, it is natural to think of priesthood as being reserved for men. However, as the revelation unfolds, it becomes more and more evident that this priesthood is for all God's children:

> For whoso is faithful unto the obtaining these two priesthoods of which I have spoken, and the magnifying their calling, are sanctified by the Spirit unto the renewing of their bodies.
>
> They become the sons of Moses and of Aaron and the seed of Abraham, and the church and kingdom, and the elect of God. (vv. 33–34)

Those who receive the priesthood receive the Lord and the Lord's servants, which leads to receiving the Father, the Father's kingdom, and all that the Father has. These teachings are also found in Section 76, describing those who inherit celestial glory, as we have seen. "And this is according to the oath and covenant which belongeth to the priesthood. Therefore, all those who receive this priesthood, receive this oath and covenant of my Father" (D&C 84:39–40). This covenant, which is without beginning, originates in the Godhead and is the new and everlasting covenant, the covenant which the Eternal Father/Mother make to bring to pass the immortality and eternal life of their children. It includes the plan of salvation, the atonement, and the ministerings of the Holy Spirit. We enter into this covenant through faith in Christ, repentance, and baptism. We then receive the Holy Spirit and, if we desire to continue our service more fully in God's kingdom, we may receive the priesthood and enter into the covenants of service that are given in the Lord's house. According to Alma, receiving priesthood ordinances is more like receiving the temple endowment than the laying on of hands. "Now these ordinances were given after this manner, that thereby the people might look forward on the Son of God, it being a type of his order, or it being his order, and this that they might look forward to him for a remission of their sins, that they might enter into the rest of the Lord" (Alma 13:16).[23]

---

23. Margaret Toscano argues convincingly that the temple endowment confers priesthood on women. See Margaret M. Toscano, "The Missing Rib: The Forgotten Place of Queens and Priestesses in the Establishment of Zion," *Sunstone* 10, no. 7 (July 1985): 16–22. For a historical perspective on this conclusion see D. Michael Quinn, "Mormon Women Have Had the Priesthood Since 1843," in *Women and Authority: Re-emerging Mormon Feminism*, edited by Maxine Hanks (Salt Lake City: Signature Books, 1992), 365–409. Concerns about gender inequity in the endowment and temple covenants are legitimate. I believe that they can be addressed by reinterpretation, reconfiguration, and, if necessary, excision. Certainly priesthood covenants should reflect the equality that

Understanding that the temple endowment confers priesthood on women leads to several important questions. How is this priesthood to be exercised? Can we use it now or do we need to wait for further light and knowledge? Can women be ordained to priesthood offices? Some who see the temple endowment as conferring priesthood on women view women's priesthood as private, as functioning outside the Church structures. Others see women's spiritual gifts as functioning outside the priesthood. While I agree that the private sphere is an important place in which priesthood is exercised and that priesthood ordination is not essential for receiving and exercising spiritual gifts, I think it is dangerous to allow these insights to become a reason for thinking that it is not necessary for women to have full priesthood rights, including holding all Church offices.

The principle of complementarity is helpful here. The spirit/body duality that forms the basis of existence also constitutes the priesthood. Section 121 of the Doctrine and Covenants defines two dimensions of priesthood. It calls them "the rights of the priesthood" and "the powers of heaven."[24] The rights of the priesthood are analogous to the body, and the powers of heaven are the spiritual dimension of priesthood. These two dimensions, according to the revelation, are inseparably connected and thus form a complementary pair. The powers of heaven are given by the Spirit of God, which is the source of all God's power. Priesthood power is not a different kind of power. The powers of the priesthood include the power of truth and the power of love. The rights of the priesthood are the structures, covenants, offices, callings, and ordinances that constitute the body of the priesthood. Priesthood is constituted when two or more beings who have covenanted with God to serve in his priesthood unite together to do God's work. Priesthood power thus adds the power of unified action to the power of love and the power of truth. Priesthood covenants are made directly with God through the Son. They are grounded in the oath and covenant of the priesthood, the everlasting covenant. Although the Church can confer the rights of the priesthood and does use these structures to organize and administer the Church and ordinances, the power of the priesthood comes directly from God. Christ, not the Church, is the mediator. Priesthood offices can be used unrighteously if they are used to cover one's sins, to gratify one's pride, or to coerce others; but priesthood power, which is authorized by the Holy Spirit, not institutional power, can be used only according to the principles of righteousness. Since the power of the priesthood and the rights of the priesthood are inseparably connected, as are the spirit and the body, telling women that they have the power of the priesthood but

---

is foundational to the work of God. For a Christological interpretation of the temple endowment see Margaret and Paul Toscano, "Rending the Veil," and "The Mormon Endowment" in *Strangers in Paradox: Explorations in Mormon Theology* (Salt Lake City: Signature Books, 1990), 265–91.

24. Alma uses "the holy calling" to refer to the powers of heaven and "the holy ordinance" to refer to the rights of the priesthood.

not the rights of the priesthood is like telling them that they have a spirit but no body in which to carry out their desires and do their work.

The primary meaning of priesthood power in Mormonism has come to mean the power to govern the Church. This view of priesthood power is not in accordance with the scriptures that discuss the nature and purpose of priesthood. According to the teachings of these texts, the main responsibilities of priesthood bearers are to teach the gospel, administer the ordinances, and exercise spiritual gifts. Priesthood holds the key to revelation, which enables members of the priesthood to carry out these responsibilities in ways that will benefit others. Priesthood work is essentially service. Although the proclamation does not mention priesthood, the gender roles it assigns to men and women clearly reflect the priesthood-motherhood dichotomy. Ironically, nurturing, the role the proclamation assigns to mothers, is closer to the scriptural meaning of priesthood as service than the roles the proclamation assigns to men. These roles—leading, controlling resources, and exercising power to define and defend boundaries—describe the functions of governance. The Church clearly sees priesthood as tied to governance and governance as the sole prerogative of men.

Jesus clearly taught his disciples how power is to be exercised in his church:

> Ye know that the princes of the Gentiles exercise dominion over them, and they that are great among them exercise authority upon them.
>
> But it shall not be so among you: But whosoever will be great among you, let him be your minister;
>
> And whosoever will be chief among you, let him be your servant:
>
> Even as the Son of man came not to be ministered unto, but to minister, and to give his life a ransom for many. (Matt. 20:25–28)

Jesus is countering a view of authority that entails the use of coercion. Section 121 makes it clear that priesthood power is never coercive. It uses persuasion, long-suffering, gentleness, meekness, love, kindness, and pure knowledge (vv. 41–42). Because governance typically has the power to enforce its directives through some form of compulsion, seeing priesthood as primarily the power to govern the Church distorts the nature of priesthood.

The structure of Church governance embeds coercion in four principal ways. First, it is structured hierarchically.[25] It has a top-down structure with no established channels for members to express their questions and concerns to the top leadership. Second, the Church teaches obedience as a primary principle of the gospel. Members are obligated to obey their leaders. Third, it teaches that leaders speak for God and will not lead the Church or members of the Church astray. Fourth, it excludes women from Church governance, thus establishing an elite class that governs and a subordinate class that has no established voice in Church

---

25. Hierarchy is not in itself pernicious. Many structures are naturally or legitimately hierarchical. Problems arise when hierarchy is combined with authoritarianism and maintained by coercion.

governance. Of course, individual leaders vary in their style of leadership. My point is that coercion is systemic in the Church, that it is built into the system.

Since priesthood is viewed as the right to govern the Church and priesthood power is structured hierarchically, authoritatively, and exclusively, the Church disempowers all women and many men. This is why Ordain Women sees priesthood ordination as crucial for women's equality. As I have shown, the primary way to achieve equality is by honoring agency. If women are excluded from the decision-making councils of the Church, they cannot be equal. The structure of Church governance should reflect the equality the gospel calls for. The principle of common consent should be honored. Coercion is contrary to the righteous use of power, and the structures that allow it to go unchecked should be uncovered and renounced. Although organizations require structures of power and authority to carry out their work, any organization based on the principle of human equality must take great care to ensure that all its members have a voice in its councils and that governance is based on the consent and participation of the governed. Certainly excluding women from Church governance violates the ideal of equality and leads to injustice.

As I have studied the texts on the nature and purpose of priesthood, I have been struck by the absence of gender markers. The texts in no way restrict priesthood to males. Indeed, they describe it as a path of service and growth that is offered to all God's children. It is only the eyes of prejudice and tradition that prevent us from seeing this. Some Church members argue that if Christ wanted women in priesthood offices, he would have placed them there in ancient times and would reveal it to our priesthood leaders now. This view overlooks the great freedom that Christ gives to the people of his Church and the promises we have been given that great revelations will be given in the last days. For many Church members, the excommunication of Kate Kelly represents a firm message from the leaders of the Church that priesthood by its very nature is for men only. But if the Church is truly the Church of Jesus Christ, his gospel and his revelations, which have been given to all the people, should be the foundation of all that we do. Leaders, even those in high offices, should not usurp them.

The fact that Christ possesses a male body is often cited as a reason for excluding those with female bodies from participating in his priesthood. But do not female bodies join with male bodies in making up the Church, the body of Christ? Symbolically, the Church is even considered female.[26] Are there not male

---

26. The scriptures symbolize Christ as the bridegroom and the Church as his bride. ". . . for the marriage of the Lamb is come, and his wife hath made herself ready. And to her was granted that she should be arrayed in fine linen, clean and white: for the fine linen is the righteousness of saints" (Rev. 19:7–8; see also Matt. 25:1, D&C 33:17, 65:3, 109:74, and John 3:27–30). A feminine metaphor taken from the Song of Solomon 6:10 is used three times in the Doctrine and Covenants to characterize the Church. The Lord describes "the coming forth of my church out of the wilderness—clear as the moon, and fair as the sun, and terrible as an army with banners" (D&C 5:14; see also D&C 105:31 and 109:73). The

bodies in the female Church? Cannot female bodies join Christ in his priesthood as they join him in his kingdom? As the Redeemer of mankind and the mediator between God and man, Jesus Christ stands for each person. Although in the flesh he has a male body, he represents each human person, male and female, embodied and distinct in the flesh, each enlivened by both the masculine and feminine principle. We each take his name upon ourselves. Cannot both men and women then represent him and serve in his priesthood? It is wisdom in God to send the Son to redeem us from a world of alienation, oppression, deceit, and injustice and lead us into their kingdom of love, truth, freedom, and justice. It is important for us to understand that establishing justice and dwelling peaceably together requires us to see that we are fundamentally human beings. Our Mother and Father God are One. There is one gospel for men and women, one Church for men and women, and one priesthood for all people. All who desire to serve are called to the work (D&C 4:3).

I would like to conclude with a personal note. I do not have any illusions that the type of theological arguments I have been developing here will influence the highest leaders of the Church to reevaluate the question of ordination for women. Some of us have been doing this work for many years and have experienced rejection of various kinds including excommunication. However, I do believe that it is important to continue developing and presenting the theological foundations for full equality in the Church. I am a follower of Jesus Christ, and I believe that the scriptures contain the word of God, which we must interpret according to our knowledge, experience, and the light God gives us. I see the gospel of Jesus Christ as it is taught to us in the scriptures and by the Spirit of God as our best hope. Although the pronouncements and actions of Church leaders have made discussion about women and the priesthood more difficult, they have not suppressed it. It cannot be suppressed as long as Church members are followers of Christ and believe and try to understand and live His gospel.

---

scriptures also characterize Zion as feminine. "And all the nations that fight against Zion, and that distress her, shall be as a dream of a night vision" (2 Ne. 27:3; see also Moro. 10:31, D&C 100:13, 101:17, and 113:8). Isaiah characterizes Zion as mother. "For as soon as Zion travailed, she brought forth her children" (Isa. 66:8).

Chapter 5

Egalitarian Marriage in a Patriarchal Church

Kristy Money and Rolf Straubhaar

March 17, 2013, in addition to being the 171st anniversary of the founding of the Relief Society, was a late night for us in our tiny UCLA Family Housing apartment. "Are we ready for this?" Kristy whispered to Rolf, careful not to wake our baby girls. We both knew Kate Kelly and her husband, Neil Ransom, from our Brigham Young University student days. We wanted the Ordain Women movement so badly for our newborn Rosie, tucked against Rolf's chest in her Moby wrap and our toddler Evie sleeping in the next room. Ordainwomen.org had gone live earlier that day, a day we both had been anticipating with excitement. Only two months ago we had both unsuccessfully petitioned our local Mormon leadership to let us participate jointly in Rosie's baby blessing, to present our daughter together to our congregation, family, and friends as a symbol of our egalitarian marriage. With Ordain Women launching now, we felt the timing was almost Jungian in its synchronicity.

"Will we ever be ready enough?" Rolf replied, as he joined Kristy at the table. We scrolled through the site and spotted many of our friends' smiling faces, accompanying beautiful and eloquent profiles proclaiming, "I believe women should be ordained." We discussed at length all the possible ramifications of our participation, including possibly only one of us going public to soften the severe reactions we expected from extended family. We talked over what this would mean for two Mormon academics on the job market, as anyone publicly supporting Ordain Women would probably never be considered for a job at BYU—a dream Kristy had had for years. She had loved her time there as a student. But as we considered all possibilities, we both knew, in the back of our minds, that this would be, like our (at that point) six years of marriage, a joint initiative. This was something we both wanted. Together. So we decided to write and put up our profiles at the same time and agreed to become public leaders and organizers for OW together. We've organized as a couple ever since.

Two weeks after the Ordain Women launch, we blessed Rosie at home together, just as we had done with our firstborn. It was Easter Sunday, March 31, 2013; and as we finished sharing our hopes and dreams for our newborn's future with Rolf's hands on her head and Kristy's arms holding her close, we both felt renewed hope in new beginnings, that change was in the wind.

Activism as a couple and our children's blessings are just two examples that illuminate the process of what we have done and the choices we have consciously made together to try to make an egalitarian marriage work. In this chapter we will draw on these and further examples from our own lives in detail, supported by citations from the current literature on successful marriages in counseling psychology (Kristy's field), to illustrate how an LDS couple can strive to pursue an egalitarian marriage even within a patriarchal culture like Mormonism.

In particular, through Kristy's training and experience as a therapist, perhaps no psychologist's work better encapsulates the principles necessary to create and maintain a functional, successful egalitarian marriage than John Mordecai Gottman,[1] professor emeritus of psychology at the University of Washington and founder of the Relationship Research Institute and the Gottman Institute. In this chapter, we will outline some of the principles he has established in his work as foundational to a successful marriage, which we will build on to illustrate how an egalitarian marriage can be pursued, even within a patriarchal cultural frame like Mormonism.

Learning Each Other: Leaving Nothing off the Table

When we first got to know each other and began dating, it was 2007, and we had both recently moved to New York City—Kristy to gain work experience for her Ph.D. in counseling psychology by working at The City University of New York's Counseling Center, and Rolf to begin teaching fourth grade in an elementary school in Washington Heights. We attended the singles ward together at Manhattan's Inwood chapel and got to know each other while visiting all of the places we'd come to know through romantic comedies: walking through Central Park and visiting the Empire State Building like Tom Hanks and Meg Ryan, visiting the Met (*When Harry Met Sally*), dancing on the FAO Schwartz piano (*Big*), and going to Ellis Island (*Hitch*). All the while, we were falling very, very hard for each other, and enjoying the romantic and dreamy haze of new love.

We had both been in serious relationships before, so parts of this one felt familiar, but one thing we both noted to each other felt quite different: There was an openness, a lack of reservation which made it feel as if nothing was off the table. Though Kristy is more naturally introverted than Rolf, neither of us felt guarded. During these walks and early dates, we would talk for hours about anything and everything; and more than we had found in previous relationships, we were genuinely and seriously interested in everything we heard. An unfortunate but common trend in relationships is for women to feel obliged to listen and feign interest in what men say, without reciprocity. In our first months together, though, the back-and-forth did not feel so imbalanced. Kristy would talk about her training in counseling psychology and offered Rolf several books to read from her Ph.D. coursework on Freud and Carl Jung. Rolf would talk about his previous experience working in adult education programs in Brazil and Mozambique,

---

1. John Mordechai Gottman, *Why Marriages Succeed or Fail: And How You Can Make Yours Last* (New York: Simon and Schuster, 1995), and his *What Predicts Divorce?: The Relationship between Marital Processes and Marital Outcomes* (New York: Psychology Press, 2014); John Mordechai Gottman and Nan Silver, *The Seven Principles for Making Marriage Work* (New York: Harmony Books, 1999).

and shared with Kristy books like William Easterly's *White Man's Burden* and his well-worn copy of Paulo Freire's *Pedagogy of the Oppressed*. While we read and talked, we found a genuine admiration and interest that hadn't often been present in our previous relationships.

John Gottman and Nan Silver refer to this process as "enhancing [each other's] love maps." In Gottman and Silver's model, a couple's love map is made up of the most personal aspects of their life, what they hope to accomplish, what they worry about, the most personal and intimate aspects of their personal and family history—in other words, the basic building blocks of their emotional world. In the most effective and productive relationships, interaction with one's partner builds those maps, and each partner uses his or her knowledge of those maps to regularly express mutual fondness and admiration. It was precisely such mutual map-building that we experienced as we walked around the Cloisters in Fort Tryon Park or rode the carousel near the City Library. While a new degree of intimacy and vulnerability came with that knowledge of each other, we also could feel the respect and admiration that made such sharing safe.

Encouraging Fondness and Admiration

This map-making led into Gottman's next principle of successful marriages, that of nurturing fondness and admiration for one another. While relatively easy when a relationship is new, continuing to nurture these feelings can become difficult as time passes and each other's faults and imperfections become increasingly apparent. Like all couples, over our seven years of marriage, we have experienced how hard it is to do this and the serious work it takes to do so.

We argue that one particular challenge to nurturing such fondness and admiration within a Mormon context is the inherent inequality between marriage partners that comes from the strict and traditional gender roles outlined in Mormon theological documents like "The Family: A Proclamation to the World." As that text states, "By divine design, fathers are to preside over their families in love and righteousness and are responsible to provide the necessities of life and protection for their families. Mothers are primarily responsible for the nurture of their children." Similarly, in his famous address "To the Mothers in Zion," President Ezra Taft Benson stated:

> In the eternal family, God established that fathers are to preside in the home. Fathers are to provide, to love, to teach, and to direct. But a mother's role is also God-ordained. Mothers are to conceive, to nourish, to love, and to train. So declare the revelations. . . . [I]n the Doctrine and Covenants, we read: "Women have claim on their husbands for their maintenance, until their husbands are taken" (D&C 83:2). This is the divine right of a wife and mother. She cares for and nourishes her children at home. Her husband earns the living for the family, which makes this nourishing possible. With that claim on their husbands for their financial support, the counsel

of the Church has always been for mothers to spend their full time in the home in rearing and caring for their children.[2]

Even though "The Family: A Proclamation to the World" tries to frame these roles in egalitarian terms by stating that each parent should "help one another as equal partners," language which stipulates that one partner should "preside" implies an inherent inequality in access to power and decision-making. In our view, such unequal power dynamics are inherently at odds with the mutual respect that is necessary for a relationship to be continually fed by mutual fondness and admiration.

Further, in cultures like Mormonism that maintain strict boundaries between male and female roles, it is very easy for marriage partners to develop and nurture a sense of resentment (or worse, contempt) if one or both partners aren't perceived as fulfilling their prescribed role. For example, if the husband were to lose his job, or for some reason encounter difficulty in meeting the family's monetary needs, he could be seen as failing in his prescribed role as "provider." On the other hand, if a woman is not perceived as being sufficiently thorough in household cleaning, demonstrating proficiency at cooking, has difficulty in dealing with day-to-day issues with her children, or, worse, encounters difficulty in conceiving or experiences infertility or child loss, she could be seen as failing in her prescribed role as primary caregiver and "nurturer." When one is taught from childhood in religious settings to expect certain things from one's life partner and then one's marital experience does not meet expectations, resentment comes quickly and easily.

However, the reality is that life happens, and no one can fully meet these societal expectations all the time. Economies sour, jobs are lost, unexpected ailments can make employment unfeasible, or even if one finds a stable job it may not be emotionally or psychologically fulfilling. On the other hand, stay-at-home mothers with gifts and talents that would lend themselves to full-time employment can yearn for careers outside the home, or experience physical or psychological problems that make it hard to "pull their weight" with kids and household chores. There are a million different ways in which individual circumstances can make living the LDS gender roles outlined in "The Family: A Proclamation to the World" (and reinforced weekly in lessons, talks, and casual conversations) impossible, leading to bitterness (or worse, if resentment is left to fester, disdain) on the part of one or both marriage partners.

Mutual respect and admiration for each other's strengths, even when these do not fit neatly into proscribed gender roles, can help to avoid such resentment. In our case, Kristy has always had a natural gift for listening that lends itself easily to her work as a therapist, as well as the investigative skills necessary for rigorous psychological research. Since the beginning of our relationship, she made clear

---

2. Ezra Taft Benson, "To the Mothers in Zion," pamphlet, address delivered at the Fireside for Parents on February 22, 1987 (Salt Lake City: Church of Jesus Christ of Latter-day Saints, 1987).

that developing those skills was a priority to her, alongside motherhood. Rolf also has an instinctual ability to understand what our children want and need and to help them feel loved and safe. He has always wanted to prioritize his role as father as well as his professional goals. Neither of these skill sets fits neatly into our respective proscribed roles as "provider" or "nurturer," but we respect and encourage each other in the development and exercise of these abilities. On the one hand, Kristy sought and gained her Ph.D. in counseling psychology, which has allowed her to work both in clinical settings and on her own as a therapist and psychological researcher. On the other, Rolf specifically sought training as an anthropologist of education because a career in academia would allow the flexibility to take an equal hand in parenting and the ability to work around Kristy's schedule.

We hardly have this all figured out—it is an iterative process, and we are doing our best to work together to solve difficulties that arise as we both pursue careers in addition to being active caregivers for our daughters. But the process of figuring these things out is only made possible through the mutual respect we consciously nurture for each other's professional passions and personal strengths. When one of us feels that our needs aren't being met, we speak up and work to find a solution so that we can both feel fulfilled in and outside the home.

Turning toward Each Other

Gottman and Silver (1999) emphasize the need for spouses to "turn toward each other," or in other words to effectively "be there" for each other in both the significant and mundane parts of each other's lives. That is, when Rolf had a particularly frustrating day with the girls, or when Kristy had an especially trying session with a client, and we reach out to one another for validation, attention, and support, we need to put down the computer or iPhone and truly listen.

In patriarchal cultures, and particularly conservative patriarchal cultures like Mormonism, we are socialized to believe that this type of listening and validation is a "woman's role." That is, in true *Mad Men* fashion, it is the wife's job to have dinner, a drink, and listening ear ready when the husband gets home from work, so that he can share his occupational dreams, struggles, and hopes—so that he can feel validated, encouraged, and loved; however, it is also her job to not unnecessarily "unload" her own stresses and worries as a homemaker and caretaker, because "he has enough on his plate" without hearing her concerns (especially if he is a partial cause of those concerns, due to working long hours, a lack of interest in the children, or the like). Women are expected to be receptive and sensitive to their husband's inner life, but men are much less often encouraged to do the same.

This sentiment has been echoed time and again in LDS general conference talks which emphasize women's inherent or natural ability to be selfless, empathic, and nurturing (unlike men). As Apostle D. Todd Christofferson stated in his October 2013 talk, "The Moral Force of Women," "Women bring with them into the world a certain virtue, a divine gift that makes them adept at instilling such qualities as faith, courage, empathy, and refinement in relationships and in cultures."[3] These are virtues associated with women in LDS rhetoric on a simply biological basis—that is, they are an inherent part of being born female and are thus expected from all women within LDS relationships.

The unfortunate result of such a 1950s U.S. cultural delineation of gender roles, as outlined heartbreakingly and eloquently in many novels (*Revolutionary Road*), films (*Far from Heaven, The Hours*) or TV series (*Mad Men* or *Masters of Sex*), is that husbands and wives lead parallel marriages characterized by built-up resentment rather than understanding and support. In an egalitarian household, the events of both partners' lives must be equally valorized and treated as equally important, no matter who is the "breadwinner." As noted earlier, a relationship in which one partner holds a larger portion of power (in particular due to the income and prestige associated with working outside the home, in contrast to homemaking) leads to an inherent inequality.

One way we have tried to counter this cultural trend within Mormon patriarchy is to make sure both of our careers are given priority. For instance, while Rolf was finishing graduate school, Kristy was working full time as a therapist. When our children were born and Kristy took some time to stay at home, Rolf still prioritized by giving Kristy sufficient time to write a number of research articles and prepare a book manuscript related to her research interests in infertility and child loss counseling. While at any given time, we had to negotiate the time we both needed for our careers and projects, in so doing we consciously tried to counter any sense that Rolf (as husband and expected breadwinner) should get priority in his career.

Accepting Influence

As noted above, patriarchal cultures and relationships have an inherent power imbalance. On the other hand, to accept the influence of one's partner, as Gottman and Silver point out, means to share power, to consider one another's feelings when making decisions. More than perhaps any of the other seven principles they outline, this principle can most successfully encourage the development of egalitarian relationships.

In our relationship, we have tried to accept one another's influence and share power in a number of different ways. With regards to our careers, we have done this by trying to prioritize Kristy's career at various decision-making points. For example, when we were still recently married, Kristy had an opportunity to pursue a clerkship working in community mental health clinics on the Navajo Reservation, particularly at one clinic where she had joined one of her mentors at BYU several years earlier in visiting and consulting. At this point, Rolf was one year into a two-year commitment to teach at an elementary school in Washington Heights in New York City through Teach For America. To make Kristy's clerkship possible, he went to Teach For America's national headquarters

---

3. D. Todd Christofferson, "The Moral Force of Women," *Ensign* November 2013, 29.

to petition for a transfer to New Mexico. While such petitions are rarely granted, with several follow-up visits, Rolf was able to secure the transfer, though he then had to seek out and apply for an elementary school position near Kristy's work on his own. Through cold-calling and a number of visits to the area, he was able to secure a position teaching third grade at an elementary school in Shiprock, New Mexico, near where Kristy hoped to work, despite the doubts expressed by many of Rolf's former colleagues in New York and acquaintances in the New Mexico school system that such a transfer would be possible. Since gaining experience in this area was a professional priority for Kristy, Rolf made it a professional priority as well.

Similarly, at several later junctions in our careers, Rolf tried to prioritize Kristy's professional needs so that she could continue to advance in her field. When Kristy had finished her Ph.D. coursework and needed a one-year clinical internship to complete her program, Rolf applied only to master's programs in areas near internship sites that fit Kristy's interests and goals. Later, when Kristy was applying to postdoctoral positions that would allow her to gain the hours of supervised clinical experience necessary for licensure as a psychologist, Rolf applied to doctoral programs in areas where she might have connections and have the ability to network with people whom she might be able to work under to gain those hours.

This power-sharing is a dynamic we have tried to continue in our personal and spiritual lives, as well. When both of our daughters were born, unlike many husbands who do not engage very directly in the pregnancy and birthing processes, Kristy and Rolf went to prenatal clinics together; and during the birthing process, Rolf served as Kristy's primary source of support. When the time came for our daughters to receive a name and a blessing in our ward settings, we consciously wanted to both be an equal part of that process, just as we had shared in every other aspect in our daughters' lives to that point. While the blessing of babies is traditionally a man's role, something we were taught is in part a father's opportunity because the mother was able to participate in the miracle of childbirth, we felt it important to both be present and active as equal partners in both of these events.

Focusing on "Solvable Problems"

One of the most constructive ideas that Gottman and Silver propose is their distinction between "solvable" and "unsolvable" problems. That is, all couples will encounter differences in preference and opinion, some of which can be reconciled and some of which cannot. If couples continually run into conflict over unsolvable problems, which by their nature do not change, conflict will become more and more common and eventually escalate into potential grounds for separation.

In patriarchal cultures like Mormonism, one of the difficulties inherent in this dynamic is that women are socialized to feel that it is their responsibility to compromise and initiate reconciliation, while men often do not because they have the final say as priesthood-holders. As Apostle Quentin L. Cook noted in his April 2011 general conference talk "LDS Women Are Incredible!," in LDS parlance women are seen as possessing an innate "willingness to sacrifice." Sheri Dew, former counselor in the Relief Society general presidency, in her October 2001 talk "Are We Not All Mothers?", similarly described all women as being divinely endowed with "complete selflessness" in their roles as wives and mothers.[4]

However, for relationships to truly be successfully egalitarian, the willingness to compromise and sacrifice for the other cannot be left entirely to one partner. Gottman and Silver describe several techniques which are crucial for *both* partners to develop in a successful egalitarian relationship: the abilities to "soften the startup" of hard conversations by leading off with something positive, to make "repair attempts" (that is, make reconciling statements or actions intended to keep tension from escalating), to soothe one's partner, to be tolerant of one another's faults, and to compromise.

In our relationship, we have found this dynamic to be poignantly captured in a passage Kristy read to Rolf at our wedding, and which we subsequently had inscribed within our wedding bands, W. B. Yeats's "Aedh Wishes for the Cloths of Heaven:"

> Had I the heavens' embroidered cloths,
> Enwrought with golden and silver light,
> The blue and the dim and the dark cloths
> Of night and light and the half light,
> I would spread the cloths under your feet:
> But I, being poor, have only my dreams;
> I have spread my dreams under your feet;
> Tread softly because you tread on my dreams.

Overcoming "Gridlock"

Gottman and Silver use the metaphor of "gridlock" to describe moments in relationships when one partner feels rejected, or when unsolvable arguments lead both partners to become entrenched in a particular position, feeling frustrated and unwilling to further engage. It is this point which most easily leads partners to resent one another, to become less and less willing to compromise, and to cut themselves off emotionally to avoid hurt.

Such times are difficult, but not unsolvable—often, the immediate problems are symbolic of larger concerns, and resolution depends on a couple's willingness to open up, become vulnerable and explore the larger, hidden issues driving the conflict. Couples need to work hard to excavate what symbols are at play in any given situation; and in a Mormon context, that process usually involves unpacking gender roles and expectations that each partner grew up with, and recognizing how those gender role-based symbols are rearing their head in a particular argument.

---

4. Quentin L. Cook, "LDS Women Are Incredible!", *Ensign,* May 2011, 18; Sheri Dew, "Are We Not All Mothers?" *Ensign,* November 2001, 97.

Usually in a Mormon context, such symbols involve one of the usual suspects: extended family (particularly in-law relationships, which can be incredibly fraught especially when there are mismatches in expectations of orthodoxy), sexual intimacy (which, particularly for Mormon women who are taught to be selfless and self-sacrificing, can feel more like a chore than a pleasure), parenting, and so forth.

However, such symbols are not always explicitly religious. For example, as Kristy was finishing her clinical postdoc and expecting our first child, Rolf was applying to Ph.D. programs. He was accepted with financial support into programs at UCLA and Columbia, and we spent a great deal of time debating this decision. As we unpacked this decision after the fact, we realized that a great deal of symbolism was guiding our decision-making—Kristy saw this as a point at which she was making a sacrifice, putting her career on hold so that Rolf could pursue his Ph.D. while she stayed home with our newborn. Since this was already going to involve a significant amount of sacrifice, we wanted it to be worth it—we both wanted to make the most strategic decision possible for Rolf's future career. We went back and forth repeatedly about the benefits of each institution for Rolf's prospects in his field, the particular financial packages of each, the faculty with which he would be working, and many other elements that we simply couldn't predict the effect of given the variability of the academic job market. Only as we discussed it after the fact did we realize how the entire episode was rather symbolic of the difficulties of making a significant sacrifice given significant uncertainties regarding the outcome. We were struggling to find the "perfect" solution when really there was none, both involved trade-offs, and we had to learn to do the best with what we were given. As much as that may not have been the most satisfying conclusion, reaching it together through dialogue represented a significant point of growth in our relationship. Even though we continue to rehash this argument over the years, we try to recognize the underlying symbol that creates the conflict: uncertainty.

Creating Shared Meaning as a Couple

Shared meaning in Gottman and Silver's framework means that a couple, to be successful, must build an inner life together: that is, they must share their own relational culture, their own in-jokes, and shared experiences. It is precisely this shared meaning and inner life that helps to bolster a relationship against the gridlock and conflicts that inevitably come with time.

While sharing the details of our shared inner life would to a certain degree spoil it, there are particulars of a shared inner life that can especially promote equality within a relationship, if a mutual commitment to equality is a part of that life. For example, Kristy and Rolf walking hand-in-hand next to our friend Kate onto Temple Square in April 2014 was an experience steeped in symbolism for us both. When the *New York Times* interviewed Kristy the month before and we both discussed what taking our OW activism to the next level would mean for our family, we deliberated and decided together to share our story of Rosie's baby blessing.

In the article, Kristy mentioned she'd be on Temple Square for the priesthood session action with Rosie in arms. We were married in the Salt Lake Temple and returned often to honor our commitment by spending time on Temple Square and in the temple. Temple Square and the Salt Lake Temple remain sacred spaces to us to this day. So, demonstrating together our desire for gender equality in that sacred space was both an important life event and symbol for us.

We embraced under an umbrella and walked determinedly past the usual evangelical hecklers who routinely show up for general conference, through strong winds, rain, a hailstorm, and a locked gate that Kate Kelly swung open when an unsuspecting tourist opened it. We walked together up to the doors of the tabernacle—right by the temple doors we had first walked out of as husband and wife years earlier—and Kristy asked the usher if she could come in from the cold and listen to the priesthood session with her husband, only to be told this session was for men and boys only. We will never forget that day together—we began our journey with Ordain Women together in 2013 because we wanted to bless Rosie together, and we walked onto Temple Square to demonstrate that desire together one year later.

As another example of shared symbols in our relationship, ever since Kristy first shared John Donne's "Valediction: Forbidding Mourning" with Rolf during one of their dates in a New York park, we have found the imagery of the compass to be a particularly compelling symbol that represents not only our mutual religious commitment, but our commitment to each other:

> Our two souls therefore, which are one,
> Though I must go, endure not yet
> A breach, but an expansion,
> Like gold to aery thinness beat.
>
> If they be two, they two so
> As stiff twin compasses are two;
> Thy soul, the fix'd foot, makes no show
> To move, but doth, if th' other do.
>
> And though it in the centre sit,
> Yet, when the other far doth roam,
> It leans, and hearkens after it,
> And grows erect, as that comes home.
>
> Such wilt thou be to me, who must,
> Like th' other foot, obliquely run;
> Thy firmness makes my circle just,
> And makes me end where I begun.

We find this passage particularly touching and compelling because it turns gender roles on their head: as the compasses here move and lean in toward each other, it's not just one (the woman) that is always pushed to compromise and lean into the man (or here, the fixed foot of the compass). In Donne's case, in fact, he referred to his wife as the "fixed foot," with him being the one to lean and harken after her as he traveled away. In other words, his world literally revolved around her. While such imagery is often evoked in romantic literature and song, what makes this passage resonate so much with us is that we both found ourselves feeling the same way—our worlds literally revolve around each other, and we both find ourselves wondering how lost we would feel without the other.

Figuring This Out as We Go: Recognizing Nobody's Perfect

Despite all that we have outlined here, we by no means intend to imply that we've figured it out. There are many things looking back that we wish we had done differently in hindsight. In particular, after Kristy finished her postdoc and we moved to Los Angeles to start Rolf's Ph.D. program, we didn't prioritize Kristy's getting licensed as a psychologist right away. Our reasons made sense at the time. We didn't plan to be in California long-term, and psychologists typically get licensed in particular states when they know they are settled there long enough to justify the fees, state exams, and other procedural steps associated with licensure. We had already planned on Rolf's expediting his Ph.D. coursework (which he did) and then doing dissertation research in Rio de Janeiro (which we did, thanks to his Fulbright-Hays Dissertation Award), so at that time it did not make much sense to launch Kristy's career while we were in transition and unsure of our long-term plans (a situation we're sure most academic couples can understand). Though this time gave Kristy a chance to study for and pass the national licensing exam for psychologists, publish her dissertation research, write her own book on infertility and miscarriage counseling, and serve on the executive board of Ordain Women, we still regretted not prioritizing her career and felt we had to some degree caved to implicit cultural pressures. That is, even given our commitment to egalitarianism, once we had our first child Kristy still felt some pressure from our cultural background to put career aspirations and continued income-earning on the back burner. As a result, she felt that those three years in which we were in flux and she was not prioritizing her clinical practice or teaching were really discouraging and difficult for her emotionally. Though we both feel parenthood is an incredibly rewarding activity and treasure the opportunity we have to do it together, we also feel strongly that earning an income by doing what you were trained to do and love doing should be a priority for every woman who so desires (and not only every man). On a personal level, Kristy has realized unequivocally that she's happier when she's working; and though balancing a dual-career household is tricky and looked too hard to do on paper at that time in our lives (especially since Rolf was earning a modest income so she didn't need to), research by one of her mentors proves that juggling two careers is a form of positive stress that couples find rewarding and worth it, even though it may seem daunting, or too much.[5] The lived experiences of other couples we know who try such a set-up have shown similarly that the benefits seem to outweigh the costs.

To provide even more context, before Kristy met Rolf she felt a lot of pressure to move through her undergraduate and graduate training quickly because family members repeatedly advised her that women "can't do everything." She worried that, if she married before finishing her coursework and decided to have children, she (like many women she had known at BYU) would never finish. As a result she sped through her education and training in ways that, looking back, she wished she hadn't. Rather she wished she'd let herself slow down and enjoy her BYU experience without always being in such a hurry. In hindsight, Kristy felt that this perspective which encouraged her to hurry because she "couldn't do everything" did not give nearly enough credit to spouses like Rolf who can and would have been a stay-at-home parent and would have made her education a priority, as he showed her while she was finishing her Ph.D. training. In the end, as we have discussed this situation after the fact, we both feel that a cultural principle such as this—that Mormon men cannot be expected to prioritize women's education—is simple misandry.

Fortunately, recent generations of Mormon men that have been raised after the many feminist gains of the last half-century have shown themselves to be capable of egalitarianism. We would encourage ambitious LDS women in their undergraduate and/or graduate education to not be in such a hurry, but rather to slow down and remain hopeful that they will be able to find a spouse (if they so choose) who will be just as accommodating of their careers as they intended to be of their spouse's. Kristy has counseled many young women at BYU's Counseling Center and has met many ambitious friends who found themselves in the same boat. We hope they prioritize their own experiences and take their time without feeling unneeded pressure. Similarly, many of Rolf's closest male friends from BYU and other LDS contexts, even those who previously expressed support for prescribed or traditional gender roles of the man as provider, have spent at least short periods of time as full-time caregivers for their children while their wives pursue careers and have found themselves surprised by how much they enjoy occupying a traditional "woman's" role. We hope that most, if not all Mormon men preparing themselves for marriage consider and plan for such opportunities.

For Our Daughters

In this chapter, we've outlined a number of reasons why we have pursued an egalitarian marriage (however fallibly): in order to strengthen our own relationship, to give each other a chance to feel fully realized both personally and professionally, and to feel as close to one another as possible. While these are all crucial

---

5. Aaron P. Jackson and Sharon V. Wilde, "Constructing Family-Friendly Work: Three Real Dreams," *Career Planning and Adult Development Journal* 15, no. 4 (2000): 37–48.

reasons we have pursued this path personally, religiously speaking there is another reason why this has been so important to us: our daughters.

Especially given the relative lack of models of egalitarian marriages within Mormonism, we have spent many hours looking into the possible futures of our daughters, whom we want to have the opportunity to also have egalitarian marriages. Through the decades we have both spent in the Church, and our own experiences in dating before finding one another, we have seen time and again the kinds of relationships and marriages our culture often produces; and as we think of our daughters we often worry: Will they be able to find spouses who are fair to them? Spouses who will let them fulfill their dreams and ambitions without saying, "My career needs to take priority?"

We know we are not alone among LDS Church members in having such concerns for our daughters. Especially among our generation, we have seen that an expectation of equal and fair treatment in marriage is increasingly the norm among LDS women. For our daughters, for Evie and Rosie, we want to model what they can and should look for, to the best of our ability. Whether we'll ultimately be successful in such egalitarian modeling is yet to be determined, but our two amazing, strong daughters give us an incredibly compelling reason to try.

Chapter 6

Trans-forming Mormonism: Transgender Perspectives on Priesthood Ordination and Gender

J. Sumerau and Ryan Cragun

The regulation of gender is central to the ecclesiastical and cultural structure of the Church of Jesus Christ of Latter-day Saints (LDS or Mormon Church).[1] The LDS Church has a long history of regulating the roles of women and men in, for example, the household, marriages,[2] Church leadership positions, the wider social world, and even the afterlife.[3] As in other patriarchal cultures, gender definitions in Mormonism function as a means for assigning and maintaining different levels of status, power, and legitimacy. Because religious interpretations of gender, like all other socially constructed systems of meaning,[4] are humanly defined distinctions that can change over time, Mormon leaders routinely reinforce and promote distinctions between women and men, one purpose of which is to socially mark who controls the Church and who does not. Given the pervasiveness of these gender beliefs[5] and the emphasis on obedience in the LDS Church,[6] it is likely that when Mormon women and men embrace these teachings they consequently feel more connected to God and their religious faith.

But what if one's gender identity does not fit neatly into the male/female distinctions taught and reinforced by most Christian denominations and in Mormonism in particular? One option would be for such individuals to conclude that the theological beliefs and institutional structure of their religion are irrelevant to their lives and leave the faith. Another option might be to change one's

---

1. J. Edward Sumerau and Ryan T. Cragun, "The Hallmarks of Righteous Women: Gendered Background Expectations in the Church of Jesus Christ of Latter-day Saints," *Sociology of Religion: A Quarterly Review* 75, no. 1 (Spring 2015): 49–71.

2. Tim B. Heaton, Kristen L. Goodman, and Thomas B. Holman, "In Search of a Peculiar People: Are Mormon Families Really Different?" in *Contemporary Mormonism: Social Science Perspectives*, edited by Marie Cornwall, Tim B. Heaton, and Lawrence A. Young, 2 vols. (Urbana: University of Illinois Press, 2001), 2:87–117.

3. Amy Hoyt, "Beyond the Victim/Empowerment Paradigm: The Gendered Cosmology of Mormon Women," *Feminist Theology* 16, no. 1 (2007): 89–100.

4. Patricia Yancey Martin, "Gender as a Social Institution," *Social Forces* 82 (June 2004): 1249–73.

5. Sumerau and Cragun, "The Hallmarks of Righteous Women."

6. Michael Nielsen and Daryl White, "Men's Grooming in the Latter-day Saints Church: A Qualitative Study of Norm Violation," *Mental Health, Religion & Culture* 11 (2008): 807–25.

gender identity in order to fit LDS definitions of women and men. However, a third option poses even greater difficulties: What if some individuals decide that changing their gender identity is not an acceptable option while still wishing to remain members of the Church? Such individuals may find themselves constantly confronted by the fact that their identity is not recognized in the Mormon faith—that their Church condemns them as moral deviants in both this life and the life to come. While challenging the denial of one's identity might help change some people's perceptions, it could also lead to further isolation or dismissal from the Church. Under such conditions, how might we make sense of other gender conflicts in the Church, like the current movement to ordain women? This is exactly what transgender Mormons must figure out in their own gendered and religious experiences. By spotlighting the current religious and moral situation of transgender Mormons as a special case in point, we hope to shed greater light on larger issues involving the complex interplay between priesthood ordination and gender in contemporary Mormonism.

Complexities of Transgender Identity

Transgender is an umbrella term that refers to all people living within, between, and /or beyond existing conceptualizations of masculinities and femininities.[7] Transgender people define and signify gender identities that may blend, reject, and/or reinvent notions of manhood and womanhood by subverting social commands to pick or maintain a gender category, and, instead, fashion their own identities as human beings with varied gender experiences, components, and tastes. While some simply refer to themselves as transgender, others adopt gender identities that speak specifically to certain locations between or beyond established gender role definitions. Some of the more common transgender labels include: *transman* (a person born female who transitions into a male); *transwoman* (a person born male who transitions into a female); genderqueer/gender fluid/gender variant/gender neutral (a person who rejects gender distinctions and lives as both woman and man or as neither); *bi-gender* (a person who lives as both man and woman, but shifts this identity in relation to different contexts and feelings throughout the life course); *intersex* (a person born with ambiguous genitalia); and agender (persons who identify themselves as having no gender). Despite the existence of different kinds of transgender people throughout history, these people are entirely absent from consideration in most religious traditions and emphatically so in LDS teachings about God and interpretations of His eternal plan.

The invisibility of transgender experience and recognition within current Mormon doctrine and practice reflects the Church's essentially dualistic understanding of gender. According to conventional exposition of LDS teachings, all

---

7. J. Edward Sumerau, Douglas P. Schrock, and Teri Jo Reese, "Transsexuals' Gendered Presentations," in Charles Edgley, ed., *Life as Performance: A Dramaturgical Handbook* (Burlington, Va.: Ashgate, 2013), 145–60.

human beings are God's spirit children and are intrinsically differentiated as being either male or female prior to their mortal births. Subsequently, in their earthly existence, they have immutable masculine and feminine selves. The implication is that God approves of the existence of only two sexes and genders, women and men, who naturally assume different role responsibilities and perform different functions during their earthly existence. Moreover, the LDS Church strongly discourages members from adopting the behaviors of another sex or gender. LDS leaders have constructed arguments that frame gender fluidity (or the ability to signify and develop both masculine and feminine selves) as an assault upon the sanctity of marriage, family, and God's eternal plan.[8] And finally, the *LDS Church Handbook of Instructions* specifies that *transsexual operations* are grounds for Church discipline,[9] which has the theological potential of disqualifying transsexuals from reaching salvation in the next life.

Such gender distinctions place transgender Mormons in an interesting position within the institutional and theological structure of the LDS Church. They are simultaneously "outside" of the religious reality assumed by orthodox members of the faith, while actively participating "within" a reality that doesn't recognize the legitimacy of their existence.[10] Accordingly, like other transgender people,[11] they often develop keen insights into the socially constructed nature of gender as a result of their daily struggles to understand and locate a space for themselves not provided by institutional authorities. In a complementary fashion, their lived experience generates a different perspective from that shared by binary male and female Mormons—a perspective that could be utilized by researchers, Church officials, or activist groups to ascertain opportunities for making the LDS Church more inclusive for all genders. Despite the potential suggested by these observations, transgender perspectives have thus far escaped notice in scholarly, activist, and official LDS debates about gender in the Mormon Church.

In this chapter, we introduce transgender interpretations of Mormonism in the hope of articulating something of value learned from this hitherto ignored

---

8. Sumerau and Cragun, "The Hallmarks of Righteous Women."

9. According to the *Church Handbook of Instructions*, 2 vols. (Salt Lake City: Church of Jesus Christ of Latter-day Saints, 2010), 1:57: "Church leaders counsel against elective transsexual operations. If a member is contemplating such an operation, a presiding officer informs him of this counsel and advises him that the operation may be cause for formal Church discipline. Bishops refer questions on specific cases to the stake president. The stake president may direct questions to the Office of the First Presidency if necessary." Note that the pronoun used in this passage is masculine (i.e., "him"), suggesting that the primary concern is with transwomen or men who become women and not vice versa. A further restriction on transgendered individuals is this policy: "A member who has undergone an elective transsexual operation may not receive a temple recommend" (p. 13).

10. Patricia Hill Collins, *Black Feminist Thought: Knowledge, Consciousness, and the Politics of Empowerment* (New York: Hyman, 1990).

11. Sumerau, Schrock, and Reese, "Transsexuals' Gendered Presentations."

TABLE 1
SELF-IDENTIFICATION OF TRANSGENDER MORMONS
TO THE MORMON GENDER ISSUES SURVEY

Gender Identification	Number of Respondents
Transgender (no details)	19
Gender queer	20
Gender fluid	18
Male to female transgender	15
Agender	10
Female to male transgender	8
Nonbinary	8
Bigender	7
Gender neutral	7
Intersex	2
Total sample	114

community. Specifically, we draw upon 114 quantitative and qualitative responses from transgender Mormons (see Table 1 for the different gender identities revealed by our sample) gathered as part of a larger, mixed methodological study of attitudes towards women's ordination in the Mormon Church. (Chapters 14, 15, and 16 also report methodology and findings from the 2013 Mormon Gender Issues Survey for summaries of the methodology used in our study).[12] In this chapter, we first examine responses from this subset of cases from the larger Gender Issues Survey to ascertain what transgender Mormons think should be changed within the Mormon Church. Next, we identify some difficult issues for LDS doctrine posed by the emergence of a growing group of transgender Mormons. Finally, we suggest some ways the Ordain Women movement might bolster its ranks and reform efforts by broadening its focus from women's equality in particular to full gender equality for all Mormons.

Transgender Attitudes Concerning Gender Reform in the LDS Church: A Quantitative Portrait

In order to ascertain the attitudes of transgender Mormons concerning gender in the LDS Church, we begin with quantitative responses to questions about contemporary gender arrangements within the Church and potential reforms that could be undertaken in the coming years. Importantly, our findings suggest that the majority of transgender Mormons in our sample (some of whom have left the Church) see the need for a number of gender policy changes in the Church. Thus, at least 50% of the survey respondents supported every proposed

---

12. The individuals whose responses we include in this chapter chose "other" to the question we asked about gender and then entered their gender identity.

TABLE 2
DEMOGRAPHIC CHARACTERISTICS OF TRANSGENDER MORMON RESPONDENTS
N = 114

Characteristic	Percentage
Religious identity	
on rolls, considers self LDS	37.7
on rolls, does not consider self LDS	43.0
not on rolls, was LDS	19.3
Age	
18–25	30.7
26–30	21.9
31–40	26.3
41–50	7.0
51–60	6.1
61–70	4.4
71+	0.9
prefer not to respond	2.6
Race	
White, non-Hispanic	75.4
Hispanic	7.0
Asian	0.9
Native American	3.5
Other	8.8
prefer not to respond	4.4
Education	
did not finish high school	0.9
high school	2.6
some college	29.8
college graduate	43.0
master's degree	11.4
PhD	6.1
JD/MD	1.8
prefer not to respond	4.4
Income	
less than $10,000	18.4
$10,001 to $25,000	14.9
$25,001 to $50,000	16.7
$50,000 to $75,000	15.8
$75,001 to $100,000	7.0
$100,001 to $250,000	8.8
$250,001 +	3.5
don't know	5.3
prefer not to respond	9.6
Political views	
very conservative	1.8
conservative	2.6
moderate, but lean conservative	9.6
moderate	5.3
moderate, but lean liberal	19.3
liberal	18.4
very liberal	20.2
other	18.4
don't know	1.8
prefer not to respond	2.6

Table 3
Attitudes of Transgender Mormon Respondents to Selected Issues
N = 114

Expression of Belief	Percentage
Some teachings of the LDS Church are hard for me to accept.	81.6
I believe wholeheartedly in all of the teachings of the LDS Church.	7.0
A good Latter-day Saint should obey the counsel of priesthood leaders without necessarily knowing why.	14.4
A good Latter-day Saint should first seek his or her own personal revelation as the motivation to obey.	85.6
Worthy women should be ordained (yes).	56.1
Concerned about different gender roles (yes).	81.3

change specified by our questionnaire and, as elaborated in the next section, also identified additional gender reforms for the Church to consider. Broadly speaking, our transgender respondents overwhelmingly agreed with the leaders of Ordain Women that existing gender policies and practices in the LDS Church are in serious need of reform.

Before assessing their views on these issues, however, it is important to note the demographic characteristics of our sample. (See Table 2.) In terms of religious identity, 38% of transgender respondents said they were on LDS rolls and identified as LDS, 43% thought their names remained on the rolls although they themselves no longer identified as LDS, and 19% said they were no longer members of record. Further, 85% of transgender respondents had been Mormon since birth and had been reared in Mormon households, whereas 13% converted to Mormonism in later life (not shown in Table 2). In terms of race, class, education, political views, and age, our sample of transgender Mormons was overwhelmingly white (75%), well educated (92% had at least some college), not particularly affluent (66% had incomes below $75,000), fairly liberal (58% self-identified as liberal or as "leaning" toward liberal), and relatively young (78% were 40 years old or younger).

Keeping these demographics in mind, a high percentage (82%) of transgender Mormons have difficulty accepting LDS teachings and 86% also tend to focus on personal revelation rather than obedience to Church authority in their religious lives. (See Table 3.) A majority of respondents (56%) were supportive of ordaining women but an even larger percentage (81%), were concerned about existing gender roles in the Church, despite the fact that some of them (33%) believed God established these roles. (See Table 4.) A substantial majority (61%), however, disagreed with the idea that God decreed that only men could hold the priesthood, and even more (76%) disagreed with assertions that women who feel unequal simply misunderstand Church doctrine. Further, a high percentage (73%) of transgender Mormons in the survey believed that feminism and Mormonism were compatible ideologies and that the treatment of women in the

TABLE 4
PERCENT OF AGREEMENT OF TRANSGENDER MORMON RESPONDENTS
WITH SELECTED ISSUES

Issue	Strongly Disagree	Disagree	Neutral	Agree	Strongly Agree
God has established different roles for men and women.	44.4	13.9	6.5	21.3	13.9
God has revealed that only men should hold the priesthood.	43.9	16.8	13.1	14	12.1
It's not fair that 12-year-old boys can pass the sacrament, but 12-year-old girls cannot.	12.8	15.6	12.8	14.7	44
Women who feel unequal to men at Church don't understand the gospel.	63.4	12.5	2.7	11.6	9.8
Feminism is incompatible with the restored gospel of Jesus Christ.	61.1	12	7.4	11.1	8.3
The way women are treated in the Church is a problem.	7.3	9.2	9.2	19.3	55
If women were given more leadership responsibilities, it would strengthen the Church.	3.8	3.8	20	18.1	54.3

current Church was a problem (74%). Many (72%), in fact, believed the Church would be stronger if more women occupied powerful positions. Tables 3 and 4 make it evident that transgender Mormons find existing gender role practices in the Church troublesome and believe strongly that reforms should be undertaken to rectify women's status within the LDS faith tradition.

We asked transgender respondents to our survey whether they supported implementation of a designated set of reforms in the coming years. As summarized in Table 5, a majority of them supported all of the listed reforms. Rather than simply focusing on women's ordination, transgender Mormons advocated a wide range of reforms—from language practices at the ward level of Church-sponsored activities to organizational changes throughout the ecclesiastical hierarchy of the Church as a whole. Despite their support for these proposals, however, a sizable percentage (39%) of transgender Mormons indicated that they thought changes in LDS doctrine resulted from conversations between God and Church authorities, while smaller percentages (not shown in our tables) attributed doctrinal changes to internal advocacy (19%) or external pressures (15%). Consequently, it appears that transgender Mormons desire significant changes in doctrine and Church policy, but many of them also believe that these changes can occur only through divine revelation to Church leaders and not as a result of pressure from advocacy groups.

Overall, it appears that transgender Mormons have much in common with groups like Ordain Women that seek change in how gender is enacted and lived in the LDS Church. While many ultimately believe that God will decide these

Table 5
Percentage of Support of Transgender Mormon Respondents for Selected LDS Policy Changes

	Fully Support	Generally Support	Neutral	Generally Oppose	Completely Oppose
Eliminate language suggesting that husbands preside over wives.	64.0	14.4	5.4	9.0	7.2
Provide equivalent budgets for the Young Women and Young Men organizations.	83.8	9.9	0.9	1.8	3.6
Balance the stories and images of males in Church publications, talks, and other media with stories and images of females.	69.6	16.1	8.9	0.9	4.5
Appoint women to serve with the stake high council.	63.1	15.3	10.8	2.7	8.1
Include the local Relief Society presidency in all bishopric meetings.	64.5	16.4	11.8	2.7	4.5
Make a greater effort to hire women to fill leadership positions at Church universities.	73.2	14.3	6.3	1.8	4.5
Hire women at equivalent rates as men in LDS Seminaries and Institutes of Religion.	70.6	17.4	7.3	0.9	3.7
Rotate the planning of sacrament services among the Relief Society presidency and members of the bishopric.	58.3	17.6	12.0	7.4	4.6
Allow women and men to serve missions of equal length at the same age.	69.6	14.3	8.9	1.8	5.4
Allow women to participate in the blessing of their children (for example, by holding their children in the circle).	66.4	16.8	7.1	5.3	4.4
Change temple marriage policies so that men and women have an equal opportunity to be sealed to their second spouses after they are widowed or divorced.	70.8	11.5	8.0	4.4	5.3
Restore the former practice of women giving certain types of blessings.	70.0	10.9	10.9	2.7	5.5

matters, they typically agree with the positions of Mormon women's rights activists about what should be done to improve LDS gender politics. At the same time, transgender Mormons represent a category of Latter-day Saints who experience parallel gender inequalities with Mormon women while also representing a potential source of support and collaboration for Mormon groups seeking reform.

Transgender Recommendations for Reforming Gender in the LDS Church: A Qualitative Assessment

Building upon information gained from their quantitative responses to the Gender Issues Survey, we sought to ascertain what lessons Mormon leaders, lay people, and activists could derive about gender reform from transgender Mormons. To this end, we collected and analyzed transgender responses to open-ended questions concerning gender in the Mormon Church. (Table 6 itemizes these questions.) We found two dominant themes in the responses. First,

Table 6
Open-ended Survey Questions

(1) Men and women are treated differently in the Church. Some of these differences are considered cultural, others doctrinal. Please describe these differences and why you feel they are beneficial or not beneficial.

(2) If women were to serve in more administrative and leadership roles in the LDS Church, how would that affect your religious/spiritual life? Please comment in as much detail as possible.

(3) What changes related to women, if any, do you hope the Church will implement over the next ten or twenty years? Describe these changes in as much detail as possible. Why do you believe these changes are important?

---

transgender Mormons identified problematic gender beliefs in the LDS Church that they believed should be doctrinally annulled and no longer formally or informally endorsed in Mormon culture. Second, our respondents concomitantly issued specific recommendations for facilitating a more egalitarian and inclusive faith community by actual revision of Church teachings about gender. While, for the sake of clarity, we discuss these related thematic concerns separately, transgender Mormons generally tied problematic beliefs and change recommendations together in their responses, suggesting that both undertakings would be necessary to accomplish true gender reform. Furthermore, despite numerous cases of each of these kinds of responses in our data, we limit ourselves to selected examples to illustrate the general patterns we discerned in the sample.

Problematic Gender Beliefs

A prominent theme in the comments we obtained from transgender respondents focused on gender beliefs commonly shared by Church leaders and lay members that helped to facilitate the subordination of women and other gender minorities. As we have noted in a previous study,[13] LDS authorities teach Church members that traditional gender distinctions are expected and should be conformed to in all aspects of life, thereby instituting a power differential that elevates men in the eyes of both God and the Church. Traditional gender beliefs that elevate men's authority and status over women also nullify the moral standing of people who do not conform to either manly or womanly norms of behavior, dress, activity, and/or self-presentation.

Echoing the experience of other transgender people in various social contexts,[14] transgender Mormons in our survey often noted painful childhood experiences of confusion and shame—not stopping short of sexual abuse and exploitation—when they were taught that they were less valued in the eyes of God and the Church. The following story from a genderqueer Mormon represents a typical case from our sample:

> Since I was a child I was taught that I was less than [males] simply because of my female body. I was taught that since I have a female body, I am a woman and there-

---

13. Sumerau and Cragun, "The Hallmarks of Righteous Women."
14. Sumerau, Schrock, and Reese, "Transsexuals' Gendered Presentations."

fore inherently subservient to each and every man. I was taught that I could not be as close to Jesus or do any of the things all of my friends that were boys did because I was not strong or smart enough. I was taught that I should allow men to touch me and use me as they pleased. I was taught that I had to dress like a girl and not a boy, even though I was more comfortable in boys' clothing. I was taught that I should not play sports, especially with other boys. I was taught that I should not speak up and voice my opinion since I was supposed to be training to be a vessel for a man's seed and make a baby because that was my only purpose in life as a woman.[15]

While this story illustrates the demeaning challenges that transgender Mormons face growing up in the Church, it also reveals some of the constraints that many females who grow up as girls, then as women, in the Church must also face. In both cases, the Church latently teaches over half its members[16] that they are valued less than straight men and enforces these beliefs by establishing "acceptable" behavior standards that appear to be based on the possession of specified anatomical characteristics.

At other times, transgender respondents noted the problematic way LDS teachings imply a black/white, either/or interpretation of reality that doesn't align with empirical evidence and can be highly damaging to people's sense of moral worth. As a gender fluid male noted: "Mormon culture tends to make things black and white. I think the gospel and the world are more gray. There is room for personal revelation and application of gospel principles in the individual lives of members and families. It is okay for women to work, it is okay for men to be 'stay-at-home-dads.' The gospel allows us to do things that best fit our needs."

Echoing this sentiment, an agender Mormon noted:

Now there is science PROVING that it is harmful for men and women to conform to gender norms, let alone the gender binary. Guys are ridiculed for being like girls, while girls can just never measure up. Here's an example in Church: girls are constantly pressured about marriage as if it's the only goal they should aspire to, while stay-at-home dads are ridiculed by other Church members for not "manning up" and getting a job. It doesn't matter if his wife makes more than enough for their family, or that they are both consenting adults and have agreed upon this on their own accord.

Rather than the freedom and personal responsibility that LDS leaders often emphasize in general conference talks,[17] many transgender Mormons are painfully aware of ways that LDS gender teachings restrict individual agency and limit people's ability to pursue God in whatever ways might mean the most for them.

---

15. We have standardized punctuation and capitalization in quotations from our respondents.
16. Rick Phillips, Ryan T. Cragun, Barry A. Kosmin, and Ariela Keysar, *Mormons in the United States 1990–2008: Socio-Demographic Trends and Regional Differences* (Hartford, Conn.: Institute for the Study of Secularism in Society and Culture, 2011), 4–5.
17. J. Edward Sumerau and Ryan T. Cragun, "'Avoid That Pornographic Playground': Teaching Pornographic Abstinence in the Church of Jesus Christ of Latter-day Saints," *Critical Research on Religion*, http://crr.sagepub.com/content/early/2015/02/05/2050303214567669.abstract (forthcoming in (2015).

While LDS leaders often posit religious devotion, faith, and even moral character as the ultimate signs of a godly life, transgender Mormons point out that, in practice, a person's assigned or presumed sexual status often plays a more powerful role than these ideals within Mormon lay culture. As an agender female observed: "Women are also the only ones who are called to serve as Primary leaders, reason being that they are women and therefore, must inherently know how to teach children. Men should also be called as Primary leaders, since having the ability to teach children doesn't have a gender boundary."[18]

Considering that LDS doctrine suggests children need fathers in their lives,[19] it seems odd that the Church would promote childhood education as primarily the role of mothers rather than fathers. This emphasis makes sense, however, when, as another agender member noted, the central place of gender in Mormonism is recognized: "The strict gender roles in the Church mean that oftentimes, when a person is being considered for a calling, the first thing that is looked at is their sex. Men are given leadership and administrative positions, while women are given care-based positions, regardless of their natural gifts, the skills they've worked hard to develop, or personality. This is ultimately to the detriment of everyone in the Church." Rather than focusing on the abilities of people to work for and with God, as their sermons and marketing materials often emphasize, one might conclude that LDS leaders operationalize judgments about people's suitability for a particular job based on their possession of a penis or vagina.

Although ward leaders may never conceptualize their identification of persons appropriate for callings in such explicitly physical terms, it seems highly unlikely that they don't sort candidates for positions by the understanding of their presentation of gender. Transgender Mormons, in contrast, who are much more keenly aware of the fluidity and element of choice in gender have no difficulty identifying points at which spiritual worth and religious qualifications in the LDS Church depend have apparently more to do with genitalia than particular skills, talents, religious devotion, or other virtues God's children might possess. Since, for a variety of reasons, some men don't have penises,[20] one might ask if Church leaders would/should rescind their priesthood? What about people whom society labels as male but who never had penises in the first place?[21] Are

---

18. According to the *Handbook 2: Administering the Church, 2010* (Salt Lake City: Church of Jesus Christ of Latter-day Saints), 88, 94, the bishop "calls and sets apart a sister" as the Primary president, but "men may serve as teachers, music leaders, pianists, activity days leaders, and Scout leaders. They may also assist in the nursery." Obviously, as this respondent's observation shows, traditional practices differ widely from ward to ward.

19. The Church of Jesus Christ of Latter-day Saints, "The Family: A Proclamation to the World," September 1995, http://perma.cc/S9TC-B58N (accessed April 7, 2015).

20. Katrina Karkazis, *Fixing Sex: Intersex, Medical Authority, and Lived Experience* (Chapel Hill, N.C.: Duke University Press, 2008).

21. Katrina Roen, "'But We Have to Do Something': Surgical Correction of Atypical Genitalia," *Body & Society* 14, no. 1 (2008): 47–66.

they allowed to hold the priesthood? Or, in such ambiguous cases, could having the priesthood simply depend on claiming maleness, thus implying possession of a penis? If this were true, could not women who identify themselves as male also receive the priesthood? Pushed to a ludicrous extreme, one might imagine the possibility that Church officials, like Olympic track and field officials monitoring male and female events, demanding evidence of a penis before conferring the priesthood on a candidate. Would this become a new ritual? What would such a ritual consist of (and how would the Church avoid lawsuits if it implemented such a ritual)? These questions seem farfetched, but we raise them to demonstrate the problematic nature of defining religious potential and spiritual roles operationalized on the presumed possession of sexual anatomical characteristics. We concur with transgender Mormons who argue that categorizing and dividing people based on such biological criteria limits the Church's ability to fulfill its proclaimed global mission to bring the restored gospel to all religious seekers.

Proposed Revisions in Teaching about Gender

Considering the implicit devaluation of women and other gender minorities embedded within contemporary Mormon teachings, transgender Mormons in our survey also proposed (or intimated) ways that these teachings could be revised to facilitate greater equity in Mormonism. In so doing, they often drew upon their own Church experiences in suggesting what leaders and lay members could do to make the LDS Church more gender-inclusive. Further, their proposals indicate ways through which activists for gender equality in both Mormonism and other religions might refocus their attention more broadly in order to promote more egalitarian religious traditions.

One of the more prominent suggestions offered by transgender Mormons is for LDS leaders and other members to reflect on their fundamental concepts of God. While the LDS theology of God radically departs from orthodox Christian conceptions,[22] it is probably fair to say that popular conceptions of God among Mormon laity approximate the views shared by most Christians, which emphasize God's absolute qualities, transcendent being, *his* (sic) gendered role as a loving father, the personal relationship one can have with God,[23] the unconditioned and immutable perfection of the created universe, and the predetermined ends of human existence. With the possible exception of a gendered God as a father figure, to the extent that these ideas concerning God and God's will dominate popular consciousness, it seems paradoxical to conclude that transgender persons and transgender experience are not part of the creation or are somehow excluded from God's plans. A transgender Mormon's comments illustrate this perplexity:

---

22. Sterling M. McMurrin, *Theological Foundations of the Mormon Religion* (Salt Lake City: University of Utah Press, 1965), esp. Part 2, "The Concept of God."

23. It is important to note here that the Mormon belief in a plurality of distinct gods means that the personal relationship is not with Jesus, which is the more common Christian perspective on this relationship, but rather with Heavenly Father or God the Father.

> I personally believe that nature makes no mistakes and that individuals who may not fit a specific gender mold should be given the liberty to experiment and decide who they want to be, or how they want to be identified. Still, how would such a person know which bathroom or locker-room to go into? Or whether or not to be ordained a deacon? The real question comes when deciding at what point an individual is educated enough or qualified to make such a decision. I suppose it would be a case by case basis, in which more information and research (and/or fasting and prayer) would be needed.

According to the way this respondent and other transgender persons who answered the survey formulated the problem, God (and by extension nature) doesn't make mistakes. They resist what they keenly perceive to be a cruel theological contradiction—that they, like other human beings, are God's spirit children, yet their human and transgender experiences typically are repudiated as deviant mistakes by ecclesiastical leaders and the Mormon lay community.

Even when Mormons and other Christians argue that transgender people are not created that way by God, as they often do with regard to sexual minorities,[24] they must still acknowledge the creation and presence of intersex people. Since intersex people have always existed in human societies,[25] those who promote the idea that there are only two sexes or genders must either deny the existence of intersex people, deny the perfection of God's creation, or deny that the existence of intersex people undermines their religious belief in the immutability of two sexes created by God. While we cannot predict how apologists will wrestle with these issues or how Mormon theology might consequently be modified, based on our research of transgender Mormons, we can say that their personal religious concerns have become important issues for the LDS community to address.

Highlighting the ambiguities in Mormon doctrine discussed above, transgender Mormons advocate for the freedom of all Mormons, independent of their designated gender categories, to pursue their own spiritual passions and personal potential. As one respondent stated:

> The gender roles taught in the Family Proclamation[26] and perpetrated through our manuals and general conference talks tell us who God says we should be. I think God wants us to discover who we should be and what our roles are in life based on the spiritual gifts that He has given us. I don't think that His plan was ever to have us try to fit into a mold instead of create our own beautiful life. I think that roles within the home should be a private matter between a husband and a wife because they know each other and can have that relationship with God. I think the gender roles that have been taught to us are age-old cultural traditions. I think men in the Church have been closed off by their own beliefs to see that.

---

24. J. Edward Sumerau and Ryan T. Cragun, "'Why Would Our Heavenly Father Do That to Anyone?': Oppressive Othering through Sexual Classification Schemes in the Church of Jesus Christ of Latter-day Saints," *Symbolic Interaction* 37, no. 3 (2014): 331–52.

25. Karkazis, *Fixing Sex*.

26. The Church of Jesus Christ of Latter-day Saints, "The Family: A Proclamation to the World," 1995.

In statements like this, transgender Mormons express concerns that LDS leaders have lost touch with God by uncritically absorbing and sacralizing a subset of cultural norms. Further, as the following statement from a gender-fluid Mormon suggests, our respondents intimate that LDS leaders should seek fresh revelations concerning their concerns—revelations that are free from the heterocentric assumptions and sexist language of existing scriptural texts: "There is definitely a lot of inequality and sexist language in both the Book of Mormon and the Bible. However, Mormonism subscribes to the idea of modern revelation, and the General Authorities use quite a bit of heterocentric, sexist language, which pushes men and women of the Church into prescribed roles." Mormons proudly maintain that, through modern revelation, the LDS Church is a "living church" that makes divinely directed policy adjustments and institutional change when worldly conditions warrant. Transgender Mormons who take seriously the potential for change inherent in the concept of modern revelation call upon Church leaders to take their concerns to God and ask for a new understanding of gender norms that matches existing earthly realities. Some also imply that theological failure to reinterpret gender identities express the human prejudices of Church authorities rather than representing a manifestation of God's will.

Elaborating these concerns, many transgender Mormons in our study surmised that existing gender roles in the Church are due primarily to the acceptance of cultural stereotypes by both the leaders and ordinary members of the faith. Many, like the following genderqueer respondent, concluded that the widespread currency of such stereotypes in the Church limits their freedom to develop the gifts God gave them:

> The gender stereotypes in the Church are simple: the man is the one who earns money for the family and is in charge of it, and the woman takes care of the kids, is amazing at all homemaking skills, and is lower than the man. In recent years, gender stereotypes have been changing a lot. I am biologically female, but I associate more with the male gender stereotype. I hate homemaking skills and taking care of young children. But I would love to work and earn money. Nowadays, I think that it is perfectly fine for couples to switch their gender roles, and even mix them up. The LDS Church seems to still be caught up in the eras before feminism. I think that it would be much more beneficial to the LDS Church if the leaders rewrote "The Family: A Proclamation to the World" to remove all of the parts that describe gender stereotypes.

In statements like this, transgender Mormons identify the limitations that LDS gender teachings impose and call for doctrinal revisions.

Moreover, as the following comments from a transwoman suggest, many of our respondents believe that reliance on cultural stereotypes ultimately undermines God's equal treatment of His children by providing the foundations for inequality in the Church: "Women are treated as second class-citizens. Their time, opinions, and talents are not valued as a man's. Additionally, the burden of maintaining the pure thoughts of men by dressing 'modestly' maintains a rape culture and victim shaming. Not conforming leads to self-hatred, depression, suicide, [and] family estrangement." Thus, in addition to limiting the opportunities of women and other gender minorities, transgender Mormons often are led to the conclusion that existing gender teachings in the Mormon Church also facilitate the subordination, marginalization, and abuse of many Church members.

Transgender Mormons not only critique existing gender teachings in the Church, but also implicitly advocate moving Mormonism past a gender focus that is operationally reduced to anatomical sexual differences to a focus on equal regard and treatment of all people regardless of gender. Since Mormon gender teachings do not currently align with empirical realities concerning the existence of many sexes and genders, contradicting common assumptions that God's plans don't include mistakes, transgender Mormons would like LDS authorities and lay members to recast their gender beliefs and teachings in ways they believe are more compatible with the idea of God's creation. In so doing, they argue that the institutional Church would ultimately be strengthened without the demeaning and exclusionary consequences of consigning people to traditional gender role categories.

Transgender Implications for Mormon Theology: A Theoretical Discussion

As discussed above, the existence of transgender people (or at the very least the existence of intersex people) as part of God's creation and as members of the LDS Church, raises some interesting questions about current Mormon teachings and practice. It appears, for example, that LDS doctrine leaves no room for the existence of transgender people in God's creation, yet these people have existed throughout history[27] and are capable of developing close relationships with God.[28] Furthermore, Mormon transgender individuals' responses to our survey demonstrate their acute sensitivity to the gender implications of LDS teachings and conceptions of God for their personal and religious lives. As more and more transgender people live openly in our society, making it harder and harder to ignore their presence in the world, it is important to consider the implications of transgender experience for the LDS Church in the twenty-first century.

Echoing the concerns raised by Ordain Women, a realistic place to start such a discussion is with conceptions of the LDS priesthood. To begin with, while personal moral worthiness is obviously an important criterion, possession of a penis (i.e., being physically male) also seems to be a requirement for priesthood ordination status. Casting the requirement in blunt terms reflects the current reality. How do LDS leaders make sense of transgender Mormons? Would a male-bodied child who became a female-bodied adult keep the priesthood, or would that priesthood be rescinded as a result of such a transition? Alternatively, would

---

27. Karkazis, *Fixing Sex*.
28. Melissa M. Wilcox, *Queer Women and Religious Individualism* (Bloomington: Indiana University Press, 2009).

a female-bodied child who became a male-bodied adult become eligible for the priesthood upon transition? If sex largely determines who is qualified to speak for God, how does the removal or addition of sex organs change one's eligibility to hold the priesthood or serve in different positions in the religion? And if such a removal or addition does shift priesthood eligibility, would this mean, *reductio ad absurdum*, that the priesthood is somehow embodied in the penis?

Building on the complications that sex transitions raise for Mormon policy and practice, another question of transgender individuals is whether priesthood is tied to biological sex or to gender presentation or performance. For example, what if a male-bodied person engages in cross-dressing or develops a gender-fluid identity that includes living at least part time as a woman? Would that male remain a priesthood holder capable of giving priesthood blessings? Can a male-bodied person utilize the priesthood while wearing a dress or other clothing traditionally considered to be feminine? Stated another way, does a male who dresses and acts as a "woman" remain a priesthood holder as a result of his biological credentials, or does the transition in gender performance render his biological credentials obsolete in the eyes of Church authorities? Inversely, what about female-bodied people who present mostly masculine selves? Would such people be eligible for the priesthood because they live as men, or would they be denied access on the basis of biological characteristics? These questions raise important issues when considering the priesthood in relation to gender variance, as such variance can involve both biological transformation or varied symbolic cues (e.g., dress, behavior, speech) associated with gender.

Another fascinating question arises in the case of intersex individuals.[29] Since intersex people are born neither biologically male nor biologically female, are they eligible for the priesthood? Or is this situation akin to racial "one-drop" rules suggesting that any female "pollution" of someone's "maleness" results in priesthood ineligibility? Another complication involves sex assignment for intersex individuals. Conventional practice in America still involves the selection of sex (i.e., placing intersex people into female or male categories and/or adjusting their natural or "God-given" bodies to fit such categories) for these people without their consent (e.g., this is usually done within their early years based on the wishes of parents and doctors). When this is done, are some of these individuals robbed of the priesthood God wanted them to have by assigning them to be female? Or are some of them granted the priesthood God didn't want them to have (and thus potentially denying God's authority) by assigning them to be male? Just as the LDS Church eventually had to address issues involving race and so-called "racial purity" in bestowing priesthood authority,[30] we anticipate that

---

29. Karkazis, *Fixing Sex*.

30. Armand L. Mauss, *All Abraham's Children: Changing Mormon Conceptions of Race and Lineage* (Urbana: University of Illinois Press, 2003), 231–44.

growing awareness of the fluid and non-binary nature of both sex and gender will eventually lead Mormon authorities to address these concerns.[31]

While we could extend this discussion further into the many ways that gender—and especially the inaccurate conceptualization of gender as composed of only two categories—is embedded within the Mormon tradition, we nevertheless hope that this chapter prompts practicing Mormons and scholars to turn their attention to these issues. Our preliminary questions reveal some ways in which the existence of transgender populations can and will continue to create significant problems for existing Mormon doctrine. For instance, the current lack of recognition of a place for transgender individuals within Mormonism allows those outside the tradition to repudiate Mormon legitimacy. Nonbelievers can point to these questions as evidence that Mormonism is a religious tradition made up by people without adequate knowledge of the world they live in. The continued lack of a place for transgender individuals in the LDS faith supports a conclusion that Mormonism is a cultural product of a particular time and place—a time and place historically where transgender individuals existed, but were considered deviant and were so oppressed that their legitimate existence was denied. Believing Latter-day Saints need to consider how to respond to these critical questions—and to the ambiguities in Mormon doctrine they reveal—if they want to construct a more inclusive and compelling sacred canopy that is inviting to all seekers of religious truth.

To this end, we suggest that LDS leaders and members may want to consider insights the Ordain Women movement has to offer, beginning with a revision of existing LDS ecclesiastical structures and traditions in relation to the empirical realities and complexities of gender and sex. If the leaders of the LDS Church restructured the religion as an inviting place for transgender individuals, Latter-day Saints would be at the forefront of the movement toward both a more equitable world in terms of gender and a conceptualization of God that does not imply that God suffers from the same inadequacies, ignorance, and prejudice as human beings. We also suggest that women's rights movements, like Ordain Women, should consider pursuing gender equality for all people instead of limiting their advocacy to one category of a fictitious binary. Doing so would arguably build a larger base of supporters, advocates, and resources for their ongoing efforts. Finally, we encourage scholars of Mormonism as well as Mormon scholars, ordinary lay members, and activists to begin grappling with these important gender questions. If the LDS Church fails to recognize the existence of transgender individuals and find a place for them within the religion, it is possible that the growing cultural awareness of the complexity and socially constructed nature

---

31. Peggy Fletcher Stack, "Transgender Mormons Struggle to Feel at Home in Their Bodies and Their Religion," *Salt Lake Tribune*, March 31, 2015 (accessed April 7, 2015), General Conference Special Section, E2, E8–10; http://perma.cc/J26H-JBZ9.

of gender will eventually pay negative dividends for the growth and vitality of contemporary Mormonism.

Conclusion

In many ways, LDS doctrines and rituals are predicated on the theological and institutional construction of gender, making it difficult for believers to entertain alternative points of view concerning the established practices of their religion. The identity concerns and experiences of transgender Mormons, however, represent an intriguing opportunity for LDS leaders, members, scholars, and activists to gain an expanded understanding of gender problems within the Church. While charged with the task of preserving the integrity of Church doctrines and policies, Mormon ecclesiastical authorities are far from immune to widespread, lasting changes in public opinion based on new knowledge and scientific information. Consequently, expansion of empirical knowledge and altered understandings concerning the complexity and socially constructed nature of gender are likely to increase pressure on Church leaders for reformulating Church doctrine and policy on a number of gender-related issues in the years to come.

For scholars, the current religious struggles experienced by transgender Mormons may be considered as a strategic case study for understanding the ways that established religious traditions are challenged to adapt and change over time in order to preserve their relevance to people's lives and ultimate concerns.[32] To maintain their legitimacy over time, religious traditions must stay close to mainstream thought and understanding, as the latter evolve and change, while simultaneously preserving enough doctrinal distinctiveness to appeal to their core constituencies. To this end, the LDS Church will have to continue wrestling with shifting gender politics among its women and transgender constituencies. Arguably, the Church could simultaneously increase its membership appeal and reduce the future waves of younger members[33] who are abandoning the faith by taking steps now to become a more egalitarian religious community for all genders and sexes.

---

32. Ryan T. Cragun and Michael Nielsen, "Fighting over Mormon: Media Coverage of the FLDS and LDS," *Dialogue: A Journal of Mormon Thought* 43, no. 4 (2009): 65–104.

33. Rick Phillips and Ryan T. Cragun, "Mormon Religiosity and the Legacy of 'Gathering,'" *Nova Religio: The Journal of Alternative and Emergent Religions* 16, no. 3 (2013): 77–94.

PART II

Historical and Cultural Context

Chapter 7

Retrieving the Keys: Historical Milestones in LDS Women's Quest for Priesthood Ordination

Margaret M. Toscano

Introduction

The Ordain Women movement made its first public appearance on March 17, 2013.[1] Its birth process was more protracted, emerging from the labor of many women. Even so, both those participating and those watching likely do not understand all the factors that have created an environment where a public debate about women's ordination is now possible in the LDS Church. Certainly no one can see the full picture or trace clear lines of cause and effect.

This chapter is my attempt to provide one perspective. I have created a chronology of events, texts, issues, struggles, and controversies relating to LDS women's claim to priesthood. Though mainly focusing on the twentieth century, I extend my timeline back into the nineteenth century to 1842 and forward to 2014 in the twenty-first century to show how antecedents and consequences overlap.[2] Let there be no mistake: The question of women's right to priesthood ordination has always been a part of the LDS experience.

I chose the chronological presentation for the following reasons. First, this linear arrangement clarifies the abundant evidence on the topic and facilitates the understanding and evaluation of source materials. Second, the timeline reveals the nature of the arguments and struggles over women's ordination in the LDS community. Third, the chronology suggests a split between (1) the early twentieth century as a period characterized by the concealment of Joseph Smith's priesthood promises to Mormon women and (2) the late twentieth century as a period characterized by the discovery of those promises. Fourth, the chronology highlights the irrepressible conviction shared by many LDS people that Mormon women have been called by God to the same priesthood fulness to which men are called, thus making women equally eligible to serve in any office of the priesthood and of the Church, notwithstanding the hostility and resistance

---

1. The first profiles were posted March 15, with the site going public on March 17, the date commemorating the founding of the Nauvoo Relief Society.
2. I have decided to focus on the twentieth century for two reasons. First, past treatments of the relationship of LDS women and the priesthood have focused on the nineteenth century. And second, I want to illustrate how the controversies of the twentieth century link the period of Joseph Smith to the present Ordain Women movement.

Cover illustration from the March 1936 *Relief Society Magazine*. Artist Joseph A. F. Everett

of many LDS Church leaders and members.³ Finally, the contemporary request for women's ordination may be based almost entirely on concepts of social and divine justice that require the equal and inclusive treatment of women and men. Nevertheless, believing Latter-day Saints need to feel that the underlying reasons for ordination are in harmony with God's revelations. Thus, a study of the historical understanding of Mormon history and doctrine is imperative.

---

3. For a detailed examination of the issues involved in women's participation in the fulness of the priesthood, see Paul James Toscano, "Restoring the Holy Order," in *The Serpent & the Dove: Messianic Mysteries of the Mormon Temple* (N.p.: Create Space Independent Publishing, 2014), 79–115.

The illustration accompanying this chapter appeared on the cover of the March 1936 *Relief Society Magazine*, which succinctly represents the crux of the controversy over LDS women's claim to priesthood. At its right, the drawing depicts the Prophet Joseph Smith standing and holding a large key in his right hand and, in his left, a book. He is shown reaching across a space to two women: one dressed in white; the other, in black. The woman in white, who is further back in perspective, looks squarely into the Prophet's face as she stretches forth her left hand to receive the key. The foregrounded woman in black reaches out with her right hand, palm forward, appearing at first glance to make a gesture of refusal; but she is actually with curved fingers grasping for the key while looking down and, in a gesture of emotion, covering her face with her left hand. Her black dress is mirrored by the Prophet's black suit. His white shirt mirrors the white dress of the other woman. The women may either be seen as two different women or the same woman. The writers of *Women of Covenant* interpret it as women moving "from darkness into light, receiving new knowledge and authority as Joseph Smith turns the key to them."[4] But perhaps an ambiguity is suggested with the woman in black reflecting the Prophet's clothing. They could represent the contemplative and active roles of women. Certainly, the woman and Prophet both in black stand prominently at equal heights, juxtaposed as two pillars of the Restoration above the scrolls beneath, flanking a middle banner bearing information about the magazine. Above this is written the Prophet's priesthood promise to Mormon women: "I now *turn the key to you* in the name of God and this Society shall rejoice, and knowledge and intelligence shall flow down from this time [emphasis mine]."

Astoundingly, this is an exact quotation of Joseph's original words as recorded in the Nauvoo Relief Society minutes. It is astounding because, in 1936, the standard version of this statement was the watered-down one found in the 1908 *History of the Church*, edited by B.H. Roberts: "I turn the key *in your behalf*," which had been changed from the original "I turn the key *to you*" found in the Nauvoo Relief Society Minutes.[5] The change is significant. The original version

---

4. Jill Mulvay Derr, Maureen Ursenbach Beecher, and Janath Russell Cannon, *Women of Covenant: The Story of Relief Society* (Salt Lake City: Deseret Book, 1991), 47. This drawing also illustrated Marianne Clark Sharp, "Relief Society Magazine," *Encyclopedia of Mormonism*, 4 vols. (New York: Macmillan Publishing, 1992), 3:1206. Also available at http://contentdm.lib.byu.edu/cdm/ref/collection/EoM/id/5426. All online sources cited in this chapter were live and available as of May 12, 2015.

5. Joseph Smith Jr. et al., *History of the Church of Jesus Christ of Latter-day Saints*, edited by B. H. Roberts, 2d ed. rev. (6 vols., 1902–12, Vol. 7, 1932; rpt., Salt Lake City: Deseret Book, 1908), 4:607. The quotation remains unchanged in the 1949 reprint and the 1976 reprint. This change has been attributed to George A. Smith, who worked on completing Joseph Smith's history in 1854. See Dean C. Jessee, "The Writing of Joseph Smith's History," *BYU Studies* 1, no. 4 (Summer 1971): 458. Also see Linda King Newell, "Gifts of the Spirit: Women's Share," in *Sisters in Spirit*, 115–16. Though the official version of Joseph Smith's statement had been changed many years before, the 1936 *Relief Society*

implies: *I give the key to you.* The doctored version implies: *I use the key for you.* The picture depicts the original language, and perhaps intent, of the Prophet to pass God's priesthood power and authority to Mormon women to be used by them independently.

This illustration and its original quotation frame the controversy over women's relationship to priesthood in the contemporary Church. In 1936, as now, some LDS people were aware that Joseph Smith at the organization of the Relief Society promised women both priesthood and keys through the temple ordinances. Nonetheless, LDS Church leaders throughout the twentieth century have repeatedly asserted that the promised priesthood and keys conveyed through the temple give women no actual power or authority in the LDS Church, except as mediated through men. These leaders have interpreted all evidence as referring only to women (1) sharing priesthood with their husbands in their homes through temple marriage, (2) receiving priesthood blessings from male priesthood holders, and (3) acting in Church callings under the direction of male priesthood leaders.

The chronology below details patterns of denial during the first half of the twentieth century when Church leaders sought to bury the memory of Smith's priesthood promises to Mormon women. And though some women continued to argue that they held priesthood through the temple endowment, leaders countered that this priesthood did not empower women to hold ecclesiastical offices. Women who claimed the right to give spiritual and health blessings on the basis of their temple priesthood were first told that they could not do so by authority of the Melchizedek Priesthood, but only on the basis of their faith. Later, they were told they could not give blessings at all.

By 1966, when BYU religion professor Rodney Turner gave his influential address telling women that they would be eternally subordinate to the leadership of their husbands and other male priesthood figures, the awareness and knowledge of women's priesthood rights had been all but lost. Yet, at about that time, LDS scholars began uncovering evidence that women had both a theological and historical claim to the same priesthood claimed by LDS men. The chronology reveals the first half of the twentieth century as a time of cover-up and the second half as a time of recovery. At least, this is my interpretation of the evidence.

This chronology is necessarily intermixed with personal milestones for me. As a scholar and activist on Mormon women's ordination issues, it has been impossible to omit my own involvement from the timeline. Rather than hide behind the mask of objectivity, I have decided to show my own journey too. Though I obviously have a bias, I make an effort to be balanced because I understand that intelligent people can differ on the question of women's ordination. Therefore, I conclude the chronology with a reference to Neylan McBaine's 2014 book *Women at Church:*

Magazine cover shows that some were aware of the original version, perhaps through Relief Society sources.

Magnifying LDS Women's Local Impact. She mentions the Ordain Women movement and references Joseph Smith's discourses to the Relief Society, now readily available online. But she wants women to concentrate on what they can do in the Church now without ecclesiastical priesthood (which she certainly does not advocate); she wants the Female Relief Society to be a powerful force in the Church. Sheri Dew, in her book the previous year, *Women and the Priesthood* (2013), acknowledges some of the priesthood implications of Joseph Smith's discourses to the Relief Society and the idea that the fulness of the priesthood is "available only to a man and woman together."[6] Still, she does not seem to believe that this gives women any right to ecclesiastical priesthood. She titled one of her chapters "God Reserved the High Privilege of Motherhood for Women," implying that motherhood is women's parallel role to priesthood. Though traditional in many ways, neither McBaine nor Dew advocates Rodney Turner's view, prevalent even through the end of the twentieth century, that women are eternal subordinates to male priesthood holders. We have all come a long way in the last fifty years. Still, it is important to acknowledge that women, as much as men, have adamantly defended the idea that priesthood is a male only responsibility.

I was born in 1949, halfway through the twentieth century, in Mesa, Arizona, the daughter of Utah and Arizona Mormon pioneers. The idea that women might have a right to priesthood never occurred to me until the early 1970s. Before that, I accepted men as the ordained servants of God and felt no desire for that status myself. By the time I graduated from BYU in 1972 with my B.A. in English, I was beginning to question women's roles in the LDS Church. No doubt I was influenced by the larger woman's movement taking place in the nation and around the world, but my restlessness occurred only on a subconscious level. What I consciously felt was dissatisfaction with the second-class roles available for me not only in the Church but in the BYU community. I began to doubt that this was the will of God because it seemed unfair and inconsistent with my perceptions of God's character. This conflict inevitably created spiritual turmoil for me as a good Latter-day Saint. I had received my temple endowments in 1971 though I was neither planning on an LDS mission nor a temple marriage at the time. But I had spiritual longings. I wanted the further knowledge promised through the temple rituals. It was during my frequent temple visits that I gained glimpses of greater possibilities for women in the restored Church, which some will see as ironic since female subordination is prevalent there too.[7]

In that eventful and long-ago summer of 1972, I read what was for me the profoundly influential book by Edward Tullidge, *Women of Mormondom*, published in 1877. His words about women's priesthood inspired me: "The sisters [at

---

6. Sheri Dew, *Women and the Priesthood: What One Mormon Woman Believes* (Salt Lake City: Deseret Book, 2013), 29.

7. I explore this tension in my essay "Myth, Ritual, and the Mormon Temple," *Exponent II* 33, no.1 (Summer 2013): 18–21.

the time of Joseph Smith] were also apostolic in a priestly sense. They partook of the priesthood equally with men. . . . Woman also soon became high priestess and prophetess. She was this *officially.*[8] Reinforced with this knowledge, I came to see my experiences in the temple as an endowment by investiture of the keys of the Holy Priesthood after the Order of the Son of God. I believed I had received the real thing. But I wondered how this fit with the priesthood to which men in the Church were ordained by the laying on of hands.

Then, in 1980, I read *The Words of Joseph Smith: The Contemporary Accounts of the Nauvoo Discourses of the Prophet Joseph*, compiled and edited by Andrew F. Ehat and Lyndon W. Cook. I had been fascinated by Joseph Smith's theological discourses ever since reading Joseph Fielding Smith's edition of *The Teachings of the Prophet Joseph Smith* during my years at BYU. What jumped out at me in reading Ehat and Cook were the unaltered and unredacted accounts of Joseph Smith's discourses, instructions, and promises given in 1842 at the organization of the Relief Society. I was stunned by what had been removed and altered. It was then I first understood that Joseph's promise to Mormon women was that "he was going to make of this society a kingdom of priests as in Enoch's day—as in Paul's day."[9] Such statements stood in stark contradiction to what I was hearing from current Church leaders: that God had decreed priesthood was only for men and that members should expect no revelation to the contrary.[10]

Over the next few years, I extensively researched Joseph Smith's statements on priesthood, his introduction of the temple endowment, and his creation of the Quorum of the Anointed that included women as well as men who had been elevated to the fulness of the priesthood. This research resulted in 1984 in my first public speech and publication on the question of women's ordination, "The Missing Rib: The Forgotten Place of Queens and Priestesses in the Establishment of Zion." In this work, I announced with naïve boldness that "women, then, can and do hold the priesthood" and that "I believe that the Church will never be organized properly until women are acknowledged as joint holders of the holy priesthood and are brought into the leading councils of the Church." At that time I worried that by demanding priesthood, women might inadvertently reinforce the corporate power rather than the spiritual power of the LDS ecclesiastical institution. So, for this reason, I was waiting for a revelation to come from the president of the LDS Church, as it had in the case of the ordination of black men in 1978. But I soon became disillusioned. The more I attempted to employ persuasion and reason, the more resistance I encountered from mainstream members and leaders, and the more I was marginalized.

---

8. Edward Tullidge, *Women of Mormondom* (New York: Tullidge and Crandall, 1877), 22–23.

9. Andrew F. Ehat and Lyndon W. Cook, eds., *The Words of Joseph Smith: The Contemporary Accounts of the Nauvoo Discourses of the Prophet Joseph Smith* (Provo, Utah: BYU Religious Studies Center, 1980), 110.

10. See President Kimball's statement below from the June 13, 1978, *Salt Lake Tribune* interview.

In 1989, after participating in a public debate about women's right to priesthood ordination, I was summarily fired from my adjunct position at BYU, where I had been teaching for fifteen years. In the summer of 1993, my stake president, Kerry Heinz, gave me an ultimatum: I must stop speaking, writing, and being quoted in the press on controversial issues. Failure to do so would result in my facing a Church disciplinary council with the potential of being excommunicated. The crux of the case against me was that I had argued the Mother God should be acknowledged as part of the Godhead with involvement in human redemption and that women had a divine calling in the priesthood. By September of that year, I was not the only one to be so threatened. My husband, Paul, and five other scholars and feminists were all disciplined. My case was put on hold for seven years after the purge of September 1993.[11]

The twentieth century came to a close in 2000. On November 30 of that year, I was brought before a high council court on grounds of apostasy and was excommunicated. This act demonstrated that LDS Church leaders had no intention to abate their century-long effort to keep women in a subordinate position; and it showed their interest in invalidating any research and writing that presented evidence for change. The high councilors at my hearing told me they needed to excommunicate me so that I wouldn't be believed.

On November 30, 2000, I could not have anticipated the Ordain Women movement that was to erupt in the early twenty-first century. By October of 2003, Mormon women's priesthood claims, along with other feminist concerns, had diminished to the point that Peggy Fletcher Stack, in a *Salt Lake Tribune* article, could rightly ask: "Where Have All the Mormon Feminists Gone?"[12] Though my sister Janice Allred and I were still running the Mormon Women's Forum and addressing women's right to ordination and the need to acknowledge Heavenly Mother, Peggy's question was nevertheless valid. Sometimes only a handful of people (maybe twenty) attended our annual conferences, and very few women were willing to advocate publicly for Mormon women's right to priesthood ordination.

But then, when interest in these issues had reached their nadir, something happened—a sea change, or rather a tiny quantum leap—for it happened at first imperceptibly on the internet. In 2004 and 2005, the Mormon community began to see a rise in feminist blogs. Feminist Mormon Housewives and Exponent were the most visible websites. At that time, I learned from many women who wrote these blogs that they believed in women's ordination but were unwilling to address these issues publicly. They said Mormon women needed to take "baby steps," to make small changes, to expand women's Church roles before addressing the "big" issue of priesthood. They did not want to face excommunication as I had.

---

11. I explain the reasons why in my essay, titled "Margaret M. Toscano," in *Transforming the Faiths of Our Fathers: Women Who Changed American Religion*, edited by Ann Braude (New York: Palgrave, 2004), 157–71.

12. Peggy Fletcher Stack, "Where Have All the Mormon Feminists Gone?" *Salt Lake Tribune,* October 4, 2003, C1, C3.

I cannot fully account for the sudden shift in thinking that took place in and after 2012, though certainly a critical mass of younger women began to see gender roles in the Church as unacceptable.[13] But everything began to accelerate. That spring, Lorie Winder Stromberg and I made our annual complaints at private feminist retreats about the lack of support for women's ordination. Women were sympathetic but still unwilling to speak out publicly. Lorie said she was determined to keep raising the issue on internet blogs, using the Roman Catholic Womenpriests movement as her inspiration. She posted concerns on the Exponent blog and received a positive response from some Mormon women. In September of 2012, Lorie arranged a dialogue between Mormon and Catholic women to discuss women's ordination at Claremont Graduate School. Mary Ellen Robertson and I also participated. (See Chapter 1 by Lorie on the rise of Ordain Women and Mary Ellen's study of ecclesiastical equality in Chapter 8.)

By January of 2013, Lorie was in communication with Kate Kelly, planning to launch Ordain Women. I was asked to speak at the Ordain Women launch meeting held on April 6, 2013, at the University of Utah. I also participated in the Ordain Women events in October 2013 and April 2014, at which supporters walked peacefully from City Creek Canyon to the Tabernacle on Temple Square to request admission to the priesthood session of the LDS General Conference. Reports of numbers vary, but there were about 200 of us on the first occasion, and about 400 on the second.[14] As an excommunicated woman who had been advocating women's ordination for thirty years, I did not expect our presence on Temple Square to be greeted well, nor did I expect that we would see a change in the Church's policy on ordaining women any time soon. But I also did not expect to feel such overpowering emotions at the sight of so many women walking courageously to express their commitment to full equality for LDS women.

By April 2014, I began to see many significant changes in the women-priesthood discussions. By then, many younger women had come to accept the rightness of women's ordination on the basis of their personal revelations and feelings alone. Many now do not rely on historical or theological justifications as did women of my generation. For these younger women, the teachings that we all have free agency and that "all are alike unto God" are sufficient justification for change.[15] Discussions are moving away from the temple endowment as the theological foundation for Mormon women's claim to priesthood. This

---

13. For a more detailed discussion of this change, see my "The Mormon 'Ordain Women' Movement," *Feminism and Religion in the 21st Century: Technology, Dialogue, and Expanding Borders,* edited by Gina Messina-Dysert and Rosemary Radford Ruether (New York: Routledge, 2015), 153–66.

14. Many of us carried proxy names for those who could not be present. There were more women than men on both occasions, and more women who were in their twenties and thirties than older women like me.

15. It is significant that some surveys show that more men than women believe in women's priesthood ordination. See Robert D. Putnam and David E. Campbell, *American*

is probably due to the temple's subordination of women to men. The Ordain Women movement focuses more on pragmatic action: the ordination of women to priesthood offices in the LDS Church. It does not concern itself so much with the theological and structural implications of change.

By the time the Ordain Women web site was launched, another shift among Mormon feminists had commenced. The shadow of fear cast by the 1993–2000 excommunications was dissipating and, with it, the perception that members would be disciplined merely for discussing women's ordination. Lorie Winder Stromberg had a difficult time soliciting the first twenty-four profiles for the Ordain Women website due to a fear of reprisal. But by the priesthood session of general conference in October 2013, hundreds of women and men were willing to make public statements and appearances on behalf of the Ordain Women movement. Mormon blogs were buzzing with discussions about women and priesthood. I was now hearing a different story. People were telling me that the day of excommunication had passed. The internet was a safety net. The Church was more open about its history. Church leaders would not muddy their image with high-profile disciplinary councils.

Personally, I was not so sure. I saw ominous portents in the press releases from LDS Church headquarters. Sadly, my fears proved to be well founded. Kate Kelly, who was the chief figurehead and spokesperson for Ordain Women, was excommunicated on June 23, 2014. LDS Church leaders were, apparently, willing to endure negative publicity to send a clear warning message to Church members. Leaders would not tolerate direct challenges to their authority. And there is no challenge greater or more fundamental to the prevailing male hierarchy than women asserting their equal right to priesthood with the possibility that women could someday preside over men.

On May 29, 2014, LDS Public Affairs manager Michael Otterson made it clear in an open letter that General Authorities would not engage with "individuals or groups who make non-negotiable demands for doctrinal changes that the Church can't possibly accept." He asserted that such demands suggest apostasy. Arguing that we do not know the reason why Christ never ordained women as apostles in the New Testament, or the Book of Mormon, or in modern times, Otterson stated: "We only know that he did not, that his leaders today regard this as a doctrinal issue that cannot be compromised." It is important to note that the LDS Church leaders ignore historical evidence and assert instead an eternal, unchanging and unchangeable doctrinal position.[16] This is a pattern in the chronology that I highlight below as well. It starts with the bold declarations

---

Grace: How Religion Divides and Unites Us (New York: Simon & Schuster, 2010), 244. I think this indicates women's conflicted feelings about wanting ecclesiastical power.

16. In addition to the work of LDS scholars documenting evidence for women's ordination in early Christianity, many other fine studies provide ample evidence. See, for example, Karen J. Torjesen, *When Women Were Priests: Women's Leadership in the Early Church and the Scandal of Their Subordination in the Rise of Christianity* (New York: Harpercollins, 1993).

of Joseph Smith that women have a right to priesthood authority and keys. Then from Brigham Young on down, male Church leaders dilute all doctrinal and ritual evidence that could give women any real priesthood power in the Church organization. Finally, Presidents Kimball and Hinckley assert that God intends priesthood only for men and that we should not expect any revelation to the contrary. Though Apostle Dallin H. Oaks concedes, at the April 2014 general conference, that women use priesthood power and authority in their Church callings, still he insists that priesthood offices and keys belong to men alone and that this is a "divinely decreed pattern."[17] Oak's explanation may show an improvement over past statements that women are only the recipients of the blessings of the priesthood. Nevertheless, he still keeps priesthood power and the right to preside, manage, and control the Church and its resources and doctrines firmly in the hands of men.

Despite Otterson's threats and Kate's publicly reported excommunication, the Ordain Women movement has persisted. Since June of 2014, the number of profiles posted on the OW website has increased. By April 2015, 612 such profiles had been posted. The debate about women's ordination has not stopped, even among believing LDS Church members. The doctrinal, historical, and ritual reasons for women's ordination powerfully outweigh the flawed assertion of Church leaders that Christ never ordained women. And in my believing moments, I feel that the Spirit of God is now moving to convince Latter-day Saints that women's equality is a principle of the restored gospel and that the Church will never be right until women apostles and prophets sit in the Church's highest councils. I think we still have many milestones to cross, but I also believe that the change will happen, even if it takes many more decades.

LDS Women and the Priesthood: A Chronology, 1842–2014

1842, March 30: Joseph Smith told Nauvoo Relief Society he was going to make them "a kingdom of priests as in Enoch's day—as in Paul's day."[18]

1842, April 28: Joseph Smith told Relief Society: "I now turn the key to you in the name of God and this Society shall rejoice and knowledge and intelligence shall flow down from this time—this is the beginning of better days to this Society."[19]

1843, September 28: Emma Smith was anointed to the "highest and holiest order of the priesthood" and became a member of the Anointed Quorum.[20]

---

17. Dallin H. Oaks, "The Keys and Authority of the Priesthood," *Ensign*, May 2014, 49–52.
18. The original is available online in the Joseph Smith papers: http://josephsmithpapers.org/paperSummary/nauvoo-relief-society-minute-book.
19. Ibid.
20. Devery S. Anderson and Gary James Bergera, "Editors' Introduction" in *Joseph Smith's Quorum of the Anointed, 1842–1845* (Salt Lake City: Signature Books, 2005), 26, 77.

1844, February 1: Heber and Vilate Kimball were anointed Priest and Priestess "unto our God."[21] The language of the priesthood anointings of both Emma Smith and Vilate Kimball indicate that they were made priestesses to God rather than to their husbands, as later became the practice.

1844, July: Brigham Young disbanded the Relief Society after the death of Joseph Smith. A few months later, he said, "When I want Sisters . . . to get up Relief Society I will summon them to my aid but until that time let them stay at home."[22]

1845, March: Brigham Young stated that LDS women "have no right to meddle in the affairs of the Kingdom of God." He also said women "never can hold the keys of the Priesthood apart from their husbands."[23]

1867–68: Brigham Young called Eliza R. Snow to reorganize the Relief Society.[24]

1870, February 12: Utah territorial legislature established general woman suffrage (but did not allow women to hold office).[25] The 1887 Edmunds-Tucker Act disfranchised all women in Utah territory. In 1896, the state of Utah's constitution reenfranchised women and gave them full political rights, including the right to hold office.[26]

1872–1914: *Woman's Exponent* magazine was published by and for women in Salt Lake City. By and large, it supported women's suffrage and women's paid employment. Its masthead read, "The Rights of Women of Zion and the Rights of Women of All Nations."[27]

1874: Brigham Young said, "The woman that honors her Priesthood, will receive an everlasting inheritance in the kingdom of God."[28]

1877: *Women of Mormondom*, by Edward Tullidge, published in New York, is addressed to world (reprints: 1957, 1965, 1973, 1975). He emphasized women's

---

21. Ibid., 54.

22. First Council of the Seventy Minutes and Early Records, Book B, 1844–48 (March 9, 1845), 78, Church Archives, quoted in Derr, Beecher, and Russell, *Women of Covenant*, 63. This history of the Relief Society gives a thorough discussion of the disruption of the general women's organization, 59–82.

23. Quoted in Quinn, "Mormon Women Have Had the Priesthood," 373; Derr, Beecher, and Russell, *Women of Covenant*, 64. Brigham Young admitted that women have a right to meddle because of their wisdom and shrewdness, but still they should not.

24. Derr, Beecher, and Russell, *Women of Covenant*, 82.

25. I include some political events in this chronology because the fundamental American belief in the equality of all people infiltrates Mormon thinking, in spite of the hierarchical nature of the Church organization.

26. For a history of women's suffrage in Utah, see Carol Cornwall Madsen, ed., *Battle for the Ballot: Essays on Woman Suffrage in Utah, 1870–1896* (Logan: Utah State University Press, 1997).

27. See Vella Neil Evans, "Empowerment and Mormon Women's Publications," in *Women and Authority: Re-emerging Mormon Feminism*, edited by Maxine Hanks (Salt Lake: Signature Books, 1992), 49–68.

28. *Journal of Discourses* 17:119.

spiritual gifts, leadership, and priestly callings. He said: "The Mormon women, as well as men, hold the priesthood."[29]

1892, March 17: Sarah M. Kimball prepared and read this statement about the founding of the Relief Society for its Jubilee celebration: "President [Joseph] Smith stated that the meeting [in Nauvoo] was called for the purpose of making more complete the organization of the Church by organizing the women *in the order of the Priesthood*" [emphasis mine].[30]

1900: Mormon women attended Susan B. Anthony's eightieth birthday and presented her with black silk fabric they had made. She said her pleasure "quadrupled because it was made by women politically equal with men."[31]

1901: January: Bathsheba W. Smith declared, with her counselors in the general presidency of the Relief Society: "We have not taken these responsibilities upon ourselves, but have been *called in the order of the holy Priesthood*" [emphasis mine].[32]

1901, April 9: Louisa Greene Richards's letter to President Lorenzo Snow challenged him about whether women have the right to seal a healing blessing. This shows the emerging debate about women's right, not just to seal blessings, but to give them at all.[33]

1903, August 8: "Gifts of the Spirit: Healing the Sick," *Young Woman's Journal*, said, "Only the higher or Melchizedek priesthood has the right to lay hands for healing of the sick."[34]

1903: Relief Society letter, "Answers to Questions," insisted that any temple-endowed woman has authority to give blessings, but women should avoid using priesthood language.[35]

1905, July-August: Bathsheba W. Smith, who was present at the Nauvoo Relief Society meetings in 1842, reviewed the original minutes in 1905 in her office as Relief Society general president who also presided over women's temple work. She reported in the *Exponent*: Joseph "said . . . he wanted to make us, as the women were in Paul's day, 'A kingdom of priestesses.' We have the ceremony in our endowments as Joseph taught."[36]

---

29. Photographic reprint, 1975, 487.

30. "Relief Society Jubilee," *Woman's Exponent* 20 (April 1, 1892): 141.

31. Quoted in Claudia Lauper Bushman and Richard Lyman Bushman, *Building the Kingdom: A History of Mormons in America* (New York: Oxford University Press, 1999), 69.

32. *Woman's Exponent* 30 (January 1902): 68.

33. Quoted in Linda King Newell, "The Historical Relationship of Mormon Women and Priesthood," in *Women and Authority*, 31–32.

34. *Young Woman's Journal* 7 (June 1896): 398; quoted in Newell, "The Historical Relationship of Mormon Women and Priesthood," 32.

35. Ibid.

36. *Woman's Exponent* 34 (July-August 1905), 14; also quoted in *Women of Covenant*, 53–54.

1905, November: The *Woman's Exponent* republished the Jubilee report from March 17, 1892, stating that the Prophet Joseph said the purpose of organizing the Relief Society was to make "complete the organization of the Church by organizing the women *in the order of the Priesthood*" [emphasis mine]. [37]

1906, January: The *Woman's Exponent* issued a "Correction" to the November 1905 report of the Jubilee statement, which had said the women of the Relief Society had been organized "in the order of the priesthood." Bathsheba W. Smith, president, and Emmeline B. Wells, secretary, stated they had found "by comparing it with the original record no such statement was made."[38]

1907, February: "Questions & Answers" in *Improvement Era*: "Does a wife hold the priesthood with her husband?" Joseph F. Smith answered, "No"; "A wife does not hold the priesthood in connection with her husband, but she enjoys the benefits thereof." He went on to say that a husband and wife can bless their children together, with the man acting as "mouth."[39]

1908: *History of the Church*, ed. and rev. by B. H. Roberts, volume 4 published, covering the Nauvoo period. Roberts, assistant Church historian and a General Authority (member of the seven-man First Council of the Seventy) changed Joseph Smith's 1842 priesthood statements to the Relief Society to remove any implication that Joseph gave women priesthood or priesthood keys. For example, Roberts's volume changed "[Joseph was] going to make *of this Society* a kingdom of priests as in Enoch's day—as in Paul's day" to "going to make *of the Church* a kingdom of priests" [emphasis mine].[40]

1910: Emmeline B. Wells, with her counselors, said, upon assuming the Relief Society presidency: "We have not taken this responsibility upon ourselves, but have been *called by the Holy Priesthood*" [emphasis mine].[41] Note the significant change of language from the 1901 Relief Society statement above.

1912: *House of the Lord*, by James E. Talmage. He said: "It is a precept of the Church that women of the Church share the authority of the Priesthood with their husbands, actual or prospective; and therefore women, whether taking the endowment for themselves or for the dead, are not ordained to specific rank

---

37. *Woman's Exponent* (November 1905): 36.
38. *Woman's Exponent* 34 (January 1906): 44. The question of why the women were complicit in altering both their history and priesthood promises needs to be examined. *Women of Covenant*, 53–54, 447–48, footnotes the alterations from 1892–1906 but, understandably, does not attempt to explain them.
39. *Improvement Era* 10 (February 1907): 308; qtd. in ibid., 35.
40. See footnote 5 above. Also see D. Michael Quinn, "Mormon Women Have Had the Priesthood since 1843," in *Women and Authority*, 365, 387 note 5, for a discussion of Roberts's changes. Quinn and Newell are both important for documenting primary sources about women and priesthood up through the 1980s.
41. "Official Announcement," *Woman's Exponent* 39 (January 1911): 44.

in the Priesthood. Nevertheless, there is no grade, rank, or phase of the temple endowment to which women are not eligible on an equality with men."[42]

1913: Joseph F. Smith said: "I believe that every mother has the right to be a prophetess and to have the gift of sight, foreseeing prescience, to foresee danger and evil and to know what to do in her family and in her sphere." "They are prophetesses, they are seers, they are revelators to their households and to their families."[43]

1913, April: *Conference Report*: Joseph F. Smith declared that the Relief Society is one of the auxiliaries that are "subject to the powers and authority" of the Church priesthood structure. It should not be viewed as independent of priesthood hierarchy.[44]

1914, February: The *Relief Society Bulletin* supported Joseph F. Smith's April statement, arguing that the male priesthood holds the presiding authority and that women should ask local priesthood leaders for advice. "Women do not hold the Priesthood."[45]

1914, October: Message of the First Presidency from Joseph F. Smith and counselors to bishops and stake presidents. They clarified that women's blessings are different from priesthood blessings and that such female blessings should relate to women's work, such as childbirth. The letter made clear that the male priesthood directs these issues, not the Relief Society.[46]

1915–70: The *Relief Society Magazine* was published by and for women. Its goal was to focus on stories and achievements of women and eventually to provide lessons for coursework.[47]

1921, April: *Conference Report*: Apostle Rudger Clawson said, "The Priesthood is not received, or held, or exercised in any degree, by the women of the Church; but nevertheless, the women of the Church enjoy the blessings of the Priesthood through their husbands."[48]

---

42. James E. Talmage, *House of the Lord*, 94; quoted in Quinn, "Mormon Women Have Had the Priesthood," 375–76.

43. Joseph F. Smith, qtd. in ibid., 377.

44. Joseph F. Smith, qtd. in Newell, "The Historical Relationship of Mormon Women and Priesthood," 36. He points out the importance that Joseph F. Smith does not see the Relief Society organization as a parallel companion to the priesthood, the tradition that dated back to Joseph Smith.

45. *Relief Society Bulletin*, February 1914, 1–3; qtd. in ibid., 36–37. Newell argues that this position breaks the chain of female authority that had existed in the Relief Society since Eliza R. Snow.

46. James R. Clark, ed., *Messages of the First Presidency*, 6 vols. (Salt Lake City: Bookcraft, 1935–51), 4:314–15, qtd. in Newell, "The Historical Relationship of Mormon Women and Priesthood," 38.

47. See Evans, "Empowerment and Mormon Women's Publications," 52–53.

48. Rudger Clawson, *Conference Report*, April 1921, 24–25.

1921, April: *Conference Report*: Charles W. Penrose said women do not hold priesthood offices: "Sisters have said to me sometimes, 'But, I hold the priesthood with my husband.' 'Well,' I asked, 'what office do you hold in the priesthood?' They could not say much more. The sisters are not ordained to any office in the Priesthood and there is authority in the Church which they cannot exercise; it does not belong to them; they cannot do that properly any more than they can change themselves into a man."[49]

1922: In a "Message of the First Presidency," President Heber J. Grant, Charles W. Penrose, and Anthony W. Ivins explained: "Women, not being heirs to the priesthood except as they enjoy and participate in the blessings through their husbands, are not identified with the priesthood quorums."[50]

1935: Letter sent from Louise Yates Robison, Relief Society general president, to Martha A. Hickman in regard to the orthodoxy of women giving washings and anointing to pregnant women prior to delivery: "This beautiful ordinance has always been with the Relief Society, and it is our earnest hope that we may continue to have that privilege.... The Presidents of the Church have always allowed it to us."[51]

1936, March: The *Relief Society Magazine* cover showed Joseph Smith giving a large key to women with this quotation: "I now turn the key to you in the name of God and this Society shall rejoice. And knowledge shall flow down from this time."[52]

1938: *Teachings of the Prophet Joseph Smith* edited by Joseph Fielding Smith. Smith followed the pattern of B. H. Roberts, taking out or altering all of the language that indicates the Prophet Joseph Smith promised women the priesthood or saw the Relief Society organization as parallel to priesthood quorums.

1939: *Priesthood and Church Government* by John A. Widtsoe. He stated that gifts of the Spirit may be used outside of male priesthood quorums. He also emphasized: "The man who arrogantly feels that he is better than his wife because he holds the Priesthood has failed utterly to comprehend the meaning and purpose of Priesthood.... [T]he Lord loves His daughters quite as well as His sons ... men can never rise superior to the women who bear and nurture them ... woman has her gift of equal magnitude—motherhood."[53]

---

49. Charles W. Penrose, *Conference Report*, April 6, 1921, 198. The fact that Rodney Turner (286), Newell (39), and Quinn (374) all quote this statement by Penrose shows its importance in documenting that, by 1921, General Authorities made the effort to show that women do not hold priesthood in any degree.

50. Clark, *Messages*, 5:216; quoted in Newell, "The Historical Relationship of Mormon Women and Priesthood," 39.

51. Louise Yates Robison, qtd. in ibid., 40.

52. Derr, Beecher, and Cannon, *Women of Covenant*, 47, uses the illustration cropped to remove Joseph Smith's words.

53. John A. Widtsoe, *Priesthood and Church Government* (1939; rev. ed., Salt Lake City: Bookcraft, 1954), 38–39, 89–90.

1940, April Conference: J. Reuben Clark, a member of the First Presidency, referred to men themselves as "the Priesthood." He also said that priesthood is "the authority of God bestowed upon men to represent Him in certain relationships between and among men and between men and God."[54]

1945, April: Belle Smith Spafford was called as general president of the Relief Society. She reported in her "Oral History" that when she was called, J. Reuben Clark told her that the Relief Society was a "companion organization of the priesthood." She commented that she saw the Relief Society as more than a women's organization; it was "a companion to the priesthood in building the kingdom."[55]

1946: Letter of Joseph Fielding Smith to Belle Spafford, Relief Society general president, officially ended women's rights to give blessings: "It is better for us to follow the plan the Lord has given us and send for the Elders of the Church to come and administer to the sick and afflicted."[56]

1946, December: J. Reuben Clark Jr. equated women's roles as mothers and sustainers as parallel with men's priesthood. He said, "This is the place of our wives and of our mothers in the Eternal Plan. They are not the bearers of the Priesthood . . . they are builders and organizers under its power, and partakers of its blessings, possessing the complement of the Priesthood powers."[57]

1952, October Conference: Stephen L Richards said, "a woman does not hold the priesthood, but she shares it with her husband, and she is the immediate beneficiary of many of its great blessings. When she unites in marriage with a man of the priesthood in one of the temples of the kingdom, the blessings pronounced upon her are of equal import to those given her husband, and these blessings are to be realized only through the enduring compact of the marriage." He also defined the roles of priest and priestess in the temple as family roles for the home.[58]

1954: *Doctrines of Salvation* by Joseph Fielding Smith. He stated, "Women do not hold the priesthood, but if they are faithful and true, they will become priest-

---

54. J. Reuben Clark, *Conference Report*, April 1940, 152–54.
55. Belle S. Spafford, Oral History conducted by Jill Mulvay Derr, 1975–76, qtd. in Derr, Beecher, and Cannon, *Women of Covenant*, 304. Spafford was released in 1974.
56. Clark, *Messages of the First Presidency*, 4:314, quoted in Newell, "The Historical Relationship of Mormon Women and Priesthood," 40–41. See also Newell, "A Gift Given, a Gift Taken: Washing, Anointing, and Blessing the Sick among Mormon Women," *Sunstone* 6 (September/October 1981): 16–25. The fact that many Mormon women have continued to feel that they have the right to bless privately shows the ongoing conflict about women's priestly functions.
57. J. Reuben Clark Jr., "Our Wives and Our Mothers in the Eternal Plan," *Relief Society Magazine*, December 1946, 800–801.
58. Stephen L Richards, *Conference Report*, October 5, 1952, 99–100; see also Rodney Turner, *Woman and the Priesthood* (Salt Lake City: Deseret Book, 1972), 292.

esses and queens in the Kingdom of God, and that implies that they will be given authority."[59]

1956, April Conference: Marion G. Romney said that "righteous men, bearing the priesthood and endowed with the gift of the Holy Ghost . . . are the only ones upon the earth with the right to receive and exercise the gifts of the spirit."[60]

1958, October Conference: "Relief Society: An Aid to the Priesthood," by Joseph Fielding Smith. He created the same confusion as above: women do not have priesthood but they have authority through the temple.[61]

1958: *Mormon Doctrine* by Bruce R. McConkie. He said: "There is no such thing in the true Church as a *high priestess*. Where this office is found in a church, it is an unauthorized and apostate innovation. Women do not hold priesthood." Then later he said: "Those women who go on to their exaltation, ruling and reigning with their husbands who are kings and priests, will themselves be *queens and priestesses*. They will hold positions of power, authority, and preferment in eternity."[62]

1966: At a BYU six-stake fireside, Rodney Turner delivered an address titled "Woman and the Priesthood," in which he said: "The stewardship of woman is encircled in the stewardship of man . . . Woman therefore finds her fulfillment in man as man finds his in God."[63]

1966: One woman's approving response to Turner made this comparison: "Women are doormats . . . They keep their men from going in / With muddy feet to God."[64]

1970, December: Last issue of the *Relief Society Magazine*. LDS women lost their independent voice in the Church.[65]

1970: The Relief Society also lost its independence, organizationally and financially, under priesthood correlation reorganization.[66] (These same subordinate conditions were imposed on the other auxiliaries as well: the Primary, YWMIA/

---

59. Joseph Fielding Smith, *Doctrines of Salvation: Compiled Sermons of Joseph Fielding Smith*, compiled by Bruce R. McConkie, 3 vols. (Salt Lake City: Bookcraft, 1954–56), 3:178.
60. *Conference Report*, April 1956, 72; cited in Newell, "The Historical Relationship of Mormon Women and Priesthood," 41.
61. Joseph Fielding Smith, *Relief Society Magazine* 46 (January 1959): 4; qtd. in Quinn, "Mormon Women Have Had the Priesthood," 383.
62. Bruce R. McConkie, *Mormon Doctrine* (Salt Lake City: Bookcraft, 1958), 326, 534. Eliza R. Snow and others were referred to as "high priestesses" in the *Woman's Exponent*. See Evans, "Empowerment and Mormon Women's Publications," 53.
63. Rodney Turner, "Woman and the Priesthood," qtd. in Newell, "The Historical Relationship of Mormon Women and Priesthood," 42–43.
64. Quoted anonymously in ibid., 43.
65. See Derr, Beecher, and Cannon, *Women of Covenant*, 340–44.
66. Ibid., 340–46.

YMMIA, and Sunday School; but they had never held "companion" status with priesthood quorums).

1972: *Woman and the Priesthood*, by Rodney Turner, BYU professor. Throughout, he emphasized the dichotomy of motherhood for women and priesthood for men, though he did acknowledge that women can give blessings in their sphere and exercise spiritual gifts. However, "the voice of the priesthood is a male voice . . . The Lord does not send women to do the work of men; it is not for women to receive instructions for the Church and kingdom and priesthood of God. The message of salvation is a priesthood message delivered by male messengers to male prophets. It is all under the direction of the Godhead—three male deities."[67]

1973: *Daughters of Light* by Carol Lynn Pearson.[68] She took a historical approach and compiles women's personal writings about spiritual gifts, such as healing, prophecy, etc., mostly from the nineteenth century.

1974, July: *Exponent II* begins publication in Boston. It is still running today, and it supports the Exponent blog, both of which have provided a forum for discussion for feminist issues.

1972, March 22: The Equal Rights Amendment passed Congress (first introduced in 1923). The date of ratification was March 1979, later extended to June 1982. It failed to pass. The LDS Church was a major opponent.

1974, December: Barbara B. Smith, Relief Society general president, took a public stance against ERA.[69]

1975: The U.N.-sponsored International Women's Year became a battleground for political and social issues. Acting through the Relief Society, Apostle Ezra Taft Benson instructed local leaders to have women in Utah and other states attend to oppose the "feminist agenda," including resolutions on equal pay, etc.[70]

1976: *Mormon Sisters: Women in Early Utah*, edited by Claudia L. Bushman. It was the first anthology of serious historical research on Mormon women, and it included essays on women's spiritual gifts, political equality, and feminism.[71]

1976, October: The First Presidency issued an official statement against the Equal Rights Amendment.[72]

---

67. Turner, *Woman and the Priesthood*, 282–83.
68. Carol Lynn Pearson, *Daughters of Light* (1973; rpt. Salt Lake City: Bookcraft, 1986).
69. Martha S. Bradley, *Podiums and Pedestals: Utah Women, Religious Authority, and Equal Rights* (Salt Lake City: Signature, 2005), 94–97.
70. Ibid., 175–76.
71. Claudia L. Bushman, ed., *Mormon Sisters: Women in Early Utah* (1976; 2d ed., Logan: Utah State University Press, 1997).
72. *Ensign*, December 1976, 79.

1977, June: At the Utah state meeting of IWY, 14,000 women packed the Salt Palace when the Relief Society sent a recommended ten women from each ward to "protect" the family from feminist attacks.[73]

1978, June 13: In an interview reported in the *Salt Lake Tribune*, President Kimball said "The church will not extend priesthood to women." After the announcement on June 8 that worthy black men could be ordained to the priesthood, President Spencer Kimball said: "We pray to God to reveal his mind and we always will, but we don't expect any revelation regarding women and the priesthood."[74]

1978, August 29: Hartman Rector Jr. sent a letter to Teddie Wood, a member of Mormons for the Equal Rights Amendment: If women were to receive priesthood, "the male would be so far below the female in power and influence that there would be little or no purpose for his existence. . . . [He] would probably be eaten by the female as is the case with the black widow Spider."[75]

1978, September: The prohibition against women praying in sacrament meetings was reversed by First Presidency. This prohibition had been a policy only since December 1967.[76]

1979, December: Sonia Johnson was excommunicated by a bishop's court for her public criticism of the LDS Church's anti-ERA stance.

1979: *She Shall Be Called Woman*, by Oscar W. McConkie. He said that male and female characteristics are more inherent in humans than personality traits. He emphasized woman's primary role as motherhood and argued that while priesthood is bestowed only on men, "its benefits and blessings are shared by their wives and families."[77]

1980: *Words of Joseph Smith: The Contemporary Accounts of the Nauvoo Discourses of the Prophet Joseph*, edited by Andrew F. Ehat and Lyndon W. Cook. This was the first publication to make available the original statements of Joseph Smith to the Relief Society.[78]

1980, February: "A Woman's Perspective on the Priesthood," by Patricia Holland, BYU Women's Conference. She argued that the womanhood-priesthood divide is

---

73. See Bradley, *Podiums and Pedestals*, 155–222.

74. *Salt Lake Tribune*, June 13, 1978, D-1.

75. Hartman Rector Jr., qtd. in Quinn, "Mormon Women Have Had the Priesthood," 381–82.

76. Lavina Fielding Anderson, "Landmarks for LDS Women: A Contemporary Chronology," *Mormon Women's Forum Quarterly* 3, nos. 3–4 (December 1992): 6. Lavina and I both kept chronologies of these women-related landmarks.

77. Oscar W. McConkie, *She Shall Be Called Woman* (Salt Lake City: Bookcraft, 1979), 4, 7, 118.

78. Andrew F. Ehat and Lyndon W. Cook, eds., *The Words of Joseph Smith: The Contemporary Accounts of the Nauvoo Discourses of the Prophet Joseph* (Provo, Utah: BYU Religious Studies Center, 1980), with preface by Truman Madsen.

not a matter of equality, but of different roles and assignments. The question is how we fulfill our responsibilities in righteousness, not who has what role.[79]

1980, December: Daniel Ludlow wrote in the *Ensign* that the spiritual gifts are available to all members of the Church, including the gift of prophecy. He quoted George Q. Cannon: "'The genius of the kingdom [is] . . . to make every man a prophet and every woman a prophetess.'"[80]

1981: Apostle James E. Faust said that priesthood reaches its potential "only in the eternal relationship of the husband and the wife sharing and administering these great blessings to the family."[81]

1981: *From Housewife to Heretic: One Woman's Spiritual Awakening and Her Excommunication from the Mormon Church*, by Sonia Johnson.[82]

1981: "Women and Priesthood," by Nadine Hansen. In perhaps the first public article to assert a belief that Mormon women should be ordained, Hansen used information from Christian feminists about early Christianity.[83]

1983: "Come All Ye Sons of God," by Boyd K. Packer. He instructed that men and women have separate roles. Men should protect and provide. "Every Mormon husband needs to feel dominant . . . . Young sisters, if you take that role from him, the one he needs, you reduce his manhood."[84]

1984, August: "The Missing Rib: The Forgotten Place of Queens and Priestesses in the Establishment of Zion," delivered by Margaret M. Toscano at the Salt Lake Sunstone Symposium. I argued that women have priesthood through the temple endowment, as promised by Joseph Smith in his 1842 discourses to the Relief Society. I also argued that the Nauvoo Quorum of the Anointed shows historical precedence for including women in Church priesthood quorums.[85]

---

79. Patricia Holland, "A Woman's Perspective on the Priesthood," *Ensign*, July 1980, www.lds.org/liahona/1982/06/a-womans-perspective-on-the-priesthood (accessed April 29, 2015).

80. Daniel H. Ludlow, "I Have a Question," *Ensign*, December 1980), 31; qtd. in Newell, "The Historical Relationship of Mormon Women and Priesthood,"43.

81. James E. Faust, "Psychotherapists, Love Your Wives," *AMCAP Journal*, January 1981, 4–6, 30–32; qtd. in Newell, "The Historical Relationship of Mormon Women and Priesthood," 43. It is significant that, although Faust was addressing the Association of Mormon Counselors and Psychotherapists, in this statement, Faust assumed that his audience consisted of men.

82. Sonia Johnson, *From Housewife to Heretic: One Woman's Spiritual Awakening and Her Excommunication from the Mormon Church* (Garden City, N.Y.: Doubleday, 1981).

83. Nadine M. Hansen, "Women and Priesthood," *Dialogue: A Journal of Mormon Thought* 14, no. 4 (Winter 1981):48–57.

84. Boyd K. Packer, "Come All Ye Sons of God," originally "Eternal Marriage," in *BYU Speeches of the Year*, BYU 1970; qtd. in Quinn, "Mormon Women Have Had the Priesthood," 408.

85. Margaret M. Toscano, "The Missing Rib: The Forgotten Place of Queens and Priestesses in the Establishment of Zion," Sunstone Symposium, Salt Lake City, August 1984, printed in *Sunstone Magazine*, July 1985, 16–22.

1984, August: Salt Lake Sunstone panel on women's relationship to priesthood: Linda King Newell, "The Historical Relationship of Mormon Women and Priesthood"; Melodie Moench Charles, "LDS Women and Priesthood: Scriptural Precedents for Priesthood; and Meg Wheatley, "An Expanded Definition of Priesthood? Some Present and Future Consequences." All three were published as a group in *Dialogue*.[86]

1984: *Mormon Engima: Prophet's Wife, "Elect Lady," Polygamy's Foe*, by Linda King Newell and Valeen Tippetts Avery. Both were banned for ten months from speaking about their book in LDS meetings.[87]

1984: The Reorganized Church of Jesus Christ of Latter Day Saints canonized as Section 156 an inspired document by its Prophet President Wallace B. Smith that extended priesthood ordination to women. Following that denomination's procedure for determining priesthood callings, the first women were ordained in 1985. (See Chapter 9 by Robin Kincaid Linkhart.)

1985: "Women, Feminism, and the Blessings of the Priesthood," by Bruce C. Hafen at the BYU Women's Conference. He said: "The one category of blessing in which the role of women is not the same as that of men holding the priesthood is that of administering the gospel and governing all things."[88]

1985, October: At the general women's meeting, Gordon B. Hinckley told LDS women not to worry or speculate about why women don't hold the priesthood. He said, "Only the Lord, through revelation, could alter that situation. He has not done so." Women should "dwell on the remarkable blessings that are yours."[89]

1986, August: Howard W. Hunter, as acting president of the Council of the Twelve, made the announcement that directives and decisions for all auxiliaries, including the Relief Society, would come through stake and ward priesthood leaders.[90]

1987: *Sisters in Spirit: Mormon Women in Historical and Cultural Perspective*, edited by Maureen Ursenbach Beecher and Lavina Fielding Anderson and published by University of Illinois Press, contains two chapters relating to priesthood: "Mormon Women and the Temple" by Carol Cornwall Madsen, and

---

86. Linda King Newell, "The Historical Relationship of Mormon Women and Priesthood"; Melodie Moench Charles, "LDS Women and Priesthood: Scriptural Precedents for Priesthood"; and Meg Wheatley, "An Expanded Definition of Priesthood? Some Present and Future Consequences," Sunstone symposium, August 1984, published in *Dialogue: A Journal of Mormon Thought* 18, no. 3 (Fall 1985): 15–42.

87. Anderson, "Landmarks for LDS Women," 1–20.

88. Bruce C. Hafen, *BYU Speeches of the Year*, 1985.

89. Gordon B. Hinckley, "Ten Gifts from the Lord," *Ensign*, November 1985. lds.org (accessed May 20, 2015).

90. Lorie Winder Stromberg, "Taking Stock: The Tenth Anniversary of the Mormon Women's Forum," *Mormon Women's Forum Quarterly* 9, no. 1 (Spring 1998): 3.

"Priesthood and Latter-day Saint Women: Eight Contemporary Definitions," by Grethe Ballif Peterson.

1988, August 23: First meeting of the Mormon Women's Forum in Salt Lake City. Margaret Toscano spoke on "Women in the Priesthood Hierarchy." "There Is Neither Male Nor Female," was written by Kelly Frame and delivered by Karen Case (now Crist). Kelly and Karen were co-founders with me of MWF.

1989, March: "Firmage Threatened after Suggesting Priesthood for Women." After Edwin B. Firmage gave a speech at the Cathedral of Madeleine "suggesting no reason why women can't be ordained," he received death threats.[91]

1989, June 8: "Should Women Be Ordained?" This public debate was sponsored by the Mormon Women's Forum at East High School in Salt Lake City; about 600 people attended. Panelists: Edwin Firmage and Margaret Toscano argued for women's ordination; Ralph Hancock and Gigi Arrington argued against it; Christine Meaders Durham, who was serving on the Utah Supreme Court, was the moderator. Local TV channels reported on debate. The *Salt Lake Tribune*'s report focused on Ed Firmage. I lost my job at BYU Salt Lake Center following this event. I had taught for BYU for fifteen years.

1989, July: "A Tribute to Women," by Boyd K. Packer. He stressed the priesthood-motherhood dichotomy as eternal, complementary roles for men and women. He explained that "the limitation of priesthood to men . . . is a tribute to the incomparable place of women in the plan of salvation."[92]

1989: *An American Prophet's Record: The Diaries and Journals of Joseph Smith*, edited by Scott H. Faulring and published by Signature Books, documented Joseph Smith's original speeches to the Relief Society.

1989, September: General Priesthood Bulletin restricted participation in Church baby blessings to Melchizedek Priesthood holders after women ask permission to participate, using the argument that non-member fathers were standing in blessing circles.[93]

1989, October: *The Mormon Women's Forum Newsletter* (later *Quarterly*) began publication.

1990: *Strangers in Paradox: Explorations in Mormon Theology*, by Margaret Toscano and Paul Toscano (Signature Books). Our book extensively explored issues of women's relationship to priesthood, arguing that there is no historical or

---

91. Item published in *Salt Lake Tribune*, March 11, 1989, D-1; reprinted in Hanks, *Women and Authority*, 335–51.

92. Boyd K. Packer, "Tribute to Women," *Ensign*, July 1989, 74.

93. 1989–3 *Bulletin* (the Church's publication distributed to priesthood, but not auxiliary, leaders), cited in Anderson, "The LDS Intellectual Community and Church Leadership," 13.

theological reason why women should not be ordained. We also connected the Heavenly Mother doctrine with women's right to priesthood.

1990, April 10: Changes in the LDS temple ceremony softened the requirement for women to obey their husbands.[94]

1992: *Women of Covenant: The Story of Relief Society*, by Jill Mulvay Derr, Janath Russell Cannon, and Maureen Ursenbach Beecher, published by Deseret Book. This was a very thorough, well-documented work that presented abundant evidence for expansive views of LDS women's authority from 1842 to the contemporary world. But it also veiled the implications of Joseph Smith's statements and promises to the Nauvoo Relief Society.[95]

1992: *Encyclopedia of Mormonism*, edited by Daniel Ludlow and published by Macmillan. The illustration from the 1936 Relief *Society Magazine* that leads this chapter was reprinted with the entry on "Relief Society Magazine." The entry on the "Heavenly Mother" acknowledged her godhood and legitimized her as orthodox doctrine.

1992, April: "The Relief Society and the Church," by Dallin H. Oaks. He asserted: "No priesthood keys were delivered to the Relief Society. Keys are conferred on individuals, not organizations." He further claimed that "priesthood keys were delivered to the members of the First Presidency and the Quorum of the Twelve Apostles, not to any organizations." He added that women laying hands on other women should be confined to the temple.[96]

1992: *Women and Authority: Re-emerging Mormon Feminism*, edited by Maxine Hanks and published by Signature Books. Forty-one percent of the book dealt with women and priesthood issues, including an influential article by D. Michael Quinn extensively documenting evidence of LDS women having priesthood since 1843.

1993, April: "The Temple, the Priesthood," by Boyd K. Packer. He explained that priesthood can be conferred only by the laying on of hands, not by the temple ceremony.[97]

1993, June: Cecilia Konchar Farr was denied continuing status as a BYU English professor for expressing feminist and political views.

1993, August: "If Women Have Had the Priesthood since 1843, Why Aren't They Using It?" Salt Lake Sunstone Symposium panel with Maxine Hanks, Michael Quinn, Linda King Newell, and Margaret Toscano was broadcast live. I had already

---

94. See ibid., 13–14, for how the press treated these changes and the consequences for those who talked about them publicly.
95. Derr, Beecher, and Cannon, *Women of Covenant*, 23–58.
96. Dallin H. Oaks, "The Relief Society and the Church," *Ensign*, May 1992, 36.
97. Boyd K. Packer, "The Temple, the Priesthood," *Ensign*, May 1993, 20.

been sent a letter by my stake president forbidding me to talk publicly about the issue of women's ordination, or I would face a Church disciplinary council.[98]

1993, September: Excommunications and Discipline of September Six. Lynne Kanavel Whitesides was the president of the Mormon Women's Forum; Maxine Hanks edited *Women and Authority*; D. Michael Quinn published on controversial topics, including women and priesthood; Paul J. Toscano had critiqued the LDS hierarchy and supported Mormon feminism, and Lavina Fielding Anderson had chronicled instances of ecclesiastical abuse in the LDS Church.[99]

1995, May 9: Excommunication of Janice Merrill Allred for apostasy. Her article on God the Mother was cited, as well as her speech that challenged the infallibility of top Church leaders.[100]

1996, April 7: President Gordon B. Hinckley declared that it is God's will that only men hold priesthood in a TV interview with Mike Wallace on *60 Minutes*: MW: "The current issue is whether Mormon women will ever be priests." GH: "Men hold the priesthood in this Church." MW: "Why?" GH: "Because God stated that it should be so. That was the revelation to the church. That was the way it was set forth." MW: "Fact is, most Mormon women don't want to be priests."[101]

1996, June 6: English Professor Gail Turley Houston was denied continuing status at BYU for publicly questioning gender roles and advocating prayer to Heavenly Mother.[102]

1997: The Relief Society presidency of Elaine Jack, Aileen Clyde, and Chieko Okazaki was released after serving since 1990. Many considered them feminist friendly. Aileen Clyde had been part of a task-force examining equality in Utah's justice system, which she reported on in a meeting of the Mormon Women's Forum.

1998: The Reorganized Church of Jesus Christ of Latter Day Saints ordained its first two women apostles: Gail E. Mengel and Linda L. Booth. (The church's name changed to Community of Christ in 2001.)

2000, October: "We Are Instruments in the Hands of God," by Mary Ellen Smoot, Relief Society general president. She emphasized the unique roles of women as seen in their Relief Society service.[103]

---

98. My speech was published in *Dialogue* 27, no. 2 (Summer 1994): 219–26.

99. Avraham Gileadi, who was also excommunicated, had done an apocalyptic critique of the Church based on his personal translation and analysis of Isaiah. He was later reinstated.

100. For a detailed account of the process, see Janice Allred, "My Controversy with the Church," *Mormon Women's Quarterly* 6 no.1 (Spring 1995): 1–16.

101. From transcript on www.lds-mormon.com/60min.shtml, accessed April 19, 2015.

102. Stromberg, "Taking Stock," 4.

103. Mary Ellen Smoot, "We Are Instruments in the Hands of God," *Ensign*, November 2000, https://www.lds.org/ensign/2000/11/we-are-instruments-in-the-hands-of-god (accessed May 30, 2015).

2000, November 30: Excommunication of Margaret Merrill Toscano by South Cottonwood stake high council. The chief issue was women's ordination.[104]

2003, October 4: "Where Have All the Mormon Feminists Gone?" by Peggy Fletcher Stack. This lengthy article in the *Salt Lake Tribune* asserted that while Mormon feminists were likely "to quietly slip into inactivity or simply go underground," this did not indicate that women's issues were dead. Claudia Bushman was quoted: "Issues that electrified earlier activists have slowly declined. . . . Female participation and visibility in the church are on the rise."

2004: Lisa Butterworth began her blog Feminist Mormon Housewives, which remains the most prominent and most visited website dealing with LDS women's issues.

2004, March: Margaret Toscano was only woman who participated in the first meeting of the Society of Mormon Philosophical Theology conference at Utah Valley University. Some male organizers tried to exclude me because I had been excommunicated. My talk, "Is There a Place for Heavenly Mother in Mormon Theology?" looked at the underlying reasons women are subordinate in the LDS Church, including their exclusion from priesthood.[105]

2004, November: "Power Hungry," by Lorie Winder Stromberg. Women who want priesthood ordination are considered "power hungry," according to Stromberg. She analyzed the faulty logic of this criticism against feminists. She first gave a version of this speech at the Mormon Women's Forum Counterpoint Conference, also in November.[106]

2004, November: "Is Priesthood Only for Men? Utilizing Women's Gifts in the Church." Panel discussion at the annual Mormon Women's Forum Counterpoint Conference at the University of Utah. Panelists were Vickie Stewart Eastman, Mira Green, Mary Ann Morgan, and Margaret Toscano.

2004, December 26: President Hinckley and Larry King discussed the question of women's ordination in King's interview of Hinckley on CNN. King asked about: "The Mormons' public image in dealing with stereotypes . . . women are regarded less in the Church." GH: "Oh, there's no substance to it. Ask the women. You'll get the answer." LK: "They can't get your job, though." GH: "No, they can't. They've got one of their own, and that's a very responsible job. They have their own organization. They have their own board. It's the largest women's

---

104. I have documented my story from notes I took shortly after the event in my unpublished essay, "The Problem with Niceness: My Excommunication from the Mormon Church."

105. Margaret Toscano, "Is There a Place for Heavenly Mother in Mormon Theology? An Investigation into Discourses of Power," in *Discourses in Mormon Theology: Philosophical & Theological Possibilities*, edited by James M. McLachlan and Loyd Ericson (Salt Lake: Greg Kofford Books, 2007), 193–223.

106. Lorie Winder Stromberg, "Power Hungry," *Sunstone Magazine*, December 2004, 60–61.

organization in the world with four million members. There's nothing like it anywhere else in the world. And they run a tremendous organization."[107]

2005: "Are Boys More Important than Girls? The Continuing Conflict of Gender Difference and Equality in Mormonism," given by Margaret Toscano at Utah Valley University's "Mormonism and Social Justice Conference." I cited women's exclusion from priesthood as one evidence of structural inequality in the Church. I argued that equality cannot be based simply on women's feelings.[108]

2005: Establishment of other Mormon feminist blogs, such as the Exponent. They mostly avoided the topic of women's ordination and relationship to priesthood until 2013. But they have been crucial for the upsurge of interest in feminist issues, for the international networking that gives questioning women support, and for the kind of community building that has been necessary to promote feminist activism for the past few years.[109]

2005, October: "Priesthood Authority in the Family and the Church," by Dallin H. Oaks. He explained that the equal partnership of men and women is for the home, not the Church organization, which is a male hierarchy.[110]

2005, October 29: "Mormon Women to Push for Priesthood Power at Counterpoint Conference," Peggy Fletcher Stack reported in the *Salt Lake Tribune* article.[111]

2009, August: "Is Priesthood Necessary for Women to Have Full Equality in the LDS Church?" Participants on this panel presented by the Mormon Women's Forum at Salt Lake Sunstone Symposium were Margaret Toscano, Janice Allred, Sonja Farnsworth, and Taryn Nelson Seawright. Someone criticized the panel, telling symposium organizer, Mary Ellen Robertson, that the topic of women and priesthood is passé.

2010: WAVE founded—Women Advocating for Voice and Equality. Their approach was to be both feminist and faithful, and to work for change in the LDS Church in a way that is "compatible with LDS beliefs in the divinity of all humans" and "the worth of all souls." In private discussions with women on their board, I was told they have made a deliberate decision not to address the issue of women's ordination.[112]

---

107. CNN.com transcript: http://transcripts.cnn.comTRANSCRIPTS/0412/26/lkl.01.html; Youtube video: https://www.youtube.com/watch?v=jAsNMWwRXvs.

108. Margaret M. Toscano, "Are Boys More Important than Girls? The Continuing Conflict of Gender Difference and Equality in Mormonism," *Sunstone Magazine,* Issue 146 (June 2007): 19–29.

109. Other important feminist blogs are Zelophehad's Daughters, Young Mormon Feminists, and I'm a Mormon Feminist.

110. Dallin H. Oaks, "Priesthood Authority in the Family and the Church," *Ensign,* November 2005, 24–27.

111. *Salt Lake Tribune,* October 29, 2005. http://www.sltrib.com/lifestyle/ci_3162675.

112. See www.ldswave.org.

2010, August: "Two Trees" given by Valerie Hudson Cassler at the FAIR conference. She argued for what she sees as equal but separate roles for men and women, triggering an energetic discussion of complementarianism as a way of dealing with female ordination issues.

2012: Joseph Smith's 1842 discourses to the Relief Society became available online through the Church History Department's Joseph Smith Papers project with their original priesthood language.[113]

2012, June 8: "Sacred Disobedience: Women's Call to Ordination" posted by Lorie Winder Stromberg on the Exponent blog. Using the Roman Catholic Womenpriests movement as inspiration, Lorie asked Mormon women to consider acts of sacred disobedience and to begin aspiring to ordination.[114]

2012, July: "Priesthood Matters: Should Mormon Women Follow the Example of the Roman Catholic Womenpriests Movement?" My Sunstone speech pled with the LDS leaders and members to accept that we already have a revelation about women's legitimate right to priesthood ordination. The question should not be "if?" but "how?"

2012, August–August 2013: On her popular blog, "Ask a Mormon Girl," Joanna Brooks wrote a series of posts on the question of Mormon women's ordination.[115]

2012, September: "All Are Alike unto God" website asked top LDS leaders to pray about women's ordination and also in the meantime to consider twenty-two other changes that would create more equality for women within the institutional Church. The online site asked people to sign the title document.[116]

2012, September 19: Mormon/Catholic dialogue on the topic of women's ordination at Claremont Graduate School. Participants were: Lorie Winder Stromberg, Margaret Toscano, Mary Ellen Robertson, Victoria Rue, Christine Haider-Winnert, and Jennifery O'Malley.

2012, December 16: "Wear Pants to Church Sunday." The website for the group announced that it is concerned with gender inequality and wants to celebrate inclusiveness.[117]

2013, January: "Let Women Pray in General Conference" website encouraged people to write to Church leaders to ask that women might be allowed to pray in the general sessions of the LDS. The specific goal was for gender inclusiveness in the Church that shows "all are alike unto God."[118]

---

113. http://josephsmithpapers.org/paperSummary/nauvoo-relief-society-minute-book.
114. http://www.the-exponent.com/sacred-disobedience-womens-call-to-ministry.
115. http://askmormongirl.com.
116. http://whatwomenknow.org/all_are_alike/index.html; 1,991 signatures were reported as of April 30, 2015.
117. http://pantstochurch.com.
118. http://letwomenpray.blogspot.com.

2013, March 17: "Ordain Women: Mormon Women Seeking Equality and Ordination to the Priesthood." The website (Ordain Women.org) officially went live, eliciting thousands of hits on the first day.

2013, March: The Mormon bloggernacle exploded with discussions about the ordination of women, from the more conservative to the more liberal, with people taking sides all along the spectrum.[119]

2013, April 5: Top women leaders in the LDS Church gave their views on women's ordination to Ruth Todd, senior manager of the Church's Public Affairs Department. When asked in the video interview what she would say to women who are concerned about not holding the priesthood, Linda K. Burton, Relief Society general president, said that most women don't desire the authority of the priesthood and are happy with the blessings of the priesthood because they understand that men and women have "complementary roles." They acknowledged that women have priesthood power, but not offices.[120]

2013, April 6: Ordain Women launch meeting, University of Utah. Speakers Kate Kelly, Lorie Winder Stromberg, Hannah Wheelwright, Margaret Toscano, Debra Jenson, and Mary Ellen Robertson explained why they think Mormon women should be ordained and what they hope to do with the organization. About 100 people attended, along with newspaper and TV reporters.[121]

2013, April 6: Jean A. Stevens became the first woman to offer a prayer in LDS General Conference.[122]

2013, October 5: Ordain Women priesthood session action. Over two hundred people, mostly women but some men, walked from City Creek Park to the Tabernacle on Temple Square to ask for admission to the general priesthood meeting. As men filed into the building, woman after woman was turned away. Cameras, cellphones, and videos recorded the event, with some women weeping as they were denied entrance.

2013, November: *Women and the Priesthood: What One Mormon Woman Believes*, by Sheri Dew, published by Deseret Book. Though Dew took the expected conservative position that men and women have complementary roles in the LDS Church, this book gave more equality to women than Rodney Turner did in 1972.

---

119. For an overview of the internet reaction in spring 2013, including the national press, see Toscano, "The Mormon 'Ordain Women' Movement: The Virtue of Virtual Activism," 153–66.
120. www.mormonnewsroom.org/article/women-leaders-insights-church-leadership.
121. The media attention to the Ordain Women movement has been significant.
122. Joanna Brooks reported the event on April 8, 2013, on Religion Dispatches: http://religiondispatches.org/historic-prayer-by-woman-at-lds-general-conference-signals-growing-concern-with-gender-equality/

2014, April 5: Ordain Women second priesthood session action. Once again a group walked to Temple Square to ask for admission to the general priesthood meeting. Participants numbered between 400–500 people, mostly women. Before all of the women in the group had made their way to the Tabernacle door, the LDS Church had released a statement condemning the action as a "disappointing" and disruptive "protest."[123]

2014, April: "The Keys and Authority of the Priesthood," by Dallin H. Oaks. He said that women use priesthood power and authority in their Church callings. "We are not accustomed to speaking of women having the authority of the priesthood in their Church callings, but what other authority can it be?" Still, he emphasized that men alone hold priesthood offices and the keys to direct the Church. He called this a "divinely decreed pattern" that cannot be altered. Oaks also stated that men "hold the priesthood" but "are not the priesthood."[124]

2014, May 29: Press release by Michael Otterson about feminist groups: "Yet there are a few people with whom Public Affairs and General Authorities do not engage, such as individuals who make non-negotiable demands for doctrinal changes that the Church can't possibly accept . . . . Such demands come across as divisive and suggestive of apostasy."[125]

2014, June 23: Excommunication of Kate Kelly from LDS Church "for conduct contrary to the laws and order of the Church."[126]

2014: *Women at Church: Magnifying LDS Women's Local Impact*, by Neylan McBaine, published by Greg Kofford Books. She said her purpose is "not an attempt to challenge or redefine gender doctrine." Rather, her goal is to "help improve gender-cooperative practices on the local levels so as to relieve unnecessary tensions caused by cultural or historically normative practices."[127]

Conclusion

This chronology clearly indicates that many people over the past 172 years have seen legitimate doctrinal and historical reasons for ordaining women to priesthood within the LDS tradition. I believe this fact contributes as much to keeping the question and possibility of women's ordination alive in the Church as does the drive for gender equality that infiltrates from the larger American culture. Forces from the inside are as significant as those from the outside because they fuel the

---

123. http://fox13now.com/2014/04/05/lds-church-actions-of-those-who-demonstrated-on-temple-square-disappointing/.

124. Oaks, "The Keys and Authority of the Priesthood," 49–52.

125. Posted May 29, 2014 on Millennial Star blog. http://www.millennialstar.org/the-lds-church-responds-to-criticism-and-details-efforts-to-reach-out-to-women/.

126. This language is a direct quotation from the *Church Handbook of Instructions*. See Nadine M. Hansen's analysis of LDS excommunication policies in Chapter 12.

127. McBaine, *Women at Church*, xvi.

kind of religious commitment that is needed to keep people in the organization to work for change. Women and men feel empowered by the spiritual realities they experience in their everyday lives, which makes them feel committed to remaining in the Church even when they see deep and widespread problems. They need to feel similar kinds of spiritual stirrings about the need for women's ordination. This is what an awareness of the history of past debates can bring to the current discussion.

Questions that have arisen in the past can also make us think in a more nuanced way about the nature and purpose of priesthood. How do the keys, authority, power, offices, gifts, and blessings of the priesthood differ and relate? What is the difference, if there is any, between the priesthood given in the temple and the ecclesiastical priesthood? What is the difference between private priesthood and public priesthood? Would extending priesthood ordination to women make men lose interest in and commitment to Church service? Is there any way priesthood can be gendered and still promote equality? Could the Relief Society continue to function if women also had roles in the Church priesthood quorums? Is there a place for sisterhood and brotherhood, as well as the united community of Saints? Why are healings and blessings at the forefront of the woman and priesthood debate? Does this show a desire to emphasize the spiritual as well as managerial side of priesthood power?[128]

Past debates also help us think more clearly and creatively about priesthood structures and their purpose within the worldwide Church organization. This is important. If and when women are ordained to offices within the LDS priesthood structure, there are still many issues that would need to be worked through to create equity and spiritual wholeness. Incorporating women into priesthood structures could make us rethink what the priesthood is, how it should be used, and where it needs to be restructured and reconceptualized to create a less hierarchical, more open Church community that works on the principles of common consent and spiritual, social, and economic equality.

---

128. It is important to note that on the OW website the photographs depicting women exercising priesthood are almost all about healing or laying on of hands.

Chapter 8

Ecclesiastical Equality: Women's Progress in Contemporary Churches

Mary Ellen Robertson

Introduction

On Sunday, March 8, 2015, an eclectic group of speakers gathered at the Salt Lake City Community of Christ chapel for the third annual Equal in Faith interfaith service. Many attendees spent the day fasting, praying, and contemplating their role in advancing gender equity in their religious communities. Women clergy talked about their experiences with gender justice advocacy in the faith communities they lead. They represented a cross-section of faith traditions: Presbyterian, Unitarian Universalist, United Church of Christ, and a rabbi from a Reform and Conservative-affiliated Jewish synagogue. Also speaking informally during the service were representatives of other faith groups including the Latter-day Saint chair of the Ordain Women board, Community of Christ, and a Zen Buddhist priestess, addressing the issues they see as pivotal in the struggle for gender equality.

The diversity on the Equal in Faith program was a microcosm of the larger conversations occurring in women's ordination and gender equality in faith communities throughout the world and in North American churches in particular. The women clergy and audience participants who shared their thoughts during the Equal in Faith worship service reflected how expansive and multidimensional the conversation about gender equity in faith communities has become. The growing interest in and advocacy for women's ordination—and for ways to visibly involve women in church leadership, worship, and congregational life—is shaping and reshaping contemporary religions in significant ways.

One of the co-founders of Equal in Faith, Lorie Winder Stromberg, describes the reasons for putting gender equity issues front and center for religious people to contemplate. Stromberg says, "It's time—past time, really—that we gather as an interfaith community to state, unequivocally, that equality for women shouldn't stop at the doors of our churches, shrines, synagogues, and mosques."[1] The Equal in Faith website poses questions about the acceptance of inequities in religious communities and distills the main drivers of the organization's gender equity work:

> While women serve as priests and in positions of religious and ritual authority in a growing number of faiths, they still are denied ordination to the priesthood and equitable inclusion in far too many religious traditions. We refuse to tolerate

---

1. "Equal in Faith 2015" video, 12:28, posted by Ordain Women Now, March 7, 2015, https://www.youtube.com/watch?v=dgyeGjAPkzo and http://www.equalinfaith.org/.

discrimination against women in our secular institutions. Why, then, do we accept it in our religious institutions?

We have faith that religion can be interpreted to liberate rather than subjugate women. Like many, we ask, which will we choose? Through a series of interfaith initiatives, we want to ignite a conversation about maintaining what we value in our religious traditions while transforming them—and our communities—into more inclusive and equitable places.[2]

As faith communities grow, change, and adjust to a modern world where women have fewer limits on their interests or achievements, the traditional arguments for continuing to exclude women from religious spheres are no longer accepted without question. Instead women and men who encounter such arguments are thinking critically about them and asking both "why?" and "why not?" While some churches actively seek to make their congregations open and welcoming places, those who don't run the risk of alienating members and being seen as less than hospitable spiritual homes. Fewer people are staying involved in the churches they were born into, and a greater percentage of Americans now identify as having no religious affiliation.[3] With such a significant denominational exodus happening in North America and around the world, church leaders, scholars, and activists are no doubt asking what might stem the outmigration from religious organizations and keep people involved in church life. Could women's ordination and greater gender equity be one approach to keep people connected to contemporary religious communities?

In this chapter, I explore the dimensions of the growing movement toward gender equity in twenty-first-century religious communities, the struggles that advocates of gender equity and women's ordination face, and the progress various religious groups have made toward paving the way for women in faith leadership. The lessons learned from other faith communities can be instructive to more recent ordination movements such as Ordain Women, whose mostly LDS members may not be as well acquainted with ordination advocacy in other religious spheres. Specifically, I examine women's ordination in three main case studies focused on churches with a significant presence in North America: Catholicism, the Episcopal Church, and Community of Christ (formerly the Reorganized

---

2. Lorie Winder Stromberg, address at Equal in Faith, March 9, 2015, http://www.equalinfaith.org/ (accessed April 30, 2015).

3. Pew Research Center, "'Nones' on the Rise," October 9, 2012, http://www.pewforum.org/2012/10/09/nones-on-the-rise/ (accessed May 3, 2015). The 2014 Pew Research Center report, announced on May 12, 2015, showed basically the same trend: more "nones" than ever and essentially flatline growth for Mormons in the U.S., except that Mormons stand out for marrying and having children at rates higher than the average U.S. population. Pew Research Center, "America's Changing Religious Landscape," May 12, 2015, http://www.pewforum.org/ (accessed May 15, 2015).

Church of Jesus Christ of Latter Day Saints).[4] For each group, I examine the denominational stance on women's ordination, the locus of the struggles and skirmishes over women's ordination, and the inroads and progress that advocates for women's ordination have made. In conclusion, I apply the "lessons learned" from other religious communities to the Ordain Women movement and examine some of the possible implications for Mormonism.

Contended Issues of Gender Equality and Ecclesiastical Reform in Contemporary Religions

Establishing gender equity and reforms necessary for women's ordination brings many contended issues to the forefront. How can traditional churches create an environment hospitable to women in clergy positions? As patriarchal practices give way to more progressive ones, how does social change intersect (or clash) with church doctrine? How can efforts to include women in church leadership and governance go beyond "add women and stir"—so they are not just figureheads or tokens but are meaningfully involved? How can women's ordination advocates convincingly demonstrate that traditional priesthood is often rooted in sexist doctrine and praxis? Should women want priesthood as it is currently constituted, advocate for a parallel women's priesthood, or scrap priesthood as we know it and create something new?

Most women advocating for ordination want to maintain their connections to the religious traditions they were born into or those they have chosen to affiliate with as adults. The desire to serve in their home churches and the transformation this often requires are key factors in working toward women's ordination. Many women who feel drawn to ministry want to work within their own faith traditions; for them, becoming ordained in those faith communities is a homecoming of sorts—a way to give back to the faiths that shaped them and to connect more deeply with and reiterate the values and teachings of those communities. This deep spiritual attachment to one's religious heritage is well exemplified by Mormon feminists active in their home wards who ardently support Ordain Women's goal of priesthood ordination for LDS women.

As women and men advocate for greater gender equality in religious spaces, many face resistance—both covert and overt—to changing the status quo. There are continuing struggles for acceptance in churches that do ordain women; there are struggles to overcome centuries of entrenched bias and sexism in theology, history, and religious praxis; and in many conservative patriarchal groups, there are struggles in even starting a conversation about women's ordination—let alone opening the door for women clergy. Some obstacles are structural. In churches that do ordain women, male clergy members often outrank women clergy members, and thus women may ascend the ranks of leadership more slowly. Ordained

---

4. The RLDS Church changed its name to Community of Christ effective in April 2001. For the sake of clarity, I use its current name retrospectively.

women may not be treated as peers and must work harder to prove themselves in leadership positions.

Some obstacles are theological. Centuries of religious and scriptural commentary created by male theologians failed to address women's presence and leadership[5] in early Christian communities and often enjoined women's participation or demanded their silence. Creators of canon law and theological commentary certainly didn't anticipate that women might desire or feel called to perform roles in religious leadership. In addition, more conservative groups take a hard-line stance against women's ordination and employ scriptural passages to justify their position of excluding women: Jesus didn't call female apostles; Paul said women should be silent in churches; Eve is the source of sin and corruption in the world; therefore no woman is equipped to be a religious authority or direct the religious lives of others, etc.

In spite of the daunting obstacles complicating the path of most women's ordination advocates, there is also progress toward more balanced and equitable participation for women. More mainline Christian denominations have started ordaining women clergy and are finding ways to incorporate women's voices and visible participation in religious and congregational leadership. More women are entering divinity schools[6] and working to develop more inclusive theology, liturgy, and ecclesiastical practices. More liberal interpretations of scripture show clear support for equality between women and men in religious and spiritual settings. Other churches are slowly cracking the doors open by bringing women into more entry-level clergy position or offices; if the door to ordination isn't all the way open, they find other meaningful ways to involve women.[7] Chaplaincy[8] is also a path into religious service that doesn't always require ordination, and a growing number of women are entering chaplaincy training to work in health care settings,[9] hospice, bereavement care, and military chaplaincy.

The questions raised by women's ordination and gender equity advocates may be profitably illuminated by case studies of three different, contemporary religions that have experienced organized movements for women's ordination and the sub-

---

5. Karen Jo Torjesen, *When Women Were Priests: Women's Leadership in the Early Church and the Scandal of Their Subordination in the Rise of Christianity* (San Francisco: Harper San Francisco, 1993).

6. "Women in Seminary," Women Priests website, http://www.womenpriests.org/classic2/howe08.asp (accessed May 1, 2015). This post is excerpted from E. Margaret Howe, *Women and Church Leadership* (Grand Rapids, Mich.: Zondervan Publications, 1982), 161–84.

7. Neylan McBaine, *Women at Church: Magnifying LDS Women's Local Impact* (Salt Lake City: Greg Kofford Books, 2014).

8. "History: A Brief History of the Association of Professional Chaplains, Association of Professional Chaplains website, http://www.professionalchaplains.org/content.asp?pl=24&sl=31&contentid=31 (accessed May 11, 2015).

9. "Catholic Women Chaplains," posted by Mariam, Mariam's Well blog, http://mariamswell.blogspot.com/p/catholic-women-chaplains.html (accessed May 11, 2015).

sequent outcomes of these efforts: the Roman Catholic Church, the Episcopal Church, and the Community of Christ. I summarize the progress toward women's ordination and/or the resultant attention given to this issue in these three traditions.

Women and Priesthood in Contemporary Roman Catholicism

Given the all-male makeup of Catholic clergy, the denominational leadership's stance on women's ordination is clear: an unequivocal no. Centuries of canon law and communal practice relegate Catholic laywomen's participation to the pews or doing charitable work and strictly proscribes the roles of women serving in religious orders. While Catholic nuns do have visible leadership roles in religious education, hospitals, health care, and charitable organizations that care for the poor, priesthood ordination is not deemed necessary by the church to carry out such work. Additionally, nuns in the United States have been subjected to particular scrutiny from the Vatican, and only recently did the Leadership Conference of Women Religious (LCWR) reach a resolution with the male clergy tasked with reviewing their activities.[10]

Hope for new directions in the Catholic Church came with the election of a new pope in 2013. So far, Pope Francis's leadership has publicly broken from past traditions of papal ceremony and aloofness in favor of a simpler life in office and emphasis on caring for the poor. A telling example occurred when he washed the feet of prison inmates—including two women—on the Maundy Thursday before conducting his first Easter Mass.[11] One CNN reporter commented: "There's already been one substantive change that has annoyed traditionalists: the way he included two women in a Holy Week ceremony representing the moment when Christ washed the feet of his twelve disciples—all men. Was the Pope hinting that he was intending to elevate the role of women in the church? It was something that raised hopes among Catholic women at the Easter Mass even if some remain skeptical that he can or will be able to bring about major change."[12] People are responding positively to Pope Francis's approach and the substance of his leadership in the twenty-first-century Catholic Church. However, the one area where Pope Francis has toed the party line is with regard to women's ordination. In a *Time Magazine* article discussing the Pope's views on women's ordination, the reporter noted:

> On two occasions when Pope Francis has been asked about possibly admitting women to the ranks of the clergy, he has given a firm no.

---

10. Sarah Posner, "Pope Does Little to Upend Status Quo on Gender and Sex, Say Advocates," April 21, 2015, http://america.aljazeera.com/articles/2015/4/21/pope-does-little-to-upend-status-quo-on-gender-and-sex-say-advocates.html (accessed April 23, 2015).

11. Heather Alexander, "Pope Washes Feet of a Young Muslim Woman Prisoner in Unprecedented Twist on Maundy Thursday," March 28, 2013, http://www.telegraph.co.uk/news/worldnews/the-pope/9960168/Pope-washes-feet-of-young-Muslim-woman-prisoner-in-unprecedented-twist-on-Maunday-Thursday.html (accessed May 2, 2015).

12. Jim Bittermann, "New Pope, New Legacy," March 31, 2013, CNN, http://www.cnn.com/videos/world/2013/04/01/pkg-bittermann-pope-easter-mass.cnn (viewed May 2, 2015).

At the same time, he has said that he wants to see a "greater role" for women in Catholicism, including participation in the "important decisions . . . where the authority of the Church is exercised." He has also said that he wants a "deeper theology" about the place of women in the faith, one that will emphasize the critically important contributions they make. During his first two years in office, however, there were relatively few steps forward in either regard.

. . . Despite his talk of expanded roles for women in the Church, Francis is still firmly against ordaining women as priests or, for that matter, as clergy of any kind. He has even rejected the idea of reviving an older tradition of lay cardinals that would include women. (A lay cardinal is a nonclerical member of the College of Cardinals.) The proposal has drawn influential support from the likes of Lucetta Scaraffia, a historian and columnist for the Vatican newspaper *L'Osservatore Romano*, but Francis has unambiguously shot it down. Francis's clearest statement on the ordination issue came during an airborne press conference in July 2013, when he was returning from Rio de Janeiro. "The Church has spoken and says no. . . . That door is closed," he said.[13]

In spite of being in the best position to establish a greater role for women in the Catholic Church, Pope Francis has disappointingly failed to initiate more action in this regard—and has, in fact, strongly reiterated the traditional exclusion of women.

The *National Catholic Reporter* quoted Pope Francis's statement: "The church says no," then continued:

"Pope John Paul [II] said so with a formula that was definitive. That door is closed." [Pope Francis] was referring to Pope John Paul's 1994 document, *Ordinatio Sacerdotalis*. In it, John Paul said the church has no authority to ordain women, and this view must be held by all as a definitive belief. Then the Congregation for the Doctrine of the Faith, headed by then-Cardinal Joseph Ratzinger, issued a clarification, stating that while *Ordinatio Sacerdotalis* was not an infallible statement, *it is the constant and clear tradition of the church that makes the ban on women priests infallible*.[14]

Although the official position from the Vatican shows no wavering, Catholic supporters of women's ordination remain tenacious in their commitment to advocacy. Activists have made little headway with the institutional church, but their grassroots activities have grown in scope and are drawing attention from more women who see the imbalance in an all-male patriarchal leadership style. More Catholic women are becoming advocates for substantive change.

One organization that has made inroads in the Catholic community is the Women's Ordination Conference (WOC). Since its founding in 1975, the

---

13. John L. Allen Jr., "Why Pope Francis Won't Let Women Become Priests," March 6, 2015, Time.com., http://time.com/3729904/francis-women/ (accessed May 3, 2015). Excerpted from John L. Allen Jr., *The Francis Miracle: Inside the Transformation of the Pope and the Church* (New York: Time Books, 2015) (accessed May 3, 2015).

14. Robert McClory, "Pope Francis and Women's Ordination," September 16, 2013, *National Catholic Reporter,* http://ncronline.org/blogs/ncr-today/pope-francis-and-womens-ordination (accessed May 4, 2015), emphasis mine.

Women's Ordination Conference has been prayerfully advocating for ordination and women's greater inclusion in ritual life and church decision-making. Periodic conferences connect WOC supporters, and the organization has grown to encompass resources and networking groups for young Catholic feminists, greater outreach to people of color, social justice on topics of race, class, and gender, efforts to build international coalitions of women's ordination supporters, and support for the activities of Roman Catholic Women Priests.[15] Some extra-church developments during the past fifteen years include the "illicit" ordinations of women on the Danube River in 2002 and 2004, independent Catholic congregations that have ordained women to priesthood, diaconate, and other offices, and the first women's ordinations in the United States beginning in 2006.

Women's Ordination Conference also launched the Three Ministries in 2003 in order to provide a variety of ways that ordination advocates could be involved in their work. The most publicly known of the three is the Ministry of Irritation, the purpose of which "is to challenge the Church's policies regarding women by engaging the hierarchy and organizing on a grassroots level to publicly witness for women's ordination into a renewing priestly ministry. . . . Although most of the U.S. bishops have made it clear they do not want to talk with us," according to a spokesperson, "through this ministry, we continue to make attempts to dialogue with them."[16] Some examples of the Ministry of Irritation's grassroots work include showering church leaders with rose petals and holding Pink Smoke events to protest the absence of women in papal conclaves and high levels of church decision. A Women's Ordination Conference group has staged events outside a Philadelphia cathedral for thirty-five years, petitioning for greater inclusion and ordination of women. Group president Regina Bannan explains the progress she sees: "When we started, 27 percent of Catholics [in the US] favored women's ordination. Now it is always two-thirds or more. Among young people it is 87 percent."[17]

Joining the women activists in the struggle are sympathetic priests—some actively working in the church who have had a change of heart about the denial of priesthood to women. Still other priest-advocates, such as Fr. Roy Bourgeois, have been removed from office.[18] Other supporters' identities remain secret to avoid reprisals or jeopardizing their standing in church leadership. For instance, Fr. Bill Brennan of Milwaukee, Wisconsin, had a friend record a video statement

---

15. "Our Story," Women's Ordination Conference, http://www.womensordination.org/about-us/our-story/ (accessed May 2, 2015).

16. "Ministry of Irritation," http://www.womensordination.org/programs/ministry-of-irritation/ (accessed May 2, 2015).

17. Hadas Kuznits, "Annual Vigil outside Phila. Cathedral Demands Ordination of Women as Catholic Priests," April 2, 2015, http://philadelphia.cbslocal.com/2015/04/02/annual-vigil-outside-phila-cathedral-demands-ordination-of-women-as-catholic-priests/ (accessed May 3, 2015).

18. See Fr. Roy Bourgeois, *My Journey from Silence to Solidarity*, edited by Margaret Knapke, 2d ed. (Yellow Springs, Ohio: fxBear, 2013).

about Brennan's support for women's ordination which was made public after Brennan's death. In this statement, Brennan said: "I don't see my position as a defiant position of authority in my attitude. . . . I just see this as my conscience." Brennan went on to say he was torn between supporting women's ordination and his duty of obedience to the authorities of the Catholic Church, but he wanted to go on the record as following his conscience: "I wish to be remembered as one who's basically pleading for equality for women in administrative and spiritual functions of the Holy Catholic Church. . . . I think this is a call of the spirit."[19] More Catholics are expressing sentiments like Fr. Brennan's and following the calls of spirit and conscience with regard to supporting women's ordination.

Noted blogger and commentator on Catholicism Damon Linker predicts that churches unwilling to adapt to changes in the larger world should prepare for emptying pews. "Sooner or later," Linker writes, "and probably sooner—egalitarian-minded Catholics are going to lose their patience with the hierarchy's unpersuasive defenses of the status quo. And they are stunningly unpersuasive."[20] Elsewhere, Linker has written, "I think it's likely that over the coming years these churches are going to confront a stark choice: Reform themselves in light of equality or watch their parishioners opt for the exits, in droves . . . The contradictions are unsustainable."[21] The growing interest in and support of women's ordination within Catholicism would seem to bear out Linker's assertions. Younger adherents see the many opportunities for women outside church settings and are not as attached to traditional ways that limit women's involvement in church leadership. As Linker points out, parishioners may simply bow out of churches that don't demonstrate equality in their pulpits.

Although Catholic supporters of women's ordination appear to have growing support in the pews, papal leadership continues to be unyielding on the subject. Nevertheless, the ways that grassroots demonstrators have made progress in shifting attitudes about ordination and have been organizing to achieve extraordinary ordinations of women to the Catholic priesthood is inspiring. Even the most conservative and hierarchical faith groups have the option to implore leaders to seek answers from God regarding women's ordination according to whatever channels they consider orthodox to receive further divine wisdom. Among all Christian denominations, Christ's promise, "Ask, and it shall be given you; seek, and ye shall find; knock, and it shall be opened unto you" (Luke 11:9) is still a living promise.

---

19. Joyce Garbaciak, "Dying Catholic Priest Records Videos Declaring Women Should Be Ordained," updated March 7, 2015, http://www.wisn.com/news/dying-catholic-priest-records-videos-declaring-women-should-be-ordained/31663242 (accessed May 3, 2015).

20. Damon Linker, "Why Churches Should Brace for a Mass Exodus of the Faithful," March 24, 2014, *The Week*, https://web.archive.org/web/20140603081641/http://theweek.com/article/index/258520/why-churches-should-brace-for-a-mass-exodus-of-the-faithful (accessed May 4, 2015).

21. Ibid.

Women and Priesthood in the Episcopal Church

The denominational stance on women's ordination in the Episcopal/Anglican church has a long and complex history. Although the General Convention first considered women's ordination in 1970,[22] and eleven women were ordained to the priesthood in Philadelphia on July 29, 1974,[23] the story stretches back much further. The earliest permissions to ordain women to the role of deacons occurred in late 1880s. However, this development was then followed by a setback: In the Episcopal Church, the 1889 General Convention agreed to allow the ordination of deaconesses. During the twenty-four years preceding that decision, the bishops of Maryland, London, Alabama, and New York agreed to "set apart" deaconesses by the laying on of hands. But in 1919 the board of the Church Pension Fund ruled that deaconesses were not considered clergy.[24] Although it was a step forward to have women ordained as Episcopal deaconesses, the later decision to retract clergy status demonstrated that there was not yet parity for women in ministerial leadership.

Historically in the Episcopal Church, only men were eligible to participate in the "apostolic succession" process and were "ordained in the threefold ministries of deacon, priest, and bishop."[25] Tradition was difficult to supplant: "Although women's ordination was not specifically prohibited, by practice it had never been allowed."[26] Opposition to women's ordination in the twentieth century came from two sources: "those who believed it impossible for women to be priests and (2) those who believed the General Convention . . . had no right to decide this question." Instead, those who held this position asserted that the appropriate method to evaluate women's ordination was "by catholic consensus or in some kind of ecumenical

---

22. Bruce A. Robinson, "Female Ordination in the Episcopal Church USA, (ECUSA)," updated June 22, 2006, Religious Tolerance website, http://www.religioustolerance.org/femclrg14.htm (retrieved May 4, 2015).

23. "Eleven Women Ordained Episcopal Priests," July 31, 1974, press release, *Diocesan Press Service,* http://www.episcopalarchives.org/cgi-bin/ENS/ENSpress_release.pl?pr_number=74200 (retrieved May 4, 2015).

24. Mary Frances Schjonberg, "Toward Columbus: Movement for Full Inclusion of Women's Ministries Has Long History," April 24, 2006, 2006 General Convention News, Episcopal News Service, http://web.archive.org/web/20110116104628/http://www.episcopalchurch.org/75383_73867_ENG_HTM.htm (accessed May 5, 2015).

25. Frank S. Mead, revised by Samuel S. Hill, *Handbook of Denominations in the United States,* 10th ed. (Nashville: Abingdon Press, 1995), 128–38. The departures were not just over women's ordination issues. There is also a long history of more traditional and conservative members departing from the main body of the church in order to stay true to Anglican traditions.

26. Pam Strickland, "Two of the Philadelphia 11 Say It's Still a Struggle for Women in the Church," April 16, 2015, Episcopal News Service, http://episcopaldigitalnetwork.com/ens/2015/04/16/two-of-philadelphia-11-say-its-still-a-struggle-for-women-in-the-church/ (accessed May 1, 2015).

council."²⁷ Pondering women's ordination in the 1970s led to the breaking away of new splinter groups wanting to retain tradition and separatist congregations—a response to changes that is not unusual in the Episcopal church.²⁸

Though initially denied to women on procedural and theological grounds, once the issue of women's ordination was brought to the General Convention, it persisted. Proposals of ordination for women were put forward and rejected twice—in 1970 and again in 1973. Following the first rejection, there was movement among the church's women to organize and advocate for women's ordination:

> The Episcopal Women's Caucus was formed on October 30, 1971, during a meeting of professional lay women and deacons. Notified that the House of Bishops had created yet another study committee on the ordination of women, without having taken action on its previous studies, the women informed the Presiding Bishop of their refusal to cooperate further and constituted themselves as the EWC.
>
> Regional organizing conferences were held in 1972, and EWC chapters were created in many parts of the country.²⁹

The third time women's ordination was brought before the General Convention proved to be the proverbial charm: "In 1976 the Episcopal General Convention at long last amended church law so that women as well as men could participate in all orders of ministry (deacons, priests, and bishops)."³⁰

However, in July 1974—two years before the General Convention approved women's ordination—a group of eleven women in Philadelphia made headlines through an "irregular" ordination to Episcopal priesthood:

> On July 10, 1974, four bishops and seven women deacons met to discuss a possible ordination. The date of July 29th was set, and there was agreement to be as quiet about it as possible. Each woman told her diocesan bishop, and Bishop Ogilby of Pennsylvania immediately sent a letter to "his" clergy forbidding their participation. . . . Meanwhile, one of the four bishops withdrew, and four additional women agreed to join the original seven.³¹

News of the planned ordinations began to travel, and 2,000 people were in the congregation at the historic event.³² Credited with helping to shatter the "stained

---

27. Mead and Hill, *Handbook of Denominations,* 136.

28. Ibid., 137.

29. "History," http://www.episcopalwomenscaucus.org/history.htm.

30. Virginia Ramey Mollenkott, "The Feminist Reformation, Episcopal Style," review essay, *Christian Feminism Today,* http://www.eewc.com/BookReviews/feminist-reformation-episcopal-style/ (accessed May 2, 2015).

31. "The Story of the Episcopal Women's Caucus 1971–1996 with an Update 1996 to 2003," 2, Episcopal Women's Caucus website, http://www.episcopalwomenscaucus.org/history/EWD-Hist-2003-StraightPages.html (accessed May 3, 2015).

32. Ibid., 2.

glass ceiling,"[33] the Philadelphia Eleven[34] represented a groundswell of support for women's ordination in the Episcopal tradition. Additional "irregular" ordinations occurred the next year. "Following the ordinations in Philadelphia and Washington, D.C., in 1974 and 1975, a special conference was called to develop strategies for the 1976 General Convention. These strategies contributed to the action of the 1976 Convention making the ordination canon equally applicable to women and men."[35] After the General Convention decision, Rev. Jacqueline Means was the first regularly ordained woman Episcopal priest on January 1, 1977.[36] In February 1989, Barbara C. Harris was the first woman ordained to the office of bishop.[37]

The fortieth anniversary of Episcopal women's ordination was celebrated widely in 2014. That year, three books were published recounting the varied paths to ordination for women in the Episcopal tradition: *The Story of the Philadelphia Eleven* by Darlene O'Dell (New York: Seabury Books); *The Spirit of the Lord Is upon Me: The Writings of Suzanne Hiatt* edited by Carter Heyward and Janine Lehane (New York: Seabury Books); and *Looking Forward, Looking Backward: Forty Years of Women's Ordination,* edited by Frederica Harris Thompsett (New York: Morehouse Publishing). Surviving members of the Philadelphia Eleven have been interviewed about their experiences and have spoken at conferences and events commemorating this historic step.

Forty years later, women are represented in all levels of Episcopal clergy and governance. Katharine Jefferts Schori's 2006 election as the Church's first female Presiding Bishop again marked a milestone in women's ordination. Inroads and progress made through grassroots efforts, women's coalitions, male allies, retired bishops who performed the first "irregular" ordinations, and eventual growing lay support for women clergy demonstrate a potential pathway for women's eventual ordination in other denominations.

---

33. Heather Adams, "The 'Philadelphia 11' Who Shattered the Stained-Glass Ceiling: 40 Years Later, Where Are They Now?" July 23, 2014, Religion News Service, http://www.religionnews.com/2014/07/23/philadelphia-11-shattered-stained-glass-ceiling-40-years-later-now/ (accessed May 5, 2015).

34. The women who became known as the "Philadelphia Eleven" were Merrill Bittner, Alla Bozarth-Campbell, Alison Cheek, Emily Hewitt, Carter Heyward, Suzanne Hiatt, Marie Moorefield, Jeannette Piccard, Betty Schiess, Katrina Swanson, and Nancy Wittig. The most concise list of names and biographies on the Philadelphia Eleven is posted on Wikipedia: http://en.wikipedia.org/wiki/Philadelphia_Eleven.

35. "The Story of the Episcopal Women's Caucus 1971–1996 with an Update 1996 to 2003," p. 2.

36. "First Woman Regularly Ordained to Episcopal Priesthood," January 6, 1977, Episcopal News Service archives, http://www.episcopalarchives.org/cgi-bin/ENS/ENSpress_release.pl?pr_number=77002 (accessed May 4, 2015).

37. "Leadership Gallery: The Right Reverend Barbara C. Harris," Episcopal Archives, http://www.episcopalarchives.org/Afro-Anglican_history/exhibit/leadership/harris.php (accessed May 4, 2015).

Of particular note, the tenth Bishop of the Episcopal Diocese of Utah, Carolyn Tanner Irish, had deep roots in the LDS Church. A *Deseret News* profile traced Bishop Irish's unique spiritual path. In her mid-thirties, she started attending Episcopal Church services. Within a few years, she followed the call to ministry and enrolled in Virginia Theological Seminary in 1983. Her decision to pursue the ministry coincided with the Episcopal Church's opening ordination to women. Soon after graduation from seminary, she was ordained a deacon, then a priest, and served congregations in dioceses in Washington, D.C., Virginia, and Michigan.[38] "Who knew," marveled a reporter, "[that] she would grow up a Utah Mormon and decades later return as a member of the Episcopal Church, as the *bishop* of Utah's Episcopal Church, as the first female ever to lead a church in Utah."[39] She served as the Episcopal Bishop of Utah for fourteen years (1996–2010)—"the fourth woman in the Episcopal Church to hold the office of bishop."[40] In returning to Utah as Episcopal Bishop, Carolyn Tanner Irish was a groundbreaking figure in both traditions—the Mormonism of her youth and her spiritual home as an adult.

Women and Priesthood in the Community of Christ

Community of Christ dramatically changed its stance on women's ordination in 1984 when Church Prophet President Wallace B. Smith brought a revelatory document to the World Conference that opened the church's lay priesthood to women. The first women were subsequently ordained in November 1985. (For the story of the "long and onerous walk" leading up to that point and the developments since then, see Chapter 9 by Robin Kincaid Linkhart.) Thirty years later, women are represented in all governing bodies of the church—from the First Presidency and the Quorum of Twelve Apostles to quorums of the Seventy, mission center leaders, pastors, and other offices in individual congregations.[41]

Questions about women's ordination in Community of Christ had been surfacing since a resolution was first put forward at the church's World Conference in April 1970. However it took another fourteen years for women's ordination to become a reality.[42] Historian William D. Russell explained the impact of President Smith's revelation in 1984: "That revelation was accepted by the delegates at the conference as a revelation from God and became Section 156 of the

---

38. Ibid.

39. Doug Robinson, "Bishop Irish Comes Full Circle," March 22, 2004, *Deseret News*, http://www.deseretnews.com/article/595045756/Bishop-Irish-comes-full-circle.html (accessed May 23, 2015).

40. http://en.wikipedia.org/wiki/Carolyn_Tanner_Irish (accessed May 23, 2015).

41. "RLDS Church Calls 2 Women to Serve among 12 Apostles," March 21 1998, *Deseret News*, http://www.deseretnews.com/article/619962/RLDS-Church-calls-2-women-to-serve-among-12-apostles.html (accessed May 3, 2015).

42. William D. Russell, "Ordaining Women and the Transformation from Sect to Denomination," *Dialogue: A Journal of Mormon Thought* 36, no. 3 (2003): 61–64.

RLDS Doctrine and Covenants, but with 20% of the delegates dissenting. It soon became clear that the largest schism in the history of the Reorganization was in the making. In the six years following the approval of Section 156, about one-fourth of the active RLDS members ceased their involvement in the church."[43]

The church struggled for some time with the fractures that women's ordination caused among members, most seriously including a substantial schismatic movement of conservative RLDS members who either organized their own independent congregations or simply dropped out of their RLDS religious affiliation altogether. The decision to ordain women was thus, at the outset, very costly to the church, but the majority of those who remained celebrated the expanded opportunities for women's service in church office. Barbara Higdon, who had focused for many years on expanding opportunities for unordained members prior to her own call to ministry, commented that "the Community of Christ is blessed immeasurably by the ministerial gifts of all of its members who are willing to participate."[44]

Ordination to priesthood in the Community of Christ is not universal for men or women but rather is based on a "calling" to ministry that is discerned by ecclesiastical leaders.[45] While this process would seem to pave the way to more easily expanding priesthood opportunities for women, the immediate aftermath of the revelation brought considerable resistance from more conservative members and congregations. Although women in ministry have been the norm for twenty to twenty-five fruitful years, those involved at the earliest stages recall painful moments. A panel discussion at the 2011 Restoration Studies Symposium, featuring some of the first women candidates for ordination, focused on some of the struggles the women faced. The revelatory source of the change did not automatically win the hearts and minds of everyone in the church. Some delegates even attempted to rescind the 1984 revelation at a subsequent World Conference. Russell explained:

> Many fundamentalists still believed Wallace B. Smith was a prophet—he had just made a mistake and it would be corrected, probably at the next World Conference in 1986. They came to the 1986 conference determined to get the conference to formally rescind Section 156. But President Smith ruled that a motion from a stake to rescind a revelation in the Doctrine and Covenants was out of order. Since he reasoned that only the prophet can propose a revelation only a prophet can initiate a move to rescind a revelation. About 90 percent of the conference delegates supported his ruling.[46]

Continued opposition came from male leaders who were reluctant to share power, from congregations that rejected women's ordinations and were hostile to-

---

43. Ibid., 63. This disaffiliation figure applies primarily to U.S. members. Worldwide, resistance to the revelation was much less significant—about 3 percent.

44. Barbara Higdon, "Present at the Beginning: One Woman's Journey," *Dialogue: A Journal of Mormon Thought* 36, no. 3 (2003): 65–69.

45. Ibid., 68. See also http://en.wikipedia.org/wiki/Priesthood_%28Community_of_Christ%29 (accessed May 6, 2015).

46. William Dean Russell, "Defenders of the Faith: Varieties of RLDS Dissent," *Sunstone* 77 (June 1990): 16.

ward women candidates, and sometimes from family members who were unsupportive or who feared community disapproval.[47] Those first ordained women dug deep, endured, and prevailed. The battle was essentially won within five years.

Today, women's priesthood ordination in the Community of Christ is firmly established. Portraits of the Twelve Apostles in the temple in Independence, Missouri, depict a church and members that are committed to gender equality and inclusivity. Ordination happened within the lifetimes of many women who long hoped for it but weren't sure they would live to see it become a reality. While the path to women's ordination was not smooth, ultimately the Community of Christ has clearly benefitted from adapting to a changing social and religious landscape through its decision to open priesthood ordination of women. Perhaps most significantly, ordaining women brought a deeply spiritual dimension to Community of Christ. Robin Linkhart, a young mother when the revelation was first announced, sees the church's willingness to embrace ordination as an identity issue: "It was about being a people who listen intently to God's voice through continuing revelation and understanding that the gospel of Jesus Christ is radically inclusive. We believe that Section 156 revealed God's will that we move a few steps closer to that core message of the gospel."[48]

Conclusion

Again, I return to the example of Equal in Faith, the interfaith group organized in 2013 to bring about greater awareness of the last bastion of gender inequity in the United States: our churches. Equal in Faith co-organizer Lorie Winder Stromberg writes, "At a time when many are leaving organized religion, we want to ignite a conversation about maintaining what we value in our religious traditions while transforming them into more inclusive, equitable and welcoming communities."[49] Indeed, it is often women's religious values which drive their participation in ordination advocacy—the desire to effect positive change within their religious communities, rather than abandoning the church in which they are rooted for more inclusive congregations elsewhere.

What can we learn from these case studies highlighting interfaith activism on ordination? How are the journeys of other advocates of women's ordination useful or applicable beyond those traditions? What could a fledgling movement such as Ordain Women learn from examining the ordination histories and advocacy work of other churches? I believe religious feminist activism provides an important template for creating change in religious communities. There are

---

47. Barbara Lee Collins, Barbara Howard, and Gwendolyn Hawks-Blue, "Initially Rejected: Pioneers Reflect on the Early Struggle for Women's Ordination in the RLDS Church," Panel discussion, Restoration Studies Symposium, Independence, Missouri, April 15–16, 2011.

48. Robin Linkhart, email, May 21, 2015. See her Chapter 9 for a fuller explanation of how this spiritual quest unfolded in Community of Christ.

49. Stromberg, http://www.equalinfaith.org/

many creative approaches and lessons to glean from the work of other advocates for women's ordination. These explorations may be of particular interest to Mormon feminists who are committed to greater gender equity in their religious communities—even if they don't yet advocate women's ordination. Because the LDS community is so insular and its adherence to gender traditionalism is so firmly entrenched,[50] Mormon feminists may not be aware of the long histories of agitation and change-seeking by faithful insiders or of religious feminist activism that has occurred or is happening in other churches. I therefore summarize some exploratory ideas from the case studies, apply them to the advocacy happening in Mormonism via Ordain Women, and examine some possible implications for contemporary Mormonism.

Catholic women have set the bar high in advocating women's ordination. They have been organizing and making their desire for ordination known for the past four decades. In recent years, the Women's Ordination Conference has made a point of involving younger women in the ordination movement and of reaching out to women of color as part of a larger vision of social justice and gender equality. Catholic women are pioneers of creative direct actions that tie into existing ritual and practice—such as the Pink Smoke campaigns during papal conclaves.[51] Their creativity extends to riverboat ordination events in order to circumnavigate restrictive church ordination rules, and other ways of agitating faithfully through the Ministry of Irritation. Catholic feminist activism is worthy of study and emulation. Theirs is, perhaps, the women's ordination playbook that is currently most applicable for the LDS Ordain Women movement—and the most consistent play is women showing up to advocate their position whether anyone in church leadership will talk to them or not. Catholic feminists keep helpful organizational histories of grassroots efforts; and along the way, they have modeled the thoughtful inclusivity they seek from their church leaders.

Episcopal women are consummate community organizers as well. The Episcopal Women's Caucus was established in 1971—the year after women's ordination was first brought before the church's General Convention—with the intention of helping to educate and advocate for women's issues in the church. The caucus and other grassroots groups worked to strategize for future conventions and position themselves to make progress toward ordination. Although the first two attempts were contested and did not result in ordination, the caucus built an important foundation for future advocacy; eventually, the changes necessary for women's ordination did prevail.

Episcopal women also have a long track record of direct actions to further the cause and a history of working with sympathetic male allies to achieve shared

---

50. David E. Campbell, John C. Green, and J. Quin Monson, *Seeking the Promised Land: Mormons and American Politics* (New York: Cambridge University Press, 2014), 112–15.

51. For more information, I highly recommend the award-winning documentary *Pink Smoke over the Vatican,* http://romancatholicwomenpriests.org/pinksmoke.htm.

goals. The Philadelphia Eleven were "irregularly" ordained by retired Episcopal bishops two years before the General Convention approved women's ordination—an act of faith coupled with defiance against conventional methods that weren't making headway. The irregular ordinations essentially forced clergy, the General Convention, and the larger church to examine whether there were canonical reasons for not ordaining women, or whether refusal simply reflected a longstanding, unquestioned, and prejudicial practice.

Community of Christ's history of women's ordination is instructive and inspirational when one considers the progress made in just thirty years. As a Restoration church that grows out of the same historical roots as the Latter-day Saints and preserves continuous revelation as an on-going process, Community of Christ provides a roadmap for the revelatory process to play a role in changing church policy and longstanding practices with regard to women's ordination. Although many in this tradition are quick to acknowledge that the path was not smooth or free from contention, the experiences of the earliest Community of Christ ordained women are also helpful to study. One of the dominant messages is to be prepared for resistance, even in one's own congregation or family. Barbara Higdon, who was one of the women who was early ordained to priesthood in Community of Christ, noted that there were also opportunities for the unordained and encouraged women to focus on those opportunities as preparation for the additional leadership roles that ordination provided.[52]

What are the observable implications for Mormonism in these three case studies? First: women can organize for advocacy work, provoke conversations about ordination, and educate others in their faith traditions long before any ecclesiastical change takes place. In many instances, women's advocacy in other churches helped build the foundations necessary for ordination. Ordain Women has begun this work of organizing by asking ordination advocates to post their personal profiles stating why they support LDS women's ordination; by calling on their sister supporters to show up at direct actions, such as petitioning for admission to the male-only priesthood session of general conference in October 2013 and April 2014; and by directing their pleas to LDS Church leaders to prayerfully take the matter of women's ordination to God—the accepted channel for seeking and receiving revelation.

While the rogue or irregular ordinations in Catholic and Episcopal traditions are examples of another type of outside-the-box advocacy, such extra-institutional ordinations of women would probably not carry the same weight in Mormonism[53] as they did forty years ago in the Episcopal Church when there was a growing tide of support for women clergy within more liberal denominations.

---

52. Higdon, "Present at the Beginning," 67.

53. Jackie Robinson, "LDS Woman Ordained to Elder," YouTube video, 6:35, July 4, 2012, https://www.youtube.com/watch?v=EvX2qP_F13I (accessed April 29, 2015). Mainstream Mormons condemned this rogue ordination. Many Ordain Women supporters felt that this act mocked an important ordinance and was out of alignment

Mormons have a lay priesthood, which suggests practically and theologically that barriers to entry are lower than in many other Christian denominations. However, the act of "irregularly" ordaining LDS women would not be viewed as efficacious/valid by most mainstream members.

Could Mormonism be on the verge of having its own breakaway groups espousing women's ordination and more progressive values? There have been past schisms in Mormon history over leadership succession and the abandonment of plural marriage; there are also groups that want to continue or even return to more conservative and fundamentalist values. Could the modern LDS Church end up with similar fragmentations over women's ordination? I suspect that, within the mainstream LDS Church, there would be as little tolerance for ordination-related schisms as there is for polygamy-related schisms. It's possible that some women's ordination advocates may grow impatient or give up on their LDS faith rather than wait for leadership to take an affirmative direction on gender equity and ordination.

Although there have been Mormon feminists advocating for women's ordination over the past thirty to forty years, Ordain Women is a comparatively young organization. Its leaders and supporters can point to many successes since the March 2013 Ordain Women launch. Hundreds of profiles have been posted on the OW website. Two successful direct actions on Temple Square during the LDS Church's general conference have attracted broad media coverage, and many more people are now joining the conversations about women's ordination, regardless of their current position on the issue.[54]

Perhaps the best lesson from other faith groups is to take the long view. Women's ordination hasn't happened quickly in other churches, and there is a lot of community building and groundwork necessary to prepare a critical mass of support—people in the pews as well as the pulpits—for a change this significant. Ordain Women has experienced triumphs, progress, and setbacks in its two-year history. It will definitely be interesting to see what's next for this intrepid group of faithful Mormon women and their male allies. Carter Heyward, one of the Episcopalian Philadelphia Eleven, reflected on the underlying principles guiding this type of activist work: "The four principles are[:] women should seek the primary role in bringing change about, learn how institutions work that they

---

with their faith-based pleas to LDS Church leaders to prayerfully consider the question of women's ordination.

54. In the 1980s and 1990s, it was rare for a Mormon feminist to admit an interest in women's ordination. Instead, drawing a line in the sand about one's stance on ordination seemed to be a way to establish faithful feminist credibility. Saying "I'm a Mormon feminist—but I don't want the priesthood" appeared to somewhat legitimize the feminist side of the equation and be seen as a more defensible position.

wish to change, be united in struggling together and avoid horizontal violence, and remember that the church needs them more than they need the church."[55]

Mormonism needs its feminists, its loyal opposition provoking conversations about women's ordination. Continuing revelation is a core belief in this tradition—the heavens are not closed to additional guidance from the divine. Mormonism is therefore uniquely positioned with regard to the possibility of religious innovation through continuing revelation in an organization based on a lay priesthood. Perhaps this trifecta will serve as catalysts for the changes sought by faithful, active, churchgoing women involved in the Ordain Women movement.

---

55. "Two of the Philadelphia 11 Say It's Still a Struggle." Heyward co-edited a book of Suzanne Hiatt's writings, *The Spirit of the Lord Is upon Me,* in which she articulated these four principles.

Chapter 9

Ordination of Women: The Community of Christ Story

Robin Kincaid Linkhart

Community of Christ has been blessed by the ordained ministry of men and women for thirty years (1985–2015). Prior to 1985 only men were considered for ordination to priesthood. Although prophetic revelation given in 1984 cleared the way for women to hold priesthood, it by no means occurred in that one prophetic action. Rather the journey to ordination of women was a long and onerous walk involving generations of people both in and out of the Church.

When I was a little girl, only men held priesthood. It never occurred to me that I might someday join their ranks. Very simply it was not even a remote possibility in the world I knew. In my late teens and early adult years that began to change.

When the Church made history by approving Section 156 for inclusion in the Doctrine and Covenants, I was drowning in diapers, caring for our twenty-one-month-old daughter and six-month-old twin boys. Priesthood for women in my mind, then, meant "other" women.

After the historic 1984 World Conference, things were very tense in our local congregation. Nearly half of our membership opposed ordination of women and eventually chose to leave. Deeply committed to the church, our dedicated pastor led with love and grace while he privately struggled with the change. At the 1986 Kirtland Temple 150-year celebration, as the gathered congregation sang "The Spirit of God like a Fire Is Burning," he received spiritual confirmation that ordaining women was God's will. Upon his return from Kirtland, he began processing priesthood calls in our congregation for women. Young mothers, however, were not on his list of consideration.

In the years that followed, a growing sense of call began to stir my soul. In September of 1995, that same pastor visited our home and presented my call to the office of elder. I was shocked and a little overwhelmed that my first call was to Melchisedec Priesthood.

I was ordained in March 1996 and immediately served in the pastorate as counselor to the pastor. In January 1997 I was set apart as the pastor of my home congregation and served for seven years. In 1999 the church employed me to devote my time to church work in my congregation and outreach in the local community. In 2003, I was ordained to the office of high priest and assigned to the Rocky Mountain Mission Center serving thirty congregations spread across Colorado and Wyoming and into parts of Kansas, New Mexico, and Nebraska. In 2003 I began my graduate studies in religion receiving my master of arts in

Christian ministry in 2007. Also in 2007, I was ordained to the office of seventy and called to serve alongside our apostle in the West Central USA Mission Field. In 2010, I was called and set apart to serve as a President of Seventy (my current office) and, with my apostle, support the Western USA Mission Field which covers close to half of the United States including Alaska.

In many ways, my experience serving the Church as member and then as priesthood parallels the Community of Christ journey to ordaining women. It was not without heart-wrenching challenge, angst, and struggle. It required dogged determination, courage, grace-filled love, and vulnerable authenticity. It resulted in the freedom to discover the ALL of who God created me to be, and the opportunity to fully live into the many dimensions of possibility resident in God's gift of life. And it called me into life-changing relationship with God, community, creation, and self.

Three things were key to realizing this monumental change in Community of Christ: (1) continuing revelation, (2) common consent, and (3) the guiding principle of "All Are Called." Understanding more about each is imperative to understanding how our story brought us to gender-inclusive priesthood.

Continuing Revelation

Revelatory experiences in Community of Christ continue to be foundational and formative to our journey just as they were in the early days of the Restoration. Continuing revelation calls us into an ongoing encounter with God revealed through Jesus Christ made known to us through the continuing presence of the Holy Spirit. It involves God disclosing God's self, followed by our best human efforts of interpreting what God reveals. It is not predicting the future. It is experiencing the prophetic voice, which speaks truth with prophetic vision, even truth to power, and increases our ability and capacity to partner with God to create the future, even Zion, God's dream for the world.[1] Each revelation is received through the Prophet President of the Church and requires approval of the world conference legislative body for inclusion in the Doctrine and Covenants. Community of Christ has received fifty-one revelations since the Reorganization in 1860.

Common Consent as Practiced in Community of Christ

As defined in the 2005 Community of Christ *Church Administrator's Handbook*, "Common Consent is a goal that all decision-making processes in the church seek to achieve. It is not confined to one specific process. In common consent, there is general agreement that a decision has been made by the appropriate person or body, that all relevant perspectives have been considered,

---

1. Stephen M. Veazey, *Listening Guide: Ways of Discovering God's Will*, http://www.cofchrist.org/common/cms/resources/Documents/Ways-of-Discovering-Gods-Will-Listening-Guide.pdf 11–12 (accessed April 14, 2015).

and that the process used to arrive at the decision fosters the spirit of community within the Church."[2]

The current understanding and definition of common consent stands on the foundation and very roots of our movement. Although in general terms it involves majority vote approval at a properly called conference utilizing an agreed-upon parliamentary process, it speaks to something deeper as stated in one of Joseph Smith Jr.'s earliest revelations found in Doctrine and Covenants 25:1b (LDS 26:2): "And all things shall be done by common consent in the church, by much prayer and faith; for all things you shall receive by faith."

More contemporary Community of Christ leader Maurice L. Draper[3] illuminates the meaning of common consent in an article he wrote for the *Saint's Herald* stating, "The phrase 'common consent' has a very rich meaning—to think or to feel together about shared responsibilities. Those who exercise common consent are learning to think and to feel together about responsibilities which they share through response to the divine will."[4]

Community of Christ calls this theocratic democracy.[5] Using parliamentary process to insure the rights of the body and encourage the free expression of all voices and opinions, as a prophetic people we also seek to claim our unity in the midst of diversity within the body of Christ. We achieve common consent when all perspectives have been received and considered in a spirit of love and prayer, and an appropriate level of support is expressed by the church body assembled, which provides the approval needed to proceed and take action.[6]

The journey to ordination of women in Community of Christ stretched and tested our resolve to faithfully practice common consent and oneness in Christ.

The Guiding Principle: All Are Called

From our sacred text we read "All are called according to the gifts of God unto them . . . for the accomplishment of the work entrusted to all."[7] From

---

2. *Church Administrator's Handbook,* 2005 ed. (Independence, Mo.: Herald House, 2005), 6.

3. Maurice L. Draper (1918–2012) served as counselor to Reorganized Church of Jesus Christ of Latter Day Saints (Community of Christ) Prophet-President W. Wallace Smith in the First Presidency 1958–1978.

4. Maurice L. Draper, "Common Consent in the Church," *Saint's Herald* 108, no. 9 (February 27, 1961): 5–6.

5. The Church, as defined by President Joseph Smith III, is a theocratic democracy. It was brought into being by divine initiative, is guided and administered by divine authority, is sustained by the light of the Holy Spirit, and exists for divine purposes. In response to divine initiative, members share responsibility for governing the church: "All things must be done in order and by common consent in the church, by the prayer of faith" (Doctrine and Covenants 27:4). Bylaws of Community of Christ, Article III - Theocratic Democracy , Section 1, Definition 1.

6. Veazey, *Listening Guide.*, 13–14.

7. *Book of Doctrine and Covenants* 119:8b (Independence, Mo.: Herald Publishing House, 2007), 159. This admonition was given in 1887.

early in the Reorganization "All Are Called" has been a guiding principle. Our challenge has been to recognize and utilize the giftedness of each one. Over time we recognized that we, like others, are sometimes blinded by the cultural norms of our day and time. Even as we stumbled toward a deeper understanding, we continued to come back to this principle seeking God's direction in gaining full understanding. All people have divinely appointed gifts and opportunities to do good and participate in God's work. Jesus Christ invites all people to follow him and share his life and ministry. As followers of the Christ and with the support of the Holy Spirit, we respond faithfully to our best understanding of God's call. All are called, no exceptions.

Cultural Context

The historical context of Community of Christ's journey to ordination of women cannot be separated from the cultural context. To understand the trajectory of events it is imperative to understand the role of patriarchy not only in the Church, but in the world.

Patriarchy is a social system that promotes and perpetuates male privilege. It is male-centered, -identified, and -dominated. Patriarchy has existed as the social norm in our world for over 7,000 years and is a system based on control and power. Patriarchy systemically oppresses women.

It is no surprise that the world's major religions reflect patriarchal structures based on male authority and power. Christianity expressed across the globe through a multitude of denominations is no exception. Neither is the Restoration Movement.

Nineteenth-century American women lived the way women had for thousands of years before them. A woman's place was in the home bearing and caring for children, tending the household, and doing chores inside and working on the garden and farm outside. Even wealthy women were considered second-class persons with no right to vote, hold property, or enter legal contracts. Some historians describe these perspectives as the "cult of true womanhood" which spelled out a rigid gender role for women, often unrealistic, and always oppressive.[8]

The ecclesiastical structure of the American-born church led by the charismatic young prophet Joseph Smith exhibited a patriarchal hierarchy. Priesthood was held exclusively by males, and the different offices were associated with different levels of authority. The nature of God was understood through a male lens, just as it had been for thousands of years before, passed down from Judaism to Christianity.

Although the Restoration church was, from the beginning, a peculiar people navigating the borderlands of the religious landscape in nineteenth-century America, it still bore the fingerprints of patriarchy and American nineteenth-cen-

---

8. Barbara Welter, *Dimity Convictions: The American Women in the Nineteenth Century* (Athens: Ohio University Press, 1976), 21–41, quoted in Madelon L Brunson, *Bonds of Sisterhood: A History of the RLDS Women's Organization, 1842–1983* (Independence, Mo.: Herald Publishing House, 1985), 17.

tury culture. Even after the Reorganization in 1860, the dominant culture prevailed and colored perspectives on the role of women in the church as evidenced in this article reprinted from the *Gleason's Literary Companion* in the RLDS 1868 *Saints Herald*, entitled, "What a Woman Can Do":

> As a wife and mother, woman can make the fortune and happiness of her children; and even if she did nothing else, surely this would be sufficient destiny. By her thrift, prudence and tact, she can secure to her partner and herself a competence in old age. . . . By her cheerfulness she can restore her husband's spirits, shaken by the anxieties of business. By her tender care she can often restore him to health, if disease has seized upon his over-tasked powers. By her counsel and her love, she can win him from bad company, if temptation in an evil hour had led him astray. By her example, and her precepts, and her own sex's insight into character, she can mould her children, however diverse their dispositions, into good men and women. And by leading in all things a true and beautiful life, she can refine, elevate and spiritualize all who come within reach, so that with others of her sex emulating and assisting her, she can do more to regenerate the world than all the statesmen or reformers that ever legislated. She can do as much—alas! perhaps even more—to degrade man, if she chooses to do it.
>
> Who can estimate the evil that woman has the power to do? As a wife, she can ruin her husband by extravagance, folly, or want of affection. She can make a devil and an outcast of a man, who might otherwise have become a good member of society. She can bring bickerings, strife and perpetual discord into what has been a happy home. She can change the innocent babes whom God has entrusted to her charge, into vile men, and even viler women. She can lower even the moral tone of society itself, and thus pollute legislation at the spring head. She can, in fine, become an instrument of evil, instead of an angel of good. Instead of making flowers of truth, purity, beauty and spirituality spring up in her footsteps, till the whole earth smiles with loveliness that is almost celestial, she can transform it to a black and blasted desert, covered with the scorn of all evil passions, and swept by the bitter blasts of everlasting death. This is what a woman can do for the wrong as well as for the right. Is her mission a little one? Has she no "worthy work," as has become the cry of late? Many may have a harder task to perform, a rougher path to travel, but he has none loftier or more influential than woman's.[9]

The brutal murders of Joseph and his brother Hyrum in 1844 left the fledgling Church grief-stricken. It was a dark and cloudy time in Nauvoo. Under the leadership of Brigham Young, the vast majority of the Church began heading west in 1845; and by 1846, the once booming, beautiful city of Nauvoo was a virtual ghost town.

My people were among the ones who stayed behind, scattered here and there, labeled by some as outliers, heretics, and apostates. Though few in numbers, a sprinkling of congregations continued to meet and area leaders banded together to shepherd the flocks. Although faithful to inspired instruction given by Joseph

---

9. "What a Woman Can Do," from *Gleason's Literary Companion* n.d., as reprinted in *Saints Herald* 14, no. 6 (September 15, 1868): 95. This column, titled "Selections," featured a number of pieces reprinted from other publications.

Smith Jr., the 1850s leadership style differed from that of the mid-Nauvoo period (1843–44), which over time had developed into political and religious power centralized in one person surrounded by an inner circle of ecclesiastical elite who, more often than not, yielded absolute rule.[10] Those who stayed behind vehemently opposed polygamy and also recognized the danger resident in a one-man rule of church and state.

Emma Smith refused Brigham Young's repeated requests to go west and stayed in Nauvoo with all of her children. Joseph Smith III, only eleven years old when his father died, eventually practiced law in Nauvoo serving as the Justice of the Peace for many years. At age twenty-seven, he received divine confirmation that he was called to lead the Church. Much to the joy of interim leaders, Joseph Smith III attended the Amboy Illinois Conference. When he addressed the conference, he stated, "I came not here of myself, but by the influence of the Spirit. . . . I come in obedience to a power not my own, and shall be dictated by the power that sent me."[11] On April 6, 1860, the hopeful, little band of Saints officially established the Reorganized Church of Jesus Christ of Latter Day Saints with Joseph Smith III as Prophet President.

The Reorganization set out, determined to honor the deep ties of the Church community while also protecting individual agency, responsibility, and freedom.[12] It would prove to be a formidable process, but one well worth the effort. The Reorganizers did not want to repeat the mistakes of Nauvoo. They continued to navigate the borderlands. Small in numbers, they were a struggling, "peculiar people" (Titus 2:14), striking out to forge a new but familiar path: to claim their authentic selves and live into a future they called Zion. Still labeled outliers, heretics, and apostates by many, misunderstood and marginalized, they persevered. The stage was set for amazing possibilities, including the reevaluation of women's role in the life of the Church.

The History of Women's Roles in the Church

From the beginning of the Reorganization, just as they had before, women eagerly participated in the life of the Church. Records show that, as early as 1864, women were included in the voting body at district and local levels. They wasted no time getting organized.

The earliest women's group of record, the Society of Gleaners, was officially founded July 11, 1867, in Sandwich Illinois. The founding of the Sisters of Dorcas in St. Louis, Missouri, and the Kewanee Sisters Mite Society in Kewanee, Illinois, soon followed.

Patterned after the first formal women's organization in the early Church, the Nauvoo Ladies' Relief Society, the women's groups in the early years of the

---

10. Richard P. Howard, *The Church through the Years*, 2 vols. (Independence, Mo.: Herald Publishing House, 1992), 1:44.

11. Ibid., 1:371–74.

12. Ibid., 1:56.

Reorganization exemplified charitable efforts and worked diligently to support the mission of the Church and help build the kingdom. Side by side they created and sold needlecrafts and handiwork, generously contributing the proceeds to the Church.[13]

While these groups accomplished much good in their communities and indeed benefitted the mission of the Church, they also provided a valuable venue for women to cultivate and develop a broad range of leadership and organizational skills beyond the confines of the traditional domestic role. Women flourished in mutual support of one another. Not surprisingly, women organizing themselves into productive, effective groups also provoked controversy, which was expressed in a variety of *Saints Herald* articles representing various perspectives on the topic of women's roles in society and the Church.

The right of women to vote in a general conference came to the floor for discussion in 1868 general conference. After two days of extensive debate and dialogue, a substitute motion was approved by the conference, which provided for women to vote only on issues "that the elders may deem of sufficient importance to bring before the church."[14]

The topic of women's voting rights at general conference continued to be controversial for several years. In April 1873, the general conference passed a resolution affirming voting privileges for all members. Furthermore, the conference took action requesting the String Prairie Conference and Nauvoo District Conference to rescind a resolution they had adopted which stated: "None had a legal right to vote on the business before the body except the Elders, or Melchisedec Priesthood."[15] It was rescinded.

When the 1881 general conference accepted rules of representation, it was a pivotal moment for women in the life of the Church. This new approach instituted the representation of districts and branches through elected delegates. The elected delegates joined the voting ex officio Church officers, appointees, high priests, and elders at general conference. Qualifications and eligibility remained the same. To serve as a voting delegate required the status of member in good standing. There were no exclusions based on gender.

Women's voices gained a new avenue for expression and soon their skills and giftedness were having a huge impact on the life of the Church. Bit by bit, the Church began to chip away at the "cult of true womanhood" and see the world through another lens. It continued to be a process of two steps forward and one step back as women soared in their endeavors to serve the Church and advance the cause of Zion, then experienced the resulting tension and fear from men who felt their priesthood authority was being challenged, even threatened. Women

---

13. Brunson, *Bonds of Sisterhood*, 24–28.
14. Ibid., 28.
15. "Minutes of the General Annual Conference," *Supplement to the True Latter Day Saints Herald* 20, no. 9 (May 1, 1873): 288.

learned to navigate the landscape of changing culture with great patience and precision, always ready to express their giftedness whenever possible.

Women made key contributions in creating a Churchwide Sunday School Program and curriculum. The outstanding leadership and quality resource production of Marietta Hodges Faulconer Walker cannot be overstated. In 1869 Walker produced "Questions on the Holy Scriptures Designed for the Use of Scholars in the Latter Day Saints Sunday Schools," quickly followed by *Zion's Hope*, a resource for which she eventually served as sole editor (1892). Walker was also owner, publisher, and editor for the first youth paper, *Autumn Leaves*, and in 1913 issued *Stepping Stones* for older children.

Women served on the forefront to develop the General Sunday School Association (1890–91) as well as the older youth program, Zion's Religio Literary Society. By 1910, 550 schools belonged to the association which supported over 25,000 teachers and students. Women served as writers and editors for a significant portion of the curriculum. Women and men worked together successfully as near equals. Eventually these and other programs were incorporated into the general departmental structure the Church adopted in the 1920s.

Women across the Church longed for connection with their sisters. Marietta Walker's "Women's Home Column," featured regularly in the *Saints Herald*, met that need; and for the next two generations, women supported one another, sharing common concerns and interests. Diverse opinions about the role of women continued to push against prior established norms supporting the "cult of true womanhood." Others dug in their heels to maintain and preserve the status quo, noting that a change in women's roles would certainly be a threat to women's true happiness.

Important male voices supporting equality for women began to emerge; and by 1920, men like Samuel A. Burgess, a lawyer who served as president of RLDS Graceland College and later as Church Historian, voiced support for the ordination of women.[16]

Prophet President Frederick M. Smith cleared the way for the organization of the Women's Department in the early 1920s. In 1934 Smith created the General Council of Women, even though he continued to hold the opinion that women's primary ministry was in the home and with other women.

Led by women, the General Council of Women connected hundreds of women departments across the Church at all jurisdictional levels. With nearly full autonomy, the women wrote and published their own resource materials, and also led women's classes and retreats. Sisterhood flourished, meeting deep needs and rekindling dreams and new visions of what could be. Women's groups also raised significant funds to support the mission of the Church during a very difficult time.

---

16. Richard P. Howard, *The Church through the Years*, Vol. 2 (Independence, Mo.: Herald Publishing House, 1993), Howard, *The Church through the Years*, 2:386–94.

At the 1970 world conference[17] members of both genders began to advocate for equal representation for women on commissions and committees. The following resolution came to the floor: "Resolved, That all those in administrative positions within the church be encouraged to appoint, hire, and nominate more women for positions not scripturally requiring priesthood so that women who constitute over half of the church membership, may be more adequately and equally represented in the administrative decision making of the church."[18]

It was tabled in 1970, but the 1972 world conference passed a resolution stating a nearly identical resolve.[19] The floodgates opened as awareness of women's issues deepened. Articles and letters to the editor streamed into the *Saints Herald*, and members worked tirelessly to increase the level of consciousness across the Church. Minds and hearts began to open.

In 1971, Marjorie Troeh was hired to serve as the Consultant on Women's Ministries for the World Church. Her title was later changed to Women's Ministries Commissioner. Her responsibilities included "(1) cultivating the giftedness of women, (2) resource production, (3) research regarding needs of women, (4) member understandings about women, and (5) education for members about women."[20] She also served as a consultant to Church leaders at all levels including the First Presidency. For the next eleven years, Troeh advocated for women during a period of intense debate over gender equity and ordination of women. Some women vehemently supported no change in the status quo, while others passionately addressed issues of inequity.

Lois Braby's 1971 letter to the First Presidency captured the sentiment of many women.

WHERE IS THE PLACE OF THE WOMAN IN THIS CONTEMPORARY WORLD CHURCH????? Are we to accept calmly the traditional role: punch and cookies, potlucks and bazaars, and 21 friendly visits per month?

Do you really believe that we are not worthy to walk with you into the "holy of holies," to hear the voice of the Lord in high places, to stand with the servants of God in the temple of God? Who among you have more often taken the servant's role? Where is our consolation? Are we to be forever content with the crumbs from the table of the "feast of the High Priests"?

What makes us unworthy? An accident of birth? A misplacement of chromosomes? By an act of God we have been created female. By the acts of man we have been delegated inferior. Only man, who has created the chains of our bondage, can release them and give us the freedom to stand as equal.

---

17. After major expansion into multiple nations, the Reorganization began using the term "world conference" instead of "general conference."
18. Howard, *The Church through the Years*, 2:397.
19. Ibid., 2:395–97.
20. Becky Savage, "A Journey toward the Ordination of Women in Community of Christ: A Historical Literature Review" (M.A. thesis, Graceland University Community of Christ Seminary, 2005), 62.

Is it too much to hope that the church which professes revelatory leadership could move in this day towards <u>full personhood</u> for women?

It is contrary to my inner belief in the stewardship of person resource that the intelligence and creativity of thousands within this "fellowship of membership: is not touched alive nor utilized but is neglected, rejected and wasted merely because their name is WOMAN!

…When will the moment come when we shall have full opportunity to offer our "acceptable offerings"—our lives—to the service of the Kingdom of our Lord. How can I teach my children? How can I honestly perpetuate a tradition which is contrary to the worth and dignity of all humankind. A tradition which says to my daughter, "You are woman, you are not wanted," but says in the same breath to my son, "You are man, you are worthy to serve."

It is impossible to write in a few words the emotions and concerns of a lifetime and I realize it is also impossible for you who have not lived through these concerns to sense how very deep-seated and vital they are. . . . I have cursed my very creation as woman and asked my Lord in bitter tones, "If you have created me woman (second-class, servant citizen) why have you also planted restless stirrings in my heart and desires for that which cannot be mine?" My Lord has not answered my question. Perhaps He has left that answering to you!

"Man was created to act and not to be acted upon. . . ." Is this true for woman also? "If ye have desires to serve . . . ye are called." Is there limitation to this statement? We, the women of the church are bound by you, the men of the priesthood. Our lives and futures await your pleasure. WE ARE NOT FREE TO ACT . . . but must consciously play the role that you define for us.

We are concerned what role you are planning for us in the future of this church. . . . You hold our lives literally in your hands. May we discuss the shape in which you are molding these lives for the woman of this moment and the moments to come???[21]

And so the dialogue continued for nearly a decade. At the 1976 world conference, the First Presidency brought a resolution calling for the legislative conference to rescind general conference resolution (GCR) 564 which was passed in 1905 and stated: "[We] do not see our way clearly to report favorable [sic] upon ordination of women."[22] Furthermore the resolution to rescind offered by the First Presidency included a resolve that the consideration of women's ordination be deferred until such time that the First Presidency judged that the Church, by common consent, was ready to accept the ordained ministry of women. The action to rescind GCR 564 passed, with amendments calling for *prophetic direction* prior to consideration of the ordination of women.

The biennial world conferences continued to receive resolutions to address women's ordination. Most were written to encourage including women in priesthood, but some were not. A motion to officially prohibit the ordination of wom-

---

21. Lois Braby, Letter to the First Presidency, October 15, 1971, RG24-1, f 33, Community of Christ Archives; Administration: Correspondence Lois and Ruth Braby 1971–1973, quoted in ibid., 63–64. All ellipses in this document are Braby's.

22. "Minutes of the 1905 General conference," 755, quoted in ibid., 73.

en was submitted to the 1980 world conference. An objection was received from the floor and sustained by the vote of the delegates, killing the motion.

During the 1982 world conference, a motion of referral calling for the First Presidency to form a task force to assess Church members' perspectives on ordination of women was passed. The resulting task force launched a survey which revealed a high level of general support for the increased participation of women in Church life. On the topic of ordination of women, the survey reported that a third of the responders supported it, and one half opposed. The neutral 13% indicated their willingness to support the direction of Church leaders regarding the ordination of women.[23] It is interesting to note that, when the First Presidency published the survey report, they also "called the church to see the incongruity of following God's prophetic message and mission while being entirely comfortable in the ways of the past."[24]

On April 3, 1984, President Wallace B. Smith presented an inspired document to the world conference. The ninth paragraph of what would become Section 156 of the Doctrine and Covenants provided for the ordination of women:

> I have heard the prayers of many, including my servant the prophet, as they have sought to know my will in regard to the question of who shall be called to share the burdens and responsibilities of priesthood in my church. I say to you now, as I have said in the past, that all are called according to the gifts which have been given them. This applies to priesthood as well as to any other aspects of the work. Therefore, do not wonder that some women of the church are being called to priesthood responsibilities. This is in harmony with my will and where these calls are made known to my servants, they may be processed according to administrative procedures and provisions of the law. Nevertheless, in the ordaining of women to priesthood, let this be done with all deliberateness. Before the actual laying on of hands takes place, let specific guidelines and instructions be provided by the spiritual authorities that all may be done in order." (Doctrine and Covenants 156:9a-d)[25]

Enid Irene Stubbart Debarthe (1912–2005) shared her experience as the revelation was read and the conference deliberated before approving its inclusion in the Doctrine and Covenants:

> I remember when the document was read on Tuesday morning. . . . I saw some of my friends so thrilled and elated, and I saw others so shocked and hurt, and almost distraught. I went home that night. My mother . . . wept until she could hardly talk. She cried herself to sleep that night. She was convinced it was wrong, wrong, wrong. She still feels that way. I got up and walked the floor, got out the *Interpreter's Bible*, read and studied and prayed. We all did for all the hours until the day of the voting—Thursday afternoon, April 6.
>
> That afternoon, Garland Tickameyer stood, and said that one afternoon Fred M. Smith (Prophet President 1915–1946) had said, "The day will come in the Reorganized

---

23. Howard, *The Church through the Years*, 2:401–2.
24. Ibid., 2:402.
25. *Book of Doctrine and Covenants* 119:8b (2007), 207–8.

Church of Jesus Christ of Latter Day Saints when women will be ordained." Garland T. was a close associate of Fred M. Smith, and I did not doubt his testimony.

As we sat there, there was such a sweet spirit that swept through the whole congregation, it seemed to me. I felt it vibrating around me. When the meeting was over, I went out and got in the car with my sister-in-law, who was a delegate for the first time.

She said, "Enid, did you hear that rush of the Spirit?"

And I said, "No, but I felt it."

My sister-in-law, up in the balcony, and her aunt turned to each other and asked simultaneously, "Do you feel that?"

Since that time, I've had letters from several parts of the county and one from Australia. That dear friend said she had been sitting there with her hands clenched so tense because of what she was afraid people would say—the hurts that were being expressed. Her district president reached over and touched her hands, and said, "Vera, relax. Feel the Spirit in this place." She said, "I relaxed and I felt such a breeze. I looked both ways, at both doors, to see if somebody had opened them, and they were both closed."

Many people have borne testimony to me of that "rush of the Spirit" that they experienced, and the vote was approximately seventy percent in favor.[26]

The document was read on a Tuesday morning. In an attitude of constant prayer and sincerity of heart, the conference deliberated over the document guided by the principle of common consent and theocratic democracy. Two days later, on April 6, 1984, it was approved for inclusion in the Doctrine and Covenants and accepted as revelation. Priesthood calls for women were processed according to Church policy, following specific guidelines and instructions provided by Church leaders after the conference. Those women called began study and preparation for ordination. The first women were ordained on November 17, 1985.

It had been a long journey to this point, but there was yet much work to be done. Now came the hard work of living into the new reality we had created.

Although the vast majority of the Church supported the change, a significant number did not. Some people chose to leave the Church immediately. Others stayed and dug in their heels, resolved to keep up the good fight to maintain the old way. Some resisted in very vocal and visible ways like organizing allies to attend stake and district conferences in order to vote in blocks against priesthood calls presented for women. Others took a more passive approach, preferring to quietly ignore ordained women by refusing to utilize their ministry in congregational life preaching, presiding, serving the sacrament of communion, or providing pastoral care to members.

Gratefully, many women were warmly received in their new priesthood roles. Countless men and women across the Church did everything they could to ease the transition and support the newly ordained women.

Still there were the cultural shifts, and culture is slow to change. As women's avenues of service expanded in the Church, things at home did not necessar-

---

26. Danny L. Jorgensen and Joni Wilson, *Herstories: Ten Autobiographical Narratives of RLDS Women* (Independence, Mo.: John Whitmer Books, 2013), 208–9.

ily adjust accordingly. Women often found themselves doing everything they had done before along with the new responsibilities of priesthood. Child care, cooking for potlucks, cleaning up at home and at Church, preparing for public ministry, conducting meetings, presiding at worship, counseling with members, teaching classes, and selecting hymns were just a few of the items on the list. Over time, living into more gender equity at Church helped open the door to more gender equity at home and at the work place.

The priesthood structure remained unchanged. One office required a name change for obvious reasons. The office of "patriarch evangelist" was renamed simply "evangelist." Priesthood calls were discerned and processed with all the same criteria and guidelines as before. In the process of preparing women for ordination, it became clear to the Church that all of the priesthood would benefit from specific coursework and ministry training prior to ordination. Soon there were courses available for each office as well as additional courses in scripture, pastoral care, ministry, the sacraments, and other related content. Since priesthood was not automatic for all males in the Reorganization, all females were not automatically called to serve. Just as men had been called according to their giftedness, so too were women.

I recently reviewed a list of objections voiced in the early 1980s in response to the prospect of women's ordination in the Reorganized Church. This list is not all-inclusive but does represent commonly noted concerns of the day. Objections included: (1) A sense that women were unqualified to hold priesthood; (2) A perception that it would be a direct violation of the longstanding tradtion of male-only priesthood; (3) The possible negative impact on the male ego and/or a sudden drop in men's church participation; (4) The potential ramifications of men and women working together in a variety of ministerial settings; and (5) The general repercussions a shift in authority might have in the home.[27]

At this juncture it feels breathtakingly liberating to read the words above and recognize that one by one we either overcame the challenges or what feared might happen did not materialize. For example, men did not stop participating in church, and ordaining women to priesthood did not cause the Church to implode or God to stop speaking. Men from all perspectives on the issue experienced transformation. An eyewitness to the proceedings at World Conference 1984, as delegates spoke in response to Section 156 providing for women's ordination, reports, "For over an hour that first day, one man after another rose to tell of his experience. They were often seriously opposed to women in the priesthood—sometimes had spoken against it hostilely—but now testified that they found the change valid and felt it should be made. Men I respected, and whom I knew to be more conservative than I, dug deep into their own souls and saw

---

27. Paul M. Edwards, "Women and Priesthood, RLDS Priesthood: Structure and Process," *Dialogue: A Journal of Mormon Thought* 17, no. 3 (Autumn 1984): 9–10.

a truth."²⁸ Hearts and minds changed and, for the most part, the people of the church stepped into a new future together.

Women brought a lifetime of experience to their new roles in priesthood much of which had never before been expressed through these offices. Additionally they took classes and studied diligently to increase their capacity to serve. Each congregation worked out the challenges of men and women serving in priesthood together, in culturally appropriate ways across the globe. As we overcame obstacles and learned new ways of doing things, fears began to ease and comfort in this new way of being grew.

The more difficult aspect of women's ordination had to do with the pressures of patriarchy to assimilate rather than integrate women into the system, especially as women were called to serve in midlevel judicatory positions and as general officers in the world church. Women had to learn how to navigate a male-dominated culture. Many found themselves patterning their behaviors after men, whether or not that was their natural leadership or communication style. Eventually this strategy led to a sense of inner disconnect for many women, and they began to realize that part of their journey into this new way of being meant claiming their whole personhood and expressing the true identity of their souls as a beloved child of God. Many explored the question, "Who am I and what does it look like to express all of who I am in every aspect of my life?" Rather than adapt to the existing patriarchal heirarchy, women began to redefine ministry, priesthood office, and authority from their own unique persepctive as women. This cracked the door open for women to discover autonomy and individuality as opposed to "sameness."²⁹

A pebble plopped into a still pond and sent ripples all across the water. As women accepted the challenge of introspection, growth, and transformation, men began to do the same. Peeling back the layers of patriarchy, a social system perpetuated by both women and men, takes time. It requires dedication to a truer way of being and vigilance to mutual accountability on behalf of the greater community.³⁰

There have been some rough spots along the way, especially in those first years after the approval of Section 156 of the Doctrine and Covenants. This year (2015) marks thirty years since the first women were ordained in Community of Christ. No one thinks twice about women holding priesthood. An entire generation in the Church knows nothing different than men and women serving side by side in all offices of the Church. Congregations and mission centers across the world are blessed through the ordained ministry of women and men. The

---

28. Ibid., 10.

29. L. Madelon Brunson, "Stranger in a Strange Land: A Personal Response to the 1984 Document," *Dialogue: A Journal of Mormon Thought* 17, no. 3 (Autumn 1984): 16.

30. To read about the author's personal experience and the experience of other women before and after Section 156 of the Doctrine and Covenants, see Robin K. Linkhart, "Women and the Priesthood: The Community of Christ Experience and the Invisible Ties that Bind" in *Restoration Studies, Vol. XI*, edited by Peter A. Judd (Independence, Mo: John Whitmer Historical Association and Community of Christ Seminary Press, 2010), 151–63.

first women apostles were ordained in 1998. In 2007 Becky Savage was ordained into the First Presidency as counselor to the prophet president. As of the 2013 world conference, the Council of Twelve Apostles included five women, one of whom serves as the president of the Council of Twelve. Two women serve on the Council of Presidents of Seventy, and the president of the High Priests Quorum is a woman.

At this juncture women are clearly moving into their own sense of identity and being as whole persons offering their lives in service to the Church and Christ's mission. As the faces around the table include men and women of many cultures, languages, and races, all are learning how to integrate the authentic presence of each person as we celebrate the beautiful diversity resident in the body of Christ. In the space of this new reality we can truly say the fullness of priesthood has been restored as reflected in the faces of God's creation.

It is difficult to be a people who celebrate diversity, the worth of all persons, and invite the voice of each one to be shared at the table.

It is difficult to be a people who earnestly strain forward, hungry and listening for the voice of continuing revelation articulated through a modern-day prophet.

It is difficult to be small, sometimes isolated and alone, in the face of overwhelming challenges, yet still feel deeply compelled to advocate for peace—to be the voice of those who have no voice, to speak truth to power and make a difference in the world—in hopes that at least one less child goes to bed hungry, one more stranger is welcomed, and one more weapon is pounded into a plowshare.

It is difficult to be a people willing to talk about highly charged issues—issues that have the potential to cause tension, precipitate conflict, damage relationships, and even divide us—issues like ordaining women and full inclusion for our LGBT sisters and brothers.

It is difficult . . . . and it is a beautiful life-giving journey.

"The Spirit of the One you follow is the spirit of love and peace. That Spirit seeks to abide in the hearts of those who would embrace its call and live its message. The path will not always be easy, the choices will not always be clear, but the cause is sure and the Spirit will bear witness to the truth, and those who live the truth will know the hope and the joy of discipleship in the community of Christ. Amen." (Doctrine and Covenants 161:7)

PART III

LDS Organizational Structure and Ecclesiastical Dynamics

PART II

Chapter 10

Organizational and Doctrinal Change in a Prophetic Religious Tradition

Gregory A. Prince

In 2010, I participated in an interfaith symposium at the University of Southern California entitled "Mormon Engagement with the World Religions." Among the LDS speakers were both laity—including myself—and hierarchy, in the person of Elder Bruce Porter of the First Quorum of Seventy. Elder Porter stated, with emphasis, "Mormon doctrine has not changed one millimeter!" His statement surprised me on two levels. The first was definitional, for it was an apparent contradiction of one of our Articles of Faith that states, "We believe all that God has revealed, all that He does now reveal, and we believe that He will yet reveal many great and important things pertaining to the Kingdom of God." In other words, "We believe in continuing revelation." It is a bedrock belief of Mormons, so much so that one would be hard pressed to find a congregation that would not vote unanimously in favor of it even while many in those congregations would hesitate to vote in favor of continuing *change*. But we can't have it both ways. Continuing revelation *means* continuing change. It does not mean God saying daily, "Nine o'clock, and all is well."

The second level on which his statement surprised me was historical. Not only has Mormon doctrine changed by millimeters; it has changed by meters and even kilometers, depending on when you are looking and what doctrine you are examining. Indeed, one of the ironies of early Mormonism was that the characteristic that attracted many of its first converts—a restoration of primitive Christianity in its simplicity—was jettisoned early on by Joseph Smith as he boldly plowed new doctrinal and organizational ground, in the process producing "new wine" that some of the "old containers" couldn't handle.[1] Our past informs our future, and so an examination of change in Mormonism's past can provide clues as to where things may head in the future, and how they will get there.

I have divided this chapter into three parts. The first, "The Joseph Smith Era," will examine in detail the way in which changes in *doctrine* and changes in *organization* occurred during the ministry of Mormonism's founder. Doctrinal change

---

1. David Whitmer, one of the Three Witnesses to the Book of Mormon, lashed out strongly against the "new wine" in an autobiographical pamphlet published decades after Joseph Smith's death: "The church never heard of or thought of having in it any of these offices, until we moved to Kirtland, Ohio, in the days of Sidney Rigdon. The Church of Christ upon either continent had no such offices in it." *An Address to All Believers in Christ* (Richmond, Mo.: David Whitmer, 1887), 60.

will be seen through the lens of changing accounts of the First Vision, which coincided with an evolving theology of the nature of Deity; and organizational change will be seen through the lens of a cascade of new offices and ordinances that continued throughout Smith's lifetime. I discuss these changes in considerable detail for the reason that the *changes* themselves are far less relevant to the topic of this chapter than the *process* by which the changes occurred—for that process remains intact today. Understanding it in its earlier iteration facilitates an understanding of how change continues to occur in the Church today and a prediction of how it may change in the future with respect to women and priesthood.

The second part, "The Post-Joseph Smith Era," shows that, although the pace of change slowed dramatically after Smith's death, important organizational and doctrinal changes continue to the present time. The dynamics of change evolved in a different direction as more and more changes at the top were driven by changes effected at the grassroots level—that is, "trickle-up revelation" became at least as important as "trickle-down revelation," until the correlation movement that began in the 1960s largely shut it down. I describe several examples of organizational change, most of which occurred in the twentieth century. One doctrinal change, the 1978 revelation on priesthood that removed the longstanding ban on the ordination of black men, will be examined in detail, as it is the best illustration of doctrinal change since the death of Joseph Smith. The examples, while illustrative, are not intended to be comprehensive; indeed, if one looks deeply enough there is scarcely a doctrinal or organizational component to Mormonism that has never undergone change.

The final part, "The Future," will examine the evolving landscape of two issues directly affecting women in today's Church: homosexuality and priesthood, with the latter issue receiving more attention.

Doctrinal and Organizational Change in the Joseph Smith Era

First Vision Narratives and the Doctrine of Deity

A stumbling block for many Latter-day Saints is the fact that the story of Joseph Smith's First Vision changed over the years. While apologists have sought to gloss over the changes, they are highly significant. If one compares just two versions—the 1832, which was the only one written in Smith's own hand; and the 1839, which is the canonized version in the Pearl of Great Price—one sees remarkable and mutually contradictory differences.[2]

The first is the question of religious authority. In the 1832 account Smith wrote, "By Searching the Scriptures I found that mankind did not come unto the Lord but that they had apostatized from the true and living faith and there

---

2. Dean C. Jessee, "The Early Accounts of Joseph Smith's First Vision," *BYU Studies* 9, no. 3 (Spring 1969):): 275–94. See also Gregory A. Prince, "Joseph Smith's First Vision in Historical Context: How a Historical Narrative Became Theological," *Journal of Mormon History* 41, no. 3 (October 2015), forthcoming.

was no society or denomination that built upon the Gospel of Jesus Christ as recorded in the new testament." In other words, the Bible, itself, gave the authoritative answer to the question, "Which church is true?" The issue that took him to the grove was not which church he should join, but his own sinfulness: "I felt to mourn for my own Sins . . ." and thus, "I cried unto the Lord for mercy."

But in the 1839 account, to his own question, "Who of all these parties are right?" he replied, "The different sects understood the same passage of Scripture so differently as to destroy all confidence in settling the question by an appeal to the Bible. . . . My object in going to inquire of the Lord was to know which of all the sects was right. . . . [A]t this time it had never entered into my heart that all were wrong." In other words, the Bible was incapable of providing the answer, and getting the answer directly from God was his motivation for going to the grove.

A second difference is the message that Smith received in response to his prayer. In 1832 it was, "Joseph my Son thy Sins are forgiven thee." The question of religious authority was moot, since he had already determined from his study of the Bible that all churches then in existence fell short of the truth. But in 1839 the central message of the vision was, "I must join none of them, for they were all wrong," a message that would not have fit into the 1832 account, since he already had the answer and thus had no reason to ask the question.

A third difference, which at first seems less significant but which is actually the key to understanding doctrinal evolution within Mormonism, appears by comparing the nature of Deity portrayed in the 1832, 1835, and 1839 accounts. In the 1832 account, "the Lord opened the heavens upon me and I Saw the Lord." One personage. In 1835 there was a change: "a pillar of fire appeared above my head," and "a personage appeard in the midst, of this pillar of flame." Soon thereafter, this first personage was joined by a second personage. And in 1839 there was yet another change: "two personages (whose brightness and glory defy all description) [stood] above me in the air."

If one juxtaposes these three portrayals of Deity with other documents produced by Smith, the evolutionary process is apparent. For instance, Smith's earliest understanding of Deity is contained in the Book of Mormon. If one reads the 1830 edition of the book, several passages stand out as differing from current LDS orthodoxy, one of which will illustrate the point: "Behold, the virgin which thou seest, is the mother of God, after the manner of the flesh" (p. 25, line 3).[3]

Such a view of Deity is termed modalism, wherein there is "one God, in one part or person at a time, performing various offices, but not simultaneously."[4] It is consistent with the 1832 account, in which only one personage is described. It is

---

3. The 1830 edition of the Book of Mormon was not divided into verses. Equivalent passages are found on p. 25, ln. 10; p. 26, ln. 9; and p. 32, ln. 9.

4. Rick Grunder, *Mormon Parallels: A Bibliographic Source* (LaFayette, N.Y.: Rick Grunder—Books, 2008), 1933.

also consistent with a verse in the "Articles and Covenants," an unpublished revelation from 1831 that states, " . . . which Father & Son & Holy Ghost is one God."[5]

In 1835, however, a shift in theology occurred, moving the Church to binitarianism.[6] The newly published Doctrine and Covenants, in a section titled "Lectures on Faith,"[7] reflected the shift:

> We shall, in this lecture speak of the Godhead: we mean the Father, Son and Holy Spirit. There are two personages who constitute the great, matchless, governing and supreme power over all things. . . . They are the Father and the Son: The Father being a personage of spirit, glory and power: possessing all perfection and fulness [sic]: The Son, who was in the bosom of the Father, a personage of tabernacle, made, or fashioned like unto man . . . possessing the same mind with the Father, which mind is the Holy Spirit. . . . How many personages are there in the Godhead? Two: the Father and the Son.[8]

Several weeks later, Smith related an account that described the appearance of one personage who did not speak, followed by the appearance of a second personage who said, "Thy sins are forgiven thee"—a marked contrast with 1832, which described only one personage. The sequential, rather than simultaneous appearance of the two personages is consistent with their different natures: the Father being a personage of spirit, and the Son being a personage of tabernacle (flesh).

The shift to a binitarian theology was further signaled when the second edition of the Book of Mormon was published in 1837. The previously cited passage from the book of 1 Nephi was changed to reflect a binitarian understanding (change highlighted in italics):[9] "Behold, the virgin whom thou seest, is the mother of *the Son of* God, after the manner of the flesh" (p. 27).

Other verses in the 1837 Book of Mormon were not similarly revised, leaving the careful reader of the current edition with a confusing, patchwork theology of Deity that incorporates both modalism and binitarianism.

The final step in Smith's evolving doctrine of Deity was tritheism, a belief in three separate personages comprising the Godhead. The 1839 account describes two personages who appear simultaneously, both of whom speak to Smith. Thus, the evolving accounts of the First Vision, while inconsistent in crucial aspects with earlier accounts, always portray Deity in a manner consistent with Smith's evolving theology as represented in other writings from the same time point.

---

5. This wording was preserved in the first published version of the revelation: *Evening and the Morning Star* 1, no. 1 (June 1832):):1–2. This same wording appears in the 1833 Book of Commandments 24:18.

6. Grunder, *Mormon Parallels*, 1934: "Binitarians taught one God only (the Father), with a god-like, literal Son created in pre-mortal existence, and fully divine through that inheritance. Only the Son (as Jesus) had a physical body. The Holy Spirit was an influence rather than a being, operating from the Father through the Son."

7. The "Lectures on Faith" remained in the LDS Doctrine and Covenants until 1921.

8. Doctrine and Covenants (1835), pp. 52–53, 55.

9. The other three passages were similarly changed.

The take-home message from this lengthy and laborious trek through history is that a prophetic tradition not only allows for, but mandates continual change, even in matters as important and seemingly immutable as the very nature of God. Indeed, if *that* can change, the good Saints should be open to any other kind of doctrinal change—otherwise, what is revelation?

Evolution of Priesthood Offices

Coincident with Smith's theological evolution were major changes in Church structure. The original Church of Christ—the Church's name when it was founded in 1830—was patterned after the Book of Mormon and contained three offices: teacher, priest and elder.[10] Early converts were satisfied with that structure, and some who later left the Church complained of Joseph Smith having added to it, among them being David Whitmer, one of the Three Witnesses, as described above.

The first additions were bishop and deacon, and they coincided with the late-1831 arrival in New York of Sidney Rigdon, a recent convert from the Disciples of Christ. Rigdon had been a bishop in that tradition—a tradition that accepted only two offices as being legitimate: bishop and deacon. High priest—the one that stuck in Whitmer's craw—was added late in 1831, followed by patriarch in 1833, and seventy and apostle in 1835. The umbrella term "priesthood" came into being gradually, and after 1831; and the terms "Aaronic Priesthood" and "Melchizedek Priesthood" were not adopted until 1835.

Evolution of Priesthood Ordinances

A similar evolution can be seen by examining ordinances. Baptism, bestowal of the gift of the Holy Spirit, ordination to offices of authority, and blessing of the sacrament of the Lord's Supper were the first ordinances of the Restoration, coinciding with the translation of the Book of Mormon in 1829 and described within it. Other practices, all of which were considered ordinances at the time, were added throughout the remainder of Smith's ministry: the blessing of children (1830), administering to the sick (1830), cursing (1830), casting out evil spirits (1830), endowment (1831), raising the dead (1831), general blessing of adults (1831), sealing (1831), washing of feet (1833), patriarchal blessing (1834), marriage (1835), washing and anointing (1836), baptism for the dead (1840), and second anointing (1843).[11] The complexity of the subject is highlighted not only by the variety of ordinances that were added, but also by the fact that there is no simple definition for "ordinance" in the LDS lexicon. It is not simply an official act performed by one holding the priesthood, for administering to the sick was performed by and for women for nearly a century, and washings and anointings are still performed in LDS temples by women. As inadequate as it sounds, an

---

10. A comprehensive treatment of the evolution of offices and ordinances in the early LDS Church can be found in Gregory A. Prince, *Power from On High: The Development of Mormon Priesthood* (Salt Lake City: Signature Books, 1995).

11. Ibid., chaps. 3–6.

ordinance is whatever tradition has defined as an ordinance. This circular definition, while clumsy, connotes flexibility. As we will see in the next section, the adoption of a new ordinance as recently as 1968 suggests that we not become agitated about the possibility of further change.

Thus, in matters both doctrinal and organizational, Joseph Smith moved the Church in a direction of continual change throughout his fifteen-year ministry. Change was not arbitrary, for it responded to perceived needs of a growing church, to visionary experiences (his 1836 "Vision of the Celestial Kingdom," later canonized as Section 137 of the Doctrine and Covenants, opened his eyes to the possibility of salvific ordinances in behalf of the dead), and to Smith's continuing interaction with the Bible (his re-reading of I Corinthians 15:29 informed the introduction of baptism for the dead in 1840). The constant throughout his ministry was that change was a prophetic process—that is, the Prophet alone could implement institutional change, regardless of the source of input that triggered the process.

Organizational and Doctrinal Change in the Post-Joseph Smith Era

"Trickle-Up" and "Trickle-Down" Modes of Revelation

Although the pace of change slowed drastically following the death of Joseph Smith, organizational and doctrinal changes continue to characterize the Church. The auxiliary organizations that still exist within the Church—Relief Society, Sunday School, Young Men/Young Women, and Primary—were products of the nineteenth century, and *all* were examples of "trickle-up revelation"—that is, individuals acting at the grassroots level. Even in the case of the Relief Society, which Smith immediately coopted by saying, "I have something better for you," laity took the initiative to do something that fulfilled a local need, and success at the local level led to adoption at the general level, including the names of the organizations.

Although no new auxiliary organizations were added in the twentieth century, organizational evolution continues to this day. Much of it is "trickle-down," including the introduction of Regional Representatives of the Twelve in 1968; the reconstitution of the First Quorum of Seventy and the concomitant dissolution of the office of Seventy at a local level in 1975; the dissolution of the office of Presiding Patriarch in 1979; and the creation of the office of Area Authority in 1995.

LDS Organizational Innovations through Trickle-Up Revelation

During the depths of the Great Depression, a stake president in Salt Lake City created a program to address the economic problems within his stake. Within three years it was adopted churchwide, initially named the Church Security Program and subsequently renamed the Church Welfare Program. That stake president, Harold B. Lee, became its director, then an apostle, and ultimately the president of the Church.[12]

In 1932, at about the same time Lee was focusing on economic needs within his stake, a bishop in Salt Lake City's 28th Ward, A. P. A. Glad, recognized that adult males in his ward who had never been ordained to an office in the Melchizedek Priesthood were stigmatized. Church policy did not allow them to meet with the elders' quorum, yet meeting with Aaronic Priesthood quorums, often with boys one to two generations their junior, was socially awkward and even humiliating. So Bishop Glad created a separate class for these men, with the hope that they would eventually be ordained to an office in the Melchizedek Priesthood. In 1936 the *Improvement Era* described "Adult Aaronic Priesthood" classes—what Glad had already implemented in his ward. With unusual candor the article acknowledged, "Many plans have been tried throughout the Churh in an effort to arouse the interest of men who are still members of the Aaronic Priesthood. . . . None of these plans has succeeded."[13] The program lasted nearly four decades, and by 1968 it was directed by a 262-page course of study.[14] In 1975 it was replaced by "Prospective Elders," who "join with elders for quorum meeting instruction and all appropriate social activities and service projects."[15]

In 1947, Richard L. Anderson, then a full-time missionary serving in the Northwestern States Mission, wrote his own series of lessons for teaching investigators. Prior to that time there had been no systematic method for such teaching. Entitled *A Plan for Effective Missionary Work* and first published by the Northwestern States Mission in 1949,[16] it was soon reprinted by other missions.[17] In 1952 it served as a template for the Church's first system-wide lesson plan for missionary work.[18]

In the early 1970s I became not only a first-hand witness, but also a participant in a far-reaching example of "trickle-up revelation." I was a graduate student at UCLA and was the regional president of the Latter-day Saint Student

---

12. An overview of twentieth-century organizational changes, several of which are described in this chapter, is W. Keith Warner and Edward L. Kimball, "Creative Stewardship," *The Carpenter* 1, no. 4 (1971):17–26.

13. "Adult Aaronic Priesthood Classes to Be Urged in 1936," *Improvement Era* 39 (February 1936): 107–8.

14. *Aaronic Priesthood/Adults. Priesthood Study Course. Series A, Revised* (Salt Lake City: Presiding Bishopric, 1968).

15. *Melchizedek Priesthood Handbook* (Salt Lake City: Church of Jesus Christ of Latter-day Saints, 1975), 2.

16. Anderson reprinted the lessons in booklet form in 1954 (Kaysville, Utah: Inland Printing Co.).

17. For example, it was published in the New Zealand Mission in 1950 under the title, *Notes for Effective Missionary Work*, with full attribution to Anderson.

18. *A Systematic Program for Teaching the Gospel: Prepared for the Use of Missionaries of the Church of Jesus Christ of Latter-day Saints* (Salt Lake City: Corporation of the President, 1952).

Association. At about the same time I became involved in LDSSA in Los Angeles Stake, young adults in nearby Long Beach Stake approached stake leaders and asked permission to organize a program for twenty-somethings who were neither college students nor married. Changes in society had continually expanded the population of single adults in the Church, but until then there had been no institutional response to address their needs. With the blessing of stake leaders, the young adults in that stake began a program that they called, not surprisingly, Young Adults. Within months, our stake followed suit.

The success of the program in the two stakes caught the attention of Church headquarters; and on July 9, 1972, Thomas S. Monson, then a junior apostle, met with twenty-eight local people including one Regional Representative, six stake presidents, and LDSSA and Young Adult leaders. The agenda for the meeting was simple: "Tell me what you're doing here." Monson asked questions to clarify specifics of what we were doing, took notes, and returned to Salt Lake City.

Three weeks later I was summoned to another meeting that had the same list of attendees, except for Monson; but Church headquarters was represented by J. Thomas Fyans, chairman of the Church's Department of Internal Communications, and two of his subordinates. The three-hour meeting consisted of two-and-a-half hours of their listening to everyone in the room tell what the local Young Adults program was doing and a half-hour of clarifying questions. They made no recommendations for us to change anything we were doing, even though we were acting entirely on local initiative, and their parting words were, "Do as you have been doing so long as you meet the needs of those over whom you have jurisdiction." Within months the Church rolled out a new program, Young Adults. Both the name and the structure were lifted, without change, from what we had initiated on our own.

Evolutionary Changes in LDS Policies and Doctrines

In addition to organizational changes, the Church has undergone significant doctrinal changes in the twentieth and twenty-first centuries. (I am including policy changes in this discussion, as many of the changes in policy have had important doctrinal implications.)

One of the most intriguing changes in policy, and one with strong doctrinal implications, has been the practice of dedicating graves at the time of burial. The practice apparently began spontaneously and locally with no clear documentation about its origins. None of the editions of the *Handbook of Instructions* (later called *General Handbook of Instructions*, and currently *Church Handbook of Instructions*) prior to 1940 mentioned the dedication of graves, even though they dealt with procedures to be followed upon the death of a Church member.

The 1940 edition contained the first mention of what was obviously an already-ongoing practice:

> The graveside prayer should include thanksgiving for the safe committal of the body to earth and reverent acknowledgement that it shall come forth, reanimated by

the immortal spirit to which it once gave tenancy, at a time appointed for its resurrection. The grave may be designated as the resting place of the body of the deceased. Any suitable person may offer this closing prayer, *whether he be a bearer of the priesthood or not*; though, naturally, if the service has been conducted by men ordained to the priesthood, one of them would be chosen to thus officiate at the grave.

It is not advised, however, that one so ministering should use words to the effect that he is officiating by virtue of any power or authority pertaining to the Holy Priesthood, nor that by any such authority or power he dedicates the grave.[19]

Note that the practice was not an ordinance, nor was the officiator required to hold the Melchizedek Priesthood—indeed, the language left open the possibility of a woman giving the graveside prayer.

Four years later, an evolutionary step occurred when Church leaders *recommended* that the officiator hold the priesthood: "The person appointed to offer the prayer *should* be a worthy brother holding the Melchizedek Priesthood."[20]

The final evolutionary step occurred in 1968, when the dedication of graves was first listed as an "Important Priesthood Ordinance" that should be overseen personally by a member of the bishopric and that it "should be done by one holding the Melchizedek Priesthood."[21] Thus, in a period of twenty-eight years the practice went from a non-ordinance that could be performed by anyone, to a non-ordinance that should be performed by one holding the Melchizedek Priesthood, to an ordinance.

Another policy with strong doctrinal overtones concerns birth control. In the nineteenth century, when the understanding of reproductive medicine advanced to the point where birth control first became effective, Church leaders lashed out at it in unambiguous tones. Brigham Young set the stage when he made it a duty for couples to have as many children as they could—and thus not to engage in birth control: "I have told you many times that there are multitudes of pure and holy spirits waiting to take tabernacles, now what is our duty? . . . It is the duty of every righteous man and woman to prepare tabernacles for all the spirits they can."[22]

As the practice of birth control became more common among Church members, leaders called it out in strong terms, with none stronger than those of George Q. Cannon, a member of the First Presidency, who said that those who engaged in it "will be damned and go to hell."[23]

---

19. *Handbook of Instructions for Stake Presidencies, Bishops and Counselors, Stake and Ward Clerks and Other Church Officers, No. 16, 1940*, 127–28; emphasis mine.

20. *Handbook of Instructions for Stake Presidents and Counselors, Bishops and Counselors, Stake and Ward Clerks and Other Church Officers, No. 17, 1944*, 77; emphasis mine.

21. *General Handbook of Instructions, No. 20, 1968*, 89.

22. Brigham Young, September 21, 1856, in *Journal of Discourses*, 27 vols. (London and Liverpool: LDS Booksellers Depot, 1855–86), 14:56.

23. Rudger Clawson, Diary, June 13, 1893, Ms 481, Box 4, Book 3, Special Collections, Marriott Library, University of Utah.

Later, Church president Joseph F. Smith, addressing the Relief Society in 1917, virtually repeated Cannon's condemnation when he said, "I think that [curtailing the birth of children] is a crime whenever it occurs. . . . I have no hesitancy in saying that I believe this is one of the greatest crimes in the world today."[24]

Gradually, however, Church leaders distanced themselves from the condemnation of birth control, with that evolution accelerating in the later decades of the twentieth century. It is instructive to chart the final changes as they were published in the *General Handbook of Instructions*, the Church's official guidebook for leaders. In 1976 the *Handbook*, while appealing to husbands to "be considerate of their wives who bear the greater responsibility not only of bearing children, but of caring for them through childhood," specifically encouraged large families and condemned birth control:

> We have been commanded to multiply and replenish the earth that we may have joy and rejoicing in our posterity.
>
> Where husband and wife enjoy health and vigor and are free from impurities that would be entailed upon their posterity, it is contrary to the teachings of the Church to artificially curtail or prevent the birth of children.[25]

The subsequent edition of the *Handbook*, published seven years later, removed completely—and without explanation—the entire paragraph condemning birth control, while retaining the exhortation to "multiply and replenish the earth."[26] The 1985 edition preserved the same wording, but the 1989 edition deleted the "multiply and replenish" exhortation, again without explanation,[27] and left the matter entirely in the hands of the husband and wife—the polar opposite of George Q. Cannon's blanket condemnation a century earlier.

While the policy regarding birth control, along with its doctrinal implications, took a century to change, the most sweeping change in the twentieth-century church took place in only one day. On June 8, 1978, Church president Spencer W. Kimball met in the Salt Lake Temple with all of the General Authorities of the Church. He said to them, "There were days when you brethren went home at night, and I had come over here night after night after night; and I have poured my heart out to the Lord to know why. Last week he answered me. He said, 'The time has come.'" After allowing each man to express his feelings, Kimball asked for a sustaining vote, which was unanimous. "He sat down and then he leaned over and put his hand on Eldon Tanner's knee, and he looked at him. I will never

---

24. Joseph F. Smith, Address, *Relief Society Magazine* 4 (June 1917): 317–18. For a comprehensive treatment of the subject of birth control, see Lester E. Bush Jr., *Health and Medicine among the Latter-day Saints* (New York: Crossroad Publishing, 1993), chap. 6.

25. *General Handbook of Instructions, Number 21* (Salt Lake City: Corporation of the President, 1976), 105.

26. *General Handbook of Instructions, Number 22* (Salt Lake City: Corporation of the President, 1983), 77.

27. *General Handbook of Instructions, Number 24* (Salt Lake City: Corporation of the President, 1989), 11–14.

forget that look. He said, 'Eldon, go tell the world.'"[28] With that, the policy of withholding priesthood ordination from males of black African ancestry was abolished.

While the change was effected in one day, the process by which the change occurred was lengthy and complex. The policy had bothered Kimball for decades. On one occasion in the early 1960s, while visiting mission president J. Thomas Fyans in Uruguay, he said, "Tom, some way we've got to solve this problem of 'the blood.' They are worthy people."[29]

Shortly before Kimball became Church president in December 1973, Lester Bush published a monograph with the title, "Mormonism's Negro Doctrine: An Historical Overview."[30] It marked the first time that a scholar had dug deeply enough into the historical record to determine that the policy was initiated by Brigham Young after Joseph Smith's death, that it emerged in an atmosphere of pre-Civil War racism, and that it never had the imprimatur of revelation to justify it, despite a long-held tradition to the contrary.[31] The monograph weighed heavily on Kimball, who digested it thoroughly, as related by his granddaughter-in-law:

> My husband, Jordan Kimball, and I were visiting with his dad, Ed Kimball [son of Spencer W.], yesterday. . . . Ed brought up that he had been contacted regarding a rumor floating around about a Kimball grandson having discovered the Lester Bush landmark article in *Dialogue* heavily marked up in Spencer Kimball's home office after his death. It stood out because it was the only article among the *Dialogue* issues heavily underlined in red, which was consistent with SWK's style of marking up. We told Ed that we could confirm that rumor.[32]

Bush's article was but one element of a complex picture that included the construction of a temple in Brazil, a country whose racial homogenization defied attempts to document black African ancestry; and Kimball's strong impulse to extend proselytizing activities to sub-Saharan Africa. And while the final piece of the picture came from above and not below, Kimball also relied on grassroots Church members for crucial—and back-channel—input prior to effecting the change in policy. On two occasions in the 1990s I spoke with people in the Washington DC Stake who had reported directly to Kimball in the months preceding the revelation, none of whom had been aware of what the others were doing.

---

28. Paul H. Dunn, interviewed by Gregory A. Prince, May 21, 1996.

29. J. Thomas Fyans, interviewed by Gregory A. Prince, June 3, 1995.

30. Lester E. Bush, Jr., "Mormonism's Negro Doctrine: An Historical Overview," *Dialogue: A Journal of Mormon Thought* 8 (Spring 1973): 11–68.

31. Bush's groundbreaking findings have been expanded in subsequent years by other scholars. For an in-depth treatment of the subject, including the 1840s implementation by Brigham Young of the policy, see Russell W. Stevenson, *For the Cause of Righteousness: A Global History of Blacks and Mormonism, 1830–2013* (Salt Lake City: Greg Kofford Books, 2014).

32. Rebecca England to Gregory A. Prince, April 14, 2014.

Jack Carlson, a Washington insider who became a confidant of Kimball during the 1976 election cycle, and his wife, Renee, had an extraordinary meeting with Kimball early in 1978. Renee described the discussion:

> Jack was lobbying for change, because at that time it was outrageous. It was so awful. And so, President Kimball said to him, "Well, what do you think would happen if we changed the policy? Give us a scenario." I was in there then, and we talked for maybe an hour....
>
> President Kimball was very rational about changing the policy on blacks, and he asked all the right questions. For instance, he asked what we thought would happen with the Southern parts of the Church, and we batted it around for quite a while....
>
> The other thing was that they talked about how it should be done. Jack's advice was, "You should do it fast. Take advantage of the fact that you are the Prophet." He needed consensus, obviously, but when it happened, he did it pretty fast.[33]

At the same time as Carlson's meetings, Kimball directed that another member of the same stake, John Baker, participate in a covert study of potential Church leadership in certain African nations, in the form of African nationals who had attended BYU and were then living in Africa.[34]

The point here is that the process of revelation, including the changes that result from it, is complex and involves—indeed, may *require*—trickle-up input, some of which may be requested, as in the case of the Carlsons and John Baker, and some of which may be unsolicited, as in the case of Lester Bush. To shut off the trickle-up component, essentially saying, "When we want your opinion, we'll tell you what it is," runs contrary to our institutional history, and carries the significant risk of impeding what that history has shown to be the revelatory process.

Even more than the evolving policy regarding birth control, the change in the priesthood ban carried strong doctrinal overtones. When the policy was first instituted by Brigham Young, he invoked neither a revelation nor a doctrinal underpinning to justify it. Subsequent apologists, including many General Authorities, constructed a doctrinal scaffolding in an effort to support the policy. One example that by today's standards is particularly jolting came from Apostle Mark E. Petersen. Given to employees of the Church Education System in 1954, his address stands as landmark of dogmatic self-assurance: "This Negro, who in the pre-existence life lived the type of life which justified the Lord in sending him to the earth in the lineage of Cain with a black skin, and possibly being born in darkest Africa—if that Negro is willing when he hears the gospel to accept it, he may have many of the blessings of the gospel.... If that Negro is faithful all his days, he can and will enter the Celestial Kingdom. He will go there as a servant, but he will get a Celestial resurrection."[35]

---

33. Renee Carlson, interviewed by Gregory A. Prince, June 2, 1994.

34. John Baker, interviewed by Gregory A. Prince, October 26, 1994.

35. Mark E. Petersen, "Race Problems—As They Affect the Church," given at Brigham Young University on August 27, 1954. As shocking as such statements are to many contemporary readers, similar views are still held by many Latter-day Saints—including Dr.

The change in policy clearly undercut its doctrinal scaffolding, and yet that scaffolding has been difficult to disassemble even six decades later.

In reviewing these and other examples of changes in Church organization, policy, and doctrine, it becomes apparent that there is no single formula that can describe the process of change. However, in the instances where sufficient data exist to allow a comprehensive picture to be assembled, there has been interplay between central institutional priorities, cultural milieu, and grassroots initiative and input. It is reasonable to assume that similar interplay will inform future changes.

Prospects for Future Revelatory Changes Affecting LDS Women

The internet has democratized data in a bidirectional manner. That is, data flow smoothly and in abundance from internet servers to the user and equally smoothly and in abundance from one user to another. The data points of Mormonism's past are available at the stroke of a computer key, and the writings and voices of those who digest the data are disseminated instantaneously to a worldwide audience whose magnitude cannot accurately be determined. Church members who in prior years felt—and were—isolated now find themselves in vibrant, virtual communities with other Church members of similar stripes. A Church that once controlled the message because it controlled the data now finds that it controls neither, and thus the potential power of the grassroots membership is at an all-time high.

It is with that backdrop that I now explore two major issues affecting Latter-day Saint women, and how they may change: homosexuality, including same-sex marriage; and priesthood.

Homosexuality and Same-Sex Marriage

Homosexuality was closeted in the Church and in the United States until the late 1960s. In 1968, one year before the Stonewall Riots brought homosexuality out of the closet nationally, the word first appeared in the *General Handbook of Instructions*—and then only as one among a list of transgressions that might be cause for convening a Church court.

By the mid-1970s mere self-identification as a homosexual (rather than committing homosexual acts), became a transgression meriting excommunication. The distinction between *being* homosexual and self-identifying as such was crucial, because until 2012 the Church considered homosexuality a chosen life-

---

Randy Bott, a BYU professor who in 2012 made similar claims to reporter Jason Horowitz. See "The Genesis of a Church's Stand on Race," *Washington Post*, February 28, 2012. The story resulted in a swift and unprecedented statement by the Church that called out Bott by name and stated flatly that his doctrinal explanations "absolutely do not represent the teaching and doctrines of The Church of Jesus Christ of Latter-day Saints. . . . We condemn racism, including any and all past racism by individuals both inside and outside the Church." "Church Statement Regarding 'Washington Post' Article on Race and the Church," mormonnewsroom.org, February 29, 2012 (accessed March 21, 2015).

style—and thus, something that could be "unchosen"—rather than a biological imprint. Church officials—and more notably, BYU security officers—became proactive in trying to identify and excommunicate homosexual members, often employing coercive tactics to identify them, and invasive and damaging tactics such as electroshock therapy to "cure" them of their homosexuality.[36]

In the early 1990s, a lawsuit in the State of Hawaii suddenly made same-sex marriage (SSM) a national issue. Having been denied marriage licenses, three same-sex couples filed a lawsuit against the state, alleging that they had been denied equal protection under the state constitution. The local court ruled against the plaintiffs; but when they appealed the case to the Supreme Court of Hawaii, the higher court remanded the case to the trial court with a requirement that the lower court demonstrate a compelling state interest in forbidding SSM.[37]

Hawaii's state Supreme Court ruling in 1993 caused a shock wave that spread throughout the country. Fearful that legitimization of SSM in Hawaii would compel other states to recognize such marriages if couples moved from Hawaii, state after state passed laws or constitutional amendments forbidding SSM. The LDS Church, members of whose hierarchy had been strongly against SSM, joined with the Catholic Church to conduct trench warfare against the issue in Hawaii. When anti-SSM legislation passed in Hawaii, the Church took action in Alaska by contributing $500,000 in cash to pass an anti-SSM initiative,[38] and then to California to join the campaign for anti-SSM legislation. Known as Proposition 22, the legislation passed in 2000, thanks in large measure to the support of the Church. This time, however, the Church employed a new strategy—one that it would use again. Church president Gordon B. Hinckley explained, "We've put no institutional funds into that effort. That effort has all been financed by the contributions of local Californians."[39]

Eight years later the California Supreme Court struck down Proposition 22, which was in the form of a state law, saying that it was unconstitutional. Immediately, anti-SSM forces gathered signatures to place the exact same wording on the ballot that November, this time as an amendment to the state constitution. Thus, Proposition 8 became a household term.

While the Church shied away from direct financial contributions to the Prop 8 campaign, it deployed an unprecedented ground game that, according to some

---

36. The granting of statewide police powers to BYU security officers received national attention in an Associated Press article in the autumn of 1979. See "Utah Church Police Controversial," *Times-News* (Hendersonville, N.C.), October 19, 1979. Electroshock therapy was described in "Homosexuality at BYU," *Seventh East Press*, April 12, 1982.

37. *Baehr v. Miike*, "Hawaii Supreme Court Decisions," http://law.justia.com/cases/hawaii/supreme-court/1996/18905-2.html (accessed August 17, 2014).

38. "Mormons Join Alaska Campaign to Ban Gay Marriage," Reuters, October 1, 1998. See http://www.lds-mormon.com/gaylds.shtml (accessed March 11, 2015).

39. "Transcript of the Interview with Gordon B. Hinckley," *Salt Lake Tribune*, February 26, 2000.

estimates, resulted in the contribution of over $20 million by Church members to the "Yes on 8" campaign and engaged thousands of Church members in phone banks and in-person get-out-the-vote efforts. The Church won its battle, as Prop 8 passed by a slim margin; but the resulting backlash caught Church leaders totally by surprise.[40] National surveys showed a deep-seated animosity toward the Church,[41] and many people linked the word "Mormon" with "homophobia." The linkage was not without merit, for it is estimated that 40 percent of homeless youth in Utah are lesbian, gay, bisexual, or transgender (LGBT), and 60 percent of homeless youth are from conservative religious families.[42]

Prop 8 was a wakeup call to LGBT[43] and their allies, and in the years since 2008 there has been an unprecedented shift in social attitudes within the United States, such that SSM is now favored by a majority of the voters and is the law of the land in three dozen states. It was also a wakeup call to LDS Church leaders, who realized belatedly that taking such a high-profile—indeed, decisive—stance on Prop 8, which it viewed strictly as a *marriage* issue, had cemented in the public consciousness an opinion that Mormonism was homophobic in general. Most recently, Apostle Dallin H. Oaks attempted to separate the two issues when speaking in the Church general conference:

> Like the Savior, His followers are sometimes confronted by sinful behavior, and today when they hold out for right and wrong as they understand it, they are sometimes called "bigots" or "fanatics." Many worldly values and practices pose such challenges to Latter-day Saints. Prominent among these today is the strong tide that is legalizing same-sex marriage in many states and provinces in the United States and Canada and many other countries in the world. . . . We should be persons of goodwill toward all, rejecting persecution of any kind, including persecution based on race, ethnicity, religious belief or nonbelief, and differences in sexual orientation.[44]

Slowly, things began to change at Church headquarters. The Public Affairs Department took the lead in reaching out to local and national LGBT communities, agreeing to agree on some issues of substance such as anti-discrimination

---

40. An overview of negative reaction to Prop 8 is a report from the Heritage Foundation. Thomas M. Messner, "The Price of Prop 8," http://www.heritage.org/research/reports/2009/10/the-price-of-prop-8 (accessed March 1, 2015).

41. A recent Pew Research poll showed that among major religious traditions in the United States, only the Muslims engendered more negative feelings than the Mormons. "How Americans Feel about Religious Groups," Pew Research Religion & Public Life Project, July 16, 2014, http://www.pewforum.org/2014/07/16/how-americans-feel-about-religious-groups/ (accessed December 28, 2014).

42. These estimates are from Marian Edmonds Allen, executive director of Ogden OUTreach, communicated to me on December 23, 2014.

43. While other abbreviations are sometimes used, including LGBTQ—"Queer" or "Questioning"—and LGBIT—"Intersex"—I employ the one most commonly used.

44. Dallin H. Oaks, "Loving Others and Living with Differences," October 4, 2014, https://www.lds.org/general-conference/2014/10/loving-others-and-living-with-differences?lang=eng (accessed March 2, 2015).

ordinances,[45] while agreeing to disagree on SSM. After gaining buy-in from the ecclesiastical line, Public Affairs employees began to invite local and national LGBT officials to the annual Tabernacle Choir Christmas Program, including VIP seating and meetings with Church officials. For example, in November 2012, I was contacted by LDS Public Affairs and asked to extend, on behalf of the Church, an invitation to Rick Jacobs (founder and executive director of the Courage Campaign in California) and his partner to attend the Mormon Tabernacle Choir Christmas concert and with my wife to fly to Salt Lake City and host them. We hosted a banquet for two dozen people prior to the concert, including Public Affairs personnel, and watched barriers drop as people who had been enemies four years earlier during the Proposition 8 campaign now dined side by side and became friends.

Just one week prior to our banquet, in December 2012, the Church launched a new website, mormonsandgays.org. Just putting the words "Mormons" and "gays" in the same phrase was an unexpected and unprecedented move, but even more remarkable was the content of the website. By stating on the home page, "individuals do not choose to have such attractions," the Church implicitly abandoned its prior and unbending position—all but canonized by Spencer W. Kimball during his apostolic assignment[46]—that homosexuality was a matter of choice, and not biology, while at the same time it had held homosexuals responsible for their actions because "they do choose how to respond to them." It is highly significant, and in accord with the current policy that homosexuality itself is no sin, that openly gay young men and women may, if celibate, serve full-time proselytizing missions. One need only go back to the 1970s and 1980s, when *being* homosexual was grounds for excommunication, to see how far the Church has come.

Affirmation, an independent LDS/LGBT support group that was founded nearly four decades ago, changed its course some three years ago away from an adversarial stance toward the Church. It now works to achieve a guarantee that LGBT members who choose to worship in LDS congregations will be able to do so without punitive actions, even if they are in same-sex relationships. Affirmation's task has been assisted by the work of Dr. Caitlin Ryan, published in the same year that the Church website went up, that shows the rate of gay suicide to be eight-fold higher in unsupportive families than in supportive families.[47] Policies that save people's lives are better than policies that kill people.

---

45. Perhaps the most dramatic example of a changed atmosphere at Church headquarters was the last-minute endorsement by the Church of a Salt Lake City non-discrimination ordinance, which was the crucial link to unanimous city council approval. "Mormon Church Backs Protection of Gay Rights in Salt Lake City," *Deseret News*, November 10, 2009, http://www.deseretnews.com/article/print/705343558/Mormon-Church-backs-protection-of-gay-rights-in-Salt-Lake-City.html (accessed April 23, 2015).

46. Spencer W. Kimball, *The Miracle of Forgiveness* (Salt Lake City: Bookcraft, 1969).

47. Caitlin Ryan and Robert A. Rees, *Supportive Families, Healthy Children: Helping Latter-day Saints Families with Lesbian, Gay, Bisexual & Transgender Children* (San Francisco: Family Acceptance Project, 2012).

While the Church has not taken any steps toward acceptance of SSM and while most of the changes towards LGBT involve policy rather than doctrine, the implicit acknowledgement that homosexuality is biologically based represents a *de facto* shift in doctrine. And biology will continue to inform both policy and doctrine as more is learned about the complex interactions of genetics (the nucleic acids that make up individual genes) and epigenetics (factors that influence the functioning of genes) that underlie homosexuality.

Many questions remain concerning LGBT and Mormonism. Will there be a formal guarantee that congregations will be zones of safety in which to worship? Will legally married same-sex couples be welcomed as members in full fellowship, even if denied temple recommends? Will they be given callings? Will same-sex weddings ever be performed in LDS meetinghouses, or will LDS bishops or other officers officiate at such unions—a possibility that currently is formally prohibited both as to locale and officiator? Will SSM ever be performed in LDS temples, and will children of such couples be sealed to their parents? Some of these questions could be answered just by changes in policy, but the more compelling ones would likely require significant theological changes—and particularly afterlife theology, for currently LDS doctrine has no place for homosexuals in the afterlife. The implicit acknowledgement on mormonsandgays.org that homosexuality is biological has not been extended to include the afterlife, and by prohibiting same-sex marriage, the Church is effectively consigning gays to a subservient status, since habitation of the highest level of heaven requires marriage.[48]

If, how, and when any of these questions may be answered is a matter of speculation, but if past is prologue, the process by which such answers may be achieved is likely to be a combination of central institutional priorities, cultural milieu, grassroots initiative and input, and, unlike past changes involving other issues, the influence of the internet. The tacit admission that the foundation of all prior Church policies—that homosexuality is a chosen behavior that can merely be un-chosen—is faulty, and that new policies will have to be built on a foundation of biology, is the real game changer. Nonetheless, the pace of change is unpredictable. The recent walking back of apparent support for statewide anti-discrimination laws in Utah[49] suggests that LGBT issues continue to be divisive among General Authorities, and the scriptural mandate that changes in policy must be ratified by unanimous vote bodes ill for rapid change (D&C 107:27).

---

48. "In the celestial glory there are three heavens or degrees; And in order to obtain the highest, a man must enter into this order of the priesthood [meaning the new and everlasting covenant of marriage]; And if he does not, he cannot obtain it." Doctrine and Covenants 131:1–3.

49. Eric Ethington, "Mormon Church Walks Back Statement of Support for Non-Discrimination Laws," http://www.thenewcivilrightsmovement.com/ericethington/mormon_church_walks_back_statement_of_support_for_non_discrimination_laws (accessed December 21, 2014).

Women and Priesthood

While same-sex marriage is a fascinating and important topic, its direct effect is quite limited in comparison to the subject of women and priesthood, which touches most households in the Church. The current debate within Mormonism as to whether women should be ordained—either to the male priesthood or to a female counterpart—is complicated by the silence of Joseph Smith on the subject, for he never explicitly confirmed or denied the possibility of women assuming a role equal to that of men at all levels of Church ministry and administration;[50] and also by the ambiguity of the biblical record, which gives no clear guidance on the subject. Church officers generally have avoided the subject completely, although on occasion they have at least left the door open. For example, in 1963 William Critchlow Jr., an Assistant to the Quorum of the Twelve, said in general conference, "Infrequently a sister asks: Why can't we (sisters) hold the priesthood? My answer: If and when he whose business priesthood is wants you to hold it, he will let his prophet know. Until then there is nothing we can do about it."[51]

The current debate about ordination of women, which has been thrust into the national consciousness by OrdainWomen, with Kate Kelly as its most prominent spokeswoman, generally bypasses a detailed discussion of the essential nature of LDS priesthood, which has evolved greatly both in form and substance since 1829. An in-depth historical examination may inform that debate.

On the surface the definition appears simple and straightforward: "It is the power and authority by which The Church of Jesus Christ of Latter-day Saints is organized and directed."[52] And yet, both the form and the definition of priesthood were evolutionary.

The motivation for Joseph Smith and Oliver Cowdery to go to the banks of the Susquehanna River in 1829 was to obtain authority to baptize. A short time thereafter, they obtained a different level of authority, one that allowed them to confer the gift of the Holy Spirit. There was no indication on the part of either man that their authority was incomplete at that point, and less than a year thereafter they founded the Church, confident that they had full authority to do so. They gave no name to their authority, and the three canonical prayers from that time period, contained both in the Book of Mormon and in Latter-day Saint revelations, either invoke "authority" as a stand-alone term (the baptismal prayer states, "Having authority given me of Jesus Christ") or are silent as to authority (the prayers for blessing the bread and wine). The word "priesthood" appears in

---

50. For an expanded treatment of the subject, see Prince, *Power from On High*, chap. 8.

51. William J. Critchlow Jr., October 4, 1963, in *Conference Report* (Salt Lake City: Church of Jesus Christ of Latter-day Saints, October 1963), 29.

52. Richard G. Ellsworth and Melvin J. Luthy, "Priesthood," in *Encyclopedia of Mormonism*, 4 vols. (New York: Macmillan Publishing, 1992), 3:1134.

none of them, and it was not used as a descriptive term relating to authority until well over a year following the founding of the Church.[53]

The landscape changed dramatically in late 1830 when Sidney Rigdon was converted in Kirtland and traveled to New York to meet Joseph Smith. Rigdon, who had been a bishop in the Campbellite tradition, had parted ways with Alexander Campbell over the issue of gifts of the Spirit. Whereas Campbell held that such gifts, while present in the ancient church, had no place in its modern counterpart, Rigdon insisted that the gifts were signs of the true, modern Church. Within weeks of his arrival in New York, Rigdon was Joseph Smith's scribe for what became Section 38 of the current Doctrine and Covenants, a revelation that instructed the fledgling Church to move to Ohio, where they would be "endowed with power from on high" (v. 32).

The revelation drew on the last chapter of the Gospel of Luke, wherein the resurrected Jesus instructed his disciples—who already had received authority from him—that in order to preach the gospel to the entire world it was necessary that they "tarry in Jerusalem" until they received a divine endowment of "power from on high" (Luke 24:49). In other words, authority was only one part of a bipartite entity, and power was the other part. The ancient endowment occurred at the day of Pentecost (Acts 2); its Latter-day Saint counterpart occurred in a schoolhouse in Kirtland in June 1831. Elders who received the endowment of power from on high—and only twenty-two of the forty-four elders present were so endowed[54]—were thus empowered to preach the gospel and perform other works, while elders who did not receive it were of a lesser status.

The distinction between authority and power is highly significant. A priesthood officer has the *authority* to perform ordinances that, even though he may be personally unworthy at the time, are fully recognized by the Church. In other words, a baptism that he performed on Saturday morning would be recognized by the Church even though it turned out that he had committed adultery on Friday night.

For other functions that he might perform, however, divine *power* is necessary. Think of a man who, in giving a blessing of healing, promises a full restoration of health to someone dying of cancer. The fulfillment of that blessing is not automatic, unlike the recognition of baptism. It depends upon the ability of the officiator to draw upon divine power, and that ability is contingent.

Thus, in its ideal formulation, priesthood is the harmonious blend of authority and power, a blend that depends upon personal rectitude as well as ordination. But what about the component parts standing alone? Is it possible for someone who is not ordained to the priesthood to tap into "power from on high"? That was pre-

---

53. See Prince, *Power from On High*, chap. 1, for an in-depth treatment of this subject.
54. "Far West Record," June 3, 1831, in Donald Q. Cannon and Lyndon W. Cook, eds., *Far West Record: Minutes of the Church of Jesus Christ of Latter-day Saints, 1830–1844* (Salt Lake City: Deseret Book, 1983), 6–7.

cisely the question that was addressed in an extraordinary—and almost universally unknown—article that was published in the Church's *Improvement Era* in 1931. With the provocative title of "Why Priesthood at All?" the article was "prepared under the direction of the Council of the Twelve"[55]— and hence, carried a quasi-canonical status. I include it here in its entirety because of its importance:

> Can any one, without the Priesthood, pray and have his prayers answered? Or receive the Holy Ghost, with its gifts and manifestations?
>
> The answer is Yes. Men, women and children who do not hold the Priesthood have had their prayers answered millions of times in the history of Christianity the world over and in the history of this dispensation. Men, women and children also receive the Holy Ghost after baptism through the laying on of hands.
>
> May one have revelations and visions of heavenly beings, without the Priesthood?
>
> Joseph Smith and Oliver Cowdery did so. In May, 1829, John the Baptist appeared to them, and that was before either of them had been ordained. It was John, in fact, who conferred the Priesthood upon them. This function of having visions, of course, was exceptional in their case.
>
> If, then, one may pray, may have his prayers answered, may have the Holy Ghost bestowed upon him, and may exercise many of its gifts, without holding any Priesthood, what is the place of Priesthood on the earth?
>
> Chiefly Priesthood functions in connection with organization. That is, the greatest need of Priesthood is where there is a service to be performed to others besides ourselves.
>
> Whenever you do anything for, or in behalf of, someone else, you must have the right to do so. If you are to sell property belonging to another, you must have his permission. If you wish to admit an alien to citizenship in our government, you cannot act without having been commissioned to do so by the proper authority.
>
> Now, a religious organization, or the Church, is in the last analysis a matter of service. You baptize someone, or you confirm him, or you administer to him in case of sickness, or you give him the Sacrament or the Priesthood, or you preach the Gospel to him—what is this but performing a service?
>
> Now, when it comes to earthly power to perform a definite service, we call it the power of attorney in the case of acting legally for someone else, or the court and the judge where it is a question of acting for the government.
>
> But in the Church of Christ this authority to act for others is known as Priesthood.[56]

Published at the centennial of the Church's founding, the article reflects a legalistic definition of priesthood, essentially setting aside the "power from on high" element by saying that the gifts of the Spirit are available to all, and not just to priesthood holders. While extraordinary to today's reader, it sits well within the context of its time.

Since the earliest years of the Restoration, women had exercised spiritual gifts, including healing, prophesying, and speaking in tongues, with the full knowledge,

---

55. The Quorum of the Twelve at that time consisted of Rudger Clawson, Reed Smoot, George Albert Smith, George F. Richards, David O. McKay, Joseph Fielding Smith, James E. Talmage, Stephen L Richards, Richard R. Lyman, Melvin J. Ballard, John A. Widtsoe, and Joseph F. Merrill.

56. "Why Priesthood At All?" *Improvement Era* 34, no. 12 (October 1931): 735.

and often the explicit encouragement of, Church leaders including Church presidents.[57] But in the early years of the twentieth century, the Reed Smoot hearings in the U.S. Senate shook the foundations of the Church and resulted in what was essentially a reinvention of Church structure.[58] Disappointed at the performance of priesthood quorums, which in general had been non-functional for decades, Church president Joseph F. Smith was characteristically diplomatic in calling them to a higher level of function, while implicitly signaling that women's role would be downgraded in order to allow space for that level of function: "We expect to see the day . . . when every council of the Priesthood in the Church of Jesus Christ of Latter-day Saints will understand its duty, will assume its own responsibility, will magnify its calling, and fill its place in the Church. . . . When that day shall come, there will not be so much necessity for work that is now being done by the auxiliary organizations [including Relief Society], because it will be done by the regular quorums of the Priesthood."[59]

In the afternoon session of general conference the same day, J. Golden Kimball was characteristically blunt in addressing the same subject: "The Priesthood quorums are apparently weary in well doing, and the officers and members seem to think that their organizations can run themselves. They have become lax in their work, and let loose their hold. While the auxiliary organizations have taken the right of way, the Priesthood quorums stand by looking on awe-struck. . . . Perhaps you don't like that picture, you men of the Priesthood quorums, but I tell you there is a lot of truth in it."[60]

The efforts to get priesthood quorums to function meaningfully took decades and involved much trial and much error.[61] Lesson manuals were written for the first time, with the goal of having quorums meet on a weekly basis, something they had not done regularly in the first eight decades of the Church's existence. By the late 1920s the goal had generally been reached, but results fell short of expectations: "A quorum, which meets merely to study lessons, only partially accomplishes its purpose," its manual chastized, adding, "A quorum that is not more attractive to its members than any club, has missed its opportunity."[62] And so, the emphasis became outward activity, rather than inward spirituality as manifested

---

57. See Linda King Newell, "A Gift Given, a Gift Taken: Washing, Anointing, and Blessing the Sick among Mormon Women." *Sunstone* 6, no. 4 (1981):16–25.

58. See Kathleen Flake, *The Politics of American Religious Identity: The Seating of Senator Reed Smoot, Mormon Apostle* (Chapel Hill: University of North Carolina Press, 2004).

59. Joseph F. Smith, April 6, 1906, *76th Annual Conference of the Church of Jesus Christ of Latter-day Saints* (Salt Lake City: Deseret News, 1906), 3.

60. J. Golden Kimball, in ibid., 19.

61. See William Hartley, "The Priesthood Reform Movement, 1908–1922," *Brigham Young University Studies* 13, no. 2 (Winter 1973): 137–56; and Richard O. Cowan, "The Priesthood-Auxiliary Movement, 1928–1938," *Brigham Young University Studies* 19, no. 1 (Fall 1978): 106–20.

62. *A Guide for Quorums of the Melchizedek Priesthood* (Salt Lake City: Deseret Book, 1928), 3.

through gifts of the Holy Spirit. (Perhaps it was no coincidence that Heber J. Grant, who was a businessman prior to becoming Church president in 1918, emphasized easily quantifiable metrics instead of spirituality.) And along the way, the exercise of such spiritual gifts was gradually de-emphasized among the women.[63]

Conclusion

In looking at options and hopes, it is instructive to examine the closest historical parallel to the ordination of women, and that is the ordination of blacks. The comparisons are intriguing:

- In each case there has been an on again/off again aspect. With blacks, there was ordination through the lifetime of Joseph Smith, then no ordination for over a century (although the priesthood of previously ordained blacks continued to be honored), and then, in 1978, ordination once again became part of Church functioning. With women there was the exercise of gifts of the Spirit and the performance of ordinances, albeit not to the same extent as the male priesthood, throughout the nineteenth century, followed by the curtailment of those functions in the early twentieth century, although some functions such as washings and anointings in temples have continued uninterrupted. Thus, in neither instance has there been a consistent policy through time.

- Full ordination was not the only option in either case. In the case of blacks, as the First Presidency was considering, in the early 1960s, if and how to establish a mission in Nigeria, Hugh B. Brown, First Counselor in the First Presidency, suggested a halfway position:

    > I wonder if the time is coming when we will give the Lesser Priesthood to them. Whether the prohibition or direction with respect to the priesthood upon which we rely applies to both the Melchizedek and the Aaronic priesthood I have never thought of it before, but I wonder if we give them the Aaronic Priesthood, and then they could administer the Sacrament and baptize under the direction of the missionaries, but that is a matter I do not know about.[64]

There is far from a consensus as to the status that women should achieve within the Church. A 2011 survey by the Pew Research Center showed that 90 percent of Mormon women opposed the ordination of women,[65] although many more favor a greater voice than they are now allowed,

---

63. Newell, *A Gift Given*.

64. Hugh B. Brown, First Presidency minutes, January 9, 1962, in David O. McKay diaries of the same date, Special Collections, Marriott Library, University of Utah.

65. Michael Lipka, "Big Majority of Mormons (including Women) Opposed Women in Priesthood," Pew Research Center, October 8, 2013, http://www.pewresearch.org/fact-tank/2013/10/08/big-majority-of-mormons-oppose-women-in-priesthood-including-women/ (accessed December 26, 2014). For critiques of this survey and its interpretation, see Chapters 14–16 in this volume.

as described in other chapters of this book. Options short of ordination either to the male priesthood or to a female counterpart are offered in Neylan McBaine's recent book.[66]

- In both instances, Church leaders all the way to the top said with confidence that the *status quo* would be maintained. One statement by Brigham Young is sufficient to illustrate the case with respect to blacks and priesthood: "That curse will remain upon them, and they never can hold the Priesthood or share in it until all the other descendants of Adam have received the promises and enjoyed the blessings of the Priesthood and the keys thereof."[67] Similarly strong statements concerning ordination of women are described in other chapters of this book. (See, esp. Chapters 1, 4, and 7.)

- Finally, it is instructive to note that forces external to the Church hierarchy were not effective in ending the ban on ordination of blacks. Neither the opposition from the NAACP, nor boycotts of BYU athletic events, nor countless pleas from Church members were sufficient to move the needle. Indeed, one could make a case that the reaction of the hierarchy to actual or perceived "frontal assaults" was to dig in deeper in order to preserve a *status quo* that they felt to be divinely sanctioned. Only when *internal* forces—in the form of the announced Brazilian temple,[68] and Spencer Kimball's compulsion to take the gospel to all of the world, including black Africa—did he challenge the policy in a way from which it had previously been immune. Similarly, external forces pushing for female ordination have thus far been met by opposition that is both reactive—that is, digging in and restating orthodoxy in a loud voice—and repressive, as exemplified by the excommunication of Kate Kelly. But at the same time Church leaders are reacting negatively to the external forces, internal pressure for change is mounting, perhaps most persuasively in the form of quiet defections from Church activity and even Church membership, as detailed in other chapters of this book. It is the internal pressures that are likely to summon the prophetic voice, in the same manner that earlier internal pressures summoned that voice in 1978.

Two points emerge from this walk through history. One is that both the nature and the structure of priesthood have been fluid since the Restoration began in 1829; and although the pace of change was quickest in the earlier years, substantive change continued throughout the twentieth century—and, indeed,

---

66. Neylan McBaine, *Women at Church: Magnifying LDS Women's Local Impact* (Salt Lake City: Greg Kofford Books, 2014).

67. Brigham Young, October 9, 1859, *Journal of Discourses* 7:290–1.

68. Because most ordinances performed in LDS temples require that the male hold the Melchizedek Priesthood, and because Brazil is so thoroughly mixed race, it would have been cumbersome at best and impossible at worst to keep the temple operating.

continues to this day. The implication should be obvious: There never was a time when priesthood was an unchangeable monolith.

The second point is that priesthood has always been a sum of its parts, but those parts have changed over time and have not always been restricted to ordained men. Witness the gifts of the Holy Spirit that were openly exercised by women for over a century, and the ordinances that today are performed in temples by women who are set apart for that purpose. Things that have or have not been considered ordinances at one point have moved in the opposite direction at other points—consider the dedication of graves, which moved from no to yes; and cursing, which moved from yes to no—and the gender of the person performing the action has not always been male. Therefore, options for women in the Church today are not limited to the simplistic request/demand: "We want to be ordained to the priesthood." And if past is prologue, the certitude of former prophets regarding an outright ban on ordination of blacks suggests caution in predicting the future of women, for current revelation trumps previous revelation.

Chapter 11

Disciplinary Councils: Excommunication and Community in the Modern Church

Robert A. Rees

This [Magna Carta] has been forced from the King. It constitutes an insult to the Holy See, a serious weakening of the royal power, a disgrace to the English nation, a danger to all Christendom, since this civil war obstructs the crusade. Therefore, we condemn the charter and forbid the King to keep it, or the barons and their supporters to make him do so, on pain of excommunication. —Pope Innocent III originally Lotario de' Conti di Segni , Papal Bull, August 24, 1215

I

"Excommunication" is word that can stir fear in the heart of a believer or of someone who finds herself at significant odds with her faith community either because of serious transgression or resulting from a dramatic departure from established doctrine and practice. Although considered by some "a medieval anachronism,"[1] excommunication nevertheless is an established ecclesiastical punishment among some religions, including in the Catholic, Lutheran, Jewish, and Latter-day Saint traditions. According to Matt Slick, in the Christian tradition, excommunication is defined as "the action . . . administered upon a Church member who has refused to repent of his sin and/or who has refused to recant of heretical teaching. This action is the final step of a formal and public removal of the person from the Christian church where the Lord's Supper (Communion) is denied to the person and where pronouncement [is made] that the person is not a member of the body of Christ."[2]

Excommunication carries the weight of history including the dark days of the Inquisition when popes excommunicated kings, emperors, and high Catholic clergy and the internecine conflicts of the Protestant Reformation when the list of excommunicants included such luminaries as Martin Luther, Henry VIII, Queen Elizabeth, and Thomas Cranmer, the Archbishop of Canterbury. Other

---

1. Lester Bush Jr., "Excommunication and Church Courts: A Note from the General Handbook of Instructions," *Dialogue: A Journal of Mormon Thought* 14, no. 2 (Summer 1981): 75. Bush attributes the quotation to Catholic television host Phil Donohue.

2. Matthew Slick, "What Is Excommunication?" https://www.google.com/search?q=matthew+slick+excommunication&rlz=1C1CHFX_enUS563US563&oq=matthew+slick+excommunication&aqs=chrome..69i57.6396j1j1&sourceid=chrome&ie=UTF-8 (accessed February 12, 2015).

famous excommunicants include Napoleon, Fidel Castro, Juan Peron, Jacqueline Kennedy Onassis and a host of bishops, archbishops, and cardinals. And in 1054, the Catholic Pope Leo IX and Orthodox Patriarch of Constantinople, Michael Cerularius, actually excommunicated one another. More recently, Pope Francis excommunicated an entire class of Catholics—the Mafia.

Excommunication also has a long history among the Latter-day Saints beginning early in the Church's history when a number of top leaders, including seven members of the original Quorum of the Twelve Apostles, were excommunicated.[3] Since then excommunication has been a part of the repertoire of the LDS Church's disciplinary actions. As with Catholics and other religions, Mormons have their list of illustrious excommunicants. In addition to a number of apostles and other top leaders, these include Samuel Brannon, Butch Cassidy, Fawn Brody, Sonia Johnson, a group known as "the September Six,"[4] and, most recently, feminist Kate Kelly.

II

Instructions and guidelines governing the holding of disciplinary councils are found in Chapter 6 of the *Church Handbook of Instruction, Volume 1: Stake Presidencies and Bishoprics* (Salt Lake City: Church of Jesus Christ of Latter-day Saints, 2010). This volume is severely restricted to priesthood leaders above a certain status level, in contrast, while *Handbook 2: Administering the Church*, provides instructions for managing meetings and leading the auxiliaries. It is readily available at Church Distribution Centers and online.

The restricted *Volume I* specifies three categories of ecclesiastical punishment: "Mandatory," "may be appropriate" and "is not appropriate." Transgressions listed under "Mandatory" include murder, incest, apostasy, and "serious transgression while holding a prominent church position." Such transgressions are defined as "attempted murder, rape, sexual abuse, spouse abuse, intentional serious physical injury of others, adultery, fornication, homosexual relations, deliberate abandonment of family responsibilities, robbery, burglary, theft, embezzlement, sale of illicit drugs, fraud, perjury, and false swearing." Some may find it disturbing that some of the transgressions requiring mandatory councils for leaders (including attempted murder, rape, and sexual abuse) are optional for ordinary members.

Formal "Church councils" may be necessary for "serious transgression (as defined above), abortion (but only under certain conditions), and transsexual operations. They are not appropriate for non-payment of tithes and debts, laxity in observing the Word of Wisdom, and not attending meetings.

A disciplinary council has four possible outcomes: no action, probation, disfellowshipment, and excommunication, which "is the most serious sanction a

---

3. See William Shepard and H. Michael Marquardt, *Lost Apostles: Forgotten Members of Mormonism's Original Quorum of Twelve* (Salt Lake City: Signature Books, 2014).

4. http://www.lds-mormon.com/sepsix.shtml (accessed February 14, 2025).

disciplinary council can impose and is generally reserved for only the most severe offences."[5] The handbook is regarded by some leaders as a set of guidelines and by others as a list of instructions. Although Latter-day Saints have a top-down leadership, with the exception of mandated transgressions, excommunications are, by and large, left up to local ecclesiastical leaders, which means that one bishop or stake president may excommunicate a number of members during his tenure while leaders in another ward and stake may excommunicate few or none.

III

When I became bishop of the Los Angeles First (Singles') Ward in 1982, I didn't know much about being a bishop, but I did know that, except under the most extreme circumstances, I wasn't going to excommunicate anyone. I did hold disciplinary councils during my tenure as bishop and, given human nature and the nature of singles' wards, placed some members on probation and disfellowshipped a few others, but I did not excommunicate anyone—nor, in the case of serious transgressions by a Melchizedek Priesthood holder, refer such an action to a stake council.

I had three reasons for making such a decision about excommunication. The first, knowing something of the history of disciplinary councils in the Church, was based on my awareness that when someone is excommunicated, it often leads to a *de facto* excommunication of his or her family and, in some cases, even friends and acquaintances. This is especially so when the excommunication involves ideology or matters of doctrine and policy rather than sexual or moral transgression. A serious sexual or moral transgression often involves a breach of trust within the family, while an excommunication over doctrinal or policy issues involves a break with the Church itself. Thus, it is not uncommon in the latter case for the spouse, children, and other family members of the excommunicant to feel that they, too, have been excommunicated (and sometimes their congregations treat them so). That is, since excommunication severs eternal bonds or sealings, others in the family besides the person being excommunicated are dramatically affected (and, one could argue, in some cases even punished) by such disciplinary action. While such severing may be justified in cases of the serious violation of marital covenants or family relationships (for example, serial adultery, incest, or abuse), it is less true for other kinds of issues.

My second reason for taking a cautious stance toward excommunication, again based on my knowledge of Church history, is that an excommunication in one generation often leads to successive generations being disconnected or disassociated from the Church, which is a very high price for both the family and the Church to pay, although, again, this may be a price that has to be paid in extreme cases. For example, I would consider such a case to be a member who is

---

5. http://en.wikipedia.org/wiki/Disciplinary_council#When_a_disciplinary_council_is_mandatory (accessed February 11, 2015).

in open, public rebellion against the Church. The main reason for such an effect is that the person who is excommunicated generally constructs a narrative that, fairly or unfairly, casts the Church in an unfavorable light. Thus, in perpetuating the justification for alienation, the effects of excommunication can be kept alive from generation to generation. An extreme spiritual example is the hostility of Laman and Lemuel toward Nephi in the Book of Mormon which shows how hatred infected the descendents of these brothers for nearly a thousand years. While some who have been accused of apostasy and excommunicated on that charge return to the Church, most, especially if they feel they have been wrongly accused or unjustly treated, never come back.

I haven't checked the records of the Church for verification, but it is likely that my great-grandfather, David L. Rees, was excommunicated from the Church. I speculate that he suffered this action because he had serious conflicts over doctrine (including the temple ceremony) at a time when such conflicts were not well tolerated. Also, he possessed some kind of seer stone through which he saw "strange manifestations," including an angelic apparition, which Brigham Young dismissed as "a swamp angel." Unhappy with Brigham's scoffing response, David left the Church, affiliated with the "Josephites" (Reorganized Church), and later joined Sidney Rigdon's splinter group, becoming one of Rigdon's twelve apostles.[6] Any one of these actions might have been grounds for excommunication. I cite David Rees because, in contrast, his brother, Joseph Alexander Rees, remained faithful to the Church and has a large, active LDS progeny. Only a small handful of David's descendants are members of the Church—all, by the way, as a consequence of later, independent conversions, not because of his spiritual or religious influence.

I cite this personal family example not to argue that excommunication under certain circumstances may not be justified, but rather to illustrate how such disciplinary action can negatively affect future generations of the excommunicant. In this case, it was my great-grandfather's behavior, not the Church's, that has caused the vast majority of his descendants to be outside the Church.

The third reason for my attitude toward excommunication was that I also knew from both Christian and Latter-day Saint history that some excommunications, or even the threat of such action, seem (and in the judgment of history are proven to be) unjust and even arbitrary. One thinks of the Jewish philosopher Baruch Spinoza who was excommunicated for "evil opinions" and "abominable heresies," and of Mormon youth Helmuth Huebener, who was excommunicated for his opposition to Hitler and the Third Reich. While it is not possible to know all the facts of any given case, based on the best available information, some ex-

---

6. Holograph autobiography of Joseph Alexander Rees, copy in my possession.

communications seem capricious, others disproportionately punitive (as was the case for Spinoza), and, in the case of Huebener, still others politically motivated.[7]

The possibility of these almost random outcomes among Latter-day Saints is increased by the fact that the Church has a lay, professionally untrained priesthood which sometimes leads to individuals being unexpectedly thrust into positions requiring wise ecclesiastical and even psychological counseling and judgment for which often they are unprepared. A psychotherapist friend from Southern California who has twice served both as a bishop and as a member of a stake presidency, and who thus has been involved in a large number of Church councils, says he has serious reservations about councils as they are conducted in the contemporary Church: "I think we [the leadership in the wards and stakes in which he was a leader] made a fair number of mistakes or at least didn't use the occasions to optimal advantage in helping people," he commented. "When I reflect upon the whole business in some depth, I'm not sure that they are more helpful than just plain spiritual counseling, except in extreme cases. I no longer have access to the Church manuals, but the ones I had were not too helpful with respect to the redemptive process. On balance, based on my experience, I think such councils cause more problems than they cure."

For a good example of the arbitrary and inconsistent nature of Church discipline, one need look no further than the treatment of California Latter-day Saints during Proposition 8 in 2008. Some members were excommunicated for open opposition to Proposition 8,[8] while others lost their temple recommends, were put on probation, or were disfellowshipped for seemingly minor expressions of dissent (for example, wearing a rainbow pin to Church with the slogan "All Families Matter"), which in other stakes resulted in no disciplinary action—or even comment. In some stakes, individuals were disciplined for voicing opposition to Proposition 8 (which discipline was clearly counter to official Church directives), while the same behavior was ignored in other stakes. Other examples of such inconsistency are not difficult to find. At one time, adultery was often considered grounds for excommunication; today, depending on the circumstances and the ward and stake, it is less so, except in extreme cases (the person holds a high position or is unrepentant). Also, right up to the 1970s, homosexuals were excommunicated simply for being gay or lesbian, something that, hopefully, no longer happens.

Even when serious transgression is involved, justice seems to be meted out unequally, even if one accounts for individual circumstance. A number of years ago I met a man who had been a mission president in South America. As it turned out, he was gay and, by his own confession to me, had been sexually

---

7. "The Boy Who Dared," http://theboywhodared.blogspot.com/2010/11/biography-of-helmuth-hubener.html; see also Thomas F. Rogers's powerful play, *Heubener*, in his collection *Heubener and Other Plays* (Orem, Utah: Poor Robert's Publications, 1992).

8. http://www.calitics.com/showDiary.do?diaryId=7020; http://www.mindonfire.com/2009/09/09/excommunicated/ (accessed February 17, 2015).

involved with his second counselor (a young missionary) for an extended period (six months, according to my recollection). Following the young missionary's release, his continued attachment to this leader led him to have an emotional breakdown and to confess his transgression. This happened shortly after the mission president's own release (not for transgression but because his tenure had ended). When I asked what had happened to him as a result of such a serious transgression, the former mission president replied that he had been certain he would be excommunicated and was therefore surprised that he had only been disfellowshipped. This sentence seemed far too lenient a discipline, both because of his prominent position and the asymmetrical nature of their relationship, although, I am quick to add, I don't know all the particulars of this case.

Two contrasting stories with which I am personally familiar from the years I served on the Los Angeles Stake high council further illustrate the unequal administration of justice meted out in high council courts. The first involved a young gay man in his early twenties. He had been involved in a sexual relationship and was clearly conflicted about how to handle it. On the one hand, he seemed truly regretful of his behavior; on the other, he was still emotionally attached to his former lover. These events took place when the Church was teaching that homosexuality was a chosen and, therefore, a changeable condition. During the council's interrogation of this man, he revealed that he had tried to overcome his sexual feelings but had been unsuccessful in doing so. It was clear to me that he was still deeply attached to the Church and that his being called before the council was painful and embarrassing. He made it clear that he did not want to be excommunicated.

After the council had finished its questioning, as the procedure requires, the young man was excused while the stake president asked the high councilors for their observations. (The council had followed scriptural instructions to draw lots with half of the council charged with ensuring that no injustice be done to the Church and the other half ensuring that no injustice be done to the individual.) Some members of the council felt that, since the young man had been unsuccessful in disentangling himself from the relationship, he should be excommunicated. Others, including me, argued for leniency, especially since the young man professed both his regrets and his devotion to the Church. This happened during a period when gays and lesbians often were excommunicated, sometimes simply for being homosexual.[9] After listening to the high councilors, the stake presidency withdrew to deliberate on the young man's fate, then returned to announce that their decision was excommunication. When they asked the council to sustain

---

9. Beginning with the 1998 *Church Handbook of Instructions*, the language of the policy was altered significantly to specify that it it was "homosexual behavior" that might be considered grounds for a disciplinary council (see, e.g., pp. 96, 159). However, when I queried Randall Thacker, the current president of Affirmation, he responded that homosexual Saints were "still" being excommunicated simply for "being homosexual."

their decision, mine was the lone dissenting vote. Nevertheless, the young man was excommunicated and wept inconsolably as he heard this sentence.[10]

Not long after this, we held another court. This time the subject was a high councilor who had been assigned as liaison to a branch with a minority population of which he had been the previous president. He had become sexually involved with a young woman in his congregation. In this case, the decision was to put this brother on probation, which seemed to me far too lenient a discipline, again considering his ecclesiastical position and the differences in their ages. I concluded that the level of discipline was likely influenced by our close association with this brother.

Another factor that complicates excommunications is that conditions that might justify such an action during one period may seem (and actually be) trivial in another. For example, an ancestor of my late wife was excommunicated in southern Idaho for buying diaper flannel for their new baby from the gentile store instead of at ZCMI, the Church's store. He had, in fact, attempted to buy the material from ZCMI, but the store did not have the fabric in stock. He therefore purchased it from the only other supplier available, pointing out the obvious defense: "Caroline [his wife] needed flannel for our baby, and I bought her flannel."

Church history is replete with examples of such excommunications. I acknowledge that such things happened at a time and place and under conditions very different from those that prevail in the modern Church and that excommunicants were often quickly rebaptized; nevertheless, examples in the modern Church sometimes recall that earlier period. For example, when I was teaching at UCLA in the 1970s, a friend, one of the best reference librarians I have ever known, was excommunicated because of the insensitivity (really, stupidity), of an aggressive home teacher. My friend came from a Latter-day Saint family of some distinction. She was of pioneer heritage, one of whose relatives eventually became president of the Church. When she hadn't been to church in some years (she was married to a non-member), her home teacher offended her by saying that if she didn't choose to be active, perhaps she should have her name removed from the records of the Church. Hurt by his bullying challenge, she replied that perhaps she should. He promptly followed up by seeing that the bishop's court took place. Dismayed and deeply hurt, she told me that she didn't really want to be excommunicated and that the action left her alienated from the Church and broke her mother's heart.

IV

Church disciplinary councils require those who conduct them, especially bishops and stake presidents who make the ultimate decision, to have both sound judgment and abundant charity, especially because few things (including some

---

10. Some years later, a son of one of the leaders committed suicide. Some of those close to the family speculated that he was gay.

particulars of Mormon doctrine) remain constant. On some subjects, the truth is rarely perfectly settled—even for prophets—as a cursory review of Church history confirms. We need to remind ourselves that, as a Church, our doctrines and teachings have not always been consistent or constant. For example, in the nineteenth century, the Quorum of the Twelve tried to excommunicate one of its members, Orson Pratt, for teaching that God was omniscient since Brigham Young and the rest of the Quorum contended that God was still progressing in knowledge.[11] A little over a hundred years later, Apostle Bruce R. McConkie, in harmony with Orson Pratt's understanding, condemned as one of the seven heresies of Mormonism what Elder Pratt's fellow apostles and the prophet himself believed and taught. One can find similar dichotomous official positions over time, including those on blacks and the priesthood and the etiology of homosexuality, to name just two.

Given human nature and the evolution of thought, such a phenomenon should not be surprising. Joseph Smith's contemporary, Theodore Parker, observed in his treatise, *A Discourse on the Transient and Permanent in Christianity*, "The heresy of one age is the orthodox belief and 'only infallible rule' of the next. Now Arius, and now Athanasius [third century disputants over the nature of the Trinity] is Lord of the ascendant. Both were excommunicated in their turn, each for affirming what the other denied. Men are burned for professing what men are burned for denying."[12] Women too, as the case of Joan of Arc exemplifies: She was excommunicated and burned at the stake in 1421, beatified in 1909 and canonized in 1920. With the Maid of Orleans, Huebener and Galileo (who, although not excommunicated, was "vehemently suspected of heresy" and required to "abjure, curse and detest " his own scientific findings under the threat of excommunication), the justification for excommunication was ultimately reversed. For Hubener, it took decades and for Galileo and Joan of Arc centuries.

Not long after I became bishop, I interviewed a woman who was living with a non-member. Finding that she was a returned missionary and therefore endowed, I called her to repentance and told her that she had to either marry the man or end the relationship. She replied that she was willing to marry but that her lover was not. She also said that she felt she should stay in the relationship. As a new bishop, I understood that it was my duty to press her to decide between two moral choices, neither of which included maintaining the status quo. I gave her time to make her decision and, when she refused to end the relationship, told her that I had no choice but to hold a court, thinking that in this instance I might have to surrender my previous inclination against excommunication. However, surprisingly, I did nothing. I was not completely comfortable doing so, but some-

---

11. D. Michael Quinn, "150 Years of Truth and Consequences about Mormon History," *Sunstone* 16, no. 1 (February 1992): 13.

12. "Theodore Parker," American Transcendental Web; http://transcendentalism-legacy.tamu.edu/authors/parker/transient.html (accessed February 26, 2015).

thing prevented me from taking disciplinary action against this woman. Not long afterward, this sister passed the age qualifying her for membership in a singles' ward and moved to another ward in the stake. A number of years later while visiting that ward, I attended a Sunday School class that I found particularly inspiring and well taught and afterwards took time to convey my sentiments to the teacher. When I was finished, she said, "You don't remember me, do you?" I told her I didn't, and then she reminded me of our earlier encounters. I told her about my ambivalence regarding her case. She said, "I'm glad you didn't do anything. The man I was living with joined the Church and recently we were married in the temple." I cite this example not to validate my inaction (since action is often required) or even to assert that it was inspired, but rather to illustrate that in such matters one cannot always rely on precedent or the *Handbook of Instructions*, as useful as both might be in particular cases.

V

What I worry about with the recent excommunication of Kate Kelly and the threatened disciplinary actions against others is the negative impact such actions likely will have on these Saints, their families and friends, and also on the Church itself. Of course, I do not know all the particulars of their individual cases and am not their ecclesiastical leader, but my impulse is to defend the process in which these Saints and many others like them are engaged as faithful expressions of their devotion to both the Church and the gospel and therefore not classifiable as rebellion or heresy.

Based on available information (which I admit may not be complete or completely accurate), it seems that Kate Kelly's behavior and actions do not fit the *General Handbook*'s definition of apostasy: Members who can be considered apostate are those who: "repeatedly act in clear, open and deliberate public opposition to the Church or its leaders; persist in teaching as Church doctrine information that is not Church doctrine after they have been corrected by their bishop or higher authority; continue to follow the teachings of apostate sects (such as those that advocate plural marriage) after being corrected by their bishop or higher authority; or formally join another church and advocate its teachings" (*Handbook*, Section 6.7.3; reformatted from list to paragraph). From what Kelly herself reports, she was not engaged in teachings contrary to Church doctrine or acting in "in clear, open, and deliberate public opposition to the Church or its leaders," but rather was calling on leaders to seek divine guidance concerning the question of women's ordination.

Hugh Nibley translated John 1:1 as: "In the beginning was the Logos (counsel, discussion), and the Logos was in the presence of God, and all things were done according to it."[13] It was a desire to engage in dialogue that led Joseph into

---

13. Hugh Nibley, "Beyond Politics," publications.maxwellinstitute.byu.edu/publications/review/23/1/S00011-51769fefbeee911Nibley.pdf (accessed February 28, 2015).

the Sacred Grove. It was the same desire that caused him to say, "We deem it a just principle . . . that all men [and women] are created equal, and that all have the privilege of thinking for themselves upon all matters relative to conscience. Consequently, then, we are not disposed, had we the power, to deprive any one of exercising that independence of mind which heaven has so graciously bestowed upon the human family as one of its choicest gifts."[14] Relative to disputes over matters of doctrine, the Prophet said, "It looks too much like the Methodists [although, one hastens to add, not today's Methodists], and not like the Latter-day Saints. Methodists have a creed which a man must believe or be asked out of their church. I want the liberty of thinking and believing as I please. It feels so good not to be trammeled. It does not prove that a man [or woman] is not a good man [or woman] because he [or she] errs in doctrine."[15]

Perhaps it would be helpful if the Church were to make a distinction between transgressions against others (such as adultery, rape, abuse, and embezzlement) and the kinds of activities having to do with doctrine. The first kind is rarely ambiguous; the second often is. In situations where a spouse has been unfaithful or a serious crime has been committed, the individual generally knows he or she has done something wrong and may be looking for forgiveness and reconciliation. A council called for such a person might indeed be experienced as a court of love.

The principles governing councils convened to excommunicate someone for heresy or apostasy may be entirely different. Those accused of such transgressions generally do not believe they have done anything wrong. In fact, it is not unusual for them to express sincere love for the Church and feel that their actions are a reflection of devotion rather than rebellion. Many in this category act out of what they consider integrity of thought and belief. They often feel, or at least hope, that they are making a positive contribution to the Church. An example from the past is those who were excommunicated over opposition to the Church's stand on blacks and the priesthood. If disciplined, especially harshly, such members are not likely to be open to changing their minds, especially if they are excommunicated and their excommunication made public. Generally, such people leave the Church; but even if they continue to attend, they are unlikely to recognize that what they have done constitutes grounds for draconian punishment and, if excommunicated, are unlikely to consider rebaptism. Being cast out, such per-

---

14. Joseph Smith et al., *History of the Church of Jesus Christ of Latter-day Saints*, 7 vols., edited by B. H. Roberts, 2d ed. rev. (Salt Lake City: Deseret Book, 1902–32), 2:6–7. The document reproduced is from "The Elders of the Church in Kirtland, to Their Brethren Abroad," January 22, 1834, published in *The Evening and the Morning Star*, February 1834, 135; and reproduced in *Teachings of Presidents of the Church: Joseph Smith* (Salt Lake City: Church of Jesus Christ of Latter-day Saints, 2011), 339–48; e-edition at https://www.lds.org/manual/print/teachings-joseph-smith/chapter-29?lang=eng#12-36481_000_033 (accessed March 1, 2015).

15. *History of the Church*, 5:340; also available at https://byustudies.byu.edu/hc/hcpgs/hc.aspx (accessed March 1, 2015).

sons are more likely to act defensively and in fact may feel compelled to retaliate against the Church for what they consider unjust treatment.

Perhaps the current cases are more complicated than what has been reported in the media and on the internet. One could argue that these cases are not about heterodoxy per se—not about freedom of conscience, freedom of expression, or an unwillingness by the Church to engage in dialogue. Rather, it may seem that they have generated movements that challenge the authority of the apostles and prophets. If what has been done rises to the level of apostasy (however these individuals' leaders choose to define it),[16] then how to address their future relationship with the Church is a matter of extreme importance, complicated by the fact that some under consideration for discipline have large constituencies who may come to the defense of the accused making the Church's response more challenging.

At a time when the Church is dealing with what some characterize as a "crisis of faith," any decision could have broad and possibly dramatic consequences. The excommunication of such individuals has the potential to engender an eruption of invective against the Church. An example of such negative publicity can be seen in Cadence Woodland's op-ed piece, "The End of the 'Mormon Moment,'" in the *New York Times* shortly after Kelly's excommunication. Woodland, a disaffected Mormon, writes,

> The church will continue to lose members like me until it realizes that messages about diversity and inclusion are hollow when excommunication and censorship are the responses to dissent. While the church invests in missionary work, especially overseas, an unwelcoming posture is likely to hinder its growth. The true legacy of the Mormon Moment might just be that the church was given the chance that many religious institutions desperately need to stay relevant in the 21st century: the opportunity to open itself to criticism and inquiry. The church has chosen not to. And it has killed its own moment by doing so.[17]

Whether Woodland's assessment is correct, I think it reflects the sentiments of a growing number of people both inside and outside the Church. Excommunication in the age of the internet clearly has consequences that it didn't have before that technological invention.

Mormonism emerged from a context of doubt and dissent which opened the way for heavenly visitations and revelations. Much of Mormonism's progress has been propelled by this same process—the human quest for truth, which is always slow, stumbling and imperfect but which leads to the eventual opening of the heavens. Revelation does not happen in a vacuum; the heart and soul must be

---

16. According to the Church's website, "Church authorities excommunicate a person from the Church only when he has chosen to live in opposition to the Lord's commandments and thus has disqualified himself for further membership in the Church." https://www.lds.org/scriptures/gs/excommunication (accessed February 11, 2015).

17. Cadence Woodland, "The End of the 'Mormon Moment," *New York Times*, July 15, 2014, http://www.nytimes.com/2014/07/15/opinion/the-end-of-the-mormon-moment.html (accessed March 12, 2015).

prepared to receive them, and that often means the messy process of doubting and questioning, of sifting and winnowing, and even at times challenging authority.

I was not called to be Kate Kelly's ecclesiastical judge; but from all I have read and understood, had I been so, I would not have found that she merited excommunication In fact, I suspect I would have been, like most bishops, relieved when she moved out of my ward and therefore my jurisdiction. Like many in our history, she was asking her leaders to seek revelation on a subject of legitimate concern to a large segment of Latter-day Saints: Is it possible for women to be ordained to the priesthood? It was a question, not an assertion or a declaration. It seems to have been asked both sincerely and respectfully, although I hasten to add that not everyone agrees with such a characterization. It was certainly a challenging question given the long history of patriarchy and male priesthood dominance, especially in light of the lessons we have learned "by sad experience"—that "it is the nature and disposition of *almost all men*, as soon as they get a little authority, *as they suppose*, they will immediately begin to exercise unrighteous dominion" (D&C 121:39; emphasis mine).

"The nature *and* disposition" of the majority of men. In other words, given this revealed reality of male propensity, it is inevitable that many priesthood holders (the ones at whom this revelation was directed) will exercise unrighteous dominion. And in a world of historical asymmetrical power between men and women, it is inevitable that women have been the subject of much of that dominion. Anyone who doubts this has not listened to the laments of Latter-day Saint women—not all women, by any stretch of the imagination, but enough so that those cries constitute a collective *crie de coeur*, one which God expects us, especially the holders of the priesthood, to listen to, understand, and respond to—with all of the specified, required virtues of the priesthood: "by persuasion, by long-suffering, by gentleness and meekness, and [especially] by love unfeigned; by kindness and pure knowledge, which shall greatly enlarge the soul without hypocrisy and without guile" (D&C 121:41–42). And it is only *after* a priesthood leader manifests all of these virtues that he is permitted to reprove "betimes" (meaning "while there is yet time"[18]) "with sharpness" ("discernment," "understanding," and "perception").[19] And then this powerful caveat—"when moved upon by the Holy Ghost" and, even more important, "showing forth afterwards an increase of love toward him [or her] whom thou hast reproved" (121:43). Lest

---

18. S.v. "betimes," *Oxford English Dictionary*, 1887; OED Online version, September 2014. http://www.oed.com/view/Entry/18317?rskey=KKgOZU&result=7&isAdvanced=false# (accessed March 11, 2015). According to Kent P. Jackson and Robert D. Hunt, in Joseph Smith's time a common connotation of "betimes" was "in good season or time." Jackson and Hunt, "Reprove, Betimes, and Sharpness in the Vocabulary of Joseph Smith," *Religious Educator*, 6, no. 2 (2005), http://rsc.byu.edu/archived/volume-6-number-2-2005/reprove-betimes-and-sharpness-vocabulary-joseph-smith (accessed March 10, 2015).

19. Among the definitions Jackson and Hunt cite from Webster's 1828 dictionary, the following seem to be most in keeping with the spirit of this revelation: "acuteness of intellect; the power of . . . discernment; quickness of understanding" and "quickness of sense or perception."

we forget the other conditionals associated with the exercise of priesthood, even after all of these requirements of the priesthood, there is yet one more: "Let thy bowels be full of charity towards all men [and women], and to the household of faith [the Church]." "Household" in the Greek likely meant, a place like the home.[20] That is, a congregant should be treated with the same kindness, respect, and love she deserves to receive in her home.

We are a church that believes in continuing revelation and that Christ's followers "should be engaged in a good cause, and do many things of their own free will and . . . bring to pass much righteousness" (D&C 58:27) because God will "yet reveal many great and important things pertaining to the Kingdom of God" (Articles of Faith 9).

VI

I think it is safe to say that most Latter-day Saints know bishops and stake presidents who likely would not have taken action against some of those recently excommunicated or who have been served with notice of councils, just as we know leaders who likely would not have taken action against some high-profile cases from the past. In other words, as in all human endeavors, there is often less than perfect judgment in such matters (which is not to say that judgment in any particular case has been or will be faulty). This is why, whoever is in the place of making such an ultimate decision regarding Church discipline must call upon the powers of heaven and have pure intent to receive whatever direction comes, erring on the side of compassion for the individual under threat of discipline.

Whatever a given case and whatever its outcome, I believe that it is enjoined upon all of us to pray for hope, faith, and charity—for them, for their families, and for their ecclesiastical leaders. Especially to pray for charity, which, as Moroni reminds us, is the "pure love of Christ." If Church councils are indeed "courts of love," as they were earlier known and are often still called, then there may be no greater call for the pure love of Christ to be manifest than in such councils.

In my classes at Graduate Theological Union, my students and I often talk of things in one another's religion for which we have "holy envy." One Catholic practice I envy has to do with excommunication. In most instances, a Catholic can be excommunicated (meaning experiencing certain limitations imposed on his or her religious practice and behavior), but he or she does not cease to be Catholic. In other words, excommunication suspends but does not sever one's relationship with the Church, which leaves the way back into full fellowship easier and therefore more likely.[21] This

---

20. "Galatians 6:10," *Bible Hub,* http://biblehub.com/commentaries/galatians/6-10.htm (accessed March 8, 2015).

21. In an article titled, "Getting Excommunicated Is Much Harder Than You Think," Fr. Alexander Lucie-Smith writes, "The excommunications above [those of Queen Elizabeth and Archbishop Joseph Lefebre] are unambiguous, in that they are made so by a papal decree. The Code of Canon Law lays down that there are two forms of excommunication. The first is *sententiae ferendae.* This is where the person excommunicated is subject to a

understanding of Catholic excommunication is the result of a 1983 change in canon law and represents to me a more enlightened and compassionate view of this extreme form of ecclesiastical discipline. Under such a system, "Catholics—unless they cease for some other reason to belong to the Church—are still Catholics and remain bound by obligations such as attending Mass, even though they are barred from receiving the Eucharist and from taking an active part in the liturgy (reading, bringing the offerings, etc.). They are urged to retain a relationship with the Church, as the goal is to encourage them to repent and return to active participation in its life."[22] According to the *Catholic Encyclopedia*, excommunication is "a medicinal rather than a vindictive penalty, being intended, not so much to punish the culprit, as to correct him and bring him back to the path of righteousness. It necessarily, therefore, contemplates the future, either to prevent the recurrence of certain culpable acts that have grievous external consequences, or, more especially, to induce the delinquent to satisfy the obligations incurred by his offence."[23]

Given the more complicated world in which we live, it seems to me that redefining excommunication is something the Church of Jesus Christ of Latter-day Saints should consider. Following the example of Catholics, Latter-day Saints who are deemed guilty of a significant violation of Church doctrine or practice could be subject to severe restrictions on their membership, but not lose their membership and therefore not be required to be rebaptized. Based on the experience of many who have been excommunicated in the past, when a Latter-day Saint is excommunicated, often he or she is shunned or ostracized, and thus experiences the literal meaning of ex-communication—cut off from communion (meaning both the communion of the sacrament and the community itself). Often such individuals are treated as strangers and foreigners, or even as enemies or contaminated members to be avoided. But according to the Savior's seminal sermon in Matthew 25, Jesus puts himself in the place of the excommunicant—who often is among those considered "the least." Whatever happens with current and future cases, my earnest hope is that, by both fellow members and the Church itself, the subjects will be seen not as "strangers and foreigners, but fellow citizens with the saints, and of the household of God" (Eph. 2:19), as we, their brothers and sisters, enfold them in the arms of our love and fellowship them, mourning with them and thus witnessing to them the abundance of both God's love and ours.

---

canonical process or trial, and if found guilty of misdemeanors meriting excommunication is duly sentenced. Once the sentence is published, that person is no longer a member of the Catholic Church. But this is a rare event." *Catholic Herald*, posted July 12, 2013, http://www.catholicherald.co.uk/features/2013/07/12/getting-excommunicated-is-much-harder-than-you-think/ (accessed March 1, 2015).

22. "Excommunication," http://en.wikipedia.org/wiki/Excommunication (accessed March 15, 2015).

23. "Excommunication," *Catholic Encyclopedia*, http://www.newadvent.org/cathen/05678a.htm (accessed February 1, 2015).

Chapter 12

Church Discipline and the Excommunication of Kate Kelly

Nadine McCombs Hansen

Excommunication from the Church of Jesus Christ of Latter-day Saints is often an act of spiritual violence masquerading as an act of "love." In fact, Church leaders euphemistically call disciplinary councils "courts of love."[1] While voluntary participation in such proceedings for a recognized and regretted act, such as adultery, can be a healing process for some, when done on grounds of "apostasy" over matters of conscience, its primary purpose is to silence and marginalize, not to love or redeem.[2] As an attorney, I have been engaged for much of my adult life with the rule of law—with its attempts to impose justice, invoke mercy, and bring order to the complicated and competing claims of individual rights brought face to face with larger demands of society. The two branches of civil and criminal law have their own rules, their own judges, and their own appeals and limitations. Most Americans have at least a rough idea that obedience to law safeguards the obedient, that breaking the law must be proved by the due process of law, and that the right to a vigorous defense aspires to fairness. But this American understanding of law and justice for Latter-day Saints subjected to Church discipline, growing out of three thousand years of Judeo-Christian religious law, can leave them handicapped. Other churches have developed full systems of "canon law" to interpret claims and work toward justice. Latter-day Saints have stopped far short of Church lawyers and skilled pleaders in canon law, by assigning the role of "common judge in Israel" to a bishop or stake president who can easily be mystified, baffled, and thwarted in an attempt to deal justly

---

1. Although the official term has been "disciplinary council" since 1989, Mike Otterson, managing director of LDS Public Affairs, was quoted on August 26, 2014, as saying: "He will not speak specifically about Ms Kelly's case, but he insists that the excommunication process is always fair, conducted locally, and decided only after careful consideration. 'We often refer to these proceedings as courts of love.' he says." Qtd. in Jane Little, "Push to Ordain Mormon Women Leads to Excommunication," BBC News, August 26, 2014, http://www.bbc.com/news/magazine-28890069.

2. *Church Handbook of Instructions*, Vol. 1 (Salt Lake City: Church of Jesus Christ of Latter-day Saints, 2010), 57; hereafter cited as *CHI* or *Handbook*, and by the relevant section in Chapter 6. All quotations are from the 2010 version. The second volume focuses on the workings of auxiliary organizations, describes the meetings held in a ward, and provides policies on music, conducting funerals, holding field trips for youth and children, etc. In contrast to Vol. 1, this second volume is readily available at Church distribution centers and at the Church's website. I do not quote from it in this chapter.

even if they themselves are practicing attorneys by trade. Power is seldom if ever equally distributed between the parties. Individuals are not equal before the law when one of them holds an ecclesiastical position that makes the judge, who is nearly always the accuser as well, much more powerful than the person on trial. And finally, fear, greed, and unworthy motives can swiftly capture principles of justice, making them serve the sheer demands of power.[3]

Church courts, or disciplinary councils as they have been known since the last quarter of the twentieth century, have deliberately avoided the kind of daily negotiations and mediations that were common in earlier periods, confining themselves strictly to matters involving Church membership. The excommunication of Kate Kelly on June 23, 2014, provides a very contemporary and troubling case of Church discipline brought on charges of apostasy. It demonstrates the nature of the Church's obscure and unenforceable "rules" that make arbitrary outcomes inevitable.

Robert A. Rees's chapter immediately preceding mine focuses on how excommunication impacts community in the contemporary Church, with Rees candidly and carefully exploring his own experiences as a bishop and raising troubling questions about both the strengths and weaknesses that a "common judge" must deal with. Like other Mormon women—until the policy against ordaining women to priesthood office is overturned—I will never be called to preside over or participate in one of these disciplinary councils, except perhaps as a witness or as a defendant. I was honored that my friend, Kate Kelly, herself an attorney, allowed my participation in preparing a defense when she was accused of behavior that could have left her charged with apostasy and stripped of her membership in the Church.

This episode caught tremendous media attention. (See Appendix compiled by Pamela A. Shepherd.) Kate courageously chose to step into the public spotlight, describing events as they unfolded, while her bishop and stake president confined themselves to issuing muted, restrained, and carefully drafted statements. Kate and her husband, Neil Ransom, had left their home ward in Vienna,

---

3. Historically, the Latter-day Saints had a long nineteenth-century history of having civil and criminal law used against them by religiously hostile neighbors to defraud them of money, appropriate property, and evade the consequences of physical assault, rape, and even murder. Scholarship on Mormons and the law has focused overwhelmingly on the unequal contest during the Utah period between the federal government's attempt to stamp out plural marriage and the Saints' resistance against abandoning their socially despised martial system. The best study of that period, beginning with Joseph Smith's much-contested legal affairs is Edwin B. Firmage and R. Collin Mangrum, *Zion in the Courts: A Legal History of the Church of Jesus Christ of Latter-day Saints, 1830–1900* (Urbana: University of Illinois Press, 1988), which described bishops' and high council courts. That record showed that, for the most part, Mormon communities accepted that these courts made a good-faith effort to achieve fairness, even when some of the parties were not Mormons. Comparable studies for later periods have been hard to come by, especially since most of the twentieth century has attempted to safeguard the privacy of contestants.

Virginia, and were staying with Kate's parents, Jim and Donna Kelly, in Provo, Utah, while waiting for visas to arrive. They were en route to Kenya where Neil would conduct fieldwork for his PhD. This move from Virginia to Utah made the situation geographically awkward due to the distance.

In this chapter, I discuss Church disciplinary policies from the *Church Handbook of Instructions* (*CHI* or *Handbook*), describe how those rules and policies applied to Kate Kelly, and make suggestions about the future of Church discipline.

Church Discipline Policies

Most members of the Church will have little or no need to understand how the rules of Church discipline govern a case like Kate's. Church discipline is ostensibly governed by procedures set forth in Doctrine and Covenants 102; but as a practical matter, the applicable rules are spelled out in the *Church Handbook of Instructions*, Chapter 6. By strict policy, the *Handbook* is distributed to defined Church leaders, only nine of whom–the Relief Society general presidency, the Young Women's general presidency, and the Primary general presidency—are women.[4] Instructions strictly forbid duplicating the *Handbook*, making access to most Church members, including almost all women, difficult if not impossible.[5]

The *Handbook* states that Church discipline has three purposes: (1) to "save the souls of transgressors," (2) to "protect the innocent," and (3) to "safeguard the integrity of the Church" (Section 6.1).

Discipline designed to "save the souls of transgressors" is deemed to help transgressors repent from their wrongdoing so that they will not be subjected to the eternal demands of justice. The purpose is to help them forsake sin, make restitution, and make positive changes in their lives. The assumption seems to be

---

4. *CHI*, 1:vi. Specified recipients are one copy each to General Authorities, Area Seventies, presidencies of auxiliaries, Church department heads, directors of temporal affairs; four copies to temple presidencies; three copies to mission presidencies, stake, or district presidencies and bishoprics; and one copy to stake and ward clerks and branch presidents.

5. Although the Church restricts access to the *Handbook*, it is available on the internet, via a search engine. What is not generally available are periodic updates that are distributed by letter to local Church leaders. This article uses an online version of the *Handbook* (http://www.scribd.com/doc/99798549/LDS-Church-Handbook-of-Instructions-Vol-1-2010-pdf#scribd), but I do not know whether any of the policies discussed herein have been modified by such updates. To the best of my knowledge, however, the 2010 *Handbook* is the one currently in use. The Church has gone to great lengths to protect the secrecy of this first volume of the *Church Handbook of Instructions*. In 1999, the Church's intellectual property arm, Intellectual Reserve, sued Utah Lighthouse Ministry for posting seventeen pages of the *Handbook* online without permission. The case was settled with an agreement that not only would the Lighthouse Ministry refrain from publishing quotations from the *Handbook*, but it would also refrain from posting links to any website that posts the Handbook. See Wikileaks, http://www.wikileaks.org/wiki/Mormon_Church_attempts_to_gag_Internet_over_handbook. As of April 28, 2015, all e-documents cited in this chapter were available on the internet.

that they would be unwilling to undertake such changes unless they are subjected to Church discipline (Section 6.1.1).

"Protecting the innocent" means that ecclesiastical officers use Church discipline to try to shield innocent people from predators who would inflict physical harm, sexual abuse, fraud, or apostasy (Section 6.1.2).

The Church's integrity requires disciplinary action in an attempt to "safeguard the purity, integrity, and good name of the Church," when transgressions "significantly impair the good name or moral influence of the Church." The *Handbook* gives no examples of behavior that might threaten the Church's integrity, but these behaviors apparently include "a serious transgression" by an individual "holding a prominent Church position." The purpose presumably is an effort to distance the Church from the wrongdoer's behavior (Section 6.1.3).

The *Handbook* lists various forms of Church discipline under two categories: "Informal Church Discipline" and "Formal Church Discipline." As members do not normally have access to the *Handbook*, it is very possible that they could be subjected to the initial level of informal Church discipline without even realizing that any "discipline" is actually taking place.

Informal discipline consists of "Private Counsel and Caution" (Section 6.8.1) and "Informal Probation" (6.8.2). Private counsel and caution is for "minor" transgressions for those who are "genuinely repentant." It is designed to help people take "preventive action to resist specific temptations." Such "counsel and caution" may blur the line between typical pastoral counseling and disciplinary counseling, and may or may not convey to members whether their standing in the Church is in jeopardy and whether they risk further Church discipline.

Informal probation is typically administered by the bishop and consists of restricting certain privileges of Church membership—for example, instructions to spend time daily praying and/or reading the scriptures, withdrawal of one's temple recommend, or being forbidden from praying publicly or speaking in church. It can essentially impose most of the restrictions associated with disfellowshipment, but without a formal disciplinary procedure. If the "transgressor" makes sufficient progress as a result of informal probation, the bishop can lift the probation with no further action by anyone else. If the transgressor fails to make progress, the person can be summoned to a disciplinary council.

Formal Church discipline is action taken as the outcome of a disciplinary council. It includes "Formal Probation" (Section 6.9.1), "Disfellowshipment" (Section 6.9.2), and "Excommunication" (Section 6.9.3). A disciplinary council could also decide to take no action (Section 6.10.4).

Formal probation restricts privileges of Church membership. The *Handbook* does not specify the restrictions but it could include all of the same items deployed in informal probation. The primary difference between formal and informal probation is that formal probation is the result of a disciplinary council, the bishop's counselors or stake president's counselors and high council are present for the discussion and imposition of the action, and its provisions cannot be reversed or modified unless the disciplinary council is reconvened. Also, the provisions of formal probation go on the member's record and go with him or her when he or she moves to another Church unit.

Disfellowshipment includes mandatory restrictions on Church privileges. A disfellowshipped member may not hold a temple recommend, serve in a Church position, offer a prayer in a Church meeting, take the sacrament, give a talk, teach a lesson, or participate in sustaining Church officers. Male members may not exercise the priesthood in any way. Other conditions may also be imposed, such as staying away from "evil influences," which the disciplinary council specifies, and engaging in positive conditions such as church attendance, scripture reading, personal prayer, and meeting at regular, specified intervals with the bishop. Disfellowshipped members are encouraged to wear garments, pay tithing, repent, and return to full fellowship.

Excommunication is the most severe form of Church discipline. It removes all privileges of Church membership, including revocation of all ordinances and temple blessings. Oddly, if the excommunicated member is sealed to a spouse, the transgressor's sealing blessings are revoked, but those of the "innocent spouse" are not, despite the fact that the sealing is no longer deemed to be in effect. That policy specifies:

> After a husband and wife have been sealed in the temple, if one of them is excommunicated, or has his or her name removed from Church membership records, his or her temple blessings are revoked. However, the sealing blessings of the innocent spouse and of children born in the covenant are not affected.
>
> Children who are born to a couple after one or the other has been excommunicated or had his or her name removed are not born in the covenant. (Section 3.6.2)

The *Handbook* lists situations in which a disciplinary council is not necessary, transgressions which "may" require one, and transgressions for which a disciplinary council is "mandatory." A disciplinary council is not necessary for failure to comply with such Church standards as Word of Wisdom violations, engagement with pornography, "self-abuse," and failing to pay tithing, attend Church meetings, or neglecting Church duties. Civil disputes, business failures, nonpayment of debts, and the passage of time since a past offence that could be considered serious may also render a disciplinary counsel unnecessary (Section 6.7.1).

A disciplinary council may be necessary for a "serious transgression," an abortion, or a transsexual operation. A "serious transgression" is defined as a "deliberate and major offense against morality," and includes, but is not limited to "attempted murder, forcible rape, sexual abuse, spouse abuse, intentional serious physical injury of others, adultery, fornication, homosexual relations, deliberate abandonment of family responsibilities, robbery, burglary, theft, embezzlement, sale of illegal drugs, fraud, perjury, and false swearing." Church leaders have considerable flexibility in cases of abortion. A disciplinary council is not mandatory if the abortion occurred prior to baptism, if the pregnancy resulted from forcible rape or incest, if the woman's life or health was in serious jeopardy, or if the fetus had severe and non-survivable birth defects (Section 6.7.2).

Elective transsexual operations are "discouraged." If a member contemplates such an operation and a presiding officer counsels against it, disregarding that counsel may be grounds for a disciplinary council (Section 6.7.2).

Disciplinary councils are mandatory for murder, incest, child sexual abuse, apostasy, serious transgression while holding a prominent Church position, a transgressor who is a predator, a pattern of serious transgressions, and serious transgression that is widely known (Section 6.7.3).

Those being subjected to Church discipline for matters of conscience, rather than for sinful behavior, are classed as "apostates" and are placed in the same category as murders and sexual predators. While Church authorities may believe they are acting with a redemptive motive toward such "transgressors" with the goal of helping them see the error of their ways and therefore repent, the *Handbook* is explicit that the primary motive is to protect others from what is deemed predatory behavior. It states: "The Savior taught the Nephites that they should continue to minister to a transgressor, 'but if he repent not he shall not be numbered among my people, that he may not destroy my people' (3 Nephi 18:31; see also Mosiah 26:36)" (Section 6.7.3).

The *Handbook* gives a four-part definition of apostasy. Such members:

1. Repeatedly act in clear, open and deliberate public opposition to the Church or its leaders.
2. Persist in teaching as Church doctrine information that is not Church doctrine after they have been corrected by their bishop or higher authority.
3. Continue to follow the teachings of apostate sects (such as those that advocate plural marriage) after being corrected by their bishop or higher authority.
4. Formally join another church and advocate its teachings. Priesthood leaders must take disciplinary action against apostates to protect Church members (Section 6.7.3).

Kate Kelly's Excommunication

The first public act of Ordain Women was the launch of its website. Gordon Shepherd and Gary Shepherd, intrigued by this bold new move, began copying and pasting these profiles into their own document file, updating that file weekly by checking the OW website and pasting in new profiles as they accumulated. (See Chapter 18). On March 15, 2013, the first two profiles were posted, with the site going live two days later on March 17, the highly symbolic date of the founding of the Female Relief Society in Nauvoo. Twenty-two profiles had been posted by the day's end. In October 2013, and again in April 2014, hundreds of Mormon feminists and their male allies gathered at Temple Square on the Saturday afternoon of general conference. The women were seeking admission into the all-male priesthood meeting held a half-block away in the Conference Center. The events received extensive media coverage with reporters making videos and listening as woman after woman, neatly dressed in Sunday best, approached the ushers stationed at the "standby-seating" doorway, requested admission, and were turned away one by one. The women each respectfully left the premises in turn. Since that point, Ordain Women has continued to do online organizing and educational efforts in addition to direct actions.

Kate, in keeping with her founding rold in Ordain Women, engaged in organizational activities. Mark M. Harrison was the bishop of Vienna Ward, and Scott Wheatley, was president of Oakton Virginia Stake. Prior to Ordain Women's website launch—in other words, more than six months before the public event in Salt Lake City—Kelly had emailed Harrison, Wheatley, and her Vienna Ward Relief Society president, informing them about the website and inviting them to discuss it with her. The only response she got from them was that they would let her know if they had any questions. No one accepted her offer for discussion, nor did anyone even ask her any questions at that time.

In December of 2013, President Wheatley asked Kate and Neil to meet with him and Bishop Harrison. Kate did so and blogged about the meeting soon afterward, specifically noting that Wheatley repeatedly told her two things, which she phrased as follows:

> The most important, immediate takeaways from my encounter with leadership were:
> 1) They explicitly and emphatically assured me that I was not facing any type of disciplinary action for my founding of, and participation in, Ordain Women.
> 2) They told me there was no directive from any area authority or higher-level Church leader instructing them to meet with me, interview me or punish me in any way. Hence, they assured me when I asked, there is no concerted effort on the part of the Church to "crack down" on members of Ordain Women or target us specifically for our unequivocal calls for female ordination. [6]

Kate sent an email to President Wheatley requesting tickets to the April 2014 priesthood session of general conference, which he declined. President Wheatley did not request any further meetings until May 4, when Kate and Neil were literally packing up for the move to Utah where they would stay with Kate's parents until their Kenya visas arrived. This meeting request was a full month after the second public Ordain Women event of petitioning in person on Temple Square for admission to the priesthood session. The initial request to meet came via a stake secretary who had no idea why Wheatley was requesting the meeting. Kate declined to meet since she was packing to move. Wheatley sent Kate an urgent email, saying he wanted to meet with her, "any time of the day or night." When she declined because she was in the last stages of packing, he informed her that he was instructing her bishop to place a hold on her membership records. Under this duress, she met with him on May 5. In a complete reversal of his prior position, he placed her on informal probation and said he was retaining her records.[7]

---

6. Kate Kelly, http://www.feministmormonhousewives.org/2013/12/excommunicating-sexism/.
7. President Wheatley's letter is available at http://ordainwomen.org/wp-content/uploads/2014/06/2014-05-22-Informal-Probation-Letter-to-Kate-Kelly.pdf.

Subsequently, Kate and Neil continued their plans and moved to Provo where they had no further communications with her former leader. Then Bishop Harrison sent Kate an email announcing that he had scheduled a disciplinary council for June 22. He thus ignored the *Church Handbook of Instructions* which requires that such notifications be personally delivered or sent by certified mail (Section 6.10.2). Although Kate and Neil could not have given Harrison and Wheatley the exact date of their departure to Kenya, since they could not predict when their visas would arrive, these two ecclesiastical leaders had, in essence, decided to impose Church discipline on a woman who had moved thousands of miles away, before an all-male council, *in absentia*, over her advocacy for gender equality, using a rule book that is available to only nine women in the entire Church. In fact, given this scenario, it would not have mattered whether Kate and Neil had already gone to Kenya.

Using an internet download of the *Church Handbook of Instructions*, I prepared and submitted a Statement of Support, resembling a legal brief. The brief pointed the procedural errors Kate's leaders had made, starting with the retention of her records while simultaneously saying that Salt Lake had no involvement in her discipline. Although the *Handbook* allows for bishops to retain records for purposes of Church discipline in certain circumstances, it forbids retention of records without the express permission of the Office of the First Presidency, or at least "Church headquarters."[8]

The brief argued that (1) the rules in the *Handbook* are unfair in general, (2) they are unfair to women in particular, and (3) Kate's leaders disregarded them in any case. The brief deconstructed the assertion that she committed apostasy and argued that there was no basis for her excommunication. Over a thousand people submitted statements to her bishop in her support. Despite the huge surge of support, or perhaps in part because of it, Bishop Harrison excommunicated Kate on June 23. She was accused initially of apostasy but in accordance with language taken directly from the *Handbook*, was excommunicated for "conduct contrary to the laws and order of the church."[9] Again, the communication came via email with a follow-up letter by certified mail, also dated June 23.

Following Kate's excommunication, the bishop notified her of her right to appeal, but only on procedural grounds. This restriction was particularly puz-

---

8. Section 6.2.7 allows bishops of prior and new wards to decide where Church discipline will take place, but Section 13.6 requires involvement of the Office of the First Presidency when records are retained. The policy reads: "Membership records include members' names and addresses, as well as ordinance and other vital information. The ward should have a membership record for each member living within the ward boundaries. Membership records are to be kept in the ward in which the member lives. Exceptions, which should be few, require the consent of the bishops and stake presidents involved *and the approval of the Office of the First Presidency* [emphasis mine]."

9. Section 6.10.7 directs the presiding officer to issue a notice consisting of a general statement that the discipline is "for conduct contrary to the laws and order of the church."

zling. How could she know how her trial had proceeded since it took place in her absence and she received no information about it from those in attendance? Despite the directive to rely only on procedural grounds, I wrote an appeal brief to the stake president that also made substantive arguments.[10] The following discussion includes excerpts and/or summaries of some of the arguments made in the appeal to the stake president.

One argument about the procedural unfairness highlights both the basic unfairness of the rules, and the unwillingness of Kate's leaders to follow them:

> Section 6.10 [of the *Handbook*] provides that "Procedures in a disciplinary council must be fair and considerate of the feelings of all who participate." That is a baseline rule that has not been observed thus far and is not observed in the appeal process. As noted in the prior Statement of Support, the willingness of Bishop Harrison to violate the already-unfair procedures stated in the CHI is troublesome, as is the willingness of President Wheatley to also violate, or allow violation of, the rules. What good are rules, even flawed ones, if they can be disregarded at the whim of those who call the shots, with no further consequence? The failure to follow notice procedures, the retention of Sister Kelly's records at the last minute before she moved away, and now the requirement of appealing Bishop Harrison's decision to Sister Kelly's initial accuser [Wheatley] all demonstrate complete disregard of any semblance of fairness. For that reason, President Wheatley should reverse the excommunication outright. If he is unwilling to do that, he should take his action promptly and allow for a speedy appeal to the First Presidency, in accordance with Section 6.10.10.

One of the most troubling aspects of Church discipline is the secrecy that surrounds it. The rules expressly prohibit making any kind of recording, and the only record is made by the ward or stake clerk. Clearly, the quality of the record depends on the skill of the clerk in taking notes, yet skill in shorthand or its equivalent—even fluency in the language used in the disciplinary council—is not one of the requirements for such an appointment. That record, such as it is, is never shown to the person being disciplined. It is impossible to draft an effective appeal from a nonexistent record. Indeed the appeal process is hopelessly flawed, not only because there is no record on appeal, but also because the appeal has to be made to individuals who placed those conducting Church discipline in their positions of authority. As noted, in the case of Kate, her appeal went to her stake president, who was her initial accuser.

Another problematic aspect of Church discipline in apostasy cases is that the accused is given very little information about the charges. That makes defending against them difficult. The *Handbook* specifically instructs the ecclesiastical officer to leave the charges vague and to use the following language (the brackets are in the original): "The [stake presidency or bishopric] is considering formal disciplinary action in your behalf, including the possibility of disfellowshipment

---

10. The brief can be found here: Nadine Hansen, "Statement in Support of Appeal," http://ordainwomen.org/wp-content/uploads/2014/07/Kate-Kelly_-Statement-in-Support-of-Appeal-_Nadine-Hansen.pdf.

or excommunication, because you are reported to have [set forth the charge in general terms, such as 'been in apostasy' or 'participated in conduct unbecoming a member of the Church,' but do not give any details or evidence]."

This practice leaves the member uninformed about what he or she did that constitutes alleged "apostasy." It is impossible to defend against charges that are intentionally hidden. After the announcement that she had been excommunicated, Kate had asked Bishop Harrison for information about her disciplinary council, which she had not been able to attend. He specifically told her: "Unfortunately, I am not in a position to answer questions about the disciplinary council, my preparations for it, or the discussions that occurred as a part of it." He did not explain why he was "not in a position" to do so—whether his inability was because he had been forbidden to, because he had not been present, or for some other reason.

My brief supporting Kate's appeal also raised the issue of "substantive unfairness." The aspects of "apostasy," as defined by the *Handbook* apparently consisted of teaching "false doctrine" and perhaps of openly opposing the Church or its leaders. In the brief, I raised the issue of teaching "false doctrine" in part as follows:

> The only reference in Bishop Harrison's excommunication letter to "doctrine" is the statement that at the December meeting, "We talked with you about the doctrine of the priesthood." It is impossible to tell, from the letter, what this "doctrine of the priesthood" is. Unless "doctrine" is clearly stated in canonized scripture, it cannot be deemed "doctrine" that is binding on the membership of the Church.
>
> [. . .]

We cannot know what President Wheatley and Bishop Harrison think the "doctrine of the priesthood" is, but nowhere to be found is any statement from Sister Kelly teaching anything whatsoever as "doctrine" about priesthood. Her message, and the message of Ordain Women, is *not* that women hold the priesthood, but simply that we sincerely ask the leaders of the Church to pray about whether women might be ordained. Because she never taught "as doctrine," about priesthood, she cannot have committed the act of apostasy through anything she taught, and to the extent that her excommunication was based on an erroneous finding or belief that she taught "false doctrine," the excommunication must be reversed.

Regarding whether public actions regarding women's ordination could constitute "apostasy," the brief made the argument that "talking about the possibility that women might one day be ordained is not apostasy, because many aspects of Mormon belief and practice support the idea that women may have priesthood." In support of that assertion, the brief argued:

> a. Women have priesthood authority.
>
> At April 2014 General Conference, Elder Dallin H. Oaks stated:
>
>> We are not accustomed to speaking of women having the authority of the priesthood in their Church callings, but what other authority can it be? *When a woman—young or old—is set apart to preach the gospel as a full-time missionary, she is given priesthood authority to perform a priesthood function.* The same is true when a woman is set apart to function as an officer or teacher in a Church

organization under the direction of one who holds the keys of the priesthood. Whoever functions in an office or calling received from one who holds priesthood keys exercises priesthood authority in performing her or his assigned duties. (Emphasis added.)

b. Women are endowed with priesthood power in the temple:

Elder Oaks also stated: "*When men and women go to the temple, they are both endowed with the same power, which is priesthood power.* . . . Access to the power and the blessings of the priesthood is available to all of God's children. (Emphasis added.)

c. Women perform priesthood ordinances in the temple.

Elder Oaks also noted: "With the exception of the sacred work that sisters do in the temple under the keys held by the temple president, which I will describe hereafter, only one who holds a priesthood office can officiate in a priesthood ordinance. And all authorized priesthood ordinances are recorded on the records of the Church."

Elder Oaks further explains: "A person may have authority given to him, or a sister to her, to do certain things in the Church that are binding and absolutely necessary for our salvation, such as the work that our sisters do in the House of the Lord. They have authority given unto them to do some great and wonderful things, sacred unto the Lord, and binding just as thoroughly as are the blessings that are given by the men who hold the Priesthood."

Taken together, these statements from Elder Oaks establish that all authority is priesthood authority, and that women can perform binding priesthood ordinances using that priesthood authority, under the direction of men who hold the priesthood keys to authorize the performance of those ordinances. Elder Oaks clearly pointed out that all who exercise priesthood authority—both men and women—do so under the direction of those who hold the priesthood keys to authorize the work they do, and that only men hold those keys.

The brief summarizes the point of Oaks's statements, saying that: "Given that women exercise priesthood authority, and have a long history of faithful Church services, it would be a small step to fully enfranchise women and incorporate women's services into all aspects of Church governance." It further states that asking Church leaders to pray about this matter "is not an act of apostasy. It is an act of faith."

Finally, the matter of Kate's public activism was addressed. On June 28, following Kate's excommunication, but prior to her appeal, the First Presidency and the Quorum of the Twelve had issued a public statement that was widely viewed as a response to Ordain Women's activism. In its entirety, the statement said:

In God's plan for the happiness and eternal progression of His children, the blessings of His priesthood are equally available to men and women. Only men are ordained to serve in priesthood offices. All service in the Church has equal merit in the eyes of God. We express profound gratitude for the millions of Latter-day Saint women and men who willingly and effectively serve God and His children. Because of their faith and service, they have discovered that the Church is a place of spiritual nourishment and growth.

We understand that from time to time Church members will have questions about Church doctrine, history, or practice. Members are always free to ask such questions and earnestly seek greater understanding. We feel special concern, however, for members who distance themselves from Church doctrine or practice and, by advocacy, encourage others to follow them.

Simply asking questions has never constituted apostasy. Apostasy is repeatedly acting in clear, open, and deliberate public opposition to the Church or its faithful leaders, or persisting, after receiving counsel, in teaching false doctrine.[11]

The brief argued:

Despite President Wheatley's and Bishop Harrison's attempt to turn Sister Kelly's request to Church leaders to ask the Lord a question about women's possible ordination into a "campaign" against Church leaders, and therefore into "apostasy," all she was really doing was to ask a reasonable question of Church leaders—the question of whether they would pray about women's ordination. That she did it in a very public way, and that she provided a forum for other women and men to ask the same question in a very public way, does not convert the act of questioning into the act of apostasy.

Kate's appeal to her stake president did not change the outcome of her disciplinary council. The stake president affirmed the decision, and it was subsequently reaffirmed by the First Presidency as well. Whether the affirmance means that the First Presidency agrees that Kate is indeed an "apostate," or whether it simply demonstrates that the First Presidency is unwilling to reverse a decision made by local leaders cannot be known.

Ordain Women remains a growing movement, which was granted 501(c)(3) status in late 2014. Profiles continue to be submitted and in October of 2014, women in several places around the world attended local broadcasts of the priesthood session of conference. A few profile holders and one Ordain Women board member have been called to task for their involvement, but no further formal disciplinary actions have occurred. Some activists and bloggers have been excommunicated or threatened with Church discipline for their writings on a variety of LDS-related topics, and discussions of the actions on social media complain of "Leadership Roulette," a situation in which some leaders tolerate speech and activities that result in threats of discipline or actual disciplinary actions at the hands of other leaders.

While it is possible that some ecclesiastical leaders enjoy threatening punishment and inflicting pain, I find it more probable that they prefer prayerful, pastoral counseling—healing rather than hurting. Some Church members who

---

11. This statement has no title but is headed "The Church of Jesus Christ of Latter-day Saints, Office of the First Presidency, 47 East South Temple Street, Salt Lake City, Utah 84150, followed by the date June 28, 2014. It is signed by the "Council of the First Presidency and Quorum of the Twelve Apostles of the Church of Jesus Christ of Latter-day Saints," https://www.lds.org/prophets-and-apostles/june-first-presidency-statement (accessed May 13, 2015).

recognize that they have made serious mistakes may want to make it right by going through the traditional process of a Church court; but such individuals would probably find faster, more whole-hearted healing by focusing early, with a priesthood leader's guidance on Christ's atonement. I find it doubtful that individuals like Kate Kelly, who take action based on the call of their conscience, will change that call because of punishment. When summoned to her disciplinary council, Kate repeated, "I'm just really, really, really heartbroken."[12] Ten months later, speaking at the Tribeca Disruptive Innovative Conference in New York City, Kate still responded emotionally, comparing her excommunication to "'an execution, a spiritual death,'" but rallied to add that, because of the way she stood up to the unjust disciplinary system, "I think I'm much happier, much more authentic, a much more invigorated person."[13]

The excommunication of Kate Kelly, followed by that in February 2015 of John Dehlin, ripped open an old wound that many Mormons believed had healed given the existence of a free and open "Bloggernacle." I suggest a better approach for the twenty-first century.

Broader Church Discipline Considerations

As I pointed out earlier, the stated purposes of Church discipline are to (1) save the souls of the transgressors; (2) protect the innocent; and (3) safeguard the purity, integrity, and good name of the Church.

How effective is Church discipline in accomplishing these goals? Do the established policies and procedures benefit "transgressors"? Do they protect "innocent" Church members or others from harmful practices? Do they "safeguard" the Church?

If Church discipline effectively accomplishes these goals, does it do so in a way that is fair, and in a way that minimizes harm? Are there better ways of accomplishing the goals of Church discipline? Is Church discipline even necessary in the twenty-first century, or is the idea of Church discipline a relic of the past that should be abandoned in favor of the private counseling of "transgressors," public prosecution and/or exposure of predators, and open discussion of matters that affect the "purity, integrity and good name of the Church"?

On June 16, 2014, a week before Kate's court, NPR's Doug Fabrizio interviewed LDS Public Affairs spokeswoman Ally Isom on KUER's Radio West

---

12. Laurie Goodstein, "Two Activists in Mormon Church Threatened with Excommunication," *New York Times*, June 11, 2014, http://www.nytimes.com/2014/06/12/us/twoactivistswithinmormonchurchthreatenedwithexcommunication.html?_r=1 (accessed June 23, 2014).

13. Thomas Burr, "Mormon Activist Kate Kelly Says She Feels 'Happier' and 'Invigorated' after Excommunication," *Salt Lake Tribune*, April 27, 2015, http://www.huffingtonpost.com/2015/04/27/kate-kelly-excommunication-happier_n_7152174.html?cps=gravity_2677_-9024076533172604217 (accessed May 1, 2015).

in Salt Lake City.[14] She took the position that Church discipline could be positive, even "transformative," in helping people change their lives. Perhaps in some cases it is. In other cases, however, Church discipline is punitive, intrusive, and alienating. In public cases, such as the recent excommunications of Kate Kelly and of Mormon podcaster John Dehlin, like those of the "September Six" who were disciplined in 1993 for their scholarly writings or their critiques of Church "spiritual abuse," the "good name" of the Church has taken a public beating, as the media has focused on a secretive and oppressive practice designed to silence dissent instead of addressing the reasons for the dissent.

As I see it, different aspects of Church discipline need to be addressed in different ways. For people whose lives are troubled by sin and guilt, the strict confidentiality of the traditional confessional needs to be honored. I suggest, however, that spiritual counseling by appropriate local leaders and professional counseling from trained therapists are better suited to encouraging life-changing thinking and behavior than the current mechanism of Church discipline. Such counseling needs to involve not only "transgressors," but also those whose lives are affected by the "transgressor's" behavior where appropriate.

For sexual or financial predators whose predatory practices place others in jeopardy, appropriate law enforcement action need to be taken to expose and prosecute the wrongdoers, thereby protecting future potential victims. Public knowledge of predatory acts would almost certainly be a much more effective deterrent than Church discipline, especially if such predators are serving the prison terms appropriate to their crimes.

For those whose study of Church history, doctrine, and contemporary practices has led them to feel the need to speak out to encourage honesty and reform, I suggest that the problems lie in the fact that existing mechanisms for discussion and debate are woefully inadequate. That inadequacy has led to robust online discussions of troublesome questions, but the discussion now takes place under a cloud of fear due to recent excommunications and threats of excommunication. This is not a healthy way for a faith community to resolve difficult questions and problems. We are long past the time when questions can be silenced or swept under the rug. I suggest that open discourse with "persuasion," "meekness," and "love unfeigned" (D&C 121:41) is a much more effective tool for reaching consensus than are excommunications or uncomfortable Public Affairs "spins" that sometimes do not stop short of name-calling and near-slander designed to marginalize and label as "apostates" those who speak their truth with integrity and candor.

Suggestions for Restructuring Church Discipline

I suggest that, at a minimum, the following seven Church discipline problems need to be addressed:

---

14. Ally Isom, interviewed by Doug Fabrizio, June 16, 2014, http://radiowest.kuer.org/post/latter-day-saints-and-excommunication-part-ii (accessed June 17, 2015).

1. Church discipline should never involve a man discussing intimate details of another person's sexual behavior, especially if that person is young, female, emotionally vulnerable, or a victim of abuse. Such discussions are wholly inappropriate for anyone who is not a trained and licensed professional.

2. The secrecy surrounding Church discipline needs to be discarded. It is unfair and unreasonable to hide the rules of Church discipline in a book that is unavailable to those who are subjected to those rules. A full and complete recording or transcript should be made of every disciplinary council so that an appeal can be made based on the actual record, not on a clerk's notes. The recording could, and in most cases should, be kept confidential at the discretion of the accused, but it should be fully available to the accused in case of an appeal.

3. To the extent that Church discipline involves fact-finding, the process needs to be fair and the "judge" should not be the accuser. Some aspects of Church discipline hearken back to a time in the nineteenth century when Church courts adjudicated disputes among Church members, but the fairness provisions of the Doctrine and Covenants that require half of the stake high council to speak for the accused have been, in essence, abandoned and replaced with a decision announced by the person convening the council. This convener is usually the accuser, and everyone else involved is expected to rubber-stamp his decision with a sustaining vote.

4. Appeals should be presented to a neutral third party, not to a superior with a vested interest in upholding a subordinate's decision, and certainly not to the member's initial accuser. Appeals to the First Presidency should be tried "de novo" with a completely new proceeding on the merits. This provision is already mandated by scripture, which instructs that either party, if "dissatisfied," may appeal to the First Presidency "and have a re-hearing, which case shall be conducted . . . as though no such decision had been made" (D&C 102:27). Wheatley convened the high council, but there is no way of knowing, without access to that record, whether he did an entirely new hearing/review of Kate's case.

5. Trials for "apostasy" should be abandoned altogether in favor of a meaningful way for Church members to discuss their concerns publicly and have them addressed, or at least acknowledged, by the Church's top leaders, not by local lay leaders who themselves lack awareness of problems and who have no ability to affect policy or obtain official answers. Much of today's discontent arises because there is no mechanism for members to be heard by those who set policy, other than to take their concerns to the public square of the internet.

6. If disciplinary councils for apostasy are going to continue, they need to have consistent, identifiable, and predictable procedures and standards.

Secret trials instigated by arbitrary local leaders who may be acting out of personal pique, concern about their own reputations, or obedience to what they interpret as instructions—or even strong hints—from an ecclesiastical superior can never effectively address the underlying problems that lead to dissent, nor can they define the boundaries of acceptable discourse and dissent. They cannot set precedents or have consistent outcomes. Church members should not be excommunicated because a local leader defines "doctrine" or "public opposition" in a way that would be wholly foreign to a different local leader in another place. Such inconsistency is arbitrary and capricious.

7. Privacy concerns are not applicable to "apostasy" and should be entirely discarded. By the Church definition, "apostasy" is a public act and it should be discussed in public where the give and take of discourse can define what is and what is not "doctrine." If there are going to be "apostasy" trials, they should be public, they should apply only to "core doctrines" which are clearly stated and defined, and the accused person should be entitled to representation by a person well-versed in those core doctrines. "Apostasy" trials should be rare and should be conducted by an "apostasy" court, one with expertise in the meaning of "apostasy" and a thorough understanding of what constitutes core Church doctrines. That approach would remove the problem of arbitrary decision-making by ill-informed or angry local leadership. In short, if there must be "apostasy" trials, there should be a fair process in a public forum that can build a publicly identifiable body of canon law and provide clear notice to all Church leaders and members of exactly what constitutes "apostasy."

Mormon scripture mandates that "no power or influence can or ought to be maintained by virtue of the priesthood, only by persuasion, by long-suffering, by gentleness and meekness, and by love unfeigned; by kindness, and pure knowledge, which shall greatly enlarge the soul without hypocrisy, and without guile" (D&C 121:41–42).

This scripture calls for persuasion, not punishment, of those disagree with contemporary policies, those who discover troubling historical facts, or those who think the Church they love could do better in serving the needs of its members.

PART IV

LDS Women in a Twenty-First-Century Church

Chapter 13

The Great Lever:
Women and Changing Mission Culture in Contemporary Mormonism

Courtney L. Rabada and Kristine L. Haglund

This great social upheaval, this woman's movement that is making itself heard and felt, means something more than that certain women are ambitious to vote and hold office. I regard it as one of the great levers by which the Almighty is lifting up this fallen world, lifting it nearer to the throne of its Creator. —Orson F. Whitney[1]

On Saturday, October 6, 2012, the Church of Jesus Christ of Latter-day Saints made the historic announcement "that able, worthy young women who have the desire to serve may be recommended for missionary service beginning at age nineteen, instead of age twenty-one," while young men could now serve one year earlier at age eighteen.[2] To say that the response has been overwhelming is an understatement. Within two weeks of the announcement, missionary applications jumped from an average of 700 per week to 4,000, with at least half of those new applications coming from women.[3] According to the most recent Church statistics, there are now over 85,000 full-time Mormon missionaries around the world, and in the two-and-a-half years since the announcement, the percentage of sister missionaries in the field has almost doubled from 15 to 28 percent, going from fewer than 9,000 women in the field in 2012 to nearly 30,000 today.[4]

Note: Limited portions of this chapter were previously published in *Dialogue: A Journal of Mormon Thought*: Courtney Rabada, "A Swelling Tide: Nineteen-Year-Old Sister Missionaries in the Twenty-First Century," *Dialogue: A Journal of Mormon Thought* 47, no. 4 (Winter 2014): 19–45.

1. Orson F. Whitney, "Elections and Suffrage," speech, Proceedings and Debates of the Convention Assembled to Adopt a Constitution for the State of Utah, March 30, 1895, transcript, http://le.utah.gov/documents/conconv/27.htm (accessed May 25, 2015).

2. President Thomas Monson, "Welcome to Conference," general conference, October 6, 2012, transcript, https://www.lds.org/general-conference/2012/10/welcome-to-conference (accessed May 25, 2015).

3. Church of Jesus Christ of Latter-day Saints: Newsroom, "Response to Mormon Missionary Age Announcement Remains Enthusiastic and Unprecedented," March 27, 2013, http://www.mormonnewsroom.org/article/mormon-missionary-age-announcement-response (accessed May 25, 2015).

4. LDS Church Growth Blog, "Statistical Reports," April 10, 2015, http://ldschurchgrowth.blogspot.com/search/label/Statistical%20Report (accessed May 25, 2015); Tad Walch, "LDS Missionary Numbers to Peak at 88,000; More to Use and Pay for Digital Devices," *Deseret News*, Thursday, July 3, 2014, http://www.deseretnews.com/article/865606271/LDS-

Not enough time has passed to know whether the numbers of sister missionaries will continue to grow after the initial novelty of the age-change wears off. But even if fewer women serve in the coming years, the structure of missions around the world and the overall mission culture has been forever changed. Women are now official and active members of mission leadership councils. Women who want to serve missions are immediately accepted and encouraged by their communities, rather than being questioned and considered unusual. Sister missionaries are no longer viewed as "old maids" who chose mission service only because they had no prospects for marriage. Additionally, the sisters' experiences may have significant implications for Mormon marriages as a whole. From marrying later to the experience of working in companionships to newfound confidence in their place in the Church, these women will presumably bring different expectations to their relationships. Future generations of sister missionaries are more likely to have older sisters and/or mothers who served missions. And perhaps most significantly, all indications point toward the idea that these women feel they are living through history in the making. They believe the age-change was a pivotal moment for their Church and for Mormon women, and that their participation has made them a part of a movement that is larger than their individual experiences.

We can usefully compare this "swelling tide" with the process of other significant policy changes within the Church, and particularly with another movement for change among Mormon women that began around the same time. In this article, we will consider the missionary age as a case study of incremental and organic change, in contrast to the more dramatic change sought by the Ordain Women organization. We will examine doctrinal and historical warrants for change, enumerate changes that have occurred and are occurring as a result of the age change, and speculate about possibilities for future developments as the effects of this policy ripple outward.

The Past:
Doctrinal and Historical Precedents

The history of women's proselytizing efforts in the Church of Jesus Christ of Latter-day Saints reveals a willingness to adduce diverse theological and scriptural resources in support of pragmatic responses to institutional concerns. Frequent changes in the rules governing sister missionaries suggest that the most contested issues with regard to women's roles in Church work have less to do with the substance of the activity, and more to do with the process by which change is achieved and who controls that process.

---

missionary-numbers-to-peak-at-88000-more-to-use-and-pay-for-digital-devices.html?pg=all (accessed May 25, 2015). The number of male missionaries has also increased significantly, which is why the percentage has doubled, but the number of female missionaries has more than tripled.

More than 200 married women served as missionaries in various assignments before the first single full-time female missionaries were called in 1898.[5] Tania Rands Lyon and Mary Ann Shumway McFarland note that, over the course of almost seven decades of informal, self-motivated missionary work, women "served with and without their husbands, official calls, having been called or set apart, and they served for a variety of reasons."[6]

Since then, policies about length of service, age requirements, and the number of sisters in the field have changed in response to circumstances, seemingly quite pragmatically, without expressed concern about a need to provide doctrinal warrant. This may be, of course, because a requirement for scriptural warrant would almost certainly exclude women from proselytizing efforts—the scanty record of women's lives in scripture offers no precedent for female missionaries. Nonetheless, Mormonism's open canon and commitment to ongoing revelation could in theory provide canonical support or at least doctrinal justification for women's involvement in proselytizing work. The fact that these warrants have not been perceived to be necessary may tell us something important about the possibilities for an expansion of women's roles in the Church: in some significant areas like missionary work, increasing women's participation is more a matter of pragmatic policy change than revising doctrine. Resistance to change is largely located in questions about process, rather than about the *content* of contemplated changes. That is, women are not seen as incapable of performing certain ecclesial functions, but merely (and perhaps temporarily) enjoined from participation.

The lack of articulated doctrinal reasons for changes in policy may obscure the potentially radical implications of this most recent change for female missionaries. As Lyon and McFarland point out, throughout the twentieth century, policies with regard to sister missionaries seemed designed with the implicit goal of keeping the number of sisters small relative to the number of elders. President Gordon B. Hinckley explicitly acknowledged this intention in his address to the priesthood session of the October 1997 general conference: "We do not ask the young women to consider a mission an essential part of their life's program. Over a period of many years, we have held the age level higher for them in an effort to keep the number going relatively small."[7] While President Hinckley's statement was the most explicit, other leaders have hinted at the concern for limiting the number of female missionaries for decades. Maintaining a gendered division of

---

5. Tania Rand Lyon and Mary Ann Shumway McFarland, "'Not Invited, But Welcome': The History and Impact of Church Policy on Sister Missionaries," *Dialogue: A Journal of Mormon Thought* 36, no. 3 (Fall 2003): 73; Calvin S. Kunz, "I Have a Question," *Ensign*, January 1981, https://www.lds.org/ensign/1981/01/i-have-a-question/i-have-a-question (accessed May 25, 2015).

6. Lyon and McFarland, "'Not Invited, But Welcome,'" 73.

7. Gordon B. Hinckley, "Some Thoughts on Temples, Retention of Converts, and Missionary Work," *Ensign*, November 1997, https://www.lds.org/ensign/1997/11/some-thoughts-on-temples-retention-of-converts-and-missionary-service (accessed May 25, 2015).

missionary labor, and giving primacy to young men, was an overriding goal of policies about sister missionaries, even though no clear reason for this goal was officially articulated.[8] The recent change in policy and apparent willingness to welcome sisters as a dramatically larger fraction of the missionary force represents a seismic shift in attitudes about women's relationships to a major element of the Church's purpose. The fact that the particulars of this attitudinal and policy change are not explicitly grounded in doctrinal pronouncements should not blind us to the radical implications of the announcement.

It is also important to note the ways in which this shift came about in the context of other notable changes in LDS practice. A combination of factors may have been involved: concern about the slowing growth in membership, conflicts in some countries with national service requirements that made it impossible for young men to leave school for mission service at age nineteen, and concern about rising inactivity rates of young people after high school graduation.[9] Importantly, though, we can only speculate about the decision-making process because it is almost entirely opaque to the general membership of the Church. This is in keeping with established conventions of revelatory policy change in the Church—decisions as momentous as the lifting of the priesthood and temple ban for black members of the Church and as mundane as the change to a three-hour block of meetings on Sunday are announced *ex cathedra*, with little or no public discussion of the process by which decisions are reached. This official silence about deliberations among Church authorities has the effect of sacralizing all policy pronouncements and allowing members to impute revelatory significance to all innovations. (This is not at all to say that revelation is not involved in the process, only that the occurrence of revelation is often left implicit, and that the mechanism of revelation is described in only the vaguest terms.)

The Present:
Immediate Changes in Missionary and Church Culture

If the patterns of the past are any guide, more information (and probably some misinformation) about the factors General Authorities considered while changing the policies about missionary age will become available over time, in

---

8. Lyon and McFarland, "'Not Invited, But Welcome,'" 88–92. Lyon and McFarland make an important point about the "inherent contradictions" of the policy that may shed some light on why the Church has never fully articulated the reasoning behind the age gap: "[Hinckley] intimates with his choice of [the word 'confession'] . . . that having sister missionaries in his own family was a secret to be confessed rather than an accomplishment to be proud of" (89). It is likely that the women who have reacted so enthusiastically to the age-change are responding not only the opportunity to serve, but also to the Church's (perhaps unintended) shift towards more openly celebrating sister missionaries.

9. Peggy Fletcher Stack and Kristen Moulton, "Some Mormon Men Can Go on Missions at Age 18," *Salt Lake Tribune*, August 25, 2011, http://www.sltrib.com/sltrib/blogsfaithblog/52458313-180/mormon-mission-age-academy.html.csp (accessed May 25, 2015).

remarks and reminiscences by participants in the process, allowing future historians to construct a more robust and less speculative record of this moment in Mormon history.

However, there is little debate that this moment is critically important for Mormon women and for the LDS Church as a whole. Elder David F. Evans, executive director of the Missionary Department, stated, "Because of President Monson's announcement, the Church has fundamentally changed, and as far as we can see, there will always be more missionaries than there were before the age change."[10] As such, it is essential to consider the immediate effects of the policy in the few years since its implementation.[11]

Convenience, Perceptions, and Mormon Marriages

There is little doubt that the age-change makes serving a mission significantly easier for women in the Church. It is ultimately a much more convenient time for young women to disengage from school or work, and their romantic relationships are likely to be more casual at age nineteen. There is no longer a sense of having to wait to serve, which was always at least implicitly part of the dynamic when men could leave for their missions two years before women.

The lag between the time men and women could serve before the age-change also fostered a perception of sister missionaries as "old maids," who only chose to serve a mission because they had no prospects for marriage. This attitude changed instantaneously upon the announcement. This is not to say that marriage and relationships no longer factor into a woman's decision to serve a mission, nor that the Church's strong pro-marriage stance has changed. In fact, no fewer than six talks directly addressed the importance of marriage during the April 2015 general conference, including one in which an apostle explicitly told returned missionaries, "You single adults need to date and marry! Please stop delaying!"[12] However,

---

10. David F. Evans, untitled speech, 2014 mission presidents' seminar, June 22, 2014, qtd. in Gerry Avant, "Missionary Work Broader Than Ever; Includes before and after Baptism," *LDS Church News*, June 25, 2014, https://www.lds.org/church/news/missionary-work-broader-than-ever-includes-before-and-after-baptism?lang=eng (accessed May 25, 2015).

11. The theories and conclusions within this chapter are based on a series of one-on-one interviews with returned sister missionaries by Courtney Rabada, as well as ongoing and less formal conversations with other Mormon women by both authors. Formal interviews were conducted November 2014–March 2015 in Claremont, California, and Provo, Utah. While this sample cannot be considered as representative of the full female missionary force, their experiences and recollections provide enough similarities that trends in current missionary culture can be identified and theories about the Church's future can be generated.

12. M. Russell Ballard, "The Greatest Generation of Young Adults," general conference, April 4, 2015, transcript, https://www.lds.org/general-conference/2015/04/the-greatest-generation-of-young-adults?lang=eng (accessed May 25, 2015).

women are no longer faced with a stark either/or decision between serving a mission and getting married, and instead see both as equally viable options.

The age-change will likely also have long term implications for Mormon marriages. With the majority of missionaries returning from missions at age twenty-one (give or take a year) and with a few years of college to complete, it is possible that the average age at which Mormon couples marry will increase slightly. There may also be a shift toward returned missionaries preferring partners who also served missions, as well as an even stronger inclination to marry only fellow Mormons. In the past, many Mormon women viewed men who had served missions as more desirable mates than those who did not serve—it was not unusual to hear women say, "I only want to marry a returned missionary"—and this has not changed. Many young women have now experienced the benefits and hardships of living with a constant companion. They see a direct correlation with how they will approach their marriage partnerships and highly value that same experience and outlook from their potential spouses. The shared experience and the strengthening of one's testimony while serving a mission are also factors that may lead to more dual-returned missionary couples in the future. There are also some indications that men are beginning to feel the same way about returned sister missionaries. While this is certainly not an inherently bad thing, it will be interesting to see the long-term implications for and trends within Mormon marriages, and particularly whether there are any negative effects for women who choose not to serve missions.[13]

Sister Missionaries as the New Norm

One notable effect of the revelatory significance members assign to such policy changes is the possibility of dramatic and immediate changes in attitudes and discourse at the grass roots. As soon as the age-change was announced, there was a major shift in attitudes throughout the Church about female missionaries. Women who decided to serve were no longer viewed as exceptions to the rule, and they were no longer questioned, second-guessed, or put in the position of having to defend their decision to a Church membership that generally viewed a mission as a last resort—or at the very least, an abnormality—for women.

Church authorities continue to stress that women are not required, nor expected, to serve missions. President Monson explicitly said as much when he

---

13. It is also possible that the larger number of sister missionaries, paired with the smaller age gap between female and male missionaries, will lead to more on-mission romances. However, such developments are strictly frowned upon by Church leaders and can be cause to send missionaries home early. Some mission presidents have instituted stricter fraternization rules, such as restricting interactions between sisters and elders on Preparation Days and limited contact outside the ward meetinghouses. It is possible these concerns were part of the reason for the larger discrepancy in minimum serving ages before the change was made. See Gary Shepherd and Gordon Shepherd, *Mormon Passage: A Missionary Chronicle* (Urbana: University of Illinois Press, 1998), 31.

made the original announcement, and the official rhetoric has not changed. However, there seems to be a subtle shift among members of the Church toward the expectation that women will serve missions. Some women have spoken of feeling peer pressure to go on a mission since the announcement, though this could very well dissipate as time passes and the initial enthusiasm generated by the age-change dies down. Personal accounts indicate that women who chose not to serve missions may feel defensive about their decision. Women have been heard saying things like "I know I didn't serve a mission but that wasn't part of God's plan for me," or prefacing their statements with a kind of apology for not serving, which clearly indicates they do feel at least some cultural pressure regarding missionary service.

One thing that has not changed yet is the comparison of males and female missionaries, often used as a tactic to motivate them (and elders in particular). There has long been a general impression among the Church leaders and members that women are more successful missionaries, as demonstrated by David O. McKay's 1921 statement: "Almost without exception, the women [missionaries] have proved to be not only equal but superior to the men."[14] Sisters are characterized as harder working, more mature, and more likely to be able to gain an audience with potential investigators. The larger numbers of female missionaries seems to have only increased this rhetoric. Sisters continue to be held up as the shining examples of hard work and obedience, while elders are chided for not working hard enough. There has been some friction caused by these gender-based comparisons, but it does not seem to impact interpersonal relationships between sisters and elders as much as one might expect. It is possible that comparisons will lessen as time passes, though the differing minimum ages and maturity levels of women and men may foster a continued rhetoric of sisters excelling and elders needing to work harder. On the other hand, an increased focus on not just "finding, [but] retaining, reactivating, and enduring" members, and away from numbers and statistics as success indicators, may also lead to fewer comparisons and less competition among sisters and elders.[15]

An Opportunity to Lead

Shortly after the age-change announcement, the Church created the role of sister training leader (STL) to instruct, lead, and support the growing number of sister missionaries. STLs are part of the mission leadership council (MLC) and are included in all district, zone, and council meetings. It was a much-needed addition

---

14. David O. McKay, "Our Lady Missionaries," *Young Woman's Journal* 32 (1921): 503, quoted in Lyon and McFarland, "'Not Invited, But Welcome,'" 82. Lyon and McFarland also quote Elder John G. Allred, who stated, "I can't speak too highly for the young ladies of our mission. . . . They can get into the homes of people and find an opportunity for explaining the gospel where the elder cannot go. Send us more lady missionaries" (77–78).

15. Evans, untitled speech, 2014 mission presidents' seminar, quoted in Avant, "Missionary Work Broader Than Ever"; and interviews conducted by Courtney Rabada.

to the mission structure given the massive influx of sister missionaries, and is generally considered by sisters and Church members as an extremely positive change.

While the exact role and responsibilities of STLs have not been completely codified yet, and they receive no formal training for the position, officially their primary duty is to act as a liaison between the mission leadership and the female missionaries—as a kind of "eyes and ears" of the mission president—through their participation in the MLC meetings and interactions with sisters during monthly exchanges. Ultimately, they are tasked with discerning and conveying the needs and concerns of the sisters in their areas, and sharing news and information regarding decisions made and information disseminated in MLC meetings with the women in the field. In a more unofficial capacity, the STLs main purpose is to provide emotional support to their fellow sisters. Exchanges and ongoing communication via phone calls and texting give the women under their care an opportunity to unload some of their troubles, get advice, take a break from their companions, and simply enjoy themselves outside the normal confines of their mission routine. Given the stressful nature of missionary work, sisters have reported fairly high levels of depression and anxiety, and keeping a watchful eye on their mental states is another aspect of being a STL.[16]

It is likely that the exact role and responsibilities of STLs will continue to evolve over the next few years, but will also be solidified and systematized at some point given the LDS Church's penchant for worldwide standards and correlation. These changes may include a more widespread use of sister training coordinators, particularly in missions with a large number of female missionaries. Sister training coordinators oversee and organize the efforts of STLs, go on exchanges with them, and also participate fully in the mission leadership councils. Though currently not a broadly implemented change, if the position is expanded to more missions, the effects of the additional leadership options for women and their increased presence in the councils will be an important aspect of missionary culture to follow.

As mentioned above, sister training leaders are also members of the mission leadership council, which meets on a regular basis to discuss the needs of the overall mission, the sisters and elders, and their investigators. Councils are made up of the mission president, the mission president's wife, assistants to the president (male only), zone and district leaders (male only), sister training leaders, and sister training coordinators (where applicable). It is only since the age-change announcement that women have officially been a part of this council, with the addition of STLs and mission presidents' wives.

The STLs participation in the MLC also provides an important opportunity for women to be on equal footing with men in the Church and to see other women participating in councils in an official capacity, perhaps for the first time.[17] Of

---

16. Interviews conducted by Courtney Rabada.

17. Gender equality in the Mormon Church is an obviously complicated topic, made more so by the fact that in surveys of LDS women, a majority report feeling equal

course, even in the position of STL, women are not technically equal with their male "counterparts" who hold the positions of district and zone leaders. These two positions have authority over both male and female missionaries, and the STLs officially answer to them, while women have no jurisdiction or authority over any of the men with whom they work, regardless of how long they have been in the field or in the STL position.

There is little doubt that the women who take part in the MLC strongly appreciate being part of the decision-making process, having an opportunity to voice their opinions, and interacting with the mission leadership on a regular basis. These experiences lead to increased feelings of confidence in both their interpersonal and leadership skills, as well as having more assurance in their own spiritual inspiration. While it would be easy to assume that most women will eventually develop this type of confidence and learn similar skills as they mature, there is at least some sense among sisters that being able to freely share one's thoughts comes with an official title. Not only does this point to an almost automatic sense of empowerment felt when a woman is given an official calling, but it also hints at how she may feel before being called: uncomfortable speaking her mind, unable to relate to those in leadership positions, and inadequate because of the lack of a calling.

On a similar note, both those women called to the job and their fellow missionaries (female and male) tend to view the STL position as prestigious and authoritative. STLs' involvement in councils and their personal relationships with the mission presidents are viewed as privileges, which set them apart from—and above—the other sisters. While the female missionaries look up to STLs as leaders and examples, what is perhaps more interesting is that male missionaries also tend to treat women called as STLs with a noticeably higher level of respect. Multiple returned sister missionaries have mentioned that their treatment "changed overnight when I became sister training leader. . . . Leaders never told me what to do or corrected me. . . . I was above reproach all of a sudden."[18]

Ultimately, the recognition, confidence, and authority that come with an official title should not be underestimated, and these factors are important to remember when discussing the discrepancy between the number of official leadership positions available to men versus women within the Mormon Church at all levels. It also informs the Church's ongoing discussion of priesthood authority. In a society that often treats authority and power as identical, it can be difficult to divorce priesthood callings, and the influence they bring, from concepts of power, particularly for young men and women who are just beginning to truly understand and experience priesthood power. LDS rhetoric includes regular references

---

with Mormon men. However, given that all worthy Mormon men are ordained to the priesthood at the age of twelve, and women cannot hold the priesthood regardless of worthiness or age, to be called to sit on the MLC with their peers may very well technically be the first time these young women have been given an equal seat at a leadership table.

18. Interviews conducted by Courtney Rabada.

to the idea that priesthood offices do not confer status or prestige, but among members there is a clear cultural hierarchy of perceived rank.[19] It is particularly evident among competitive young male missionaries, for whom being called as a district or zone leader or assistant to the mission president is treated as an indicator of achievement or even of greater righteousness.[20] It remains to be seen whether female missionaries will be fully assimilated into this subtly competitive culture, but the changes sisters experience in how they are treated once being called to a leadership position would indicate that it is not a gender-specific phenomenon and, as such, ought to be included in future observation and analysis.

Both the creation of the STL position and women's inclusion in the mission leadership councils are positive and important steps for the LDS Church in making sure sister missionaries are fully incorporated in the new mission landscape. They not only create opportunities for women to gain leadership skills but also ensure that the needs and concerns of the sisters are directly heard by the mission leadership (rather than passed from sister to district leader to mission president, for example). Though it is unlikely that STLs' membership in the leadership council will change, it will be interesting to follow the council dynamics as time progresses. When large numbers of sister missionaries become the norm, rather than a relatively recent occurrence, will mission presidents continue make overt efforts to hear their voices? Will sisters take on additional responsibilities in some way? Will the position of STL grow in stature and become more highly competitive and coveted, or will it be sidelined into a primarily support position? And perhaps most important, how will the Church nurture these women's newly acquired skills when they return home from their missions?

One obvious way to continue creating and fostering female leaders is through embracing the Church's increased emphasis on the use of governing councils at the ward and stake level throughout the Church. Beginning with Elder M. Russell Ballard's conference address in April 1994, a recurrent theme has been the instruction and encouragement of bishops and other priesthood leaders to in-

---

19. This is a regular theme in Sunday services. Additionally, numerous general conference talks on the topic of hierarchy, priesthood authority, and how they should be understood outside the context of Church governance indicate that there is a misunderstanding that Church leaders are attempting to correct. See Elder Dallin H. Oaks, "Priesthood Authority in the Family and the Church," general conference, October 1, 2005, transcript, https://www.lds.org/general-conference/2005/10/priesthood-authority-in-the-family-and-the-church?lang=eng (accessed May 25, 2015); Elder Dallin H. Oaks, "The Keys and Authority of the Priesthood," general conference, April 5, 2014, transcript, https://www.lds.org/general-conference/2014/04/the-keys-and-authority-of-the-priesthood?lang=eng (accessed May 25, 2015); and Elder Boyd K. Packer, "Called to Serve," general conference, October 4, 1997, https://www.lds.org/general-conference/1997/10/called-to-serve (accessed May 25, 2015).

20. Personal accounts shared with both authors support this claim and indicate that it remains a current issue, but it has been an ongoing facet of missionary life for many years. See Shepherd and Shepherd, *Mormon Passage*, 233–40.

clude women in decision-making meetings and to be solicitous of women's opinions.[21] The most recent iteration of the *Church Handbook of Instructions* (2010) that governs Church bureaucracy elevated the ward council (in which several women participate) to a much more significant role in the governance of local congregations than it had previously occupied. As Rosalynde Welch pointed out in a perceptive blog post after the publication of the new guidelines, "One of the practical effects of this change is that, for the first time, women have full access to a venue in which they participate in an executive (rather than merely advisory or auxiliary) capacity at the highest ward level. . . . Any member of the council, male or female . . . can receive inspiration for the entire ward in the context of that body's deliberations."[22] She further noted the possibility of this change extending from the ward level to the stake and even general level of Church government: "Without having to touch on the vexed topic of female ordination, the same mechanism that has extended authority to women at the local level through the ward council could bring women into executive councils at the stake and area levels. The framework—and indeed the doctrinal justification—for a larger scale integration is already in place in the new handbook."[23]

The increased participation of sisters in councils on their missions will prepare them to be full participants in ward councils upon their return. Young men who have been encouraged to listen to the voices of sister missionaries and who have seen their mission presidents modeling such attentiveness will be more prepared to truly collaborate with women in their future Church service. While such change is not as measurable and in some ways not as satisfying as the structural change that would occur if women were ordained to the priesthood, it is nonetheless a necessary element of cultural change that ordination alone would not inevitably enact.

Feelings of Isolation

The Church's ability to incorporate returned missionaries back into their wards and to use their skills and talents has long been deemed an important aspect of missionary service. Almost twenty years ago, President Gordon B. Hinckley stated, "I am satisfied that if every returning missionary had a meaningful responsibility the day he or she came home, we'd have fewer of them grow cold in their faith. I wish that [the bishops] would make an effort to see that every returned missionary receives a meaningful assignment. Activity is the nurturing

---

21. M. Russell Ballard, "Counseling with Our Councils," general conference, April 2, 1994, transcript, https://www.lds.org/general-conference/1994/04/counseling-with-our-councils (accessed May 25, 2015).

22. Rosalynde Welch, "Handbook and Help Meet," Patheos.com: Salt and Seed, November 23, 2010, http://www.patheos.com/Resources/Additional-Resources/Handbook-and-Help-Meet (accessed May 25, 2015).

23. Ibid.

process of faithfulness."[24] And yet the returned missionaries' frustrated desire for purpose remains a problem today, and may only grow more troublesome now that a significantly larger portion of the Mormon population is dealing with the difficult shift back home from the mission field.[25]

Though not a new nor gender-specific phenomenon, painful transitions are certainly widespread among returned sister missionaries.[26] They have reported feeling depressed, isolated, lonely, purposeless, selfish, guilty, worthless, and alienated from God and the Spirit—no trivial list of issues.[27] These troubles may only be exacerbated by the high levels of depression and anxiety many women experience while serving their missions. The sisters' reactions should give Mormon leaders pause, since these are likely some of the important factors behind the reasons many returned missionaries drift away from the Church. Additionally, the relative paucity of Church callings available to women due to priesthood requirements might contribute to attrition as young women feel unneeded. But beyond retention, it seems that the Church owes it to these women and men, who have just dedicated years of their lives to serving their faith, to do as much as possible to help them feel whole, valued, and celebrated.

A New Identity

Missionaries do not only set aside their day-to-day lives in order to serve; they also set aside their identities. It is not unusual to hear a sister speak of letting go of "Jane" in order to become "Sister Smith." While some of these changes are part of shifting the focus away from themselves and toward the work of a missionary and to serving the Church and the people they meet, this change has additional dimensions. The sisters experience their mission as a life-changing event that shapes them into an altogether new person; when they return, they are not interested in going back to how things were before. The difficulty in letting go of their "old selves" while struggling to define their "new selves" is certainly one of the factors that makes the transition home so hard.

It is true that men also return from their missions greatly changed, and as mentioned above, they also face internal hardships in making the transition. But it is likely that the experience is different for women in one very important way: In a Church that assumes young men will serve a mission and begins preparing them for that role from a very young age, Mormon men are fulfilling an expecta-

---

24. Gordon B. Hinckley, "Latter-day Counsel: Selections from Addresses by President Gordon B. Hinckley," *Ensign*, March 2001, 65, quoted in Richard J. McClendon and Bruce A. Chadwick, "Latter-day Saint Returned Missionaries in the United States: A Survey on Religious Activity and Postmission Adjustment," *BYU Studies* 43, no. 2 (2004): 131.

25. Interviews conducted by Courtney Rabada; also discussed in depth in McClendon and Chadwick, "Latter-day Saint Returned Missionaries in the United States."

26. This theme is also explored in McClendon and Chadwick, "Latter-day Saint Returned Missionaries in the United States."

27. Interviews conducted by Courtney Rabada.

tion, while women are challenging traditional expectations in choosing to serve. Male returned missionaries have completed a familiar rite of passage; women are breaking new ground and may therefore have a more difficult time reconciling their new post-mission identities.

Consequently, the Church's ability to recognize and embrace the new identities of these women could have a significant impact on their relationship with the Church in the future. Sister missionaries have been empowered, educated, and enlightened. They have assumed larger roles in Church service, and cannot be expected to return home and revert to being the same people they were before they left.

The Future:
The Long-Term Impacts of the Age-Change Announcement

In addition to changing the lives of the sisters, the massive influx of missionaries could very well have a significant impact on the growth of the overall Church. Though current statistics show only a small increase in the number of convert baptisms since the age change, the numbers do suggest increases in convert retention and member activity rates. While more data would be necessary to draw definite inferences, it is possible that this growth is due to the missionaries' expanded focus on continued interaction with new and current members, and renewed efforts to bring lapsed members back to the Church.[28]

However, it is almost certain that the current surge of sister missionaries will have a lasting and powerful impact on future generations of Mormon women. Young women today will grow up in a Church in which serving a mission is not only more convenient but is culturally accepted. Most will have interacted with, and been taught and led by, returned sister missionaries who will not only have broken through barriers in their wards, but will also be able to serve as role models. Women serving missions will be a part of conversations and lessons in a way that they simply were not before the age-change announcement. Of course, this influence will also extend to the children of returned missionaries, more of whom will grow up in households in which their mothers and older sisters served missions.

As mentioned above, the age change could have a long-term impact on Mormon marriages in general. As one counselor stated, "Missionary service typically leads to temple marriage and the establishment of loving eternal family relationships. Couples sealed in the temple place greater importance on eternal families. They tend to have more children, and those children are more likely to become faithful adult members in the Church."[29] The lessons learned through

---

28. LDS Church Growth Blog, "Statistical Reports": "Convert Baptisms: 296,803 (increase of 13,858 from 2013; a 4.90% annual increase) . . . . The average number of converts baptized per missionary inched upward from 3.4 converts baptized per missionary in 2013 to 3.5 converts baptized per missionary in 2014."

29. Kevin W. Pearson, "The Value of a Returned Missionary," The Church of Jesus Christ of Latter-day Saints: Area Presidency Messages, August 2012, http://www.lds.org/pages/areapresidency/2012/aug (accessed May 25, 2015).

eighteen months of working with a constant companion will almost certainly have consequences for how wives and husbands interact and communicate with one another, and both Church authorities and members have long said that a returned sister missionary will "become a better wife, a better mother, a better Relief Society president."[30] Finally, the 2015 Pew Research Center study on the American religious landscape confirms that out of all Christian faiths, Mormons are the most likely to be married and "also tend to have larger families than [those] in other religious groups."[31]

Whether they are serving as a Relief Society president or in another calling, returned sister missionaries have also learned invaluable leadership skills. Mission service gives women confidence to deal with difficult situations, enlarges their scriptural and doctrinal knowledge, and empowers them to lead and assist other women. It also gives them a taste of what it will be like to serve in the Church through various callings or participation in ward councils, and there is some anecdotal evidence that a woman's missionary service has become a factor when leaders consider candidates for ward callings. Sisters report that their mission presidents speak to them explicitly about their futures as leaders of the Church, and they feel they have been given opportunities as sister training leaders and senior companions to hone these skills.[32]

These feelings of confidence and empowerment may also lead to women feeling more comfortable advocating for change within their wards. Whether it is pushing to be included in ward councils and other meetings, speaking up about discrepancies in the budgets or activities for the Young Women and Young Men organizations, or questioning the practice of calling only men to positions which do not specifically require priesthood authority (such as ward mission leader), returned sister missionaries will have the tools to instigate real and major changes within their Church.

However, it is very likely that most of these efforts for change will remain focused at the local or ward level. While returning sisters are uninterested in returning to the status quo on a personal level, there does not seem to be a strong

---

30. Franklin D. Richards, "Have a Dream," *New Era* 8 (January 1978): 4; quoted in Lyon and McFarland, "'Not Invited, But Welcome,'" 84. This idea is also mentioned in Jodi Kantor and Laurie Goodstein, "Missions Signal a Growing Role for Mormon Women," *New York Times*, March 1, 2014, http://www.nytimes.com/2014/03/02/us/a-growing-role-for-mormon-women.html (accessed May 25, 2015); and Associated Press, "More Women Expected to Serve Mormon Missions," *USA Today*, January 18, 2013, http://www.usatoday.com/story/news/nation/2013/01/18/mormon-women-missionaries/1844423/ (accessed May 25, 2015).

31. Pew Research Center, "Marital Status and Family Size of Religious Groups," *Religious Landscape Study*, May 12, 2015, http://www.pewforum.org/2015/05/12/chapter-3-demographic-profiles-of-religious-groups/ (accessed May 25, 2015).

32. Interviews conducted by Courtney Rabada.

interest in pushing for change in the Church hierarchy.³³ This response could be influenced by myriad factors: their relative youth, their focus on finishing school, marrying, and starting families, their recently strengthened testimonies which in turn reinforces their faith in the relative infallibility of the leaders of the Church, or the "distance" between their day-to-day experiences and the concerns of the larger institutional Church. Moreover, the post-correlation structure of the Church's organization does not provide mechanisms for women to interact with women or men above them in the hierarchy.³⁴ Women's opportunities to offer new ideas and perspectives are confined to the ward councils, with no analogous councils at the stake or general level.

Somewhat surprisingly, the Ordain Women movement may also have an impact on this generation of sister missionaries' interest in effecting change within their Church. First, the movement has spurred the Church leaders to focus on the topic of priesthood in a new, more gender-inclusive way, most notably in Elder Dallin H. Oaks's April 2014 general conference talk: "Priesthood keys direct women as well as men, and priesthood ordinances and priesthood authority pertain to women as well as men."³⁵ By changing the conversation about priesthood and emphasizing that it is available to women (though in explicitly limited forms), the imbalances have, in some ways, been neutralized. This message is strongly reinforced to the women and men serving missions during widespread conversations about priesthood power; and as such, it is not unusual to hear sister missionaries disclaim their desire for, or a woman's need to hold, the priesthood.³⁶ This conservative attitude regarding women's priesthood ordination is indicative of most LDS women's general reluctance to promote institutional-level changes. Second, the Church's handling and negative rhetoric surrounding the Ordain Women movement and its public actions, including requesting admission to the priesthood sessions at general conferences, have emphasized the otherness and minority status of Mormon feminists (and opened the door to making "feminism"

---

33. Interviews conducted by Courtney Rabada.

34. Until the mid-1960s, ward-level leaders of women's and children's organizations reported to their counterparts in the stake auxiliary presidencies, who in turn reported to the general presidencies and boards of those organizations in Salt Lake City, creating a female hierarchy that functioned with a great deal of independent control over curriculum, budgets, etc. The movement to streamline Church governance functions which came to be called "correlation" eroded the power of those auxiliary presidencies and changed the organizational structure of the Church so that ward auxiliary presidencies reported to bishops and stake auxiliary presidencies reported to stake presidents, thus severing lines of official communication and influence that had previously been the prerogative of the female leaders. See Matthew Bowman, *The Mormon People: The Making of an American Faith* (New York: Random House, 2012), 192–95.

35. Dallin H. Oaks, "The Keys and the Authority of the Priesthood," general conference, April 5, 2014, transcript, https://www.lds.org/general-conference/2014/04/the-keys-and-authority-of-the-priesthood?lang=eng (accessed May 25, 2015).

36. Interviews conducted by Courtney Rabada.

a dirty word again), thus rendering suspect and even threatening almost any suggestion for change that can be construed or understood as gender-motivated.[37]

However, there is at least some informal evidence that the patriarchal nature of the Church is less acceptable to younger generations of women. Taunalyn Ford Rutherford relates the following example given by one oral history subject: "The priesthood is the ruling power. . . . Even though you've got a Relief Society president it is still under the authority of priesthood. It doesn't bother me in the least. My eldest daughter is horrified at that sort of thing. But I'm not."[38] It is possible that many returning sister missionaries will begin to feel the weight of their Church's institutional patriarchy more heavily as time passes. Rather than feeling comfortable in inhabiting the Church's strictly defined gender roles, these young women could begin to experience a sense of disquiet and dissatisfaction, and a yearning for more opportunities, much like the "feminine mystique" that initiated second-wave feminism.[39]

The mere fact that tens of thousands of Mormon women have joined the missionary force points toward major changes for the LDS Church. They may take the shape as the influence returned sister missionaries will have on their children's decisions to serve missions. Perhaps there will be a shift toward the expectation for women to serve, with a focus on duty rather than just a desire. The Church could devote more resources to awareness and treatment of mental health issues

---

37. Interviews conducted by Courtney Rabada. After the April 2014 general conference, Church spokesperson Cody Craynor stated, "Despite polite and respectful requests from church leaders not to make Temple Square a place of protest, a mixed group of men and women ignored that request and staged a demonstration outside the Tabernacle on General Conference weekend, refusing to accept ushers' directions and refusing to leave when asked. . . . While not all the protesters were members of the church, such divisive actions are not the kind of behavior that is expected from Latter-day Saints and will be as disappointing to our members as it is to church leaders." Qtd. in Kristin Moulton, "Mormon Women Again Turned Away from Priesthood Meeting," *Salt Lake Tribune*, April 11, 2014 (http://www.sltrib.com/sltrib/news/57778960-78/women-church-square-ordain.html.csp (accessed May 25, 2015).

A similar sentiment was expressed by another Church spokesperson, Ruth Todd, in 2013: "Millions of women in the church do not share the views of this small group who organized today's protest, and most church members would see such efforts as divisive." Qtd. in Whitney Evans, "Women Hear Priesthood Session, but Not in Conference Center," *Deseret News*, October 5, 2013, http://www.deseretnews.com/article/865587795/Women-hear-LDS-Priesthood-meeting-but-not-at-conference-center.html?pg=all (accessed May 25, 2015).

38. Taunalyn Ford Rutherford, "Relief Society," in *Mormon Women Have Their Say: Essays from the Claremont Oral History Project*, edited by Claudia L. Bushman and Caroline Kline (Salt Lake City: Greg Kofford Books, 2013), 243.

39. Betty Friedan, *The Feminine Mystique*, edited by Kirsten Fermaglich and Lisa M. Fine, Norton Critical Editions (New York: W. W. Norton & Company, 2013), 12–13. First published in 1963.

in order to combat the anxiety and depression experienced by so many Mormon women, both in the mission field and elsewhere.[40] It is possible that women will begin to be called to those leadership positions that have traditionally been held by men but that do not require priesthood authority; at least one returned sister missionary has been called to the position of co-ward mission leader, though her official title is "sister training leader."[41] Perhaps the Church's future bishops, stake presidents, and apostles will bring their experiences in serving side-by-side with sister missionaries to their callings and will create more opportunities for women to participate in the decision-making process at all levels. But it seems most likely that Mormon women will speak out, both more clearly and more frequently, about their needs and concerns, and will push for the changes they want to see in their Church. These are all possibilities.

But what is certain is that the current generation of Mormon women has been empowered. They have been heard, they have deepened their testimonies, and they have experienced significant hardships and blessings. They are imbued with a wonderful sense of optimism about their futures, and the future of their Church. They believe, as one sister beautifully stated:

> The age change was intentional on God's part in progressing equality in the Church. This will have a huge impact on women feeling more empowered, and in seeing women feel equal with men. . . . It will promote women feeling entitled to have a voice in the Church. It will affect the way men see women in the Church. Women aren't apologizing anymore. They are confident in their knowledge and skill set and their ability to contribute. They won't be pushed aside or let someone look down on them. More women with this attitude will help push the Church in the direction of equality, and open-mindedness to the female perspective.[42]

In other words, they just might be unstoppable.

---

40. Ben Lockhart, "UVU Professor's Study Puts Focus on LDS Women and Depression," *Deseret News*, January 31, 2013, http://www.deseretnews.com/article/865571984/UVU-professors-study-puts-focus-on-LDS-women-and-depression.html?pg=all (accessed May 25, 2015); and James Thalman, "Utah Leads the Nation in Rates of Depression," *Deseret News*, November 29, 2007, http://www.deseretnews.com/article/695231614/Utah-leads-the-nation-in-rates-of-depression.html?pg=all (accessed May 25, 2015).

41. Interviews conducted by Courtney Rabada.

42. Caroline (pseud.), interviewed by Courtney Rabada, March 6, 2015, Brigham Young University, Provo Utah.

Chapter 14

An Insider Account of the Mormon Gender Issues Survey: Why We Did It and Why a Vocal Minority Hated It

Brent D. Beal, Heather K. Olson Beal, and S. Matthew Stearmer

On Sunday morning, November 16, 2014, we launched an online survey about gender issues in the Mormon Church. We were hoping, fingers crossed, that a few hundred fellow Mormons would click on the links we'd posted in several online groups and forums. If we were patient, we thought, we might get a thousand respondents.

Survey research is generally a pretty staid affair. Researchers often associate it with the cavernous quiet of libraries, the muffled shuffling of paper, and the barely audible scraping of pencil lead. This survey was different. We launched the survey on Sunday morning and by Monday afternoon, more than 50,000 respondents had completed it. We included three optional open-ended questions at the end of the survey. By the end of the second day, we'd received the equivalent of more than 5,000 single-spaced pages of text from more than 15,000 individuals. Utah Public Radio picked up the story.[1] So did KUER, a National Public Radio (NPR) member station licensed to the University of Utah in Salt Lake City.[2] The Mormon blogosphere (aka, the Bloggernacle[3]) was abuzz. We spent a few days giving each other virtual high-fives on our group's Facebook page. It was exciting.

It wasn't all good news, though. Hundreds of respondents left critical comments on a Google form we'd put up to collect feedback. Lengthy comment threads debating the survey's merits popped up like daisies on Facebook and on a number of Mormon blogs. Complaints were lodged with the institutional review boards of the universities that had approved the survey. Several members of our research group spent hours responding to angry emails. Although we disagreed with the bulk of criticism, we were struck by the negative emotions our survey evoked from a number of respondents. Some indicated, for example, that it made them "feel sick," that it felt "like a trap," and that negative emotional responses experienced while taking it were "warnings from the Holy Ghost" that we were

---

1. http://upr.org/post/mormon-gender-issues-survey-snowballs-social-media. All web addresses were last accessed in March 2015.
2. http://kuer.org/post/new-survey-lds-gender-issues-piques-interest-liberal-conservative-mormons.
3. http://en.wikipedia.org/wiki/Mormon_blogosphere.

up to no good. (See Appendix A). Others claimed that the survey was "anti-Mormon," "completely biased," designed to make Mormons look bad, and that it asked respondents to "throw their pearls before swine."

We suspect that our survey went viral[4] because it probed an increasingly sensitive issue for Mormons: the growing gap between gender egalitarianism in American culture and Mormonism's earnest attempts to protect and perpetuate a modified version of the "culture of domesticity" in which men naturally assume leadership and administrative responsibilities while women provide support as wives, mothers, and caretakers of the home.[5] In what follows, we describe the origins of the Mormon Gender Issues Survey Group, revisit our internal discussions and debates about the format, substance, and launch of our survey, and reflect on the intensely negative reactions of a vocal minority of survey respondents.

Why We Did It

It started with a post by Ryan Hammond in a private Facebook group on Thursday, March 27, 2014, at 8:06 A.M. "Do any of you know of any undergrad students who are looking for an undergrad project in a social science or statistics class? I would love to have them try and get some sort of random survey that mimics the Pew/American Grace ordination question and then asks some alternative/in-depth follow ups." Early participants in this thread included Brent D. Beal, who was planning to organize a group to conduct a similar survey and was in the process of setting up a Kickstarter page to raise money for it, Heather Olson Beal and Nancy Ross, both of whom were involved with Ordain Women and were interested in seeing a survey like this done, S. Matthew Stearmer, a PhD student in sociology interested in the study of networks and the diffusion of ideas and culture identity, and Jessica Finnigan, who had also been discussing the possibility of doing a similar survey with several colleagues. After a short discussion, we decided to create a Facebook page and call ourselves the Mormon Gender Issues Survey Group.

We started looking around in various online groups and forums for other people who might be interested in contributing to a survey that focused on equality issues in contemporary Mormonism. "The more the merrier," we thought. By the time we launched the survey, our group had grown to sixteen.[6] We were an eclectic mix of academics and professionals, including a senior research scientist in health and education studies, a business professor, a professor of secondary education, two graduate students in political science, two sociology professors and a sociology graduate student, a psychology professor, a PhD and two doctoral candidates in counseling psychology, and an art history professor. Some of us studied religion for a living and others had experience in survey work; all of us were Mormons or former Mormons.

---

4. The final count was 91,698 survey attempts. Excluding incomplete surveys and removing duplicate submissions based on IP address yielded 61,066 usable responses.

5. http://en.wikipedia.org/wiki/Cult_of_Domesticity.

6. http://mormongendersurvey.org/researchers/.

Two things brought the group together. First, we sensed that this was a timely topic. Ordain Women had recently pushed the broad issue of gender equality into the Mormon consciousness by directly engaging Mormon religious leaders on the specific proposition that women should be ordained to the lay Mormon priesthood—an issue central to the organizational structure and functioning of the LDS Church. Ordain Women had staged several public "actions" that had drawn media attention to the Church's patriarchal structure and had paired these actions with earnest petitions to the Church's all-male leadership to seek divine revelation sanctioning the ordination of women. Because Ordain Women intentionally balanced its criticism of the patriarchal status quo with an explicit appeal to the Church's all-male leadership for redress, the group was able to characterize its activities as "faithful" agitation—agitation that demonstrated a sincere belief in Mormonism and in the revelatory process, but that also maintained its commitment to spotlighting fundamental gender inequalities in the contemporary LDS Church.

Within the space of a few months, Ordain Women was featured in *USA Today*, *The New York Times*, *The Washington Post*, and *The Atlantic*, among numerous other outlets, and was discussed on *Good Morning, America*. As a group, Mormons are sensitive to external perceptions of their faith, and this concentrated media coverage had the effect of raising awareness in the Mormon community of the fact that many people outside the Church view the religiously relegated role of Mormon women as problematic. In addition to timeliness, we also sensed that there was a need for additional data. Several members of the group had noticed that it was routine for different media outlets, when covering gender issues in the Mormon Church, to cite the results of a 2011 survey of Mormons in the United States by the Pew Research Center.[7]

This was the question that Pew asked: "Should women who are dedicated members of the LDS Church be ordained to the priesthood? Eighty-seven percent said "no." Interestingly, women were more opposed than men (90% compared to 84%). For those with high religious commitment, 95% said "no." Opposition to female ordination was significantly lower for those with lower religious commitment (69%). Pew researchers derived these data from interviews conducted in October and November of 2011 with 1,019 self-identified Mormons. The interviews did not include individuals whom the Church still counted as members but who no longer self-identified as Mormon, nor did it include Mormons living outside the United States.

Members of our survey group were interested in challenging and updating the Pew findings in a number of different ways. Several of us, for example, wanted to know if the Pew numbers still held three years later in 2014. Several others argued that the phrasing of the survey question itself needed to be probed. Many Mormons believe that significant changes in Church policy, organizational struc-

---

7. "Mormons in American – Certain in Their Beliefs, Uncertain of Their Place in Society," http://www.pewforum.org/2012/01/12/mormons-in-america-executive-summary/.

ture, and doctrine are explicitly dictated by God through revelation to the Church's prophet-president. In this context—given that women are not currently eligible for priesthood ordination—asking Church members if women "should" be ordained is tantamount to asking them if they disagree with God's prophet and, by extension, with God himself. We felt that this question could be altered in a number of interesting ways to yield more nuanced responses. For example: "If the prophet were to receive a revelation indicating that women should be ordained, would you support it?" "If the prophet were to receive such a revelation, do you believe other members would support it?" "Do you believe the prophet will eventually receive a revelation giving women the priesthood?" "Do you believe that women will be given the priesthood sooner if the prophet actively petitions God for such a revelation?" "Do you believe that women will be given the priesthood sooner if women actively petition male Church leaders to seek such a revelation?"

Some of our survey group members wanted an opportunity to assess the way gender inequality is experienced within the Church and to gauge support for more incremental changes, such as equalizing the budgets for male and female youth activities, or allowing men and women to serve missions at the same age. Others were interested in documenting different justifications offered for gender differences and examining individual beliefs regarding the nature of revelation and the process of change within the Church. Finally, although the Pew study purported to answer the question of how much internal support exists in the Mormon Church for female ordination, the study included only self-identified Mormons in the United States, even though that subset of Mormons demographically and geographically represents a statistical minority of the 15+ million global membership formally claimed by the LDS Church.[8] Based on the Church's own definition of membership, gauging member support for female ordination should also include inactive and disaffiliated Mormons, as well as members residing in other countries.

Once we determined that there was enough commitment by those in our group to carry through with the survey, we wrote a short organizational document, which we discussed, refined, and approved by consensus. We collected professional biographies and, on April 27, 2014, we launched a Kickstarter campaign to raise funds for the project.[9] We ended the campaign a month later with pledges from 107 individuals totaling $4,727.00 (more than 150% of the initial fundraising goal of $3,000). Here's how we represented ourselves on our Kickstarter page:

> The Mormon Gender Issues Survey Group is a group of academics and other interested individuals that will design, outsource (to the degree possible, given resource constraints), oversee, and then publicize a survey of Mormons about their views on gender issues in the Mormon religious community. . . . This survey will capture the views of a wide range of Mormons (not just "active" Mormons), given that dissatisfaction with

---

8. http://www.mormonnewsroom.org/facts-and-stats.

9. https://www.kickstarter.com/projects/371903876/gender-and-equality-in-the-mormon-Church.

gender inequality in the LDS Church often plays a significant role in disaffiliation. The design and administration of the survey will be overseen by Dr. Michael Nielsen.

Group Dynamics

We introduced this chapter by noting the overwhelming response to our survey and then commenting on the intensely negative reactions of a vocal minority of respondents. (See Appendix A.) A good way to begin assessing negative reactions to the survey is to review what we did as a group for five and a half months between the end of the Kickstarter campaign and the survey launch on November 16, 2014.[10] We began by discussing and debating different strategies for ensuring the representativeness and the validity of our survey data. We concluded early on that if we wanted to know what members of the LDS Church thought about gender issues we would have to do two things: (1) define what we meant by "member" of the Church (i.e., we needed to define our population), and (2) figure out how to get a group of people to take our survey who "looked" like, or accurately reflected, this population.

The LDS Church regularly publishes membership statistics,[11] so initially it appeared that the appropriate population might be the group of people that the LDS Church currently considers to be members. Several of our survey group, including one of the authors of this chapter, were adamant about providing at least a tentative answer to the question of what percentage of Church members— i.e., members as defined by the LDS Church—were in favor of female ordination. In retrospect, this was a fairly naive hope that probably annoyed the more experienced religious scholars in the group. No truly definitive answer can be provided to this question. The LDS Church claimed, for example, 6,398,889 U.S. members at the end of 2012. Large-scale surveys indicate, however, that a smaller number self-identify as Mormon in the U.S. population.[12] Being listed as a member on the rolls of the LDS Church is not contingent on attending or even self-identifying as a Mormon. Anyone familiar with local ward membership rosters can attest that a significant percentage of the "members" of local congregations are "less active," have not attended the LDS Church in years, or, not infrequently, attend other local denominations.

---

10. Prior to launching the survey, we put up a web site that lists the names of individuals in the Mormon Gender Issues Survey Issue Group, along with phone numbers, emails, and short bios. For more information about individual members of the group, please visit http://mormongendersurvey.org/.

11. http://www.mormonnewsroom.org/facts-and-stats. The Church of Jesus Christ of Latter-day Saints, *Deseret News 2013 Church Almanac* (Salt Lake City: Deseret Book, 2013), http://en.wikipedia.org/wiki/The_Church_of_Jesus_Christ_of_Latter-day_Saints_membership_history.

12. Rick Phillips and Ryan T. Cragun, "Mormons in the United States 1990–2008: Socio-Demographic Trends and Regional Differences," 2011, http://commons.trincoll.edu/aris/publications/2008-2/mormons-in-the-united-states-1990-2008-socio-demographic-trends-and-regional-differences/ .

Outside the United States, the conflated problem of membership counts, inactivity rates, and disaffiliation is particularly evident. For example, in Mexico, the LDS Church reported approximately 1,200,000 in 2010,[13] but the 2010 national census found only 314,932 individuals in the population who self-identified as Mormon.[14] Similarly, in Brazil, the Church claimed approximately 1,100,000 members, but a 2010 census found only 226,509 Mormons in the population.[15] Similar discrepancies between Church-reported membership numbers and census data in Chile, New Zealand, and elsewhere, have been identified and discussed by several scholars and bloggers.[16] The degree of divergence between LDS membership numbers and census data in these countries is startling. These kinds of statistical discrepancies are not universal, however. Seventh-day Adventists, for example, claimed approximately 700,000 members in Mexico and 1,300,000 in Brazil,[17] and the same 2010 census data cited above found 661,878 and 1,561,070 Adventists in these countries, respectively. Jehovah's Witnesses, who employ a much stricter definition of membership, consistently report membership numbers that are significantly lower than figures typically reported in census data. For example, the Jehovah's Witnesses claimed approximately 700,000 members in Brazil, but 1,393,208 individuals self-identified as Witnesses in Brazil's 2010 census.[18]

So what does it mean to claim, based on the Pew survey, that "87% of Mormons are opposed to female ordination"? What population of Mormons is being referenced? In this case, a more accurate statement would be: "87% of individuals in the U.S. population that self-identify as Mormon are opposed to female ordination." As a survey team, we agreed to conceptualize "representativeness" as the actual number of individuals worldwide (not just in the United States) who self-identify as Mormon, excluding those on Church rolls who no longer consider

---

13. http://en.wikipedia.org/wiki/The_Church_of_Jesus_Christ_of_Latter-day_Saints_in_Mexico.

14. http://www.inegi.org.mx/prod_serv/contenidos/espanol/bvinegi/productos/censos/poblacion/2010/panora_religion/religiones_2010.pdf, see p. 3.

15. ftp://ftp.ibge.gov.br/Censos/Censo_Demografico_2010/Caracteristicas_Gerais_Religiao_Deficiencia/tab1_4.pdf.

16. Lowell C. Bennion and Lawrence A. Young, "The Uncertain Dynamics of LDS Expansion, 1950–2020," *Dialogue: A Journal of Mormon Thought* 29 (Spring 1996): 8–32; David C. Knowlton, "How Many Members Are There Really? Two Censuses and the Meaning of LDS Membership in Chile and Mexico," *Dialogue: A Journal of Mormon Thought* 38, no. 2 (2005): 53–78; Rick Phillips, "Rethinking the International Expansion of Mormonism," *Nova Religio: The Journal of Alternative & Emergent Religion* 10, no. 1 (2006): 52–68; Phillips and Cragun, Mormons in the United States 1990–2008." Also see the case studies on LDS growth worldwide on http://www.cumorah.com/.

17. http://www.adventiststatistics.org/.

18. ftp://ftp.ibge.gov.br/Censos/Censo_Demografico_2010/Caracteristicas_Gerais_Religiao_Deficiencia/tab1_4.pdf.

themselves to be Latter-day Saints.[19] At the same time, we included a few questions in the survey that we hoped would allow us to construct an educated guess about the hypothetical opinions of the 15+ million members officially recorded on Church rolls. One such question was: "According to its records, the Church of Jesus Christ of Latter-day Saints (LDS Church) has approximately 15 million members. Do you think your name is on the Church records?" Possible responses were: "(a) Yes, and I currently identify as LDS, (b) Yes, but I do not identify as LDS, (c) No, but I was LDS, and (d) No, I have never been LDS." By combining the results of this question with other questions related to Church activity, and then weighting responses based on demographic estimates of Church membership, we hoped to calculate a reasonable approximation of what this hypothetical population would say in response to our questions concerning gender and the priesthood. It is important to note, however, that religious scholars are generally more interested in the views of the actual Mormon population (defined by the common-sense notion of self-identification) than the theoretical group of "official" Mormons defined by Church membership records (particularly when the characteristics of the former diverge significantly from the latter).

Once we agreed on how to define our target population, we took three steps to maximize the representativeness of our sample. First, we contracted with a survey firm to administer a shortened version of our survey to a random national sample of U.S. Mormons. Second, we decided that after finishing the survey, respondents would receive a unique link encouraging them to email the survey to friends and/or share it on social media, a practice commonly called "snowball sampling." We anticipated that these links would allow us to track respondent referrals and reconstruct the respondent network. We generated approximately forty different starter links with the intention of placing them in different Mormon-related online groups and on a number of Mormon-themed blogs. We anticipated treating these starter links as network nodes, analyzing the responses associated with each and, based on the length of the network referral chain, assessing how average responses evolved. As a group, we shared and discussed research literature suggesting that data derived from individuals more than two or three levels deep in a referral (or snowball) network are generally representative of the larger population, regardless of the biases that may be associated with the starting nodes of the network.[20] And third, we elected to include a number of

---

19. Although we initially conceptualized our population this way, the survey was only available in English, and we cannot therefore claim that we successfully targeted this population.

20. M. A. Eland-Goossensen, Leo A. Van De Goor, E. C. Vollemans, V. M. Hendriks, and H. E. L. Garretsen, "Snowball Sampling Applied to Opiate Addicts outside the Treatment System," *Addiction Research* 5, no. 4 (1997): 317; L. A. Goodman, "Comment: On Respondent-Driven Sampling and Snowball Sampling in Hard-to-Reach Populations and Snowball Sampling Not in Hard-to-Reach Populations," *Sociological Methodology* 41, no. 1 (2011): 347–53; Douglas D. Heckathorn, "Comment: Snowball Versus Respondent-Driven Sampling," *Sociological Methodology* 41, no. 1 (2011): 355–66.

questions from other representative surveys of Mormons so that we could directly compare our results with the results of those previous surveys.[21]

In addition to the potential representativeness and validity of our data, we also debated the purpose of our survey, its objectives, and how best to achieve them. We worried about transparency, and we anticipated (perhaps, naïvely) that being clear about who we were and what we wanted up front would make respondents feel more comfortable. We wrote the survey as a group, collectively deciding which questions to include, determining how it should be formatted, and taking turns revising and editing the final set of questions. We recognized that how a question was worded was crucial. Because many Mormons believe that significant changes in the LDS Church will occur only if God instructs Church leaders to implement them, soliciting individual perceptions and beliefs is often difficult, particularly if those perceptions and beliefs can be interpreted as critical of the status quo, or are at odds with official Church policy.

To illustrate, the following comment received from an unhappy respondent confirmed that our concerns about how we worded the questionnaire were well-founded:

> Several of your questions involved a scenario regarding the First Presidency announcing a change that women could hold the priesthood. You asked if I would be supportive. My honest answer is yes, but that is because if it comes from the First Presidency, it is coming from God. On the survey, I answered no. Because what you asked was manipulating your data. I don't believe that the First Presidency will ever make that change, because it is not essential to God's plan, and I did not want to even remotely make it appear that I would support the idea. (capitalization standardized)

"How," we asked ourselves, "do we get at the personal perceptions and beliefs of individuals with these kinds of concerns?" Not only did this respondent answer "no" to a question to which she should have answered "yes," but she makes it clear that she would support female ordination if it were implemented by Church leadership (and therefore sanctioned by God). She proceeds, however, to conflate official Church doctrine ("not essential to God's plan") with her own beliefs that Church leaders will never advocate ordination of women. Instead of simply answering the question, she reframes it as a "trick" and answers in the negative in order to emphasize that her personal beliefs coincide with current Church teaching and policies that she believes are immutable. In the final analysis, despite the convoluted reasoning, these kinds of responses reflect an emphatic rejection of the possibility of any policy or doctrinal changes with respect to the Mormon priesthood.

In constructing the survey, we also wanted to include questions that would allow us to distinguish between respondents' desires to show solidarity with current Church doctrines and practices and any personal attitudes of misogyny. For

---

21. Questions were taken from the Pew 2011 National Survey of Mormons, http://www.thearda.com/Archive/Files/Codebooks/MORMON_CB.asp, and D. E. Campbell, J. C. Green, and J. Q. Monson. *Seeking the Promised Land: Mormons and American Politics* (New York: Cambridge University Press, 2014).

example, there are two ways to interpret the Pew data. One way is to infer that more devout members—and women in particular—were more concerned about showing solidarity with the Church's current position on gender roles than men or less devout members. An alternative (and less flattering) interpretation of the Pew data is that Mormon women and devout members in general are more misogynistic than Mormon men and less devout members. We debated at length about which of these interpretations was most plausible.

In the interest of transparency, we built a website (http://mormongendersurvey.org/) that explained who we were and what we were trying to accomplish with the survey. Two of our group members, Michael Nielsen at Georgia Southern University and Ryan Cragun at the University of Tampa, submitted proposals to their respective institutional review boards for approval, which was subsequently granted. Although Nielsen and Cragun were clearly competent in their roles, we did some hand-wringing about how, as a survey team, our own group dynamics in some respects seemed to mirror typical Mormon gender roles, with older and more experienced male researchers frequently assuming leadership roles. We worried about how the involvement of individual members of our team in other Mormon groups, podcasts, and blogs might be perceived. For example, two of our members, Heather Olson Beal and Nancy Ross, had served on the executive board of Ordain Women. Would respondents who checked our team biographies still consider the survey to be legitimate? We spent time debating the timing of the survey, second-guessing ourselves about how the Church's excommunication of Kate Kelly, one of the founders of Ordain Women, on June 23, 2014, might affect the results. We debated how long we needed to wait: three or four months after Kelly's excommunication? until October to coincide with the Church's general conference and another planned public action by Ordain Women? or until after the U.S. general elections in November? In the meantime, Matthew Stearmer, aided by several other group members, uploaded and formatted the survey in Qualtrics (the platform we planned to use to launch the survey online), and both Nancy Ross and Matthew Stearmer worked behind the scenes putting together a list of Mormon Facebook groups, discussion boards, blogs, and web pages where we intended to post links to the survey once we launched it. During all of this preparatory work, which lasted about five and a half months, we periodically informed our Kickstarter backers of our progress.

Why a Vocal Minority Hated It

A common rule-of-thumb in business is that for every customer who complains, there are probably ten more who are equally dissatisfied but who didn't take the time to voice their concerns. Although there are obvious differences between customers and survey respondents, in this case, the same rule likely applies. We received approximately 150 comments on a Google form that we set up to collect feedback on the survey, and collected approximately another three hundred critical comments from different Facebook groups, online forums, and blogs. A significant number of respondents also took advantage of the optional open-ended response items at the end of survey to complain about different aspects of the survey. An unscientific guess, based on the volume of this feedback and the loose application of the one-to-ten "iceberg" rule-of-thumb mentioned above, is that 5–10% of survey respondents were, for various reasons, unhappy with our survey. As the comments we received demonstrate, for a significant percentage of this vocal minority, taking our survey was a particularly distressing experience. (See Appendix A.) We believe that there were three primary reasons this was the case: (1) our "home court" advantage, (2) our indifference about whether or not survey results would support existing Mormon narrative or beliefs, and (3) a sense of betrayal engendered by our Mormon backgrounds.

Home Court Advantage

One common refrain in the criticism we received in response to the survey after its launch was that our questions were biased. Initially, this complaint puzzled us. Although there are different kinds of bias (researcher or experimenter bias, selection bias, response bias), which can be attributed to different causes (e.g., leading questions, social desirability attribution), we felt we had taken adequate precautions against these potential problems. In more than five and a half months of active discussion among survey group members, no consistent preference for any particular outcome had been expressed. In fact, as a group, we were unable to decide what outcome might be more or less "favorable" for the LDS Church. If a high number of Church members, for example, opposed female ordination, then Mormonism as a religion might appear to sustain a sexist culture out of step with contemporary gender norms. On the other hand, if a relatively large number of Church members supported ordination, then the (all-male) leadership of the Church, in particular, might look out of touch with the modern world. Because we didn't have a preference for a particular outcome, the accusation that we designed a survey that was intended to produce a particular outcome (i.e., that reflected researcher bias) was particularly frustrating.

One of the authors of this chapter recalls a particular exchange with an unhappy survey respondent who, in response to being asked if he felt that we would purposely tamper with the results of the survey to produce a particular outcome, responded by asserting that "it's not the results that are biased, it's the survey itself." Upon reflection, we think we understand what this respondent, and a number of others who complained about the survey, meant when they accused us of bias. (See Appendix A.) As a research team, we were comfortable defining gender equality in a way that explicitly included the level of input (or influence) that women have in structuring the relationships and institutions around them. For us, there is no hedging on this basic principle. If women's participation in the governance of a particular group or organization is restricted based on their gender, then the principle of gender equality is violated. Defining gender equality in these terms is consistent with our professional training and our academic experience, and we are comfortable acknowledging this bias. From our perspective, an essential component of gender equality is the concept that men and women, despite any other biological or cultural differences, should be equal in one critical respect: They should be afforded the same rights and opportunities for institutional authority and political influence.

As one Mormon blogger put it, defining gender equality this way implies that "equality is not a feeling":[22] it can be quantified, analyzed, and assessed. Given our concept of gender equality, men and women in the LDS Church are not treated equally. For example, virtually all of the top leadership positions in the Church are reserved exclusively for men; women cannot administer the same religious rites routinely administered by lay males, including boys and male youths; men monopolize most of the speaking time during annual general conference sessions; many more men than women are professors and administrators at the Church's flagship university (Brigham Young University); the number of active men in designated localities is a determining factor used to determine if new congregations are formed (the number of women in these localities is irrelevant); access to the restricted parts of the *Church Handbook of Instructions: Book 1* is available to approximately 100,000 men, but to only nine women;[23] male youth have more organizational duties and responsibilities, more opportunities for public recognition, and more resources and money devoted to their activities than their female counterparts; men are over-represented in stories and images in Church manuals; women are not allowed to participate in Church disciplinary councils except as defendants and witnesses, and so on.[24]

Given our understanding of gender equality, one of the primary objectives of the survey was to assess the degree to which Mormon respondents shared this view and, correspondingly, the degree to which they found existing gender roles in the Church to be problematic. Although we included optional open-ended questions at the end of the survey allowing respondents to explain and/or defend their views, the constrained-choice questions part of the survey did not allow for this possibility. For example, one constrained-choice question explicitly asked if respondents were "concerned" about existing gender roles. Another question listed a number of situations involving gender discrimination (e.g., women not being included in congregation decision-making processes, women's exclusion from the naming and blessing of infants) and asked respondents to check those they have personally witnessed in the prior three months. Another set of ques-

---

22. http://www.dovesandserpents.org/wp/category/columns/equality-is-not-feeling/.

23. Beginning in 1998, the handbook was divided into two volumes. Book 1 is available only to stake presidencies and bishoprics (hence, approximately 100,000 men), but only to the Relief Society, Young Women, and Primary general presidencies (nine women). The second volume, *Book 2: Priesthood and Auxiliary Leaders*, is readily available to anyone through regional distribution centers and online at http://www.ldsChurch.org.

24. See http://www.dovesandserpents.org/wp/category/columns/equality-is-not-feeling/; also see http://www.ldswave.org/?p=402.

tions asked respondents to provide their opinion about the likelihood of these gender policies being changed.

The constrained-choice format of the main portion of the survey was designed to assess agreement with our conception of gender equality. We wanted to know how many (and to what extent) members of the LDS Church viewed gender inequality to be problematic, and how many (and to what extent) members viewed female ordination as a viable solution. In other words, we asked respondents to agree or disagree with an egalitarian critique of gender roles in contemporary Mormonism, and a vocal minority didn't like it. Many of those who didn't like our approach aired their complaints in the optional, open-ended questions at the end of the survey or in a Google form we had set up to collect voluntary feedback.[25] Respondents offered both negative critiques of the integrity of our survey and defended traditional Mormon justifications for an all-male priesthood. These justifications generally fell into the following categories: (1) separate-but-equal arguments (often grounded in appeals to biological differences between the sexes); (2) arguments that conflated gender equality with importance or worth (i.e., we all have equal worth in God's eyes; ergo, men and women are "equal"); (3) assertions that because one doesn't "feel" unequal, gender inequality isn't a problem; (4) arguments that hinge on women's exercise of "soft" power (e.g., through personal persuasion, or by virtue of their relationships with their husbands or other men in decision-making positions in the priesthood hierarchy); and (5) variations on the "because-God-wants-it-this-way" appeals to divine authority. Similar justifying explanations can be easily accessed on LDS.org (the official Church website) where one can see that Church leaders have been repeating these same arguments in different forums for decades.

Viewed from this perspective, many of the critical comments in Appendix A make sense. Did the survey imply that "there is something wrong with how our Church does things"? Yes, it did. Could respondents have gotten a "bad feeling" while taking the survey? It's entirely possible, because, in order to assess discontent with a perceived problem, the problem has to be explicitly referenced, and for some individuals this was a jarring experience. Were we "leading the witness"? Not in the sense that we wanted a specific outcome, but yes, in the sense that the survey demanded that respondents consider, at least temporarily, our view of the nature of gender inequality inherent in existing Church practices (even if they disagreed with our framing of it). Does it make sense for respondents to claim that "something feels amiss?" Yes, because we were implicitly encouraging respondents to think critically about gender roles, and this line of thought can

---

25. To be specific, quite a few respondents failed to complete the survey, although statistically, it's not clear why, because the completion rate wasn't significantly different across different nodes, i.e., first-wave completion rates were the same for liberal and conservative nodes. Another consideration is that respondents didn't know they would be presented with the option of responding to open-ended questions, unless they had talked to someone who had taken the survey before them.

feel subversive in a top-down hierarchical organization run by leaders who are believed to be in direct communication with Deity. We therefore infer that the first reason a vocal minority of respondents were unhappy with the survey was because of our "home-court" advantage. It was our survey and we picked the questions. And yes, the questions were grounded in our definition of gender equality and our assumptions about gender practices in the Mormon Church.

Empirical Accuracy versus Support for Existing Beliefs

The second reason we believe we received a relatively large number of critical comments about our survey is more subtle. Conversion to Mormonism is a two-step process. The first step is usually characterized, at least retrospectively, as a search process in which individuals consider different religious and spiritual options, carefully weigh Mormon truth claims, and then appeal directly to God to confirm, through some sort of spiritual experience, that these claims are "true." This step is often described as "gaining a testimony." It is important to note that the typical Mormon narrative normally stresses the role of agency and the careful consideration of different spiritual options before claiming receipt of divine confirmation of Mormonism's truthfulness. Once one has "gained a testimony" of Mormon truth claims, the second step involves committing to do what Church leaders say to do, or what they report God has revealed for us to do (e.g., pay tithing, attend the temple, do genealogy work, serve in various "callings" in local congregations, and so forth). The reward for being obedient to official Church counsel consists of immediate blessings (e.g., a happy family, professional success, a healthy spiritual life, and personal happiness and contentment,) and eternal rewards (e.g., entry into the celestial kingdom, possessing an intact family unit for eternity, and the opportunity to continue progressing in various ways in the afterlife). Members are warned that disobedience will result in God's withdrawing his protection and guidance, ultimately leading to a reduced sense of fulfillment and/or happiness in this life, and to a lesser reward in the afterlife.

Understanding how this two-step process is conceptualized by many Church members is important because it explains the frequent juxtaposition of what might appear to outsiders to be two mutually incompatible Mormons precepts: (1) personal agency and responsibility, and (2) unwavering obedience.[26] It can be argued that Mormons are able to preserve their commitment to the ideal of personal agency by focusing on its exercise in the first step of conversion, then ignoring the fact that they surrender it in the second. Members of the Mormon Church often occupy a tentative space between these two steps, alternatively emphasizing one, then the other, in a self-reinforcing pattern of commitment and obedience. For example, spiritual experiences that led one to the conclusion that Mormonism is "true" are often recalled later on to strengthen one's resolve to be

---

26. http://www.dovesandserpents.org/wp/2012/04/28-mcs-dissonance-101/.

obedient to religious dictates. This obedience often results in spiritual experiences that, in turn, can be leveraged to motivate future obedience.

In general, many Church members who have taken the first step in the conversion process by interpreting personal spiritual experiences as evidence of the Church's truthfulness do their best to avoid situations in which their testimony of the Church is brought into explicit conflict either with their own ideas or beliefs or with new ideas or information. This tendency is not uniquely Mormon, of course, and is explained by the psychological principle of cognitive dissonance—defined as the mental stress or discomfort derived from holding contradictory ideas or beliefs.[27] One conclusion that might be drawn is that our survey, by explicitly conveying negative ideas about Mormon gender roles, forced respondents to confront two contradictory ideas: (1) the Mormon Church is true, and (2) the Mormon Church treats women unfairly. Arguably, this implicit contradiction created cognitive dissonance, which prompted a number of survey respondents to adopt an attitude of righteous defensiveness.

Although this explanation may apply in a number of cases, we prefer a more subtle explanation. Mormons are accustomed to employing a number of different coping strategies in order to preserve perceptions of themselves as rational and volitional actors and also to make sense of their own ongoing commitment to the LDS Church. One of the strategies that members employ is to avoid reassessing the process of assigning meaning to the spiritual experiences that led them to gain a testimony of Mormonism's truth claims. They intentionally treat these conclusions (i.e., their testimony) as "settled" and therefore inviolate. Mormon youth learn to employ this strategy when they are taught to distinguish between "questioning" (or "doubting") and "asking questions."[28] As often framed by Church leaders, the act of questioning involves rethinking and reassessing the chain of assumptions and attributions at the core of one's commitment to Mormonism. Questioning, in this sense, represents an effort to allow new ideas and experiences to shape one's religious beliefs, and is therefore framed by Church leaders as a perilous process that can have unforeseen and long-lasting spiritual consequences. In contrast, "asking questions" assumes that the foundational truth claims of Mormonism are valid (and therefore don't need to be reexamined), and focuses instead on resolving apparent contradictions by finding suitable ways to interpret new experiences and ideas that are compatible with one's existing faith commitment. Asking questions, therefore, is about making new experiences and ideas conform to existing beliefs (instead of the other way around).

Once an individual has taken the first step in the conversion process by interpreting spiritual experiences as confirmation of the validity of Mormonism, there is a natural tendency to avoid situations in which this conclusion is challenged

---

27. http://en.wikipedia.org/wiki/Cognitive_dissonance.

28. https://www.lds.org/youth/article/when-you-have-questions; see also Adam Kotter, "When Doubts and Questions Arise," *Ensign*, March 2015, 37–39.

or called into question. This avoidance often leads to an emphasis on identifying and empathizing experiences that support these *a priori* religious beliefs, an approach that can quickly devolve into a self-reinforcing pattern of confirmation bias.[29] New experiences or new ideas are judged by whether or not they can be interpreted in a way that supports existing beliefs. If they can't, they are ignored, suspected of being unreliable, or set aside for possible additional consideration at some point in the future. For example, information about the growth of the Church (converts, number of missionaries, new temples, etc.) confirms Mormon truth claims and is therefore readily accepted as valid. Information about high levels of "inactivity," large discrepancies between census data and official membership numbers in different countries (e.g., in Mexico, Brazil, Chile), and high rates of disaffiliation are often ignored or treated as unreliable. This selective focus creates a situation in which information about the Church is assessed and placed on one of two extremes on a moral continuum; either information confirms Mormon narratives and beliefs (and is therefore valid and worthy of praise), or it challenges and undermines these narratives and beliefs (and is therefore illegitimate and is treated with suspicion, if not derision).

As a group of researchers, we didn't operate on this same continuum. We were not concerned about whether or not the results of our survey would support or undermine Mormon narratives or beliefs. We understood that our survey would be judged by the degree to which our results could be defended as an accurate description of a social reality that is assumed to be empirically (and reproducibly) accessible to other researchers. Instead of asking ourselves if the results of our survey would support or undermine Mormon narratives or beliefs, we asked ourselves this question: "Will our results accurately reflect what the actual population of self-identified Mormons think about gender equality (as we define it) in the LDS Church."

Several of the comments in Appendix A illustrate these differences. If respondents didn't anticipate that the results of our survey would support current Mormon belief and practice, then they concluded that we were "anti-Mormon," as indicated by these kinds of statements: "Your voice will not be heard unless you are anti-Mormon"; "I felt it was written (or heavily influenced) by an anti-Mormon"; "it was definitely a trap," and so on. Because our survey (and our research group by extension) couldn't be comfortably assigned to the "supportive" end of the continuum used by many Mormons to determine the utility and/or reliability of new ideas or experiences, we were immediately viewed with suspicion and mistrust.

Sense of Betrayal

Nearly everyone in the Mormon Gender Issues Survey Group grew up in the Mormon faith, and many of us had served full-time missions and/or served in various Church leadership roles. Although our familiarity with Mormonism

---

29. http://en.wikipedia.org/wiki/Confirmation_bias.

was an asset in a number of respects, we believe it also worked against us. Because we knew what to ask (and how to ask it), we believe that the survey effectively "outed" us as ostensible insiders (a fact that a simple Google search using our names would have confirmed). Because of this, we weren't given the same leeway that a tight-knit community might afford to "outside" investigators.

Mistrust of our survey by many Church members was further compounded by the fact that we adopted a "foreign" (i.e., an external and more generally accepted) view of gender equality and were prepared to assess the value of our work by a different set of criteria than that employed by many members of the Mormon community. This, we conclude, created a palpable sense of "betrayal" for some of our respondents. Consequently, we were perceived as turncoats by some survey respondents, and our motives were explicitly questioned on a number of different Mormon blogs and in different Mormon-related groups and forums.

Now What?

On the one hand, we sympathize with respondents who were distressed by our survey. We believe that their negative feelings and reactions were authentic. On the other hand, we believe that their experience should also serve as a cautionary tale. Unreflective acceptance of the Church's truth claims can lead to an unhealthy rigidity of belief and a worrisome commitment to "obedience," with potentially negative consequences for both individuals and the groups to which they belong. It can lead to insularity, reliance on confirmation bias to reduce cognitive dissonance, and an insider-versus-outsider mentality. It can also lead to the conclusion that a survey on gender issues written by a group of academics is a conspiratorial and sinister attempt to undermine the faith of true believers.

Gender issues in the LDS Church are a weighty business—messy and complex. As you read this, we are probably still wading through the data produced by the survey. With close to a hundred different response items, hundreds of different interconnections and relationships between these data points, and thousands of pages of text from our three open-ended questions, we'll be able to occupy ourselves for years trying to make sense of it all.

So what, in fact, were the primary findings of the survey, you might ask? The two following chapters in this volume are dedicated to answering that question (as are a number of different chapters and academic articles currently in progress). We sincerely thank those who donated to our Kickstarter campaign and who took the time to respond to our survey. Please access our website (http://mormongendersurvey.org/) for future updates and links to our findings.

Appendix A
A Sample of Critical Comments

Note: The responses quoted below are excerpted from, in many cases, much longer and more detailed responses, but which focused repeatedly on the same concerns (tone, perceived bias, anti-Mormon agenda, etc.). Punctuation and capitalization are standardized; typographical (e.g., "prefect" instead of "perfect") and grammatical errors are silently corrected. We changed respondents' trailing periods to dashes to eliminate confusion about whether we had edited the responses. All ellipses in the quotations below are ours.

- I started taking the survey and then felt wrong about it and stopped answering the questions.
- I am reading that a lot of women on here feel bad about taking this survey. Listen to that feeling! It is the Holy Ghost warning you against it!!!
- It was definitely a trap. I smell a rat! I know a thing or two about how surveys are formed. You don't need to be an expert to know that that survey is bad news.
- This is not written as a legitimate survey. It reads more like a propaganda piece. You can get that faithful women in the Church will be made to look subservient and brainwashed.
- The priesthood is ordained of God and had been passed down through the male line! I do not believe women need to challenge and waste their time to change what has always been! . . . We do not need to take on the priesthood because of our drive to be an exact equal. That is absurd.
- To take this survey is to enter the devil's playing ground in the hopes of fair play. It has already come forth that this is the Ordain Women's movement and that they are manipulating the survey. Counting the number of people partaking REGARDLESS of your answer . . . is being reported as in favor of their stance. The Lord did not do anything in secrecy, or anonymity nor shall I. That should have been the first clue that something was amiss.
- None of us understands gender issues from God's point of view. It would be foolish for anyone to truly believe that they do. My guess is that THERE ARE NOT GENDER ISSUES from God's point of view.
- Completely biased. These questions are worded to make us fail. There were multiple questions where the answer that best fits the Church doctrine is between the two answers or not present at all. I preferred not to respond to many of them because they felt like AMMO. As if you were thinking, "How can we use these stats to misquote the Mormon population and make them look bad?"
- I felt a bit as if I was throwing my pearls before swine.
- I took it. I felt it was written (or heavily influenced) by an anti-Mormon and some of the questions were worded wrong (you had to choose to answer what you thought it intended to ask or to answer what it literally asked—either way it would be easy for the answers to be manipulated to imply incorrect things).
- I don't feel that Mormons have "issues" regarding gender and the title of the survey alone told me that the questions were going to be open ended and biased in an effort to skew the world['s] view toward the Church.
- After taking it, something feels amiss. I will not be sharing it with my large LDS friend groups. Something seems quite wrong.

- Needless to say, I was disappointed in you guys for trying to make this look legit when it is so obviously biased to the hypothesis that Mormons have a "bad" view of gender roles.
- Several of your questions involved a scenario regarding the First Presidency announcing a change that women could hold the priesthood. You asked if I would be supportive. My honest answer is yes, but that is because if it comes from the First Presidency, it is coming from God. On the survey, I answered no. Because what you asked was manipulating your data. I don't believe that the First Presidency will ever make that change, because it is not essential to God's plan, and I did not want to even remotely make it appear that I would support the idea.
- I hated this survey because the whole implication was that there is something wrong with how our Church does things.
- If you take this survey, your voice will not be heard unless you are anti-Mormon. This survey is sponsored by anti-Mormons who have a track record of using surveys to distort the Church's position on issues and to generate negative publicity for the Church. No matter what you answer, it will not turn out well, so there's no point in participating. The people behind this have proven themselves dishonest on previous surveys. Don't bother.
- As a former test maker (teacher) these questions would get me nowhere in determining the knowledge (or feelings in this matter) of my students. Whenever I was tempted to ask questions like this, I always just took a minute to think how it might be worded better, in order to not to lead my student. You can also think about it in a different way. I am a law student; and when I found myself reading some of your questions, I yelled out, "Objection, Your Honor, the opposition is leading the witness."
- The questions are completely biased and skewed to try to get people to answer the way that you want them to, instead of how they really feel about things. How can you ever get real answers from members of our Church if the questions aren't neutral? Oh, that's right, you probably aren't concerned about real answers. You just want answers that fit your agenda. Yes, I am miffed. Yes, I am irritated. Yes, the Ordain Women movement is crap from a garbage heap. That is how I really feel.
- We don't need trained social scientists to give us the opportunity "to see, hear, learn, and understand the truth" of who we are. We have scripture, prophets, prayer, and personal revelation to reveal all of that to us. And that comes from the Lord, not a survey.
- I took the survey so my voice would be heard. But a lot of those questions made me feel sick.

Appendix B:
Sample Survey Questions*

- According to its records, the Church of Jesus Christ of Latter-day Saints (LDS Church) has approximately 15 million members. Do you think your name is on the Church records? [Responses: Yes, and I currently identify as LDS; Yes, but I do not identify as LDS; No, but I was LDS; No, I have never been LDS; Don't know; Prefer not to respond]
- Take a moment and think of the individuals with whom you have socialized during your leisure time during the past month. Indicate below the rough percentage of these individuals who are members of the Church. [Responses: Sliding Percentage Scale]
- How active are you in the LDS Church? [Responses: Very active; Somewhat active; Not too active; Not at all active; Don't know; Prefer not to respond]

- Do you hold a current temple recommend? [Responses: Yes; No; Don't know]
- Is believing that Joseph Smith literally saw God the Father and Jesus Christ essential for being a good Mormon? [Responses: Essential; Important, but not essential; Not too important; Not at all important; Don't know; Prefer not to respond]
- Which statement comes closer to your own view, even if neither is exactly right? [Responses: Some teachings of the LDS Church are hard for me to accept; I believe wholeheartedly in all the teachings of the LDS Church; Don't know; Prefer not to respond]
- Which statement comes closer to your own view, even if neither is exactly right? [Responses: A good Latter-day Saint should obey the counsel of priesthood leaders without necessarily knowing why; A good Latter-day Saint should first seek his or her own personal revelation as the motivation to obey.]
- Have you personally observed any of the following within the LDS community in the last three months? (please check all that apply): Women, young women, and/or young girls . . . being told that they should dress a particular way to help boys/men have pure thoughts; feeling that they cannot express their opinions about how ward organizations are run; not being consulted about important ward decisions; feeling left out of baby blessings; feeling uncomfortable talking with male priesthood authorities in private settings; limiting career goals to conform to cultural expectations; feeling that they cannot ask questions important to them; feeling that they do not want to come to Church because of the pressure to conform to cultural expectations.
- Please carefully read each of the following statements and indicate your level of agreement or disagreement: God has established different roles for men and women; God has revealed that only men should hold the priesthood; It's not fair that 12-year-old boys can pass the sacrament, but 12-year-old girls can not; Women who feel unequal to men at church don't understand the gospel; Feminism is incompatible with the restored gospel of Jesus Christ; The way women are treated in the Church is a problem; If women were given more leadership responsibilities, it would strengthen the Church. [Responses: Strongly disagree; Disagree; Neutral; Agree; Strongly agree; Don't know]
- Do you, personally, believe that women who are dedicated members of the Church should have the opportunity to be ordained to the priesthood? [Responses: Yes; No; Other; Don't know; Prefer not to respond]
- We are interested in your open-ended responses to a few additional questions. . . Would you like to answer the open-ended questions or would you prefer to end the survey?
    A) Men and women are treated differently in the Church. Some of these differences are considered cultural, others doctrinal. Please describe these differences and why you feel they are beneficial or not beneficial.
    B) If women were to serve in more administrative and leadership roles in the LDS Church, how would that affect your religious/spiritual life? Please comment in as much detail as possible.
    C) What changes related to women, if any, do you hope the Church will implement over the next ten or twenty years? Describe these changes in as much detail as possible. Why do you believe these changes are important?

*This is not a complete list of questions. A number of standard demographic questions were asked, none of which are reproduced here.

Chapter 15

The Mormon Gender Issues Survey: A Quantitative Analysis of U.S. Respondents

Ryan T. Cragun and Michael Nielsen

Introduction

While women's roles in religions have long been debated,[1] a growing body of research in recent decades has turned to issues surrounding gender inequality in religions.[2] Some of this research has focused on the roles of women in the LDS Church. For instance, scholars have noted that Mormon women used to hold and utilize the priesthood[3] on a regular basis,[4] and have detailed how the male leaders of the Church removed Mormon women's priesthood gradually over time, centralizing authority in the male priesthood bodies of the Church.[5] Other

---

1. R. Emerson Dobash and Russell P. Dobash, "Love, Honour and Obey: Institutional Ideologies and the Struggle for Battered Women," *Contemporary Crises* 1, no. 4 (October 1977): 403–15; Ronald G. Stover and Christine A. Hope, "Monotheism and Gender Status: A Cross-Societal Study," *Social Forces* 63, no. 2 (1984): 335–48; Tim B. Heaton and Marie Cornwall, "Religious Group Variation in the Socioeconomic Status and Family Behavior of Women," *Journal for the Scientific Study of Religion* 28, no. 3 (1989): 283–99.

2. Mark Chaves, *Ordaining Women: Culture and Conflict in Religious Organizations* (Cambridge, Mass.: Harvard University Press, 1997); Jimi Adams, "Stained Glass Makes the Ceiling Visible: Organizational Opposition to Women in Congregational Leadership," *Gender & Society* 21, no. 1 (February 2007): 80–105; Jaime Kucinskas, "A Research Note on Islam and Gender Egalitarianism: An Examination of Egyptian and Saudi Arabian Youth Attitudes," *Journal for the Scientific Study of Religion* 49, no. 4 (2010): 761–70; John P. Bartkowski and Lynn M. Hempel, "Sex and Gender Traditionalism among Conservative Protestants: Does the Difference Make a Difference?" *Journal for the Scientific Study of Religion* 48, no. 4 (December 2009): 805–16, doi:10.1111/j.1468-5906.2009.01487.x; John E. Hoffmann and John E. Bartkowski, "Gender, Religious Tradition and Biblical Literalism," *Social Forces* 86, no. 3 (March 2008): 1245–72.

3. Grethe Ballif Peterson, "Priesthood and Latter-day Saint Women: Eight Contemporary Definitions," in *Sisters in Spirit: Mormon Women in Historical and Cultural Perspective*, edited by Maureen Ursenbach Beecher and Lavina Fielding Anderson (Urbana: University of Illinois Press, 1992), 249–68.

4. Carol Cornwall Madsen, "Mormon Women and the Temple: Toward a New Understanding," in *Sisters in Spirit: Mormon Women in Historical and Cultural Perspective*, edited by Maureen Ursenbach Beecher and Lavina Fielding Anderson (Urbana: University of Illinois Press, 1992), 80–110.

5. Jennifer Huss Basquiat, "Reproducing Patriarchy and Erasing Feminism: The Selective Construction of History within the Mormon Community," *Journal of Feminist Studies in Religion* 17, no. 2 (October 1, 2001): 5–37; Linda King Newell, "Gifts of the

research has shown that conceptions of gender in the Church, while changing slightly over the last fifty to sixty years, remain highly unequal, with women cast in subordinate and subservient roles to men.[6]

As most if not all of the chapters in this book illustrate, there is growing interest in gender issues in the LDS Church today. In this chapter, we present some of the findings of the 2014 Mormon Gender Issues Survey, focusing on basic descriptive statistics from the survey. In the process, we answer certain questions but also make it clear that there is a great deal still to be investigated when it comes to gender issues in the LDS Church.

Background on the Survey

The preceding chapter detailed the motivations behind fielding the Mormon Gender Issues Survey. In this chapter, we focus on the methodology employed in gathering the data.

The Mormon Gender Survey Group fielded two surveys to examine attitudes and views concerning gender issues in the LDS Church. Prior to data collection, Institutional Review Board (IRB) approval was obtained from The University of Tampa and Georgia Southern University. The first survey was designed to be a nationally representative, random sample of members of the Church. For this sample we contracted with Qualtrics, a survey company that has a database of individuals who have agreed to participate in surveys for compensation. Among the demographic data that Qualtrics has identified in its potential pool of survey participants is religious affiliation. Thus, for our survey, Qualtrics chose a random sample of individuals from its database who had identified their religious affiliation as the Church of Jesus Christ of Latter-day Saints, LDS, or Mormon, and asked them to participate in the survey. Qualtrics indicated that they could guarantee a final representative sample of roughly 500 responses from people identified as LDS or Mormon. This survey was launched in November of 2014 and remained open for just under a week. During that time, 624 individuals clicked on the survey link Qualtrics sent them. However, after reading the informed con-

---

Spirit: Women's Share," in *Sisters in Spirit: Mormon Women in Historical and Cultural Perspective*, edited by Maureen Ursenbach Beecher and Lavina Fielding Anderson (Urbana: University of Illinois Press, 1992), 111–50.

6. J. Edward Sumerau and Ryan T. Cragun, "The Hallmarks of Righteous Women: Gendered Background Expectations in the Church of Jesus Christ of Latter-day Saints," *Sociology of Religion* 76, no. 1 (2015): 49–71, doi:10.1093/socrel/sru040; Laurence R. Iannaccone and Carrie A. Miles, "Dealing with Social Change: The Mormon Church's Response to Change in Women's Roles," *Social Forces* 68, no. 4 (1990): 1231–50; Carrie A. Miles, "LDS Family Ideals versus the Equality of Women: Navigating the Changes since 1957," in *Revisiting Thomas F. O'Dea's* The Mormons: *Contemporary Perspectives*, edited by Cardell K. Jacobson, John P. Hoffman, and Tim B. Heaton (Salt Lake City: University of Utah Press, 2008), 101–34; Laura Vance, "Evolution of Ideals for Women in Mormon Periodicals, 1897–1999," *Sociology of Religion* 63, no. 1 (March 20, 2002): 91–112, doi:10.2307/3712541.

sent statement, eight individuals did not agree to take the survey. Additionally, thirty-three of those invited to participate were excluded from the survey because they had never been members of the LDS Church. Another fifty-eight participants were dropped from the final sample based on either the speed with which they took the survey or their failure to respond accurately to an "attention question," suggesting they were not paying close attention to the survey items. After removing all of the above individuals, the final sample size was 525 participants. Throughout this chapter we will refer to this sample as the "random" sample.

The second survey we fielded was a purposive sample,[7] which we refer to in this chapter as the "purposive" sample. There were two reasons for gathering a purposive sample in addition to the random sample. First, given the cost of the random sample, we were limited in the number of items we could include. With a self-hosted online purposive sample, we could expand the number of survey items we included without increasing the cost. Second, the purposive sample allowed us to gather qualitative data, which we were unable to do with the random sample. (See Chapters 16 and 17 for findings based on the qualitative data.)

Uncertain of how many responses we would get for the purposive survey, we initially planned to keep the survey up for a month, hoping for roughly 5,000 responses. We launched the survey on November 16, 2014, posting initial links in a variety of locations on the internet, including Facebook groups, blogs, and forums covering a wide spectrum of Mormonism-related websites. We deliberately tried to include a spectrum of orientations from progressive to conservative. (See Chapter 18 for a discussion of the critical role these blogs and other internet forums have played in the resurgence of twenty-first-century Mormonism.) To say that the response was much larger than we anticipated is an understatement. By the end of the first day, the survey had over 30,000 completed responses. As a result of the large response, we decided to close the survey early (December 4) rather than keeping it up for an entire month.

Cleaning the purposive sample data was a complex task for a number of reasons. First, we opted to refrain from restricting the number of times the survey could be taken from a single IP address or computer in the interest of allowing multiple members of the same household to take the survey. However, after careful scrutiny of the data, it became apparent that some individuals took the survey multiple times. We had to find and remove those data. Additionally, we were concerned with whether certain individuals were more or less likely to complete the survey. A careful analysis of the incomplete responses suggested that more active members of the LDS Church were more likely to complete the survey than were former members or less active members. This finding helped alleviate our concern that more devout Church members would find the survey questions

---

7. Purposive samples are selected for their possession of a known characteristic, in this case, their affiliation with the LDS Church. They are used most often to locate respondents from specialized samples, rather than from the general population.

more disturbing and might be less likely to complete it.[8] When we ended the survey, we had 71,309 completed responses, and 20,389 incomplete responses. After all of our data cleaning procedures (removing incomplete questionnaires, duplicates, and those who were screened out of the survey), the final sample size for the purposive sample was 61,066.[9]

To ensure that the random sample and the purposive sample data are more readily comparable, for this chapter we have excluded from our analyses survey respondents in the purposive sample who do not currently live in the United States (n = 3,634 respondents, or 5.95 percent of the total respondents in the purposive sample). We plan to analyze responses from those individuals in other publications. We have also limited our analyses in both data sets to only individuals who reported that they are on the rolls of the Church and who identify as LDS (see below). In the random sample, 5.6 percent of respondents indicated that they were still on record as members but no longer identified as LDS, and 1.9 percent of respondents indicated they were no longer on the rolls but had been LDS in the past. In the purposive sample, 11.2 percent of respondents indicated that they were still on the rolls but no longer identified as LDS, and 2.6 percent of respondents indicated that they were no longer on the rolls but were LDS. We also plan to analyze data from these respondents in other publications. After excluding the above respondents, the random sample included 476 respondents, and the purposive sample included 49,568 respondents.

Methods

Participants in both surveys were shown an informed consent screen before they could continue taking the survey. At the bottom of this first screen, they indicated whether they agreed to participate before continuing the survey. We included in both surveys a screening question about religious affiliation. The question asked

---

8. That devout members were more likely to complete the survey is likely the result of our questions and the wording of those questions, which was designed to reflect the perspective of an active member of the LDS Church. See Chapter 15 for how people responded to the survey. In building the survey items, the Mormon Gender Survey Group tried to frame the questions such that they would reflect the view of a moderate Mormon. Thus, we were not entirely surprised that there was criticism from both conservative and liberal Mormons. Additionally, we did not field the survey with the intent of learning about the views of former Mormons. We knew that former Mormons would likely experience some difficulty answering some of the questions because they were framed from the perspective of current, self-identifying, active Mormons. Even so, our aim with the survey was to gain a better understanding of the views of current members of the LDS Church. In future research, we will likely take a different approach, branching the survey in such a way that the questions former Mormons are shown are more appropriate for them.

9. Although purposive samples are not used for probabilistic generalizations, this is nevertheless an unusually large sample for this kind of social science survey, and it may be the largest single Mormon sample ever surveyed. Comparing its results with those of other surveys is one way to assess the representativeness of its data.

participants, "According to its records, the Church of Jesus Christ of Latter-day Saints (LDS Church) has approximately 15 million members. Do you think your name is on the Church records?" Response options included, "Yes, and I currently identify as LDS," "Yes, but I do not identify as LDS," "No, but I was LDS," "No, I have never been LDS," "Don't know," and "Prefer not to respond." Individuals who chose one of the last three options were sent to a screen where they were told that their interest in the survey was appreciated but that the target audience was current or former members of the LDS Church. For our analysis in this chapter we are interested only in those who are on the rolls of the LDS Church and who self-identify as Mormon. Furthermore, in this chapter we limit ourselves to presenting simple descriptive statistics from the survey. We are in the process of analyzing the data using more complex inferential analyses and plan to submit findings based on those analyses to a variety of peer-reviewed, scholarly journals.

Results

Demographics

Participants in both surveys were asked their gender (with an option for "other" that is not analyzed in this chapter. (See Chapter 6 for data from transgender respondents.) In line with some prior research,[10] we found that men were a substantial minority in both our surveys, making up about 30 percent of the respondents in the United States. Whether this is due to higher rates of religious exiting among men—which is common in the United States[11]—or some other factor, is uncertain, but it does have intriguing implications for the LDS Church. A gender imbalance in the Church could result in higher rates of religiously heterogeneous marriages, which cannot be solemnized in Mormon temples. It could also result in greater difficulty staffing the many, exclusively male leadership positions in the Church. It is possible, though less likely with the random sample and more likely with the purposive sample, that women were simply more interested than men in participating in the survey because of its topic.

Participants in our purposive sample were quite a bit younger than the participants in our random sample. However, both of our samples were substantially younger than Pew's sample of Mormons.[12] Our samples—particularly the random sample—more closely mirror the age structure of the state of Utah than does the

---

10. Rick Phillips et al., *Mormons in the United States 1990–2008: Socio-Demographic Trends and Regional Differences. A Report Based on the American Religious Identification Survey 2008*. (Hartford, Conn.: Institute for the Study of Secularism in Society and Culture, 2011).

11. Joseph O. Baker and Buster G. Smith, "The Nones: Social Characteristics of the Religiously Unaffiliated," *Social Forces* 87, no. 3 (2009): 1251–63, doi:10.1353/sof.0.0181; Darren E. Sherkat, "Beyond Belief: Atheism, Agnosticism, and Theistic Certainty in the United States," *Sociological Spectrum* 28, no. 5 (2008): 438–59.

12. Pew Forum on Religion & Public Life, *Mormons in America: Certain in Their Beliefs, Uncertain of Their Place in Society* (Washington, D.C.: Pew Forum on Religion & Public Life, January 12, 2012).

TABLE 1
DESCRIPTIVES FOR DEMOGRAPHIC VARIABLES
FROM RANDOM AND PURPOSIVE SAMPLES.

	Random Sample %	Purposive Sample %
Gender		
man	30.9	27.7
woman	69.1	72.3
Age		
18-25	15.1	20.2
26-30	15.5	22.6
31-40	24.6	33.5
41-50	14.1	11.5
51-60	13.2	7.8
61-70	12.4	3.5
71+	5.0	0.9
Education		
did not finish high school	0.8	0.2
high school	9.9	3.3
some college	35.4	26.6
college graduate	40.6	47.4
master's degree	10.7	16.3
PhD	0.8	2.5
JD/MD	1.7	3.7
Income		
less than $10,000	6.1	5.5
$10,0001 to $25,000	11.4	9.5
$25,001 to $50,000	29.8	19.9
$50,000 to $75,000	28.0	21.6
$75,001 to $100,000	13.7	18.5
$100,001 to $250,000	10.0	21.2
$250,000+	0.9	3.8
Race/ethnicity		
white, non-Hispanic	89.7	93.2
black, non-Hispanic	1.1	0.4
Hispanic	3.6	2.6
Asian	2.1	0.8
Native American	0.8	0.6
other	2.1	2.0
Pacific Islander	0.6	0.5
Political views		
very conservative	19.2	7.9
conservative	31.4	27.6
moderate, but lean conservative	21.5	29.2
moderate	16.5	12.5
moderate, but lean liberal	5.7	11.4
liberal	3.4	5.9
very liberal	1.8	1.5
other	0.5	3.8
State		
Utah	27.1	37.2
California	9.2	9.0
Idaho	6.1	5.6
Arizona	4.8	5.5
Texas	5.3	5.0

TABLE 2
DESCRIPTIVE STATISTICS FOR MORMON RELIGIOSITY VARIABLES IN RANDOM AND PURPOSIVE SAMPLES

	Random % or Mean (sd)	Purposive % or Mean (sd)
Activity level		
very active	62.6	79.0
somewhat active	18.3	14.5
not too active	10.5	4.2
not at all active	8.6	2.2
How became member		
child of record, baptized at 8	67.8	85.8
child of record, baptized after 8	3.8	2.0
converted as youth	8.1	4.7
converted as adult	20.3	7.4
Mormon network density	59.65	65.71
	(29.73)	(26.40)
Hold temple recommend		
yes	65.9	84.3
no	34.1	15.7
View on teachings		
some hard to accept	31.6	42.3
I believe in all of them	68.4	57.7
View on obedience		
obey counsel	34.2	34.2
seek revelation first	65.8	65.8
Believe Joseph Smith saw God		
essential	67.7	60.9
important but not essential	29.5	31.1
not too important	1.1	2.7
not at all important	1.7	1.9

Pew sample, which leads us to believe that Pew may have over-sampled elderly Mormons in Utah. This may also be the result of different methodologies, as Pew relies heavily on phone surveys while both of our surveys were conducted online.

In the random sample, participants' educational attainment was very similar to national levels of educational attainment. In our purposive sample, educational attainment was substantially higher than national averages, suggesting that our purposive sample was made up of a particularly well-educated segment of the Mormon population,[13] which is consistent with the finding that internet surveys field more highly educated samples in general. Likewise, incomes in our purposive sample were higher than in the random sample.

---

13. R. M. Merrill and A. L. Thygerson, "Religious Preference, Church Activity, and Physical Exercise," *Preventive Medicine* 33, no. 1 (July 2001): 38–45; Tim B. Heaton, Stephen J. Bahr, and Cardell K. Jacobson, *A Statistical Profile of Mormons: Health, Wealth, and Social Life* (Lewiston, N.Y.: Edwin Mellen Press, 2005); Phillips et al., *Mormons in the United States 1990–2008: Socio-Demographic Trends and Regional Differences.*

In both samples, the predominantly white makeup of the Church is apparent; based on our surveys, close to 90 percent of Mormons in the United States are white, which is similar to what other surveys have found.[14]

Also in line with previous surveys,[15] we found that Mormons are politically quite conservative, with more than 70 percent of participants in the random sample and nearly 65 percent of participants in the purposive sample indicating they were on the conservative end of the political spectrum.

As previously noted, we tracked participants' IP addresses, which allowed us to determine the country in which they took the survey as well as the state for those who were in the United States. At the bottom of Table 1 are the percentages of respondents from the two surveys from the five states with the highest number of participants: Utah, California, Idaho, Arizona, and Texas. These five states account for over half of U.S. Mormons. Based on the two surveys, between one in four and one in three Mormons in the United States live in Utah.

Religiosity

We asked our survey participants a variety of questions in an attempt to capture their level of religious devotion. Results from these questions are shown in Table 2. Thus, for example, we asked participants, "How active are you in the LDS Church?" The majority of respondents chose "very active" in both samples, with nearly 80 percent of participants in the purposive sample indicating they were very active. Concomitantly, close to 20 percent of the participants in the random sample indicated they were not too active or not at all active.

We also asked participants how they became members of the Church. More of the participants in the random sample were adult converts (20.3 percent) than in the purposive sample (7.4 percent). A substantial majority of the participants in both surveys were born into LDS families.

We also asked participants a question to capture the composition of their social network, "Take a moment and think of the individuals with whom you have socialized during your leisure time during the past month. Indicate below the rough percentage of these individuals who are members of the Church." Averages are somewhat deceptive on this question because the distributions were negatively skewed,[16] but in both surveys close to 60 percent of respondents' social networks were made up of other Mormons.

---

14. Pew Forum on Religion & Public Life, *Mormons in America: Certain in Their Beliefs, Uncertain of Their Place in Society*; Phillips et al., *Mormons in the United States 1990–2008: Socio-Demographic Trends and Regional Differences*; Heaton, Bahr, and Jacobson, *A Statistical Profile of Mormons*.

15. Robert D. Putnam and David E. Campbell, *American Grace: How Religion Divides and Unites Us* (New York: Simon & Schuster, 2012).

16. "Skewness" refers to the shape of a distribution of scores. In both samples, the distributions were similar. The most common response (or modal response) was 50 percent. But in the purposive sample there were just as many people who reported that

In order to compare our data to previous surveys,[17] we also asked participants, "Do you hold a current temple recommend?" About two-thirds of participants in the random sample did while almost 85 percent of participants in the purposive sample indicated that they were recommend holders. The percentage of temple recommend holders we found in our random sample was very similar to the one found in Pew's survey of Mormons.

Again for comparison purposes, we included two questions that had appeared in the Pew survey of Mormons.[18] The first question asked, "Is believing that Joseph Smith literally saw God the Father and Jesus Christ essential for being a good Mormon?" Response options included, "Essential," "Important, but not essential," "Not too important," and "Not at all important." Even though this question does not clearly measure our respondents' personal beliefs, their responses were similar to those Pew found, with between 60 percent and 70 percent of participants in the two samples indicating that they consider belief in the literal truth of Joseph Smith's "first vision" account to be essential for good Mormons.

The second question from the Pew survey that we included asked, "Which statement comes closer to your *own* view, even if neither is exactly right?" Participants in the survey were offered just two options, even though not everyone liked the two options offered. (See Chapter 15 for critical responses to the wording of various questions.) More participants in both of our surveys (31.6 percent in the random survey; 42.3 percent in the purposive survey) chose "Some teachings of the LDS Church are hard for me to accept" than was the case in the Pew survey, in which just 22.5 percent chose that option. The majority in all three surveys chose the other option, "I believe wholeheartedly in all of the teachings of the LDS Church." We included a similarly structured question that also asked, "Which statement comes closer to your own view, even if neither is exactly right?" On this question, the options were, "A good Latter-day Saint should obey the counsel of priesthood leaders without necessarily knowing why" and "A good Latter-day Saint should first seek his or her own personal revelation as the motivation to obey." In both surveys, 34 percent of respondents chose the former—obeying without questioning, while 66 percent chose the latter.

Considered collectively, responses to our religiosity questions indicate that majorities in both the random and purposive samples were faithful, believing Latter-day Saints. This is important to know when considering respondents' opinions on contemporary gender equality issues.

---

their social network was more than 89 percent LDS as there were who reported that their social network was less than 50 percent LDS. In the random sample, the corresponding results were 85 percent and 40 percent. Thus, most Mormons have social networks that are primarily made up of other Mormons.

17. Pew Forum on Religion & Public Life, *Mormons in America*.
18. Ibid.

TABLE 3
DESCRIPTIVE STATISTICS ON GENDER ISSUES QUESTIONS.

	Random Sample %	Purposive Sample %
Concerned about gender roles		
yes	11.2	24.2
no	88.8	75.8
Differences between women and men in the Church are		
cultural	4.3	6.7
doctrinal	42.8	24.7
a mix of culture and doctrine	52.9	68.6
Dedicated women should be ordained		
yes	9.9	8.3
no	80.7	71.3
other	3.6	11.3
don't know	5.5	7.7
prefer not to respond	0.4	1.2
If leaders received revelation, a typical member would be		
strongly supportive	17.9	13
supportive	44.1	50.6
neither supportive nor opposed	16.7	11.4
opposed	16.0	18.6
strongly opposed	5.3	6.4
If leaders received revelation, I would be		
strongly supportive	27.1	34.7
supportive	40.0	42.4
neither supportive nor opposed	17.9	14.2
opposed	8.8	4.8
strongly opposed	6.2	3.9
If women were allowed, primary reason behind change		
a revelation from God		48.2
a response from God to inquiries by the leaders of the LDS Church		36.3
a response from Church leaders to pressure from inside the LDS Church		6.6
a response from Church leaders to pressure from outside the LDS Church		4
other		4.9
When blacks were allowed, primary reason behind change		
a revelation from God		40.7
a response from God to inquiries by the leaders of the LDS Church		45.8
a response from Church leaders to pressure from inside the LDS Church		2.6
a response from Church leaders to pressure from outside the LDS Church		7
other		3.9
If ward member supported ordination of women, what would you do?		
do nothing		25
encourage him/her to express their views		11.5
encourage him/her to express their views, but remind him/her to refrain from trying to persuade others to accept them		28.8
acknowledge his/her private beliefs, but discourage him/her from publicly expressing them		19.3
refer the individual for formal disciplinary council		2.5
other		13

Gender Issues

Our primary focus in the survey, of course, was on gender issues in the LDS Church. At a very broad level, we wanted to find out whether members of the Church were concerned about gender roles. Thus, we asked participants, "Are you personally concerned about the different roles men and women are expected to play in the LDS Church?" In the random sample, just 11 percent of respondents indicated concern about gender roles in the Church, while a much higher percentage, 24 percent, expressed concern in the purposive sample. In both samples, however, a substantial majority of respondents indicated little concern about LDS gender role norms. But there are more layers to consider in Mormon gender debates than this.

Digging deeper into LDS gender issues, we asked participants to respond to this question: "Differences between the roles of women and men in the LDS Church are . . . " Participants could choose between the following three options, "Cultural," "A mix of culture and doctrine," and "Doctrinal." Very few participants chose just the "cultural" option—only 4.3 percent in the random sample and 6.7 percent in the purposive sample. Most Mormons appear to believe that what the Church teaches about gender and how gender roles are performed in the Church are a mixture of culture and doctrine, while a sizable percentage (43 percent in the random sample and 25 percent in the purposive sample) believe the differences are exclusively doctrinal. These results suggest both challenges and possibilities when it comes to advocating for gender equality in the LDS Church. The challenge is that external pressures[19] to ordain women (and other genders; see Chapter 6 on transgender Mormons) will likely be perceived by members as a threat to their doctrine and beliefs. Even so, there is the possibility of change resulting from the fact that Mormons believe in ongoing revelation, which means that doctrines can change. At the same time, *how* doctrinal change comes about is a critical question. Several of our key questions allowed us to examine the challenges of religious change in greater detail.

We included two questions in our survey to capture attitudes toward the ordination of women. The first question replicated the survey question used by Pew: "Do you, personally, believe that women who are dedicated members of the Church should have the opportunity to be ordained to the priesthood?" Our results were fairly similar to those of Pew (though we also allowed participants to choose an "other" option, which many, in fact, chose). In the Pew survey,[20] 10.7 percent of respondents indicated that they thought women should be ordained, while 86.9 percent said they should not, with 2.4 percent responding that they didn't know. In our random survey, 9.9 percent supported the ordination of women, 80.7 percent opposed it, while 3.6 percent chose "other," and another 5.5 percent reported that they didn't know. In our purposive sample, 8.3 percent supported the ordination of women, 71.3 percent opposed it, 11.3

---

19. Chaves, *Ordaining Women*.
20. Pew Forum on Religion & Public Life, *Mormons in America*.

percent chose other, 7.7 percent said they didn't know, and another 1.2 percent chose not to respond. Individuals who chose "other" could write in a response that better reflected their views. Many of these responses suggested that participants thought women may eventually receive the priesthood, but indicated that they did not think it was currently the right time, since that has to be revealed by God. In other words, many of the "other" responses were qualified support for the ordination of women that was contingent upon Church leaders receiving a revelation. The sizable number of "other" responses suggests that questions about the ordination of women need to reflect the ways that change in the Church is perceived to take place by members.

Correspondingly, our second question attempted to capture how change occurs in the LDS Church by asking participants in the surveys their views toward a top-down change. The question asked, "If the First Presidency and the Quorum of the Twelve Apostles were to receive a revelation allowing women to hold the priesthood, *the typical member* would be . . . " In both samples, the majority of respondents believed that members would support such a change (62 percent in the random sample; 63.6 percent in the purposive sample). Immediately following this question, we asked a nearly identical question but replaced "the typical member would be . . . " with "*I would be* . . . ." Our findings indicate that many Mormons are more likely to support such a change (67.1 percent in the random sample; 76.1 percent in the purposive sample) compared to what they think would be true for their fellow members.

This is a fascinating finding for multiple reasons. First, two-thirds to three-fourths of Mormons would support women being ordained if the leaders of the religion announced such a change. This is a substantial difference from the 10 percent of Mormons who indicated that they think dedicated women should be ordained (a bottom-up approach). This disjunction between attitudes toward ordination, depending on how the change comes about, illustrates the importance of taking into consideration how change actually takes place in a religion. Second, it illustrates just how submissive and obedient members of the Church are to the dictates of their leaders. If roughly half of Church members (~65 percent who would support a top-down change minus the ~10 percent who support a change regardless) will support whatever their leaders say, just how far would this obedience to authority (i.e., authoritarianism)[21] persist? What would it take for members of the LDS Church to oppose their leaders on a given issue?[22] Third, this finding also indicates that Church members think other members are even more resistant to gender equality than they are. This has interesting implications for understand-

---

21. Bob Altemeyer, *The Authoritarians* (Cherry Hill, N.J.: Cherry Hill Publishing, 2008); Bob Altemeyer and Bruce Hunsberger, "Authoritarianism, Religious Fundamentalism, Quest, and Prejudice," *International Journal for the Psychology of Religion* 2, no. 2 (1992): 113–33.

22. We are obviously not the first to point this out. Jon Krakauer, for instance, explored the problems with religious obedience in the LDS Church and some of its splinter groups in his *Under the Banner of Heaven: A Story of Violent Faith* (New York; Doubleday, 2003).

ing conformity in religious settings. Why do many Mormons think *other Mormons* would be more opposed to a top-down change than they would be? Perhaps this is due to a culture of conformity in the LDS Church (and possibly in conservative religion more generally) wherein dissent is not tolerated. Because dissent from the official pronouncements of General Authorities is not tolerated in Mormonism and is enforced through either informal or formal sanctions,[23] members of the Church who may hold more liberal or progressive views, particularly toward the ordination of women, may feel obligated not to share those views with other members.[24] As a result, it is possible that there is greater *perceived* opposition to the ordination of women in the Church than there is actual opposition. Alternatively, research on social norms suggests that it is rather common for individuals to believe that their group's position is more extreme than it actually is. This tendency has been the focus of extensive investigation in such areas as college students' perceptions of drinking.[25] From a social-psychological perspective, a review of that literature could be applied usefully to the question of attitudes toward women's ordination by both its supporters and its detractors.

Due to space limitations, we asked some questions in the purposive survey that we did not ask in the random sample. Two of those questions attempted to get at precisely how Mormons believe policy changes occur in their religion. The first asked, "If a decision were made to allow women to hold the priesthood in the LDS Church, what would you describe as being the primary reason behind the change?" Almost 85 percent of participants in the purposive sample indicated that such a change would come about as a revelation from God that might or might not have resulted from an inquiry by the leaders of the religion. Just 4 percent believe that such a change would result from external pressure exerted on Church leaders.

Given the hypothetical nature of the above question, we asked a follow-up question that was less hypothetical, "In 1978, the Church extended the priesthood to all worthy males. What would you describe as being the primary reason behind this change?" Participants could choose from the same options as in the previous question, and the options they chose were nearly identical. Almost all of the participants (86 percent) indicated that it was a revelation from God, possibly in response

---

23. Formal sanctions would be disfellowshipping and excommunication. Informal sanctions would be negative comments made by other members, dirty looks, or informal interviews with leaders during which members are told not to express dissenting views.

24. Paul Malan, "Op-Ed: Mormon Fringes Should Speak Up to Take Us beyond Monoculturalism," *Salt Lake Tribune*, April 11, 2015, http://www.sltrib.com/opinion/2382761-155/op-ed-mormon-fringes-should-speak-up (accessed April 14, 2015).

25. H. W. Perkins and A. D. Berkowitz, "Perceiving the Community Norms of Alcohol Use among Students: Some Research Implications for Campus Alcohol Education Programming," *International Journal of the Addictions, 2*, nos. 9–10 (1986): 961–76; Melissa A. Lewis and Clayton Neighbors, "Social Norms Approaches Using Descriptive Drinking Norms Education: A Review of the Research on Personalized Normative Feedback," *Journal of American College Health* 54, no. 4 (2006): 213–18.

to inquiries by Church leaders. These two questions illustrate the importance of understanding the role of what Peter Berger called a "sacred canopy"[26] in thinking about religious change for members of conservative religions. A "sacred canopy" is the collection of beliefs and values through which believers view the world. Berger described religion as a social construction that requires the existence of a plausibility structure to hold up that sacred canopy. The plausibility structure holding up that canopy is made up of the many faith-promoting and mutually reinforcing elements of people's everyday lives, from the shared meanings and assumptions of family and friends to individuals' own socially acquired beliefs and behaviors. The leaders of the Church help to prop up the members' sacred canopy by framing changes in policy and practice as resulting from divine guidance rather than from external and secular forces. This is how LDS leadership has framed the two best-known major changes in Mormon history—ending the practice of polygamy and allowing black men to be ordained into the priesthood.[27] In both cases, there was substantial pressure on Church leaders—both internally and externally—to make these changes.[28] But when these changes were presented to the members, they were framed as inspired revelations from God and there was very little recognition of other contributing factors.

The implications of understanding other factors contributing to religious change in the debate over the ordination of LDS women are two-fold. Activists who want Mormon women to gain equality and be ordained should continue to increase the pressure on LDS leadership to enact such change. But activists should also keep in mind that taking credit for such changes threatens the plausibility structure that upholds Mormonism's sacred canopy. When small changes do occur—like a woman being allowed to offer a prayer in general conference or when a formal statement is issued about the acceptability of women wearing pants to church—activists are likely to garner additional support among other members if they suggest that the changes resulted from revelation from God rather than from the pressure such activism exerted on the Church. From the perspective of the institution, emphasizing the role of revelation in making change is also advantageous, as this formulation helps to maintain Berger's notion of a sacred canopy while change is nevertheless gradually occurring.

Related to the above discussion concerning how members of the Church might respond to someone who expressed support for the ordination of women, in the purposive sample we asked participants: "Church leaders have indicated that each congregation is responsible for conducting its own disciplinary courts. If a member

---

26. Peter L. Berger, *The Sacred Canopy: Elements of a Sociological Theory of Religion* (New York: Anchor, 1990).

27. Matthew Burton Bowman, *The Mormon People: The Making of an American Faith* (New York: Random House, 2012); Armand L. Mauss, *All Abraham's Children: Changing Mormon Conceptions of Race and Lineage* (Urbana: University of Illinois Press, 2003).

28. Gregory A. Prince and Wm Robert Wright, *David O. McKay and the Rise of Modern Mormonism* (Salt Lake City: University of Utah Press, 2005).

Table 4
Agreement of Transgender Respondents on Various Issues.

	Strongly Disagree	Disagree	Neutral	Agree	Strongly Agree
Random					
God has established different roles for men and women.	1.7	3.2	4	21.6	69.6
The way women are treated in the Church is a problem.	55	26.1	8.3	6.8	3.8
If women were given more leadership responsibilities, it would strengthen the Church.	26.1	19.5	33.1	12.9	8.4
Purposive					
God has established different roles for men and women.	2.9	3.3	4.5	24.3	64.9
God has revealed that only men should hold the priesthood.	5.2	7.5	7.8	21.6	57.9
It's not fair that 12-year-old boys can pass the sacrament, but 12-year-old girls can not.	62.4	19.6	8.1	5.3	4.6
Women who feel unequal to men at Church don't understand the gospel.	15.6	17.7	13.7	27.7	25.2
Feminism is incompatible with the restored Gospel of Jesus Christ.	32.5	35.3	16.3	9.6	6.3
The way women are treated in the Church is a problem.	42.9	24.4	11	12.5	9.2
If women were given more leadership responsibilities, it would strengthen the Church.	18.5	19.2	29.8	17.1	15.5

of your LDS ward were to publicly express his/her support for the ordination of women to the priesthood, what would your response be?" One in four participants said they would do nothing. About 40 percent of respondents indicated they would encourage this person to express their views, but about two-thirds of this group only indicated support with the caveat that they would also tell this person not to try to persuade others. Another 19 percent of respondents indicated that they would not encourage the expression of these views publicly but would tolerate it in private. In other words, about 50 percent of the participants in the purposive sample would either try to convince other members not to express their views publicly or counsel them not to attempt persuading others to accept their views.

Given the LDS Church's heavy emphasis on spreading Mormonism throughout the world and the necessity of trying to convince others of Mormonism's ultimate truth, it might seem odd that such a sizable percentage of Mormons would discourage fellow members from sharing their views with others and trying to convince others of their opinions. However, this finding becomes less odd when viewed in light of the culture of conformity implied by the results of this survey. The top-down, hierarchical nature of the Church results not only in members obediently following the dictates of Church leaders but also in members enacting sanctions against fellow members who question the positions of their leaders.[29] Nevertheless, just 2.5 percent of participants in the purposive sample indicated that they would refer the individual for formal discipline. This finding suggests that many lay Mormons in the United States may privately accept that other Mormons have doubts and question leaders—likely because many of them also do so in secret. Yet, many Mormons feel that publicly expressing those doubts crosses an unacceptable line. While these individuals would probably not use such terms as "sacred canopies" and "plausibility structures" to describe their rationale for why that line shouldn't be crossed,[30] there is some evidence that members see vocal proclamations of doubt and disbelief as threats to the faith of others.[31] In other words, Mormons recognize that public dissent undermines Mormonism's culture of obedience and conformity, even if they would not use that exact language.

In addition to the single-item questions we asked above to measure attitudes on gender issues in the Church, our research team came up with several sets of questions that attempted to do so in a systematic way. For instance, the Mormon Gender Survey Group generated a series of statements that attempted to capture perceptions of gender equality in the LDS Church. Participants were asked to carefully read each statement and indicate their level of agreement or disagreement. (See Table 4 for response options.) Because of space limitations, we only included the first three statements in the random sample. All of the statements were included in the purposive sample survey. In both samples, over 80 percent of participants agreed that God established different roles for men and women. Likewise, in both samples, close to two-thirds of participants disagreed that the way women are treated is a problem. There was also strong consensus (82 percent) that it is fair for twelve-year-old boys to pass the sacrament but not twelve-year-old girls, that God has revealed that only men should hold the priesthood (80 percent agree), and that feminism is incompatible with the gospel (67.8 percent). Results were more mixed on two other items. While a majority (52.9 percent) agrees that women who feel unequal to men at Church don't understand the gospel, a sizable minority disagreed (33.3 percent). Likewise, views on the last item in this section of the survey—that giving women more leadership responsibilities would strengthen the Church—also resulted in split views, with 37.7 percent disagreeing and 32.6 percent agreeing.

---

29. Malan, "Op-Ed"; Michael Nielsen and Daryl White, "Men's Grooming in the Latter-day Saints Church: A Qualitative Study of Norm Violation," *Mental Health, Religion & Culture* 11 (December 2008): 807–25, doi:10.1080/13674670802087286.

30. Berger, *The Sacred Canopy*.

31. Peggy Fletcher Stack, "Did Mormon Podcaster Go Too Far? Dehlin Faces Possible Excommunication," *Salt Lake Tribune*, January 15, 2015, http://www.sltrib.com/lifestyle/faith/2063440-155/did-mormon-podcaster-go-too-far (accessed April 12, 2015).

Given that the above items reflected broad-level perceptions of inequality, the Survey Group also asked about a list of policy changes that could take place in the Church that would not actually require women to be ordained to the priesthood but which would result in greater gender equality.[32] Specifically, the question stated, "The following are some suggestions that people have made for changes in the Church that do not include ordaining women to the priesthood. Please indicate the degree to which you support the following changes." As with the previous series of items, a subset (five of the eleven) were included in the random sample, while all of the items were included on the purposive survey. The results are shown in Table 5. Given the number of items in this set, it is possible to see a general pattern to the responses. On more practical items where inequality can be tangibly measured, there is support for changes in policies. This pattern emerged for questions regarding budgets for Young Women and Young Men (81.2 percent supported this change in the purposive sample), in hiring policies at universities (57.6 percent supported this change in the purposive sample), and seminaries (62 percent supported this change in the random sample; 64.8 percent did in the purposive sample), or in the proportion of images of females to males in Church media (50.8 percent supported this change in the purposive sample). However, when policies are largely symbolic in how they empower men over women, there was more opposition to those changes. For instance, more Church members opposed eliminating language that suggests husbands "preside" over wives than supported eliminating such language (46.5 percent opposed this in the random sample while just 26.3 percent supported it; in the purposive sample it was 43.6 percent opposed and 34.5 percent in favor).

Of course, there is a mixture of support and opposition on all of the items, but the general pattern we observed does suggest something interesting about how many Mormons think about gender, and it is not unique to Mormons. As Mark Chaves noted in his book about the ordination of women in Christian denominations in the United States,[33] there is a loose coupling between ordination and women's involvement in religions. In many religions that do not allow women to be ordained, women are heavily involved in many leadership aspects in the religion (though, typically, not at the highest levels). Inversely, in many religions where women are allowed to be ordained, there has not been much interest among women to be ordained. The data in Table 5 support Chaves's findings in the sense that there is more support for policies that would allow women to make practical contributions to the running of the Church, like working in seminaries and institutes. More opposition occurs when it seems as though the policy changes would grant women equality with men—for instance removing language

---

32. We based our list of policy changes on the list generated by the creators of this website: http://www.whatwomenknow.org/all_are_alike/index.html (accessed April 22, 2015). For a permanent copy of this site, see http://perma.cc/9Z7X-95QC.

33. Chaves, *Ordaining Women*.

Table 5
Support for Policy Changes That Do Not Require Ordination of Women But Increase Gender Equality

	Fully Support	Generally Support	Neutral	Generally Oppose	Completely Oppose
Random					
Eliminate language that suggests husbands preside over wives.	10.0	16.3	27.2	25.6	20.9
Hire women at equivalent rates as men in LDS Seminaries and Institutes of Religion.	29.0	33.0	27.2	7.6	3.1
Allow women and men to serve missions of equal length at the same age.	16.9	24.1	34.5	15.0	9.5
Allow women to participate in the blessing of their children (for example, by holding their children in the circle).	10.7	12.9	20.8	24.6	30.9
Change temple marriage policies so that men and women have equal opportunity to be sealed to their second spouses after they are widowed or divorced.	15.0	20.3	26.3	16.2	22.2
Purposive					
Eliminate language that suggests husbands preside over wives.	18.8	15.7	21.9	24.3	19.3
Provide equivalent budgets for the Young Women and Young Men organizations.	57.2	24.0	13.7	3.0	2.1
Balance the stories and images of males in Church publications, talks, and other media with stories and images of females.	27.6	23.2	35.4	8.4	5.4
Appoint women to serve with the Stake High Council.	16.1	10.5	18.6	19.4	35.4
Include the local Relief Society presidency in all bishopric meetings.	18.9	17.0	19.7	23.7	20.7
Make a greater effort to hire women to fill leadership positions in Church universities.	30.1	27.5	33.1	5.7	3.5
Hire women at equivalent rates as men in LDS Seminaries and Institutes of Religion.	39.4	25.4	25.6	6.6	3.0
Rotate the planning of sacrament services among the Relief Society presidency and members of the bishopric.	11.7	8.7	20.9	25.2	33.6
Allow women and men to serve missions of equal length at the same age.	23.1	17.6	32.2	17.2	9.8
Allow women to participate in the blessing of their children (for example, by holding their children in the circle).	18.7	12.0	20.9	20.2	28.2
Change temple marriage policies so that men and women have equal opportunity to be sealed to their second spouses after they are widowed or divorced.	27.6	16.6	21.6	12.5	21.7
Restore the former practice of women giving certain types of blessings	19.7	11.7	30.4	16.4	21.8

indicating that men "preside" over women. In other words, it appears as though a number of Mormons support women having prominent roles in running the day-to-day operations of the Church, but only so long as these "prominent" roles are at least symbolically subordinated to the roles of men. This finding exemplifies what might be considered a way to negotiate change while maintaining the status quo. This type of "status quo bias," in which people prefer things to remain

Table 6
Men Observing and Women Experiencing Inequality Acts
(Purposive Sample Only)

Behavior	%
Men observing women, young women, or girls	
being told that they should dress a particular way to help boys/men have pure thoughts	9.3
feeling that they cannot express their opinions about how ward organizations are run	3.7
not being consulted about ward decisions	4
feeling left out of baby blessings	2.1
feeling uncomfortable talking with male priesthood authorities in private settings	4
limiting career goals to conform to cultural expectations	5.6
feeling that they cannot ask questions important to them	3.6
feeling that they do not want to come to church because of the pressure to conform to cultural expectations	5.5
Women personally experiencing	
being told that they should dress a particular way to help boys/men have pure thoughts	24.8
feeling that they cannot express their opinions about how ward organizations are run	10.3
not being consulted about ward decisions	7.8
feeling left out of baby blessings	3.8
feeling uncomfortable talking with male priesthood authorities in private settings	9.3
limiting career goals to conform to cultural expectations	11.6
feeling that they cannot ask questions important to them	10.7
feeling that they do not want to come to church because of the pressure to conform to cultural expectations	14.3

the same,[34] might be desirable from the perspective that it allows for change while at the same time maintains some traditional norms or policies.

Our final set of questions in the survey asked participants about specific acts that reflect gender inequality. (See Table 6.) We included these questions only in the purposive sample. For those who indicated their gender as male, we asked: "Have you personally observed any of the following within the LDS community in the last three months? Women, young women, and/or young girls . . . " What followed was a list of possible actions that would suggest gender inequality, such as women being told to dress a particular way to keep men from "sinning," or women being left out of important ward decisions. For women, we asked the question more directly, "Have you personally experienced any of the following within the LDS community in the last three months?" Responses are detailed in Table 6. Not surprisingly, a smaller proportion of men reported observing acts that demonstrated inequality when compared with the proportion of women who reported experiencing them. That men were less likely to observe these acts is probably due to their dominant status in society. Since they don't experience

---

34. Daniel Kahneman, Paul Slovic, and Amos Tversky, "Anomalies: The Endowment Effect, Loss Aversion, and Status Quo," *Journal of Economic Perspectives*, 5, no. 1 (1991): 193–206.

subordinating and discriminatory gender actions, they don't perceive these actions when in fact they do occur.[35] Likewise, women's enhanced ability to perceive discriminatory acts is likely due to their subordinate status. It may also be the case that women's personal experiences supports their perceptions that these acts reflect gender subordination. However, it is also worth noting just how few Mormons report observing these acts of inequality. We note this because most of these acts are very common in Mormon religious life. This suggests that, despite being surrounded by (and likely participating in) acts that subordinate women on a weekly and even daily basis, many Mormons do not perceive such acts to be manifestations of gender inequality. Until greater numbers of Mormons begin to perceive the pervasive gender inequality in the LDS Church, it is unlikely that major reformative changes will occur.

Conclusion

Understanding the dynamics of gender inequality in the LDS Church is, in many ways, just beginning to unfold. We are only beginning to collect data that will help us better understand why LDS gender dynamics are the way they are (i.e., emphatically patriarchal), why they continue to be that way, and why there is such manifest opposition to gender equality among both Church leaders and many lay members. However, the Mormon Gender Issues Survey provides some important, early insights into these dynamics. In what follows, we highlight several key findings from our survey.

Perhaps the most important finding from our survey is the enormous difference in support for the ordination of women that results from a change in questionnaire item wording. When the question is asked in such a fashion that it fails to reflect the top-down, hierarchical structure of the Church, most Mormons oppose the ordination of women. But when the question reflects how change is believed to take place in the Mormon faith tradition, most members of the Church indicate they would support or strongly support the ordination of women. While there is a methodological lesson to be learned here for those who plan to study gender issues in Mormonism in the future, there are also important lessons for those advocating for change in gender dynamics in the Church (as well as for those who resist change). First, if LDS authorities wanted gender equality in the religion and took the necessary steps to implement it, the majority of members would likely support that change. This puts much of the responsibility for effecting gender inequality in the LDS Church on the highest levels of Church leadership. It may also explain why leaders have gone to such great lengths in the past to try to convince members that gender roles are innate

---

35. Eduardo Bonilla-Silva, *Racism without Racists: Color-Blind Racism and the Persistence of Racial Inequality in the United States* (Lanham, Md.: Rowman & Littlefield, 2010); Patricia Collins, *Black Feminist Thought: Knowledge, Consciousness, and the Politics of Empowerment* (New York: Routledge, 2008).

and divine.[36] So long as members believe that gender role differences are innate and divinely intended, pressure on Church leaders to take the necessary steps to implement gender equality will be limited, since it is from leadership that change has to be perceived as originating. Also, as noted above, activists for gender equality in the Church should try to depict progressive changes toward equality as resulting from revelation rather than from their activism. If they don't emphasize this point, both leaders and members will feel threatened by external pressure to change, potentially slowing progress toward gender equality.

Another important finding is that many Mormons support policy changes that do not include the ordination of women but which increase women's participation in the running of the day-to-day affairs of the Church. Most Mormons, however, want to retain symbolic patriarchy in the Church. In other words, even if women contribute substantially to the work in the lay-based operations of the LDS Church, most Mormons still want to believe that men are in charge. This finding strongly supports previous research that shows a loose coupling between the ordination of women and their participation in religions.[37] Much of the opposition to the ordination of women results from the symbolic disempowerment of men. Activists should keep this fact in mind as they frame their activism. The openly stated goal does not have to be the "disempowerment" of men, since many Mormons are opposed to that outcome, but the goal could be framed instead as an issue of "human rights" or a raising of "religious standards" for *both* women and men.

Finally, the substantial differences in perceiving gender inequality acts according to the actor's gender—men are less likely than women to see these acts—remain to be addressed. However, so, too, does the fact that most LDS Church members fail to see how common Mormon behaviors reinforce gender inequality. Consider, for instance, the contrasts evident between interviewing a subordinate in the work world and in the LDS Church. In work settings, it is unusual for interviews to be conducted exclusively by men, but in Mormonism this is the unexceptional norm, even when interviews encompass personal sexual issues. Nonetheless, very few women protest such "worthiness interviews" being conducted exclusively by men. If women were to request that they be accompanied in such interviews by another woman, it might help raise awareness about the power dynamics operating in such interviews. With this recommendation, we do not mean to suggest that the onus of addressing gender inequality is solely on women. However, if just one woman in each LDS ward requested that she be accompanied by another woman in all interviews with priesthood leaders, that could have the effect of raising the consciousness of local leaders regarding the power dynamics that exist in such interviews and thereby encourage them to change their interviewing policy for all women members. The onus for implementing policy changes is on men, but women can

---

36. Sumerau and Cragun, "The Hallmarks of Righteous Women."
37. Chaves, *Ordaining Women*.

help them see the inequality by refusing to be interviewed one-on-one by a male official. Ultimately, advocates of change would benefit from remembering that Mormonism's sacred canopy relies on internal plausibility structures. Changes that are perceived as coming from within the structure are more likely to be adopted and maintained, especially if they address objective differences, such as comparing the discrepancy between budgets available to the Young Men and Young Women programs in the LDS Church.

There are many other important findings from the Mormon Gender Issues Survey, and we are just beginning to explore the interrelationships between the questions described above. Yet even with this cursory overview, it is clear that our initial foray into the gender dynamics operating within the LDS Church sheds some light on an increasingly important and timely topic. Additionally, our findings have helped us realize the need to gather even more data on LDS gender issues, as our findings make us aware of just how little we currently know about these topics.

Chapter 16

Finding the Middle Ground: Negotiating Mormonism and Gender

Nancy Ross, Jessica Finnigan, Heather K. Olson Beal, Kristy Money, Amber Choruby Whiteley, and Caitlin Carroll

The open-ended response questions on the Mormon Gender Issues Survey (see Chapters 13, 14, and 15 for more explanatory information about this survey) were designed to gather information about how Mormons view gender, to identify any changes that members would like to see with regard to gender, to ask them to envision increased leadership roles for women, and then to respond to that idea. We expected to find a majority of survey participants reiterating statements made in general conference and LDS Church curricular materials. Certainly, many responses reflected the language that the Church uses to talk about gender, but we were surprised to find that progressive and conservative Mormons tend to think about gender in different terms. A major finding of the data used in this chapter shows LDS Church members trying to reconcile Church teachings with lived experiences.

The data tell a story that is not reflected in the polarized discussions you might hear in Sunday meetings in the American West. That story is not reflected in conservative or progressive Mormon blog posts on the internet. It is not echoed in general conference talks. Instead, the data analysis reveals a substantial and previously unrecognized middle ground on the subject of gender.

Data Analysis Concerns

It was not feasible to carefully examine the open-ended response questions for all 61,066 respondents, which amounted to more than 3 million words. Instead, the Mormon Gender Issues Survey team randomly selected 500 responses, and this study analyses that subset of the data. Our review identified one duplicated response, thus changing the N to 499. Not all 499 randomly selected respondents answered all of the qualitative questions, and the total number of respondents for each question will be noted below and in the discussion.

Coding the responses proved to be a challenging task. Participants in this survey tended to write long and complex answers to the questions, which is not typical for most surveys. Initially, the responses were coded for straightforward binary answers (yes/no, agree/disagree, etc.) to the survey questions. In reviewing the data, we found that the coding did not reflect the mixed nature of many responses, so we then recoded the data to account for greater complexity.

Surveys on gender and religion tend to focus on a single demographic, like conservative women. This survey is unusual in that it is broader in its demographic focus. This survey targeted Mormons who use the internet and gathered data from LDS Church members from a variety of backgrounds, nationalities, genders, incomes, political persuasions, and Church activity levels.

Findings from this chapter are based on data obtained from three open-ended questions at the end of the Mormon Gender Issues Survey. The three questions were as follows:

1. Men and women are treated differently in the Church. Some of these differences are considered cultural, other doctrinal. Please describe these differences and why you feel they are beneficial or not beneficial. (N = 446)
2. If women were to serve in more administrative and leadership roles in the LDS Church, how would that affect your religious/spiritual life? Please comment in as much detail as possible. (N = 475)
3. What changes related to women, if any, do you hope the Church will implement over the next ten or twenty years? Describe these changes in as much detail as possible. Why do you believe these changes are important? (N = 448)

We performed content analysis through the use of open coding.[1] In doing this, we were looking to highlight the diversity of responses to understand both the range of responses and their complexity. This method revealed natural categories and themes, and the structure of this chapter follows these.[2]

The scholarly literature on gender and religion tends to revolve around the idea of agency (or personal choice) and the effect that religious belief, practice, and community have on an individual's ability to act.[3] Early agency research was based on feminist assumptions about individuals who participate in patriarchal religion.[4] More recent agency research has worked to dispel the common stereotypes used to describe religious women, including domesticity, submissiveness, and lack of self-determination.[5]

Recent agency literature, and especially the work of Orit Avishai, shaped our initial and follow-up coding procedures. Because feminist scholars have a tendency to make value judgements about the statements of their more conservative

---

1. Anselm Strauss and Juliet Corbin, *Basics of Qualitative Research: Techniques and Procedures for Developing Grounded Theory* (2nd ed.). Thousand Oaks, Calif.: Sage Publications, 1998).

2. Ibid., M. Q. Patton, *Qualitative Research & Evaluation Methods* (3rd ed.). London: Sage Publications, 2002).

3. Orit Avishai, "'Doing Religion' in a Secular World: Women in Conservative Religions and the Question of Agency," *Gender and Society* 22 (2007): 409–33; Kelsy C. Burke, "Women's Agency in Gender-Traditional Religions," *Sociology Compass* 6, no. 2 (2012): 122–33; Saba Mahmood, *The Politics of Piety: The Islamic and the Feminist Subject* (Princeton, N.J.: Princeton University Press, 2004).

4. Burke, "Women's Agency in Gender-Traditional Religions."

5. Avishai, "'Doing Religion' in a Secular World"; Jeanette S. Jouili and Schirin Amir-Moazami, "Knowledge, Empowerment and Religious Authority among Pious Muslim Women in France and Germany," *The Muslim World* 96, no. 4 (2006): 617–42.

research subjects, they sometimes end up categorizing and judging people instead of analyzing actions. Orit Avishai, Lynne Gerber, and Jennifer Randles insisted that researchers have to look past their own academic, political, and feminist bias in studying women in gender-traditional religions.[6] In working on this project, we took this advice to heart.

When we tried to understand the survey responses in terms of agency, however, we ran into some problems. Existing literature on agency is limited to the ways in which people perform their religion.[7] Researchers tend to focus on binary measures of orthopraxy, placing individuals into pre-existing categories.[8] When we started to look at the agency literature more broadly, we realized that researchers resisted asking subjects about their thoughts and instead focused on action. Agency framework did not work with our survey because our three questions asked about thoughts and not actions. Nor did the responses, once coded, fit neatly into pre-existing categories. Simply put, literature that explains the complexity of how religious people view gender does not currently exist and there is no established framework to understand this topic.

Negotiating the Meaning of Religious Teachings with Personal Experience

We propose that the appropriate theoretical underpinning of the data presented here is one of *negotiation*. We define negotiation as the process through which individuals integrate religious teachings and lived experiences. Negotiation can be an internal thought-based process and/or an external process that involves interacting with other individuals. Although these two categories of negotiation are complementary in actual experience, the questions in this survey dealt primarily with internal negotiation. By using the concept of negotiation, we avoided categorizing people according to presumptive binaries while still coding and analyzing the diversity of an individual's thoughts and behaviors. This new framework assists in understanding the complexity of thought that an individual holds about a particular issue, like gender and religion.

Negotiation theory helps us to better understand that, while many Mormons hold conservative views on gender, these are not their only views on gender. The

---

6. Orit Avishai, Lynne Gerber, and Jennifer Randles, "The Feminist Ethnographer's Dilemma: Reconciling Progressive Research Agendas with Fieldwork Realities," *Journal of Contemporary Ethnography* 20, no. 10 (2012): 1–33; Lori G. Beaman, "Molly Mormons, Mormon Feminists and Moderates: Religious Diversity and the Latter Day Saints [sic] Church," *Sociology of Religion* 62, no. 1 (2001): 65–86; Sirma Bilge, "Beyond Subordination vs. Resistance: An Intersectional Approach to the Agency of Veiled Muslim Women," *Journal of Intercultural Studies* 31, no 1 (2010): 9–28; Amy Hoyt, "Beyond the Victim/Empowerment Paradigm: The Gendered Cosmology of Mormon Women," *Feminist Theology* 16 (2007): 89–100.; Mahmood, "Politics of Piety."

7. Avishai, "'Doing Religion' in a Secular World."

8. Beaman, "Molly Mormons, Mormon Feminists, and Moderates."

data from this survey show that the story of Mormons and gender is one of tangled views. These findings seem to run counter to other kinds of research on Mormons.[9]

Campbell, Green, and Monson demonstrated that Mormons are among the most conservative religious groups in America.[10] Their research suggests the hypothesis that our survey respondents would also express acute gender binary paradigms. Visible political involvement in such issues as the ERA, Proposition 8, and recent so-called "religious freedom" legislation has clearly demonstrated that the LDS Church has formed conservative alliances concerning gender issues in American society.

While gender and religion in the United States have not always been seen as a political issue, Mark Chaves argued that gender has become the benchmark political issue within religious communities.[11] He set forth the idea that a religious organization's views on gender are a proxy for the larger issues of modernization and secularization. In doing charitable and political work, religious organizations form alliances with other organizations that share their views on gender. If a church changes its stance on gender, it risks losing those inter-denominational relationships. In this way, gender issues have helped defined the American religious landscape and have contributed to political polarization both within and between American churches.

This process of gender-issue alignment among American religious groups has helped to facilitate black-and-white thinking about the roles and religious responsibilities of men and women. This is generally reflected in the official language and teachings of these churches. The result is that if you ask conservative American Christians (Mormons included) straightforward questions about gender, you are likely to get straightforward conservative responses. However, if you ask more complex questions whose answers are not easily quantified, you will get more mixed results.

This is the case with the open-ended questions we used in our survey. The quantitative data from the survey (see Chapter 15) points to a strong alignment with traditional ideas about gender, because participants had to choose categorical positions. The qualitative data is much messier and many individual responses articulate a range of ideas, as will be discussed later. This is the benefit of qualitative analysis, as it allows for a much deeper examination of the negotiation process.

---

9. The Pew Research Center produced a report in 2012 titled *Mormons in America*. Its results showed that most Mormons in the U.S. hold traditional beliefs about gender roles. Fifty-eight percent of Mormons thought that marriage was more satisfying if the husband provided while the wife stayed home. Eighty-seven percent thought that women should not be ordained to the priesthood.

10. David E. Campbell, John C. Green, and J. Quin Monson, *Seeking the Promised Land: Mormons and American Politics* (Cambridge, England: Cambridge University Press, 2014).

11. Mark Chaves, *Ordaining Women: Culture and Conflict in Religious Organizations* (Cambridge, Mass.: Harvard University Press, 1999).

To address the challenging intersection of gender, religion, political alliances, and the need to capture its complexity, we turned to the work of Jonathan Haidt, which highlights the difficulties inherent in creating dialogue between conservative and liberal individuals and groups.[12] Haidt has illustrated how individuals negotiate moral and ethical issues. His work showed that religion complicates the negotiation process because religion is often about in-group/out-group dynamics and researchers do not always take this into account. Conservatives, in particular, tend to be drawn to absolutes and may resist negotiation. He suggested that it may not be possible for individuals from either side to agree, but that the goal should be to create balance and space for each position.

We agree with Haidt that Mormonism needs to develop more space for respectful and constructive discussion about gender issues from a range of viewpoints. Unfortunately, the range of perspectives is quite limited in LDS Church discourse. The conservative and liberal spaces of online Mormonism are also relatively polarized. There are, however, a few attempts on both sides to find this elusive balance: the work of Terryl and Fiona Givens, the work of Neylan McBaine, the new Gospel Topics essays from the Church History Department, the work of Richard and Claudia Bushman, Sunstone's "Why I Stay" annual panel of speakers, and a recent blog post by Paul Malan on the problems of the Mormon monoculture[13]—all of which are good examples of recent Mormon efforts to seek greater balance in the contemporary debate over gender issues in the Church.

Survey Demographics

Before discussing the survey responses, it is helpful to know some demographic information about the respondents. Seventy-two percent were women, and 27 percent were men.[14] One percent responded "Other" or preferred not to respond. The responses skewed young, with 41 percent of respondents ages eighteen through thirty and 33 percent aged thirty-one through forty. Ninety-six percent lived in America at the time of the survey, and 36 percent lived in Utah specifically. The overwhelming majority of respondents identified their race/ethnicity as white (91 percent) and the second-largest group was Pacific Islanders (3 percent).

Forty-six percent were college graduates and a further 26 percent had graduate degrees. When asked to identify their political beliefs on a scale from "very conservative" to "very liberal," the largest group (26 percent) identified as "mod-

---

12. Jonathan Haidt, *The Righteous Mind: Why Good People Are Divided by Politics and Religion* (New York: Vintage, 2012).

13. Paul Malan, February 15, 2015, "Wetlands: The Future of Mormonism," https://medium com/@ungewissen/wetlands-the-future-of-mormonism-f1c1b3b62256.

14. These percentages are very closely aligned with the gender demographics obtained from a content analysis of individuals who have submitted profiles to the Ordain Women website in which 70.4 percent of profilers were women and 29.6 percent were men. For this and other related demographic statistics to those obtained in our Gender Issues Survey, see Chapter 18.

erate, but lean conservative." The second-largest group (19 percent) identified as "conservative," and the third-largest group (14 percent) as "moderate, but lean liberal." Eighty-six percent told us that they are LDS and currently identify as LDS while a further 11 percent think that their names are still on Church records but do not identify as LDS. Most of the remainder reported that they used to be LDS but that their names are no longer on Church records.

Different Treatment: Doctrine or Culture?

The first open-ended question asked respondents to consider whether differences in the way that men and women are treated in the Church stem from LDS doctrine or Mormon culture, with a follow-up question asking if these differences in treatment are beneficial or not. Of the 500 randomly selected respondents, 446 answered this question. Seventeen percent of respondents reported that different treatment of men and women by the Church stemmed from doctrine and 23 percent reported that it stemmed from culture. The largest group of respondents, 47 percent, believed that different treatment of men and women in the Church was rooted in both doctrine and culture. Thirteen percent did not address the doctrine/culture divide on the issue of gendered treatment in the Church.

In asking whether gendered treatment by the Church was beneficial or not, 32 percent felt that different treatment was beneficial. Twenty-eight percent thought it was not beneficial. Thirty-one percent expressed mixed feelings, and 9 percent did not comment on this part of the question. In looking at both doctrine/culture and beneficial/not beneficial questions, 24 percent of respondents had mixed feelings about both parts of the question, which was the single biggest category.

Researchers anticipated that a majority of respondents would clearly identify doctrine as the root of gendered treatment in the LDS Church and express an opinion that it was beneficial. This did not happen. Mormons who participated in this survey demonstrated a thoughtful process of negotiation that integrated official Church teachings with lived experiences. This process of negotiation is a compelling example of how Mormons do not actually perceive their lives in terms of either/or binaries but use their lived experiences to draw lines between those teachings that are seen as central to the Church (doctrine) and those that are not (culture).

The following response demonstrates this process of negotiation and, while very long, represents many of the mixed doctrine/culture responses.

> First is the difference regarding the Priesthood. Men hold it. Women do not. This is a very doctrinal difference, and it's important to note that women don't need to hold it in order to access it. So long as they are faithful, they can have all the benefits of the priesthood despite not holding it. The reason men hold the priesthood ties into the next difference in treatment: in the home. Men preside over the home. They hold the priesthood keys and they have that responsibility. This is a good thing. However, this does not mean that every decision in the home is made by the man. On the contrary, decisions need to be made by both the husband and the wife. The

wife is an equal to her husband in this regard. It's her life too. The wife's duty is to raise the children, should there be children, with the help of her husband. There are really a million differences I could list, but ultimately, I think most of them boil down to being beneficial. To a certain point. And in their purest form. The problem is that they can easily get taken out of context or twisted by extremists of either direction. Just because a wife should raise the children doesn't mean that the husband shouldn't be bothered with that. It also doesn't mean that she can't get a job. Or get a higher education. Or that the roles can't be reversed between husband and wife. These are all ultimately decisions that should be tackled by the husband and wife together, for their household and it's not for anyone else to dispute. I think a lot of people forget that last part. And that's when the differences can seem not beneficial. And this can go for virtually any difference. There a good side, and bad side. The good side is the doctrinal side, and the bad side is how people who have no right to take part in the decision of an individual or their opinion of the difference spin it and condemn the person/people involved.

This respondent started off by reiterating Church teachings on gender with regard to the priesthood and men presiding in the home, both of which were described as beneficial. The respondent then went on to identify specific situations in which gendered treatment was not beneficial. This was a pattern that many of the mixed doctrine/culture responses followed. This person finished the response by stating that good outcomes are related to doctrine and bad outcomes are related to culture. Throughout the survey, gendered treatment stemming from doctrine correlated with feelings that this treatment was beneficial, while gendered treatment stemming from culture correlated with feelings that this treatment was harmful.

The survey responses did not form a consensus on what constituted doctrine or culture, with some expressing certainty about their attributions and others not. Representing the doctrine-only set, one respondent wrote: "I believe that God has set up his Church the way He has for a reason. The differences in the Church aren't meant to degrade or undermine the men or women. We each have our roles that are of equal importance. I believe the roles men and women play in the Church are purely doctrinal." This individual identifies as doctrine all of the ways men and women and are treated differently and does so with confidence. However, respondents also made the opposite claim with equal confidence. One culture-only respondent wrote: "Gender roles are a social construct and they hurt both men and women (though they hurt women more). For instance, men staying at home and women working outside the home are both stigmatized."

This second respondent is direct in stating that gender roles are a product of society and not of doctrine. While neither the first nor the second quotation is typical of those in the survey, they demonstrate the range of opinions on the doctrine/culture issue.

Instead of expressing certainty in separating doctrine and culture, a few respondents addressed this difficulty directly: "I have always lived in Utah and so it is very difficult for me to separate what is cultural and what is doctrinal because seminary teachers, institute teachers, bishops, etc. also have a hard time separating the two." This respondent acknowledges that she does not know how to interpret Church teachings as received from her leaders over time, because she is sure that they did not understand these differences. Another respondent wrote: "The Church, like every other religion in the world, suffers from a distinct divide between official doctrine as taught by the church and doctrine as believed by members." This response speaks to the difficulty of teaching and learning. The LDS Church works hard to teach its members about LDS values and priorities, but it cannot control how members receive and understand that information, which seems to be a very individualized outcome.

While respondents did not come to a consensus on what was doctrinal or cultural about gendered treatment in the church, 28 percent of respondents referenced priesthood as a key concern. The responses referred to and viewed priesthood in a variety of ways. These selections do not represent full responses, but snippets of what people had to say about priesthood:

> Women are given nurturing authority while men are given priesthood authority.
>
> If for some reason the church decided to give the priesthood to women I really wouldn't mind. It doesn't change the principles by which I try to live my life one bit.
>
> The Relief Society has become pros at recognizing those in need and providing care while the Priesthood is used to spiritually bless the members and receive revelation for a larger group.
>
> Women [are] categorically excluded from various positions within Church leadership—even those that do not require the priesthood.
>
> I have been taught that the priesthood trumps womanhood. I should have equal opportunity to preside, and decide in my home at the very least.
>
> I am not threatened by men holding the priesthood and women not. Statistically women tend to be more religious and righteous and men have a harder time haha, therefore I feel it is in God's wisdom to have men "in charge" to keep them valiant and true. I feel more valued as a woman in the gospel than if I were a man.
>
> As stated, having held a Stake Calling and having participated in Stake Council, I honestly would not want to have to deal with the issues the Presiding Priesthood Leaders need to deal with on a daily and weekly basis. Such a calling would take me away from my family and my family is my #1 priority.
>
> The only real difference that I see is the difference in priesthood and some callings. Otherwise it's equal. Women can't hold the priesthood.

In these responses, priesthood is positioned opposite womanhood and then characterized in positive, neutral, and negative ways. Of the 28 percent who referenced priesthood, many of them agreed that men holding the priesthood was a doctrinal principle and not a cultural practice.

Of the participants who referenced priesthood, some specifically discussed how priesthood impacted women:

> "If two of us are the same, one of us is not necessary" (unknown source). Different roles are needed, even necessary. Women not holding the priesthood is a doctrinal

difference. The differences allow for organization as well as personal growth. I personally just don't see the big deal at all. The priesthood is not designed to be self serving in any manner, so why the craving to have it? One can serve others in myriad ways without it. One can be plenty busy within the church without it. Why the craving to be in positions that are more visible or prominent?

This response argues that women perform a role in the Church that is entirely separate from priesthood. This individual also highlights the tension between the institutional view that only men hold the priesthood and those who want women to be ordained to the priesthood.

Another respondent observed that priesthood is used to exclude women from participation in Church ordinances and to encourage women to stay at home with children:

It is atrocious that women are excluded from baby blessings. There is no doctrinal reason behind this. Many men in the circle are not even "worthy" members. Boys are elevated to priesthood "power" at age 12 and given budget, attention, activities, that girls aren't. Girls are taught to marry young, have children and be a stay at home mom—a recipe for disaster in many circumstances. Girls should be taught to have careers that enable them to support themselves and their families and then they have choices.

A third participant negotiates women and the priesthood differently than the previous two, stating her belief that men and women do not need the same responsibilities while showing how priesthood is often used in ways she feels are inappropriate to exclude women from particular callings:

I do not think women need to have all the same responsibilities and roles in order to be treated equally, but I do feel like women's opinions and abilities are not equally utilized or respected in the church, currently. I think there are spectra in callings at this time that are only open to one gender or the other that are only that way due to cultural expectations and not doctrinal necessity. I think women would make fantastic ward clerks, Sunday school presidents and ward mission leaders, locally and on a stake level it makes no sense to me that the stake technology specialist must be a Melchizedek Priesthood holder. I also think a man could make an excellent primary president or a compassionate service leader. I don't understand why PEC meetings take place regularly and discuss needs in the ward without consulting the RS President. Other than Bishopric meetings, I think all ward planning meetings should include female leaders along with the men.

A fourth respondent expressed a different understanding of the priesthood, seeing it as being used to include women and not being gendered in the same way that the first three women described:

Being an adult convert, I have seen very little difference as far as men and women are treated. Women have the same priesthood authority as men, as all priesthood authority comes from Heavenly Father. Any calling a person gets, whether male or female, comes from the same priesthood authority. As the president of an auxiliary of the church, I am involved in leadership meetings, teach the gospel, and administer to others the same as our bishop or any other "man" in our ward. Women have a more nurturing role and men more administrative role, but each are equal in the doctrine of the church.

The issue of how Church members view women's relationship to the priesthood is a difficult one to parse. Many associate priesthood with the ability to lead and perform a wide variety of ordinance-based and administrative roles, but like the last woman quoted, believe that both men and women act with priesthood authority in their different capacities.

Effect on Spiritual/Religious Lives

In the second open-ended question, respondents considered how an expansion of administrative and leadership roles for women would affect their religious and spiritual lives. We anticipated that a majority of responses would be either negative or positive, in keeping with our understanding of the scholarly literature and the tendency for the LDS Church to represent belief in terms of binary distinctions. When the responses were coded, the largest group (31 percent)[15] was those who supported increased leadership roles for women and/or felt that an increased role would have positive results. One woman wrote: "I would feel more comfortable sharing my concerns with female leaders. I would be more comfortable with my daughters having interviews. I feel like I would be taken more seriously as a disciple and follower of Christ." Her response lists three ways that she will benefit from increased women's leadership: receiving spiritual guidance from women, greater security in having women interview her daughter, and a sense that women will be taken more seriously in the Church. This respondent supports increased leadership roles for women and expressed her reasons without hesitation.

Within this first group, we also included those who would support changes if Church leaders announced a new policy. These individuals do not necessarily see a need for change but endorsed Church leadership and affirmed their decisions. These respondents, like the one below, engaged in a thought experiment and negotiated their own feelings with potential future direction by Church leaders: "If that revelation came from Heavenly Father, I would accept and follow it. I believe women add a rich diverseness and great value to the Church. I personally have felt that my opinion was very valued and often implemented when I served as a Young Women's president."

Surprisingly, the second-largest group (27 percent) felt that increased leadership roles for women would have no effect on their spiritual or religious life. One woman wrote: "I do not feel it would affect my spirituality in any way. It would only affect how I serve the church with my spirituality. My views about the church, my belief in the doctrine, my testimony, and my willingness to work for God would be exactly the same as it ever was." This type of comment, which appeared frequently in the responses, is outside the anticipated binary of for/against responses. Another respondent indicated that her spiritual life would not be impacted because, "My spiritual life is my own responsibility. The Church can help me have spiritual experiences, but men and women are equally able

---

15. Eight percent of respondents gave answers that did not address the question.

to facilitate my spiritual experiences. Having women serve in more leadership callings wouldn't affect me more than having men, because we are equal." Both respondents see themselves as spiritually independent—an independence that remains unaffected by Church policies.

Those who expressed mixed feelings about increased leadership roles comprised the third-largest group (21 percent). Many of these responses reveal the process of negotiation as participants tried to think through the effects of increased leadership roles for women. In these cases, the respondents separated priesthood from administrative/leadership positions in a way that mirrored the discourse on the separation between doctrine and culture. Respondents again identified the priesthood as a doctrinal and administrative change as cultural. One individual wrote:

> I view the priesthood and administration of the church as separate things generally. For example, I believe that the role of the bishop is more of a spiritual role than an administrative role. I wouldn't have a problem with women organizing/conducting meetings, setting budgets, giving trainings, handling tithing, and other administrative functions. Without a revelation from God through his prophet, I am opposed to women trying to take on spiritual roles of the priesthood, such as the bishop responsibilities of being a judge, sacrament ordinances, blessings, etc. That being said, if the prophet did have a revelation that would grant women the priesthood, I would accept it as a commandment and it wouldn't affect my spirituality.

This respondent described a belief in a separation between administrative and spiritual leadership; she agreed with others who felt that expanding administrative leadership roles to women would not require a revelation, but that expanding women's roles to include calling them as bishops would requires a specific revelation. Other respondents affirmed:

> It would depend on what roles you are asking about. Serving as a Sunday School President would a good thing, serving as a bishop—unless directed by revelation, would put the Church at odds with God and doom the Church to the fate that other men/women lead [sic] Church's are facing.

> As far as it doesn't pertain to the ordination of the priesthood, it wouldn't affect my spiritual life and testimony at all. Women should take a more active role in leadership, but they shouldn't try to force obtaining callings that require the priesthood. Because that's not going to happen. Ever.

These two respondents agreed that such changes without revelation would place the Church at odds with God. The very firmness of their support for the status quo, unless changed by revelation, suggests that they found such a revelation unlikely. Ironically, their expressed faith in a revelation-only change is a factor that would apparently keep them from seeking or asking for such a revelation.

Other respondents weighed the benefits and drawbacks of increased women's roles and how such an expansion would impact women, men, and boys. One participant wrote:

> If women were called to be ward clerks and executive secretaries it would not affect my spiritual life. If the bishop's wife were asked to call speakers on Sunday that would not change my faith. My grandma recently told me that the daughter of a friend of hers "who was made a trainer at 2 months on her mission, is now in some supervisory position equivalent to zone leader or such. . . . [T]hat is a step toward equality, priesthood not required, position added to sister's opportunity." I think there is room for women to serve in leadership and administrative roles in the church—to be Sunday School presidents and to fulfill other roles that don't require the priesthood. There are many callings traditionally given to men that don't necessarily need to be restricted to men. At the same time, I believe that many men, especially younger men, need church responsibilities and callings to keep them on a straight path. I think a balance could be struck, especially under the guidance of an inspired leader.

This respondent outlines the ways in which more equality would be beneficial yet negotiated the potential social cost for men and boys without leadership calling.

Another common concern in the internal negotiation process was related to the time women would be required to spend away from home and family responsibilities and the possible confusion of roles. Some noted that the time commitment required by the lay leadership structure can be intense. Many respondents expressed that such callings would take them out of the home. Two respondents found the prospect dismaying:

> I personally know that I would be called to higher positions and that is not something I seek after or even desire at all. My main calling and concern is that of my family and children and to be called away, more than I already am, would be very hard for me. I would do any calling I am asked, but do I want to, no.

> I guess that would give me and my daughters more opportunities to serve others. Or it would probably just mean more meetings! It might help me be a bit more consistent religiously, but I really don't see it doing much but adding more responsibility/time away from my family. Mormon leaders have stated that no failure in the home can compensate for success elsewhere (find quote).

Respondents also indicated that women holding certain positions could cause confusion regarding the order of the Church and issues related to priesthood keys. One male respondent described his personal roadblocks to successfully negotiating seeing women in leadership positions:

> For women to hold these positions would require a doctrinal paradigm shift. The current doctrine is very much entrenched in the history and plays a significant part in our understanding of what the eternities will be like. A change in this doctrine will require a lot of explaining to members if the Church doesn't want to alienate its members. For me personally, I admit I'd find it hard to accept simply because I have a preconceived vision of what life will be like after this life, and women holding the priesthood isn't currently part of that vision. I'd hate to say that my vision is so rigid that it couldn't adapt to a more greater understanding of the gospel if that's really what God had intended from the beginning.

Those who stated that expanded priesthood ordination would be positive often concluded that their daughters would have more opportunities to serve, develop more spiritual gifts, and represent a broader spectrum of ideas and perspectives. Two respondents stated:

> Female leaders would understand my circumstances, needs, and feelings much better. They would "speak my language." As a result, I would feel greater support. Female leaders would bring more visibility to women, which would provide more role models for girls and women. More positive role models would give women more confidence and more ideas about how to serve others in and out of the church. Women would feel more valued for their efforts and ideas. When we are invisible to church leaders, it is easy to project those feelings onto God. Women would have more opportunity to feel God's guidance more strongly and frequently. I believe this is the case because of the many stories I hear men telling about their experiences in calling and counseling church members under their stewardship.

> It would show me that God and his leaders understand the importance of the female voice in the church. It would show that there is compassion for the women that don't necessarily have a connection with a man, but still require assistance and support in a way men don't understand.

The smallest substantive group included those who had negative feelings about expanded leadership roles for women (13 percent). Many women objected to this possibility because they felt that women already had enough responsibility in the Church. One woman expressed this view succinctly, "I feel women are given enough responsibilities within the church and without. I think it would be too much on my plate personally." Another woman expressed concern that increased Church responsibilities would take time away from her family:

> In my opinion, women already have administrative and leadership roles. We are Primary, Young Women, and Relief Society Presidents. These roles are administrative leadership roles. We administer to the members of each of these organizations. We are part of Ward Councils which allows us to report on our organizations. We work together with all other organizations to minister to members in our congregations. We have counselors and secretaries to assist in these roles. We oversee a large number of members. Many of us also have the responsibility of raising our families. Some of us, myself included, are single parents. To say that women should have more administrative and leadership roles is going against the laws of Heavenly Father. Women have many more roles than just in church and I am happy giving our brethren the roles that oversee our congregations. Personally, I am grateful for the organization of the gospel. I do feel that my religious/spiritual life would not be as rich if women were to have more administrative and leadership roles. It would lead to being burnt out and eventually I would feel I have to make a choice about the importance of church or family. Given the direction of society today, we need a balance of home/family and religion/spirituality. We need less feminist perspective!

Anticipating Change in the Next Two Decades

The third qualitative question in our survey asked respondents to propose desirable changes that would positively affect women in the LDS Church in the next ten to twenty years. It should be noted that approximately a quarter of respondents indicated that they were happy with the way the Church currently treats women. Of that quarter, roughly half of the respondents indicated that they were not interested in change and generalized from their experiences. One respondent stated: "I am perfectly happy as a female member of the church so I do not really think about or want any particular change." Another individual said: "I don't want any changes! I am happy the way things are." A third respondent highlighted how she identified her own equality and the importance of women in the Church in relation to men:

> I don't need any changes. I have never felt less important than my husband in the church. If anything I have constantly felt the opposite. I feel like if women would stop picking it apart and look around . . . I haven't met one bishop or presidency member that thinks they could do what they do without their wife by their side. I feel like a lot of women need to be in those roles to feel important. It's a self worth thing. In reality they are already more important then they will apparently ever know. If they married a good man with a good heart he knows that the wom[a]n standing beside him keep him standing. So the only thing I think that needs to be fixed is women realizing they don't need those roles to be just as important if not more important than the men holding them.

This woman has harmonized Church teachings and her own experiences, a negotiation that has led her to a conservative position on the roles of men and women in Church leadership. Not all internal negotiation ends in a middle-ground position.

The other half of this group indicated that they would not like to see changes in the Church but, during the process of negotiating this position, incorporated the experiences of others without generalizing from their own experience. Some of these answers negotiated again between culture and doctrine. One respondent highlighted this tension between culture and doctrine and her own personal experiences of feeling valued. She wrote:

> I don't have specific requests or goals for women in the Church. I trust God to know what men and women need, and I hope the Church leaders will be open to any changes God wants us to make, and to constantly seek His will. I think those changes will mostly happen gradually. I've already seen small steps in the right direction (as mentioned in a previous question). I feel that many members are ready for radical change, but the Church as a whole may not be ready right now. I trust God to know when changes need to happen, and our leaders to facilitate it when it's appropriate.

The majority of respondents in this group qualified their responses with the desire to follow the prophet and expressed a belief in continuing revelation, thus indicating a degree of flexibility in their positions.

In addition to the group who did not want any change, approximately an additional 10 percent indicated that they did not want policy changes but that they did want the Church's current position to be better articulated by Church leaders and curriculum materials. They were distinguished from the previous group because they listed and expressed concrete changes they would like to see enacted within the Church but stopped short of suggesting cultural, policy, or doctrinal changes. One respondent expressed her desire for changes in training:

> I hope that Church leadership training will improve with regards to engaging everyone, men and women, in the process of their own salvation. That personal responsibility for applying the doctrine is increasingly taught. I hope that the men are taught that holding the priesthood doesn't give them all the answers, revelation is a process, and answers come from many sources, and that when a woman approaches you with a concern, listen. They need to understand that the phrase "God is no respecter of persons" (Acts 10:34) means that the role of men is no more important than that of women, and he has given women important stewardship, too. These responsibilities are different, but no less important, and because women have different responsibilities it is only by working together that God's purposes are achieved. Equality is not the same as being identical.

The respondents in this group expanded upon the need for better instruction from the top leadership to the local level, often indicating their faith that the General Authorities operated from doctrine, while local leaders often were influenced by culture. One respondent wrote:

> I think it would be good if bishops were encouraged to trust the personal revelation of women, especially those in leadership roles. I've known a few bishops who felt the need to "check" the revelation of the Young Women President about who she wanted as advisors, rather than just trusting that she knew who was right for the job. Little things like that could be changed if the Church leadership spoke more about the value of women in Church leadership. But for myself, I don't feel undervalued and don't feel the need for any major changes.

Over half of the respondents to this question listed specific aspects of either Church culture (defined as unrelated to the priesthood) and doctrine (especially priesthood and temple work) that they would like to see clarified. Two-thirds of this group suggested culture-related changes including: equal budgets for the Young Men and Young Women's programs, expanded administrative callings for women, expanded autonomy for the Relief Society, and changes in gendered teaching concerning modesty, chastity, and roles. One-third of this group indicated that they would like to see changes in doctrine, including ordination for women, changes in temple ceremonies, and revised and more flexible gender roles.

Conclusion

If this chapter were a newspaper article, the headline would be something like "Mormons More Moderate Than Previously Thought." In negotiating gender and religion, the respondents for this survey combined both official Church teachings and personal experience to understand issues of gender. We feel that this process of internal negotiation creates a fertile middle ground for understanding gender in a variety of different ways. In tackling gender, it is clear that Mormons understand Church teachings as reflecting both essential truths (doctrine) and cultural practices, but that both forces are understood and delineated on an individual level without universal guidelines, highlighting the relative absence of a systematic theology of gender.

Much of the official Church discourse on gender emphasizes the differences between men and women while drawing on gender essentialism and complementarianism.[16] Mormons have internalized some of these ideas, but there is clearly more space for a larger discussion of men's and women's roles in family life and in Church organization. Many members are ready for increased women's leadership and desire specific changes in Church policy so that men and women will have more positive interactions with the institutional Church organization. In thinking and discussing gender at church, many members are ready for a more nuanced discussion of gender—one that moves away from absolutes. The Church may benefit from listening to and understanding the different ways that members negotiate gender and could use that new understanding to inform Church policy.

---

16. According to Margot Badran, "Feminism and Conversion: Comparing British, Dutch, and South African Life Stories," in Karin van Nieuwkerk, ed., *Women Embracing Islam: Gender and Conversion in the West* (Austin: University of Texas Press, 2009), gender complementarianism is the idea that men and women have separate but complementary roles in public and private life. Gender essentialism is the idea that men and women are fundamentally different and that those differences stem from biology. Diana Fuss, *Essentially Speaking: Feminism, Nature, and Difference* (New York: Routledge, 2013).

Chapter 17

Mormon Feminists in Social Media: A Story of Community and Education

Jessica Finnigan and Nancy Ross

On the afternoon of Saturday, April 5, 2014, 509[1] Ordain Women supporters gathered at City Creek Park in Salt Lake City, Utah. This was the second time that Ordain Women had asked supporters to meet at the park, walk to Temple Square, and wait in line for standby tickets to the priesthood session of general conference. Nancy moved next to Kate Kelly as we walked out of the park with a small army of media photographers, videographers, reporters, and observers clearing the way in front of us. In the following days, those images illustrated news stories about the event.

What was not visible on that day were the thousands of Mormon feminists and allies who were watching and waiting for news of what was happening. Nor could one see the social media volunteers who sat in Jessica Finnigan's living room seven time zones away. In Cambridge, England, this remote team had access to Ordain Women's accounts on Twitter and Instagram, as well as the official Facebook page. They were ready to repost content with predetermined hashtags from multiple sources and platforms in real time. For two hours the small group worked quickly to collect information, photos, and videos and to share them as widely as possible through official Ordain Women channels and progressive Mormon Facebook groups.

Previous Ordain Women actions had demonstrated the need for real-time updates for those who could not physically attend. Social media played a central role in organizing, promoting, and documenting this particular action. Multiple individuals created event-related Facebook pages, twitter announcements, memes, and blog posts that encouraged and invited people to participate. Ordain Women raised money through social media to facilitate travel to and from the event for supporters. Social media also made it possible to collect real-time data on participation numbers, to document the stages of the action, and to follow the reactions of other Mormons.

In this chapter, we (1) provide a brief review of scholarly literature on religious feminism and the new social media; (2) describe the methods we employed in conducting our own surveys of online Mormon feminism; (3) offer a summary comparison of key findings from our 2013 and 2015 surveys of Mormon social media participants; (4) review online Mormon feminism and LDS racial issues

---

1. Newspaper estimates ranged from 200–400 for both Ordain Women events, but our actual count was 509.

as an example of "spiral" education though internet discussion groups; and (5) discuss social media participants' learning needs for coping with the tension and negative consequences of supporting Mormon feminism.

Scholarly Literature on Social Media and Religious Feminism

Typically, sociological studies of women in religion address topics of agency, resistance, coercion, oppression, submission, voice, identity, power, tradition, ritual, and ambivalence.[2] Our study diverges from much of the literature on women and religion in that it focuses on the benefits of participating in online religious feminist spaces. Most obviously, social media provides Mormon feminists with a virtual community, but it does more than that. The social media community doubles as teaching and learning environments for individuals to engage with social issues and feminist theory. While many Mormon feminists engage in campaigns to encourage institutional change within the Church, they most often create change within themselves.

The single biggest contribution to understanding contemporary religious feminism and the internet, and the most relevant to this chapter, has come from a collection of essays titled *Feminism and Religion in the 21st Century: Technology, Dialogue, and Expanding Borders,* edited by Gina Messina-Dysert and Rosemary Radford Ruether (New York: Routledge, 2014). This book was the first interfaith text on religious feminism and an excellent model of dialogue and investigation. The book's essays demonstrated how Jewish, Muslim, Catholic, Mormon, and other religious feminist groups have used the internet to create new and flexible spaces for religious participation.

Studies have shown that the internet has increased participation in online and offline activism.[3] Marouf Hasian Jr. explored how the internet quickly and powerfully facilitated social connections in comparison with offline relationships,

---

2. Orit Avishai, "'Doing Religion' in a Secular World: Women in Conservative Religions and the Question of Agency," *Gender and Society* 22 (2008): 409–33; Margot Badran and Mathias Rohe, *Feminism beyond East and West: New Gender Talk and Practice in Global Islam* (New Delhi: Global Media Publications, 2007); Sylvia Barack Fishman, *A Breath of Life: Feminism in the American Jewish Community* (Lebanon, N.H.: University Press of New England, 1995); Yael Israel-Cohen, *Between Feminism and Orthodox Judaism: Resistance, Identity, and Religious Change in Israel* (Boston: Brill, 2012); Irit Koren, "The Bride's Voice: Religious Women Challenge the Wedding Ritual," *Nashim: A Journal of Jewish Women's Studies & Gender Issues* 10 (Fall 2006): 29–52; Christel Manning, *God Gave Us the Right: Conservative Catholic, Evangelical Protestant, and Orthodox Jewish Women Grapple with Feminism* (New Brunswick, N.J.: Rutgers University Press, 1999); and Valentine M. Moghadam, "Islamic Feminism and Its Discontents: Toward a Resolution of the Debate," *Signs: Journal of Women in Culture and Society* 27 (2002): 1135–71.

3. Caroline Kline, "The Mormon Conception of Women's Nature and Role: A Feminist Analysis," *Feminist Theology* 22, no. 2 (2014): 186–202; and S. Leizerov, "Privacy Advocacy Groups Versus Intel: A Case Study of How Social Movements Are Tactically Using the Internet to Fight Corporations," *Social Science Computer Review* 18, no. 4 (2000): 461–83.

creating connections that would have been impossible in pre-internet days.⁴ Mia Lovheim and Alf Linderman demonstrated that the internet impacts the formation of both individual and collective religious identities.⁵

In 2013, we conducted a survey of the online Mormon feminist community.⁶ Our initial research sought to set a baseline for this relatively new online community and to examine how it used social media to organize and negotiate the historical dangers of activism within the LDS Church.⁷ We conducted a new survey in 2015 that repeated many of the original survey's questions and added some reflective questions so that Mormon feminists could tell us how the community has changed over time. In this chapter we will document the changes within the online Mormon feminist community and the growing use of social media since late 2013. This is the first longitudinal sociological study of online Mormon feminists and adds to the growing body of literature on religious feminism.

Research Methods for Surveys of the Online Mormon Feminist Community

For this study, we have combined quantitative and qualitative methods. The findings we report in this chapter are the result of three years of ethnographic and survey-based research. The first survey was conducted on July 7–14, 2013, and received 1,862 complete responses. The second survey was conducted January 30–February 19, 2015, and received 937 responses from those who self-identified as Mormon feminists or allies of Mormon feminism. These projects were entirely digital in their conception and execution. Thus, we organized and conducted our research through Facebook and Google chat, Google Hangouts, and Skype. The surveys, responses, analysis, and write-ups were transacted in Google Forms, Sheets, and Docs. In these digital surveys we have attempted to capture a sense of Mormon feminist identity, religiosity levels, activist participation, and reactions to Mormon feminist activism over time.

Online progressive Mormonism is conducive to digital study because of the wealth of born-digital online primary sources, including podcasts, blogs, and other social media. Familiarity with these sources helped fill in the gaps of our knowledge and make it possible to conduct more nuanced research. Closed and

---

4. Marouf Hasian Jr., "The Internet and the Human Genome," *Peace Review* 13, no. 3 (2001): 375–80.

5. Mia Lovheim and Alf G. Linderman, "Constructing Religious Identity on the Internet," in Morten Hojsgaard and Margit Warburg, eds., *Religion and Cyberspace* (New York: Taylor and Francis, 2005), 121–37.

6. Nancy Ross and Jessica Finnigan, "Mormon Feminist Perspectives on the Mormon Digital Awakening: A Study of Identity and Personal Narratives," *Dialogue: A Journal of Mormon Thought* 47, no. 4 (2014): 47–84.

7. Jessica Finnigan and Nancy Ross, "'I'm a Mormon Feminist:' How Social Media Revitalized and Enlarged a Movement," *Interdisciplinary Journal of Research on Religion* 9, no.12 (2013): 1–25.

private Facebook groups, which became available in 2011, provided activists with the necessary support community and the virtual space to organize activist events.[8] These spaces are different from public blogs with potentially anonymous comments, because individuals use their real names and engage in conversations behind virtual closed doors, which minimize the potential social costs of disapproval and opprobrium. While participants may not have known each other in real life, Facebook brought together previously isolated Mormon feminists.

Within Mormon feminism, the quick adoption of Facebook closed and private groups in late 2011 changed the nature of Mormon feminism.[9] In 2012, Mormon feminists began organizing online and carrying out activist campaigns both online and offline. The blog community has been discussing culture and gender grievances since 2004, but the protected spaces of Facebook facilitated new kinds of discussions that led to online activism and ultimately to direct actions in the public sphere. We found that the difficult work of Mormon feminist activism happened in the closed spaces afforded by private Facebook groups.[10] By observing these formative discussions and the topics that come up in these kinds of protected spaces, scholars can gain unprecedented insight into feminist religious activism. Researchers may gain some insight into activism by reading public social media but will not understand the diversity of beliefs within a religious activist group and the processes of resolving tension and navigating ambivalence unless they also study private spaces. We considered these factors as we analyzed the archived material from the two largest Mormon feminist blogs: Feminist Mormon Housewives and The Exponent.

Comparative Findings of 2013 and 2015 Surveys of Mormon Social Media Participants

Of particular interest to the subfield of Mormon studies today are the approximately 100 Facebook groups dedicated entirely to progressive Mormonism. There are more than fifteen active group blogging sites, twenty regular podcasts, numerous Twitter feeds, and countless individual blogs. Because these spaces are highly reactive to current events and tied to the larger online and offline Mormon community, they are continually in flux and we have had to adapt our research methods accordingly.

Our 2013 study briefly outlined the demographics of those who participated in the survey. The demographics for the 2015 are mostly similar but differ in important ways. In 2015, only 14 percent of respondents identified themselves as men, compared with 19 percent in 2013. Seventy percent of respondents were aged 18–30, compared with 79 percent two years ago. In both surveys, the overwhelming majority of participants (95 percent plus) lived in the United States. A

---

8. Ibid.
9. Ibid.
10. Ibid.

larger percentage (96 percent) of white people participated in the survey this year than in 2013 (91 percent). Those who identified as Hispanics/Latinos made up the second-largest racial group.

The 2015 survey shows a marked difference in Church participation. Sixty-five percent reported that they attend LDS meetings at least two or three times per month or more—a significant reduction from 2013, when 81 percent of respondents reported attending church at those levels. Two years ago, the percentage of surveyed Mormon feminists who held a calling was 70 percent; this year it is down to 58 percent. Two years ago, the overwhelming majority of respondents likely came from Mormon families, as evidenced by baptismal age. This recent survey includes far more adult converts. In 2013, survey respondents had a belief profile that was consistent with mainstream Mormons in America, but the belief profile of respondents in 2015 does not match the mainstream and may indicate that belief among our respondents has declined somewhat.[11] The survey did not explicitly ask people to explain their Church participation or belief, but other open-ended responses indicate that Mormon feminists may have shifted their behaving and belonging patterns as a result of Kate Kelly's excommunication in June 2014. This particular issue warrants further investigation and follow-up surveys should ask about factors that affect respondents' beliefs and religious activity.

In 2013, we asked Mormon feminists what they believed in terms of the potential ordination of women, and we asked that question again this year. In 2015, 63 percent of our respondents believed that women will be ordained in this life or the next life, compared with 59 percent in 2013. The percentages of those who believe that women already hold the priesthood were similar: 26 percent this year and 24 percent two years ago. The percentage of respondents who believe that women will *never* hold the priesthood has declined a little, from 16 percent in 2013 to 9 percent in 2015.

In 2015, 68 percent of participants thought that future changes in the LDS Church would be more inclusive of women, a percentage which is down from 74 percent in 2013. The percentage of respondents who reported that they felt local leaders were including women in ward-level decisions also declined significantly—from 58 percent to 43 percent. It appear that the 2015 online survey population is slightly older, whiter, and less involved with the Church than those we surveyed in 2013, making it difficult to determine the representative nature of the sample.

The 2015 survey asked participants to respond to the open-ended question: "What have been the benefits to you, if any, of participating in online Mormon feminism?" Two themes appeared consistently throughout the answers: community and education. Online Mormon feminism helped respondents to feel less

---

11. Pew Research Center, *Mormons in America: Certain in Their Beliefs, Uncertain of Their Place in Society,* 2012, www.pewforum.org/2012/01/12/mormons-in-america-methodology. All of the internet sources cited in this article were live as of May 9, 2015.

lonely and isolated in both their feminist and Mormon views and participating in the community taught them about the intersection of gender and Mormonism.

In writing about community, about a quarter of all respondents said that their participation made them feel less isolated. One person wrote: "I have felt like I am not alone in my feelings, and have found a community to truly emotionally invest in." Many respondents indicated that feelings of belonging to the online community brought relief to the emotional distress of feeling out of place at church. One woman wrote; "I can sleep more peaceful knowing that I am not alone in this journey. There is a place for me. There are others who understand me."

More than just finding a sense of belonging, many Mormon feminists indicated that they had established lasting friendships through their participation online. A woman wrote: "I have made some of the most valuable friendships in my whole life. I have come to love these women, despite being on the other side of the world, and coming from different backgrounds. It is wonderful." Another woman wrote: "The only reason I can remain engaged in the LDS Church is because I have friends to help me vent and tell me I'm not crazy."

Others wrote of how the online community empowered them and offered a safe place for open discussion. One woman commented, "I've had an increase in empathy from and for those who have had the same and similar experiences. I've felt validated in knowing I'm not the only one upset by gender imbalances at church. It's empowering to know I'm not alone." Another respondent elaborated on this idea and indicated that she felt empowered to examine her belief and the Church: "It has empowered me where I felt powerless. Knowing that there was a community out there helped me confront issues I've had with the church in a more open and honest way. . . . If my parents dislike/disown me, that's fine. I'm not alone. I have a community." A third respondent discussed empowerment in terms of creating change: "[Online Mormon feminism] helped me not feel alone. It empowered me to be part of change. It kept me in the church for years." Throughout the survey, other respondents echoed the idea that participation in the online community helped Mormon feminists maintain a relationship with the institutional Church.

The survey asked respondents about their friends in the online community. Had they met their Mormon feminist friends in real life or spoken to them by phone? Fifty-six percent of respondents had met their friends in person, but just 16 percent reported seeing their Mormon feminists friends regularly. Thirty-four percent had never met their Mormon feminist friends in person. Seventeen percent had telephone conversations with their Mormon feminists friends. These numbers speak to the ways in which the relationships that form the contemporary Mormon feminist community are rooted primarily in social media and not in face-to-face interactions.

We asked Mormon feminists how they participated in the online community. The top three social media platforms were Facebook, with 79 percent of respondents participating there, blogs (70 percent), and podcasts (42 percent).

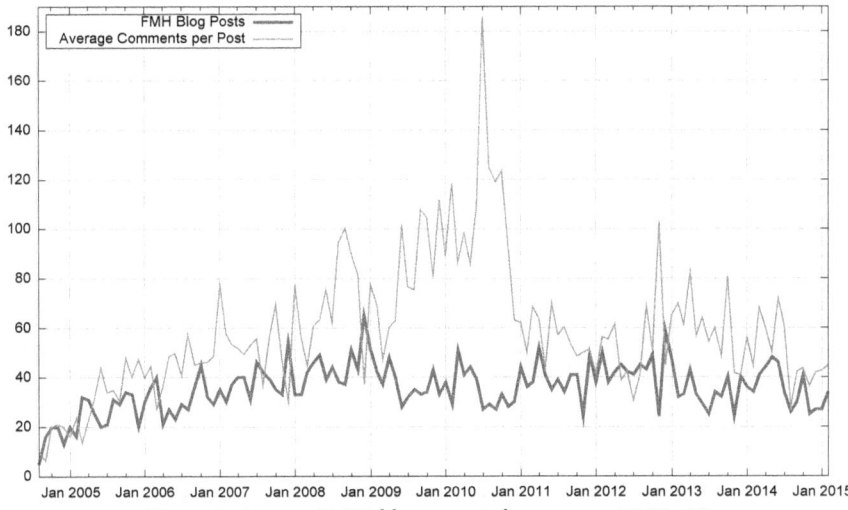
Figure 1. Average FMH blog posts and comments, 2005–15

Mormon feminists participated on other social media platforms, but at much smaller rates: Twitter (15 percent), Instagram (7 percent), and Pinterest (6 percent). Just under 5 percent reported engaging in other ways, including real-life meetups and retreats, email lists, subscribing to *Exponent II* magazine, Sunstone, Reddit, Tumblr, and various professional activities. We asked respondents how they interacted with Mormon feminists in these online spaces. The five main modes of interaction were Mormon feminist-themed Facebook groups (65 percent), blog comments (45 percent), Facebook messaging (33 percent), email (22 percent), and tweets (eight percent). By both of these measures, Facebook and blogs are the main spaces for Mormon feminists online.

Before blogs, online Mormon feminism existed in private listserves, which sent out emails to a group of users.[12] The Feminist Mormon Housewives (FMH) blog was founded in 2004. Giving Mormon feminism a more public face, it grew in number of posts and comments over time. (See Fig. 1). Today, it is the central blog for the Mormon feminist community. Over the last year, the FMH blog has received an average of 47,477 unique users per month, an increase from 2013. (See Fig. 2.) It is unclear what these numbers suggest about the size of the Mormon feminist community, as there are likely some readers of the blog who do not identify as Mormon feminists or their allies.

---

12. Lorie Winder Stromberg, "The Sacred and the Mundane: Mormon Feminism on the Internet," *Mormon Women's Forum Quarterly* 7, nos. 1–2 (1996): 1–15, http://66.147.244.239/~girlsgo6/mormonwomensforum/wp-content/uploads/2011/10/MWfVol7Num12.pdf .

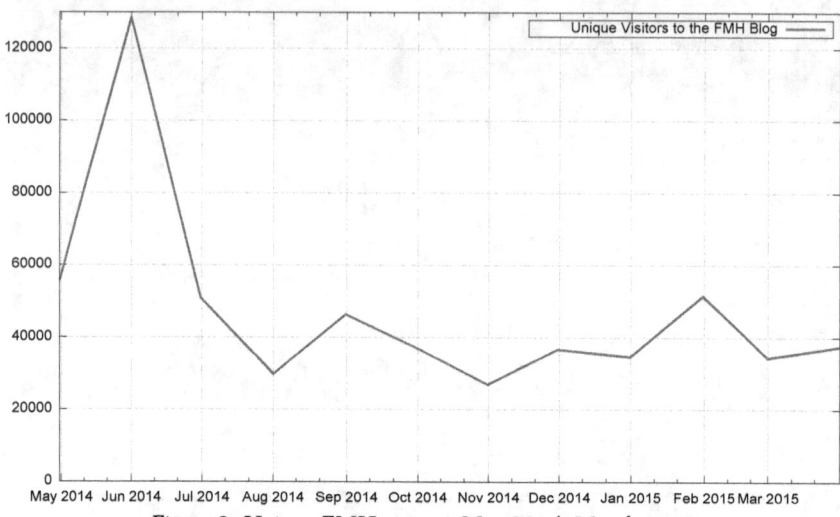

Figure 2. Unique FMH visitors, May 2014–March 2015

There may be another way to approach this question. Self-identified Mormons make up just 2 percent of the population of the United States,[13] and an estimated 15 percent of them are progressive in their political values,[14] though the researchers did not ask about feminist beliefs or attitudes toward gender equality. From our research and experience within progressive Mormon blogs and Facebook groups, not all progressive Mormons identify as feminists and there are perhaps 948,300 progressive Mormons in America. At this stage, it is not possible to count all of the self-identified Mormon feminists in America or to get a rough idea of how many progressive Mormons self-identify as Mormon feminists. Our best guess is that less than half do. Even within the progressive Mormon community, many see women's issues as a niche issue or do not recognize that there are problems with the way that the institutional Church treats women. Thus, while the actual number of Mormon feminists is unknown, if we make a conservative assumption that roughly 20 percent of progressive Mormons probably self-identify as Mormon feminists, then there may be about 190,000 Mormon feminists in the USA.

Bloggers from FMH founded a closed Facebook group in September of 2011. It is from this and other Mormon feminist groups that individuals began to brainstorm and organize activist campaigns. For privacy's sake, we can write in only general terms about that group, but it was possible to identify the date when each member joined the FMH Facebook group and chart the growth of

---

13. Gallup, "Religion Poll, 2014," http://www.gallup.com/poll/1690/religion.aspx (accessed April 13, 2015).

14. David E. Campbell, John Clifford Green, and J. Quin Monson, *Mormons and American Politics: Seeking the Promised Land* (New York: Cambridge University Press, 2014), 65.

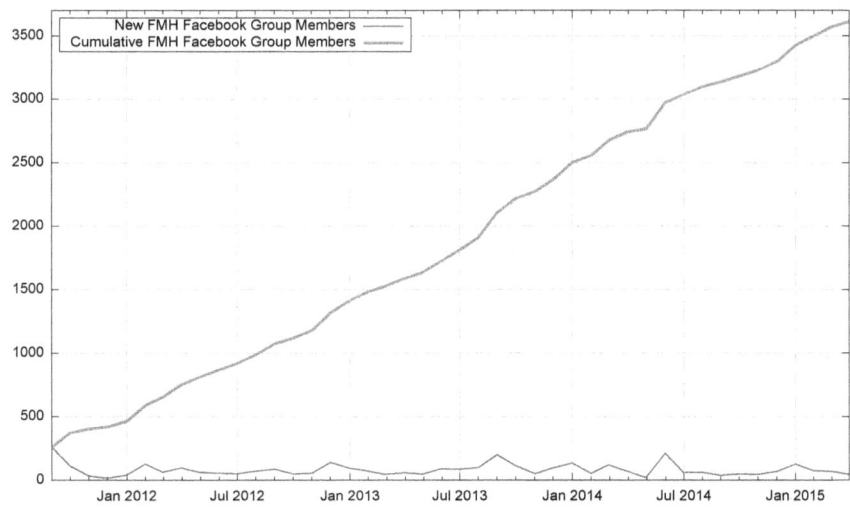

Figure 3. New/cumulative FMH Facebook members, 2012–15

the group over its lifespan. (See Fig. 3). The growth of the group is surprisingly linear. Perhaps the idea of gender equality is one that is compelling and enduring. It is difficult to get to the heart of the linear growth, but it may continue as the number of FMH's Facebook members is far smaller than the much larger online community that surrounds it.

We experimented with graphing various combinations of the number of FMH and Exponent II blog posts and comments (see Fig. 4), the growth of the FMH Facebook group, Ordain Women profiles, and overlaying that data with a rough timeline of significant events. From these graphs, we can make a few general comments about the online community. (See Fig. 5.) The internet provides a fast and low-cost platform for informal mass communication; as a result it allows the online community to be highly reactive to media coverage of emerging news stories or swiftly developing events. Peaks in Mormon online activity can distinctly be observed in conjunction with Church-related activism or official LDS Church announcements.

A planned campaign will increase the number of blog posts and comments. If the action has been directly related to Ordain Women, profile submissions increase during the run-up to that event. A large planned event, like Ordain Women's October and April priesthood actions, is frequently followed by a sharp drop in online activity. (For additional confirmation of these findings, see Chapter 19.) Ordain Women appears to be the most responsive online site to public events and Exponent II seems to be the least. Perhaps the growth of the FMH Facebook group remains steady precisely because individuals who have not yet joined are not part of the ebb and flow of daily events and activity.

We expected to find that respondents benefitted from the social elements of the online community, but we did not anticipate large numbers of Mormon

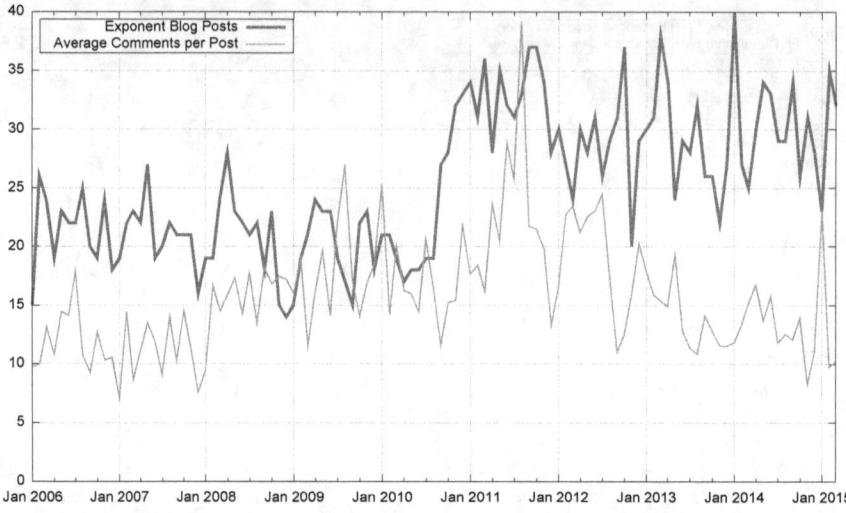
Figure 4. Exponent blog posts and average comments, 2006–15

feminists referencing education as an important outcome. In outlining the benefits of participating in the online community, one woman wrote: "I've met a lot of wonderful women who . . . educate and lift their sisters." Many respondents articulated the specific nature of this learning process. One woman wrote: "I have been able to flesh out my beliefs more solidly and determine where I stand. I have also found a forum in which I can air my concerns and use the group as a sounding board for some of my questions and concerns. We also share positive experiences or ideas to bring up in ward situations, like Young Women's leaders ask for ideas for youth activities that are less stereotyping and more diverse." This respondent felt that the educational environment of the online community provided for a sharing of practical ideas related to negotiating feminism and Church callings and helped her determine her own beliefs. Another respondent discussed this same outcome in more detail:

> Online Mormon feminism has been a complete re-education and reshaping of my LDS framework. I have been active LDS for 59 years, and I can finally, clearly identify the cognitive dissonance, thanks to my LDS feminists sisters/scholars. I have come to reject notions of the infallibility of leaders, the "one true church," the follow-the-prophet rhetoric, and the excessive obedience rhetoric. As I have mentally discarded these dogmas I have grown so much stronger in my testimony of Jesus Christ and the Holy Ghost. I believe the Holy Ghost is female. My inner spirituality and commitment to the Savior is stronger than it has ever been. This has spilled over in my lessons to my 12-year-old Sunday School class, lessons that are full of the Spirit and love of the Savior. I appreciate the positive values and habits I have gained from Mormonism, like service, Word of Wisdom, etc. But I clearly identify how seriously, emotionally damaging the patriarchy is to my psyche. I no longer attend RS [Relief Society], the most psychologically harmful place for me in my ultra-conservative ward. I can NOT listen to any general conference talks. Those male voices intoning

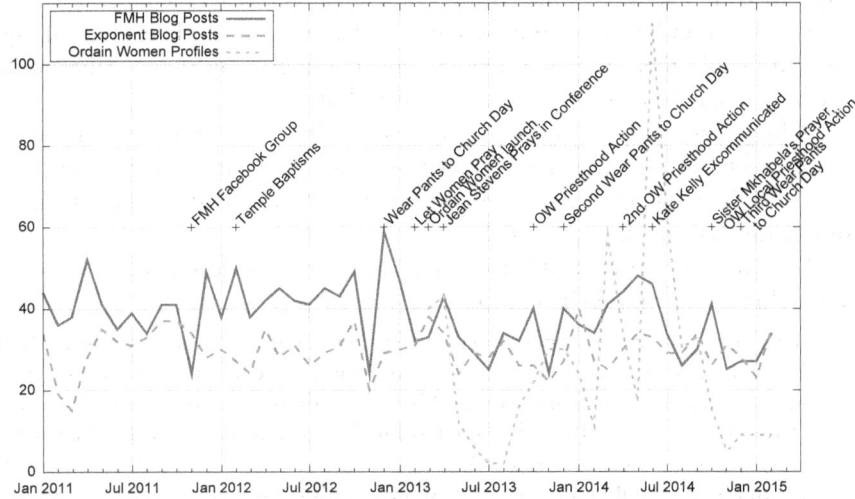

Figure 5. Blog posts at FMH, Exponent, and Ordain Women, 2011–15

the rigid, controlled roles of women from their position of male privilege, power, and prestige, [are] just too painful. I even have a hard time hearing the women speakers because they are mostly rubber-stamps of the male view, a requirement of LDS women who move up the leadership ladder. Another big benefit to me is finally coming to terms with polygamy. I have always been so troubled that my husband is still sealed to his first wife. Through FMH's Year of Polygamy, I have come to understand that polygamy is but a construct of men. In moments of strength, I know it is a crock. In moments of weakness, I still have fleeting thoughts that maybe just maybe it's true. But then my reason and discernment takes over and I can see that it is all just a power structure to enable men control over women. Online Mormon feminism has been central to my maturation and individuation away from corporate church structure, patriarchy, and dogma, to a personal sense of discernment, enlightenment, and empowerment. My prayers have improved, I have grown closer to Christ, and more fully realize my value to my Heavenly Parents.

Respondents learned more about themselves by participating in online Mormon feminism, but they also learned more about others: "I personally am fairly conservative, compared to most of the Mormon Feminists I know. I am grateful to be made aware of how others think and perceive various issues. It broadens my own scope and makes me think more closely about what I feel to be right and true. It also has increased my capacity for empathy, which I feel is an essential part of charity." This sense of empathy was also expressed by another respondent in a different way. "[I have learned about] checking my privilege and recognizing more feminist issues that arise."

In a closely related vein, the online community gives women the opportunity to learn from each other, as indicated by this comment: "I've learned a greater vocabulary and met many wonderful people. It's given me a voice that I've never had. I read the thoughts and ideas of other feminists, and it helps me shape my own. I see how other strong women handle situations, and it gives me the know-how and courage to handle things that way myself. I've seen, through the example of other feminists, how to continue to be a faithful member of the Church while holding strong to my feminist ideals."

A huge part of the learning in this community comes from role-modeling. Mormon feminists get the opportunity to brainstorm solutions to various problems, and their interchanges give other women the knowledge and courage to confidently make their own decisions.

One male ally articulated his learning and growth process and how it helped him evaluate his own role in a patriarchal system:

> The Mormon feminists I know and love best have taught me invaluable lessons about their concerns and have forced me to continually engage in introspection about my own role in our patriarchal society and how I can most ethically participate therein. I have grown in empathy and in my passion for social justice. As the father of two daughters, I have been able to think long and hard about what I want for my daughters and how I should raise them. Mormon feminism has also given me and my wife some common ground in our discussions about the church and the things that I've found challenging. She hasn't necessarily been concerned about some of the things that have contributed to my distancing myself from Church activity, but feminism is one area where we are very much on the same page and in which I have been able to relate to her. This has been invaluable to our marriage.

Another male ally put it more simply when he wrote "[Participating in the community has given me] a greater appreciation of the challenges that women face. I have always seen something amiss. Now I can put a finger on it."

Perhaps we should have anticipated that Mormon feminists would identify education as a benefit of participation. In our 2013 study, we referenced the issue of education in terms of spiraling. In that article, we noted that some respondents complained that online Mormon feminists often rehash the same topics again and again. We previously stated:

> Mormon feminist blog topics from the last nine years form a cyclical pattern as the community continually revisits particular issues in Mormonism. The blog comment sections often display the disdain some readers have for the repetitive nature of the topics. However, a careful comparison of blog posts from FMH's early years with posts since 2012 show that the same topics are discussed on a semi-regular basis but that the conversations surrounding the topics have evolved significantly since 2004. The tone and style of writing have become more professional, posts reveal a more thoughtful composition, and the arguments are more complex, producing a more sophisticated conversation. The repetitive conversations appear to be creating an upward spiral rather than an infinite loop. This improved articulation is useful to Mormon feminists as they practice their conservative religion while embracing feminist principles.

Today, we can compare the survey results from 2013 and 2015 and analyze blog data to identify the "spiraling" process by which, through repetitive discussion, issues are clarified, refined, and evolve over time.

In both surveys, we asked respondents to answer the open-ended question; "What changes would you like to see in the LDS Church?" The comparative differences in responses illustrate the education process within the online community. In the 2013 survey, roughly 10 percent responded with extensive answers, but many others responded in fairly general ways. One respondent said that changes should be made in "everything enumerated in the All Are Alike Unto God Document." Another individual wrote, "Priesthood and all that entails." Additional change recommendations included women being more involved in Church leadership, equal callings for women and men, moving away from the Church's "The Family: A Proclamation to the World" and its position on traditional husband-wife roles, and giving more emphasis on the teachings of Jesus Christ.

More than half of the 2,015 survey responses were lengthy and demonstrated greater specificity and articulation for change. The range of topics covered within each response was more extensive than in 2013. One respondent, for example, itemized all of the following recommendations for change in LDS women's participatory roles:

> Inclusion in all blessings: baby blessings, healings, mother/father blessings, blessings of comfort. Inclusion in blessing and passing the sacrament — the YW can participate! Women in bishoprics. Women bishops. Women in stake presidencies. Women as a stake president. Women high council members. Women offering women/girls temple recommend interviews. Women approving bishop's storehouse orders without the bishop scrutinizing the grocery list. Women leading a temple session. Women checking temple recommends at the front desk. Women setting apart other women.

This respondent articulated a variety of themes including blessings, ordination, callings, leadership callings, women's autonomy in welfare food orders, and activities in the temple. The following quotation reiterates many of the same themes but adds additional examples to this respondent's articulation of what she felt needed to be changed:

> Fund programs for the girls equally with funding for programs for boys. Encourage education and career development for women and girls on par with the encouragement provided for men and boys. Give girls visible opportunities to serve their faith community. Include women in decisions that affect them. Give women authority to run their own programs, manage their own budgets, and write their own manuals, without intrusive priesthood interference. Include women's voices in our manuals. Include Heavenly Mother. Have women leaders interview women and girls in worthiness interviews. Have female representation on disciplinary councils. Increase the female representation in general church leadership. Give wives of mission presidents a title representative of the work they do instead of "wife of mission president."

This respondent expressed the need to include Heavenly Mother in Church teachings, expanded examples of how women should become more autonomous and how specific callings should be addressed.

All of these examples of changes in the results of our two surveys over time demonstrate the potential of the spiraling process to help Mormon feminists better understand and articulate gender issues within the LDS Church.

Mormon Online Feminism and Race Issues

We also would like to look at how the spiraling process has impacted Mormon feminists' understanding of race issues. We chose race because respondents mentioned it repeatedly in the 2015 survey but less than 1 percent of respondents mentioned it in the 2013 survey. This topic has proved to be difficult because the Mormon feminists who participate in the online community are overwhelmingly white, and Mormonism has a complicated history with race. As an example, many members of the FMH Facebook group struggled to understand why Mormon feminists of color were excited by seeing Sister Mkhabela, an African woman, pray at the October 2014 general conference. It took a number of tense conversations between women of color and white women for white women to acknowledge their insensitivity to the concerns of Latter-day Saint women of color.

In the 2013 survey, respondents who made comments regarding race tended to be well-educated white women, who referenced race in response to the question: "What would you like to see changed in the LDS Church?" These Mormon feminists included, without elaboration, race in lists of things that they wanted changed. One respondent wrote that she wanted to see "More honesty about church history. Willingness to admit the huge mistakes in the church's past. Complete equality for all genders and races." The 2013 survey garnered a total of fourteen references to race.

One of those comments on race was made by a woman of color. She stated that she did not participate in Mormon feminist activism because of the problematic handling of racial issues within the online community. She wrote: "It is my belief that the Mormon feminist campaigns have issues with race and this played a part in my decision to not participate." However, other women of color in the community feel differently when they encounter racism in Mormon feminist spaces. In the 2015 survey, one black/African-American woman wrote: "I started as a casual observer but started to see race issues within FMH and was compelled to participate more. That group has a long way to go and it's hard with so many members and the church culture being so whitewashed."

In the 2015 survey, respondents addressed the issues of racial prejudice in low numbers, but more frequently (6 percent) than they had in 2013 (less than 1 percent). Consequently, we observed two additional areas where racial issues were discussed. The survey included the question: "What has changed in the online Mormon feminist community since you started participating?" One white respondent stated that one of the changes had been "A lot more focus on inclusivity and intersectionality with race, LGBT issues, other –isms . . . " Another white respondent pinpointed what she believed to be the catalyst for the discussion surrounding race and intersectionality conversations: "The discussion of race issues has increased dramatically, in part precipitated by the events surrounding the deaths of Michael Brown and Eric Garner and the subsequent protests. People talk a lot more about how we should include the perspectives of women of color."

White Mormon feminists perceived an increase in inclusivity with race-related conversations; people of color, however, perceived a gap in understanding. This is an area that we plan to study further in our next survey.

Even though the gains are small, as demonstrated by comparing references to race in both surveys, there are other ways to measure the educational process taking place in Mormon online communities. A close analysis of the FMH and Exponent II blogs demonstrated this process of educational spiraling. The early blog posts about race show a desire to engage with the issue, but the writing does not reflect a depth of understanding of current problems of racism either in American society or in the Church. Thus, the Exponent II blog posts discussed race in relation to Black History Month with little commentary.[15] In 2008, the Exponent blog tackled the issue in a blog post titled "How Do I Talk about Race?"[16] This post, by a white woman, began by raising the issue of race in relation to the 2008 Obama presidential campaign. She mentioned the fear that (white) people have in discussing the issue and some personal experiences related to race. The author was clearly trying to address what she saw was an important matter, but the discussion was limited because it revolved around her personal experiences. She did not possess or reference a critical framework necessary for a thorough understanding of the racial issues involved. One of the commenters, a self-identified white mother of black children, raised the issue of privilege three times in the discussion, but none of the other commenters engaged in response. This pattern is one that has been repeated a number of times in blogs and Facebook groups as white Mormon feminists try to write about and discuss race. These initial spirals raised the issue but did not provide Mormon feminists with the necessary historical or conceptual framework for learning about race.

In December 2013, the LDS Church published an online essay highlighting the racial undertones to the priesthood and temple ban of individuals of African descent.[17] The blog posts and conversations that followed were significant in the spiraling process. Most significantly, these included the first guest posts (many of whom have become permanent bloggers) by women of color who shared their stories related

---

15. EmilyCC, "Search Results Black | The Exponent," February 5, 2014, http://exponent.com/?s=Black&x=0&y=0 (accessed April 22, 2015).

16. Zenaida, "How Do I Talk about Race?" March 28, 2008, http://exponent.com/how-do-i-talk-about-race/ (accessed April 28, 2015).

17. Max Perry Mueller, "An Evolving Mormon Church Finally Addresses a Racist Past," December 12, 2013, http://religionandpolitics.org/2013/12/12/an-evolving-mormon-church-finally-addresses-a-racist-past/ (accessed April 23, 2015).

to racism in the LDS Church.[18] The subsequent conversations provided the online community with a better framework for understanding institutional racism.

Still, the conversations in the Facebook groups were tense. As white individuals tried to reconcile the Church essay, their own experiences, the experiences of women of color, and issues of privilege, they used the FMH Facebook group to try and reach a better understanding of these matters and how to integrate them. Women of color noted that there was a lot of pressure on them to explain race and racism, and they were often dismissed when they did so. Some Mormon feminists, in their desire to demonstrate their new knowledge, labeled individuals and their comments as racist. Some felt that this approach was shaming beyond the necessary discomfort in confronting bias. These binary labels of racist/antiracist disrupted the process of negotiation and learning for many individuals who were openly discussing their thoughts and feelings.

These conversations became more intense following the shooting of Michael Brown by police in Ferguson, Missouri, and the police shootings of other black men afterward. Following this turbulent period, many people continued to post articles and blog posts about race in the FMH group, but fewer people commented. It is likely that members of the community saw the potential dangers of some of these more open conversations and instead opted to process the issues internally or in other arenas.

This prolonged period of continually spiraling back to the issue of race produced hard-won learning. This is not to say that white Mormon feminists are all good anti-racism allies; rather, many have started to realize the gap between our own experience in understanding racial issues in the Church and the lived experiences of women of color. We are more likely to acknowledge that existence of a large gap.

Perhaps the best demonstration of this gap was when Reyna Aburto, a woman of color, prayed in the women's general session of LDS general conference in April 2015. Many white Mormon feminists immediately recognized and celebrated her prayer as a step forward.[19] Many white Mormon feminists have linked to the new FEMWOC (Feminist Mormon Women of Color) blog founded in

---

18. Janan Graham, "Hearing Black Mormon Women, 2: Coming to Grips with the Multigenerational Impacts of Mormon Institutional Racism," December 15, 2013, http://www.feministmormonhousewives.org/2013/12/hearing-black-mormon-women-2-coming-to-grips-with-the-multigenerational-impacts-of-mormon-institutional-racism/ (accessed April 25, 2015); Moana Uluave, "'The Most Dangerous Person in the US Is a Brown Body Armed with a Pen': Moana Uluave Remembers Siale Angilau," May 1, 2014, http://www.feministmormonhousewives.org/2014/05/the-most-dangerous-person-in-the-us-is-a-brown-body-armed-with-a-pen-moana-uluave-remembers-siale-angilau/ (accessed April 29, 2015); Tinesha. "Mormon, Biracial, Feminist . . . and Creating My Own Identity," February 25, 2013, http://www.feministmormonhousewives.org/2013/02/mormon-biracial-feminist-and-creating-my-own-identity/ (accessed April 29, 2015).

19. Jerilyn Hassell Pool, "Women's Session Live Blog," March 28, 2015, http://www.feministmormonhousewives.org/2015/03/womens-session-live-blog/ (accessed April 14, 2015).

March 2015. Mormon feminists attended and have linked to the audio files of Sunstone's recent conference titled "Theology from the Margins," which featured the voices of people of color. The online Mormon community has continued to expand its understanding of racial issues and recently created a closed Facebook group dedicated to understanding race in the LDS Church.

A 2015 survey respondent made an observation regarding the increased attention to various intersectionalities within the Mormon feminist community. "I feel we are progressing as feminists as well as in our feminist goals." These gains are small but significant, as they represent a shift from blindness on racial issues (among others) to a recognition of the problem. Perhaps these are signals that at least some Mormon feminists are initiating a transformative educational and learning process.

A traditional classroom with a teacher, syllabus, and textbook create learning in a linear way. By continuing to circle back to the issue of race and by finding better inputs into this process, like the voices of women of color, spiraling has created learning within the Mormon feminist community in a nonlinear fashion. We have observed that, as white individuals have been able to step back and integrate the lived narratives of others into their own understanding, they are able to move beyond the language of racial binaries and unexamined preconceptions regarding race.

Learning to Cope with the Tension and Negative Consequences of Being a Mormon Feminist

We have observed that blogs were a more productive place for individuals to share and navigate through the topic of race. While the use of Facebook was helpful in spiraling the feminist community toward activism,[20] the Facebook group discussions often broke down and, at times, inhibited growth. We saw that the Facebook platform can become a volatile learning space when a majority of the participants have not yet internalized the necessary phases and outcomes of the learning process. Spiraling is not simply a rehashing of topics but an internalization of those conversations, an elevation of understanding, and a refinement of argument.

In both the 2013 survey and in the 2015 survey, researchers asked participants a multiple-choice question with four possible answers, focusing on questions regarding their communication with leaders concerning gender issues. This question was designed to measure over time how members of the Mormon feminist community integrated their online community with their lived experiences. The first question asked respondents if they had "ever approached your local leaders with feminist concerns?" In 2013, 38 percent reported that they had approached their leaders. In 2015, the percentage increased to 48 percent. The next question asked, "How do you feel your comments were received?" In 2013, 37 percent of respondents indicated that they had been listened to and that their

---

20. Finnigan and Nancy Ross, "I'm a Mormon Feminist."

leader had made a change, while in 2015 the percentage dropped to 24 percent. The percentage of respondents indicating that they had spoken to a leader and had been heard, but no change had occurred, increased from 32 to 37 percent between 2013 and 2015. In 2013, 12 percent indicated that they felt that they had not been heard by their local leaders; in 2015 that figure increased slightly to 16 percent. The final option allowed respondents to indicate if they felt they had not been heard and, as a result, had received a negative consequence. Between 2013 and 2015, the percentage of respondents affirming this outcome increased only slightly from 17 percent to 22 percent.

The next question in the survey spoke to respondents' experiences more broadly: "Do you feel that you have ever faced negative consequences as a result of expressing feminist views?" In 2013, 56 percent responded "Yes" and in 2015 that figure increased to 61 percent. An open-ended follow-up question asked respondents to identify those consequences. In 2013, fifteen individuals (slightly less than 1 percent of respondents) said that their temple recommends were taken away or that their bishop had threatened to take them away. That number increased to 27 individuals in 2015 (2.8 percent of respondents). Respondents in 2013 usually indicated that the negative consequences they had faced consisted of tensions with family and close friends in the Church. The 2015 survey indicated that these kinds of social tensions were still present, but the respondents also indicated more specific forms of Church discipline being employed against them, including temple recommends being revoked, loss of Church callings, being put into the children's Primary organization as a "safe" place to prevent trouble, never being asked to speak or pray even in small Church gatherings, and a loss of trust and social capital among other ward members when speaking up about their beliefs.

Conclusion

The online Mormon feminist community provides a place for individuals to navigate through their own negative Church experiences via blogs and Facebook groups. These online sites provide a more expansive forum for dealing with the negative consequences of being a Mormon feminist or ally voicing critical questions about their faith tradition and especially for initiating online and direct actions to call attention to gender norms, such as the "wear pants to Church" campaign.[21] The blogs also provide a platform for minority voices to express their concerns without the direct confrontation that can take place in Facebook groups.

---

21. Anne Peffer, "Archive Sunday: Finding Your Inner Pants," December 15, 2013, http://www.feministmormonhousewives.org/2013/12/archive-sunday-finding-your-inner-pants/ (accessed January 3, 2015); Anne Peffer,. "Finding Your Inner Pants: Empowerment through Self-Understanding and the Language of Authority," December 15, 2012, http://www.feministmormonhousewives.org/2012/12/finding-your-inner-pants-empowerment-through-self-understanding-and-the-language-of-authority/ (accessed January 3, 2015).

Facebook groups, however, provide instant solidarity and support for those who are facing negative consequences or social ostracism for voicing concerns about current Church practices. This dynamic again demonstrates the need for multiple platforms to fulfill the needs of the online Mormon feminist community.

As the Mormon feminist community grows, each social media platform offers a different set of strengths and weakness in the education, activism, empowerment, and community-building processes. The internet and social media are vital to helping the Mormon feminist community capture and promote important events and issues. There is increasing evidence that the online community spills into the offline world. As the Mormon feminist community continues to grow and as technology develops, new platforms will expand the spiraling process. Currently, the community is bound together because it provides continual social interaction and learning opportunities. New technology and ways of interacting online will undoubtedly cause the Mormon feminist community to develop even further, providing other new benefits to participants.

Our first social media report[22] explored how Mormon feminism became an online social movement. We traced the different campaigns that Mormon feminists engaged in and examined Mormon feminists' reactions to those campaigns, including whether or not survey participants thought that the actions were successful. Existing literature measures the success of social movements in narrow ways, based primarily on whether or not activists achieve institutional change.[23] Our follow-up study of online Mormon feminism demonstrates additional ways in which the success of the movement can be measured in terms of the benefits that participants experience and how those benefits shape their lives. These benefits empower individuals to tackle their fears and engage in new forms of learning on a variety of levels. This includes the kind of learning that may create personal discomfort in dealing with issues of inequality and demonstrates how social movements can change and strengthen individuals to better navigate the tensions invariably generated by critical challenges to the status quo.

---

22. Finnigan and Ross, "I'm a Mormon Feminist."
23. Jennifer Earl and Katrina Kimport, *Digitally Enabled Social Change: Activism in the Internet Age* (Cambridge, Mass.: MIT Press, 2011).

Chapter 18

What Ordain Women Profiles Tell Us about Mormon Women's Hopes and Discontents

Gary Shepherd and Gordon Shepherd

The first two profiles on the Ordain Women website {ordainwomen.org} were posted on March 15, 2013, and the site went live on March 17, in honor of the founding of the LDS Relief Society. As of May 1, 2015, the number of profiles posted had reached 614. What are these profiles? What are their internet functions and who takes them seriously? What can they tell us about the people who post them? These are questions we propose to address in this chapter.

In what follows, we review OW guidelines for composing and submitting profiles, summarize the personal dilemmas for active Latter-day Saints who publicly support women's ordination on the OW website, outline the methods we developed for doing a content analysis of the profiles, report the statistical results of our analysis and discuss their significance for understanding current gender issues in the LDS Church.

Ordain Women Profile Guidelines

The banner on the cover screen of the OW website[1] defines Ordain Women simply as "Mormon women seeking equality and ordination to the priesthood." Under the banner are both a slideshow (a photo illustration campaign projecting images of women performing different priesthood ordinances) and a set of twelve color photographs of individuals who recently have submitted their profiles. Adjacent to the pictures of "Our Most Recent Profiles" is a link to a complete listing of all the profiles that have thus far been submitted to the Ordain Women website. Clicking this link takes the viewer to all profile pictures on file. Profile pictures themselves can be clicked on, which takes the viewer to a particular person's profile. Profiles (for which writing and submission guidelines are given via another link) are supposed to be approximately 500 words or fewer and typically consist of brief biographical information that humanizes the profiler, including recounting her or his connections with Mormonism and specific Church service,

---

1. The OW Website platform is divided into a number of different topical categories which can be accessed by clicking on various site links. Site links include: "About Us" (featuring a mission statement, news items pertinent to the organization's interests, informational resources in the form of articles and videos on women's concerns, and organizational contact information); "OW Conversations" (teaching tools concerning feminist principles in a series of didactic lessons); "Actions" (information about planned activities and actions to promote OW's goals); "Commentary" (periodic essays posted on topics related to gender equality issues); and, as already noted, "Submit a Profile" (with guidelines for profile contents and submission procedures).

if any. Thus, every profile listed at ordainwomen.org shows a picture of the profiler, informally begins by saying, "Hi, I'm Eliza," or, "Hi, I'm Brigham" (only first names are used as identifiers), gives some personal background information, and is followed by the profiler's reasons for why she or he thinks women should be ordained to the priesthood. Each profile is concluded by the affirmation, "I believe women should be ordained."

Profile guidelines make it clear that submissions are welcome from all quarters of the religious spectrum—including "faithful Mormons, those who might return to the Church but for gender inequality, or those who care deeply about the Church and its members and are concerned about how gender inequality affects all of us." At the same time the guidelines stipulate that, as an organization, Ordain Women does not solicit nor does it support "diatribes against the Church of Jesus Christ of Latter-day Saints." Instead, the guidelines emphasize "thoughtful submissions on what the ordination of women would mean to you personally and/or for the institutional church."

Finally, the guidelines caution potential profilers that there is no way to predict the reaction of local Church authorities to their postings on the OW website and advise respondents to "carefully weigh the personal consequences you might face and take them into account before submitting a profile." Those who submit profiles may withdraw them if they become "problematic for you" and are given assurances that "your full name and contact information will be kept completely confidential."

Dilemmas of Personal Conscience in Posting OW Profiles

The internet has become a place where a considerable amount of anonymity is possible. It's possible to post observations online, comment on postings by others, and carry on virtual conversations while remaining both faceless and nameless. However, the Ordain Women website is not a private domain; it is open to public scrutiny. Its conceived purpose is, in fact, to be global in its outreach as a means of publicizing and attracting support for its goal of seeking Mormon women's equality through ordination to the LDS priesthood. While those who post profiles are identified only by their first names, they are certainly not faceless and would be easily recognizable to their family, friends, local Church members, and local ecclesiastical lay leaders. For this reason, the OW website guidelines for posting profiles anticipate that profilers cannot assume anonymity and may potentially experience reprisals—including ostracism and official Church disciplinary action—for the decision to publicize their support for Ordain Women in such an open, personal way.[2]

---

2. Significant ostracism from other Church members for publicly expressing support for Ordain Women has, in fact, been commonly experienced by many who have submitted their profiles. See, for example, http://www.the-exponent.com/no-discipline-cases-elder-oaks (accessed January 30, 2015). Official ecclesiastical pressure exerted by local bishops and/or stake presidents on supporters to withdraw their profiles from the OW website has not been uncommon either, especially for women in Ordain Women leadership roles. Prior to her excommunication on June 23, 2014, Kate Kelly (then chair of the OW Executive Board)

For Mormons tentatively sympathetic to Ordain Women's cause (or to different aspects of their cause), the open invitation to submit a profile in support of priesthood ordination is a call to personal conscience. For many, the stirrings of personal conscience are trumped by priority allegiance given to family, kin, and the superordinate authority of their religious inheritance. It is the priority values of their relationship to their faith community that seem most threatened and put at risk when participants take a personal stand that can be interpreted as opposition to deeply engrained religious traditions and orthodox LDS doctrinal interpretation. A putative majority of Mormons, of course, are not currently sympathetic with the goals—and especially not with the organizational tactics—of Ordain Women.[3] These opponents constitute the families, local ward members, and lay ecclesiastical leaders who disapprove even carefully thought-out action based on the call of conscience. Their affectionate understanding and respect may erode in the face of a loved one's decision to publicly support Ordain Women. Potentially, those who are closest to Ordain Women supporters are precisely those who might most painfully shun and rebuke rather than kindly tolerate and respect alternative voices of personal conscience.

Our point is to emphasize that it is no small thing for the small number of faithful and active Latter-day Saints who have submitted OW profiles to do so. It is also fair to say that there are other like-minded Church members who might wish to join them but who are deterred because of their divided loyalties and apprehensions concerning family and religious reprisals or, in other cases, by their sheer

---

was specifically instructed by her stake president to cease her active involvement with Ordain Women and to remove her profile from the website. She refused to do either. See http://www.deseretnews.com/article/865605659/Ordain-Women-releases-LDS-bishops-letter-giving-reasons-for-Kellys-excommunication.html?pg=all (accessed June 23, 2014). Other OW members also have been warned or cautioned. As another specific example, on January 15, 2015, April Young Bennett of the OW Executive Board was forced to resign her board position under pressure from her stake president who would not renew her temple recommend unless she did. While Bennett negotiated with her stake president to maintain her profile on the OW website, he also required her to withdraw eleven articles she had posted on the blog site of Exponent II that dealt with the subject of women's ordination. See http://www.the-exponent.com/an-announcement-from-april-bennett-young/ (accessed January 15, 2015).

3. Chapters 14–16 of this book are derived from a large-scale survey (the Mormon Gender Issues Survey) of over 60,000 Mormon respondents worldwide concerning gender equality issues in the LDS Church, including priesthood ordination of women. The initial impetus for this survey was a Pew Research Center report published in 2011 of a national survey of U.S Mormons. Among other things, the Pew survey concluded that only a small fraction of Mormons were concerned about the issue of female ordination and that the vast majority of Mormons—especially Mormon women—were opposed to it. Chapters 15–17 critique the Pew survey and its conclusions regarding the overall satisfaction among Latter-day Saints with current priesthood practices. In contrast, the key findings of the Mormon Gender Issues Survey discussed in these chapters demonstrate much greater complexity and controversy over the issue of female ordination and related gender concerns among Latter-day Saints.

obliviousness to Ordain Women and the channel it represents by which individuals can express their personal beliefs concerning gender issues in the LDS Church.

What are the profile characteristics of those individuals who have thus far made a decision of personal conscience to post their profiles on the OW website? How many of them are, by their own lights, faithful and active Latter-day Saints? What are their hopes and concerns? How many are estranged from the faith or have renounced their memberships? What are their grievances and criticisms?

Content Analysis Methods in the Study of OW Profiles

The accumulation of profiles on the OW website is an on-going process, so to conduct a study of these profiles we had to stipulate a more or less arbitrary ending date for collecting the profiles to be included in our analysis. The closing date we chose was December 31, 2014. When we commenced recording profiles on June 11, 2014, a total of 363 profiles had already been posted on the OW website. We began copying and pasting these profiles into our own document file, updating that file weekly by checking the OW website and pasting in new profiles as they accumulated. According to our count, between March 15, 2013, when the first two profiles were posted, and December 31, 2014, when we stopped counting, a total of 588 profiles had accumulated.[4] It is these 588 profiles that constitute our data collection and to which we refer in the following discussion of our methods and analysis. Although activity on the site has continued in 2015, our spanning dates include the launch of the OW website; the enthusiasm but also the cautions concerning OW's first public action in October 2013 of requesting admittance to the priesthood session of general conference; determination in the face of continued official resistance to again requesting admittance to the April 2014 priesthood general session; and the anxiety and sadness associated with Kate Kelly's excommunication in June 2014.

In studying the profiles posted on the OW website, we have conducted a statistical content analysis. By this, we mean that we developed a coding rubric consisting of particular category items for analyzing all of the profiles and recording the results in a data software file for statistical processing.[5] Our coding rubric was divided into two major parts. We used the first part to collect various demographic and personal background items of information that profilers voluntarily included in their profiles. The second part of the rubric contained a list of more than sixty prototypical reasons that profilers offered for their support of the ordination of women. In what follows, we first outline the protocols followed in coding the profiles for demographic information and then summarize our find-

---

4. As indicated above, some early supporters of Ordain Women (approximately a dozen) have removed their profiles from the OW website under pressure from their local bishops and/or stake presidents.

5. Credit and our thanks for systematically coding the OW profiles for our content analysis go to Natalie Shepherd and Chandler Gaines.

ings. We subsequently do the same with respect to coding and analyzing profilers' reasons for supporting priesthood ordination of women in the LDS Church.

Coding Demographic and Personal Background Information

Demographic and personal background information offered by profilers about themselves varies greatly from one profile to another. The guidelines do not specify that such information items are required, so those who submit profiles are at liberty to disclose as much or as little about themselves as they see fit. Nonetheless, by scanning all of the profiles in our collection before coding them, we extracted a set of twenty-eight potential coding categories, including gender, race, age, nationality, residence, education, marital status (including temple marriages), children, Church membership, Church activity indicators (including callings and missionary experience), and, when mentioned, a spouse's Church affiliation and activity level as well. Given liberty to provide or not provide this kind of personal detail, the most commonly recorded information item for some of our coding categories was missing or "not given." At the same time, much of the kind of background information we were interested in *was* provided in the profiles and, for certain key demographic categories (e.g., gender and age) a coding judgment (or estimation, in the case of age) was made for every profile or profile photograph in the collection. Despite the missing information on some of the profiles, we were able to construct a reasonably valid demographic portrait of the individuals who have submitted profiles on the OW website in support of ordaining women to the priesthood.

By and large, who are these Ordain Women profilers? Beyond their support for women's ordination, do they share any social characteristics in common? If so, what are they? Do they represent demographic outliers in global Mormonism? Collectively speaking, are they from the margins of LDS culture and its institutional history or closer to its center? If they are demographically marginal (or not), in what ways is this true?

Demographic Analysis of Ordain Women Profiles

Table 1 summarizes selected demographic characteristics of our set of 588 profiles submitted to the OW website between March 13, 2013, and December 31, 2014.

As we already have noted, individuals who make the decision to submit OW profiles are at liberty to provide as much or as little personal information as they choose. Thus, for many of the profiles in our data set, pertinent demographic information was missing or not given. Because of this pattern, in our summary description of the data which follows, we will alternatively refer to simple frequencies (number of cases in a particular category) and to percentage values (or proportional frequencies)

Bearing this in mind, several elementary conclusions about those who have submitted profiles are immediately clear: While the LDS Church claims a worldwide

TABLE 1
SELECTED SUMMARY DEMOGRAPHICS OBTAINED FROM ORDAIN WOMEN PROFILES

Nationality	N	%	Residence	N	%	Gender	N	%	Race	N	%	Age	N	%
USA	556	94.6	Utah	39	6.6	Female	414	70.4	White	553	94.0	Youth	9	1.5
Other	32	5.4	West states	27	4.6	Male	174	29.6	Other	35	6.0	Y. Adult	262	44.6
Totals	588	100	Other states	36	6.1	Totals	588	100	Totals	588	100	Adult	257	43.7
			Outside U.S.	29	4.9							Sr. Adult	60	10.2
			Not given	457	77.8							Totals	588	100
			Totals	588	100									

Marital Status	N	%	Children	N	%	Education	N	%	Academic Major	N	%	Women's Occupation	N	%
Married	323	54.9	None	58	9.9	H. School	6	1.0	Lib. Arts	58	9.9	Stay Home	21	5.1
Divorced	16	2.7	1–3	208	35.4	College	95	16.2	Helping	41	7.0	Employed	135	32.6
Single	36	6.1	4+	64	10.9	Post grad	66	11.2	Applied	39	6.6	Not Given	258	62.3
Not given	213	36.3	Not given	258	43.8	Not given	421	71.6	Not given	450	76.5	Totals	414	100
Totals	588	100	Totals	588	100	Totals	588	100	Totals	588	100			

membership of over 15 million members in 155 countries,[6] a substantial majority of OW profilers in our collection were American (94.6 percent), white (94.0 percent), and female (70.4 percent). At the same time, a sizeable fraction (29.6 percent) consisted of men who wanted to add their voices in support of priesthood ordination for women. This latter statistic supports the conclusion that the ordination movement appeals to a fair number of Mormon men as well as to their female counterparts.

While mainly residing somewhere in the United States, many profilers (77.8 percent) neglected to indicate their state or region, making more specific conclusions about the geographical location of Ordain Women supporters less easy to ascertain. Nonetheless, among those who specified their residence, only 6.6 percent lived in Utah, while roughly the same combined proportion (4.6 percent) reported residences in the adjacent western states of Arizona, California, Colorado, Idaho, and Wyoming. The remainder of those reporting their residence were distributed throughout the United States and a small number of foreign countries, ranging from Australia to Uganda (not shown in Table 1). One plausible inference to cautiously draw from these numbers is that OW supporters are not especially concentrated in the Mormon heartland of Utah, nor in the larger Mormon cultural region of the western United States, but are widely dispersed throughout the United States and, to a much lesser degree, in other countries in different parts of the world.

---

6. See Chapters 15–16 for the issues affecting how to define membership for the purposes of counting numbers of members. For other studies focused on the problem of defining and counting membership in the LDS Church, see David C. Knowlton, "How Many Members Are There Really? Two Censuses and the Meaning of LDS Membership in Chile and Mexico," *Dialogue: A Journal of Mormon Thought* 38, no. 2 (2005): 53–78; Rick Phillips, "Rethinking the International Expansion of Mormonism," *Nova Religio: The Journal of New and Emergent Religions* 10, no. 1 (2006): 52–68; and, Rick Phillips and Ryan T. Cragun, "Contemporary Mormon Religiosity and the Legacy of Gathering," *Nova Religio: The Journal of New and Emergent Religions* 6, no. 3 (2013): 77–94.

Additional characteristics of Ordain Women supporters, such as age, marital and parental status, education levels, and types of occupations, also appear in our profile data. The great majority of profilers fall into one of two middle-age categories that we identified: Thus, we classified 44.6 percent as young adults (ages twenty-one through thirty-five) and a comparable number (43.7 percent) were classified as middle-age adults (ages thirty-six through fifty-five). Using current popular terminology for American age cohort groups since World War II, these age brackets include an admixture of Generation-Xers and Millennials. Only 10.2 percent of those posting profiles in our data set were over age fifty-five, representing either Baby Boomers or elderly members of the "Silent Generation."[7] At the same time, among those volunteering biographical information, a majority (323) were married and only a few (16) reported being single or divorced. Of those who reported themselves as married, a substantial number were also parents: Among self-identified parents, 208 reported having between one and three children and sixty-four had four or more children. Less than 10 percent of OW profilers were definitely classified as not being parents.

A majority of profilers did not specify their educational attainments; but among those who provided educational information, (161) had at least some college education and, among the college educated, sixty-six had postgraduate degrees. Interestingly, as one important indicator of their religious backgrounds, 154 of the profilers in our survey reported having attended Brigham Young University at the Provo, Rexburg, or Hawaii campuses (not shown in Table 1). Academic majors at college ranged from liberal arts fields of study (e.g., history, religion, art, or music, etc.) to applied disciplines (e.g., law, engineering, health science/medical related, etc.) and the helping professions (e.g., education, social work, counseling, etc.). The one general category of studies notably lacking any mention in our collection of profiles was in business-related fields.[8] Of those providing information about their occupations, one out of three specified occupations, which included education, medical/health care, counseling, and law. Focusing particularly on women profilers in our survey (n = 414), of those who said something about their working

---

7. The Pew Research Center defines twentieth-century age cohorts as follows: *Greatest Generation*, born before 1929; *Silent Generation*, born 1928–45; *Baby Boom Generation*, born 1946–64; *Generation X*, born 1965–80; and *Millennial Generation*, born 1981–97. See http://www.pewresearch.org/files2015/01/FT_gnerations-defined.png (accessed April 15, 2015).

8. In a purely speculative vein, we surmise that many OW supporters were drawn to fields of study other than business because of already formed value priorities that placed humanistic concerns ahead of financial remuneration or material acquisitions through successful careers in the business world. For a review of literature confirming the "attraction-accentuation hypothesis" in higher education, which predicts that most students are attracted to college majors that are consistent with and reinforce values they already possess, see Gordon Shepherd and Gary Shepherd, "Civic Tolerance among Honors Students," *Journal of the National Collegiate Honors Council* 15, no. 1 (2014): 85–113.

lives, 135 pursued occupational careers in which they were gainfully employed and only 21 described themselves as stay-at-home moms.

Extrapolating from the figures reviewed so far, we would characterize many if not most of Ordain Women supporters as follows: They are relatively young adults to middle-age professionals, dispersed throughout the United States, who are well educated and married with children. As we will see later in this chapter when we review profilers' reasons for supporting the ordination of women, many young parents are concerned about raising their children in a religious tradition that they see as fostering gender role inequality.

In addition to their marital, parental, and educational/professional working lives, what do OW profiles reveal about the religious commitments and Church activity of those who post them? The numbers shown in Table 2 confirm that the vast majority (93.0 percent) of OW profilers were, in fact, Latter-day Saints, along with a smattering of profiles coming from people of other faith traditions who have an interest in supporting the ordination of women. We should also point out that twenty-six profilers in our survey were either excommunicated Mormons or Mormons who, for a variety of reasons, no longer affiliate with the LDS Church but who wished to add their voices in support of the cause of women's ordination.

Table 2 also demonstrates that a considerable number of profilers had family roots in the LDS tradition. While 11.4 percent of those submitting profiles were converts to Mormonism, close to two-thirds (65.6 percent) were born to LDS parents and hence considered themselves members since birth; 20.6 percent did not indicate their LDS generational standing. Having observed this pattern, it is also relevant to point out that, among those reporting Latter-day Saint heritage, the largest proportion (46.6 percent) were second-generation Mormons, with a smaller but still sizable fraction (19.0 percent) who traced their Mormon roots back three or more generations.

In addition to their Mormon heritage, arguably the single most important descriptive finding of our survey is the level of Church activity that profilers imputed to themselves: Close to three-fourths of them (72.1 percent) described themselves as active members of the Church, while only 14.1 percent described themselves as inactive, and approximately the same number (13.8 percent) did not mention the subject of Church activity. While a majority of profilers did not list or specify their lay callings in the Church, an appreciable number did. Female supporters of priesthood ordination included women who had served (or are currently serving) in non-priesthood callings, such as stake and ward Relief Society presidencies, stake and ward Primary and Young Women's presidencies, as seminary or institute teachers, gospel doctrine teachers, and temple ordinance workers, to name the most prominent examples. Among male supporters of Ordain Women were bishops (or former bishops), bishop's counselors, branch presidents, high councilors, high priest group leaders, elders' quorum presidents or counselors, and members of Young Men's presidencies, to name some of the more prominent priesthood callings identified in our survey. Furthermore, a total

TABLE 2
INDICATORS OF LDS CHURCH INVOLVEMENT FOR INDIVIDUALS
SUBMITTING PROFILES TO THE OW WEBSITE, MARCH 2013-DECEMBER 2014

Church Membership	N	%	LDS Generations	N	%	Church Activity	N	%
LDS	547	93.0	Convert	67	11.4	Active	424	72.1
Former LDS	26	4.4	2nd generation	274	46.6	Not active	83	14.1
Other religions	14	2.4	3+ generations	112	19.0	Not given	81	13.8
None	1	0.2	None	14	2.4	*Totals*	588	100
Totals	588	100	Not given	121	20.6			
			Totals	588	100			
Church Callings	N	%	Temple Marriage	N	%	Missionary Service	N	%
Non-priesthood	191	32.5	Yes	134	22.8	Yes	154	26.2
Priesthood	45	7.6	No	42	7.1	Not given	434	73.8
Not given	352	59.9	Not given	412	70.1	*Totals*	588	100
Totals	588	100	*Totals*	588	100			

of 154 profilers had served LDS missions; and among those who included particular mention of their marital status (a majority did not), 134 had been married in Latter-day Saint temples.

While many individuals submitting profiles to the Ordain Women website chose not to include personal information about their own religious involvements in the areas we have just reviewed, a sufficiently large enough number did to warrant this summary conclusion: OW profilers are not merely disconnected dissenters on the Mormon margins. Collectively they are (or have been) actively involved Latter-day Saints with significant family ties and religious attachments to the Mormon faith community.

Coding Reasons for Supporting the Priesthood Ordination of Women

Individuals publicly supporting women's ordination to the priesthood by posting profiles to the Ordain Women website do so for a variety of reasons. An important part of our content analysis was to determine the range and relative frequency of the different kinds of reasons the profilers offered to validate their support.

We inductively identified a range of reasons in support of women's ordination by reading through a large sample of profiles and listing specific reasons as we encountered them. Many of the reasons presented in the profiles varied in their wording but essentially constituted a common justification, which made it possible for us to begin classifying particular statements into more general categories with a shared emphasis. Inductively classifying reasons for supporting ordination resulted in a still-lengthy list of sixty-four categories. Evaluating this list for further classification possibilities, we recognized two primary types of reasons, which we labeled as positive affirmations and critical grievances.

Positive affirmations consisted of avowals of belief in gender equality; God's equal love for His children; a belief in Heavenly Parents and/or more specifically a Mother in Heaven; the value of gender inclusiveness and equal partnerships;

TABLE 3
RELATIVE FREQUENCY OF AFFIRMATION AND GRIEVANCE STATEMENTS
IN OW PROFILES SUPPORTING THE ORDINATION OF WOMEN
(N = 3,232)

Rank	Frequency	Percent	Affirmations
1	135	4.2	Belief in equality
2	119	3.7	Female ordination will strengthen the Church
3	107	3.3	Value of inclusiveness and equal partnerships
4	103	3.2	Women's gifts and talents
5	99	3.1	Raise children in a Church that values equality
6	90	2.8	God's equal love for all his children
7	82	2.5	Value of having female leaders
8	73	2.3	Desire for equal decision-making authority
9	71	2.2	Desire to give blessings, administer ordinances
10	56	1.7	Revelation given when readiness is expressed
11–41	972	30	[Remaining 31 affirmative profile reasons not shown]
Subtotals	1,907	59.0	

Rank	Frequency	Percent	Grievances
1	179	5.5	Gender discrimination/exclusion in the Church
2	136	4.2	Injustice of gender inequality
3	113	3.5	Need for greater equality and inclusiveness
4	101	3.1	Dissonance with traditional LDS gender norms
5	87	2.7	Church losing members because of inequalities
6	71	2.2	Deprivation of spiritual/service opportunities
7	66	2.0	Dissatisfaction with focus on wife/mother roles
8	59	1.8	Lack of priesthood damages girls' self-worth
9	59	1.8	Lack of priesthood teaches female inferiority
10	57	1.8	Lack of priesthood is spiritually demeaning
11–23	397	12.4	[Remaining 13 critical profile reasons not shown]
Subtotals	1,325	41.0	
Grand totals	3,232	100	

recognition of women's talents and spiritual gifts; realization of women's divine potential; the righteous desire to bestow blessings and to administer ordinances; the exercise of equal decision-making in Church councils; strengthening the Church and its mission; strengthening families; raising children in a religious culture that values gender equality; finding scriptural support and supportive historical evidence; priesthood change through prayerful petition; and continuous revelation in a living Church committed to the restoration of all things, etc.

In rhetorical contrast, *critical grievances* consisted of statements concerning the injustice of gender discrimination; practices of discrimination and inequality in the LDS Church; unequal institutional support of boys and young men over girls and young women; how lack of priesthood ordination is spiritually demeaning to women and teaches female inferiority; how women's auxiliary status belittles and unfairly limits women's potential; dissatisfaction with narrow LDS gender norms; how lack of priesthood deprives women of spiritual experiences as well as service and leadership opportunities; the waste of women's organizational talents and underutilization of their leadership potential; Church leaders' failure

TABLE 4
SPECIFIC REASONS FOR SUPPORTING WOMEN'S ORDINATION
GROUPED INTO THEMATIC CATEGORIES OF AFFIRMATION AND GRIEVANCES

Rank	Frequency	Percent	Thematic Affirmation Categories
1	405	12.6	Doctrinal and historical support
2	394	12.2	Values of equality and inclusiveness
3	220	6.8	Priesthood change through revelation
4	191	5.9	Shared authority and participation
5	185	5.7	Women's abilities and talents
6	143	4.4	Strengthening Church and family systems
7	118	3.7	Moral exemplars and teachers of equality
8	117	3.6	Changing cultural traditions
9	78	2.4	Personal conscience and free agency
10	56	1.7	Women's equal empowerment and respect
Subtotals	1907	59.0	

Rank	Frequency	Percent	Grievances
1	664	20.5	Gender discrimination/exclusion in the Church
2	361	11.2	Injustice of gender inequality
3	200	6.2	Need for greater equality and inclusiveness
4	100	3.1	Dissonance with traditional LDS gender norms
Subtotals	1325	41.0	
Grand totals	3,232	100	

to listen to women's concerns; the disillusionment of youth and the loss of members because of gender inequality in the Church, etc.

What are the most common of these reasons reiterated in the profiles? Are critical grievances cited more often than positive affirmations? Do these women and their male supporters' discontents outweigh their hopes for affirmative change in the religion of the Latter-day Saints, or can ultimate optimism be discerned from their profiled testimonials?

Data Analysis of OW Profile Affirmations and Grievances

In Tables 3 and 4 we summarize the statistical results of our content analysis of the reasons that OW supporters identified in their online profiles. In Table 3 we have identified the ten most frequently stated affirmations and critical grievances; in Table 4 we have consolidated the range of specific reasons extracted from the profiles into broader, thematic categories, yielding summary sets of major affirmation and grievance themes in support of the ordination of women to the LDS priesthood.

To measure the relative frequency with which different reasons or theme categories in support of women's ordination appeared in the profiles that we studied, we simply recorded and counted every reason offered in all 588 of our profiles. Some profiles expounded numerous reasons in support while others only cited one or two reasons. The sum total of statements we counted in the profiles came to 3,232, with a mean of 5.5, indicating that the typical OW profile contained between five and six different reasons in support of priesthood ordination. The conclusion that we drew from this finding is that most of those posting profiles saw multiple and widespread consequences of gender inequality. We decided to use the total number of 3,232 statements produced by our content analysis as the base number for calculating the relative frequency (or percentage) of particular reasons and more general thematic categories appearing in the profiles.

Table 3 shows that the ten most frequently expressed affirmative reasons and grievances for supporting female ordination that we identified in the profiles represented a substantial majority (57.6 percent) of all the reasons offered. Without elaborating on any of the supporting reasons specified in Table 3, we see that the most commonly offered *affirmations* were: (1) belief in the principle of equality, (2) belief that female ordination will strengthen the Church; (3) belief in the value of religious inclusiveness and equal partnerships between men and women; (4) belief in women's gifts and talents; (5) belief in the importance of raising children in a church that values equality; (6) God's equal love for all his children; (7) the value of having female leaders; (8) the desire for equal female decision-making authority in Church councils; (9) women's desire to bless their children and administer other priesthood ordinances; and (10) belief that divine revelation for change is given when people openly express their readiness to receive it.

Shifting attention to criticisms, we see that the most common *grievances* expressed in the profiles were: (1) observing or experiencing gender discrimination and exclusion in the Church; (2) the moral injustice of gender inequality; (3) the need for greater equality and inclusiveness in the Church; (4) dissonance experienced in conforming with traditional LDS gender norms in contemporary society; (5) perception that the Church is losing members because of gender inequality norms and practices; (6) spiritual and service opportunities requiring priesthood authority from which women are deprived; (7) dissatisfaction with a one-sided focus on wife and mother roles for LDS women; (8) the perception that lacking priesthood ordination damages girls' self-worth; (9) the perception that the lack of female priesthood ordination teaches and reinforces female inferiority in the Church; and (10) the perception that the lack of female priesthood ordination is spiritually demeaning to women.

One very noteworthy observation to make about the relative frequency of positive affirmations and critical grievances expressed in the OW profiles is the wider range of affirmative reasons offered compared to grievances. In our coding we recorded a total of forty-one different affirmative reasons in contrast to only twenty-three different grievances. This discrepancy in the larger number of affirmative reasons is mirrored by the overall percentage of affirmations relative to grievances in the profiles: Three out of five (59 percent) of all profile statements we coded were positive affirmations in support of ordaining women to the LDS priesthood.

Many of the reasons enumerated in Table 3 are clearly interrelated, which is equally true for other reasons in the profiles that are not enumerated. By identifying and consolidating the most closely related reasons offered by OW profilers in support of women's ordination, we produced a summary set of thematic categories, which are displayed in Table 4. As with the previous support reasons listed in Table 3, we used the total number of 3,232 recorded profile statements as the base for computing the relative frequencies of affirmative and critical thematic categories itemized in Table 4.

The overall prevalence of affirmative themes (59 percent) compared to grievance themes (41 percent) in Table 4 replicates the results we have just reviewed and, for the same reason. Affirmations were distributed over a wider range of particular reasons offered compared to grievances. Thus, there were almost twice as many affirmative reasons (forty-one) identified in the profiles compared to grievances (twenty-three). Consequently, as shown in Table 4, we derived a total of ten thematic categories expressing general affirmation themes and only four that expressed general grievance themes.

In order of their relative frequency, the principal thematic affirmation categories we derived by consolidating closely related reasons offered in the profile statements included: (1) *Doctrinal and historical support* for women's ordination cited in the form of scripture references,[9] quotations from Church leaders, historical references to Mormon women exercising priesthood authority in the nineteenth century, and contemporary temple scripts and ordinances also linking women to the exercise of priesthood authority; (2) belief in the *values of equality and inclusiveness* in the Church; (3) belief in *priesthood change through revelation* as the mechanism for changing current priesthood rules of eligibility (especially including by way of a historical precedent, the 1978 reversal of the ban on ordaining males of African descent to the priesthood); (4) the righteousness of *shared authority and equal participation* by women and men in the Church; (5) the spiritual and organizational value of *women's abilities and talents*; (6) the benefits of female priesthood ordination for *strengthening the Church and family systems*; (7) selected references to *moral exemplars and teachers of equality* (both Church authorities and secular leaders)[10] who advocate for justice and equality; (8) affirmative prospects for *changing cultural traditions* of gender inequality that reflect prejudicial human customs and practices rather than God's will; (9)

---

9. Scriptural citations included verses from the Old and New Testaments, the Doctrine and Covenants, and the Book of Mormon. The most commonly cited verse from the Bible was Matthew 7:7: "Ask and it shall be given you; seek and ye shall find; knock and it shall be opened unto you." From the Doctrine and Covenants 12:41: "No power or influence can or ought to be maintained by virtue of the priesthood, only by persuasion, by long-suffering, by gentleness and meekness, and by love unfeigned;" and from the Book of Mormon, 2 Nephi 26:33: "he denieth none that come unto him, black and white, bond and free, male and female; and all are alike unto God." Also frequently quoted was the LDS Ninth Article of Faith: "We believe all that God has revealed, all that he does now reveal, and that he will yet reveal many great and important things pertaining to the kingdom of God."

10. Among those individuals most commonly quoted or referenced as exponents of equality in support of profilers' claims were Joseph Smith and an assortment of more recent LDS General Authorities, especially former Church presidents Gordon B. Hinckley and Spencer W. Kimball. Among the non-Mormon voices most frequently cited in support of equality was the Reverend Martin Luther King Jr.

commitment to the principles of *personal conscience and free agency* that mandate moral responsibility for supporting efforts to eliminate inequality; and (10) aspirations for *women's equal empowerment and respect* in their Church, family, and personal relationships with men.

While fewer in number, the thematic grievance categories we adduced from the profiles demonstrate the extent to which Ordain Women supporters have struggled with and grieved over problems of gender equality in their personal experiences and religious lives as Latter-day Saints. The single most prevalent thematic category (identified in 20.5 percent of all profile statements we examined) in fact consisted of: (1) an assortment of references to *LDS gender discrimination and inequalities* observed and/or personally experienced by OW profilers. Other major thematic grievances, in order of their relative frequencies in the profiles, included: (2) perceptions or experience of *individual deprivation and harm* (whether spiritual, psychological, or social) for both women and men as a result of gender inequalities in the Church; (3) *disillusionment with and/or criticism of Church leaders* for their failure to acknowledge gender inequalities and/or act justly in the performance of their religious duties; and (4) the *institutional deprivation and harm from inequality* done to the Church itself (such as loss of both members and potential converts and the underutilization of women's lay leadership potential as a result of depriving them of priesthood authority).

Conclusion: The Dilemma of Democratic Values and Obedience in the LDS Church

In summary, who are the people who openly support the priesthood ordination goal of Ordain Women by posting their profiles on the OW website? What are their hopes for the future and their discontents with the present state of affairs in the LDS Church? What are the prospects that their religious discontents will be subdued by their hopes or, conversely, their hopes overwhelmed by their discontents?

Our content analysis of OW profiles reveals that the great majority who submit them are Latter-day Saints with substantial generational ties and family connections in the Mormon faith tradition. They reside primarily in the United States but many are scattered throughout the country rather than being concentrated in the Mormon cultural region of the Intermountain West. A majority of profilers are women, but they are supported by a significant number of men as well. As a group these women and men are not Mormon outliers on the margins of LDS lay culture and Church participation. To the contrary, a majority are believing, active Mormons who have lengthy records of service in a wide range of Church callings. A large number of them have served LDS missions and most are well educated, with many attending or receiving degrees from LDS Church schools. They tend to be relatively young (overlapping Gen-Xers and Millennials) and married (many were married in LDS temples), who are still having or raising their children but are concerned about the models of gender inequality to which they are exposed in the contemporary LDS Church.

These concerns are clearly seen in our data analysis of profilers' thematic grievances, especially with respect to (1) observing and experiencing different forms of gender discrimination in the context of administering and participating in LDS worship settings and Church-sponsored programs, and (2) dismay over archaic gender norms that devalue contemporary women's aspirations and achievements outside of domestic family roles as Mormon wives and mothers. The core value shared and expressed both directly and indirectly in virtually all of the profiles is the value of human equality. When this core value is undermined by different forms of racial, gender, or LGBT discrimination in the Church (and by teachings that justify and reinforce discriminatory practices) it produces tremendous dissonance for many modern Latter-day Saints—especially those with the same or similar demographic characteristics to those described above. Most young, educated Mormons with children do not, of course, submit profiles to the Ordain Women website to publicly announce their support for the ordination of women. But it would be a mistake to think that only those who speak out in this particular way are troubled by gender inequalities in the contemporary LDS Church—by the apparent contradiction between the core value of equality shared by many Church members and discriminatory religious practices that perpetrate inequality.

Perhaps those Latter-day Saints who feel compelled by personal conscience to submit OW profiles are set apart from other Latter-day Saints who share their dissonance but don't submit profiles by their positive belief in the ultimate efficacy of a united moral movement for change, even in a patriarchal religious tradition that is governed by echelon priesthood authority in a hierarchical church. A key finding of our content analysis was that positive affirmation themes outnumbered grievance themes expressed in OW profiles by a ratio of 3:5. One inference to draw from this statistic is that a majority of profilers believe that changing LDS gender norms for priesthood eligibility is both justifiable and possible. They articulate the reasons for their optimism by equating democratic principles of equality with the justice of God's will and by enumerating scriptural, historical, ethical, and practical reasons to support this supposition. (We should note that these equality themes coincide with the theology of justice propounded in Chapter 12). Their optimistic understanding of how the process of revelation works for changing traditional beliefs and practices in a prophet-centered religion is also democratic: They argue for the validity of "trickle-up" revelation (see Chapter 10 on this topic)—which is to say that the people must unitedly be willing and ready to change and that their readiness must be expressed to God through prayer and petitioning of God's anointed spokespersons to seek and obtain divine guidance.

It is their apparent commitment to democratic values that paradoxically stimulates both dissonance and optimism among supporters of Ordain Women, while simultaneously polarizing the issue of women's priesthood ordination within the LDS Church community. OW supporters experience dissonance and the pangs of personal conscience when the core values of human equality before a just God appear to be routinely ignored or transgressed with respect to gender discrimination in God's church. At the same time, supporters are optimistic that a legitimate religious remedy is at hand by democratically petitioning their leaders who are recognized and sustained as prophets to seek new revelation on the issue of gender and the priesthood.

The principal problem and source of cleavage concerning contemporary gender issues within the LDS community is, of course, that the modern LDS Church is not a democratic institution. It is, rather, a top-down, theocratic institution in which religious authority to convey God's word to the people is vested in its hierarchical, male priesthood organization. As we emphasize in Chapter 2, there are no authorized procedures or institutional mechanisms in the LDS Church that permit and channel the expression of dissent or minority views in opposition to official priesthood policies and pronouncements. The LDS Church does not countenance—in fact, strenuously discourages—organized dissent and the public expression of minority views, so essential to the functioning of a democracy. For Latter-day Saints who repudiate Ordain Woman and its supporters, the idea of forming dissent organizations in order to publicly agitate for reform and, in the process, seeming to question the superordinate value of obedience to the echelon authority of its priesthood leadership, is deeply offensive and contradicts their fundamental faith commitment to the prophetic premise of the restored Church of Jesus Christ. (The vitriolic backlash expressed by many nominally devout Latter-day Saints toward their sisters and brothers in the faith who openly advocate for greater gender equality in the Church is reviewed in Chapters 14 and 19.)

The optimistic views of democratic equality and belief in the legitimacy of their dissent expressed by supporters of female ordination in the profiles they submit to the OW website stand in sharp contrast to the views of those Mormons who embrace obedience to prophetic authority as their religion's priority value. As religious scholar Thomas O'Dea has said, there is "an inherent dilemma involved in the relationship between a religion of transcendence and democratic institutions." While recognizing the essential contributions which prophetic religion made to the development of Western democracies, O'Dea observes that, once the doctrines and organizational forms of a new prophetic religion congeal into the institutional arrangements of a church, "the church as a sacred entity tends to inhibit criticism of itself and of the social order with which it has become accommodated. Thus, the original source of the prophetic element—the transcendental reference—which made possible criticism and protest, is transformed into a sacralization of established forms and becomes an inhibiting mechanism with respect to both protest and criticism."[11]

The organization of Ordain Women and its public supporters who have submitted their profiles and reasons for supporting the ordination of women to the priesthood are but a very small fraction of the worldwide membership of the LDS Church. Nonetheless, their tactical actions to bring renewed attention to issues of gender equality in the Church have stimulated both controversy and widespread discussion among other Latter-day Saints and the attention of the national media as a major news story, a topic which we review in a research note at the end of this chapter. Largely as a result of resurgent Mormon feminism, small changes toward greater gender equality are currently underway in Mormonism's lay ecclesiastical culture, as reported and assessed in other chapters of this book. The intrinsic tension between democratic values and theocratically structured religious institutions is simultaneously a source of both functional and dysfunctional consequences for different segments of the religious community and for the Church as a whole. In the Mormon equation over the short run, the priority value of obedience to ecclesiastical leaders prevails. But in the long run, to the extent that the women and male allies of Ordain Women and other contemporary Mormon feminists have substantially expanded the debate over priesthood eligibility, stimulating a process of reformative change, we are witnessing in action the priority value of human equality on the democratic side of the equation in the Mormon faith tradition. For the would-be reformers of Ordain Women, it is this evidence of change and the prospects for yet greater change that lift their religious hopes over their grievances for their own and their children's futures as Latter-day Saints in a twenty-first-century church.

RESEARCH NOTE ON OW SUBMISSIONS AND OW ACTIONS THAT ATTRACT MEDIA ATTENTION

with Pamela A. Shepherd

---

11. Thomas F. O'Dea and Janet O'Dea Aviad, *The Sociology of Religion*, 2d ed. (Englewood Cliffs, N.J.: Prentice-Hall, 1983), 115. O'Dea was a Catholic sociologist with a general interest in the sociology of religion and a particular interest in Mormon studies. He was the author of *The Mormons* (Chicago: University of Chicago Press, 1957), a groundbreaking sociological analysis of Mormon institutions circa mid-twentieth century. Fifty years later, in recognition of O'Dea's contributions to Mormon studies, the University of Utah Press published an anthology of essays assessing and critiquing the relevance of his work for twenty-first-century Mormonism: Cardell K. Jacobson, John P. Hoffman, and Tim B. Heaton, eds., *Revisiting Thomas F. O'Dea's 'The Mormons': Contemporary Perspectives* (2008).

TABLE 5
MONTHLY NUMBER OF OW PROFILE SUBMISSIONS AND U. S. MEDIA STORIES
RELATED TO ORDAIN WOMEN AND MORMON FEMINISM, MARCH 2013-DECEMBER 2014

Month/Year	OW Profiles	Media Stories	Month/Year	OW Profiles	Media Stories
3/13	39	51	2/14	10	4
4/13	42	94	3/14	54	249
5/13	12	9	4/14	34	359
6/13	6	3	5/14	15	59
7/13	2	26	6/14	112	2,644
8/13	2	30	7/14	63	106
9/13	19	60	8/14	29	33
10/13	21	417	9/14	28	40
11/13	28	10	10/14	14	658
12/13	27	4	11/14	4	93
1/14	22	2	12/14	6	9
			Totals	OW Profiles	Media Stories
				588	4,960

Summary of Descriptive Statistics
OW monthly profiles mean = 26.7; median = 22.5; standard deviation = 25.1
Media stories monthly mean = 225.5; median = 36.5; standard deviation = 565.9
Pearson Correlation between monthly OW submissions and media stories = .756

In coding our set of 588 OW profiles, we recorded the date when each profile was submitted to the website. This gave us the ability to keep track of monthly submissions for the twenty-two months covered by our study (March 2013–December 2014). At the same time, with the assistance of Pamela A. Shepherd, we collected data on the number of U.S media stories appearing during this same period of time related to the topics of LDS women, Mormon women/Ordain Women, and Kate Kelly.[12] In an appendix at the end of the book we itemize the initial, originating articles identified in our search, many of which were republished numerous times and circulated in multiple media outlets. For statistical purposes, in Table 5 we display the combined frequency counts of both originating and replicated articles published or broadcast monthly in multiple media sources, along with monthly OW profile submissions.

The numbers for both profile submissions and media stories focusing on Mormon women topics show a great deal of fluctuation during the designated time period of our study. Thus, OW profile submissions ranged from lows of two in the months of July and August of 2013 and peaked at 112 in June 2014, with a mean of 26.9 per month. Media stories also ranged from a low of two in January 2014 and peaked with 2,644 stories posted in June 2014. In between

---

12. An online news service called Meltwater News (http://www.meltwater.com/products/?gclid=CITnpImi-cQCFQmTaQodCWkA8g) has developed software that monitors the internet and can be used to search news sources for keywords relevant to its customers' research needs. Among other things, Meltwater provides counts for the total number of stories posted or published that contain designated keywords by name of the media source (e.g., *Deseret News, Salt Lake Tribune, Los Angeles Times, New York Times*, etc.), and date of publication.

the highs and lows for both variables, we see substantial monthly fluctuations, with some months showing relatively high frequencies and others with very low frequencies. The average amount of variation for both our variables is measured by the standard deviation,[13] which shows a large monthly variation of 25.1 OW profile submissions and a huge average variation of 565.9 media stories over the span of 22 months.[14] To what extent are the fluctuations of profile submissions correlated with media stories and why?

Our research hypothesis was that fluctuations in OW submissions would be correlated with monthly variations in media stories. To test this, we computed a Pearson correlation coefficient,[15] which yielded a strong, positive correlation of .756 between monthly submissions to Ordain Women and U.S. media stories posted on topics related to Mormon feminism. In other words, when media stories increased, so did profile submissions. This correlation does not, of course, "prove" that media stories caused increases in profile submissions (and certainly not the other way around). The common denominator between these two variables has to do with *actions or events deemed newsworthy* by the media and which, correspondingly, attract the attention of concerned publics.

What were the actions or events that captured the attention of both news media outlets and a concerned public with respect to issues of gender equality in the LDS Church? The dominating news story in the month of June 2014—the high-water mark for both OW profiles submissions and media stories—was the Church's excommunication of Kate Kelly for her leadership in planning and carrying out public actions on Temple Square in Salt Lake City during April 2014 general conference in support of the ordination of women. (See Chapter 12 for a discussion of the Church's action against Kelly.) The announcement that Kelly's bishop in Virginia summoned her to a disciplinary council created intense interest—both the expectation that she would be ecclesiastically punished but also suspense and hope/dread for both Mormons and interested non-Mormons around the country.

---

13. The standard deviation is a statistic that measures the average amount that different frequencies in a distribution deviate from the mean of the distribution.

14. The monthly means for both OW profile submissions and media stories were inflated by the much larger frequencies recorded in certain months compared to others throughout the time period we observed. This was especially true for media stories dealing with LDS gender issues and Ordain Women-related events. As an alternative measure of the average, which is not skewed in the direction of the more extreme values in a frequency distribution, the monthly *median* for OW profiles (mdn = 22.5) was somewhat smaller than the mean number of 26.7 submissions, while the monthly median of media stories (mdn = 36.5) was radically smaller than the mean of 565.9 stories. This latter comparison reinforces the point that heavy media coverage is primarily a function of dramatic or controversial action/events deemed newsworthy by media outlets.

15. A Pearson correlation is a statistical calculation that measures both the degree of correlation between variables (ranging between 0.000 and 1.000), and the direction the correlation takes (either positive or negative).

The decision of the bishop's court—excommunication—was announced on June 23, 2014.[16] Kelly's excommunication appears to have been a tipping point for an undetermined number of Latter-day Saints in sympathy with Ordain Women's efforts and plausibly explains the surge of 112 new OW profiles submissions in June, closely followed in July by sixty-three additional new profiles, the second largest number registered by Ordain Women in a single month.

Beyond Kelly's excommunication, we see accelerated frequency clusters for both profile submissions and media stories at different intervals between March 2013 and December 2014. One such cluster of profile submissions (March-April 2013) is correlated with the inauguration of the OW website and related publicity that attended the formation of a Mormon "radical flank" organization (as discussed in Chapter 2) committed to full priesthood equality for Mormon women. Fast-forwarding from there to October-December of that same year, we see another cluster of submissions submitted during and after October conference, when Ordain Women staged its first public action at the Mormon Tabernacle on Temple Square. The next cluster of submissions swells again in March-April of 2014, coinciding with the anticipation of OW's second (and larger) gathering of supporters during the April priesthood session of general conference. From there we arrive at the surge of submissions in June-August 2014, in reaction to Kelly's excommunication. In October 2014, however, Ordain Women did not organize a concentrated action in downtown Salt Lake City but instead encouraged supporters to seek admission to the priesthood session of general conference shown on television at their local ward chapels or stake centers.[17] At the same time, OW submissions dwindled to relatively small numbers in the final months of October, November, and December covered by our study.

Looking at media stories over this same span of time, we see frequency clusters that are in relatively close alignment with spurts of OW submission increases. Thus, significantly increased media attention occurred in connection with: (1) the inauguration of Ordain Women as a feminist organization and the launching of its website; (2) just prior to and during the October 2013 general conference; (3) just prior to and during the April 2014 conference, and (4) especially the weeks up to and following Kate Kelly's excommunication in June. The one major discrepancy between OW profile postings and media stories related to Mormon feminist activism occurred in the fall months of October–December 2014, when OW profile submissions dwindled significantly. Media stories, however, once again surged, especially in the month of October conference, presumably in continued antici-

---

16. For the announcement of Kelly's excommunication, see http://www.deseretnews.com/article/865605659/Ordain-Women-releases-LDS-bishops-letter-giving-reasons-for-Kellys-excommunication.html?pg=all (accessed March 30, 2015).

17. The intent and rationale for the 2014 October OW action at local wards or stake centers can be found at http://ordainwomen.org/october-2014-priesthood-session-action-faq/ (accessed March 30, 2015).

pation of newsworthy statements from either LDS authorities or OW supporters related to the issues of Mormon gender equality and priesthood eligibility.

What lessons can be gleaned from the data accumulated thus far? In particular, what appears to be reducing OW profile submissions over the past six months?[18] Has an early plateau been reached signaling the declining appeal of Ordain Women's brand of feminist activism among more liberal-minded Mormons? Does increasing public attention and support for feminist change require continuing to plan and stage large-scale media events, rather than working more quietly behind the scenes online or in the local congregational units of members' wards and stakes? The OW social media committee has been vigorously promoting a photo illustration campaign of women exercising the priesthood since January 2015, which appears to have eclipsed other activities that have stimulated submission of new profiles in the past. Also worth considering is a potential factor for which we lack statistical evidence: Have excommunication and other threatened disciplinary measures effectively stifled continued or even greater support for the OW movement?

If nothing else, we may safely conclude that present and future leaders of Ordain Women are confronted with their fair share of organizational challenges as they nurture their hopes of maintaining forward momentum in the years ahead toward ultimately realizing full parity with men in the priesthood administration and direction of the LDS Church.

---

18. From October 2013 through April 2014, only forty-nine new profiles were posted, averaging a little more than eight profiles per month during this period. As of May 1, 2015, only twenty-five new profiles have been added to the OW website.

Chapter 19

From the Kotel to the Square: The Rhetoric of Religious Feminism

Debra Elaine Jenson

On Saturday, April 5, 2014, more than 400 women and men gathered in a park in Salt Lake City, Utah, to sing hymns and pray for courage. These individuals carried with them the names of 500 more souls who could not make the trek to the Beehive State but who shared the same desire: to see women ordained to priesthood authority in the Church of Jesus Christ of Latter-day Saints (or LDS Church). We lined up, hoping to gain admission to the men-only priesthood session of general conference; we walked to Temple Square, the symbolic home of the Mormonism and the LDS Church. We saw ourselves as faithful members of the Church. Overwhelmingly, these men and women were faithful members of the Church. Our internal survey showed that more than 70 percent of those who participated in Ordain Women actions attended church at least two to three times a month.[1] Long before the general conference, we had asked for tickets to attend this meeting. Denied because of our gender, we next informed our leaders of our intention to wait in the standby line. Again, we were rebuffed and invited to stand in the "Free Speech Zone" with anti-Mormon protestors.[2] These same protestors, to whom our leaders had compared us, saw us as Mormons and had yelled offensive things at us as we walked quietly by. We were too Mormon for them—but we were not Mormon enough for the General Authorities of the LDS Church.

The question of whether Ordain Women supporters are faithful members of the LDS Church or on the road to apostasy is key to understanding the progress the group has made so far. It is the same question of insider/outsider status that impacts all social movements in the effort to create change but is particularly important in faith-based movements. This chapter will review theories on social movements and communication and then apply those theories to past research on two prominent religious social movements and Ordain Women in particular.

Social Movement Theory

The term "social movement" can be applied to any group or groups working to create change in a community. Researchers define a social movement as

---

[1]. Ordain Women, internal survey conducted October of 2013 by Jessica Finnigan and Nancy Ross.

[2]. Jessica Moody, letter to Ordain Women on behalf of the Church of Jesus Christ of Latter-day Saints, March 17, 2014.

a "sustained challenge to authority."[3] The community within which movements emerge to bring about change can be both geographic and socially constructed. A socially constructed community is one that crosses geographic boundaries but unites individuals around a common identity. Each community operates in what Habermas called the "public sphere" or "the domain of our social life in which such a thing as public opinion can be formed."[4] The public sphere is where we establish shared understanding. Habermas maintained that the importance of the public sphere and public opinion is that the two form the "sediment of history,"[5] the foundations for understanding our surroundings and our community. Or as Andrew Jamison described them: "Social movements . . . have periodically served as important contexts for the reconstitution of knowledge."[6]

Social movements matter because they create meaning, but they also serve to *change* meaning. History often shows that movements that embodied critical oppositional voices from within a community "later came to participate in reconstituting the form and content of socially organized knowledge."[7] In every cultural community there are foundational ideas or beliefs. These beliefs are often seen as irrefutable facts: America is the greatest country in the world, democracy is good, women are instinctive nurturers, men are born providers and leaders, etc.. These beliefs become normative and prescriptive. They inform the rhetoric that defines a culture and its people, establishing what is acceptable and unacceptable. According to William Gamson, "Definition of issues, actors, and events is a matter of constant contention. A central part of the symbolic struggle, then, is about the process of constructing specific meanings."[8] Gamson argues that this contested process is "a constant, uphill struggle for those who would sustain collective action in the face of official myths and metaphors."[9] Individuals who challenge official norms typically are seen as deviants and outsiders.

Understanding the cultural language of a community is vital to a social movement. Social movements are part of a larger conversation with multiple participants and overlapping constituencies, attempting to define contested ideas.[10]

---

3. Marco Giugni, Doug McAdam, Charles Tilly, *How Social Movements Matter: Past Research, Present Problems, Future Developments* (Minneapolis: University of Minnesota Press, 1999), xxii.

4. Jürgen Habermas, *Jürgen Habermas on Society and Politics: A Reader*, edited by Steven Seidman (Boston, Mass.: Beacon Press, 1989).

5. Habermas, *Jürgen Habermas on Society* 232.

6. Andrew Jamison, "Social Movements and Knowledge-making," *Making of Green Knowledge* (Port Chester, N.Y.: Cambridge University Press, 2002), 46.

7. Ibid., 53.

8. William A. Gamson, "Political Discourse and Collective Action," *International Social Movement Research* 1 (1988): 219.

9. Ibid.

10. Robert D. Benford and David A. Snow, "Framing Processes and Social Movements: An Overview and Assessment," *Annual Review of Sociology*, 26, no. 1 (2000): 611–39.

Because persuasive messages are built on shared understandings, certain arguments will "have a natural advantage because their ideas and language resonate with larger cultural themes.... They appear natural and familiar."[11] The ability to craft a meaningful narrative around an issue is largely dependent on familiarity with the issue in the context of a community's history and culture. Within this context, communications scholar Robert Cialdini identifies several fundamental elements of persuasive communication, especially including social validation: an audience or public is more likely to respond to a message and act if people feel that they are part of a community. Beyond a sense of belonging, the "bandwagon effect" gives them a sense of collective protection such that they feel they can act with less personal risk.[12]

Though the potential ability of social movement groups to influence policy is not in doubt, scholars have debated how and when this influence is at its peak. Research suggests that social movements may be more influential in some stages of their history than others. "Interest groups ... help frame issues, weigh the importance of information, and draft bills, but their influence on voting decisions is minimal."[13] The informational stage of an issue is when social movements have the best chance to shape and guide a conversation. Movements can work on "drawing attention to an issue, educating legislators, and provoking legislators to take some form of action."[14] This is when the opportunity to focus the public eye is the greatest.

The power of social movements also lies in their ability to define the scope of a debate or create a conceptual frame for specifying priority issues. Cultural framing involves couching arguments in the dominant narratives of the community.[15] When crafting persuasive messages, George Lakoff reiterates that the social, cultural, and political contexts always matter and that they should be used to shape the frame for discussing a topic.[16] It is crucial for the leaders of social movement organizations to frame the meaning of events in ways that are significant to members and supporters by drawing upon shared understanding and cultural themes that are already prevalent in the community.[17] This meaning is

---

11. Gamson, "Political Discourse and Collective Action," 227.

12. Robert B. Cialdini, "The SCIENCE of Persuasion," *Scientific American Special Edition* (January 2004): 70–77.

13. Brayden G. King, Marie Cornwall, and Eric C. Dahlin, "Winning Woman Suffrage One Step at a Time: Social Movements and the Logic of the Legislative Process," *Social Forces*, 83 (2005): 1214.

14. King, Cornwall, and Dahlin, "Winning Women Suffrage One Step at a Time," 1215.

15. Ibid., 1217.

16. George Lakoff, "Simple Framing: An Introduction to Framing and Its Uses in Politics," *Rockridge Institute* 14 (2006), http://www.rockridgeinstitute.org/projects/strategic/simple_framing, (accessed April 6, 2015).

17. David A. Snow and Robert D. Benford, "Ideology, Frame Resonance, and Participant Mobilization," *International Social Movement Research* 1 (1988): 197–217.

created by using shared patterns of understandings and themes. Dennis Chong and James Druckman have argued that meaningfully constructed frames have the ability to help influence audiences to the point of changing their behaviors.[18] The question is not what we talk about, but *how* we talk about what we talk about. If Gamson is correct and the ultimate value of social movements is in creating new meanings, then the way a group frames an issue is crucial. As social movement scholars Robert Benford and David Snow conclude, effective framing is "a central dynamic in understanding the character and course of social movements."[19]

Snow and Benford's theory describing the importance of framing in social movements is named collective action frame theory (CAFT), which emphasizes that the success of campaigns for social change depends on the ability to "drum up support for their view and aims and activate individuals who already agree with those views and aims."[20] According to Benford and Snow's CAFT analysis, groups aiming to enact policy change must first diagnose the problem they are addressing. This step requires group leaders to identify a cause of the problem and assign blame or responsibility. The second and third steps are for leadership to identify solutions and then communicate to supporters a rationale for action to supporters.

Effective frames function alternatively as tools for diagnosis (identifying a problem), prognosis (solving the problem), mobilization (a call to arms or rationale for active engagement).[21] While on the surface the principles of frame theory might not seem obviously to be applicable to a religious movement, they are in fact a key to understanding successful religious movements. Oftentimes religious people do not initially see a problem in their faith. This is particularly true when it comes to gender inequality, as gender roles typically are built into foundational texts (written by men in ancient patriarchal societies). Contemporary religious social movements challenge the biblical narratives upon which present-day Christian and Jewish religious structures are built and for many, are the way they have ordered their lives. Even more challenging to the status quo is the proposed solution to contemporary issues of religious gender equality. Many of the faithful view movements of religious social justice as an attempt to tell God how to run his religion. In some ways this challenge raises the cost for religious social justice action, because traditionalists perceive it not only as a challenge to the status quo, but also as a challenge to deity. And as discussed in Chapters 11 and 12, the contemporary LDS Church disciplinary councils have functioned to punish lay members who mobilize or attempt to initiate reformative change of its ecclesiastical structure. I will discuss the difficulty in framing or creating meaning around religious issues as it relates to feminist religious movements later in this chapter.

---

18. Dennis Chong and James N. Druckman, "Framing Theory," *Annual Review of Political Science* 10 (June 2007): 104.

19. Robert D. Benford and David A. Snow, "Framing Processes and Social Movements: An Overview and Assessment," *Annual Review of Sociology*, 26, no. 1 (2000): 612.

20. Snow and Benford, "Ideology, Frame Resonance, and Paricipant Mobilization," 199.

21. Ibid.

Here, however, I simply want to emphasize that an issue must be ripe for media and public attention for religious activists to be successful. They cannot force an issue to be of compelling concern to members of a religious community in which grievances don't already exist.

One example of an ultimately effective framing strategy is the women's suffrage movement. According to King, Cornwall, and Dahlin, the most powerful impact of the suffrage movement came from its ability to frame the issue. The easiest, quickest movement toward this objective occurred in states that had already shifted their cultural norm. Where rates of women in the workplace were already higher, the right to vote was won earlier and faster.[22] In other words, once the conversation was no longer about redefining the role and place of women in society, it became easier to discuss women as citizens and voters.

In another example, Fabio Rojas examined the efforts of campus groups to establish African-American studies programs at various colleges and universities across the United States. Rojas found that while disruptive tactics have occasionally resulted in the movement's success in achieving its goals, they have also damaged the movement's reputation. On the other hand, non-disruptive protest, such as rallies and demonstrations, were more likely to produce successful outcomes and preserve the movement's image.[23] Rojas came to two important conclusions. First, by employing non-disruptive tactics, "the movement indirectly changes an organization by showing how behavior contradicts stated ideologies, policies and social mores."[24] Non-disruptive tactics demonstrate respectful demeanor and defuse organizational claims that protestors are disrespectful or outsiders. And second, that social movements are successful because they "create uncertainty for organizations."[25]

Of the various options open to a social movement, public protest poses a threat to the reputation and legitimacy of established institutions.[26] The definition of protest is difficult to pin down but often includes some form of action that disrupts the public order. Often, this action is taken by a group or subgroup that lacks authority in the community. This definition is important in a conversation about Ordain Women because OW leaders have struggled to define their activities *not* as protests, but as "actions," in an effort to avoid being painted as outsiders. That said, protest typically is directed against "targets in which hierarchy is the dominant mode of governance."[27] It is important to note that researchers have found that protest does not have to create a financial threat

---

22. Brayden King, Marie Cornwall, and Eric Dahlin, "Winning Woman Suffrage One Step at a Time," *Social* Forces 83 (March 2005): 1217.

23. Fabio Rojas, "Social Movement Tactics, Organizational Change, and the Spread of African-American Studies," *Social Forces* 84, no. 4 (2006): 2147–66.

24. Ibid., 2149.

25. Ibid., 2150.

26. King and Soule, "Social Movements as Extra-Institutional Entrepreneurs: The Effect of Protests on Stock Price Returns," *Administrative Science Quarterly* 52 (2007): 413–442.

27. Ibid., 415.

to target organizations, but rather a threat to their reputation and legitimacy.[28] Probably the most important thing to remember when considering movement tactics, though, is the caution offered by Soule and King about organizations becoming too radical to effectively mobilize other potential allies.[29]

A social movement is successful after it garners media attention, which increases influence because it is a threat to a target organization's reputation.[30] According to King, "Boycotts and other movement tactics present alternative messages about a target that threaten its efforts to build a positive image among constituents."[31] Groups that challenge the existing narratives that justify traditional practices become a threat when they influence the way other groups think about or frame what is now being defined as an issue. If a small gang of rogue "misfits" sees a problem, an organization need not necessarily feel any concern; however, once the ideas espoused by the misfits resonate and gain traction with constituents who matter, concern is heightened. But how do organizations decide which constituents matter?

As discussed earlier, the language and rhetoric about an emerging issue creates new meanings. These meanings, with their accompanying lingo and mindset, help form collective identities. William Gamson emphasizes: "A collective identity is more cultural than cognitive, demonstrated both by language and symbols, and by other forms of participation in movement actions and culture."[32] The importance of this identity is its power to define what it means to be a part of the movement—establish a collective "we." This identity helps "create boundaries between an 'us' and a 'them.'"[33] The verbal cues incorporated in the cultural rhetoric of different groups allow a community to determine who is a legitimate player and who is an outsider.

In the study of social movements, scholars use the term "stakeholders" to identify individuals who have power to influence an organization, have a legitimate relationship to the organization, and have an urgent claim on the organization.[34] While each of these is important, stakeholder claims can be legitimate regardless of influence. The stakeholders who have urgent claims and a legitimate relationship to the organization but have no power to influence are defined as

---

28. Ibid.
29. Sarah A. Soule and Brayden G. King, "The Stages of the Policy Process and the Equal Rights Amendment, 1972–1982," *American Journal of Sociology* 111 (May 2006): 1871–1909.
30. Brayden G. King, "A Political Mediation Model of Corporate Response to Social Movement Activism," *Administrative Science Quarterly* 53 (2008): 413.
31. Ibid., 399.
32. Gamson, "Political Discourse and Collective Action," 42.
33. Ibid.
34. Ronald K. Mitchell, Bradley R. Agle, and Donna J. Wood, "Toward a Theory of Stakeholder Identification and Salience: Defining the Principle of Who and What Really Counts," *Academy of Management Review* 22 (1997): 853–86.

"dependent" stakeholders.[35] For organizations the problem is to identify which stakeholders matter or need to be included in decision making and policy formation. Theories of stakeholders include distinctions between those who are active or latent, while researchers have argued that "the *potential* relationship can be as relevant as the actual one."[36] Yet another way of distinguishing among stakeholders is to identify primary and secondary stakeholders. Because they lack a direct voice in decision making "secondary stakeholders must find other means to influence organizational change."[37]

Stakeholders' attributes significantly increase (or decrease) their ability to influence organizational decision-making.[38] For those whose organizational concerns fall outside the norms of standard practice or procedure, the challenge is to be recognized as *legitimate* dissenters. Traditional narratives and conventional communication are heavily laden with symbolism that can minimize their effectiveness. Furthermore, organizations tend to ignore secondary stakeholders, who have little to no authority. Nonetheless, research has shown that secondary stakeholders can be incredibly effective at attacks on organizations.[39] In the business world, organizations with leadership that does not include stakeholders in decision-making must deal with the consequences of diminished social responsibility and decreased financial performance.[40] Compare this to religious institutions, particularly religious organizations with all-male leaders: Will male religious leaders fail to identify or understand the importance of their social responsibility toward including contemporary women in the governance of a twenty-first century church?

Some activists have attempted to move organizations by "voting with their feet." In a commercial enterprise this action would take the form of a boycott— think Montgomery bus boycotts during the civil rights era, or more recently, LGBTQIA groups that have asked supporters to refrain from frequenting Chick-fil-A stores as a punitive consequence for that company's repudiation of same-sex marriage.[41] But in religious organizations, this strategy most often takes the form

---

35. Ibid., 877.
36. Ibid., 859.
37. King, "A Political Mediation Model of Corporate Response," 395.
38. Jeffrey S. Harrison and R. Edward Freeman, "Stakeholders, Social Responsibility, and Performance: Empirical Evidence and Theoretical Perspectives," *The Academy of Management Journal* 42, no. 5 (October 1999): 479–85.
39. King, "A Political Mediation Model of Corporate Response," 399.
40. Harrison and Freeman, "Stakeholders, Social Responsibility, and Performance," 479–85.
41. Some observers have seen this boycott as backfiring from its intended purpose because it helped foment a movement in support of Chick-fil-A that dulled, and even countered, the effect of the boycott.
Bradley W. Brooks, Steven M. Cox, Karen Shearer Dunn, and Michael Kobre, "Superman: Man of Steel! . . . Or . . . Man of Boycott?" *Journal of Case Studies* 32, no. 1 (2014): 37–48.

of an exodus. The faithful leave their erstwhile religion, either officially through excommunication or resignation, or informally via inactivity. Inactivity is not a particularly effective way to create institutional change. Therefore, it is less a social movement than a personal choice to relieve pain or feelings of threat, which is also a valid choice made by reasonable people.

"When stakeholders constitute a disproportionately small share of the firm's base, business scholars have concluded, voice may be the only real option for influence-seeking stakeholders."[42] In other words, protest or demonstration may be the only avenue for marginalized or disfranchised stakeholders to influence organizational change. Women stakeholders in patriarchal religious organizations are both marginalized and disfranchised. In attempting to achieve increased recognition and authority inside those faith communities, women constitute secondary religious stakeholders who are a "disproportionately small share" of ecclesiastical apparatus and want a greater voice in administering and directing the religious life of the community. As will be seen, groups pushing for religious gender equality face strikingly similar challenges and employ common rhetorical strategies across faith groups.

Religious Social Activism for Gender Equality

The social activism the late twentieth century ushered in a new focus on gender equality. After the 1960s the women's movement gained traction in several secular policy areas, including employment, education, and reproductive rights. Social rights were not the only advancement women sought, though. Mark Chaves and James Cavendish identified a "correlation between an active secular women's movement and increased intradenominational conflict over gender equality.... Movement activists and adherents promoted change in a variety of societal institutions, including religious institutions."[43] These efforts to bring about gender equality in the religious world were not aimed solely at ordination, however. They also included campaigns about "increasing gender equality in other ways, such as winning the right for women to hold seats at General Conferences."[44]

According to Susan Sered, religious conflict is a fight over symbols and divine legitimation.[45] For women specifically, religious debate centers on the ontological question of what is *woman*. It divides females into two categories—the woman who is an individual agent, and the symbolic Woman who serves important traditional

---

42. Brayden G. King and Sarah A. Soule, "Social Movements as Extra-institutional Entrepreneurs: The Effect of Protests on Stock Price Returns," *Administrative Science Quarterly* 52 (2007): 413; punctuation edited for clarity.

43. Mark Chaves and James Cavendish, "Recent Changes in Women's Ordination Conflicts: The Effect of a Social Movement on Intraorganizational Controversy," *Journal for the Scientific Study of Religion* 36, no. 4 (1997): 577.

44. Ibid., 575.

45. Susan Sered, "Women and Religious Change in Israel: Rebellion or Revolution," *Sociology of Religion* 58 (1997) 1–24.

roles. Seen as an individual agent, each woman has her own skills and contributions to make. If she is denied that opportunity because of ancient cultural traditions, then the challenge of her contemporary protest is legitimate. Sered points to campaigns in Israel that expanded the cultural role women were allowed to play, specifically the prohibition on women serving in elected positions in Orthodox Jewish communities. Where the debate was framed as simply a municipal policy—a question of culture and not doctrine—the custom was changeable and women were eventually recognized as legitimate candidates. Conversely, when the Women of the Wall argued for the right to pray at the Western Wall in Jerusalem while wearing traditionally male religious regalia they were challenging the deeply traditional idea of Woman. The campaign was deemed an attack on fundamental rabbinical doctrine and the campaign has remained controversial for nearly three decades.

So how, then, have these women organized and mobilized in defense of their cause? The rest of this chapter will look at three movements from three very different faith traditions and at very different stages of organization: the Catholic Women's Ordination Conference (CWOC), a group pressing for women's ordination to Catholic priesthood; the Women of the Wall (WoW), a group pushing for legal access to prayer privileges at the Western Wall in Jerusalem; and Ordain Women (OW) a new group asking leaders of the Church of Jesus Christ of Latter-day Saints (LDS or Mormon Church) to pray for revelation that would expand ordination to the priesthood held virtually universally by all LDS males over age twelve, to women.

The Catholic Women's Ordination Conference

The Catholic Women's Ordination Conference has forty years experience as a "visible feminist advocate for the ordination of women as priests, deacons and bishops into an inclusive and accountable Roman Catholic Church."[46] (See also Chapters 1 and 8 for intersections with this group.) Ironically, the group emerged following the instruction of Pope Pius XII in 1952 that encouraged orders of religious women to expand their education and professional training. Providing added impetus was the Second Vatican Council in 1962 that "urged religious orders to reflect on the renewal of religious life by giving consideration to how religious communities might adjust to changed social conditions."[47] Over the course of a decade women became scriptorians and seminary graduates, gained advanced degrees, and left the convent for life amongst the community they served. All the while, the women's movement was gaining momentum, creating a new understanding of the role women could play in society. (For more background, see Chapter 8.) The first Women's Ordination Conference was held in November 1975 in Detroit, and "for the first time the galvanizing issue

---

46. Catholic Women's Ordination Conference, "About Us," www.womensordination.org/about-us/ (accessed April 6, 2015).

47. Mary Fainsod Katzenstein, "Feminist within American Institutions: Unobtrusive Mobilization in the 1980s," *Signs* 16, no. 1 (Autumn 1990): 27–54.

was women's exclusion from the priesthood."[48] For the next three years, Roman Catholic leaders issued declarations against women's ordination in terms that made it clear that negotiation was not an option.

Approaching its fortieth anniversary, the CWOC remains a vibrant organization, with an expanded focus on social justice and the claim that women in clergy will connect to larger issues and calls to social change.[49] They also have established programs dedicated to training young women in leadership and activism, thus ensuring future agitation for women's ordination. Their tactics have included staging media events at gatherings of Church officials, releasing pink smoke at the Vatican with the election of a new pontiff, and rogue ordinations of women (always leading to excommunication from the Roman Catholic Church).[50]

Women of the Wall

In December 1988, a group of women approached Jerusalem's Western Wall (the Kotel)—one of the holiest sites in Judaism and the place where, more than any other, religious Jews believe they can experience God—and began a women's prayer service, including a reading from the Torah. They prayed aloud and many of the women wore prayer shawls. They were immediately bombarded with screams and curses from the men and other women present, but the Kotel Administrator, Rabbi Yehuda Gertz, did not stop the service because the women were "not violating Halakhah (Jewish Law)."[51] This group became the Women of the Wall (WoW), or Neshot Hakotel, and has attempted to hold regular prayer services, including readings from the Torah, at the Kotel despite physical violence, threats, harassment, and repeated court battles.[52] In October of 2013 they successfully read from a miniature Torah for a bat mitzvah, but this ceremony has not been repeated.[53]

Though WoW has gained notoriety in large part because of their public demonstrations at the Kotel, the mission of the group is to help women and girls become more active in the Jewish tradition of community prayer which "empowers us to use our voices in prayer and struggle, even in the face of attempts to silence us."[54] One of the major challenges that exists for WoW is the question of whether a woman can seek greater spiritual voice and authority yet still remain

---

48. Ibid., 38.

49. Ibid., 39.

50. Catholic Women's Ordination Conference, "About Us." www.womensordination.org/about-us/our-story/ (accessed April 6, 2015).

51. Women of the Wall, "History," www.womenofthewall.org.il/about/history (accessed April 6, 2015).

52. Ibid.

53. Women of the Wall, "Bat Mitzvah," www.womenofthewall.org.il/batmitzvah/ (accessed April 6, 2015).

54. Women of the Wall, "About Us," www.womenofthewall.org.il/about/ (accessed April 6, 2015).

Jewish. Can she read from the Torah, wear a *tallit*[55] or *tefillin*[56] at the Wall, and still be a good Jewish woman? WoW has branded itself as *kosher* while its opponents have called them *Reformim* (fringe Americans). They were also accused of being *davka*, or contrary for the sake of being controversial. These challenges are intermingled with the unique experience of Israeli Jews: they are a people defined by their religion and their nationality.[57] These religious activists had the benefit of legal protections that guaranteed them certain rights to access their holy sites and express themselves; but they also faced a legal and police system largely loyal to maintaining traditional religious practices, including gender role restrictions.

While the history of Ordain Women has already been described in this book, a few points warrant review. Ordain Women (OW) officially launched in April 2013 with a mission to expand access to Mormonism's lay priesthood to women. OW's first major action was establishing the website www.ordainwomen.org, which included profiles submitted from Church members, each of whom shared their name, a photograph, and the declaration: "I believe women should be ordained." Public declarations such as this are groundbreaking for Mormons who have long connected priesthood power and authority with maleness.[58] As one woman stated, "I still remember the day I learned what the answer was supposed to be to the question, 'Would you ever want the priesthood?' And I knew I had said the wrong thing." As of this writing (April 2015) more than 650 individuals have submitted profiles and thousands have submitted letters of support for Ordain Women and their mission. (An analysis of these profiles is the subject of Chapter 18.) Though it maintains an impressive online presence, the group has also planned public actions, launched educational programming, and participated in interfaith events. It is now governed by an executive board of eleven people and eight committees staffed by scores of volunteers. Co-founder Kate Kelly was excommunicated in June 2014, and several of its leaders have been subjected to informal discipline.[59]

The Rhetoric of WoW, CWOC, and OW

The similarities between these three groups are uncanny and reflect much of the scholarship on social movements, including the importance of framing

---

55. A Jewish prayer shawl.
56. Small black boxes that contain scrolls with verses of the Torah. Each weekday tefillin are worn by Jewish men during morning prayer service.
57. Leah Shakdiel, "Women of the Wall: Radical Feminism as an Opportunity for a New Discourse in Israel," *Journal of Israeli History: Politics, Society, Culture* 21 (2010): 126–63.
58. This assumption runs contrary to the early history of the LDS Church and the priesthood, which, according to some historians and feminists, had been bestowed on women by the Church's founder Joseph Smith. Evidence of his intentions is ambiguous, making the argument fierce and contentious.
59. Informal discipline in the LDS Church includes removal from callings (positions held by lay members), the voiding of temple recommends, resulting in no access to LDS temples, and more.

pertinent issues and the relative power of stakeholders to bring about change in organizations. The final section of this chapter will discuss the rhetorical narratives generated by these three organizations—how they have been framed by their faith communities, their common themes, and how they have impacted their tactics. To be clear, this is not an exhaustive analysis, but rather a summary comparison of the rhetoric of the WoW and CWOC movements and my personal experiences with the rhetoric generated by Ordain Women. The value in this exercise is in recognizing the similarities between and across these movements, and seeing how they compare to larger theories of social movement rhetoric and communication strategy.

Though these three campaigns for women's equality have evolved in different Judeo-Christian faiths, the rhetoric surrounding them demonstrates nearly identical patterns. First, all three groups have been forced to participate in "meaning" work; second, each has been forced to defend its rights as stakeholders to contribute to raise organizational questions; and third, they have all had to engage in a debate over whether their tactics are disruptive and therefore illegitimate.

Each of the groups in this brief review has participated in Gamson's "meaning work." The groups were and are struggling to reshape the way in which their brothers and sisters in faith think about fundamental questions. A common thread of this work has been an attempt to tackle the basic question of gender roles, with each organization dealing with strikingly similar constraints. Across the three religions, traditional gender roles are staunchly defended. According to Susannah Heschel, in the Orthodox Jewish community, "Men and women are believed to be essentially different, with different natures, spiritual paths, and legal statuses. Women are seen primarily as domestic beings, whereas all public and official leadership roles (rabbis, cantors, judges, circumcisers, and ritual slaughterers) are the province of men."[60] WoW has tried to establish a new image of these ritual positions, and create space for women in sacred spaces, by approaching the Kotel. They have used their physical bodies to demonstrate a new role for Jewish women.

The LDS Church teaches these same ideas regarding differences between men and women. It preaches that God has specific roles for each gender. "By divine design, fathers are to preside over their families in love and righteousness and are responsible to provide the necessities of life and protection for their families. . . . Mothers are primarily responsible for the nurture of their children."[61] Mormon children are taught, from the earliest ages, to sing this "doctrine of the family" set to music:

---

60. Susannah Heschel, quoted in Sered, "Women and Religious Change in Israel," 4.

61. "The Family: A Proclamation to the World," The First Presidency and Council of the Twelve Apostles of the Church of Jesus Christ of Latter-day Saints," 1995.

> A father's place is to preside, provide,
> To love and teach the gospel to his children.
> A father leads in fam'ly prayer to share
> Their love for Father in Heaven.
>
> A mother's purpose is to care, prepare,
> To nurture and to strengthen all her children.
> She teaches children to obey, to pray,
> To love and serve in the fam'ly.[62]

The idea that women might desire to step outside these firmly held beliefs regarding family gender roles is not just an infringement of Mormon social conventions; it is seen as a swipe at doctrine.

In much the same way, a decade after the Catholic Women's Ordination Conference began its work, an open letter and statement on women and priesthood was published in *Crisis Magazine*.[63] The authors declared that women's "female nature affords us distinct physical and spiritual capabilities with which to participate in the Divine Plan for creation."[64] It continued by recognizing "that the specific role of ordained priesthood is intrinsically connected with and representative of the begetting creativity of God in which only human males can participate."[65] The aims and goals of CWOC were not merely viewed as an expansion of the 1970s women's movement—they were an assault on basic doctrine and corresponding gender roles.

While the idea of a lay priesthood for Mormons is different than that of Catholic clerical priesthood (for Mormons it is defined as the literal power to act for God, which is bestowed upon all "worthy" male members of the Church beginning at age twelve), the rhetoric of motherhood = priesthood crosses into both faiths. One of the most common arguments against ordination for Mormon women is that women have the gift and responsibility of bringing children into the world and that, without priesthood, men would have nothing of corresponding importance and no reason to behave responsibly. As Sonja Farnsworth explained: "So what does the coupling of motherhood with priesthood really mean for the contemporary church? It means that the 'plain and precious truth' of motherhood as a simple but authentic partnership with fathers has been buried in the perennial rhetoric about a partnership with God, which is revived whenever traditional views of women are challenged. While this rhetoric seems to protect female needs, in reality it has protected male authority and denied

---

62. Matthew Neeley, "The Family Is of God," *The Friend*, April 2014, 30–31. This song was the theme for the annual Primary sacrament meeting program for 2014.

63. *Crisis Magazine* is not an official publication of a Catholic diocese but is a privately published periodical written by lay authors and funded by donations.

64. "Affirmation of Catholic Women," *Crisis Magazine*, April 1985, http://www.crisismagazine.com/1985/affirmation-of-catholic-women (accessed April 12, 2015).

65. Ibid.

women what is properly theirs."[66] In contemporary Mormonism, the concept of "Man" is inextricably tied to "priesthood." One concrete example of this blurred line that most Mormons overlook can be found every six months in the sessions of general conference. All women and girls aged eight and older are invited to attend the general *women's* session, while all men and boys aged twelve and older are invited to attend the general *priesthood* session.[67] There is no "men's session" because priesthood is synonymous with maleness.

Ordain Women has worked to establish a narrative that separates priesthood from maleness. One of the key elements of OW talking points is to call women "prospective elders." In their public statements, both to representatives of the LDS Church and also to the press, they have claimed that their goal is "to present themselves to church leaders as potential priesthood holders."[68] It is an effort to redefine the way Mormons speak about and even think about priesthood. Untangling the idea of priesthood as inherently male is an extension of the larger cultural narrative that dictates gender roles and sees women as nurturers while men are leaders.

The simple act of reframing gender roles has resulted in labeling supporters of these groups as outsiders to their own religious communities, challenging their role as stakeholders and limiting their legitimacy in conversation regarding their faith. However, this is not the only reason WoW, CWOC, and OW possesses diminished stakeholder status. Each of these groups moves in a unique faith community, yet all three exclude women from positions of authority or power in institutional structures. In Catholicism, "the official church does not seem to recognize that women are equal in Christ."[69] They hold no power in Rome and are under the authority of bishops, cardinals, and the Pope himself.

The Women of the Wall operate largely within the Orthodox Jewish community, a community that reserves all leadership positions—secular and spiritual—for men. Their activism has challenged these areas and some changes have been made. Jewish women have won legal victories from the Israeli government, providing them with opportunities to serve on municipal councils and boards, and WoW has sued for and received police protection for their worship at the Kotel. This does not mean they have been accepted in the Jewish community, though. Quite the contrary. For the Women of the Wall, their diminished stake-

---

66. Sonja Farnsworth, "Mormonism's Odd Couple: The Motherhood-Priesthood Connection," in *Women and Authority: Re-emerging Mormon Feminism*, edited by Maxine Hanks (Salt Lake City: Signature Books, 1992), available at Signature Books Library, http://signaturebookslibrary.org/woman-and-authority-13/ (accessed April 12, 2015).

67. The general women's session was first held as a general women's meeting and not as an actual session of general conference in April 2014. As of April 2015, it became an official session.

68. OW Press Release, "LDS Women Seeking Ordaintion Will Walk to Attend General Priesthood Session," April 2014.

69. Catholic Women's Ordination Conference, "Why Ordination?" http://www.womensordination.org/resources/why-ordination/ (accessed April 12, 2015).

holder status is revealed in the names they are called, such as "protestant" and "Reform"—both terms of opprobrium. As Shakdiel described it, "WoW's supporters prefer to contain [their identity] in the 'kosher' religious camp, whereas its opponents see it as anti-religious dangerous heresy."[70] Despite their commitment to passive, peaceful actions and their repeatedly stated desire to be seen as faithful, "their struggle was and is still considered weird and objectionable."[71] They are seen as less Jewish, or not Jewish at all, and are therefore conceded no legitimacy in their argument.

Ordain Women has encountered this same problem, in that the structure of the Church of Jesus Christ of Latter-day Saints reserves all institutional power and authority for male priesthood holders. The *Church Handbook of Instruction, Volume 1: Stake Presidencies and Bishoprics* is the official instruction and policy manual for leading all Church units and Church members. Of those who have access to the *Handbook*, 118,000 are men and nine are women.[72] Those nine women are general officers of the Church, while the 118,000 men are local priesthood leaders, mission presidents, or General Authorities. Women never hold officer positions in any group that includes men—only in the groups specifically for women or children—and are never allowed to control financial resources.

Attempting to operate in this patriarchal structure, Ordain Women has experienced counter-rhetoric that diminishes their status as stakeholders both from fellow Mormons and also from official representatives of the LDS Church itself. In October 2013, Church spokesperson Ruth Todd delivered a statement on OW, declaring that "millions of women in this church do not share the views of this small group who organized today's protest, and most church members would see such efforts as divisive."[73] And six months later, yet another Church spokesperson, Jessica Moody, said, "Women in the Church, by a very large majority, do not share your advocacy for priesthood ordination for women and consider that position to be extreme."[74] These quotations demonstrate two interesting tactics the LDS Church has used to paint OW as illegitimate. First, it has consistently used women to make public statements in oppositional response to Ordain Women activities and media inquiries.[75] Second, the argument that OW does not

---

70. Shakdiel, "Women of the Wall," 137.

71. Ibid., 130.

72. April Young Bennett, "The Sealed Book," *The Exponent*, http://www.the-exponent.com/the-sealed-book-church-handbook-of-instruction-volume-1/ (accessed April 12, 2015).

73. Whitney Evans and Carole Mikita, "Debate over LDS Women's Roles Spotlighted in Protest," KSL News, October 5, 2013, http://www.ksl.com/?sid=27133883 (accessed April 12, 2015).

74. Moody, letter to leaders of Ordain Women, March 17, 2014.

75. Beyond these two examples, Ally Isom was called upon to represent the LDS Church during June 2014 when Kate Kelly was being excommunicated. To my knowledge, only one official statement from the LDS Church Office of Public Affairs directed specifically at Ordain Women was written and voiced by a man: a press release written by Cody Craynor

represent a majority, or even a significant portion, of LDS women suggests that OW activists are not truly Mormon women—or at least not Mormon women worth listening to.

In one final symbolic attempt to diminish Ordain Women as Mormons, the LDS Church, in response to OW requests to attend the priesthood session of general conference, denied the request and asked OW to not even come to Temple Square. Moody, who authored the rejection letter, then continued: "If you feel you must come and demonstrate, we ask that you do so in free speech zones adjacent to Temple Square."[76] For someone who is not familiar with LDS general conference or Mormon culture, this request may seem simple, but it is actually the ultimate insult. The free speech zones are reserved for anti-Mormon protesters who hold signs (sometimes with gruesome pictures of aborted fetuses) and shout offensive epithets at conference-goers. Church spokespersons attempted to equate OW's desire to attend the meeting—and by extension their desire for women's ordination—with protesters shouting "JOSEPH IS A FRAUD!!!"

If the reception from Church representatives has been frosty, the comments from other Mormons can be frigid. Supporters of OW are often invited to leave the LDS Church. The Ordain Women Facebook page regularly receives comments such as "End of story! Go join some other religion and stop giving us a headache!"[77] or "Why not join the Community of Christ, they allow for women being ordained."[78] Often, the comments included personal attacks: "You are a horrible and vile person. You are trying to force your deviant liberal and disgusting 'values' on the church you claim to love so much. You are a wolf in sheep's clothing. You sick feminists are just ugly women with low self esteem."[79] Supporters have been called "dishonest posers" and "a willful cancer" on their community.[80]

The official OW response to institutional and personal attacks has been to publicly express faith and disappointment in the negative characterizations; to provide extensive de-escalation training for individuals participating in public actions; and to engage in a fierce social media campaign referred to as "scattering sunshine" in which volunteers take daily, sometimes hourly, shifts leaving positive or uplifting comments on Facebook to try to drown out negative comments. Additionally, OW has tried to tie itself to an established and recognized

---

in response to the Ordain Women action at the April 2014 general priesthood session. This release is quoted extensively in Mark Green, "LDS Church: Actions of Those Who Demonstrated on Temple Square 'Disappointing,'" http://fox13now.com/2014/04/05/lds-church-actions-of-those-who-demonstrated-on-temple-square-disappointing/ (accessed April 12, 2015).

76. Moody, letter to leaders of Ordain Women, March 17, 2014.

77. Anonymous comment 1. I cite all social media comments as anonymous to protect the online identities of commenters.

78. Anonymous comment 2.

79. Anonymous comment 3.

80. Anonymous comment 4.

history of Mormon feminists and academics, declaring that "this effort is part of a decades-long campaign for women's ordination inside the Utah-based faith."[81] How successful the attempts to legitimize themselves will be remains to be seen, but the way their tactics are framed suggests it will be a long road.

Many of the arguments used against the three dissent groups I am comparing have focused on the public nature of their work. As Sered described the reaction to WoW, it was clear that "women should not act collectively, should not make noise, and should stay out of the public sphere."[82] There was an implication that faithful women would not feel this way and that, even if they did, they would certainly never air their opinions publicly. The actions at the Kotel were described as "provocative transparency . . . visibility, externalization and exhibitionism [that] cannot go hand in hand with religious faith, which 'naturally' belongs indoors and not outdoors."[83] The consequence of this public activism for WoW has been physical harm, legal action, and a loss of cultural legitimacy.

The same arguments have been used against supporters of Ordain Women but with different consequences. When it comes to their actions, OW has been chastised both for the public nature and its appearance of recruiting more supporters. The typical argument is that women are allowed to have these questions individually but that the collective spirit and tone of OW's actions, and even the name, are problematic. The declarative nature of the name "Ordain Women" first became a focus when Michael Otterson, LDS Public Affairs managing director, denounced "individuals or groups who make non-negotiable demands," accusing them of "com[ing] across as divisive and suggestive of apostasy."[84] Another Public Affairs spokesperson, Ally Isom, followed up on this theme: "When you use a grammatical ultimatum, Ordain Women . . . it presents some problems."[85] The action of naming themselves, without a question mark at the end, was itself deemed too controversial.

In what turned out to be quite a surprise to many in OW, a seemingly bland tactic has also been controversial. In May 2014, the group launched a series of "Six Discussions" designed to spur conversation around the topic of gender inequality and the history of women's ordination in the LDS Church. These discussions

---

81. Ordain Women, press release, "LDS Women Seeking Priesthood Ordination Will Try to Attend Church's General Priesthood Session," April 2014

82. Sered, "Women and Religious Change in Israel," 16.

83. Shakdiel, "Women of the Wall,"136.

84. Michael Otterson, Managing Director Public Affairs, the Church of Jesus Christ of Latter-day Saints, 2014. This was an open letter sent to several Mormon blogs. Tad Walch, "LDS Spokesman Sends Open Letter about Mormon Women," http://www.deseretnews.com/article/865604172/LDS-spokesman-sends-open-letter-about-Mormon-women.html?pg=all (accessed April 15, 2015).

85. Ally Isom, interviewed by Doug Fabrizio, KUER Radio West June 16, 2014, http://radiowest.kuer.org/post/latter-day-saints-and-excommunication-part-ii (accessed April 11, 2015).

were intended for the use of supporters who wanted to invite friends and family to learn more about gender inequality. They included quotations from Church leaders and manuals and did not introduce any doctrinal arguments. They were named "Discussions" as a play on the six missionary discussions, in use from the 1950s through the 2000s, and familiar to thousands of LDS men and women who served full-time or stake missionaries during that period. The structured "discussions" helped teach interested individuals more about the LDS Church. The parallel language was seen as offensive, however, so OW accommodated this hypersensitivity by renaming them "Conversations." The very existence of these dialogues was seen as provocative and as evidence of an attempt to recruit followers. Once again, Ally Isom explained the problem as an attempt "to recruit people to participate in something that is contrary.... A conversation is not recruitment. A conversation, a dialogue, asking questions—that's vastly different than an organized effort with six discussions."[86] Further, in what came as a shock, Ally Isom suggested that these low-key discussions might have been the grounds for holding a disciplinary council on one of OW's founders, Kate Kelly, which was held in June 2014 and resulting in her excommunication. Oddly enough, the more public act of attempting to attend the priesthood session was not cited as the grounds for her punishment.

This is not to say that the most public OW actions were without controversy. Jessica Moody, speaking for LDS Public Affairs, stressed that the problem was the public nature of the actions: "Your organization has again publicized its intention to demonstrate on Temple Square during the April 5 priesthood session. Activist events like this detract from the sacred environment of Temple Square and the spirit of harmony sought at General Conference. Please reconsider."[87] The Church insisted that a group of women standing quietly in line, waiting for a chance to request admittance to a Church meeting, was a "demonstration" that would be distracting and disruptive. Finally, Ally Isom declared in a radio interview: "Exploring questions, having doubts, discussing issues is all completely—not just important—but welcome and invited and expected. But let's do it in the right tone and with the right spirit. . . . There are many avenues to express that and discuss that. No one's questioning our ability to discuss it in a congregation, in a Sunday school class, in Relief Society class. . . . The conversation is not the problem. It is really the spirit of one's intent and one's heart that is the challenge."[88]

Thus, the women of OW are allowed to want priesthood ordination; they are allowed to hope and pray for priesthood ordination; and they are allowed to speak to others about priesthood ordination. Those acts would be considered faithful, until they crossed an invisible line, defined by their local leaders as disrespectful or recruiting (terms without clear definitions). LDS General Authorities in Salt

---

86. Isom, interviewed by Fabrizio, June 16, 2014.
87. Moody, Letter to leaders of Ordain Women, March 17, 2014.
88. Isom, interviewed by Fabrizio, June 16, 2014.

Lake City refused to declare OW apostate or not—they refused to even mention the name Ordain Women. Rather, they allowed leaders of local congregations to judge and discipline women in their home wards. The tactics of OW became the conversation, instead of the ideas in question.

Conclusion

The fight for religious gender equality has been waged for decades and even centuries. In the three faith communities I have reviewed here, it goes back at least three generations. Patterns that have emerged in the strategic communication of secular groups pursuing social change also appear to be present in the activities of religious groups, regardless of the denomination. As women and men work to expand the rights and privileges of women across faith traditions, they continue to face the trials of meaning making and legitimacy. The simple act of asking for more access to religious authority forces individuals to reexamine many of their foundational beliefs, including those that may have guided the life choices they have already made. The consequence of this challenge to the religious status quo is a massive backlash: communities that were once welcoming become wary; they begin to create barriers among themselves and find ways to label each other.

For those who continue to work for religious gender equality, the fight is nonetheless worth it. The threats of social exclusion or religious excommunication, though painful, are less anguishing than the thought of living an inauthentic life. And the long view of a future where our daughters are recognized as equal and who serve side by side with men in their church is a primal motivation. That image is the beating heart of Ordain Women, and as long as it is cherished by even one Mormon woman, Ordain Women will continue.

Epilogue:

Prospects for the Ordination of LDS Women in the Twenty-first Century

Gordon Shepherd and Gary Shepherd

As Lavina Fielding Anderson states in the preface of this book, the importance of the chapters assembled herein is to provide clear expression to a third, alternative voice in the responsible discussion of gender issues which has become increasingly ascendant in the contemporary LDS Church. This vigorous and enlivening discussion allows sufficient room for a range of perspectives—from relatively conservative to moderate to progressive points of view—concerning the rightful role of women in twenty-first century religion. By and large (excepting several of our authors' personal views), the collective weight of the essays, theological expositions, historical analyses, and empirical studies aggregated in *Voices for Equality* falls squarely on the progressive side of the debate—on the side of full gender equality for Latter-day Saint women in all aspects of religious life, including ordination to the priesthood and elevation to the governing councils of the Church.

At a minimum, all of the chapters in this book confirm, directly or indirectly, that a genuine resurgence of religious aspiration among many LDS women for greater equality with male priesthood holders in their Church is currently underway. To what extent have recent changes in Church policies and official rhetoric about priesthood resulted from Ordain Women and other allied groups raising the issue of women's ordination? The complex and complicated information and data explored in this volume suggest that the institutional impact of the current, organized ferment for priesthood equality has not been trivial. Modest ecclesiastical changes and recent rhetorical modifications notwithstanding, the ultimate outcomes of this movement have not yet been fully realized, and it may be years before scholars and lay Church members alike will recognize fundamental alterations in Mormon theology and practice where current gender issues are concerned.

While the majority of authors who contributed to *Voices for Equality* think LDS women should be ordained to the priesthood, it is not a forgone conclusion that they are equally optimistic that expanding ordination to women will happen anytime soon or, if and when it happens, what the primary reasons for this monumental change would be. Borrowing from some of the questions asked of the tens of thousands of Latter-day Saints who responded to the Mormon Gender Issues Survey discussed in Chapters 14–16, we surveyed the opinions of the book's twenty-eight authors and co-authors on the following key questions:

- How likely is it that sometime in the future the LDS Church will ordain women to the priesthood?
- When, if ever, is this most likely to happen?
- If in the future a decision allowing women to hold the priesthood is made by Church authorities, what would be the primary reason for their doing so?

Predictably, given their basic orientation, our authors overwhelmingly concluded that sooner or later LDS women will be given the priesthood. But they spanned the spectrum on when and how likely they thought such a step would be taken. Only 4 percent of our authors believed women would receive the priesthood within the next ten years, while a very substantial majority (76 percent) thought it would take between twenty and fifty years. A definitely less optimistic 16 percent concluded that such a step might take as long as 100 years, but only 4 percent said they didn't believe that women would ever be ordained to the LDS priesthood. Couching their expectations in terms of the probability or likelihood of future ordination of women, only 16 percent of our authors were pessimistic, ranging in their answers from "somewhat likely" to "unlikely" or "never." The majority of authors, however, said female ordination was "likely" (29 percent), "very likely" (13 percent), or "extremely likely" (21 percent). And, at the most optimistic end of the scale, close to a quarter (21 percent) also said they were *certain* that priesthood ordination would be bestowed on future LDS women.

In general, then, we summarize these findings by saying that contributors to this book are cautiously confident that women will be ordained to the priesthood but also recognize that it may take many years of continued aspiration and determination for this to come about. With regard to how and why they think such a fundamental change in LDS ecclesiastical policy will eventually occur, 37 percent said the primary reason for change would be a direct revelation from God to the prophet and/or a response from God to inquiries by the First Presidency and Quorum of the Twelve. A substantial 63 percent majority, however, identified multiple causes—that change would come about primarily as Church leaders responded to "insider" pressures (members desiring change), from changing trends and accumulating social pressures gathering energy from outside the Church, or a combination of both. None of these reasons are, of course, mutually exclusive. A number of author-respondents added clarifying explanations to support their answers, as the following excerpts illustrate (punctuation standardized):

> I checked both "a direct revelation" and "pressure from inside and outside" because I think that, while the Church will officially state that the decision to ordain women was due to a revelation, it will come only after increased pressures on Church leadership. This is not to say claiming it came through revelation will be untrue; rather, the Church is unlikely to admit making such a large change due to social pressures, including the pressure to pray to God about the matter.

> It will be framed the same way as past changes (i.e., as a revelation in response to independent inquiry), and it's entirely possible that those doing the inquiring (and receiving the revelation) will perceive it this way.

It may be that Mormon leaders will believe they have a revelation when they decided to ordain women. But to the extent that they do, it will be the result of pressure from the inside and outside that will make them uncomfortable enough about the status of women in the Church that they will decide to pray about it and, in addition, to listen to what women are saying. . . . But until they decide that there is something to pray about, nothing is going to change.

Several of the added comments underscored the perception that current ecclesiastical authorities are not yet seriously attuned to women's concerns in the Church and that continued pressure over the long-term will be a crucial factor in bringing about change. The following statements serve as examples of doubt concerning any immediate, positive responses in the direction of priesthood ordination from current leaders:

> While I believe in a God that supports gender equality, I'm not sure the LDS Church leaders will get the memo unless they are ASKING about women's ordination to the priesthood. I suspect they won't want to appear to be caving to pressure, but the reality is they do respond to bad PR. If OW can keep applying pressure via direct action/showing up and pressing the issue, maybe we'll see some movement.

> I believe that leaders of the Church will eventually receive revelation extending the priesthood to women. The only thing delaying it is the leaders' need to be open enough to ask the question and receive the answer. This feels like a clear case of the hubris and closed minds of men (and women) holding back the work of God

> Although I believe that the gospel and the scriptures provide grounds for giving priesthood to women, I don't believe that the present LDS leaders will be moved by these. I don't believe that these leaders will seek revelation on the question of priesthood for women. The process by which leaders are chosen and trained leads me to believe that this is likely to be true for a long time. If God gives a revelation about priesthood for women, it will not come from these leaders.

Finally, while a majority of our authors are optimistic that fundamental changes will eventually occur in how the Church views the relationship between gender and the priesthood, and many maintain their Latter-day Saint faith in God's ultimate guidance of Church leaders through the revelatory process and heartfelt petitions from faithful members, a significant minority saw Mormon patriarchy as thoroughly impervious to such concerns, as these latter statements demonstrate:

> All of the theology, doctrine, cosmology, and temple ordinances of the LDS Church are completely male centered and patriarchal. Patriarchy is the foundation. To include women fully in ordination would require a complete deconstruction and reconstruction, including the nature of the Godhead. I do not see that happening.

> As long as conservative and patriarchal religion exists, the Church will do what it can to maintain traditional gender roles. It will do this as long as it is tolerated by its membership, and as long as it does not begin to be too far outside cultural norms. If (1) current predictions that Islam will continue to grow and eventually overtake Christianity as the most common religion, and (2) Muslim cultures retain their relatively conservative dress standards and gender roles, then I think that we will see

more latitude given the LDS, Catholic, and other churches to maintain distinct differences in sex roles among their members.

The LDS Church tends to hover between 20 and 50 years behind secular society's values. While it is certainly the case that the Church could withstand the pressure to conform to the rest of society in empowering women, doing so would likely mean its demise. It will eventually relent, but not until much damage to its reputation and to the trans and cisgendered members of the religion has been done.... The LDS Church is a patriarchal institution, despite prevailing social norms, not because of them. It will change, but begrudgingly, and only after lots of external and internal pressure.

In the chapters they have contributed to this book, our authors have laid out their varying thoughts on the momentous issue of women and the priesthood, supported by evidence that ranges from historical and statistical to comparative, theological, and personal. While a majority of them share plausible hope in the eventual ordination of women to the LDS priesthood (and, by implication, hope in the parallel rise of women in the ecclesiastical structure and decision-making councils of the Church), they are not of one mind concerning why and when such a transformative change will occur. In spite of many remaining uncertainties, we nevertheless have good reason to believe that raising the issue of women's ordination in recent years has already had a tangible impact on official LDS Church rhetoric about priesthood. This impact includes at least the following rhetorical shifts, each identified in some chapters of this book: (1) The issue of women's ordination is now being directly addressed by leaders rather than simply being ignored or dismissed; (2) the implied equivalency parallel between men being privileged to hold the priesthood while women are privileged to be mothers appears to be waning as an argument in official statements; (3) maleness is no longer being equated in official rhetoric as an intrinsic quality of priesthood; it is recognized that men are not priesthood; (4) leader discourses have moved from emphasizing that women enjoy the blessings of the priesthood to allusions that in some way women already have priesthood and currently exercise some aspect of priesthood in the callings they are given.

The traditional patriarchal foundations of the Mormon religion are still with us and are unlikely to disappear anytime soon. But the world is changing, and it's a safe bet that the LDS Church will also continue changing. We conclude that, whatever the co-mingling factors and their assorted weights for change might be, they are now converging with accelerating force to push Mormon culture and the LDS Church onto a widening path of gender equality.

Appendix

Bibliography of Media Stories January 1, 2013–December 31, 2014, on Mormon/LDS Women, Ordain Women, and Kate Kelly

Compiled by Pamela A. Shepherd

This appendix provides a bibliography of media articles and news stories, both print and digital, published during a two-year period between January 1, 2013, and December 31, 2014, by U.S. media outlets on the subjects of Mormon women's issues in general and Ordain Women-related activities in particular. The search engine we used for identifying stories on the internet is available through Meltwater News, an online media monitoring service that can be accessed at http://www.meltwater.com/. The key words on which we searched were "Mormon women," "LDS women," "Ordain Women," and "Kate Kelly." Many of the articles identified by Meltwater as relevant to our topic were published or reprinted multiple times in numerous media outlets. In this bibliography, we list only originating articles and their original outlet sources. Each article is listed by its date of publication, the author or reporter's name (only first authors are listed for stories or articles with multiple authors), the name of the original media outlet, story title, online access URL, and the number of times the story or article was republished and circulated through other outlets. Stories for which a zero is recorded are stories that were not picked up by other media outlets. Stories that were republished ranged from a low of once to a high of 915 repetitions in multiple media outlets. Most of the news stories with high frequency circulation in multiple outlets originated with and/or were distributed by the Associated Press.

Date	Author/Reporter	Media Outlet	Article/Story Title	URL	Republished
1/1/2013	Brent Huntsaker	KTVX ABC 4 Salt Lake City	"Pants Protest" against LDS Church Picks Up Steam	http://tinyurl.com/k3e7sgm	0
1/5/2013	Peggy Fletcher Stack	*Salt Lake Tribune*	Mormon "Pants Day"—Debate Heats Up as Women Prepare to Dress Down	http://tinyurl.com/c3ajupx	6
1/9/2013	Unidentified	88.9 Nevada Public Radio	Mormon Women Dare to Wear Pants	http://tinyurl.com/kpd8vsh	0
1/13/2013	Piper Hoffman	Care2 Causes	Wearing Pants to Church: Mormon Women's Protest for Equality	http://tinyurl.com/ajfbuzc	2
1/18/2013	Robert Kirby	*Salt Lake Tribune*	Let Mormon Women Pray if They Keep It Short	http://tinyurl.com/axtxald	0
1/21/2013	Brady McCombs	Associated Press	Women Ask to Lead Prayers at Mormon Conference	http://tinyurl.com/m7q3ok8	38

Date	Author	Source	Title	URL	
1/23/2013	Kim Fischer Fisher	KTVX ABC 4 Salt Lake City	Remark Stirs Controversy on LDS Women's Rights and Roles	http://tinyurl.com/mwz3cf8	0
1/23/2013	Peggy Fletcher Stack	*Salt Lake Tribune*	LDS Women's Leader Stirs It Up with "No Need to Lobby"	http://tinyurl.com/kst747f	4
2/5/2013	Sara Benincasa	Take Part	Mormon Feminists Work for Change—One Pant Leg at a Time	http://tinyurl.com/lxmgxmt	0
3/16/2013	Catherine Jeppsen	*Washington Post*	A Prayer for the Progression of Mormon Women	http://tinyurl.com/ke5qa8r	0
3/19/2013	Unidentified	KUTV.com	Women to Give Prayers at LDS General Conference	http://tinyurl.com/koy5sww	0
3/22/2013	Peggy Fletcher Stack	*Salt Lake Tribune*	April Mormon Conference May Make History: Women Will Pray	http://tinyurl.com/c727zur	23
3/23/2013	Unidentified	Associated Press	Mormon Group Pushing for Women in the Priesthood	http://tinyurl.com/ltnv59o	12
3/25/2013	Unidentified	Associated Press	Correction: Mormon Women-Priesthood Story	http://tinyurl.com/lqt79yh	10
3/25/2013	Unidentified	*The Digital Universe*	New Website Promotes Giving Mormon Women the Priesthood	http://tinyurl.com/lycflzm	0
3/26/2013	Yonat Shimron	Religion News Service	Tuesday's Religion News Roundup	http://tinyurl.com/mdoab3r	0
4/2/2013	Peggy Fletcher Stack	*Salt Lake Tribune*	Mormons Launch Online Push to Ordain Women to the Priesthood	http://tinyurl.com/lcp5dld	30
4/3/2013	Noah Bond	Abc4.com	Group Pushing to Ordain LDS Women	http://tinyurl.com/mydjcet	0
4/3/2013	Brittany Green-Miner	Fox 13 Salt Lake City	Mormon Group Pushes for Women to Get the Priesthood	http://tinyurl.com/k3hmk7l	0
4/4/2013	Joanna Brooks	Religion Dispatches	"Joseph Smith Himself Viewed Women as Priesthood Holders"	http://tinyurl.com/kqdppgh	0
4/5/2013	Donald W. Meyers	*Salt Lake Tribune*	Mormon Women at U. Event: We'll Press Forward for Priesthood	http://tinyurl.com/c7o5vgo	1
4/5/2013	Unidentified	*Salt Lake Tribune*	Faith in Action: Mormon Events, Holocaust Survivor and More	http://tinyurl.com/lojw5fq	0
4/5/2013	Heidi Hatch	KUTV.com	Group Of LDS Women Looking for Equality through Ordaining Women	http://tinyurl.com/l8dyc8f	3
4/5/2013	Rachel J. Trotter	*Standard-Examiner*	LDS Church Addresses Women's Group Pushing for Priesthood	http://tinyurl.com/l8k3q9n	0
4/5/2013	Brittany Green-Miner	Fox 13 Salt Lake City	LDS General Conference Is This Weekend	http://tinyurl.com/ljaq25r	0
4/5/2013	Lisa Wangsness	*Boston Globe*	Mormon Feminists Speak Out	http://tinyurl.com/n3cetfe	0
4/5/2013	Paul Johnson	Fox 14 Sun Valley	Mormon Group Advocates Female Priests	http://tinyurl.com/ka6rw96	0
4/5/2013	Joseph Walker	*Deseret News*	Mormon Women Seek Blessings of Priesthood, Not Authority of Priesthood	http://tinyurl.com/kpe25vd	5
4/5/2013	Staff	*Standard-Examiner*	Ordain Women Plans Launch Event Today in SLC	http://tinyurl.com/n3hovok	0
4/5/2013	Ben Fulton	*Salt Lake Tribune*	Theater Review: "Suffrage" Offers a Different Take on Utah's Polygamist Past	http://tinyurl.com/kbawf7f	0

Date	Author	Publication	Title	URL	
4/6/2013	Peggy Fletcher Stack	Salt Lake Tribune	First Prayer by Woman Offered at Mormon Conference	http://tinyurl.com/mhcxavz	27
4/6/2013	Antone Clark	Standard-Examiner	Conference Highlights: Woman Saying Prayer at Session for First Time	http://tinyurl.com/kqwmfyq	0
4/6/2013	Noah Bond	Abc4.com	First Woman Prays in LDS General Conference	http://tinyurl.com/k8zbsqv	0
4/6/2013	Mark Green	Fox 13 Salt Lake City	Group Advocating Ordaining LDS Women to Priesthood Hold Launch Event	http://tinyurl.com/l5t8zl8	0
4/6/2013	Robert Kirby	Salt Lake Tribune	Kirby: The Top of My Scary List? Women Getting the Priesthood	http://tinyurl.com/mpd8psl	0
4/6/2013	Cody Clark	Daily Herald (AP)	Religion Briefs for April 6	http://tinyurl.com/n6z3sbl	0
4/7/2013	Joanna Brooks	Religion Dispatches	Historic Prayer by Woman at LDS General Conference	http://tinyurl.com/kvp25l6	0
4/7/2013	Noah Bond	Abc4.com	LDS Women Group Wants Priesthood	http://tinyurl.com/kjx6btp	0
4/7/2013	Dan Bammes	KUER 90.1	LDS Women Seek Ordination	http://tinyurl.com/kec7hnh	0
4/7/2013	Antone Clark	Standard-Examiner	Women Given Greater Role in LDS Church Mission Change	http://tinyurl.com/l55cote	0
4/8/2013	Lisa Schencker	Salt Lake Tribune	Mormon Apostle Packer Warns against "Tolerance Trap"	http://tinyurl.com/lhjle2g	0
4/8/2013	Marjorie Clark	Daily Utah Chronicle	Women's Group Says Priesthood Equality Is Necessary	http://tinyurl.com/mv74ep7	0
4/8/2013	Howard Berkes	NPR	A Woman's Prayer Makes Mormon History	http://tinyurl.com/mo4ndh7	23
4/9/2013	Karin Klein	Los Angeles Times	Mormonism and the Discussion of a Woman's Place	http://tinyurl.com/n2erjpx	0
4/9/2013	Peggy Fletcher Stack	Salt Lake Tribune	So Are Mormon Women Really Making Gains? Views Differ	http://tinyurl.com/ka4hcno	0
4/11/2013	Chris Henrichsen	RadioWest	"Mormon Women and the Priesthood" Today on RadioWest	http://tinyurl.com/me7zgyx	0
4/15/2013	Peggy Fletcher Stack	Salt Lake Tribune	Feminists Meet Opposition from Top in Catholic, Mormon, Orthodox Faiths	http://tinyurl.com/mtzad7b	0
4/15/2013	Brynn Whaley	Standard-Examiner	Changes Ongoing within Church	http://tinyurl.com/lrkb22r	0
4/15/2013	James Carroll	Boston Globe	Religious Women Press for Change	http://tinyurl.com/mvu42lx	3
4/23/2013	Rod Decker	KUTV.com	Take Two: LDS Women in Priesthood	http://tinyurl.com/kvglw9d	0
5/10/2013	Peggy Fletcher Stack	Salt Lake Tribune	First Prayer by Woman Offered at Mormon Conference (video)	http://tinyurl.com/cegceb8	0
6/19/2013	Holly Welker	Salt Lake City Weekly	Mormon Feminism	http://tinyurl.com/k6twdnj	0
8/7/2013	Holly Welker	Salt Lake City Weekly	Sunstone Symposium	http://tinyurl.com/lwvo3jc	0
8/18/2013	Hannah Wheelwright	Daily Herald	Mother's Hands Joining Father's in Priesthood Blessing	http://tinyurl.com/mdy7yt5	0
8/28/2013	Peggy Fletcher Stack	Salt Lake Tribune	Mormon Feminists Hope to Attend Priesthood Meeting	http://tinyurl.com/nswkyfh	27

Date	Author	Publication	Title	URL	Comments
8/30/2013	Kirsten Johnson	*Dame Magazine*	Mormon Feminists Take Aim at All-Male Ordination Rules	http://tinyurl.com/mlfo5wn	0
8/31/2013	Nineveh Dinha	Fox 13 Salt Lake City	Group of Mormon Feminists Push to be Part of Priesthood Meeting	http://tinyurl.com/mcc3jtd	0
9/23/2001	David Howlette	Patheos	Why LDS Women Will Not Be Ordained to the Priesthood	http://tinyurl.com/kfwnqus	0
9/9/2013	Margaret Blair Young	Patheos	Priesthood Restrictions—Shall We Protest?	http://tinyurl.com/kcwmsdf	0
9/14/2013	Margaret Blair Young	Patheos	I Return to "Ordain Women," Where Angels Fear to Tread	http://tinyurl.com/ldccsh7	0
9/24/2013	Unidentified	Associated Press	Men-only Mormon Conference Session to Be Broadcast	http://tinyurl.com/n2wvoq4	31
9/24/2013	Unidentified	KUTV.com	"Ordain Women" Work toward LDS Church Equality	http://tinyurl.com/lhpd2q6	0
9/24/2013	Joseph Walker	*Deseret News*	LDS Church Responds to Priesthood Meeting Request by Activists	http://tinyurl.com/kbbhnxs	2
9/24/2013	Bob Evans	Fox 13 Salt Lake City	LDS Church to Offer Live Stream of Priesthood Session	http://tinyurl.com/mlxfsae	0
9/24/2013	Nineveh Dinha	Fox 13 Salt Lake City	Mormon Feminists Applaud Church Decision to Broadcast Priesthood Session	http://tinyurl.com/mxszspl	0
9/25/2013	Dan Bammes	KUER 90.1	Group Seeking to Ordain LDS Women Hopes to Attend Priesthood Session	http://tinyurl.com/p7o23ub	0
9/25/2013	Billy Hesterman	*Daily Herald*	LDS Church to Broadcast Priesthood Session on BYUtv and Internet	http://tinyurl.com/mofye5t	1
9/26/2013	Unidentified	*Daily Herald*	LDS Men Encouraged to Attend Priesthood Session	http://tinyurl.com/lupcvwn	0
9/27/2013	Peggy Fletcher Stack	*Salt Lake Tribune*	Women Can See, But Not Attend, Mormon Priesthood Session	http://tinyurl.com/mcphokm	0
9/30/2013	Joanna Brooks	Religion Dispatches	Why the Women's Ordination Question Will Shape the Future of Mormonism	http://tinyurl.com/l2mp8yv	0
9/30/2013	Amy McDonald	*The Digital Universe*	Mormon Feminism about More than Ordination	http://tinyurl.com/lxnbyvn	0
10/2/2013	Eric S. Peterson	*Salt Lake City Weekly*	Restoring the Priesthood Page 1	http://tinyurl.com/k38tlk9	0
10/4/2013	Brady McCombs	*Daily Herald* (AP)	Gender Equality among Issues at Mormon Conference	http://tinyurl.com/l9gbggl	157
10/4/2013	Brady McCombs	*Daily Herald* (AP)	100K Mormons in SLC for Biannual Church Conference	http://tinyurl.com/mb78dju	9
10/4/2013	Rachel Redfern	PolicyMic	Young Mormon Feminists Are Doing It for Themselves	http://tinyurl.com/lam8b6w	0
10/4/2013	Mark Green	Fox 13 Salt Lake City	Member of Ordain Women Discusses Upcoming LDS Priesthood Meeting	http://tinyurl.com/nf9umh4	0
10/4/2013	Chris Henrichsen	Patheos	Ordain Women Is Succeeding	http://tinyurl.com/m9k6nr3	0
10/4/2013	Benito Baeza	News Radio 1310 KLIX	Women's Role in LDS Church Debated Ahead of Conference	http://tinyurl.com/l98ctjc	0
10/5/2013	Unidentified	Associated Press	Mormon Women's Group Shut Out of All-Male Meeting	http://tinyurl.com/ldourcf	153

Date	Author	Source	Title	URL	
10/5/2013	Antone Clark	Standard-Examiner	LDS Women Priesthood Crashers Rebuffed at Church Conference	http://tinyurl.com/mekswdd	0
10/5/2013	Holly Welker	Religion Dispatches	Mormon Women Knock at the Door, Are Turned Away	http://tinyurl.com/khutytg	1
10/5/2013	Cristina Rendon	Abc4.com	Ordain Women Turned Away from Priesthood Session	http://tinyurl.com/lgemje4	0
10/5/2013	Whitney Evans	Deseret News	Women Hear LDS Priesthood Meeting, But Not at Conference Center	http://tinyurl.com/l4snkdy	0
10/5/2013	Mark Green	Fox 13 Salt Lake City	Women Who Want to Attend Priesthood Session Rally	http://tinyurl.com/lkqqkr2	0
10/5/2013	Timothy Pratt	Reuters	Women Seek Access to Traditionally Male-Only Mormon Gathering	http://tinyurl.com/loxuxcn	20
10/6/2013	Peggy Fletcher Stack	Salt Lake Tribune	Leaders Say Mormons Cannot Condone Same-Sex Marriage	http://tinyurl.com/kofkhht	0
10/6/2013	Mark Green	Fox 13 Salt Lake City	Women and the Priesthood among Topics at LDS General Conference	http://tinyurl.com/kcmj4fz	0
10/6/2013	Brittany Tait	KUTV.com	Group of LDS Women Looking for Equality through Ordaining Women	http://tinyurl.com/lcrspfe	0
10/7/2013	Joanna Brooks	Religion Dispatches	"Equality Is Not a Feeling"	http://tinyurl.com/mmregjm	1
10/7/2013	Michael Allen	Opposing Views	Mormon Officials Block Female Members from All-Male Conference	http://tinyurl.com/ljkxk7n	0
10/7/2013	Katie McDonough	Salon.com	Mormon Women Line Up to Protest Exclusion of Women from Priesthood	http://tinyurl.com/qagtyhl	0
10/7/2013	Bennett Rieser	WebProNews	Mormon Women Protest All-Male Priesthood	http://tinyurl.com/lcrspfe	5
10/7/2013	Kirsten Johnson	Dame Magazine	Mormon Women's Bid to Enter All-Male Priesthood Meeting Rejected	http://tinyurl.com/jwef5qv	0
10/7/2013	Chris Henrichsen	Patheos	Not Selma, But Significant: Brief Reflections on Saturday and Ordain Women	http://tinyurl.com/kvsap8k	0
10/7/2013	Dan Bammes	KUER 90.1	Ordain Women Group Turned Away from LDS Priesthood Conference	http://tinyurl.com/k9r6ra3	0
10/7/2013	David Edwards	Raw Story	Mormon Officials Turn Away 150 Female Members from All-Male Conference	http://tinyurl.com/me2sfo5	1
10/8/2013	Aaron Clark	Daily Chronicle	"Sexism" Claims Unjustified	http://tinyurl.com/mou2f4d	0
10/8/2013	Michael Lipka	Fact Tank Pew Research Center	Big Majority of Mormons (Including Women) Oppose Women in Priesthood	http://tinyurl.com/pnzq4b7	0
10/8/2013	Nafisa Masud	Daily Utah Chronicle	Gender Roles Create Rift	http://tinyurl.com/keahx4d	0
10/8/2013	Lauren Lane	Patheos	Mormon Women Turned Away from All-Male Conference on Priesthood	http://bit.ly/1dtJELk	0
10/8/2013	Shannon Barber	Addicting Info	Sexist Pigs: Mormon Men Ban Mormon Women from Religious Conference	http://bit.ly/1PITtWR	2

Date	Author	Publication	Title	URL	Count
10/9/2013	Caryn Riswold	Patheos	"… and I Would Like to Listen"	http://bit.ly/1AuwIyI	0
10/9/2013	Justin Higginbottom	Al Jazeera America	Mormon Women March for Entry into Priesthood	http://alj.am/1KiAJGV	0
10/10/2013	Peggy Fletcher Stack	Salt Lake Tribune	Mormon Apostle Edits His Sermon, Removes Reference to "Feminist Thinkers"	http://bit.ly/1JRJxW8	0
10/10/2013	Tresa Edmunds	The Guardian	Mormon Women Are No Longer Afraid to Challenge Inequality	http://bit.ly/1EtMHZ9	2
10/11/2013	Peggy Fletcher Stack	Salt Lake Tribune	How Mormon Women Might Have Gotten into Priesthood Meetings	http://bit.ly/1J0I6E9	0
10/11/2013	Carrie Kohler	Ecumenical News.com	Lack of Female Ordination Is an Issue for Some Mormon Women	http://bit.ly/1LDdZT5	0
10/14/2013	Melissa Inouye	Patheos	Beyond Family: Women's Leadership in the LDS Church	http://bit.ly/1J0Ia6Q	0
10/14/2013	Melissa Inouye	Patheos	Multiplying Talents: Mormon Women in Global Church Leadership	http://bit.ly/1HHmJpG	0
10/16/2013	D.P. Sorensen	Salt Lake City Weekly	Power Failure	http://bit.ly/1HGIUiL	0
10/23/2013	Ralph Hancock	First Things	Progressivism among the Mormons	http://bit.ly/1Q7qgjl	0
10/24/2013	Peggy Fletcher Stack	Salt Lake Tribune	Pants Worn by LDS Women Stitched into Quilt	http://bit.ly/1HGIVmB	0
10/24/2013	Margaret Blair Young	Patheos	That "Third" Conversation? Never, No Never!	http://bit.ly/1Aq95rA	0
10/30/2013	Robert Kirby	Salt Lake Tribune	Mormon Women Would Gain Rights with Me as Relief Society President	http://bit.ly/1Bmiaws	0
11/4/2013	Christine Broussard	Daily Sentinel	Local LDS Member Joins Movement, Challenges Gender Roles in Church	http://bit.ly/1LzSf9V	0
11/5/2013	Unidentified	Daily Herald	LDS Men Encouraged to Attend Priesthood Session	http://bit.ly/1cX0KAv	1
11/19/2013	Peggy Fletcher Stack	Salt Lake Tribune	Mormon Women Plan Sequels — Pants and Priesthood Part II	http://bit.ly/1Gz4wfl	1
11/21/2013	Robert Kirby	Salt Lake Tribune	Granting Women Mormon Priesthood up to God	http://bit.ly/1RiBYK8	0
11/22/2013	Unidentified	Salt Lake Tribune	Leaders Say Mormons Cannot Condone Same-Sex Marriage	http://bit.ly/1Fc2yNu	0
11/29/2013	Unidentified	Standard-Examiner	LDS Church to Hold General Women's Meetings Twice a Year	http://bit.ly/1KvWgzc	0
11/29/2013	Brady McCombs	Associated Press	Mormon Women Asked to Wear Pants to Church	http://bit.ly/1FA8Tow	43
12/12/2013	Ben Winslow	Fox 13 Salt Lake City	Another Push for Mormon Women to Wear Pants to Church	http://bit.ly/1JRLphH	0
12/14/2013	Natalie Seid	Boise Weekly	LDS Women Suit Up for Second "Wear Pants to Church Day"	http://bit.ly/1Gz4Bjf	0
12/16/2013	Jennifer Dobner	Reuters	Mormon Feminists Don Pants to Promote Church Equality	http://reut.rs/1Fc2Dkg	8
12/17/2013	Michelle A. Gonzalez	Sojourner	Breaking the Habits of Machismo	http://bit.ly/1dtgZlo	0

Bibliography of Media Stories 407

Date	Author	Publication	Title	URL	Count
12/17/2013	Michael Gryboski	Christian Post	Mormon Women Observe "Wear Pants to Church" Sunday to Promote Equality	http://bit.ly/1eqTEFx	3
12/22/2013	Genelle Pugmire	Daily Herald	TOP 10 STORIES OF 2013	http://bit.ly/1FRD3Xn	0
12/29/2013	Carole Mikita	KSL	Religion Story Highlights from 2013	http://bit.ly/1Szj9En	0
12/31/2013	Jennifer Napier-Pearce	Salt Lake Tribune	Trib Talk: The Top Stories of 2013	http://bit.ly/1dtKRCw	0
1/3/2014	David Noyce	Salt Lake Tribune	Pope Francis to Mormon Women — Utah's Top 2013 Faith Stories	http://bit.ly/1FA9cQe	0
1/8/2014	Peggy Fletcher Stack	Salt Lake Tribune	Like Mormon Pants Day, Muslim Women Plan World Hijab Day	http://bit.ly/1fdLQ91	0
2/5/2014	Unidentified	US News - NewsCastic	Founder of Ordain Women Excommunicated from Mormon Church	http://bit.ly/1JRM1E1	0
2/7/2014	Marianne Mansfield	The Independent	OPINION: Kate Kelly Is Just Getting Started	http://bit.ly/1Aqam1G	0
3/1/2014	Tom Harvey	Salt Lake Tribune	Panelist: Internet Has Revolutionized Mormon Feminism	http://bit.ly/1HGKWiM	0
3/1/2014	Jodi Kantor	New York Times	A Growing Role for Mormon Women	http://nyti.ms/1cX0XUi	8
3/6/2014	Mark Green	Fox 13 Salt Lake City	Mormon Women Plan to Request Tickets to Historically Male-Only Meeting	http://bit.ly/1FRDGAm	0
3/6/2014	Matthew Piper	Salt Lake Tribune	Mormon Women to Try Again to Get into Priesthood Meeting	http://bit.ly/1LzV1vL	0
3/7/2014	Sigal Samuel	BuzzFeed	Feminism in Faith: Four Women Who Are Revolutionizing Religion	http://bzfd.it/1hggTff	0
3/7/2014	Jodi Kantor	CBS News	More Mormon Women Questioning Traditional Church Roles	http://cbsn.ws/1J0KUkA	0
3/7/2014	Kelly Faircloth	Jezebel	Mormon Women Want Some Changes Made around Here	http://bit.ly/1FRDO2X	0
3/8/2014	Ophelia Benson	Freethought Blogs	Pieces of Chewed Gum	http://bit.ly/1SzjgzJ	0
3/9/2014	Unidentified	KUTV.com	Women Ask LDS Church Again to Attend Priesthood Session	http://bit.ly/MZJMnT	0
3/10/2014	Carly Figueroa	Fox 13 Salt Lake City	Most LDS Church Members Oppose Ordination of Women, Study Shows	http://bit.ly/1RiCHv7	0
3/10/2014	Holly Welker	Religion Dispatches	Loyal and Not So Loyal LDS Dissent	http://bit.ly/1Fc31zc	0
3/13/2014	Maurine Proctor	Meridian Magazine	Airtime or Error Time? The New York Times and the Ordination of Women	http://bit.ly/1EtOJZ7	0
3/13/2014	Brady McCombs	Deseret News (AP)	Gender Equality among Issues at Mormon Conference	http://bit.ly/1Fc3ce6	0
3/13/2014	Kari Kenner	Daily Herald (AP)	The New York Times, Mormon Women, and Doug Fabrizio	http://bit.ly/PtBsil	0
3/16/2014	Holly Welker	Religion Dispatches	Ordain Women Transforms Mormon Feminism	http://bit.ly/1cX17uM	0
3/17/2014	Brady McCombs	Associated Press	Mormon Church Tells Women's Group Not to Protest	http://bit.ly/1PfVz97	98

Date	Author	Source	Title	URL	Count
3/17/2014	Arturo Garcia	Raw Story	Mormon Group Calling for Female Priests Barred from Appearing at Gathering	http://bit.ly/1IWshQr	0
3/17/2014	Taylor Winget	The Digital Universe	Church Responds to Ordain Women Activist Group	http://bit.ly/1cX181U	0
3/17/2014	Unidentified	KUTV.com	LDS Church Denies Ordain Women Tickets to Priesthood Session	http://bit.ly/1KiDnMG	0
3/17/2014	Tad Walch	Deseret News	LDS Church: Aims of "Ordain Women" Detract from Dialogue	http://bit.ly/1J0Lz5x	2
3/17/2014	Dan Bammes	KUER 90.1	Ordain Women Group Again Asking LDS Church to Open Doors	http://bit.ly/1JRMAh9	0
3/18/2014	Jennifer Dobner	Reuters	Mormon Church Bars Women's Group from Leadership Conference	http://reut.rs/1Bmj0cBs	28
3/18/2014	Unidentified	Rock 106.5	LDS Church Asks Feminist Protesters to Show Restraint	http://bit.ly/1cX1bLb	1
3/18/2014	Unidentified	KUTV.com	LDS Church Denies	http://bit.ly/1cX1be8	0
3/18/2014	Holly Welker	Religion Dispatches	LDS Church "Non-Negotiable" on Women's Ordination	http://bit.ly/1EtP0LE	0
3/18/2014	Unidentified	Associated Press	Despite Ban, Mormon Women to March into Temple Square and Demand Entry	http://bit.ly/1IWskM1	0
3/18/2014	Unidentified	Fox News	Mormon Church Bans Women from Clergy and All Male Meeting	http://bit.ly/1FREp4o	2
3/18/2014	Antonia Blumberg	The Huffington Post	Ordain Women, Mormon Women's Advocacy Group, Denied Access	http://huff.to/1FA9wOM	0
3/18/2014	Lauren Markoe	Religion News Service	Presto Universe * Mormon Women *	http://bit.ly/1Szjp6a	0
3/19/2014	Peggy Fletcher Stack	Salt Lake Tribune	A First: Photos of Mormon Women Leaders Go Up in Conference Center	http://bit.ly/1j76bu0	0
3/19/2014	jupiterschild	Patheos	The Problem of Gendered Voice Memo to Leaders of Ordain Women	http://bit.ly/1Ht9JBs	0
3/20/2014	Bobby Ross Jr.	Patheos	Do Mormon Women Lack Standing in Their Own Faith?	http://bit.ly/1FMz9xg	0
3/20/2014	Brady McCombs	Associated Press	Leaders Vow to Continue Pushing for Equality Anyway	http://bit.ly/1cX1e9P	0
3/20/2014	Jennifer Napier-Pearce	Salt Lake Tribune	Trib Talk: Mormon Women and the Priesthood	http://bit.ly/1eqUrGk	0
3/21/2014	Taylor Petrey	Patheos	Ordaining Women Is Not Going Away for LDS	http://bit.ly/1Cb2n7k	0
3/21/2014	Lisa Carricaburu	Salt Lake Tribune	Journalists Ask LDS Church to Reconsider Banning Photographers	http://bit.ly/1LzVKx4	0
3/21/2014	Haley Tharp	The Digital Universe	First General Women's Meeting on Saturday	http://bit.ly/1Fc3mCe	0
3/21/2014	Peggy Fletcher Stack	Salt Lake Tribune	Purple Reigns: Ordain Women to Wear That Color to Women's Meeting	http://bit.ly/1gjAVdA	0

Bibliography of Media Stories 409

Date	Author	Source	Title	URL	
3/21/2014	Jennifer Napier-Pearce	Salt Lake Tribune	Ski Interconnect Is Launched, Mormon Women's Group Rebuffed	http://bit.ly/1Bmi08l	0
3/22/2014	Unidentified	Women's eNews	Ohioans Protest Rape Law; Egyptian Victim Blamed	http://bit.ly/1Gz3m3v	0
3/23/2014	Anne McMullin Peffer	Salt Lake Tribune	Op-ed: LDS Church Letter to Ordain Women Meant to Intimidate	http://bit.ly/1Bmi08l	0
3/23/2014	Maurine Proctor	Meridian Magazine	Ordain, or Else?	http://bit.ly/1BmhQgZ	0
3/24/2014	Damon Linker	The Week Magazine	Why Churches Should Brace for a Mass Exodus of the Faithful	http://bit.ly/1gm0utC	0
3/24/2014	Melissa Inouye	Patheos	No More Strangers	http://bit.ly/1m6nux6	0
3/24/2014	Dan Bammes	KUER 90.1	Ordain Women Supporters Plan to Wear Purple at LDS Women's Meeting	http://bit.ly/1F70N3a	0
3/26/2014	Dan Peterson	Patheos	"These Are Our Sisters"	http://bit.ly/1Fc12em	0
3/26/2014	Robert Kirby	Salt Lake Tribune	When Afterlife Is Anything But Celestial	http://bit.ly/1RizZ8J	0
3/27/2014	Tad Walch	Patheos	Activist Group "Detracts" from Dialogue, LDS Church Says	http://bit.ly/1Ht66M0	0
3/27/2014	Peggy Fletcher Stack	Salt Lake Tribune	Mormon Women Seeking Priesthood May Be Blocked from Temple Square	http://bit.ly/1mdY4R0	9
3/27/2014	Debbie Mays	Herald Journal	Protesting the Protest: Local Woman Questions Ordain Women Actions	http://bit.ly/1AuwFDb	0
3/28/2014	Don Bammes	KUER 90.1	LDS Women's Meeting Will Include a Quiet Statement from Ordain Women	http://bit.ly/1KvUFZY	0
3/28/2014	Mark Gray	Davis County Clipper (AP)	The Marriage Wars: Diverse Views on Ordain Women Movement	http://bit.ly/1J0L1wA	0
3/29/2014	Unidentified	KUTV.com	LDS Women Gather in SLC for Historic Meeting	http://bit.ly/1BmiOKe	0
3/30/2014	Unidentified	Daily Journal	Mormon General Women's Meeting Brings Together Female Members	http://bit.ly/1Fc32U0	0
3/30/2014	Unidentified	Associated Press	Mormons Gather for Historic Women's Meeting	http://bit.ly/1Q7sb7q	78
3/31/2014	Peggy Fletcher Stack	Salt Lake Tribune	Mormons Again Say No to News Cameras on Temple Square	http://bit.ly/1h4nw3K	0
3/31/2014	Peggy Fletcher Stack	Salt Lake Tribune	"Most Glorious Sisterhood" of Mormons Gather in Historic Meeting	http://bit.ly/1PIVouD	0
4/1/2014	Gina Colvin	Patheos	I'll Be at the Ordain Women "Event", But . . .	http://bit.ly/1PIVq5x	0
4/2/2014	Holly Welker	Religion Dispatches	No Need For Satire When There are Quotes Like This	http://bit.ly/1FMz906	0
4/3/2014	Unidentified	Daily Herald (AP)	Herald Poll: Women at the LDS Priesthood Meeting	http://bit.ly/1HGKOQq	1
4/3/2014	Tad Walch	Deseret News	New LDS Women's Group Quickly Gains Steam on Facebook	http://bit.ly/1HHnJtV	0

Date	Author	Publication	Title	URL	Count
4/3/2014	Stephanie Lauritzen	*Salt Lake City Weekly*	Ask Not	http://bit.ly/1FMz90a	0
4/4/2014	Daniel Gross	The Toast	"Like Wearing Pants to Church": Mormon Feminists Testing the Waters	http://bit.ly/1KvWZ37	0
4/4/2014	Editorial	*Salt Lake Tribune*	Editorial: Ban on Reporters Only Hurts LDS Church	http://bit.ly/1cf6ghb	0
4/4/2014	Paul Rolly	*Salt Lake Tribune*	Beware, Salt Lake City Parking Cops Don't Give an Inch	http://bit.ly/1FMz9x3	0
4/4/2014	Dan Bammes	KUER 90.1	Reporters Excluded from Temple Square	http://bit.ly/1FMzbVI	0
4/4/2014	Unidentified	KUTV.com	Group of Mormon Women Seeking Priesthood Doubles in Size for Protest	http://bit.ly/1dtLfku	0
4/4/2014	Peggy Fletcher Stack	*Salt Lake Tribune*	Temple Square Now Off-Limits to Reporters during Mormon Conference	http://bit.ly/1Auyf7Z	0
4/4/2014	Unidentified	News 88.9 KNPR	"Ordain Women" Demonstrates in Temple Square	http://bit.ly/1J0LcYS	0
4/5/2014	Brady McCombs	*Daily Herald* (AP)	Mormon Leader Outlines Opposition to Gay Marriage	http://bit.ly/1Fc3a5T	133
4/5/2014	Mark Saal	*Standard-Examiner*	Just My Ticket: Banned from Temple Square	http://bit.ly/1EtOPAe	0
4/5/2014	Brady McCombs	*Daily Herald* (AP)	Women's Group Demonstrates at LDS Priesthood Meeting	http://bit.ly/1RiCS9u	65
4/5/2014	Whitney Evans	KSL.com	Women Seeking Priesthood March Again to Temple Square	http://bit.ly/1eqTT3p	1
4/5/2014	Natasha Helfer Parker	Patheos	General Conf. – a Mental Health Perspective	http://bit.ly/1Fc2IED	0
4/5/2014	Mark Green	Fox 13 Salt Lake City	LDS Church: Actions of Those Who Demonstrated "Disappointing"	http://bit.ly/1KvWrKI	0
4/5/2014	Mark Green	Fox 13 Salt Lake City	Hundreds Advocate for Changes to LDS Church Policies Regarding Women	http://bit.ly/1EtOihy	0
4/5/2014	Kelly Cannon	*Herald Journal*	Cache Residents among "Ordain Women" Marchers	http://bit.ly/1cX0W2D	0
4/5/2014	Kristen Moulton	*Salt Lake Tribune*	Mormon Women Again Turned Away from Priesthood Meeting	http://bit.ly/1sK6YWN	1
4/5/2014	Peggy Fletcher Stack	*Salt Lake Tribune*	Mormon Women Have Authority, Apostle Oaks Declares	http://bit.ly/1HHnFdR	0
4/5/2014	Kristen Moulton	*Salt Lake Tribune*	Mormon Women Poised to March to Temple Square	http://bit.ly/1sK6YWN	0
4/5/2014	Unidentified	*Standard-Examiner*	Ordain Women Group Rebuffed at Mormon Priesthood Meeting	http://bit.ly/1AuxY57	0
4/5/2014	Dan Bammes	KUER 90.1	Ordain Women Turned Away Again from LDS Priesthood Conference	http://bit.ly/1eqTQEy	0
4/6/2014	Bill Waters	NewsOXY	Mormon Women: Church Faces Obstacles in Equality	http://bit.ly/1cf681c	0
4/6/2014	Unidentified	The Inquisitr News	Mormon Women Are Revolting (Against Their Treatment by Mormon Men)	http://bit.ly/1RiCgki	0

Date	Author	Outlet	Title	URL	Shares
4/6/2014	Anugrah Kumar	Christian Post	Mormon Women Seeking Priesthood Demonstrate at Temple Square	http://bit.ly/1F72luf	0
4/6/2014	Jennifer Dobner	Reuters	Mormon Women, Seeking Wider Role, Denied Entrance to All-Male Meeting	http://reut.rs/1J0JW7V	88
4/7/2014	Holly Welker	Religion Dispatches	LDS Church Says Hugs and Heart-felt Conversations "Divisive"	http://bit.ly/1iqB8aK	0
4/7/2014	Oulimata Ba	Headlines & Global News	Hundreds of Mormon Women Banned from Attending All-Male Gathering	http://bit.ly/1F71idL	0
4/7/2014	Unidentified	Al Jazeera America	Women, Atheists Protest Mormon Church Conference	http://alj.am/1fYBPuE	0
4/7/2014	Dan Peterson	Patheos	A New Group for LDS Women	http://tinyurl.com/ot8oysc	0
4/7/2014	Benito Baeza	News Radio 1310 KLIX	Mormon Women's Group Allowed to Protest at Temple Square	http://bit.ly/1KiBkZ2	0
4/7/2014	Brady McCombs	Associated Press	Mormon Women: Reverent, Respectful, and Seeking a Bigger Role	http://bit.ly/1Bmijjm	2
4/8/2014	AJAM Stream	Storify	Women, Atheists Protest Mormon Church Conference	http://bit.ly/1Fc1FET	0
4/8/2014	Christine Broussard	Daily Sentinel	Group Seeks Gender Equality in Church	http://bit.ly/1Ht7j5Q	0
4/8/2014	Eric S. Peterson	Salt Lake City Weekly	Alternate Realities Roundup 4/8	http://bit.ly/1RiAM9M	0
4/11/2014	Natalie Dicou	The Atlantic	What Mormon Women Want	http://theatln.tc/1F71gSX	2
4/15/2014	Meg Sanders	Standard-Examiner	Change Religion If You Don't Like Its Tenets	http://bit.ly/1SziSkA	0
4/16/2014	Morgan Lee	Christian Post	LDS Church Lawyers Unhappy with "Mormon Match" Online Dating Site	http://bit.ly/1Ht7f6h	0
4/24/2014	Peggy Fletcher Stack	Salt Lake Tribune	Mormon Women Seeking Priesthood May Be Blocked from Temple Square	http://bit.ly/1J0IMte	0
4/25/2014	Matthew Piper	Salt Lake Tribune	Mormon Women to Try Again to Get into Priesthood Meeting	http://bit.ly/1HHmY4a	0
4/29/2014	Holly Welker	Religion Dispatches	Ordaining Mormon Women Would End Joyful Diversity	http://bit.ly/1FMz5NO	0
5/7/2014	Stephanie Lauritzen	Salt Lake City Weekly	You're Right, I'm Wrong	http://bit.ly/1cf5CQF	0
5/14/2014	Peggy Fletcher Stack	Salt Lake Tribune	Scholars Pushing for New Research on Mormon Gender Issues	http://bit.ly/1Auxhsq	0
5/19/2014	John Halstead	Patheos	Finding the Pagan Goddess in a Mormon Temple	http://bit.ly/1SziUcg	0
5/27/2014	Dan Bammes	KUER 90.1	Group Hoping "Discussions" Move LDS Church Toward Ordaining Women	http://bit.ly/1PIUaiU	0
5/27/2014	Peggy Fletcher Stack	Salt Lake Tribune	Ordain Women Launches New Effort in Push for Mormon Priesthood	http://bit.ly/1myDLMF	2
5/29/2014	Gavin Sheehan	Salt Lake City Weekly	Beehive Bugle	http://bit.ly/1FMz5NU	0
5/29/2014	Tad Walch	Deseret News	LDS Spokesman Sends Open Letter about Mormon Women	http://bit.ly/1Auxk7u	4

Date	Author	Publication	Title	URL	Count
5/30/2014	Peggy Fletcher Stack	Salt Lake Tribune	Mormon P.R. Point Man answers Critics in Debate about Women	http://bit.ly/Sj9I0s	0
5/30/2014	Genelle Pugmire	Daily Herald (AP)	LDS Church Spokesman Responds to Women's Rights Groups	http://bit.ly/1AuxnjT	0
5/30/2014	Dan Bammes	KUER 90.1	LDS Public Affairs Chief Says Church Is Listening to Women	http://bit.ly/1FA8xhq	0
5/30/2014	Peggy Fletcher Stack	Salt Lake Tribune	Ordain Women to Mormon P.R. Boss: Thanks for Writing	http://bit.ly/1tv7qHj	0
5/30/2014	Unidentified	Associated Press	Women's Group Shifts Strategy	http://bit.ly/1Ht7UEw	9
6/1/2014	Unidentified	Meridian Magazine	LDS Spokesman Responds to Online Criticisms about Women in the Church	http://tinyurl.com/ky29d3u	0
6/11/2014	Tom Harvey	Salt Lake Tribune	Panelist: Internet Has Revolutionized Mormon Feminism	http://tinyurl.com/lrel7z2	0
6/11/2014	Peggy Fletcher Stack	Salt Lake Tribune	Founder of Mormon Women's Group Threatened with Excommunication	http://tinyurl.com/lanuyk5	3
6/12/2014	Genelle Pugmire	Daily Herald (AP)	History Repeats Itself as LDS Activists Go Public	http://tinyurl.com/n46qjze	0
6/12/2014	Peggy Fletcher Stack	Salt Lake Tribune	Where Mormonism's "September Six" Are Now	http://tinyurl.com/kyjvvnh	0
6/12/2014	Jennifer Napier-Pearce	Salt Lake Tribune	Trib Talk: Censure for Ordain Women Leader, Mormon Blogger?	http://tinyurl.com/mdrq7fx	0
6/12/2014	Jennifer Napier-Pearce	Salt Lake Tribune	Trib Talk: Excommunication for Ordain Women Founder, Mormon Blogger?	http://tinyurl.com/kqdnvaj	0
6/13/2014	Robert Kirby	Salt Lake Tribune	What If Mormon Church Excommunication Fails to Have Desired Effect?	http://tinyurl.com/l5aayuy	0
6/13/2014	Robert Kirby	Salt Lake Tribune	Excommunicated from Mormon Church? Who, Me?	http://bit.ly/1dtIYpp	0
6/13/2014	Robert Kirby	Salt Lake Tribune	If I Were Excommunicated from Mormon Church	http://bit.ly/1HGHAMl	0
6/13/2014	Matt Jensen	UPR	Mormon Facing Excommunication Speaks Out	http://bit.ly/1FA7uy4	0
6/13/2014	Emily Shire	The Daily Beast	Excommunication with a Smile: Mormon Activists Face Kangaroo Courts	http://thebea.st/1p2N1KR	0
6/14/2014	Unidentified	Honolulu Star-Advertiser	Missives to Critics Assert Boundaries	http://bit.ly/1LDdjgj	0
6/15/2014	Dan Peterson	Patheos	"Changing the Church: How Ordain Women Gets It Wrong"	http://bit.ly/1J0HlLb	0
6/16/2014	Kate Kelly	The Guardian	I Was Excommunicated from My Church for Asking for Equal Rights	http://bit.ly/1lKJ9wz	8
6/17/2014	Peggy Fletcher Stack	Salt Lake Tribune	This Week's Vocabulary Word: "Excommunication"...	http://bit.ly/1FA7xdj	0
6/17/2014	Unidentified	Deseret News	LDS Spokeswoman Discusses Church Discipline with Radio Host	http://bit.ly/1Gz2UlH	1
6/18/2014	Dan Peterson	Patheos	Punished for Just Doubting? Questioning? Trying to Help?	http://bit.ly/1EtM3uK	0

Bibliography of Media Stories 413

6/19/2014	Kristen Moulton	Salt Lake Tribune	Conservative Mormons, Like Progressives, in Church Cross Hairs	http://bit.ly/1cWZRb9	0
6/20/2014	Terry Tempest Williams	Salt Lake Tribune	Op-ed: Women in Priesthood an Act of Self-respect, Not Apostasy	http://bit.ly/1l3zxZn	0
6/20/2014	Genelle Pugmire	Daily Herald (AP)	LDS Church: OK to Question, It's How	http://bit.ly/1KiA8F5	0
6/20/2014	Ashley I. Woolley	Deseret News	Ordain Women Is Not the Answer on Mormon Women's Equality	http://bit.ly/1EtMbu4	1
6/20/2014	Robert Kirby	Salt Lake Tribune	Why Mormons Should Allow Female Bishops	http://bit.ly/1dtJfbQ	0
6/21/2014	Peggy Fletcher Stack	Salt Lake Tribune	The New Debate: What (Mormon) Women Want	http://bit.ly/1PIT7PQ	0
6/21/2014	Kristen Moulton	Salt Lake Tribune	Kelly to Mormon Leaders: Don't Punish Me	http://bit.ly/1Fc0KUN	0
6/22/2014	Unidentified	Associated Press	Mormon Church Excommunicates Founder of Women's Group	http://fxn.ws/1SziAuc	711
6/22/2014	Unidentified	Associated Press	Mormon Woman Awaits Decision on Excommunication	http://bit.ly/1IWqudZ	915
6/22/2014	Kristen Moulton	Salt Lake Tribune	Kelly Awaits Verdict, Tells 250 Mormons at Vigil: "I Feel a Lot of Hope"	http://bit.ly/1F70EN6	0
6/22/2014	Wesley Robinson	Washington Post	LDS Disciplinary Council in Virginia Considers Case of Women's Activist	http://wapo.st/1KvUo9n	0
6/22/2014	Stephanie K. Baer	Chicago Tribune	Chicago Area Mormons Hold Vigil during Apostasy Hearings	http://trib.in/1J0HAG9	1
6/22/2014	Scott Neuman	NPR	Mormon Church Excommunicates Advocate for Female Priests	http://bit.ly/1BmhAie	26
6/22/2014	Whitney Evans	Deseret News	Decision Pending for Activist in Conflict with LDS Church	http://bit.ly/1Q7pToO	2
6/22/2014	Eric S. Peterson	Salt Lake City Weekly	Group Worries Leader's Excommunication Will Divide LDS Women	http://bit.ly/1cf50dY	0
6/22/2014	Dan Bammes	KUER 90.1	Hundreds Support Ordain Women Founder at Vigil	http://bit.ly/1LzRxcD	6
6/23/2014	Tracy Connor	NBC News	Mormon Women's Group Founder Kate Kelly Excommunicated	http://nbcnews.to/1sAYo0v	0
6/23/2014	Jennifer Napier-Pearce	Salt Lake Tribune	Trib Talk: The Line between Mormon Discourse and Apostasy	http://bit.ly/1KiArjg	0
6/23/2014	Jeffrey Meyer	News Busters	ABC Continues to Cheerlead for Mormon Activist	http://bit.ly/1BmhNlp	1
6/23/2014	Terry Gildea	KUER 90.1	Kelly Excommunicated from LDS Church	http://bit.ly/1Q7q1ok	0
6/23/2014	Mara Schiavocampo	ABCNews.com	Why a Woman was Excommunicated by the Mormon Church	http://abcn.ws/1nYSL76	0
6/23/2014	Genelle Pugmire	Daily Herald	Ordain Women Founder to Appeal Excommunication	http://bit.ly/1KiBKyC	3
6/23/2014	Charlotte Alter	Time Magazine	Activist Who Pushed Mormon Church to Ordain Women Excommunicated	http://ti.me/1AuxpIr	0

Date	Author	Outlet	Title	URL	
6/23/2014	Dan Bammes	KUER 90.1	In Trial, Movement to Ordain Mormon Women Approaches Defining Moment	http://bit.ly/1Ht83rA	20
6/23/2014	Kristen Moulton	Salt Lake Tribune	Kelly Excommunicated	http://bit.ly/1nC6f5D	1
6/23/2014	Dan Bammes	KUER 90.1	Kelly Says Ordain Women Movement Will Continue	http://bit.ly/1IWrleR	0
6/23/2014	Rod Dreher	The American Conservative	On That Mormon Excommunication	http://bit.ly/1KvVMsT	0
6/23/2014	Dan Bammes	KUER 90.1	Ordain Women Founder Says Movement Will Continue after Excommunication	http://bit.ly/1nC4aa3	1
6/23/2014	Unidentified	Deseret News	Ordain Women Releases Bishop's Letter Giving Reasons for Excommunication	http://bit.ly/1J0JlTU	1
6/23/2014	Brady McCombs	Daily Herald (AP)	Supporters of Mormon Woman Facing Excommunication Hold Vigil	http://bit.ly/1Aq9x93	53
6/23/2014	Unidentified	Salt Lake Tribune	What Excommunication Means to a Mormon	http://bit.ly/1RiBunm	0
6/24/2014	Whitney Evans	KSL.com	Excommunicated Mormon Activist Says She Has No Plans to Change	http://bit.ly/1HGK0ep	1
6/24/2014	Jessica Ravitz	CNN	Mormon Who Advocated Ordination of Women Excommunicated	http://cnn.it/1ruzbAq	7
6/24/2014	Steven L. Taylor	Outside The Beltway	No Female Priests for You (Mormon Edition)	http://bit.ly/1Ht8rq4	0
6/24/2014	Meredith Somers	Washington Times	Mormons Excommunicate Woman for Advocating Female Clergy	http://bit.ly/1dtKBTS	0
6/24/2014	Tracy Connor	NBCNEWS.com	Mormon Women's Group Founder Kate Kelly Excommunicated	http://nbcnews.to/1sAYo0v	0
6/24/2014	Katie Halper	Feministing	Mormon Church Excommunicates Woman for Calling Church Sexist	http://bit.ly/1J0JHtq	0
6/24/2014	Billy Hallowell	The Blaze	Critics and Supporters Respond to Excommunication of Group Leader	http://bit.ly/1Q7rmvq	0
6/24/2014	Peggy Fletcher Stack	Salt Lake Tribune	Kelly: Mormon Feminists "Galvanized" by LDS Action	http://bit.ly/1lO7ZvA	0
6/24/2014	Genelle Pugmire	Daily Herald (AP)	Supporters Mourn Kate Kelly's Excommunication	http://bit.ly/1dtKCHq	0
6/24/2014	Jennifer Napier-Pearce	Salt Lake Tribune	Trib Talk: Fallout from Kate Kelly's Excommunication	http://bit.ly/1yJN6aR	0
6/25/2014	Randal Maurice Jelks	CNN Belief Blog	Hey Religion, Your Misogyny Is Showing	http://cnn.it/1qwfA30	0
6/25/2014	Mary Emily O'Hara	VICE News	Meet Kate Kelly, the Mormon Feminist Who Was Excommunicated	http://bit.ly/1qwl8uj	0
6/25/2014	Kristine Haglund	Religion & Politics	Banishing Dissent: The Excommunication of Mormon Activist Kate Kelly	http://bit.ly/1Szj6sa	0
6/25/2014	Unidentified	CNN Belief Blog	Mormon Feminist: I'll Fight Excommunication	http://cnn.it/1Szj57r	0
6/26/2014	Jennifer Dobner	Reuters	Feminist Kelly to Appeal Excommunication from Mormon Church	http://bit.ly/1KvW82B	16

Date	Author	Publication	Title	Link	
6/26/2014	Danny Barrett Jr.	*Vicksburg Post*	Pivot Point Possible for Female Clergy	http://bit.ly/1cX0Jwy	0
6/26/2014	Emmilie Whitlock	*Standard Journal*	Ordain Women: A Call for Compassion	http://bit.ly/1EtN1qE	0
6/27/2014	Michel Martin	National Public Radio	Excommunicated Mormon Says Church Can't Take Away Her Faith	http://n.pr/1LDefRN	0
6/27/2014	Unidentified	*Salt Lake Tribune*	Harry Reid Declines Comment on Kelly Excommunication	http://bit.ly/1Ht6ZUO	0
6/27/2014	Dan Peterson	Patheos	"Faith, Community, Excommunication, and Kate Kelly"	http://bit.ly/1HHmNG6	0
6/27/2014	Robert Kirby	*Salt Lake Tribune*	Mormon Women Leaders Rarely Excommunicated in Early Church	http://bit.ly/1dtK30z	0
6/27/2014	Anne Mcmullin Peffer	*Salt Lake Tribune*	Op-ed: For Kate Kelly, It's Never Been about Gaining a Following	http://bit.ly/1Q7qxmc	0
6/28/2014	Peggy Fletcher Stack	*Salt Lake Tribune*	Top Mormon Leaders Repeat "Only Men" Qualify for Priesthood	http://bit.ly/1KvV8eJ	0
6/28/2014	Tad Walch	*Deseret News*	Priesthood Blessings Equally Available to All, LDS Leaders Say in Statement	http://bit.ly/1J0Ipi8	1
6/28/2014	Michael Muskal	*Los Angeles Times*	Feminism and Mormon Doctrine Collide and Lead to Rare Excommunication	http://lat.ms/1eqSwlf	1
6/28/2014	Mark Green	Fox 13 Salt Lake City	LDS Church Issues Statement in Wake of Excommunication of Kate Kelly	http://bit.ly/1KvV1Qy	3
6/29/2014	Unidentified	*Daily Herald*	LDS Church First Presidency Issues Statement on Priesthood and Apostasy	http://bit.ly/1AuwUxW	0
6/29/2014	Dan Peterson	Patheos	Three Reflections, More or Less on the Kate Kelly Controversy	http://bit.ly/1PITFFv	0
6/30/2014	Unidentified	*Daily Herald* (AP)	LDS Church Issues Statement on Priesthood and Apostasy	http://bit.ly/1AuwUxW	0
6/30/2014	Dan Bammes	KUER 90.1	LDS Statement Reserves Priesthood Ordination to Men	http://bit.ly/1SziMto	0
6/30/2014	Peggy Fletcher Stack	*Salt Lake Tribune*	Ordain Women Tells Top Mormon Leaders: We Sustain You	http://bit.ly/1JRJOs4	0
7/2/2014	Neil J. Young	*Huffington Post*	Kate Kelly, the LDS Church, and the Problem of Mormon Feminists	http://huff.to/1dtJR1j	0
7/4/2014	Peggy Fletcher Stack	*Salt Lake Tribune*	Fear Runs through Many Mormons in Ordain Women Ranks	http://bit.ly/1j9xh8M	3
7/6/2014	Unidentified	*Elko Daily Free Press*	ANALYSIS: Mormon Church Excommunicates Woman for Feminist Advocacy	http://tinyurl.com/k9l97qz	3
7/8/2014	Caryn Riswold	Patheos	Vocation Enmeshed	http://tinyurl.com/n5beg45	0
7/8/2014	Natasha Helfer Parker	Patheos	Is Gender Inequality Bad for Mental Health?	http://tinyurl.com/kevq3e2	0
7/8/2014	Peggy Fletcher Stack	*Salt Lake Tribune*	After Her Mormon Excommunication, Kate Kelly Hurting but "Joyful"	http://bit.ly/1FMz7Fy	0

Date	Author	Publication	Title	URL	Count
7/9/2014	Michelle Boorstein	Washington Post	Following Kelly Excommunication, Dissenters Push for Disciplinary Hearings	http://tinyurl.com/me7m4ct	0
7/10/2014	R. B. Scott	Cognoscenti - WBUR	An Excommunication, and the Future of the LDS Church	http://tinyurl.com/k2mrgh6	0
7/11/2014	Genelle Pugmire	Daily Herald (AP)	Ordain Women Founder to Appeal Excommunication	http://tinyurl.com/mj3jzgd	1
7/15/2014	Nancy Ross	The Huffington Post	Mormon Feminist Excommunicated, Sparking Rise of Digital Movement	http://tinyurl.com/m8a8ow6	0
7/16/2014	Hemant Mehta	Patheos	What the Fading "Mormon Moment" Means for Other Conservative Religions	http://tinyurl.com/oo2hm6b	0
7/18/2014	Stephanie Pappas	LiveScience	Mormon Church Hasn't Budged on Gender Roles in 40 Years	http://tinyurl.com/nufcn3x	1
7/20/2014	Gina Colvin	Patheos	A Conversation with Kate Kelly: Feminist and Optimist	http://tinyurl.com/ml96wos	0
7/24/2014	Jennifer Dobner	Rueters	Excommunicated Mormon Feminist Appeals Ejection from Faith	http://tinyurl.com/ll8tfvh	25
7/24/2014	Antonia Blumberg	Huffington Post	Group Conducts Mass Resignation from Church to Protest Excommunication	http://tinyurl.com/m88gd74	2
7/24/2014	Nate Carlisle	Salt Lake Tribune	Kate Kelly Appeals Excommunication from Mormon Church	http://tinyurl.com/ksfl6h3	6
7/25/2014	Genelle Pugmire	Daily Herald (AP)	Hundreds, Including Husband, Support Kelly's Appeal	http://tinyurl.com/m2zcoze	0
7/25/2014	Darla Isackson	Meridian Magazine	Apostasy and Divorce: An Unexpected Commonality	http://tinyurl.com/kww64a6	0
7/25/2014	Daniel Reynolds	The Advocate	Mormon Mass Resignation Held in Protest of Feminist's Excommunication	http://tinyurl.com/k2x25c5	1
7/28/2014	Peggy Fletcher Stack	Salt Lake Tribune	Ordain Women, Abuse, Defections & More on Tap for Mormon Symposium	http://tinyurl.com/mcbwvhh	0
8/1/2014	Ashley I. Woolley	Salt Lake Tribune	Op-ed: Ordain Women Distorts Quotes to Make Its Case	http://tinyurl.com/lrtgpvp	0
8/1/2014	Peggy Fletcher Stack	Salt Lake Tribune	Ordain Women Sheds Mormon Missionary-like Moniker	http://tinyurl.com/k7h6sjd	0
8/2/2014	Peggy Fletcher Stack	Salt Lake Tribune	Mormon Feminists Discuss Tone and the Patriarchy	http://tinyurl.com/lphn3z3	2
8/3/2014	Kurt Opprecht	The Daily Beast	Mormon Reformers behind the "Zion Curtain" Refuse to Be Silenced	http://tinyurl.com/q7lxt6h	1
8/5/2014	Peggy Fletcher Stack	Salt Lake Tribune	FAIR Gathering to Focus on Women, Blacks, Gays, Other Mormon Issues	http://tinyurl.com/k5gtgk4	0
8/5/2014	Al Cardwell	Napa Valley Register (AP)	Religion Complicates Gender Equality	http://tinyurl.com/mhl6yrg	0
8/8/2014	Peggy Fletcher Stack	Salt Lake Tribune	LDS Leader: Mormon Tenets Empower Women, But Some Traditions Fall Short	http://tinyurl.com/mks9ed4	0
8/12/2014	Lynette Kalsnes	Chicago Public Radio	Mormon Feminists Find Grounds for Hope, Fear in Changing Church	http://tinyurl.com/mvdllx2	1

Bibliography of Media Stories 417

Date	Author	Publication	Title	URL	
8/13/2014	George McHendry	Broomfield Enterprise	McHendry: Women Slowly Making Inroads as Clergy Members	http://tinyurl.com/kv5v6c5	0
8/13/2014	Unidentified	Storify	Morning Shift: Mormon Feminists Advocate for Change	http://tinyurl.com/k84hvr3	0
8/18/2014	James Hitchcock	Touchstone Magazine	Eyeing the Sanctuary	http://tinyurl.com/kggdz9z	0
8/19/2014	Peggy Fletcher Stack	Salt Lake Tribune	LDS Church Surveying Mormons about Women, Ordination, Apostasy	http://tinyurl.com/kkadelc	0
8/25/2014	Peggy Fletcher Stack	Salt Lake Tribune	Forget Priesthood — Moderate Mormon Feminists Seek a Middle Way	http://tinyurl.com/ko98qrs	6
8/25/2014	Jennifer Napier-Pearce	Salt Lake Tribune	Trib Talk: Moderate Mormon Women Speak Out	http://tinyurl.com/mdkwuaf	0
8/26/2014	Jane Little	BBC News	Push to Ordain Mormon Women Leads to Excommunication	http://tinyurl.com/mbpo897	4
8/28/2014	Jake Highton	Daily Sparks Tribune	Mormons Destroy Adherents Who Ask Questions	http://tinyurl.com/m2hyw7t	1
8/29/2014	Peggy Fletcher Stack	Salt Lake Tribune	Is Ordain Women an Apostate Group? Mormon Leaders Won't Say	http://tinyurl.com/jwrx4m6	2
9/1/2014	Kate Kelly	Salt Lake Tribune	Kate Kelly: As Sisters in Zion, Greater Inclusion of Women Common Goal	http://tinyurl.com/luahdjx	0
9/4/2014	Peggy Fletcher Stack	Salt Lake Tribune	For Many Black Mormons, Racism Is a Bigger Issue Than Sexism	http://tinyurl.com/ku7334b	0
9/10/2014	Jennifer Napier-Pearce	Salt Lake Tribune	Trib Talk: Kate Kelly on Finding Common Ground with Mormon Feminists	http://tinyurl.com/lgytl9d	0
9/15/2014	Kimberly Winston	Religion News Service	Mormons Embrace Social Media to Push Back against Official Church Teachings	http://tinyurl.com/mm2924h	3
9/17/2014	Peggy Fletcher Stack	Salt Lake Tribune	Mormon Group Ordain Women Won't Storm Temple Square	http://tinyurl.com/keljsog	0
9/18/2014	Tim Slover	KUER 90.1	Ordain Women Now Seeking Local Access to LDS Priesthood Session	http://tinyurl.com/mocjodk	0
9/18/2014	Genelle Pugmire	Daily Herald (AP)	Ordain Women Have New Plan for Priesthood Session	http://tinyurl.com/k8naaep	0
9/19/2014	Robert Kirby	Salt Lake Tribune	Summon the Legion for Ordain Women	http://tinyurl.com/k5n9buc	0
9/22/2014	Peggy Fletcher Stack	Salt Lake Tribune	Ordain Women Taking Its Message to Local Level	http://tinyurl.com/l7l8nyt	14
9/25/2014	Emmilie Whitlock	Standard-Journal	Holland Says "Be Firm" in Exclusive Interview	http://tinyurl.com/kct83mg	0
9/26/2014	Dan Bammes	KUER 90.1	Activists Plan to Attend General LDS Women's Meeting	http://tinyurl.com/nqhlgjc	0
9/27/2014	Alexa Mills	Boston Globe	Mormon Women Celebrate 40 Years of Faith and Feminism	http://tinyurl.com/mgz4bu9	0
9/27/2014	Peggy Fletcher Stack	Salt Lake Tribune	Press Barred from Conference Center for Mormon Women's Meeting	http://tinyurl.com/n74gnf2	0

Date	Author	Source	Title	URL	
9/28/2014	Peggy Fletcher Stack	Salt Lake Tribune	LDS Women's Meeting: Feminists Seeking Change Find it in Subtle Wording	http://tinyurl.com/n7mpthj	3
10/1/2014	Dan Bammes	KUER 90.1	Ordain Women Plans Take Shape as LDS Conference Approaches	http://tinyurl.com/n9cpfzw	0
10/3/2014	Taylor Halversen	UPR	Going Local: Ordain Women Changes Priesthood Session Tactic	http://tinyurl.com/kj2bdwp	0
10/3/2014	Erica Palmer	The Digital Universe	Ordain Women Group Enters Priesthood Broadcast at Marriott Center	http://tinyurl.com/qhkkatw	1
10/4/2014	Kristen Moulton	Salt Lake Tribune	Third Time's the Charm — Some Women Get into Mormon Priesthood Session	http://tinyurl.com/k8pvs2s	0
10/5/2014	Unidentified	Associated Press	Group of LDS Women Attend All-Male Meeting	http://tinyurl.com/m6khrwz	267
10/31/2014	Daniel Wallis	Reuters US News	U.S. Mormon Feminist Says Appeal against Excommunication Denied	http://tinyurl.com/lqzytmp	24
10/31/2014	Unidentified	Associated Report	Excommunicated Mormon Loses Her Appeal	http://tinyurl.com/p7dtbp8	86
10/31/2014	Whitney Evans	Deseret News	Appeal of Excommunicated LDS Activist Kate Kelly Denied	http://tinyurl.com/mzh3vjx	0
10/31/2014	Erica Palmer	The Digital Universe	LDS Church Denies Appeal of Ordain Women Founder	http://tinyurl.com/m9o3hy2	0
11/3/2014	Genelle Pugmire	Daily Herald	Kate Kelly to Appeal to LDS Hierarchy	http://tinyurl.com/n8utmeg	0
11/3/2014	Unidentified	Religion News Service	Mormon Ordain Women Leader Kate Kelly Lost Her Appeal of Excommunication	http://tinyurl.com/mngj36l	0
11/5/2014	Unidentified	Associated Press	Kate Kelly Loses Appeal, Pledges to Continue Ordain Women Campaign	http://tinyurl.com/nxc4yjv	5
11/5/2014	Meg Monk	The Digital Universe	I'm a Mormon Feminist: One Perspective on Women's Rights	http://tinyurl.com/m6ma6ok	0
11/14/2014	Dan Bammes	NPR	Mormon Church Publishes Essay on Founder Joseph Smith's Polygamy	http://tinyurl.com/n6jw5ts	63
11/17/2014	Genelle Pugmire	Daily Herald	Ordain Women Going Billboard Route	http://tinyurl.com/mtvmy6v	0
11/17/2014	Dan Bammes	KUER 90.1	New Survey on LDS Gender Issues Piques Interest	http://tinyurl.com/nsbpkde	0
11/20/2014	Peggy Fletcher Stack	Salt Lake Tribune	Kelly Loses Appeal, Keeps Fighting for Mormon Membership	http://tinyurl.com/l68oxor	0
12/2/2014	Kristine Haglund	Slate	What the "Mormon Moment" Actually Accomplished	http://tinyurl.com/q8qmt8f	0
12/3/2014	Kate Kelly	Salt Lake Tribune	As Sisters in Zion, Inclusion of Women Is Common Goal	http://tinyurl.com/lm2d4pn	0

Contributors

Janice Allred is an independent scholar who speaks and writes on theological topics. The author of *God the Mother and Other Theological Essays*, she has published in *Dialogue: A Journal of Mormon Thought*, *Sunstone*, and *Mormon Women's Forum: An LDS Feminist Quarterly*. She has presented papers at the Sunstone Symposium, Counterpoint Conference, and the Society for Mormon Philosophy and Theology Conference.

Lavina Fielding Anderson, president of Editing, Inc., is copy editor of the *Journal of Mormon History*, and past copy editor of *Dialogue: A Journal of Mormon Thought*, and *The Review of Higher Education*. She is a trustee of the Mormon Alliance, former editor of the *Journal of Mormon History*, former associate editor of the *Ensign*, former associate editor and co-associate editor of *Dialogue*, and past president of the Association for Mormon Letters. An honorary life member of the Association for Mormon Letters and the Mormon History Association, she is currently researching Lucy Mack Smith and J. Golden Kimball.

Brent D. Beal received his PhD in management from the Lowry Mays College and Graduate School of Business at Texas A&M University. He is currently an associate professor in the College of Business and Technology at The University of Texas at Tyler. He conducts research in the area of corporate social responsibility and has a long-standing interest in Mormonism.

Heather K. Olson Beal received her PhD in curriculum and instruction from Louisiana State University in 2008. She is currently an associate professor of secondary education at Stephen F. Austin State University, where she teaches courses in student diversity, educational foundations, classroom management, literacy, and action research. Her scholarship examines the issues of school choice, second language education, and the educational experiences of immigrant students. She is a lifelong Mormon, a feminist, and a Mormon feminist activist. She was a board member of Ordain Women in 2013–14.

Caitlin Carroll has a BA in political science from Brigham Young University and an MA in political science from the University of Wisconsin at Madison. She is beginning a graduate program in sociology at the University of Texas at Austin in the fall of 2015. Her research interests include comparative and global feminisms, gender and politics, and social movements.

Ryan T. Cragun is a husband, father, and sociologist of religion (in order of importance). Originally from Utah, he now lives in Florida and works at The University of Tampa. His research and writing focuses on religion, with an emphasis on Mormonism and the nonreligious. His research has been published in a variety of academic journals, and he's the author of several books. For more about his work you can visit his website: www.ryantcragun.com. When he's not working, he's spending time with his wife and son, cooking, watching science fiction, hiking, playing soccer, or tinkering with computers.

Jessica Finnigan is a master's student in the study of religion in the contemporary world at King's College, London. She recently completed her advanced diploma in study of religion at the University of Cambridge. Her research centers on the intersection of technology and religion, specifically the impact of the internet. She graduated from BYU in 2003 with a BS in marriage, family, and human development. Her recent work includes several collaborative articles on Mormon feminism and the impact of the internet on the LDS Church.

Kristine L. Haglund is departing editor of *Dialogue: A Journal of Thought*. Her research interests include Mormon women's and children's history, American hymnody, and religion and new media. She lives near Boston, Massachusetts, with her husband, Brad Woodworth, and their five children.

Nadine McCombs Hansen was born and raised in southern California. She attended BYU where she met her husband of forty-eight years, and married him when she was nineteen. After having four children, she went back to school and got a B.A. in economics from San Jose State University, and then a law degree from Santa Clara University. She and her husband live in Cedar City, Utah, where she practices law parttime, grows food and chickens, and enjoys hiking and driving through southern Utah's beautiful red rock country. They have four children and eight grandchildren.

Debra Elaine Jenson is an assistant professor of communication at Utah State University in Logan. Her research areas include social movements and how they impact public policy, with an emphasis in the early environmental movement. She also studies the representation of women and people with disabilities in popular culture. She has presented research at academic conferences and ComicCon. Jenson serves as a member of the Executive Board of Ordain Women and chairs the Communication Committee, helping craft materials for public release and private communication with LDS Church officials. She is an active member of the LDS Church and is especially fond of girls' camp.

Robin Kincaid Linkhart is a President of Seventy in Community of Christ and represents the Western USA on a multination council tasked with leading the church in mission. She also serves on Community of Christ Theology Formation Team and Ecumenical and Interfaith Ministries Team, chairs the International Latter-day Seekers Ministries Team, serves on the Editorial Review Board for *Restoration Studies: Theology and Culture in Community of Christ and the Latter Day Saint Movement*, and is a contributing author for the *Herald* magazine and the *Restoration Studies* journal. Linkhart and husband Kevin make their home in Longmont, Colorado. They have four children and two grandchildren.

Kristy Money received her PhD from Brigham Young University in counseling psychology. She earned her postdoctoral residency at a community mental health clinic in Massachusetts. Her clinical and research specialties revolve around women's mental health, particularly spirituality, relationships, infertility counseling, grief work during child loss, and anxiety/depression during pregnancy and postpartum. She has worked with Mormons while living around the world, including Utah, New York City, the Navajo Reservation, Texas, and Rio de Janeiro. She is currently a psychologist working in private practice and a writer on women's issues in Mormonism.

Michael Nielsen is professor and chair of psychology at Georgia Southern University, where he has taught courses in the psychology of religion, social psychology, and research methods since 1993. The focus of his research is on the psychology of religion, with Mormonism playing a prominent role. He has served as co-editor of the Archive for the Psychology of Religion and is on the editorial board of several journals including the *Journal for the Scientific Study of Religion* and *Dialogue: A Journal of Mormon Thought*. He is president-elect of the Society for the Psychology of Religion and Spirituality.

Boyd Jay Petersen serves as the program coordinator for Mormon Studies at Utah Valley University, where he teaches for the English Department and Religious Studies program. He is the incoming editor for *Dialogue: A Journal of Mormon Thought* and the outgoing book review editor for the *Journal of Mormon History*. He has served as president of the Association for Mormon Literature and on the boards of Mormon Scholars in the Humanities and *Segullah*. He has published across the range of Mormon studies, from publications like the *FARMS Review* and *BYU Studies* to *Dialogue* and *Sunstone*. He wrote the biography *Hugh Nibley: A Consecrated Life*, which won the best biography award from the Mormon History Association in 2003 and is currently writing a book about Adam and Eve in Mormon thought. He graduated from BYU and holds an MA from the University of Maryland and a PhD from the University of Utah, both in comparative literature, emphasizing romanticism and religious studies.

Gregory A. Prince earned doctorate degrees in dentistry and pathology at UCLA, moved to Maryland to work at the National Institutes of Health, and over a four-decade career in biomedical research, pioneered the prevention of RSV pneumonia in high-risk infants. He has published over 150 scientific papers, two books on Mormon history—*Power from On High: The Development of Mormon Priesthood* (Salt Lake City: Signature Books, 1995), and *David O. McKay and the Rise of Modern Mormonism* (Salt Lake City: University of Utah Press, 2005)—and over two dozen articles, chapters, and reviews in the field of Mormon studies. He and his wife, JaLynn Rasmussen Prince, are the parents of three children.

Courtney Rabada earned her master's degree in religious studies at Claremont Graduate University in 2015, with particular interests in Mormonism, women's studies, and world religions. Her research includes the study of women and gender within the LDS Church, specifically the impact of the 2012 age change for sister missionaries. She is a native of the San Francisco Bay Area and earned her BA in English literature from Indiana University, Bloomington.

Robert A. Rees teaches Mormon studies at Graduate Theological Union and UC Berkeley. Previously he taught at UCLA and UC Santa Cruz and was a Fulbright Professor of American Studies in the Baltics. He is the editor or co-editor of *Proving by Contraries* (Salt Lake City: Signature Books, 2005), *A Readers' Book of Mormon* (Salt Lake City: Signature Books, 2008), and *Why I Stay: The Challenge of Discipleship for Contemporary Mormons* (Salt Lake City: Signature Books, 2011). Currently he is editing a second volume of *Why I Stay* as well as books on discipleship and Mormons and gays. He blogs at Exploring Mormonism and Nomorestrangers: LGBT Mormon Forum. He has served as a bishop, counselor in a full-time mission presidency, and other callings.

Mary Ellen Robertson earned a master's degree in women's studies in religion from Claremont Graduate University. Her thesis project was titled: *Subordination: Mormon Women's Historical Relationship with Spiritual Gifts and Priesthood Authority*. She spoke about Mormon women's history at the Ordain Women launch in March 2013 and has been a feminist activist since her undergraduate days at Brigham Young University. The Mormon Women's Forum gave her the 2014 Eve Award at its annual Counterpoint Conference for her service to Mormon feminism. She served as Symposium Director and Executive Director of Sunstone Education Foundation for six years.

Nancy Ross is an assistant professor of art history at Dixie State University. She graduated from the University of Cambridge in 2007 with a thesis focused on the iconographic development of illustrated English Apocalypse manuscripts in the later Middle Ages. She is the contributing editor for medieval art with Smarthistory at Khan Academy. Her recent work includes several articles written in collaboration with Jessica Finnigan on Mormon feminists and related topics.

Contributors 423

Gary Shepherd obtained his undergraduate and master's degrees at the University of Utah and his PhD from Michigan State University. He is the former department chair of sociology and anthropology and professor emeritus at Oakland University. With Gordon Shepherd, he is co-author of *Mormon Passage: A Missionary Chronicle* (Urbana: University of Illinois Press, 1998), *Talking with the Children of God: Prophecy and Reformation in a Radical Religious Group* (Urbana: University of Illinois Press, 2010), *Binding Heaven and Earth: Patriarchal Blessings in the Prophetic Development of Early Mormonism* (University Park: Penn State University Press, 2012), and *A Kingdom Transformed: Early Mormonism and the Modern LDS Church* (Salt Lake City: University of Utah Press, 2015).

Gordon Shepherd obtained his undergraduate degree from the University of Utah and his PhD from the State University of New York at Stony Brook. He is currently professor of sociology at the University of Central Arkansas. With Gary Shepherd, he is co-author of *Mormon Passage: A Missionary Chronicle* (Urbana: University of Illinois Press, 1998), *Talking with the Children of God: Prophecy and Reformation in a Radical Religious Group* (Urbana: University of Illinois Press, 2010), *Binding Heaven and Earth: Patriarchal Blessings in the Prophetic Development of Early Mormonism* (University Park: Penn State University Press, 2012), and *A Kingdom Transformed: Early Mormonism and the Modern LDS Church* (Salt Lake City: University of Utah Press, 2015).

Pamela A. Shepherd holds an MA in political communication from the Johns Hopkins University and a BA in journalism from Brigham Young University. She currently works as communications director for the National Council of Higher Education Resources in Washington, D.C.

Rolf Straubhaar is a postdoctoral research associate at the University of Georgia's Center for Latino Achievement and Success in Education (CLASE). Trained as an anthropologist of educational policy, his research examines the spread, adaptation, and implementation of educational policies in Brazil, the United States, and Mozambique. His work has been published widely, and his dissertation on the spread of U.S.-based education reforms to Rio de Janeiro was awarded the 2014 Frederick Erickson Outstanding Dissertation Award by the American Anthropological Association's Council on Anthropology and Education.

S. Matthew Stearmer is a Ph.D. candidate in the Department of Sociology at Ohio State University. Prior to Ohio State, Stearmer graduated from Brigham Young University with dual master's degrees in geography and sociology. He has been a principal investigator on several prominent grants including two with the National Science Foundation. His research interests are primarily focused on access to health care, gender equality, and social movements.

Lorie Winder Stromberg has an MA in humanities from Brigham Young University. She was the managing editor of the *Journal of Modern History*, editor of the *Mormon Women's Forum Quarterly*, associate editor of *Sunstone*, co-founder and chair of the Sunstone West Symposium, and a former advisory committee member for both *Sunstone* and *Dialogue: A Journal of Mormon Thought*. She served on the board of *Exponent II* and presently serves on the executive board of OrdainWomen. org. For more than thirty years, she has written and spoken about Mormon feminism and advocated for the ordination of women. Now that her children have left home, her friends say she spends entirely too much time in cat management.

J. Sumerau is an assistant professor of sociology at the University of Tampa. His teaching and research examines the intersection of sexualities, gender, religion, and health in the historical and interpersonal experiences of religious and sexual minorities, and has been published in edited volumes and peer-reviewed academic journals including but not limited to *Gender & Society, Journal of Contemporary Ethnography, Symbolic Interaction, Journal of Sex Research, Men and Masculinities, Journal for the Scientific Study of Religion,* and *Sociology of Religion*.

Margaret M. Toscano is an associate professor of classics and comparative studies at the University of Utah. Her research centers on myth, religion, and gender in ancient and modern contexts. She is co-editor of *Hell and Its Afterlife: Historical and Contemporary Perspectives*. She has published extensively on Mormon feminism since 1984, including *Strangers in Paradox: Explorations in Mormon Theology* with Paul James Toscano (Salt Lake City: Signature Books, 1990) and "Are Boys More Important than Girls? The Continuing Conflict of Gender Difference and Equality in Mormonism" (*Sunstone,* 2007). She has been involved in Mormon feminist activist groups (Mormon Women's Forum and Ordain Women) for the past thirty years.

Amber Choruby Whiteley is a doctoral candidate in the counseling psychology program in the Educational Psychology Department at the University of Utah. She is currently an instructor and researcher for the university. Her research interests center around the topic of social justice. Her past research topics have involved women's issues, microaggressions experienced by the LGBT population in a religious setting, cultural humility, and childhood sexual assault. Amber became interested in social justice research after serving low-income families in St. Louis, Missouri.

Index

A

abortion, grounds for disciplinary council, 228, 245
Aburto, Reyna, 350
activism. *See* Ordain Women *and* Kate Kelly.
Adam and Eve.*See also* Eve.
   as ideal spouses/parents, 69
   in "The Family: A Proclamation to the World," 49
   narratives of gender theology, 79–82
Adult Aaronic program, 209
adultery, grounds for disciplinary council, 228, 245
"Aedh Wishes for the Cloths of Heaven," 119
Affirmation (LDS/LGBT), 218, 232 note 9
African-American studies program, 381
agency, 89, 289–90, 320–21, 367. *See also* theology.
Alaska, Church opposes same-sex marriage, 216
"All Are Called," Community of Christ principle, 187–88
All Are Alike unto God
   petition to Church leaders, 8, 12
   prayers for women's ordination, 163
   recommended changes for equality, 163, 347
All Enlisted, 7, 12, 17, 23
Allen, Penny, 72
Allen, Prudence, 55
Alliance for Marriage, 52
Allred, Janice Merrill
   excommunicated, 6, 160
   on panel, 158
Allred, John G., 265 note 14
Alma 13, and sanctification, 96–97
alternative narratives, in closed systems, 39–41
American Prophet's Record: The Diaries and Journals of Joseph Smith, An, 158
Andersen, Neil L., 23
Anderson, Lavina Fielding, 15, 31–32, 157, 160
Anderson, Lynn Matthews, 6–7
Anderson, Mary, 63
Anderson, Richard L., 209
Anthony, Susan B., 148

apostasy
   defined, 234–37
   discussing issues involved, 255
   four categories of, 246
   Kate Kelly charged with, 243
   mandatory disciplinary councils, 246
apostates, classed with murderers and sexual predators, 246
"Are Boys More Important than Girls?" 162
Aristotle, 55, 70
Armstrong, Susie, 64
Arrington, Gigi, 158
"Ask a Mormon Girl," 163
assimilation. *See* Armand Mauss.
Augustine of Hippo, 56
"authority," not "priesthood," in early Church, 220–21
Autumn Leaves, 192
Avery, Valeen Tippetts, 5, 157
Avishai, Orit, 320–21

B

baby, name and blessing, 103, 109, 287, 314–15, 327, 347
   restricted to Melchizedek Priesthood holders, 158
Baehr v. Miike, 50, 75
Baker, John, 214
Ballard, M. Russell, 23, 25, 268
Ballif, Arta Romney, 73–74
bandwagon effect, and sense of protection, 379
Bannan, Regina, 173
baptism for the dead, 208
Barnes, Mark, 19, 21
Beal, Brent D., 278
Beal, Heather K. Olson
   and Mormon Gender Issues Survey, 278
   and Ordain Women activities/executive board, 16–17, 21–22, 278, 285
Beck, Julie B., 8
Beecher, Maureen Ursenbach, 157, 159
Benford, Robert, 380
Bennett, April, 19, 22–23, 357 note 2
Benson, Ezra Taft, 68–69, 105–6, 150

Berger, Peter, 313
bi-gender. *See* transgender.
binary
    failure to capture complexity, 328
    limitations on coding, 321
    opposition, 86 note 11
binitarianism, 206
birth control, policy evolution, 68, 211–12
bishop's interviews, of girls and women, 255, 317
bishops. *See* local leaders.
Bittner, Merrill, 177 note 34
"black widow spider," ordained women compared to, 155
blessing of babies. *See* baby.
blessings, by women, 140, 148, 150, 152 note 56, 159, 166 note 125, 314
blogs, feminist, 143–45, 337–40, 346. *See also* Facebook *and* interent.
Booth, Linda L., 160
Bott, Randy, 215 note 35
boundary maintenance, excommunication as, 28
Bourgeois, Roy, 173
boycotts, 383
Bozarth-Campbell, Alla, 177 note 34
Braby, Lois, 193–94
Brannon, Samuel, 228
Brazil
    Church membership in, 282
    race in, 225 note 68
Brennan, Bill, 173–74
Brinkerhoff, Kimberly, 13, 18
Brody, Fawn, 228
Brooks, Joanna, 7, 12, 19, 163
Brown, Hugh B., 224
Brown, Michael, 349–50
Burgess, Samuel A., 192
burglary/theft, grounds for disciplinary council, 228, 245
Burton, Linda K.
    LDS Newsroom interview with, 18
    on covenant path, 45
    on women's complementary roles (video), 164
    quoted, 3, 23, 25
Bush, George, 51
Bush, Lester E., 213
Bushman, Claudia L., 150, 161, 323
Bushman, Richard, 323
Butterworth, Lisa Patterson, 12, 14, 161
Bynum, Carolyn Walker, 81 note 6

C

California, Church opposes same-sex in, 216
callings
    cancelled for Ordain Women supporters, 352, 387 note 59
    proposed expansions for women, 327, 333
    forbidden to disfellowshipped/ excommunicated members, 245
    influence of gender on, 127, 194
    men excluded from some, 327
Campbell, Alexander, 221
Campbell, David E., 322
Cannon, George Q., 156, 211–12
Cannon, Janath Russell, 159
canon law, 239–42
Capella, Marina, vii–ix
career goals and cultural expectations, 315
Carlson, Jack, and Renee, 214
Case (Crist), Karen, 158
Cassidy, Butch, 228
Cassler, Valerie Hudson. *See* Hudson, Valerie.
Catholic Church. *See also* Roman Catholic Women Priests.
    and LDS Church oppose same-sex marriage, 50 note 4, 216
    and women's ordination, 21, 171–74, 336
    feminists, 336
    interfaith panel, 163
    male-only priesthood, 389–90
    two forms of excommunication, 239 note 21
Catholic Women's Ordination Conference (CWOC), 385–86
Cavendish, James, 384
change. *See also* revelation *and* models of change.
    desirability of, 347
    expanded roles for women, 8–9, 42–44 note 27, 347
    external/internal forces for change, 225, 309–10, 313, 398–99
    in Mormon history, 203–15
    proposed, 320, 347, 400
    recommendations for, 333
    steps in effecting, 380
    survey responses to proposals, 313–14
chaplains, women, 170
Charles, Melodie Moench, 157
Chaves, Mark, 313–14, 322, 384
Cheek, Alison, 177 note 34

Index   427

Cheney, Dick, 10–11
child sexual abuse and mandatory disciplinary councils, 246
Chile, Church membership in, 282
Chong, Dennis, 380
Christafferson, Wilhelmina, 63
Christofferson, D. Todd, 107–8
Church Handbook of Instructions. Vol. 1: Stake Presidencies and Bishops (2010), 241 note 2
  recommended availability, 255
  restricted access, 243, 287, 391
  rules for disciplinary councils, 228–29, 235, 243–46
Church Handbook of Instructions. Vol. 2: Priesthood and Auxiliary Leaders, (2010), 241 note 2, 269, 287 note 23
Church of Jesus Christ of Latter-day Saints. *See* LDS Church.
Cialdini, Robert, 379
Claremont Graduate University, 8
Clark, J. Reuben, Jr., 67, 152
Clawson, Rudger, 150
Clayton, William, 92
Clinton, Bill, 51
Clyde, Aileen, 160
coercion, forbidden by scriptures, 99
collective action frame theory (CAFT), 380
collective identities, and social movements, 382
Committee to Promote the Status of Women. *See* VOICE.
common consent, in Community of Christ, 186–87
Commonwealth of Massachusetts v. United States Department of Health and Human Services, 52
community, 181, 335, 379
Community of Christ
  and continuing revelation, 180
  as identity issue, 180
  dissent in, 32
  establishment of, 189
  first ordinations (November 17, 1985), 196
  first women apostles, 160
  history of women's ordination (1976–84), 168–69, 178–80, 185–99
  opposed polygamy, 190
  rejected one-man rule, 190
  response to women's ordination, x–xi
  Section 156, 195–96
  voting policies: 1864, 190; 1881, 191

women's individual growth, 198
women's groups in, 190–91
complementarianism, 158, 163–64
  and equality, 88–89
  and priesthood, 98–99
  critique of, 86–90
  defined, 334 note 16
conservativism, 39, 323
Cook, Lyndon W., 142
Cook, Mary N., 45
Cook, Quentin L., 109–10
Coontz, Stephanie, 59
Cornwall, Marie, 46–47, 381
correlation movement
  and auxiliaries, 153–54
  ended female hierarchy structure, 273 note 34
  repressive effects of, 31, 46 note 30, 204
Council of the Twelve. *See* General Authorities.
Counterpoint Conference. *See* Mormon Women's Forum.
Courage campaign, 218
"court of love," 236, 239, 241 note 1
"covenant path," 45
Cowdery, Oliver, 220
Cragun, Ryan, 285
Craynor, Cody, 274 note 37, 391 note 75
crisis of faith, 237
Crowley, Gabrielle Perri, 21
"cult of true womanhood," 188
culture. *See also* doctrine basis, gender roles, *and* revelation.
  and gender roles, 130, 133, 320
  as basis of LDS practices, 306–7, 324–28
  influence on support/opposition, 332, 367
cultural framing and dominant narratives, 379–80

D

Dahlin, Eric, 46–47, 381
Dalton, Elaine S., 18
Daly, Mary, 93
Danube River, Catholic ordinations, 173
Daughters of Light, 154
De Leon v. Perry, 52, 76
Debarthe, Enid Irene Stubbart, 195–96
dedication of graves, 210–11
defections, from LDS Church, 41–42, 225, 281–83, 383–84. *See also* LDS Church, membership claims.

mandatory discipline council for joining another church, 246
not excommunicated for inactivity, 233, 245, 384
Dehlin, John
   excommunicated, 28, 77 note 1, 253
   fosters networking, 12–13
   message sent by excommunication, x, 37 note 22
democracy, and Church, 370–71
Derr, Jill Mulvay, 159
Dew, Sheri L., xi, xii, 141
   on male-only priesthood, 23–25, 164
   on women's "nature," 110
Dialogue, as forum for feminist discussion, 6
diaper flannel, excommunicated for, 233
Dilworth, Jason, 16
disaffection. *See* defections.
disciplinary councils, 227–40, 241–56
   arbitrary outcomes inevitable, 243
   as act of violence/punishment, 241, 380
   categories of, 228, 244
   charges deliberately vague, 249–50
   effect on others, 229–33
   effectiveness in achieving stated goals, 253–54
   examples of injustice, 230–33
   not helpful in cases of conscience, 236, 253
   possible outcomes, 228–29
   possibly helpful in regretted actions, 236, 241, 244, 253–54
   procedure specified in scriptures, 233–35, 255
   stated purposes of, 243, 253–54
   recommended reforms, 254–56
   secrecy of, 249
Discourse on the Transient and Permanent in Christianity, The, 234
disfellowshipment, 231, 244–45
disruptive protests, less effective, 381
dissent
   leaders' typical responses to, 41
   no channels for, 77, 256, 370
   suppressed in closed systems, 31–32, 38–39
doctrine base of LDS practices. *See also* culture basis.
   as motivation for change, 306–7
   defined, 325–26
   in Mormon Gender Issues Survey responses, 320, 324–28
doctrine of the family, 388–89. *See also* "The Family: A Proclamation to the World."

"doctrine of the priesthood," in Kate Kelly's disciplinary council, 250
Doctrine and Covenants 76, 90–92, 97
Doctrine and Covenants 84, 96–97
Doctrine and Covenants 131, 91–92
Doctrine and Covenants 132, 92–93
Doctrines of Salvation, 152
Donne, John, 110–11
doormats, women compared to, 153
Doves and Serpents blog, 16
Draper, Maurice L., 187
Druckman, James, 380
drug-dealing, grounds for disciplinary council, 228, 245
dual-career couples, 107–9, 112–14
Durham, Christine Meaders, 158

E

Eastman, Vickie Stewart, 161
education, and online participation, 344–46. *See also* feminist blogs *and* internet. online participation, personal growth, 353
Edwards, Paul M., x
Ehat, Andrew F., 142
electronic lists. *See* feminist blogs *and* internet.
Electronic Latter-day Women's Caucus—Plus Men (ELWC+), 6–7
Ellis-Clegg, Christy, 21–22
embezzlement, grounds for disciplinary council, 228, 245
embodiment of God, and Heavenly Mother, 94–95
Encyclopedia of Mormonism, on Relief Society, 159; on Heavenly Mother, 159
"End of the 'Mormon Moment,' The," 237
endowment. *See* temple endowment.
England, Rebecca, 213
Episcopal Church, 168, 175–78
Episcopal Women's Caucus, 176, 181
Equal in Faith, 21, 167–68, 176
Equal Rights Amendment. *See* LDS Church.
equality. *See also* inequality.
   and agency, 88–90, 100
   at home/church, 197
   fundamental to Atonement, 78
   gender roles diminish, 106–8
   measures of, 287, 397
   power/value of, 367, 395
Evans, David F., 263
Eve. *See also* Adam and Eve.

as model for Christ, 73
contemporary poetry about, 72–75
dual functions of, 54
influence over men, 63–64
LDS views of, 60–75
meaning of name, 81
rate of citations in conference, 66–67
rib, symbolism of, 61 note 41, 69–70
excommunication, 227–57
and Church reputation, 254
defined, 227, 237 note 16
effect on Ordain Women profiles, 375
excommunicants, as "the least," 240
fear created by, 254
history of, 227–28
mandatory for prominent leaders, 245–46
notable excommunicants, 227–28
revokes ordinances and sealings, 245
expanded involvement. *See* change.
Exponent (blog), 7, 143–44, 162–63, 339, 343–45, 349–50
Exponent II, 4, 6, 154, 341
Eyring, Henry B., 45

F

Fabrizio, Doug, ix, 253–54
Facebook
and Mormon feminists, 337–38
closed groups, 342–43, 352–53
participation in, 340–41
"Faithful Disagreement," 32
false swearing, grounds for disciplinary council, 228, 245
family. *See also* "The Family: A Proclamation to the World," *and* doctrine of the family.
abandonment of, grounds for disciplinary council, 228, 245
citations of in general conference talks, 81 note 7
as basic unit of society, 85–86, 91
structure since 1970, 56
"The Family: A Proclamation to the World"
analysis of, 82–86
and gender roles, 70, 82, 85, 105–6, 129
creedal function of, 84, 89
domination-submission model in, 86
excludes Jesus, 89
no author cited, 53 note 15. See also Packer, Boyd K.
political purpose of, 49–50, 84
quoted in general conference, 52 note 13, 53
reaction to, 347
twentieth anniversary, 71
Farnsworth, Sonja, 158, 389
Farr, Cecilia Konchar, 159
fatherhood, prioritizing, 114
Faulring, Scott H., 158
Faust, James E., 156
Feminism and Religion in the 21st Century: Technology, Dialogue, and Expanding Religious Borders, 336
feminists, Mormon
and fear of excommunication, 141, 143, 145, 237, 254
blogs, 143–45, 337–40, 346. See also Facebook.
estimated numbers of, 342
history of, 3–9
opposition to, viii–ix
swift reaction to media, 343
Feminist Mormon Women of Color (FEMWOC), 350–51
Feminist Mormon Housewives, 7, 14, 143
and race, 348–50
begins, 161
closed Facebook, 342–43
largest Mormon feminist group, 339
number of blog posts, 345
participation in, 341–43
feminization of professions, 58
Fife, Chelsea Robarge, 12
Finnigan, Jessica, 39–42, 278, 335
Firmage, Edwin B., 158, 243
First Presidency. *See also* General Authorities.
affirms Kate Kelly's excommunication, 252
and appeals in disciplinary councils, 255
approves "asking questions," 252
must approve retention of membership records, 248 note 8
on male-only priesthood, 160, 251–52
First Vision, 43, 204–7
fornication, grounds for disciplinary council, 228, 245
Fox, Ruth May, 64
Frame, Kelly, 158
framing, strategies for social change, 380
fraud, grounds for disciplinary council, 228, 245
free agency. *See* agency.
Free Speech zone and anti-Mormon protesters, 377, 392

Friedan, Betty, 68
From Housewife to Heretic: One Woman's Spiritual Awakening and Her Excommunication from the Mormon Church, 156
Frost, Robert, 74
fund-raising, through social media, 355
Fyans, J. Thomas, 210, 213

G

Galileo, 234
Gamson, William, 378, 382, 388
Garner, Eric, 349
gender
  and agency, 125–27
  as benchmark political issue, 322
  as eternal, 83 note 6
  as synonym for sex, 53, 88 note 12
  equality, 384, 388
  essentialism, 334 note 16
  in "The Family: A Proclamation to the World," 53, 70, 82, 85, 105–6, 129
  need for clarified theology, 334
  reform recommendations, 120–24
gender equality, and religious social movements, 384, 388
gender roles
  and Church's views, 54, 85–86, 118–19, 322
  doctrine vs. culture, 324–28
  history of, in Western civilization, 55–59
  in professions, 58
  pronouncements on, 105–7
  traditional, 105–9, 188–89, 298–300, 388
general conference, reactions to, 344–45. *See also* Ordain Women, events.
general priesthood session, 390
general women's session, 390
General Authorities. *See also* LDS Church, revelation, *and* Public Affairs Department.
  logic of deliberations/decisions, 47
  on ordination, 400
  on priesthood (1931), 222
  praise for women, x
  refused to meet with Ordain Women leaders, 20
  responsibility in change, 38, 316–17. *See also* revelation.
General Council of Women (RLDS), 192
Gerber, Lynne, 321
Gertz, Yehuda, 386
Gileadi, Avraham, 160 note 99
Ginsburg, Ruth Bader, 59

Givens, Terryl, and Fiona, 323
giving talk/lesson, and disfellowshipment, 245
Glad, A. P. A., 209
Gleason's Literary Companion, 189
God the Father
  as father, limitations of, 95
  gendered nature of, 128–29
  Joseph Smith's understanding of, 205–6
God the Mother. *See* Heavenly Mother.
Godhead, roles in, 95 note 22
Google Chat, 337
Google Hangouts, 337
Gore, Al, 51
gospel essay, on ordaining black men, 349
Gottman, John Mordecai, 105–12
Grant, Heber J., 150, 224
grass-roots. *See also* trickle-up effect *and* radical flank.
Great Apostasy, 33 note 15
Green, John C., 322
Green, Mira, 161
Greg Kofford Books, xiii

H

Habermas, Jürgen, 378
Hafen, Bruce C., 26, 70–71, 157
Haglund, Kristine, 31 note 11
Haider-Winnert, Christine, 163
Haidt, Jonathan, 323
Hancock, Ralph, 158
Hanks, Maxine, 7, 159–60
Hansen, Jim, 50–51
Hansen, Nadine, 4–5, 23, 156
Harris, Barbara C., 177
Harrison, Mark M.
  and Kate Kelly's excommunication, 247–48, 250
  bishop of Vienna Virginia Ward, 247
  examples of violating handbook, 248–49
  quotation from excommunication letter, 27
Harvey, Shirley Adwena, 72
Hasian, Marouf, Jr., 336
Hawaii, Church opposes same-sex marriage in, 50, 216
Hawaii's Future Today, 50 note 4, 76
healing blessings. *See* blessings.
Heavenly Mother, 93–95, 139, 160
  absent from "The Family: A Proclamation to the World," 812
  and Mormon theology, 161
  and women's priesthood, 159

as feminist issue, 143
BYU Studies article, 10
call for inclusion, 347
complement to masculine representations, 94
not considered to be God, 94
prayers to, 160
Heinz, Kerry, 143
Henry, Matthew, 61 note 41
Herbert v. Kitchen, 52
heresy. *See* apostasy.yy
Heschel, Susannah, 388
Hewitt, Emily, 177 note 34
Hewlings, Lucy M., 64
Heyward, Carter, 177, 183
Hiatt, Suzanne, 177 note 34
Hickman, Aimee Evans, 11
Hickman, Martha A., 150
hierarchical conservative settings (HCS), 39–41
Higdon, Barbara, 179, 182
high priestess, 153 note 62
Hinckley, Gordon B.
　and equality, 367 note 10
　and "The Family: A Proclamation to the World," 49, 51, 82–86
　anti-gay marriage strategy, 216
　denies women's priesthood, 17, 146, 160–62
　forbids prayers to God the Mother, 94
　on inactive missionaries, 269
　on small numbers of sister missionaries, 261–62
　revelation needed to change priesthood, 157
hiring policies, equality in, 313–14
"Historical Relationship of Mormon Women and Priesthood," 4–5
history
　and community, 379
　and ordination, 144, 166, 367
　essays, on LDS website, 323
　honesty in, 254, 348
History of the Church, changes in Nauvoo Relief Society minutes, 139, 149
Holland, Patricia, 155–56
Hollingsworth v. Perry, 52, 75
"holy envy," 240
"home-court" advantage in Mormon Gender Issues Survey, 286–89
homosexuality. *See also* same-sex marriage *and* transgender.
　and afterlife, 219
　Church policy on, 204, 215–19
　grounds for disciplinary council, 228, 231, 245
House of the Lord, 149
Houston, Gail Turley, 160
Howard, Sarah, 61
Hoyt, Amy, 59, 61
Hudson, Valerie, 25, 162
Huebener, Helmuth, 230, 234
Hunt, Robert D., 238 notes 18–19
Hunter, Howard W., 157
husbands "preside," 313–14

I

I'm a Mormon Feminist (blog), 162 note 109
Improvement Era, on priesthood, 149, 222
inactivity. *See* defections.
incest, and mandatory disciplinary council, 245–46
inclusive language, 91
individual vs. family in gospel, 91
inequality
　harm caused by, 368
　not perceived, 314–16
injustice of denying ordination, 96
insider/outsider, 28–30, 323, 382, 398–99
Instagram, 341
interfaith activities, 167, 336
International Women's Year, 150–51
internet. *See also* feminist blogs.
　and Mormon feminist discussions, 6, 143–45
　and women's relationships, 336–40, 346
　blogs, 143–45
　effects of, 215
　fear caused by excommunications, 254
　reduced fear of discipline, 141, 145
　revived interest in feminism, 143–45
intersex individuals, no place in LDS theology, 129, 131–32. *See also* transgender.
Irish, Carolyn Tanner, 178
irregular ordinations, 182–83
"Is There a Place for Heavenly Mother in Mormon Theology?" 161
Islam, and LDS Church's conservatism, 399–400
Isom, Ally, ix, 253–54, 391 note 75, 393–94
Ivins, Anthony W., 150

J

Jack, Elaine, 160
Jackson, Kent P., 238 notes 18–19

Jacobs, Rick, 218
Jamison, Andrew, 378
Jehovah's Witnesses, 282
Jensen, Marlin K., 81 note 9
Jensen, Virginia U., 71
Jenson, Debra Elaine
  biography/personal experiences, 377
  Ordain Women involvement, 15, 22, 164
  reports punishment of Ordain Women
    supporters, 38 note 23
Jesus
  as revelation of God, 95
  atonement brings equality, 96
Jewish. *See* Orthodox Jewish.
Joan of Arc, 234
Johnson, Maria Miller, 65
Johnson, Sonia, 4, 155–56
joining another Church, and mandatory
  disciplinary council, 246
justice, theology of, 369, 380
justification, and priesthood, 96

K

Kelly, Donna, 9, 243
Kelly, Jim, 10, 243
Kelly, Kate
  activism of, 12–13, 15, 20, 238, 251–52, 335
  and Ordain Women events, 19, 22–23,
    111–12, 144, 164, 247–48
  at WOC conference, 21
  biography/personal experiences, 9–12
  excommunicated, 145–46, 161, 165, 228;
    analysis of disciplinary council, 235,
    246–53; and surge in Ordain Women
    profiles, 373; priesthood event not cited
    as grounds, 393; reaction to, x, 27, 37
    note 22, 253, 339
  instructed to remove Ordain Women profile,
    357 note 2
  media bibliography about, 401–18
  message sent by excommunication, 77
  networking of, 13–14
Kelly, Natalie, 13, 15
Kempthorne, Dirk, 51
Kewanee Sisters Mite, 190
keys, priesthood (illustration), 138–40, 146,
  151, 159
"Keys and Authority of the Priesthood, The," 165
Kickstarter funding for Mormon Gender
  Issues Survey, 280, 292

Kimball, Edward L., 213
Kimball, Heber C., 60, 147
Kimball, Jordan, 213
Kimball, Sarah M., 148
Kimball, Spencer W.
  and equality, 367 note 10
  and missionary policy, 225
  and ordination of black men, 212–14
  denies women's priesthood, 146, 155
  on Eve, 68
  on homosexuality, 218
Kimball, Vilate, 147
King, Brayden G., 46–47, 381
King, Hannah Tapfield, 65
King, Larry, 161
King, Martin Luther, 48 note 34, 367 note 10
Kitchen v. Herbert v. Smith, 52, 76
Kline, Caroline, 8, 16
Kotel (Western Wall in Jerusalem), women
  praying at, 386. *See also* Orthodox Jews.
Krakauer, Jon, 308
KUER Radio West, 254, 277

L

Ladies Night Out, 18
Lakoff, George, 379
Lamont, Ruby. *See* Johnson, Maria Miller.
Lauritzen, Stephanie, 13
Lawrence, D. H., 53 note 14
LDS Church. *See also* General Authorities, "The
  Family: A Proclamation to the World," *and*
  Public Affairs Department.
  and doctrine of the family, 82–84 notes 9–10
  as closed social system, 31–34
  discourages dissent, 31–32
  files amicus curiae briefs, 50, 75–76
  gay policy, possible changes, 219
  gender. See gender roles.
  gospel topics essays, 323
  greater inclusiveness, x, 41; changes in
    rhetoric, 23–26; women speakers/
    prayers at general conference, x; general
    meeting declared a "session," x
  harmed by inequality, 368
  hires marketing firm on family, 49
  members disillusioned with, 368
  membership numbers, 281–83. See also
    defections.
  official rhetoric on gender, 322

opposes Equal Rights Amendment, 4, 11, 47, 68, 154, 322
opposes gay marriage, 50 note 4
policies affecting women, 44
power limited to men, 390
seen as homophobic, 217
service in. *See* callings.
succession in, 33–34
systemic coercion in, 99–100
theology does not recognize transgender, 131–32
Leadership Conference of Women Religious (LCWR), 171
"Leadership Roulette," 231, 252, 256
League of Women Voters, 5
Lectures on Faith, 206
Lee, Harold B., 208–9
LeHane, Janine, 177
Let Women Pray (movement), 9, 20, 163
LGBTI individuals. *See also* transgender.
and feminism, 348
excluded by "The Family: A Proclamation to the World," 85
liberalism, disapproved, 309
Lighthouse Ministry, 243 note 5
Linderman Alf, 337
Linker, Damon, 174
Linkhart, Robin Kincaid, xi–xii, 180, 185–86
local leaders
inconsistency/incompetence of, 229, 231, 239, 241–42, 255
influenced by culture, 333
response to feminist issues, 351–52
Looking Forward, Looking Backward: Forty Years of Women's Ordination, 177
Lovheim, Mia, 337
Ludlow, Daniel, 156
Lyon, Tania Rands, 261

M

Madsen, Carol Cornwall, 157
Magna Carta, 227
Malan, Paul, 323
male allies, 192, 246, 341, 346. *See also* marriage.
participation in Ordain Women activities, 7, 19, 335, 362
support for women's ordination, 173–74, 183
male/female, complexity of survey responses, 324–28

Mangrum, R. Collin, 243
Marchant, Byron, 30 note 12
marriage
egalitarian, 105–14, 126
General Authorities stress, 263–64
mission as preparation for marriage, 264, 271–72
Mason, Patrick, 37 note 22
Mauss, Armand, 28, 31, 35–39, 45
McBaine, Neylan, xi–xii, 323
and Joseph Smith, 136–37, 165
expanded roles for women locally, 43 note 27, 225
on Relief Society, 140–41
McConkie, Bruce R., 153, 234
McConkie, Carol F., 45
McConkie, Oscar W., 155
McCullough, J. E., 71
McFarland, Mary Ann Shumway, 261
McKay, David O., 71
Means, Jacqueline, 177
media coverage, 371–72, 382, 401–18
Meltwater News, 371 note 12, 401
men and priesthood
fear that ordination threatens priesthood, 191
need priesthood to remain active, 330
terms not synonyms, 24, 165, 400
Mengel, Gail E., 160
Messina-Dysert, Gina, 336
Mexico, Church membership in, 282
Miles, Carrie, 66
Ministry of Irritation, 173, 181
"Missing Rib: The Forgotten Place of Queens and Priestesses in the Establishment of Zion, The," 4, 138, 156
mission leadership council (MLC), 265–68
missionaries. *See also* sister missionaries.
male, numbers of, 260 note 4
reform in ages/service, 314
romance between, 264 note 13
missionary lessons (1947), 209
Mkhabela (prayer October 2014), 348
modalism, 105–6
models of change, 34–47
modesty, gendered teachings of, 130, 315, 333
Money, Kristy
and Ordain Women events, 21–22, 103, 111–12
as typically desirable member, 40 note 25
courtship, 104–5

dual careers, and priorities, 106–14
daughters, 103, 114–15
monoculture, Mormon, 323
Monson, J. Quin, 322
Monson, Thomas S., 210, 263–64
Moody, Jessica, 391–92, 394
Mooney, Danielle, 20, 22
Moorefield, Marie, 177 note 34
Morgan, Mary Ann, 161
Mormon Doctrine, 153
Mormon doctrine, allegedly unchanged, 203
"Mormon Engagement with the World Religions," 203
Mormon Enigma: Prophet's Wife, "Elect Lady," Polygamy's Foe, 157
Mormon Feminist Network, 7
Mormon Gender Issue Survey, 277–95, 319–53
and gender equality, 286–87
backgrounds of survey creators, 278
completion of, 288, 299
complex (not binary) answers, 319–20
demographics, 301–3, 323–24
differences in progressive/conservative responses, 319
liberal views of others, 311
media interest in, 277
methodology, 298–301
negative comments from respondents, 277–78, 285–94
number of responses, 277, 278 note 4, 299, 319
open-ended questions, 277, 319
Pew survey compared, 302–3, 305, 307
purpose of, 285, 319
quantitative analysis, 297–318
religiosity of respondents, 304–5
representativeness of sample, 283–84
responses on gender issues, 306–16
sample, 283–84, 299–300
sample questions, 294–95
target population, 281–83
timing of release, 285
unrecognized middle ground, 319
use of Mormon language, 284, 291–92, 300 note 8
Mormon legal history, 242 note 3, 243
Mormon manhood, 60
"Mormon Moment," 13
Mormon Sisters: Women in Early Utah, 150
Mormon women. *See* women.
Mormon Women's Forum, 5–6, 143, 160

activities of, 158, 160
Counterpoint Conference/meetings, 31, 158, 161
founded, 158
Mormon Women's Forum Newsletter/Quarterly, 6, 158
"Mormonism's Negro Doctrine: An Historical Overview," 213
Mormons for ERA, 5, 11
mormonsandgays.org, 218
Morrill, Susanna, 63
Morrise, Martha Pettijohn, 72–73
Mother in Heaven. *See* Heavenly Mother.
motherhood
and priesthood, ix, 42, 67, 99, 141, 151–52, 154, 158, 389, 400
as prophetesses, 150
seen as partnership with God (not fatherhood), 389
motives for/against ordination
affirmations and grievances, 363–66
affirmations outnumber grievances, 366, 369
supporters, 169, 180
murder, disciplinary council mandatory, 228, 245–46
Muslim religious feminists, 336

N

Nader, Ralph, 10–11
National Women's Equality Day, 21
nature of God, and gender roles, 188
Nauvoo Relief Society minutes, changed, 139, 149, 190
negative consequences of feminism. *See* opposition.
negotiation, and feminist theory, 321–23
Nelson, Russell M., 52, 69–70
New Zealand, Church membership in, 282
Newell, Linda King, 4–5, 157, 159
Nibley, Hugh, 235
Nielsen, Michael, 281, 285
nurturing, and servitude, 86

O

O'Dea, Thomas, 370
O'Dell, Darlene, 177
O'Malley, Jennifery, 163
Oaks, Dallin H.
men and priesthood, not synonyms, 24

men-women's partnership for home, not Church, 158
on alternate voices, 6
on priesthood keys, 273
on same-sex marriage, 49, 217
women and priesthood, 24–26, 44, 146, 159, 165, 250–51
obedience, importance of, 289–92, 308, 312, 370
Obergefell v. Hodges, 52, 57, 76
Ogilby (Episcopal bishop) 176
Okazaki, Chieko, 9 note 25, 160
"old maids," 260, 263
online communities, personal growth, 315, 337–48, 344–46, 351, 353
opposition to women's ordination, 169–71, 315, 328, 330, 332, 352–53
and family neglect, 331
and RLDS women's ordination, 179
arguments against, 169
comments on Ordain Women Facebook, 391
critique of reasons, 100–101
objections unfounded, 198
three forms of, 87 note 11
Ordain Women: Mormon Women Seeking Equality and Ordination to the Priesthood
activism, 145
and gender equality, 133–34
as "faithful agitation," 45, 279
as radical flank, 40
asks General Authorities to pray for revelation, 45, 385
bibliography about, 401–18
board burn-out, 22 note 56
collaboration in, 15–16
continued activities in 2014–15, 252
events: October 2013, vii, 22, 27, 144, 164, 247, 387
events: April 2014, vii, 18–20, 27, 111–12, 144, 164–65, 247, 355, 377, 387;
number of participants, 335 note 1
de-escalation training after public actions, 392
denied tickets to attend priesthood meeting, 22, 377
governance structure, 387
historical antecedents of, 4–9
impact of, 17–18, 43 note 27
interfaith events, 387
lessons from other denominations, 180–86
media attention, 242, 279, 401–18
opposition to:

backlash, 395
characterized as invalid stakeholders, 391
classed with evangelical anti-Mormons, 377
Church avoids response to content, 394–95
events defined as protest, 37 note 37
framed with feminist and academics, 393
informal discipline of board members, 387
personal attacks on Facebook, 392
supporters punished, 38 note 22
organizational activities, 14–16
priesthood ordination for women, 387
profiles:
content analysis, 355–75
demographics, 359–62
fluctuations in submissions, 372–74
guidelines, 355
number of, (2015), 142, 387
religiosity, 20, 362–63, 368
responsiveness to publicity, 343
support ordination, 363–69
presents women as potential priesthood holders, 390
"Six Discussions," 393–94
social media committee, 374
symbols, 383–85
"tone" seen as problematic, 393
use of Twitter, Instagram, Facebook, 335
website, 16
categories within, 355 note 1
date of launch, 164, 246, 355
demographics of profile submitters, 323 note 14
number of blog posts, 345
warns of possible negative consequences, 356–57 and note 2
Ordain Women Now (Lutheran Church-Missouri Synod), 21
ordinances, 207–8, 226
ordination of women
and family responsibilities, 330
and transgender issues, 132
compared to black men, 212–15, 224–26
effect on personal lives, 320, 328–31
eschewing as marker of faithfulness (1980s–1990s), 183 note 54
generational differences in motives, 144, 181
in other religions, lessons from, 180–83
likelihood of, 146, 339, 398
reasons for, 77

Orthodox Jewish women, 336, 393
  denied valid stakeholder status, 391
  praying at Western Wall, 385
  power limited to men, 390
Oscarson, Bonnie L., 71–72
Otterson, Michael, 145–46, 165, 241 note 1, 393
Oxley, Susan Skoor, x

P

Packer, Boyd K.
  and "The Family: A Proclamation to the World," 53 note 15, 70, 81 note 8
  on complementarian roles, 70, 156, 158
  on feminists, intellectuals, and homosexual as dangers to the Church, 6
  priesthood not conferred in temple, 159
Page, Sarah, 74–75
Parent's Guide, A, 69
Park, Lindsay Hansen, 12
Parker, Theodore, 234
"patriarch evangelist" renamed "evangelist," 197
patriarchy
  and Community of Christ, 188–90
  and control of agency, 86
  condition of post-Fall, 82
  damaging to women, 344–45
  LDS Church's commitment to, 399–400
Patterson, Sara, 59, 61
Paulsen, David L., 10
Pearson, Carol Lynn, 72, 154
Peay, Ida, 60
Penrose, Charles W., 150
perjury, as grounds for disciplinary council, 228, 245
Perry, L. Tom, 82 note 10
Perry v. Schwarzenegger, 52, 75
Petersen, Mark E., 214
Peterson, Esther, 68
Peterson, Grethe Ballif, 158
Pew Research Center reports
  2011: women oppose ordination, 224, 279, 357 note 3; critiqued, 279–80, 282, 357 note 3; on Mormons as Christian, 45 note 29, 322 note 9
  2012: Mormons support traditional gender roles, 322 note 9; growth in "nones," 168 note 3
  2014: growth in "nones," 168 note 3
  2015: Mormons have higher rates of marriage and children, 168 note 3, 272

Philadelphia Eleven, 176–77, 183–84
Phillips, John A., 81
Philo of Alexandria, 56
Piccard, Jeannette, 177 note 34
pink/blue, assigned to boys/girls, 57–58
Pink Smoke, 173, 181
Pinterest, 341
Pius XII, 385
plan of happiness/plan of salvation, 89 note 13
Pocock, J. G. A., 55
polarity. *See* complementarianism.
policies. *See* change.
polygamy, 32, 92, 93 note 17, 246, 345
Pope Francis, 171–72, 228
pornography, disciplinary council not mandatory, 245
Porter, Bruce, 203
Powell, Colin, 51
power
  and authority, 221–22
  and gender roles, 117, 125, 130
  in disciplinary councils, 243
  need to share, 7
"Power Hungry," 7, 161
Pratt, Mary Ann, 66
Pratt, Orson, 234
prayer
  and disfellowshipment, 245
  in general conference by women, 44, 313
  in sacrament meeting by women, 155
  request to General Authorities, 251. *See also* revelation.
Preach My Gospel, 52 note 13
predators, 244, 246, 254
Presidential Commission on the Status of Women, 68
priesthood
  and equality, 95–101
  defined as service, 98–99, 101
  and disfellowshipment, 245
  and sex organs, 131–32
  and women, history, 137–66, 198, 250–51; possibly less than full ordination, 224. *See also* Pew Research Center.
  arguments for ordaining women, 95–201
  as administration, 328
  as compensation for women's greater spirituality, 326, 389
  as male-only, 33, 288, 390
  black men ordained, 32, 204

Church's definition, 31, 99
current conception misrepresents gospel, 96
denied to women, 140, 327
detached from maleness, 390
doctrine/culture, 326–27
fluidity/evolution of, x, 220–21, 225–26
offices, changes in Joseph Smith's life, 207
policy historically inconsistent, 224
rhetorical developments, 24–25, 98–99
scriptures: not limited to men, 100, 250–51; rules for using, 255–56
survey responses, 326
word not cited in LDS canonical prayers, 220–21

Priesthood and Church Government, 151
"Priesthood Authority in Family and the Church," 162
priesthood session broadcast live, 22
Primary, 127, 352
Prince, Gregory A.
personal experiences, 203, 209–10, 218
on "trickle-down" and "trickle-up" revelation, 45 note 30, 208–15
privacy, in twentieth-century disciplinary councils, 243
"private counsel and caution," as disciplinary step, 244
probation, informal/formal, 231, 244–45. *See also* disciplinary councils.
Proclamation on the Family. *See* "The Family: A Proclamation to the World."
proclamations, *Church News* defines, 50
progressive Mormons, estimated numbers of, 342
Proposition 8 (2008), 216–17, 231, 322
Church opposes gay marriage, 52, 81 note 9
inconsistent reaction of local leaders, 231
Proposition 22, 216
Protect Marriage (campaign), 52
Protestants, 36 note 18
Provo Feminists, 14
proxy names, at Ordain Women events, 144 note 14
public activism, negative consequences of, 393
Public Affairs Department, 164, 241
and Ordain Women, ix, 241, 393; calls events a "protest," 165, 274 note 37; groups with anti-Mormons, 392; uses women spokespersons, 391
changes Church's homophobic image, 217–18
excommunications as local, 28
image management by name-calling, 254
perceptions of Mormon image, 45
statement on men-only ordination, 19–20
Pulido, Martin, 10

Q

Qualtrics survey, 285, 298–99
questioning, Church discourages, 290
Quinn, D. Michael, 159–60
quorum not a club, 223
Quorum of the Anointed, 142

R

race, and feminism, 181, 348–51
discrimination and legislation, 47 note 33
"Race and the Priesthood," LDS Newsroom Essay, 47 note 32
radical flank, 40–42, 48, 373
radical organizations, cannot mobilize allies, 381
Radke-Moss, Andrea, 42–46
Randles, Jennifer, 321
Ransom, Neil, 10, 16
rape
culture, 130–31
grounds for disciplinary council, 228, 245
resulting in pregnancy, 245
Ratzinger, Joseph, 172
Rector, Hartman, Jr., 155
Reddit, 341
Rees, David L., 230
Rees, Joseph Alexander, 230
Rees, Robert A., biography, 229–35
"Relief Society and the Church, The," 159
Relief Society. *See also* blessings.
and correlation, 153–54
and women's suffrage, 148
date of founding, 355
in Nauvoo, 139–40, 148–49
need for autonomy, 333
proposed expanded role, 166, 314, 326
status diminished (1906), 223
Relief Society Magazine, 150, 153
"religious freedom" legislation, 322
Reorganized Church of Jesus Christ of Latter Day Saints. *See* Community of Christ.
Restoration Studies Symposium, 179
retrenchment. *See* Armand Mauss.
revelation

importance of in change, 32, 45, 142, 239, 307, 309, 316, 322, 367, 369
and gender reform, 123, 130
and women's ordination, 155, 184, 328–29
as Article of Faith, 203
continuing, 199
in Community of Christ, 186
messiness of process, 238
not cited in sister missionary age change, 261
personal, and women's ordination, 144
schism, percentage of, 179, 179 note 43
strategy of emphasizing, 310, 317
survey: and nuanced questions, 280; responses prioritize, 398–99
Richards, Louisa Greene, 148
Richards, Stephen L, 152
Rigdon, Sidney, 221
RLDS Church. See Community of Christ.
robbery, grounds for disciplinary council, 228, 245
Roberts, B. H., change in Relief Society minutes, 139, 149
Robertson, Mary Ellen
and Ordain Women, 19, 164
on interfaith panel, 16, 144, 162–63
Robison, Louise Yates, 150
Rojas, Fabio, 381
Roman Catholic Women Priests, 8, 140, 163, 168, 173, 177. See also Catholic Church.
Romney, Marion G., 153
Romney, Mitt, 13
Ross, Nancy, 335
and Mormon Gender Issues Survey, 278, 285
and Ordain Women, 17, 21, 22 and note 56, 278, 285
surveys by, 20
Rue, Victoria, 16, 163
Ruether, Rosemary Radford, 336
Russell, William D., 178–79
Rutherford, Taunalyn Ford, 274
Ryan, Caitlin, 218

S

sacrament, and disfellowshipment, 245
"sacred canopy," 313, 318
"Sacred Disobedience: Women's Call to Ordination," 163
safeguarding Church, a purpose of disciplinary councils, 244
same-sex marriage, Church opposes, 215–18
sanctification, and priesthood, 96
Sanders, Ashley, 10–12, 14, 19
Savage, Becky, 199
Savage, Katie, 14
"scattering sunshine" campaign, 392
Schiess, Betty, 177 note 34
schism, possibility in Mormonism, 183
Schori, Katharine Jefferts, 177
Scott, Richard G., 70
scriptures, ambiguous on women's priesthood, 220; supports equality, 367 note 9
sealing, 93 note 18
Seawright, Taryn Nelson, 158
Second Vatican Council, 385
secrecy in disciplinary councils, reform needed, 255
"self-abuse," disciplinary council not required, 245
separate spheres, 62–63. See also complementarianism.
September Six, 6, 160, 228
Sered, Susan, 384, 393
serious transgressions, and mandatory disciplinary councils, 246
service. See callings.
Seventh-day Adventists, 282
sex
and gender, in "The Family: A Proclamation to the World," 82
sexual abuse, and disciplinary councils, 228, 245; ignored in "The Family: A Proclamation to the World," 85
sexual minorities. See transgender and LGBT.
She Shall Be Called Woman, 155
Shepherd, Gary and Gordon, tracking Ordain Women profiles, 246
Shepherd, Pamela A., 242, 371
Shipps, Jan, 27–28
Sidwell, Adelia B. Cox, 64
Silver, Nan, 105–12
sister missionaries, 259–75
age lowered to nineteen, 44, 46, 259
and culture change, 271
defensive about not going, 265
expansion of service without priesthood, 330
history of, 260–62
increased status of, 264
influence of Ordain Women, 273
influence on marriages, 260, 264
mental health, 266, 269–70, 274–75

Index   439

missions not expected/required, 264
numbers of, 259
policy of keeping numbers small, 261–62
post-mission, 270, 273–74
reluctant to push for change, 273–74
revelation not cited for change, 261
seen as exemplary, 265
seen as leaders, 272
value of earlier preparation, 270–71
sister training leader (STL)
  increased status, 267
  newly created position, 265–69
  limited power, 267–68
Sisters in Spirit: Mormon Women in Historical and Cultural Perspective, 157
Sisters of Dorcas, 190
Skype, and Mormon feminists, 337
Slick, Matt, 227
Smith, Alison Moore, x note 2
Smith, Barbara B., 4, 154
Smith, Bathsheba W., 148–49
Smith, Emma, 146–47, 190
Smith, Frederick M., 192, 195–96
Smith, Joseph
  and equality, 367 note 10
  and priesthood teachings, 141–42
  changes in First Vision accounts, 204–7
  discourses online, 163
  doctrinal/organizational changes during lifetime, 203–8
  evolution in portraying God, 204–7
  on common consent, 187
  on freedom of conscience, 236
  on women's priesthood, 137–39, 146, 149, 159, 220
Smith, Joseph F.
  on birth control, 212
  on women's priesthood, 149–50
  upgrades quorums, downgrades women, 223
Smith, Joseph Fielding, 142, 151–53
  ended women's health blessings, 152
Smith, Joseph, III, 190
Smith, Suzette, 20
Smith, Wallace B., 178, 195
Smoot, Mary Ellen, 160
Smoot, Reed, 223
Snow, David, 380
Snow, Eliza R., 60–61, 147, 153 note 62
Snow, Lorenzo, 148
snowball sampling, 283

social media, and Ordain Women, 335–53
social movement, defined, 377–79
social systems, closed and open, 28–30
Society of Gleaners, 190
Society of Mormon Philosophical Theology, 161
Soule, Sarah A., 381
Spafford, Belle Smith, 152
Spencer, Emily, 58, 65
Spinoza, Baruch, 230
spiraling learning, 346–49, 351, 353
The Spirit of the Lord Is upon Me: The Writings of Suzanne Hiatt, 177
spiritual gifts, 221–24
Stack, Peggy Fletcher, articles by, 6, 14, 139, 161–62
stake presidents. *See* local leaders.
stakeholders, 382–83, 388
Stearmer, S. Matthew, 39–42, 278, 285
Stephens, Carole M., 45
Stevens, Jean A., 20, 164
Stepping Stones, 192
stereotypes, and religious women, 320
Story of the Philadelphia Eleven, 177
Strangers in Paradox: Explorations in Mormon Theology, 158
Straubhaar, Rolf, 40 note 25, 103–5, 111–12. *See also* Money, Kristy.
Strayer, Chelsea Shields, 10, 11–12, 16–17, 22–23
Strayer, Mike, 11
Stromberg, Lorie Winder
  addresses/writings, 7, 161, 163
  All Are Alike unto God FAQs, 16
  and Equal in Faith, 176
  at WOC conference, 21
  commitment to women's priesthood, 144–45
  personal experiences, 3–4, 8–9
  and Ordain Women, 19, 21–23, 145, 164
  on women's equality, 167
suffrage, 46–47, 61–63, 147, 381
suicide, among gays, 218
Sunstone "Why I Stay," 323
Sunstone (magazine/symposia), and feminist topics, 6, 156–57, 159, 162–63, 341, 351
Sunstone West Symposium, 8
surveys in 2013, 2015
  and Mormon feminist online groups, 337–48
  and social media, 335
  complexity of responses, 324
  demographics, 338–39

likelihood of women's ordination, 339
methodology, 337
Pew survey compared, 144 note 15, 322 note 9
religiosity of respondents, 339
sustaining vote, 32 note 12, 245
Swanson, Katrina, 177 note 34

T

Tabernacle Choir Christmas Program, 218
tactics, legitimacy of, 388
Talmage, James E., 54 note 16, 60, 149
Tanner, N. Eldon, 213
"Taxonomy of Gender Roles," 56
Teachings of the Prophet Joseph Smith, 142, 151
Teasdale, M. E., 61
temple endowment
   and gender inequity, 97 note 23
   and priesthood, 24–25, 142–43, 149–50, 156, 251
   and women's authority, 251
   changes in (1990), 159
   less emphasized in priesthood discussions, 144
temple marriage policies, reforms, 314
temple ordinances, performed by women, 226
temple recommend
   and disfellowshipment, 245
   and Proposition 8, 231
   taken or threatened, 352, 387 note 59
temple sealings
   excludes homosexuals, transgendered, and unmarried, 90
   not required for salvation, 90–93
   subordinates women, 90
tension management, and change, 35
Thacker, Randall, 232 note 9
theocratic democracy, 187
theology, and ordination, 78, 137, 144, 170
"Theology from the Margins," 351
Thompsett, Frederica Harris, 177
Tickameyer, Garland, 195–96
tithing
   disfellowshipped members pay, 245
   failure to pay and disciplinary councils, 245
Todd, Ruth, 22, 164, 391
Toscano, Margaret
   addresses/essays by, 4–5, 11, 156, 158, 160–63
   and Catholic-Mormon panel, 16
   and Ordain Women, 15, 19, 23, 144, 164

   biography, 141–44, 160
   excommunicated, 6, 143, 161
   fired from BYU, 143, 158
   temple endowment and priesthood, 97 note 23
Toscano, Paul J., 139, 158, 160
transgender
   defined, 118
   excluded from exaltation, 90
   responses to survey, 120–33
transsexual operation
   and disciplinary councils, 119 note 9, 228, 245–46
   and Mormon Gender Issues Survey, 118–22
   demographics, 121–23
trickle-down revelation, 45 note 30, 198, 210–15
trickle-up revelation, 45 note 30, 204, 208–15, 369
tritheism, 206
Troeh, Marjorie, 193
Trotter, Scott, 17
Tullidge, Edward, 141–42, 147–48
Tumblr, 341
Turner, Rodney, 140–41, 153–50
tweets, 341
Twitter, 341

U–W

Ulrich, Laurel Thatcher, 20
unrighteous dominion, 238–39, 254
U.S. Supreme Court, Reynolds case, 49
U.S. Women's Bureau, 68
Utah Public Radio, 277
"Valediction: Forbidding Mourning," 112–13
value judgements, avoiding in research, 320
VOICE, 5, 14
Walker, Marietta Hodges Faulconer, 192
Wallace, Carolyn M., 82 note 6
Wallace, Mike, 160
ward/congregation, opposition to feminism, examples of, vii–ix, 352–53
ward council, women's influence limited to, 273
Wayne, Tiffany K., 54
We Are Women (rally), 11
Wear Pants to Church (2012), 12–13, 17, 163, 313, 352
Welch, Rosalynde, 269
welfare program, 202–3
Welker, Holly, 15
Wells, Emmeline B., 61, 65, 149

Wheatley, Meg, 157
Wheatley, Scott
　affirmed bishop's action, 252
　charges of false doctrine incorrect, 250
　examples of violating handbook, 248–49
　interviews and reassures Kate Kelly, 247–48
Wheelwright, Hannah, 13–14, 19, 22, 164
"Where Have All the Mormon Feminists Gone?" 6, 139, 161
Whiteley, Amber Choruby, 21
Whitesides, Lynne Kanavel, 6, 160
Whitmer, David, 203 note 1
Whitney, Orson F., 259
Widdison, Renae, 14
Widtsoe, John A., 151
Wittig, Nancy, 177 note 34
Wixom, Rosemary M., 18
WOC. *See* Women's Ordination Conference.
Woman and the Priesthood, 154
Woman's Exponent, 147, 149
"Woman's Perspective on the Priesthood, A," 155–56
women. *See also* gender roles.
　as property, 59
　debate on ordination, 158, 220–24, 367, 400; topic declared passé, 162
　general session of conference, 44
　giving blessings, illustrated on Ordain Women, 374
　historic use of priesthood, 297. See also Joseph Smith.
　influence on men, 63–64
　marginalized and disfranchised, 384
　media bibliography, 401–18
　percent working outside the home, 56–57
　praying in general conference, 350
　talents, under-used, 368
　traditional views of "nature," 388
　status diminished by Joseph F. Smith, 223
　suffer from unrighteous dominion, 238
Women Advocating for Voice and Equality (WAVE), 7, 9–10, 162
Women and Authority: Re-emerging Mormon Feminism, 159
Women and the Priesthood: What One Mormon Woman Believes, xi, 141, 164
Women at Church, Magnifying LDS Women's Local Impact, xi–xii, 43 note 27, 140–41, 165

"Women, Feminism, and the Blessings of the Priesthood," 157
"Women in the Priesthood Hierarchy," 158
Women of Covenant: The Story of Relief Society, 139, 159
Women of Mormondom, 141–42, 147–48
Women of the Wall. *See* Orthodox Jewish.
"Women's Home Column," 192
Women's Ministries Commissioner (RLDS), 193
Women's Ordination Conference (WOC), 21, 172–73, 177, 181
Women's Political Caucus (Utah County), 4
Women's Research Institute (BYU), 6
Wood, Teddie, 155
Woodland, Cadence, 237
Woods, M. C., 65
Word of Wisdom, 63, 245, 288
Words of Joseph Smith: The Contemporary Accounts of the Nauvoo Discourses of the Prophet Joseph, 142

Y–Z

Yeats, W. B., 110
yin/yang, as elements of reality, 87–88
Young Adult program, as trickle-up revelation, 210
Young, Brigham
　as Joseph Smith's successor, 189
　denies ordination of black men, 213 note 31, 225
　Eve as a plural wife, 60
　on birth control, 211
　on women's priesthood, 146–47
　versus Orson Pratt, 234
Young Men/Young Women, equalized budgets, 333
Young Mormon Feminist (blog), 12, 162 note 109
Young, Phoebe, 61
Young, Thelma, 14
Young Woman's Journal, 148
Young Women/Young Men, 313–14
Young Women's Retrenchment Association, 60
Zelophehad's Daughters (blog), 7, 162 note 109
Zion in the Courts: A Legal History of the Church of Jesus Christ of Latter-day Saints, 1830–1900, 243
Zion's Hope, 192

Also available from
GREG KOFFORD BOOKS

Women at Church: Magnifying LDS Women's Local Impact

Neylan McBaine

Paperback, ISBN: 978-1-58958-688-8

Women at Church is a practical and faithful guide to improving the way men and women work together at church. Looking at current administrative and cultural practices, the author explains why some women struggle with the gendered divisions of labor. She then examines ample real-life examples that are currently happening in local settings around the country that expand and reimagine gendered practices. Readers will understand how to evaluate possible pain points in current practices and propose solutions that continue to uphold all mandated church policies. Readers will be equipped with the tools they need to have respectful, empathetic and productive conversations about gendered practices in Church administration and culture.

Praise for *Women at Church*:

"Such a timely, faithful, and practical book! I suggest ordering this book in bulk to give to your bishopric, stake presidency, and all your local leadership to start a conversation on changing Church culture for women by letting our doctrine suggest creative local adaptations—Neylan McBaine shows the way!" — Valerie Hudson Cassler, author of *Women in Eternity, Women of Zion*

"A pivotal work replete with wisdom and insight. Neylan McBaine deftly outlines a workable programme for facilitating movement in the direction of the 'privileges and powers' promised the nascent Female Relief Society of Nauvoo." — Fiona Givens, co-author of *The God Who Weeps: How Mormonism Makes Sense of Life*

"In her timely and brilliant findings, Neylan McBaine issues a gracious invitation to rethink our assumptions about women's public Church service. Well researched, authentic, and respectful of the current Church administrative structure, McBaine shares exciting and practical ideas that address diverse needs and involve all members in the meaningful work of the Church." — Camille Fronk Olson, author of *Women of the Old Testament* and *Women of the New Testament*

Mormon Women Have Their Say: Essays from the Claremont Oral History Collection

Edited by Claudia L. Bushman and Caroline Kline

Paperback, ISBN: 978-1-58958-494-5

The Claremont Women's Oral History Project has collected hundreds of interviews with Mormon women of various ages, experiences, and levels of activity. These interviews record the experiences of these women in their homes and family life, their church life, and their work life, in their roles as homemakers, students, missionaries, career women, single women, converts, and disaffected members. Their stories feed into and illuminate the broader narrative of LDS history and belief, filling in a large gap in Mormon history that has often neglected the lived experiences of women. This project preserves and perpetuates their voices and memories, allowing them to say share what has too often been left unspoken. The silent majority speaks in these records.

This volume is the first to explore the riches of the collection in print. A group of young scholars and others have used the interviews to better understand what Mormonism means to these women and what women mean for Mormonism. They explore those interviews through the lenses of history, doctrine, mythology, feminist theory, personal experience, and current events to help us understand what these women have to say about their own faith and lives.

Praise for *Mormon Women Have Their Say*:

"Using a variety of analytical techniques and their own savvy, the authors connect ordinary lives with enduring themes in Latter-day Saint faith and history." --Laurel Thatcher Ulrich, author of *Well-Behaved Women Seldom Make History*

"Essential.... In these pages, Mormon women will find *ourselves*." --Joanna Brooks, author of *The Book of Mormon Girl: A Memoir of an American Faith*

"The varieties of women's responses to the major issues in their lives will provide many surprises for the reader, who will be struck by how many different ways there are to be a thoughtful and faithful Latter-day Saint woman." --Armand Mauss, author of *All Abraham's Children: Changing Mormon Conceptions of Race and Lineage*

Common Ground—Different Opinions: Latter-day Saints and Contemporary Issues

Edited by Justin F. White and James E. Faulconer

Paperback, ISBN: 978-1-58958-573-7

There are many hotly debated issues about which many people disagree, and where common ground is hard to find. From evolution to environmentalism, war and peace to political partisanship, stem cell research to same-sex marriage, how we think about controversial issues affects how we interact as Latter-day Saints.

In this volume various Latter-day Saint authors address these and other issues from differing points of view. Though they differ on these tough questions, they have all found common ground in the gospel of Jesus Christ and the latter-day restoration. Their insights offer diverse points of view while demonstrating we can still love those with whom we disagree.

Praise for *Common Ground—Different Opinions*:

"[This book] provide models of faithful and diverse Latter-day Saints who remain united in the body of Christ. This collection clearly demonstrates that a variety of perspectives on a number of sensitive issues do in fact exist in the Church. . . . [T]he collection is successful in any case where it manages to give readers pause with regard to an issue they've been fond of debating, or convinces them to approach such conversations with greater charity and much more patience. It served as just such a reminder and encouragement to me, and for that reason above all, I recommend this book." — Blair Hodges, Maxwell Institute

Latter-Day Dissent:
At the Crossroads of Intellectual Inquiry and Ecclesiastical Authority

Philip Lindholm

Paperback, ISBN: 978-1-58958-128-9

This volume collects, for the first time in book form, stories from the "September Six," a group of intellectuals officially excommunicated or disfellowshipped from the LDS Church in September of 1993 on charges of "apostasy" or "conduct unbecoming" Church members. Their experiences are significant and yet are largely unknown outside of scholarly or more liberal Mormon circles, which is surprising given that their story was immediately propelled onto screens and cover pages across the Western world.

Interviews by Dr. Philip Lindholm (Ph.D. Theology, University of Oxford) include those of the "September Six," Lynne Kanavel Whitesides, Paul James Toscano, Maxine Hanks, Lavina Fielding Anderson, and D. Michael Quinn; as well as Janice Merrill Allred, Margaret Merrill Toscano, Thomas W. Murphy, and former employee of the LDS Church's Public Affairs Department, Donald B. Jessee.

Each interview illustrates the tension that often exists between the Church and its intellectual critics, and highlights the difficulty of accommodating congregational diversity while maintaining doctrinal unity—a difficulty hearkening back to the very heart of ancient Christianity.

Excavating Mormon Pasts: The New Historiography of the Last Half Century

Newell G. Bringhurst and
Lavina Fielding Anderson

Paperback, ISBN: 978-1-58958-115-9

Special Book Award - John Whitmer Historical Association

Mormonism was born less than 200 years ago, but in that short time it has developed into a dynamic world religious movement. With that growth has come the inevitable restructuring and reevaluation of its history and doctrine. Mormon and non-Mormon scholars alike have viewed Joseph Smith's religion as fertile soil for religious, historical and sociological studies. Many early attempts to either defend or defame the Church were at best sloppy and often dishonest. It has taken decades for Mormon scholarship to mature to its present state. The editors of this book have assembled 16 essays addressing the substantial number of published works in the field of Mormon studies from 1950 to the present. The contributors come from various segments of the Mormon tradition and fairly represent the broad intellectual spectrum of that tradition. Each essay focuses on a particular aspect of Mormonism (history, women's issues, polygamy, etc.), and each is careful to evenhandedly evaluate the strengths and weaknesses of the books under discussion. More importantly, each volume is placed in context with other, related works, giving the reader a panoramic view of contemporary research. Students of Mormonism will find this collection of historiographical essays an invaluable addition to their libraries.

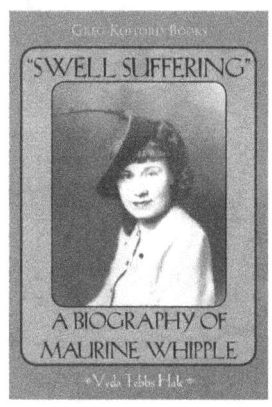

"Swell Suffering": A Biography of Maurine Whipple

Veda Tebbs Hale

Paperback, ISBN: 978-1-58958-124-1
Hardcover, ISBN: 978-1-58958-122-7

Maurine Whipple, author of what some critics consider Mormonism's greatest novel, *The Giant Joshua,* is an enigma. Her prize-winning novel has never been out of print, and its portrayal of the founding of St. George draws on her own family history to produce its unforgettable and candid portrait of plural marriage's challenges. Yet Maurine's life is full of contradictions and unanswered questions. Veda Tebbs Hale, a personal friend of the paradoxical novelist, answers these questions with sympathy and tact, nailing each insight down with thorough research in Whipple's vast but under-utilized collected papers.

Praise for *"Swell Suffering"*:

"Hale achieves an admirable balance of compassion and objectivity toward an author who seemed fated to offend those who offered to love or befriend her. . . . Readers of this biography will be reminded that Whipple was a full peer of such Utah writers as Virginia Sorensen, Fawn Brodie, and Juanita Brooks, all of whom achieved national fame for their literary and historical works during the mid-twentieth century"
—Levi S. Peterson, author of *The Backslider* and *Juanita Brooks: Mormon Historian*

"This is My Doctrine": The Development of Mormon Theology

Charles R. Harrell

Hardcover, ISBN: 978-1-58958-103-6

The principal doctrines defining Mormonism today often bear little resemblance to those it started out with in the early 1830s. This book shows that these doctrines did not originate in a vacuum but were rather prompted and informed by the religious culture from which Mormonism arose. Early Mormons, like their early Christian and even earlier Israelite predecessors, brought with them their own varied culturally conditioned theological presuppositions (a process of convergence) and only later acquired a more distinctive theological outlook (a process of differentiation).

In this first-of-its-kind comprehensive treatment of the development of Mormon theology, Charles Harrell traces the history of Latter-day Saint doctrines from the times of the Old Testament to the present. He describes how Mormonism has carried on the tradition of the biblical authors, early Christians, and later Protestants in reinterpreting scripture to accommodate new theological ideas while attempting to uphold the integrity and authority of the scriptures. In the process, he probes three questions: How did Mormon doctrines develop? What are the scriptural underpinnings of these doctrines? And what do critical scholars make of these same scriptures? In this enlightening study, Harrell systematically peels back the doctrinal accretions of time to provide a fresh new look at Mormon theology.

"*This Is My Doctrine*" will provide those already versed in Mormonism's theological tradition with a new and richer perspective of Mormon theology. Those unacquainted with Mormonism will gain an appreciation for how Mormon theology fits into the larger Jewish and Christian theological traditions.

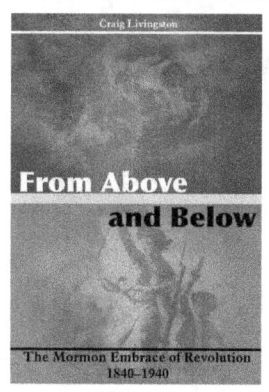

From Above and Below: The Mormon Embrace of Revolution, 1840–1940

Craig Livingston

Paperback, ISBN: 978-1-58958-621-5

Praise for *From Above and Below*:

"In this engaging study, Craig Livingston examines Mormon responses to political revolutions across the globe from the 1840s to the 1930s. Latter-day Saints saw utopian possibilities in revolutions from the European tumults of 1848 to the Mexican Revolution. Highlighting the often radical anti-capitalist and anti-imperialist rhetoric of Mormon leaders, Livingston demonstrates how Latter-day Saints interpreted revolutions through their unique theology and millennialism."
--Matthew J. Grow, author of *Liberty to the Downtrodden: Thomas L. Kane, Romantic Reformer*

"Craig Livingston's landmark book demonstrates how 21st-century Mormonism's arch-conservatism was preceded by its pro-revolutionary worldview that was dominant from the 1830s to the 1930s. Shown by current opinion-polling to be the most politically conservative religious group in the United States, contemporary Mormons are unaware that leaders of the LDS Church once praised radical liberalism and violent revolutionaries. By this pre-1936 Mormon view, 'The people would reduce privilege and exploitation in the crucible of revolution, then reforge society in a spiritual union of peace' before the Coming of Christ and His Millennium. With profound research in Mormon sources and in academic studies about various social revolutions and political upheavals, Livingston provides a nuanced examination of this little-known dimension of LDS thought which tenuously balanced pro-revolutionary enthusiasms with anti-mob sentiments."
--D. Michael Quinn, author of *Elder Statesman: A Biography of J. Reuben Clark*

Discourses in Mormon Theology: Philosophical and Theological Possibilities

Edited by
James M. McLachlan and Loyd Ericson

Hardcover, ISBN: 978-1-58958-103-6

A mere two hundred years old, Mormonism is still in its infancy compared to other theological disciplines (Judaism, Catholicism, Buddhism, etc.). This volume will introduce its reader to the rich blend of theological viewpoints that exist within Mormonism. The essays break new ground in Mormon studies by exploring the vast expanse of philosophical territory left largely untouched by traditional approaches to Mormon theology. It presents philosophical and theological essays by many of the finest minds associated with Mormonism in an organized and easy-to-understand manner and provides the reader with a window into the fascinating diversity amongst Mormon philosophers. Open-minded students of pure religion will appreciate this volume's thoughtful inquiries.

These essays were delivered at the first conference of the Society for Mormon Philosophy and Theology. Authors include Grant Underwood, Blake T. Ostler, Dennis Potter, Margaret Merrill Toscano, James E. Faulconer, and Robert L. Millet

Praise for *Discourses in Mormon Theology*:

"In short, *Discourses in Mormon Theology* is an excellent compilation of essays that are sure to feed both the mind and soul. It reminds all of us that beyond the white shirts and ties there exists a universe of theological and moral sensitivity that cries out for study and acclamation."
　　　-Jeff Needle, Association for Mormon Letters

Dead Wood and Rushing Water: Essays on Mormon Faith, Culture, and Family

Boyd Jay Petersen

Paperback, ISBN: 978-1-58958-658-1

For over a decade, Boyd Petersen has been an active voice in Mormon studies and thought. In essays that steer a course between apologetics and criticism, striving for the balance of what Eugene England once called the "radical middle," he explores various aspects of Mormon life and culture—from the Dream Mine near Salem, Utah, to the challenges that Latter-day Saints of the millennial generation face today.

Praise for *Dead Wood and Rushing Water*:

"*Dead Wood and Rushing Water* gives us a reflective, striving, wise soul ruminating on his world. In the tradition of Eugene England, Petersen examines everything in his Mormon life from the gold plates to missions to dream mines to doubt and on to Glenn Beck, Hugh Nibley, and gender. It is a book I had trouble putting down." — Richard L. Bushman, author of *Joseph Smith: Rough Stone Rolling*

"Boyd Petersen is correct when he says that Mormons have a deep hunger for personal stories—at least when they are as thoughtful and well-crafted as the ones he shares in this collection." — Jana Riess, author of *The Twible* and *Flunking Sainthood*

"Boyd Petersen invites us all to ponder anew the verities we hold, sharing in his humility, tentativeness, and cheerful confidence that our paths will converge in the end." — Terryl. L. Givens, author of *People of Paradox: A History of Mormon Culture*

www.ingramcontent.com/pod-product-compliance
Lightning Source LLC
Chambersburg PA
CBHW071824230426
43672CB00013B/2755